07569301

KT-599-823

301
POTTER
760466

...TION

B.C.H.E. - LIBRARY

00015299

Dimensions of Society

A Reader

*The Social Sciences Foundation Course Team
at The Open University*

Andrew Learmonth (course team chairman)
John Annett
Brendan Connors
Christopher Brook
F. S. Brooman
Hedy Brown
Francis G. Castles
Robert Cookson
Ruth Finnegan
Peter Hamilton
Margaret Kiloh
Frank Knox
Malcolm McDonald
Dennis Mills
Michael Philps (BBC)
Kay Pole
David Potter
Lilian Power
Graeme Salaman
Philip Sarre
Richard Stevens
Kenneth Thompson
Janet Woollacott
Vincent Worth

BATH SPA UNIVERSITY
NEWTON PARK LIBRARY

Class No. 301 POT

DISCARD

unknown

/ POT

Dimensions of Society

A Reader

Edited by David Potter and Philip Sarre

with F. S. Brooman, Ruth Finnegan,
Peter Hamilton, Andrew Learmonth,
Kay Pole, Graeme Salaman

*for the Social Sciences Foundation Course Team
at The Open University*

University of London Press Ltd
in association with
The Open University Press

ISBN 0 340 19369 7 Paper
ISBN 0 340 19370 0 Boards

Selection and editorial material
copyright © The Open University 1974
All rights reserved. No part of this publication may be
reproduced or transmitted in any form or by any means,
electronic or mechanical, including photocopy,
recording, or any information storage and retrieval
system, without permission in writing from the publisher.

University of London Press Ltd
St Paul's House, Warwick Lane, London EC4P 4AH

Printed and bound in Great Britain by
Hazell Watson & Viney Ltd, Aylesbury, Bucks

Contents

Part IV   Work

Part V   Social relations

Editors' Acknowledgments

This Reader has grown out of the planning and development of an introductory course in Social Science at the Open University. The book's general approach is therefore the product of the team of people who prepared the course. Barbara Field and Jennifer Potter helped with editorial chores in the final rush to get the manuscript to the publishers on time; we are grateful for their assistance. We wish to thank Maureen Adams and Sharon Stocker for cheerfully accepting the typing requirements involved. We also wish to acknowledge the contribution made by Roger Lubbock for handling arrangements for the manuscript's publication.

Publishers' Acknowledgments

The editors and publisher wish to thank the following for permission to reprint the articles included in this book:

The Clarendon Press for 'Demography of small-scale societies' by Colin M. Turnbull (reprinted from *The Structure of Human Populations*, edited by G. A. Harrison and A. J. Boyce, 1972, pp. 283–312); the Greater London Council for 'Population – growth or decline?' by Eivind Gilje and Terry Gould (reprinted from GLC Intelligence Unit Quarterly Bulletin number 24 (September 1973), pp. 29–35); Penguin Books Ltd for 'Eye-contact and the direction of gaze' (reprinted from *The Psychology of Interpersonal Behaviour* by Michael Argyle, 1972, pp. 80–93), 'Hours of work and the twenty-four-hour cycle of rest and activity' by Robert Wilkinson (reprinted from *Psychology at Work*, edited by Peter Brian Warr, 1971, pp. 31–54), and 'On the line' (reprinted from *Working for Ford* by Huw Beynon, 1973, pp. 109–59); Tavistock Publications Ltd for 'Interaction and inter-experience in dyads' (reprinted from *Interpersonal Perception* by R. D. Laing, H. Phillipson and A. R. Lee, 1966, pp. 9–18) and 'Productive efficiency and customary systems of rewards in rural South India' by Scarlett Epstein (reprinted from *Themes in Economic Anthropology*, edited by Raymond Firth, 1967, pp. 229–52); *Saturday Review* for 'Is literacy passé?' by Walter J. Ong sj (reprinted from *Saturday Review*, 28 November 1959); John Wiley & Sons Inc. for 'On communication, ancient and modern' (reprinted from *World Communication – Threat or Promise?* by Colin Cherry, 1971, pp. 28–53, 185–9); the MIT Press for 'Peoples, nations and communication' (reprinted from *Nationalism and Social Communication* by Karl W. Deutsch, 1966, pp. 86–106); Routledge &

Kegan Paul Ltd for 'Material conditions and economic characteristics of feudal society' (reprinted from *Feudal Society* by Marc Bloch, 1962, pp. 59–71) and 'The human situation' (reprinted from *Man for Himself* by Erich Fromm, 1949, pp. 39–50); Methuen & Co. Ltd for 'The industrial revolution – identity and beginning' (reprinted from *The First Industrial Nation* by Peter Mathias, 1969, pp. 1–18); Sir Isaac Pitman & Sons Ltd for 'The social framework' by F. C. Benham (reprinted from *Economics: A General Introduction*, edited by F. W. Paish, 8th edition, 1967, pp. 42–56); André Deutsch Ltd for 'The planning lacunae' (reprinted from *The New Industrial State* by J. K. Galbraith, originally published by Hamish Hamilton Ltd, pp. 349–56); Professor Robert L. Heilbroner for 'Economic problems of a "postindustrial" society' by Robert L. Heilbroner (reprinted from *Dissent*, 1 April 1973, pp. 163–76); Macmillan, London and Basingstoke, for 'The conditions of work' (reprinted from *The Growth of British Industrial Relations* by E. H. Phelps-Brown, 1959, pp. 98–113); The University of Chicago Press for 'Cultural approaches to childhood' by Margaret Mead (reprinted from *Childhood in Contemporary Cultures* edited by Margaret Mead and M. Wolfenstein, 1955, pp. 6–14), 'The cabdriver and his fare: facets of a fleeting relationship' by Fred Davis (reprinted from *American Journal of Sociology*, 1965, pp. 158–65) and 'The sociological roots of science' by Edgar Zilsel (reprinted from *American Journal of Sociology*, XLVII (January 1942), pp. 544–60; The American Sociological Association for 'The choice of variables in the study of socialization' by Eleanor E. Maccoby (reprinted from *Sociometry*, 24 (1961) pp. 357–71); Dr Daniel Katz and Columbia University Press for 'The functional approach to the study of attitudes' by Daniel Katz (reprinted from *The Public Opinion Quarterly*, 24 (1960), pp. 163–77); Harper & Row for 'Motive forces of the new science' (reprinted from *Science, Technology and Society in Seventeenth-Century England* by Robert K. Merton, 1970, pp. 80–110); Heinemann Educational Books Ltd for 'The Halévy thesis' (reprinted from *A Sociology of Religion* by Michael Hill, 1973, pp. 183–204); *European Journal of Sociology* for 'Millenarian movements' by Yonina Talmon (reprinted from *European Journal of Sociology*, VII (1966), pp. 159–200); Macmillan Publishing Co. Inc. for 'Power' by Robert A. Dahl (reprinted by permission of the publisher from *International Encyclopedia of the Social Sciences* edited by David Sills, Volume 12 (1968), pp. 405–15. Copyright © Macmillan Incorporated); Macmillan Publishing Co. Inc. for 'Marx as a power theorist' by Marvin E. Olsen (reprinted from *Power in Societies* edited by Marvin E. Olsen, 1970, pp. 70–6. Copyright © Marvin E. Olsen); Random House Inc. for 'The interpretation of social change' (reprinted from *Economy and Society* by Wilbert E. Moore,

1964, pp. 34–43); George Allen & Unwin Ltd for 'The development of modern Western civilization' (reprinted from *The Protestant Ethic and the Spirit of Capitalism* by Max Weber, 1962, pp. 13–31); Professor Melvin M. Webber and the Bartlett Society, University of London for 'A new concept of the future' by Melvin M. Webber (reprinted from *Town Planning Review*, **39**, number 3 (1968), pp. 179–95); and George Weidenfeld and Nicolson Ltd for 'Predictions' (reprinted from *The Art of Conjecture* by Bertrand de Jouvenel, 1967, pp. 59–81).

It has not been possible to contact the copyright holders of 'Presentation of self to others' (reprinted from *The Presentation of Self in Everyday Life* by Erving Goffman, 1959, pp. 220–31) and of 'Variability in population change in India 1871–1941' by Arthur Geddes (reprinted from *Human Relations*, volume 1 (1947–8), pp. 181–205). However, the publishers will be pleased to make full acknowledgment in subsequent editions of this book of any rights not acknowledged here.

General introduction

This book contains essential readings for students of the Open University who are taking the foundation course in social science called 'Making Sense of Society' (D101). The point of this General Introduction is to say something briefly about the strategy of the course as a whole, and how the contents of this Reader relate to it.

In thinking about how to design an introductory, interdisciplinary course in social science (and anyone who has tried to design such a course will know how difficult it is), we started, of course, with our students. Open University students are adults in full-time employment or working in the home or elsewhere. They are men and women who have not attended a conventional university, and who wish to pursue a course of studies in a university while continuing their work as mechanic or teacher or housewife or whatever. They can select from a wide range of courses in both arts and science subjects. The heart of any particular course in the Open University is a set of correspondence 'packages' sent at periodic intervals throughout the year to students by post. Integrated with these correspondence packages are radio and television programmes shown on the BBC. Short summer or weekend 'schools' are also provided, where intensive face-to-face teaching occurs during periods when students can get away from job or family commitments. There are also several hundred Open University Study Centres scattered up and down the country where students can obtain tutorial and counselling assistance in the evenings. Students are required to complete a number of assignments during the year, and to take an examination at the end of it. No formal academic qualifications are required for registration, and many of those who begin the course have not done much in the way of serious study, or the writing of essays, for a number of years. At the same time, such mature students have gained valuable experience in all sorts of different ways, and start their study with a strong commitment to learning. It is for such students that the course 'Making Sense of Society' has been prepared.

The course was designed in the light of three basic principles, which arise from the essential functions of an Open University Foundation Course. The first principle was that it should be *open* – i.e. that it should be accessible to intelligent people with no formal educational qualifications. The second was that it should prepare students for the second-level courses offered by the Faculty of Social Sciences, which include single-discipline courses in economics, geography, politics, psychology and sociology as well as interdisciplinary courses involving all five disciplines. The third principle was that the course should be genuinely interdisciplinary rather than multidisciplinary: this was indicated by saying that it would be primarily concerned to introduce social science rather than the social sciences. The general principles were built into a course structure covering thirty-two weeks of work for students.

We attempted to make the course genuinely open by adopting two strategies for the first three weeks of study. First, students start by considering several phenomena which are commonly regarded as social problems and which seem to the man in the street to be more relevant topics for study than do many of the concerns of social science theory. Second, we begin discussion of these issues in everyday language and only introduce the concepts and methods of social science as and when they are necessary to illuminate the problems. The main reason for adopting this strategy at the beginning of the course is that the literature of social science is at a different level of discourse from that of everyday discussion, even when the same subjects are being dealt with. Many beginning students find social science literature excessively abstract and vague about issues they consider important, as well as incomprehensible as a result of the use of technical terms and statistical calculations. This is, of course, a soluble problem inasmuch as the social science level of discussion can be mastered with a little effort. There is, however, a prior problem: to persuade students that the effort will be worthwhile. This is the main goal of the first three weeks of the course.

Although the analysis of social problems has advantages in suggesting relevance and generating interest, it has disadvantages in that it does not provide a systematic framework for the study of society as a whole. Because of these disadvantages, we rejected the 'problem' approach for the main body of the course.

The body of the course consists of twenty-five weeks' work. It divides into seven main parts. The topic of each of these parts is as indicated in Parts I–VII of this Reader. The seven parts attempt to provide a coherent structure to some of the most important topics covered by the social sciences without resorting to sections based on individual disciplines. We avoided a discipline-centred approach for two reasons. First, it would have had to be based on a number of abstract theoretical positions which cannot easily be grasped by beginning students and, second, it would have emphasized disciplinary structure at the cost of obscuring the links between individual disciplines and the ways of thinking which are common to all social sciences. Instead we have tried to give the course a continuous narrative based on practical ideas and to use it to introduce social science methods and to demonstrate disciplinary ideas in an interdisciplinary context. We have subdivided this narrative into seven parts, which we call dimensions. We use the term dimensions to emphasize that these are not exclusive topics with few links – that would be too much like a breakdown into disciplines. Instead, we stress that the dimensions cross-cut and intertwine in reality although we abstract and isolate them for convenience of study. We hope that this structure will demonstrate the essential unity of the social science disciplines in spite of their separation for the purposes of academic administration.

Our use of the term 'dimension' has evolved as the course has developed, and is rather unusual. An analogy may help to make our intentions clear. Imagine that we have the task of familiarizing people with a continent that contains at least five countries. Each country has its own history, way of life, dialect, institutions, literature and ideology. Each has a core territory, but some have large areas peopled by separatists. Worse, there are substantial areas where two or more countries claim jurisdiction, and other areas which are not claimed at all. How are we to communicate the nature of this continent? One option would be to provide maps which depicted the layout, together with descriptions of the areas differentiated on the maps. The problem would be that the maps, if simple, would not do justice to the reality, while if complex they would be readable only by specialists. Similarly, the descriptions would fail to convey the 'feel' of the countries and would tend to emphasize the difference between countries at the expense of the very real similarities. A preferable solution is to arrange a number of guided tours which allow foreigners to get the feel of the continent and to witness its variations for themselves. To give a reasonable picture, these tours must pass not only through the capital cities and beauty spots of the countries, but also through the small towns, industrial areas and frontier zones. If the tourists are to witness the way of life realistically, they need to acquire the rudiments of the languages spoken and get some idea of the problems which occupy the inhabitants of different areas. Once they have experienced these tours, they would be far better able to understand (and criticize) the maps and descriptions which are available and would be well placed to decide which countries they would prefer to live in for a time, or whether they would prefer more intense guided tours which range over the whole continent. The dimensions of this course are our guided tours of social science.

This analogy suggests that, in principle, the tours might be taken in any order. However, the need to learn sufficient of the local languages means that once the travel agents have worked out the programme, tourists would be well advised to follow it. Similarly with our dimensions: we might have ordered them differently but once the order was settled we built concepts and skills into the correspondence material in a roughly sequential way so that students of the course should follow the prescribed order. Other purchasers of the Reader may well choose their own sequence.

Towards the end of the course, we provide (in two weeks' work) short introductions to the individual disciplines of economics, geography, political science, psychology and sociology. These introductions are equivalent to the tourists looking at maps to see where they have been. In it we interpret the experience of the interdisciplinary narrative in disciplinary terms – pointing out that such and such a concern is peculiar to economists or that sociologists characteristically argue in this way, and so on.

The concluding part of the course (two weeks) takes up and makes explicit the theme of social change which runs through Parts I–VII of this Reader. The focus on social problems is used at the beginning of the course to highlight methods and areas of study which might contribute to an understanding of the problems. However, in common sense terms we expect consideration of problems to lead to likely solutions. When the problems are social, we are led to think about social change. The idea of social change comes out clearly in most of the seven dimensions. For example, 'Population, resources and technology' spotlights the future problems of overpopulation and resource depletion, 'Communication' and 'Production and allocation' spotlight phenomena which seem to cause social change, 'Power' is seen as involved not only in administering day to day life but in moulding the future. The last part of the course and this Reader, then, considers the major theme of social change. It underlines the importance of examining any contemporary society or aspect of it not in static terms but rather as a changing feature having a past and possible future. The point is to suggest to students that the systematic analysis and understanding of society has value because it enables one to perceive certain tendencies in present events and to make certain projections about the future. To equip men and women with an understanding of society enables them more effectively to change their society if they don't like what they see in their projections.

David Potter
Philip Sarre

The Open University
March 1974

Part I Population, resources and technology

Introduction

The first of seven dimensions of society dealt with in the course Making Sense of Society, and in this book, is a complex one made up of the interactions between population, resources and technology. This has been chosen as the first substantive content for a number of reasons. First, the size and distribution of population provides an introduction to the dramatis personae of society. Second, the technological level influences the kinds of activities which make up production and consumption and thus influences society. Third, the resource base does something to explain the current situation and constrain future developments. The fourth, and perhaps the most important immediate reason, is that the complex interaction between these three elements is a useful context in which to demonstrate some of the methods used by social scientists to analyse complex interrelationships. The fifth reason is that the study of population and technology lead inevitably to a consideration of social change in the past and future. Social change is a recurrent theme of the course and one which is taken up in Part VIII of this Reader.

Three weeks of student time are devoted to this discussion. The first sets the scene with a critical reading of C. M. Cipolla's *Economic History of World Population* and a mapping exercise. The next two weeks help students to move beyond this short overall survey through the adoption of a number of perspectives. In the course of this argument simple deterministic formulations – whether economic, technological or demographic – are criticized except insofar as they contribute to the development of multi-variate models. The analytical approaches considered range from Malthus's deductive method, through descriptive models like the 'demographic transition model' to Pearl's controlled experiments with the fruit fly. The most complex model considered is the system-model produced by Meadows *et al.* (1972). As a balance to the abstract material, three societies are examined as case studies. The intention is both to exemplify the stages of the demographic transition model and to show that real-world examples tend to contain far more variability and complexity than the best models. It is these case studies that are reproduced below. They concern a small-scale society, India in the late colonial period and Britain today.

Colin Turnbull's paper on the demography of small-scale societies deals mainly with a pygmy group, though with many cross-references to other societies. He uses the term small-scale societies because he is dissatisfied with other terms often used for groups of people living in relatively simple economies – simple societies, primitive societies, pre-industrial societies, for example. His paper is one piece of evidence that such small-scale societies have been able to achieve a kind of demographic balance with their environment. Given their particular technology, rain-forest environment, and their relations with neighbouring tribes, their customs have become adjusted to the prevailing health conditions, infant mortality and the like in such a way that their population remains steady and there is some sort of equilibrium.

Arthur Geddes's classic paper on the demographic geography of India towards the end of the British period is clearly very different in scale, bringing out contrasts within a subcontinent of 4 million square kilometres and hundreds of millions of people. In contrast with Turnbull's study, Geddes brings out particular aspects of a population evidently thrown out of demographic equilibrium and generally in a situation of rapid change. No doubt British rule in India was largely responsible. We need not pause to try to draw up a balance sheet of exploitation against benefits during the colonial phase, to see that there was sudden and enforced contact between local traditions and the European power and its technology and economy (themselves in a state of rapid movement and change). Nationalist and Marxist views would converge in pointing up ill-balanced and lopsided economic development during the period of Geddes's study. Of the contrasted demographic types Geddes recognized, his 'stagnation type' somewhat resembles the relative equilibrium in Turnbull's pygmy group. Indeed the map of areas of 'stagnation' covers some tribal territory in which somewhat comparable conditions were found. However, Geddes believed that a main factor was highly endemic malaria, that is, constantly present, as contrasted with epidemic malaria. Nonetheless, in regions of much more variable climate than that of the endemic malaria areas we find, in the period studied, Geddes's 'recurrent crisis type'. This is characterized by periods of rapid population increase, checked by periodic famine or epidemic (often of malaria, plague, cholera or influenza). This may be an alternative to the steady populations of 'stagnation' – or of Turnbull's small-scale societies. It is worth noting that 'stagnant' carries an implication of an undesirable state, like a stagnant and unattractive pool of water. Geddes deliberately chose this term. It is, to use a current phrase, value-laden. But he saw it in contrast to the term 'stable' often applied to any fairly steady population, and which he saw as carrying approval, and so also implying bias by the values held by our society. Geddes saw endemic malaria as a main factor in population 'stagnation' in densely peopled Hindu ricelands as well as in tribal country, and was reluctant to apply the term 'stability' to them. The disease then caused a very high infant mortality rate and a great deal of adult misery in these areas and he preferred to retain the term 'stability' for societies with low birth rates and low death rates. Our third case study is of our own society moving towards such a state.

The paper by Gilje and Gould has been chosen to complement discussion in the correspondence material of the 'demographic transition model'. This model presents the idea that economically developed societies with high standards of material living tend to move through the following stages, of course not excluding minor or even major fluctuations from these generalizations: 1. fairly steady population totals, with approximately equal and high births and deaths (and birth rates and death rates) roughly comparable to Geddes's 'stagnation type'; 2. a period of rapid population increase, with high birth rates and low death rates, comparable to those of nineteenth-century Britain or modern India (and some of Geddes's demographic regions, notably that of his 'high natural increase type'); 3. a period of renewed steadiness of population totals, characterized by low death rates and low birth rates, like that common in modern Britain and other developed countries – though subject to considerable fluctuations as economic circumstances and society's values change. In modern India only limited and on the whole exceptionally prosperous groups of the population show this kind of population trend. Gilje and Gould present alternative frameworks to those used by the census authorities for projection of future populations in England and Wales, and in particular for the Greater London area. They suggest that the population of England and Wales may cease to grow within a few decades, and show how this projection would modify the prediction for the rate of falling which, it is generally agreed, is likely in the population of the Greater London area.

Andrew Learmonth

Reference
MEADOWS, D. and others (1972) *The Limits to Growth* London, Pan Books.

1 Demography of small-scale societies

Colin M. Turnbull

This paper must necessarily take a limited form for two major reasons. Firstly, there simply is no adequate information upon which to base any detailed conclusions, and secondly, the data, such as they are, are not easily, if at all, quantifiable and are subject to a wide diversity of social forces that vary from society to society. While some answer is possible to the first problem, the second is inescapable and the best that can be done here is to point to the broad types of consideration that must be taken into account before any accurate assessment can be made of demography in small-scale societies.

The lack of reliable data does not mean, unfortunately, that there is also a lack of unreliable data. Assessments have too frequently been made without regard for the complex social forces at play, based on the surface appearance of populations and accepting too readily information provided by informants. Unfortunately, those in the best position to obtain more reliable data, based upon observation over a longer period of time and upon a deeper understanding of the various demographic forces at work, namely social and cultural anthropologists, have not traditionally seen much need for acquiring such data. As a social anthropologist myself I am very aware that our interests have led us in other directions, and that our time in the field tends to be occupied in trying to grapple with problems more directly related to those interests, and that it simply is not possible to devote the time to the kind of minute detail and data collection that would be required for effective demographic study. Happily, we are now increasingly aware of the intricate interplay between biological and social structure, and are more willing to cooperate and devote the time necessary for interdisciplinary work, without which our knowledge and understanding of human populations must remain, at best, partial. A few notable anthropologists are in fact devoting a major part of their energies in this direction, and it should be possible to encourage more. The major problem, then, remains the very nature of the data, and the complex social factors affecting demography in small-scale societies.

The term 'small-scale', though not entirely satisfactory, is greatly prefer-

TURNBULL, COLIN M. (1972) 'Demography of Small-scale Societies' in Harrison, G. A. and Boyce, A. J. (eds), *The Structure of Human Populations* Oxford, Clarendon Press, 283–312.

able to 'primitive', which not only has pejorative connotations but which also, even more seriously for us, has connotations of evolution and progress that, from a social standpoint, are often difficult or impossible to justify. The term is of particular importance here because of the implications of population size upon social structure. 'Pre-literate', equally if not more pejorative, indicates another facet of small-scale societies of importance to demographers, for in the absence of written records one has to gather the necessary information from census data, where available, from informants, and from on-the-spot observation. There are difficulties at every turn here, for among such populations there are frequently good reasons for avoiding giving accurate information to any census-taker, informants are notoriously willing to give the kind of answers that will please, and quick to discover just what that is, and even where this is not so, are nearly always under certain restrictions, arising from their own culture, that prevent them from providing certain classes of information. Further, with informants, there is the exceptionally difficult problem of translation, for terms such as are of the utmost significance to the demographer, and unequivocal in nature, often have no exact counterpart in the language of a small-scale society but may translate into a term representing a superficially similar category that, in fact, is radically different. Even such terms as 'family', and kinship terms such as 'father', 'mother', 'brother', and 'sister' will vary widely from society to society in the classes of people covered by such terms. Frequently they are not related at all, for in small-scale societies such terms primarily indicate social relationships rather than actual kinship relationships, the family (as we could conceive of it) merely serving as a model. In this way it is perfectly common for an informant to count several fathers, of whom some may even be female. The likelihood is, that in this case they would all be relatives on his father's side, and share the same kind of mutual obligations with him as his father. Similarly with nearly all kinship terms, they are essentially classificatory. To spell out the difference between different kinds of fathers or brothers or sisters or mothers would often either be forbidden, or considered the grossest breach of etiquette. Similarly, mention of names of the dead often is forbidden; even the fact of death in some cases may not be referred to. Thus trying to elicit, by mere question and answer, whether a woman has given birth to children that died during infancy or adolescence is frequently futile, and is likely to be worse, for in order to stop this undesirable line of questioning the woman, or the informant, will probably provide any figure that is likely to satisfy.

Families range, in the concepts of small-scale societies, from nuclear families to whole tribes, and in segmentary systems any individual will clearly define his family at three or four different levels according to the context, resolutely rejecting any other definition until the context changes. Marriage is another institution with wide variability in significance. For some, it takes place simply, as it does with us, by virtue of a ritual act. But often this act is prolonged over a period of days, weeks, months, or even years, and the marriage is not then considered final until the ritual is over, though the casual observer might consider it to have taken place on the first day if he judges just by outward appearances. With such passage of time divers rights are transferred from one group to the other, including rights to sexual intercourse, rights over children, and rights over property. Under some circumstances, a woman may address any of her husband's family as 'husband', for in the event of his death another will take his place, and perhaps even father children in the dead man's name. Sometimes a marriage is not considered effective until a child has been born and has lived beyond a certain period of time. Frequently a birth does not, so to speak, result in a child until, again, that child has shown that it has come to stay. He is then named, and assumes a social identity for the first time. If he were to die before naming there would be no way of remembering him, and no need to remember, for he had no identity. This custom of delaying the naming of a child, sometimes elaborated into the giving of a succession of names at different intervals, might in fact be of the utmost importance to a demographer as it is probably a fairly accurate gauge of the level and nature of infant and child mortality.

These, then, are some, and only a very few, of the kinds of problems to be faced in obtaining reliable demographic data, problems associated with the garnering of what, in other societies, would be the simplest and most unequivocal of facts. But when we come to consider the powerful social forces at work in affecting the structure of such a population then we face another kind of problem. Not only is there a great deal of variability from one society to another, as stated before, but there is the inescapable difficulty in any kind of quantitative assessment. How does one quantify belief, love, hate, hunger, or fear? These are just a few of the factors that come to mind as having potential significance in determining the demography of any small-scale population. Even to expect a simple rank-ordering may be asking too much, but the first step is plainly to set out what factors, as social anthropologists, we see as affecting population structure, leaving the issue of quantification for later study.

I propose, having attempted to give a broad outline of the nature of the problems, to illustrate in more detail a few of the major social factors involved, repeating only that there is an almost infinite variety of such factors.

Having done this, I will then briefly sketch one small-scale society rather more completely, to show how even in one society, allegedly one of the simplest in terms of social structure, there is great complexity. I have chosen the Mbuti pygmies for this, partly because they are best known to me, partly because as one of the few remaining viable hunting and gathering groups left in the world, and at the simplest end of the technological scale, they present not only the simplest form of social structure, but are exceptionally intimately connected with their physical environment, a factor I suggest of supreme importance with regard to the demography of almost any small-scale society, though in the case of the Mbuti we have an extreme (for references, see Turnbull 1965*a*, *b*, and *c*). I also mention, in less detail, a second society, that of the Ik of northern Uganda, who until recently were hunters and gatherers but became caught up in political change, including an enforced change of environment which has led to their decimation to the point where, once again, they are able to maintain a precarious balance with their new ecological setting.

From such sketchy information it would be presumptuous to draw conclusions, so none are drawn. The objective is merely to point to some of the factors involved, and to the very real need for much closer co-operation than has hitherto been fashionable between members of different disciplines. While mentioning other aspects, I will concentrate on environmental factors and on the problem of mobility, both social and spatial. Professor L. L. Cavalli-Sforza and his colleagues have done by far the most intensive and significant, and the most recent, physiological and genetic studies among African pygmies and neighbouring populations (see, for example, Cavalli-Sforza, Zonta, Nuzzo, Bernini, De Jong, Meera Khan, Ray, Went, Siniscalco, Nijenhuis, Van Loghem, and Modiano 1969). Similarly, Lee and De Vore have been working intensively among the South African Bushmen, also hunters and gatherers. For the Ik, unfortunately, there is no published information available at all, and my own study is not likely to be in print for over a year yet. (For descriptive analyses of other African tribal groups see Gibbs 1965.)

Environmental considerations

Any experience of small-scale societies creates a strong sense of an intimate and dynamic interplay between the two (physical and social) aspects of life, with a good deal of adaptiveness on both sides. This is partly a function of population size, and partly, perhaps even more directly, a function of the limited technology. Such societies tend to be adaptive rather than dominant, and react sensitively to even minute environmental changes. While this is particularly true for hunters and gatherers, it is almost equally true for pastoralists, and is still of prime importance among the technologically more advanced cultivators.

A general observation might be made here concerning the influence of environment on small-scale population structure. At the relatively simple technological level of such societies there is a close response to environmental influence in terms of domestic (including kinship) organization, economy, political and religious structure, and systems of beliefs and values. It is a widespread fact among such societies that the totality of human experience is closely integrated into a single system of thought and the objective of that system, if one can properly talk of objective, is survival of the society as such. Among many pastoral peoples, for instance, dispute resolution ranks equally and is closely integrated with care of and consideration for cattle, with the whole value system which pivots around cattle and pasture and water, with the consequent pattern of domestic organization, and is ultimately sanctioned by a system of religious belief that encourages the most all-round satisfactory utilization of the environment, including among the fauna and flora the neighbouring human populations and their lands and produce.

The Mbuti pygmies are perhaps one of the clearest examples of the environmental potential, but rather than being considered as an exceptional example their case might well serve as a basis for an examination of similar potential elsewhere. While they can survive, in a physical sense, outside their forest environment, that is about all they can do, if even that. The psychological shock, for some, can be fatal, as can the inadequacy of a sense of hygiene that was perfectly adequate in the forest. But equally significant for the demographer, surely, is the almost total breakdown of a morality that in the forest context contributed strongly towards an effective form of birth control, maintaining the population size in sensitive response to environmental considerations. But this morality, like all aspects of social life, was closely interwoven with the other aspects, and centred around the clear recognition by the Mbuti of their dependence upon, and intimate relationship with, the forest. Thus their forest morality had for them no significance the moment they stepped into one of the cleared enclaves cut from the forest by the village farmers. Any permanent settlement of pygmies in or near such enclaves, as being constantly proposed by divers governments, would have immeasurable demographic consequences.

Similarly with the Ik, whose relationship with their environment is different but none the less intense and intimate, their environmental conditioning has led them, in one generation, to the verge of total extinction despite a remarkable versatility and adaptability and willingness to change in all respects except in the one respect of location in their mountain environment. This was brought on by what seemed at the time an insignificant restriction on their nomadic pattern, coupled with a psychological inability to support life in the flat plains below their homeland.

Simplistic environmental determinism and the reaction against it has unfortunately obscured the subtle realities of man's relationship with the world around him, and examples of extreme cases, such as those, could well be used as springboards for the examination of urban, suburban, or rural environments in other, more complex societies, with every likelihood of discovering forces at work affecting the demography of such populations. With a more complex technology, obviously, man is able to alter and control his environment and adapt it to his will to a very great extent. This does not necessarily minimize his relationship with that environment, and it certainly does not remove the environment as a factor of major importance.

The absence of a complex technology brings other, perhaps more profound, skills into play, and calls for a flexibility of social organization perhaps only possible in small-scale societies. Above all, it encourages maximal use of the environment, and frequently causes systematic redistribution of populations and, I suspect, necessitates divers forms of population (size) control. One of the prime factors in many small-scale societies is mobility, in its widest sense. This is essential for economic reasons as well as political ones, and of course is of major concern to any demographer. I shall deal with mobility in more detail when discussing the Mbuti pygmies, but here it is worth pointing to certain forms of spatial population movement characteristic of different types of primitive society, each with different demographic implications.

Spatial movement among small-scale societies

For the demographer, as for the social anthropologist, it is not so much the quantity of movement but rather its quality that is important. Movement of any kind creates specific problems of social organization, and any changes in nomadic patterns result in changes in organization. Sometimes, as with the Ik, a slight change can result in a major shift in social organization and have drastic demographic consequences (Turnbull 1972). Movement is an essential part of nearly all small-scale societies, even of cultivators, though if measured in mere terms of distance it may seem insignificant. It creates, amongst other problems, problems of social control, and may well result in division of labour along lines of sex and age that have obvious demographic significance. I will give a brief example of the age factor but first wish to mention two types of population movement most characteristic of small-scale societies. The two types of movement referred to are nomadism and transhumance, and with regard to the latter I should say that the usage of the term by social anthropologists does not exactly correspond to its usage by geographers, but in essence remains the same. It is a form of seasonal migration of a population (or part of it) with its flocks or herds, in response to a variety of environmental conditions. But whereas for the geographer, altitude is of special importance, transhumance, for the anthropologist, also takes place horizontally, as with the Nilotic cattle herders, and the Fulani cattle herders of West Africa. The significance of transhumance remains in its essentially seasonal nature.

Nomadism is by no means the free, unpredictable, spontaneous form of movement it is sometimes said to be. A characteristic of hunting and gathering populations, nomadism obviously occurs within restricted areas, is frequently cyclic (particularly where there are marked seasonal variations), and even where it appears to be most haphazard can sometimes be shown not only to have a logic of its own, but to correspond to relatively predictable and limited movements of game. An area that contains a nomadic population might be exploited evenly by the total population, or it might be divided into territories each of which has its own nomadic cycle and contains its own nomadic sub-population. In the latter case, however, the sub-population is not necessarily stable in composition; it may be the territory that is fixed rather than the population, which may move from territory to territory as the bands undergo the process of fission and fusion. These are plainly different forms of nomadism each with different significance for the demographer as for the social anthropologist. The Mbuti pygmies whom we shall be considering, exemplify the greatest degree of mobility, each band being in a constant state of flux. Yet this fact could only be ascertained by living in one small hunting territory throughout a continuous period of twelve months and observing not only the nomadic pattern of the band, but the ever changing composition of the population. At any given moment it would have presented to an acute observer a picture of much greater stability than was in fact the case and we may suspect the same is true of other hunting-and-gathering peoples.

Transhumance, a pattern of movement characteristic of cattle herders, is more fixed in that there is generally a given starting place and a given finishing place for each leg of the back-and-forth movement. It is more predictable in that it usually corresponds to seasonal fluctuations in the availability of water and pasture. It is more stable in that while transhumant populations are often divided into sub-groups which, like the hunting band, are subject constantly to the process of fission and fusion, the process follows a lineal pattern of segmentation, and is associated with a unilineal kinship system unlike that of most hunters. During the annual cycle, then, while there is a waxing and waning of the size of the herding units, the social horizons are only temporarily altered, returning eventually to the same point. Just as the Mbuti are a clear example of the extreme flux to be found amongst hunters, so are the Nuer, of the southern Sudan, a clear example of the segmentary system and transhumance associated with cattle herding (Evans-Pritchard 1968). While during the wet season the Nuer live in isolated vilages, with communications sometimes reduced to nil by flood waters, the people of these villages, linked in innumerable associations, come together in ever increasing numbers as they herd the cattle further and further away during the dry season. At the height of the dry season the Nuer are grouped together, not in isolated villages, but in a series of large cattle camps, the composition of which, each year, is almost as predictable as that of the villages during the wet season.

The Fulani of West Africa have a similar transhumant pattern, though for them the wet season is the time for assembly in maximal groupings (Stenning 1959, 1965). But the Fulani also exhibit another form of movement, which Stenning calls '*migratory drift*'. The Fulani movement is a north/south one, and is relatively stable from one year to the next, but a diversity of conditions, ecological and political, sometimes cause a sideways shift to east or west of the total transhumant population. While this does not affect relationships within the population, it does affect relationships between that population and neighbouring ones. The drift may also, though less often, be northward or southward. Under extreme conditions the Fulani transhumant population migrates in a single, dramatic shift. Again, at any given moment, or even over a respectable period of time, say a whole year, it would be easy to misinterpret the situation as being much more stable than it actually is. Since many field studies cover only a single year, and few are conducted for a continuous period of more than two years, added to which there is not always an opportunity for remaining throughout with one single sub-group (a method that has its obvious disadvantages just as it has obvious advantages), it is plain that we do not have the facts we need. Small-scale societies that practise agriculture have on the whole been much better studied, and the data of demographic significance are more likely to be reliable. Such populations are, of course, more stable still, though by no means always as sedentary as might be expected. In the absence of the clear ecological forces that demand population movement, other forces come into play achieving at least something of the same effect.

One important corollary of the agricultural level of organization in small-scale societies is that, due to its semi-sedentary nature, a much more complex form of social control is necessitated resulting in the division of the population into a diversity of sub-groupings which may be domestic (kinship), economic, political or religious. These sub-groupings may be associated with rules of either exogamy or endogamy, the most common examples being the various lineal descent groups, class and caste groups such as nobility, which is usually hereditary, or specialized occupational castes such as black-smithing, wood-carving, ivory-working, judgement-giving, which may also be hereditary. Marital mobility, in such a relatively complex society may further be restricted by religious and political sub-groupings and, a prime factor much neglected, residential or territorial groupings (which are sometimes so important as to override other considerations, the spatial relationship plainly being more important than that of kinship which in any case is frequently hypothetical or fictional).

Spatial movement and age grouping

While in nearly all small-scale societies age is an important and vital sub-division of the population, its importance being witnessed by the elaborate rites of entry and exit, age grouping assumes special significance when related to population movement. The necessarily fissile, segmentary nature of transhumant populations calls for some kind of mechanism for balancing the tendency to fission with some kind of tendency to fusion. This is essential for social purposes, and is sometimes also necessary for military purposes (defence), though this aspect has probably been overplayed. None the less, the social, economic, political, and religious needs, any one of them, are enough to bring about the phenomenon of age grouping. The clearest examples known to me may be found among the East African cattle herders where social horizons are, to a great extent, sealed at or near puberty, having to all intents been predetermined by the date of birth. This is of particular significance for demographic purposes when it is ordained that mates shall be found within specific age-sets, or sub-sets (i.e. those who have been initiated during a given year or period), or taken from specific age-levels (i.e. youth, adolescence, early adulthood). The number of levels (or grades or groups, as they are sometimes called) varies from tribe to tribe, as does the duration of the initiation period during which individuals become age-mates in the same set. Once the set is closed, the horizons are

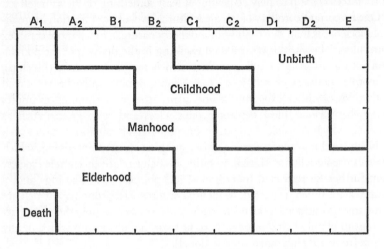

Fig. 1   Scheme of a system of age-sets in which each set is divided into two sub-sets. There are three age levels. Time is shown along the horizontal axis in five-year periods.

sealed, just as the individual family is when the parents no longer produce (or adopt) children. In such societies this social age (for there is sometimes a fair degree of flexibility designed to allow for the precocious child as well as for the backward one) becomes a major factor, in conjunction with territory, in determining the approved direction of marriage.

A generalized example is here offered, of a type of age-set system that, while it rigidly divides the population into sets, each of which is subdivided into two sub-sets, still takes care to allow for an overlapping of age levels so that each set is allowed a brief period of fraternization (and possibility of inter-marriage) with the set on either side of it. There are three basic age levels: childhood, manhood, and elderhood. Initiation marks the entry to manhood, a period which lasts from ten to fifteen years, and during which fraternization with the senior and junior sets may take place according to the scheme shown in figure 1. The horizontal scale, for simplicity, is in five-year periods; the vertical scale simply denotes the passage from childhood, through manhood, into old age. Thus, when the first subdivision of A age-set, A_1, is initiated, they enter manhood and live as age-brothers for five years before the second half of the set, A_2, is initiated. During those five initial years they were the junior men (*moran* is a common East African term) sharing the responsibilities of manhood with the previous set, who instructed them, and dropped out into elderhood as soon as A_2 was initiated. Thus, members of A_1 shared the same quarters as members of the previous set, and had access to their sisters, but A_2 did not. After a further five years, however, B_1 are initiated, and both A_1 and A_2 fraternize with that sub-set until they jointly drop out, as a unified set A, on the initiation of B_2.

During manhood the men live in special quarters, attended by their sisters, who become the lovers of other men whom they marry when the set passes into elderhood. Women are sometimes initiated into parallel sets, similarly organized.

A less formal variant is found among the Nyakyusa of Zambia, where at puberty boys leave their natal village and begin building villages of their own, into which they introduce their girl-friends as wives, 'closing' the village after a given period. It is not clear, however, along exactly what lines boys choose their village mates, male or female, but we have the clear establishment of what Wilson calls 'age villages'.

One more type of age-set system should be mentioned, which is cyclic rather than linear. In the linear system, when an age-set dies out, its name and identity die with it. In the cyclic systems the names recur, sometimes almost immediately (in which case those of age-set A who are in the old-age level, and are about to die, see children being born who, at puberty, they know will be initiated into a new A set, or into a 'shadow A' set) or sometimes after a generation has passed. In any case, the members of sets in such a system believe in a form of re-birth, and although once again the data are inadequate it would be reasonable to suppose that this might have demographic consequences. A man might, for instance, desire to have children that will be born into or initiated into a specific set or sets. Such a system is shown in figure 2.

Even in the much less complex societies, such as those of hunters and gatherers, age and residence are major factors in social organization, ranking equally and sometimes more importantly than kinship, and notions of relative age frequently are linked with mating patterns in sometimes unexpected ways. In northern Nigeria, for instance, among some of the non-Muslim tribes, there is the unusual situation in which biological motherhood is of such little significance (in organizational terms) that few men know who their mothers are. Very shortly after giving birth women leave their husbands, who have a plurality of wives in succession. The children are left with the father, and know only their foster-mothers. There is marked unconcern about the possibility of incest, which is recognized as being perfectly possible, and against which the only operative rule is an indirect one which discourages but does not prevent sexual relations between young men and older women. Such liaisons, however, are considered

Fig. 2   Scheme of a cyclic system of age-sets. Outer circle denotes fixed levels; inner circle, revolving sets.

by some as rather dashing. When questioned as to whether it would be more or less dashing if the woman turned out to be her lover's mother, the men's reaction is 'only if she is older' . . . in other words the criterion is solely one of age, even in the face of possible mother/son incest.

Another example of practised mother/son incest, known to me in my limited experience, can be found in northern Kenya and northern Uganda. Women anxious to acquire supernatural powers attempt to do so by forcing their own sons to have sexual intercourse with them. Brother/sister incest of the kind practised in ancient Egypt is relatively widespread in sub-Saharan Africa among people with comparable systems of kinship. Under those same conditions political considerations frequently compel the royal line to marry out into neighbouring populations. In some cases marriage boundaries are fixed (and followed) for the total population, in other cases they may be fixed only for a segment of the population, and in many cases, whether they are geographical, linguistic, religious, social, or kinship boundaries, they are, even within the same population, essentially flexible, serving as little more than temporary conveniences. What a population practises today is by no means necessarily an example of what it practised yesterday.

Birth control

There are many social factors affecting and controlling birth rate, some directly, some indirectly. Some, by their bizarre appearance or more obvious, superficial purpose, are not always recognized as such mechanisms. The marriage of young girls to old men, which may have a diversity of functions, may also have the effect of keeping a potential child-rearer out of action for a number of years. It may be as well to mention the fact, well enough known by now, but again perhaps of wider extent than is sometimes supposed, that polygyny does not always by any means involve childbirth; as an institution, it is frequently a way of taking care of widows, of barren women, or of young women whom it is desired to secure for the younger generation (in which case it is more a form of betrothal, via the prospective groom's father or older brother, rather than of marriage). Unfortunately, the term 'marriage' does not have the same connotations in all societies, yet is frequently used without adequate clarification as to the function of the union, which may be quite other than the rearing of children.

Similarly little discussed is homosexuality as a means of birth control which is practised among small-scale societies, usually in conjunction with various ritual taboos on sexual intercourse with women. The clearest examples of this, perhaps, come from South America, where among many of the Indian tribes the living quarters are divided into male and female sections, the women with their young children living apart from the men, and the men being sub-divided into small groups of half a dozen or so who are, in a sense, endogamous – that is, adult males of each sub-group, within its own sleeping quarters, practise homosexual intercourse with each other, but not across the partitions that divide them either from the other males or from the females. It is only when weaning is complete (again, as among the Mbuti, frequently a lengthy period of up to three years) that a man may again have sexual intercourse with his wife, until she becomes pregnant, when he rejoins his homosexual sub-group. These sub-groups act as hunting units and as divisions of warring parties, and are considered as held together by this bond, which also binds them together by strong affective bonds, and makes for a tightly knit overall society. The Mbuti do not practise this form of homosexuality, though youths and men frequently sleep together around a camp fire and openly derive mild erotic satisfaction from the physical contact. In purely affective terms, probably most African societies, if not indeed most small-scale societies, may be said to be strongly homosexual, men looking to other men for companionship, and women to women, without precluding a different quality of affective relationship between men and their wives. The close bonds between men, the often vigorous activities they undertake together (particularly drinking and dancing), and the festivals they must attend that exclude women, all contribute to a reduction in the amount of sexual intercourse that can take place between man and wife, and life in a small-scale society is frequently full of such activity. One may suspect that among some peoples institutionalized warfare or raiding serve a similar function, frequently being accompanied by periods of a month or longer during which sexual intercourse is taboo, 'to make the men strong'.

The Ituri population

In many instances, it is even difficult to decide just what constitutes a 'population' in either biological or sociological terms. Even where neighbouring populations appear to be distinct by every criterion, including physical type, we should be careful in drawing our population boundaries, for each may prove to be part of a more complex network of interconnected (and interbreeding) populations. Such is the situation in the Ituri Forest, an area of some 50,000 square miles in the north-east corner of the Congo (Kinshasa), with a total population of some 100,000.

This population, which sees itself as an interacting group of sub-populations, and feels a common identity at least by virtue of its common occupation of a distinctive territory, consists of about 40,000 Mbuti pygmies, who are nomadic hunters and gatherers, and some 60,000 semi-sedentary slash-and-burn non-pygmy African farmers and fishers, to whom I refer generally as 'villagers'. The figures are very approximate; they refer to pre-independence times, and recent civil disturbances have resulted in a reduction of the population by anything up to 50 per cent. At first sight the total population seems to be further subdivided, both the pygmy and the villager segments, into smaller discrete sub-populations, each separated from the others in terms of territory, history, culture (including major linguistic divisions), and physical type. The pygmies are apparently physically homogenous, but are differentiated in terms of economy, nomadic pattern, language, and in the nature of their relationship with their villager neighbours; their territories are similarly distinct.

The villagers are similarly divided, but into many more groups, distributed as if in a vast circle which, apart from its southern sector, runs around the periphery of the forest. The distribution is strictly linear, with one or two minor exceptions, each tribal group having only two neighbours, one at each extremity, but all of them sharing in common the total pygmy population which occupies the central forest proper. To the south lies a vast stretch of allegedly uninhabited forest (certainly there are no farmers there, and there are no signs of any substantial pygmy population); to east, west, and north the forest thins out rapidly or changes abruptly into grassland. Some of the villagers are Bantu-speaking, others are Sudanic-speaking; correspondingly some of them do circumcise and some do not, and on that count alone there should be no interbreeding and no gene flow. Some came in from the north-west, some from the south, some from the east, some from the north-east; some arrived in the approximate area almost as much as 1,000 years ago, but the bulk (in the south, east, and north-east) are recent immigrants, dating back perhaps not much more than 200 years, with a few stragglers still arriving. The Mbuti are the original inhabitants, beyond doubt, and can be dated back as far as nearly 5,000 years by the historic documentation of the ancient Egyptians.

Other barriers than size, such as cultural and linguistic, at first sight should also in themselves be enough to prevent interbreeding, and the economic situation is such that each group is self-sufficient so there is no need for trade, just as there is ample land so there is no need for aggression. In the midst of this heterogeneity the Mbuti seem to preserve a remarkable homogeneity. They adopt many of the outward customs of their neighbours but not the rules that go with them. Thus, those in the north-east do not circumcise, whereas those in the south and west do, but that does not prevent inter-marriage between those pygmies. And while there is a limited amount of intermarriage with all the villager groups, it maintains a single outward direction, village males taking pygmy females, the offspring of which are said (and seem) to never to return to the forest, but remain, with their offspring, as villagers. Thus the pygmy population contributes to the village gene pools, but is not itself affected. By their central location, their high degree of mobility, and the extremely fluid nature of their band com-

position, the pygmies actually create political links between village populations that are not adjacent, and effectively enlarge social horizons in a way
that, to my certain but again limited knowledge, leads to some inter-
marriage 'across' the forest.

The diagrams (figs 3 and 4) represent the general manner in which the

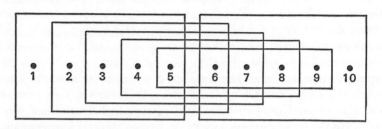

Fig. 3 Plan of Bira villages, showing the market/initiation/marriage horizon of each
one.

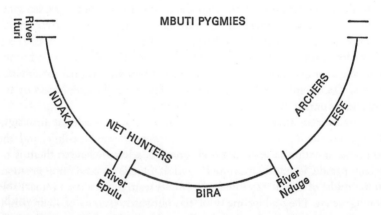

Fig. 4 Plan of the Ndaka/Bira/Lese segment of the village circle.

village populations are distributed, and in which intermarriage within these
technically endogamous tribal units takes place; the noteworthy thing being that at the extremities, as might be expected, the marital horizons are
more limited than in the centre, but at the extremities certain overlappings
of a cultural nature (shared initiations, for instance) are matched by overlapping pygmy bands, and by inter-tribal marriage. Thus the circle is com-

plete, and not divided into truly discrete segments, and instead of a number of isolated populations we get a series of overlapping populations. In terms of distance, marital horizons are limited to market horizons; villages sharing markets share initiations and share wives. This is usually about five villages, but although village 1 does not market at village 9, its horizons extend as far as that, since both market, and may meet, at village 5. One of the prime functions of markets, in an area where each village is economically independent, is to provide for courtship.

The diagrams, of course, are an over-simplification of the actual situation, but represent accurately enough the system which pertained until the post-colonial disorders in the north-eastern Congo. Although the villagers all practised a method of cultivation that necessitated their shifting their plantations every three years, and their villages every nine years, their relative position on the circumference of the circle remained the same, and each village could be regarded as a patrilineage since marriage was patrilocal (the wife taking up residence in her husband's village) and descent patrilineal (the children inheriting clan membership, status, and wealth mainly from their father). Each village of any size, however, while still retaining its lineal character, tended to incorporate several other subordinate (in that village) lineal groupings, introduced either by marriage for purposes of economy or politics, or by necessity (such as the need for a blacksmith or some other specialist), in this latter case marriage with someone from the dominant lineage nearly always sealing the arrangement. Such accretions were seldom permanent, or significant in terms of marital mobility, for members of a small subordinate lineal group tended to continue to participate in the initiations and marital circles of the village where their lineage was dominant.

By contrast with this regularity, the Mbuti pygmies, who live within the circle, are in a constant state of flux. At first sight, their organization corresponds to that of the villagers, for radiating outwards from a central neutral territory are the various hunting territories of the 250 or so bands into which the total population of about 40,000 is evenly divided. The appearance is heightened by the system, which I have described elsewhere (Turnbull 1965a), whereby the pygmies deliberately lend credence to the villager belief that each hunting territory is populated by a patrilineal band, constituted under the kind of patrilineal/patrilocal organization practised by the villagers. This deception is an integral and vital part of the mechanism by which the two potentially hostile populations maintain a well ordered and peaceful relationship.

The reality, however, is that only the territorial boundaries are fixed (and

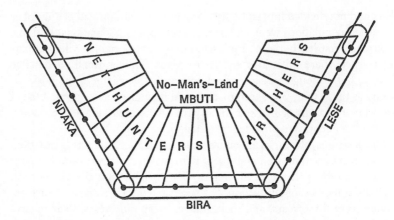

Fig. 5 Schematic relationship of hunting territories to villages. Each village and territory marked represents about five. Whereas each segment represents a marriage circle for the villagers, it has no such significance for the Mbuti. The diagram similarly defines the spatial mobility of the villagers, but not of the Mbuti.

I really have no certainty that even these are fixed beyond the limits of my own experience, which covers three field trips to the same area between 1951 and 1958). The population within each territory is very definitely bilateral, a system that allows for maximum mobility, and changes with every monthly shift of camp, and even within the duration of any one camp. Figures 5 and 6 give an idea of the territorial divisions of the Mbuti, and how they correspond to the village distribution, and of the internal fluctuations that take place within any one territory during the course of a year.

With reference to figure 6, although this is the typical pattern for a net-hunting group, an almost identical pattern of fission and fusion pertains for the archers. The major difference is that whereas for the bulk of the year the net-hunters live in relatively large-sized bands or sub-bands (six or seven nets, which is to say six or seven nuclear families, is a minimum for a successful net hunt, thirty is a maximum), splitting up into smaller units only for the honey season, the reverse is true of the archers, who for the bulk of the year live in small sub-bands, the total population for the territory uniting only during the honey season.

The change in the size of the camps is about all that can be predicted, the composition of the population is entirely unpredictable, since one major function of this process is dispute resolution, and such movement is spon-

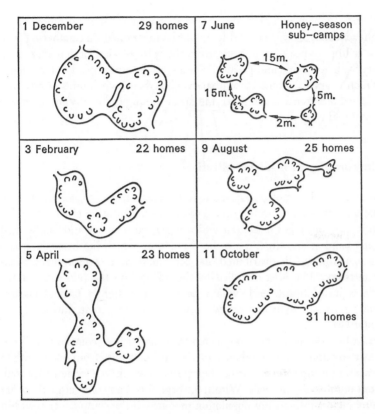

Fig. 6 Monthly fluctuations of band size and distribution within a net-hunting territory over a period of twelve months. The evident clusterings of homes within any camp do not necessarily correspond to kinship ties, but rather to bonds of friendship and cooperation.

taneous, responding to political as well as economic needs of the moment. However, men in particular come to regard certain territories (two or three) as 'theirs'; a very few spend the major part of their life in one or other of these 'home' territories. There is a sentimental attachment, but also the practical consideration that these are areas that they know best, in all the intimate ecological detail so vital to successful hunting and gathering. They are usually areas in which they grew up as children. There is, then, a slight tendency to patrilocality, for hunting conditions are more particular than gathering, which is largely the province of women. It is no more than a slight tendency, however, and it should be mentioned that gathering is of greater importance than hunting from the point of view of general sustenance. Such economic and political considerations are coupled to a tendency for men to marry women from bands other than their 'home' bands, and the stated preference is for 'marrying far', meaning spatial distance, but also implying kinship distance.

Demography of the Ituri Mbuti

Out of the total area of 50,000 square miles, about 10,000–15,000 can be said to be a no-man's-land in the centre of the overall hunting circle, in which hunting seldom takes place, but which is neutral territory and can be used by any band at any time. Thus the population, which lies between 35,000 and 40,000 Mbuti, is distributed one per square mile of recognized hunting territory. The area occupied by the villages on the periphery of the circle is insignificant, each village being a tiny, tightly packed enclave usually no more than one or two square miles in extent, including the plantations.

Each hunting territory is populated by a band whose composition is not likely to retain much more than a 40 per cent continuity from one month to the next, hunting camps shifting their position within the territory approximately at monthly intervals. Within the brief life of any one camp, there are several factors influencing population mobility. If the camp is near (within a day's return walk) to the village, individuals or families might well move radially out and back, sometimes staying overnight or even a few days. This is of little demographic significance, since the only other Mbuti they are likely to meet in that village at that time are those who constitute the band from which they came, at that moment. Mbuti may, but seldom do, move from a given hunting territory directly to a village associated with another hunting territory. If they wish to do that, they first move laterally from their own hunting territory to the other, joining that band, as a member of which they then visit the new village. However, it is during these individual visits to villages that courtship leading to mating between a village male and a pygmy female may take place, rather than when an entire band descends and settles for a week or so on the edge of the village, as it may do two or three times each year.

Any move, individual or group, from hunting camp to village may be prompted by a variety of factors. The simple desire for trade is one, though not as important as has been supposed, for any interdependence between village and forest is voluntary, a question of convenience rather than necessity. More frequently Mbuti simply feel the need of a holiday from the rigours of hunting, and when weather is bad and hunting poor then the whole band may decide to give up hunting for a week and visit the village *en masse*. During such mass visits, however, they fraternize less with the villagers than during the individual visits. Another cause may be disputation within the camp, which is most commonly resolved, if it reaches major proportions, by one party or the other leaving, either going to another territory or to the village. Sometimes if an entire camp is torn by dispute (though this generally coincides with bad weather) it will decide to take its 'noise' to the village, which is considered a proper place for 'noise' whereas 'quiet' is the ideal value associated with the forest.

Apart from moves to and from the village, the band moves about month to month within its territory, changing its composition each time. There is a basic economic necessity for this, since after a month the game gets scared away from the vicinity of a camp, the vegetable foods are gathered out and have to be fetched from an inconveniently great distance, and Mbuti sanitation is such that much longer in any one camp would tend to be unhealthy. The moves are all within the territory, and usually each camp is a full day's march from the last, that being adequate to ensure ample supplies of game and vegetable produce.

As seen in figure 6, the size of a net-hunting camp remains fairly constant throughout the bulk of the year, but towards the honey season it begins to break up into smaller sub-camps which at the height of the season may be 15 miles from each other (an easy day's march). The total population within the territory, however, remains basically unaffected in terms of size.

If an adjacent or nearby territory for some reason becomes unfavourable to hunting, the band there will reduce itself in size to whatever size can be supported, the others going to join other bands. Similarly, a territory where the hunting is particularly good is likely to attract more members. Such fluctuations are temporary, the game and vegetable supply throughout the forest is remarkably even from one end of the year to the next. However, net hunting requires a minimum of 7 nets, and above 30 nets the hunt becomes cumbersome. Only married men may have nets, so a net may be said to correspond to a nuclear family, and the size of a net-hunting band must be between 7 and 30 families. A 'family' seems to average out at about 5 and may comprise parents and unmarried children, and sometimes visiting children, and sometimes widowed grandparents.

Archer bands undergo essentially the same process, but since they can hunt best in small numbers, remain fragmented into small sub-bands for most of the year, coming together at the honey season for the communal *begbe* hunt which requires maximum strength, usually about 30 families, never less than 20.

The honey season is said to be a time of year when vegetable produce is most plentiful, though in fact it is abundant throughout the year. The net-hunting ban takes advantage of this one seasonal event, the availability of honey, to split up into tiny groups and so get relief from all the tensions that build up in the larger, tightly cooperative camps. It is noteworthy that sibling unity seems to have little value for the Mbuti, and the honey season as frequently as not sees brothers go in opposite directions. Food-gathering compatibility is a much stronger factor in determining residence, far above kinship in importance.

The archers evidently feel the need to assert their unity, having been split up for the bulk of the year, and all those in a given territory join together during the honey season for the *begbe* hunt, a beat which requires the men and youths to form a tight but large semi-circle while the women and children beat the game into the arc, hence the necessity for large numbers. But again kinship plays little part, it is rather those that happen to be in any territory at the time of *begbe* who are expected to participate; in other words it is the territory that is considered of importance, rather than the population it contains. This is seen in other realms of Mbuti life, even the most sacred festivals, *elima* and *molimo*, demand participation (in the latter case under threat of death for failure to participate) on grounds of presence within the territory where the girl's initiation or the death ceremony is being held, quite regardless of any kinship consideration.

Movement from one territory to another is plainly of more importance. To some extent this is associated with the monthly displacements of each camp within its own territory, for this is the moment at which individuals decide to go and visit another band, either to escape the 'noise' of a dispute, or simply for the sake of seeing old friends and relatives, or, if a youth, for courtship. Trespass, brought on by pursuing game across territorial boundaries, occurs but is of no demographic significance. Families often exchange visits (sometimes simultaneously, so that the total number of nets is not affected, amongst net-hunters) and generally for purely personal reasons. This serves the same function as the market does for the villagers, it enlarges social horizons and gives youths a chance to find suitable mates. Marriage with someone whose home territory is adjacent is generally discouraged, since it limits rather than expands the social horizons. A gap of several territories is preferred, though not too frequently across the central neutral area (possibly due to the different hunting techniques, spear to the north, net west and south, bow and arrow in the east).

The only stated marriage restriction is against marrying anyone 'related on either side', but given the short genealogical memory of the Mbuti this only effectively excludes first cousins. The only stated preference is equally general, for 'marrying far', meaning several territories distant. There is a fairly widespread custom of sister-exchange, whereby a man is expected to provide a classificatory sister for his wife's classificatory brother, but the classification is so general that the custom has little significance other than as yet another mechanism for setting up a complex system of inter-familial and inter-territorial relationships that can be utilized or ignored according to the needs of the moment. The net result, however, is that almost any Mbuti can find one such relationship to invoke in almost every other territory, should it suit him to move there, temporarily or permanently. It is habitual for each hunter, with his wife and possibly with his unmarried children, to exercise their rights in at least four or five other territories ranging up to ten territories on either side of his home territory, and sometimes across the neutral area. But whereas the net hunter is versed in archery, and can readily join an archer band in the east, the archer, not possessing a net, is at a disadvantage in net-hunting territory unless there is a net (or a sick man, for instance) for him to use, or unless he is content with a junior role. Youths, male and female, frequently travel on their own for purposes of courtship, though there is nothing to prevent courtship and marriage within any one camp, since there are nearly always a number of 'stranger' families present, perhaps specifically with the purpose of effecting a marriage.

Life crises: birth, adolescence, marriage, and death

The villagers state categorically that Mbuti women are more fertile than their own women, and give this as one reason for seeking intermarriage. Other reasons, economic and political, can be suspected in addition, but there is the undoubted fact that venereal disease is rampant amongst the villagers and almost totally absent among the Mbuti, so there may be some truth to the belief. It may also be that the infant mortality rate is lower among the Mbuti, resulting in an appearance of higher birth rate. On the other hand, the Mbuti practise birth control, whereas to the best of my knowledge the villagers do not.

Birth

There is no anxiety, among the Mbuti, over birth; it is treated as a normal event. Each woman will follow her own inclinations as to food restrictions and hunting restrictions, but most continue to hunt and gather with the band until the day of delivery, and it is not uncommon for women to give birth while on the hunt, pausing only for a couple of hours before returning to camp with the infant. It is not possible here to go into details of child-birth and child care; my knowledge is in any case limited, but I have observed great attention paid to post-natal care and my general impression certainly confirms the belief shared by the villagers and Mbuti that Mbuti children have a far better chance of survival than villagers. There are no reliable data on fertility or fecundity, nor on sex ratio. But there is definitely no evidence of infanticide, except in the case of monsters; stillbirths are evidently extremely rare, and yet according to Patrick Putnam, who lived in the Ituri for a quarter of a century and ran a hospital there, the population shows no sign of increase. This implies very clearly that there is some indigenous form of birth control.

The husband comes under important restrictions immediately following the birth of a child to his wife. Until that moment, he has been under no restrictions concerning sexual intercourse; some hold that during pregnancy it hurries matters along, and that towards the end it merely becomes 'uncomfortable'. Immediately following birth, the husband comes under the stated prohibition against intercourse *with his wife* until the child is weaned, a period of three years. It is, of course, difficult to be sure of what does and does not go on under cover of night in the huts of recent parents, but Mbuti leaf-huts being as flimsy and as close to each other as they are, one can occasionally hear signs of illicit activity. I suspect much of this is intentional, in the nature of a bawdy joke: only on one occasion was it taken by the Mbuti to be for real, and then it caused a major dispute on the grounds that such activity would be injurious to the health of the child. The Mbuti are much concerned about motherhood, and about lactation, for which they have several herbal medicines in case of deficiency. The women keep to the three-year weaning period, which means they do not become pregnant for three years, though I do not for a moment believe this is due to total abstinence from sexual intercourse. During this time their husbands may flirt around, everyone turning a blind eye to such flirtations provided they are discreet. Discretion is a simple matter. Only married couples have sexual intercourse inside huts, others like to have it outside, in the forest. During the weaning period the mother takes her child to introduce it to friends and relatives in other bands, while the husband may accompany her but frequently takes advantage of the occasion to go off on his own on special hunting expeditions, such as elephant hunting, on which women are not taken. The net effect is that a married woman only produces one child (twins are almost unknown; I suspect that one is allowed to die at birth) every four years. It is difficult to arrive at any reliable figure for the number of children who survive into adulthood; the critical period, from a health point of view, is up to the age of eight or nine. I know a few young families with as many as six children alive, but I know of few families where more than four siblings are themselves parents.

Adolescence

As children grow up in the intimacy of their family hut, where nothing is concealed from them, and in a band within which among their age-mates they can find many a legitimate partner, and where pre-marital sexual inter-course is considered as a healthy and indeed a delightful pastime, it is re-markable that in some four years of close contact and intimate living among the Mbuti, I know of not a single case of pre-marital pregnancy. There are potions taken by youths of both sexes to avert conception, abortion is known and, I am told, occasionally practised by unmarried girls and by married women, but more important perhaps are simpler restrictions on the ways in which an unmarried couple may lie and embrace each other. I found it diffi-cult to obtain exact details, but it is certain that such restrictions cause cer-tain difficulties (which are the subject of much mirth among the youths) and may very well effectively prevent conception. The Mbuti themselves indicate this is so, though they assert that intercourse is complete and satis-fying to both partners. At adolescence there is a major religious festival, the *elima*, which in a sense is a joint puberty festival for youths of both sexes, but which is triggered by 'the first blood' of a young girl. There is a curious and highly significant difference of opinion and attitude concerning menstrua-tion, between villagers and Mbuti. The former regard it with horror, as a sign of moral and ritual uncleanliness. Sexual intercourse is rigorously prohibited at this time, and the girl or woman is segregated, under strict taboos against handling food or fire. The 'first blood' among the villagers is said to have been caused by her rape, and they demand that the girl (shut off from the entire community) name her aggressor. This is an opportunity for her to name her would-be spouse, whether or not he raped her. He then can either accept the charge, whereupon he pays the cleansing fine and is 'forced' to marry the girl. Or else (if he does not want to marry her) he denies the charge, pays a similar fine, and the girl is asked to think again. In any event, it leads to marriage almost immediately.

Among the Mbuti the attitude is quite different. The news is broadcast to the world with joy, for a mere girl has now become, they say, a potential mother. She is the object of pride and envy. Within the band, as constituted at that moment, there may be other girls about 'to see the blood', or who have recently seen it, and the girl who has seen it can nominate friends amongst these others and all jointly enter the *elima* hut, built specially for them. There they are taught the arts of motherhood, such as they do not already know, and they openly court the young men who flock to the camp when they hear the news of the *elima*. The young men, invited by the girls, also enter the hut, and sleep with the girls. It is a free-choice arrangement, but in order to enter the hut the youth has to display considerable courage and do battle with the mothers (prospective mothers-in-law) who surround the hut and have all the power needed to prevent any youth they dislike from entering the hut, by sheer physical force. It is expected that during the *elima* (usually a month in duration, i.e. one camp's duration) the girls will settle on their future life partners, but there is no compulsion to do so, and it may be only several years later that they enter marriage. It is said that restrictions on sexual intercourse inside the *elima* hut are rigidly enforced, along the lines mentioned earlier, for the girl is in particular danger of becoming pregnant at this time. This leads us to the possibly significant belief among the Mbuti, an odd one for a people so knowledgeable about animal life, that when a woman is menstruating, sexual intercourse has the most chance of causing pregnancy. Among youths it is a question of taste; some say that intercourse is more pleasurable at this time, some say it is less so; in itself it involves no restrictions. But during married life, if a couple want to have children, they concentrate their efforts on this monthly period. The effects of this upon birth rate might be worth considering.

Marriage

For the Mbuti this is a simple matter, depending almost entirely on the desire of the partners concerned. The question of locality is determined in part by the groom's knowledge of certain hunting territories, and in part by the strength of the bands in those territories at that time. The tendency is for patrilocality; but it is by no means universal, and if the couple has encountered any opposition to their marriage they are likely to go to a remote territory where, after all, they can learn speedily enough all they need to know about the new environment. Marriage takes place when the couple are about 16 or 17 years old, seldom earlier, sometimes later. The only qualification is that the young man should have proven himself capable of supporting a family, which he does by killing one of the larger antelopes from his position on the periphery of the hunt, or by single-handed tracking.

It is plain that economic and political considerations are paramount. In my own experience I know of only two cases in which kinship was raised as an issue, and only one of those involved a potential marriage, the other was merely a mildly incestuous affair. It is considered important that both partners should be approximately the same age; thus again age and residence are prime factors, superseding those of kinship. Companionability is a factor, and brothers and sisters who have grown up in the same territory, as usually happens, are often to be parted at marriage. Sister-exchange marriage, with both couples settling in the same territory, moving together as hunting companions, makes separation unnecessary, and is said to create the strongest bonds and make for the best hunting.

Polygyny occurs, but is relatively rare (perhaps one in thirty). It usually occurs by chance rather than design, for a couple of newly-weds who have not produced children are not considered as fully married, and do not have full marital status. If, after a year of living together, the girl has not shown signs of pregnancy, the couple usually separate, and seek new partners. It sometimes happens that after the boy has settled down with a new girl, which he has to do almost immediately in order to be able to operate as a net hunter (the alternative being to give up his net and rejoin the youths), his former bride finds that she is, after all, pregnant, and comes to rejoin him. I only know of one case where a man, by design, took three wives. This was considered as an invitation to 'noise', and held in disfavour. Sociological parenthood is of much more importance than biological parenthood; if a woman is so unfortunate as to bear no children, friends or relatives who already have four children will give their next child to the childless couple. It is extremely difficult, even by the most diligent enquiry, to know for sure when this has happened, and this is (though sometimes to a lesser extent) true of all the small-scale societies known to me. Even clan membership of the wife, in a patrilineal society, is often concealed, and it may be considered indelicate to enquire too closely into her lineal origins since this implies distance between her and her husband. There are societies where she is formally adopted into her husband's lineage, thus giving her security and status in a society in which she would otherwise remain a foreigner. This is perhaps a little unusual, though even where there is no such adoption a woman may well give her husband's clan when asked for hers. Even in a classical segmentary society, where lineage plays so dominant a role, socio-logical membership is the vital concern, although this usually coincides with biological descent in such a society. The Mbuti present an extreme example of wide-range marital mobility, yet I suspect that the range is much wider than is often supposed in many other more formally and tightly organized small-scale societies.

Death

As with other demographic factors, for the Mbuti little is known of mor-bidity and mortality. Accidental death is rare; pygmies are seldom injured during the hunt, and very rarely fall from trees or fall victim to attack by animal or snake. One of the few forms of accidental death that can be ex-pected to repeat itself, infrequently, arises from the habit of waking at night and sitting close to a fire for warmth. On such occasions the Mbuti are likely to smoke, and to inhale with extra depth, and they have been known to fall unconscious as a result and fall into the fire and die as a result of their burns. There is no warfare or murder or feud, either amongst themselves or between themselves and the villagers. Disease is minimal, since on the forest floor there are neither flies nor mosquitoes to carry disease, and the nomadic life ensures sanitary living conditions. Mbuti associate the village with premature death, and with good reason, for in the villages they are subject to heat stroke and they have little resistance to various diseases against which the villagers have immunity. The villagers similarly associate the forest with premature death, and this reciprocal fear in itself is an effec-tive demographic force encouraging the continued separation of the two populations.

The Mbuti recognize that the first 8 or 9 years of life are relatively hazard-ous, but having passed that period they can look forward to living a healthy life into their sixties. They accept death with equanimity as a natural if regrettable event. The ensuing festival in itself is part of the overall birth-control mechanism, while its symbolism clearly indicates a recognition of the necessity for regeneration of life. The *molimo*, or death festival, is accompanied by certain restrictions on sexual intercourse, and in any case is a period (of a month at least) of such intensive nocturnal activity, allowing the married men a mere one hour, just before dawn, when they can try and snatch some sleep before getting ready for the next day's hunt, that most men admit that sexual intercourse is just about unthinkable. Even the youths (who in any case would not produce children) find their ardour dampened. The ritual, significantly enough, is a dramatic symbolization of

Mbuti notions about life and death, and the role of men and women in procreation, and their power to create, preserve, and destroy life. The sexual conflicts of interest are openly manifest, and there is a ritual dance performed at this time in which ritual reversal takes place, the men dressing and behaving as women, the women as men, culminating in an imitation of the act of copulation, each sex playing the opposite role. I confess I do not clearly see how this dance, *ekokomea*, is associated with population control or other demographic issues, but in conjunction with the rest of the *molimo* festival symbolism it may give us a clue to attitudes that do lead to effective control.

Environment, identity, and population

By way of summary I use another population, the Ik of northern Uganda, as an example of the fundamental and dynamic yet potentially disastrous interplay between these three elements. The potential for disaster cannot be dealt with here, other than to point to the Ik as a clear example of such disaster arising from the interference by technologically more advanced peoples in the delicate balance of life among a technologically limited people until then living satisfactorily in an extremely restrictive environment. It would not be correct to blame the technological limitations of the Ik, for until such interference in their life they evidently had no difficulty in surviving, though their population size probably waxed and waned according to contextual changes. The point being made is sharpened, perhaps, by referring to the clear indications in our 'civilized' world that technology itself is directly inviting even greater disaster by making even greater disruption of this vital relationship possible. And again, the ultimate fault is not with technology *per se*, but rather with this dislocation that it encourages and causes, and with us for assuming that our technological mastery (limited as it is) over the environment, our highly individualistic and independent sense of identity, and our arbitrary and artificial and essentially politico–economic division of the world into 'national' populations, are all beyond question right and proper. However we might define 'ecological success', it would be difficult to consider the modern nation as ecologically successful, and it is significant that success seems further removed in proportion to the increasing size of the 'population', or nation.

Survival is surely a major component of ecological success, as is a reasonable anticipation of continued survival given similar ecological circumstances, and given a technology that can adapt to predictable changes in such circumstances. Small-scale societies, by such definition, are demonstrably far more successful than the larger more complex societies, and in analysing such success the interplay between the three elements under consideration is most evident. The intimate relationship of man to his environment we have already discussed, and obviously his identity is involved with it. It is not a romantic invention of the anthropologist that the pygmies refer to themselves as 'children of the forest', and that the Ik similarly refer to themselves as *kwarikik*, or 'mountain people'. And the identification itself is more than a mere intellectual exercise; it is real and full, for such people make themselves a living, responsive part of the environment they identify with, one might almost say a parasitic part, and therein lies the secret of their success.

One of the problems that the anthropologist, as also the demographer, has to face is how to define 'population', where to draw the boundaries between one population and another. Obviously, boundaries can be drawn at will, for purposes of analysis, but if we think again in terms of ecologically successful populations, we find that they tend to be those defined by common identity of this kind. Thus for the Mbuti it is not a question of size, colour, language, or culture that separates them from their village neighbours, it is their conscious identification with the forest, just as the villagers' conscious rejection of the forest provides them with *their* identity. Yet in so far as all live within the same overall forest they all perceive a wider identity, as different forms of parasites living off the same host. This corresponds, as has been seen, to both the anthropological and demographic facts.

Looking at the larger nations in the same way, we might be tempted to say that they do not form populations let alone societies in any meaningful sense, they are merely administrative or governmental conveniences at best. They have lost their intrinsic viability and are held together by man's fallible artifice. Yet by analysis we could perceive viable societies and populations within such nations, very often overlapping the artificial boundaries. Environment and identity again provide valuable clues.

It seems that among small-scale societies the individual sees himself differently than among large-scale societies, and that this must be understood before we can properly comprehend their thoughts or their actions, or, perhaps, their demography. The so-called kinship systems prove, on close inspection, to be by no means as closed and inflexible as they appear when stated. Kinship terms are a great deal broader (more classificatory) than our own, and designate social relationships rather than actual kinship. Among hunters and gatherers such as the Mbuti, such terms designate age levels, specifically, utterly ignoring kinship, so that all individuals of the same age

regard each other and address each other as brother and sister, and all those
younger as child, all those of a generation higher as mother or father, and
those older still as grandparent. Even the sex differentiation only occurs in
the parental terms, a single term equivalent to sibling (or, perhaps better,
'friend') being used rather than brother or sister. The terms are as follows:

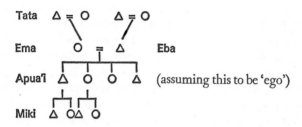

(assuming this to be 'ego')

This clearly shows the sociological orientation of the people. They are concerned with the society as a whole, rather than with individuals. And just as
these terms of address and reference indicate this concern, so do personal
names and lineages and clan names. The individual only exists as part of a
complex interlocking system of social relationships, by himself he has no
identity and no value. Good and bad are judged by what is good and bad
for the society as a whole. It was therefore perturbing for me, at first, when
I found myself working amongst a group of hunters-turned-cultivators (the
Ik of northern Uganda) whose only stated value was *ngag*, or food; whose
only notion of goodness (*marangik*) was the individual possession of food
in the stomach; and whose definition of a good man (*yakw ana marang*)
was 'a man who has a full belly'. The Ik are barely surviving under conditions of extreme starvation, in an environment they refuse to leave and
which is incapable of supporting them at their previous population size. Individualism was cultivated, it seems, in response to this situation, as a
mechanism for reducing the population to a reasonable size, by making the
frequency of death, and the fact of death, perfectly acceptable to the sur-
vivors. Neighbouring African tribes look on the Ik with horror, and denied
that they were human, and said they were more like Europeans. This was
no mere insult, it was a perceptive comparison between two peoples who
practised the essentially un-African (and un-small-scale society) custom of
allowing people to grow up as individuals, without any social consciousness
(which is how Europeans appeared to these Africans, at least). Villages
were still built, as a symbol of social solidarity, but the nuclear family, as a
viable institution, simply ceased to function, in all but the most general

way. Children, born with reluctance, maintained by reluctant mothers with even less grace until weaned at three (unless the mother has managed to leave the infant where it would be eaten by a leopard, an occasion for much rejoicing), had to find their own way in life from 3 years old onwards. They grow up, reasonably enough, without any great sense of filial devotion, and were as amused to see their parents die as their parents would have been to see them die, for after all, death by definition was a good thing, it meant more *ngag* for the others. Couples get married only in case there should be need for cooperation (the same reason that mothers bother to feed their children until weaned), in the unlikely event of the hunt or the fields ever being productive enough to require cooperation. But for the most part, food-getting for adults is an individual affair, and any tactics are justified by the supreme (because it is solitary) value of goodness, the individual possession of food in the stomach. One sees children opening the mouths of old people to extract food, should the old people manage to find any. Certainly nobody would give them any. Younger children get beaten up by older children if found with food. Food must be transferred to the stomach as rapidly as possible, so it is frequently not cooked, since the smoke from the fire would give the game away. The result of eating uncooked grains (rounded off with smooth pebbles and tree bark) is not infrequently fatal.

Sexual activity is minimal, few have the energy. The breeding group (that is the teenagers, for in the early twenties one begins to age rapidly) is the healthiest and takes food from adults, elders and children alike, and indulges in limited sexual activity. It is considered as a chore, however, and likened, as only the Ik could liken it, to the mildly pleasurable chore of defaecation. Rather than intercourse, which is more tiring and leads to demands of payment in food (even between wives and husbands) by the female who knows she can sell what energy she has among the neighbouring herders, masturbation is practised. It is sometimes combined with a more important activity, such as keeping an eagle eye open for tell-tale signs of food – smoke, circling vultures, and so forth. The lesser activity is immediately abandoned.

In times of extreme shortage (such as the 18 months I spent among the Ik) these sad but functional practices are most obvious. But the situation being of over 30 years duration now, it has become established so that even in times of plenty, which I witnessed on a subsequent visit, the individual good is still the only good.

It is a remarkable achievement that the Ik have found a way of surviving *as a society*, in such abnormal situations. It is significant that their technique involves the retention of their 'environmental identity' even at the cost of their social consciousness. This would seem to be a last resort, for as little as two generations ago the Ik were, as far as we can tell, hunters and gatherers organized very similarly to the Mbuti. Both societies, in their extremes of abundance and insufficiency exhibit the same intensely sensitive adjustment to the environment, a characteristic, I suggest, of all small-scale societies, and perhaps more a characteristic of our own large-scale industrial societies than we might suppose; the comparison between ourselves and the Ik being uncomfortably close.

References

CAVALLI-SFORZA, L. L., ZONTA, L. A., NUZZO, F., BERNINI, L., DE JONG, W. W. W., MEERA KHAN, P., RAY, A. K., WENT, L. N., SINISCALCO, M., NIJENHUIS, L. E., VAN LOGHEM, E., and MODIANO, G. (1969) Studies on African Pygmies, I. A pilot investigation of Babinga Pygmies in the Central Africa Republic (with an analysis of genetic distances), *Am. J. hum. Genet.* 21, 252–74.

EVANS-PRITCHARD, E. E. (1968) *The Nuer* Oxford, Clarendon Press.

GIBBS, J. L. (1965) *Peoples of Africa* New York, Holt, Rinehart, and Winston.

LEE, R. B. and DE VORE, I. (eds) (1968) *Man the Hunter* Chicago, Aldine Press.

STENNING, D. J. (1959) *Savannah Nomads. A Study of the Wodaabe Fulani of Western Bornu Province, Northern Region, Nigeria* Oxford, Clarendon Press.

STENNING, D. J. (1965) The pastoral Fulani of northern Nigeria. In *Peoples of Africa* (ed. Gibbs, J. L.) New York, Holt, Rinehart, and Winston.

TURNBULL, C. M. (1965a) The Mbuti Pygmies: an ethnographic survey, *Anthrop. Papers, Am. Mus. Nat. Hist.* 50, 139–282.

TURNBULL, C. M. (1965b) The Mbuti Pygmies of the Congo. In *Peoples of Africa* (ed. Gibbs, J. L.) New York, Holt, Rinehart, and Winston.

TURNBULL, C. M. (1965c) *Wayward Servants. The Two Worlds of the African Pygmies* New York, Natural History Press.

TURNBULL, C. M. (1972) *The Mountain People* New York, Simon and Schuster.

2 Variability in population change in India 1871–1941

Arthur Geddes

In this paper examples of the four best-marked types of change and variability of population are given, chosen from Indian village communities known to the author.

By 'net change' is simply meant the net difference, positive or negative (and expressed as a percentage), between the first and last of two or more census enumerations; but 'variability' requires a fuller definition. To estimate the variability, a smoothed curve (assumed to be exponential) was calculated, passing through the first and last available points, which were the populations of Indian regional units in 1881 and 1931. The deviations from this 'expected' curve, derived from the actual numbers at intervening censuses, were then summed, averaged, and expressed as a percentage of the mean population between the two dates. The greater the deviations, the greater their average expressed in the resulting percentage variability. This ranged from a minimum of 0·1 per cent to extremes of over 11 per cent which in one or two colony districts approached 20 per cent. One also noted the year (or years) of greatest deviation, with its negative or positive sign, the *minus* of disaster or the *plus* of recovery. In some provinces the census goes back to 1871, certain major facts being also known for earlier dates, while the last census carries on our knowledge up to 1941. Thus, while the calculations dealt only with six censuses and a fifty-year period, as shown in the six graphs (figure 1), conditions can be plotted, at least approximately, for seventy years. It need hardly be emphasized that statistics of health and of births and deaths are extremely inadequate in India; hence it is necessary to depend greatly upon the decennial census.

Let us briefly consider these differences of variability and net change of population, and the types into which they fall, in India during the half-century between 1881 and 1931. Where – so exceptionally for India without the help of immigration – population had virtually doubled in these fifty years, as in the annually flooded and silt-enriched eastern half of the deltaic

GEDDES, ARTHUR (1947–8) 'The Social and Psychological Significance of Population Change, with Examples from India 1871–1941', in *Human Relations*, 1, 181–205.

Bengal plain, the steeply-rising curve of population was practically indistinguishable from the 'ideal' curve drawn to join the number first enumerated in 1881 to that of the last census in 1931. In this instance, increase was very high while variability was minimal. This may be termed high steady increase or simply 'high increase' forming Type 1 (fig. 1(a)). Where, on the other hand, endemic malaria had already taken hold of a population before the first census date, as in the western Delta of Bengal, the low net increase or arrest of population, recorded at the end of the period, actually corresponds to stagnation of the population throughout. Here the conditions of life from decade to decade, and even from year to year, have been almost as moribund as that of the rivers of this region which, in the peasants' own telling phrase, are 'dead' or 'dying'. The increase is low (or non-existent), and the variability is slight or minimal. 'Stagnation' may best describe this condition, forming Type 2 (fig. 1(b)).

For other regions, the change and 'variability' differed. Passing by intermediate examples of low increase but moderate variability, which may be described as 'intermediate' and classed as Type 3 (fig. 1(c)), let us consider the next well-marked type.

Where famine has repeatedly taken violent toll, as in the western Deccan or Rajputana, there are jagged graphs of population, in which relatively prolonged ascents are interrupted by the short, steep falls that tell of catastrophe. The increase is low or non-existent, but the variability is high to extreme. This is the type of 'recurrent crisis', Type 4 (fig. 1(d)). Before coming to the last type to be considered, we pass through examples of moderate increase and moderate variability, Type 5 (fig. 1(e)), which may simply be called 'Variable Increase'.

Finally, where, through the immigration of colonists, increase occurred as high as or even higher than that of Type 1 (perhaps to many times the initial population), the graph shows a definite change from the time colonization began. The graph, flatter at first than the postulated curve, steepens sharply from the year (or census date) following the creation of a new and revolutionary factor. In an arid district this factor might be the extension of perennial irrigation to an area of steppes, which, as in the southern Punjab, brought forthwith an inflow of burly Sikhs, Jats and north-western Muslims. In upper Assam after 1911 the new factor was the commencement of mass immigration by sturdy Muslims from over-populated eastern Bengal. In such cases the actual curve taken is very different from the smooth 'expected' one; we find a notable and an extreme variability with the high to extreme increases; hence we know that this extreme variability marks, not a catastrophe but a demographic revolution, bringing in a new sequence of rising change. This may be described as 'immigration' or simply 'colonization', Type 6 (fig. 1(f)).

Two maps accompany the graphs of the six selected administrative districts of provinces, or states, which are given in this paper (fig. 2). While the inset map shows the location of these six districts, the large map outlines the distribution of the six demographic types throughout India. Now the statistics for the whole country were compiled from administrative units such as the six districts here chosen to exemplify the 'types', each example chosen presenting homogeneity in the environmental conditions of human life throughout its area. But the boundaries of many other districts or units enclose territories each one of which may be highly diverse in physical environment and way of life. Yet an uncorrected administrative map assumes a uniformity of conditions throughout each unit, however diversified it may be in reality.

Ignoring in this paper the intermediate types (Nos. 3 and 5) – whose shades of difference I found highly informative and suggestive, as a geographer surveying the country as a whole – let us concentrate on one example of each of the four best-marked types: Nos. 1, 2, 4 and 6. For each type in turn, the people of a village and region which I came to know in India will be described, in order to show how the index of variability and change may reflect what struck me most in the condition of the people. We shall begin with 'recurrent crisis' (Type 4), as seen in a semi-arid tract of the Deccan lava region, and contrast it with 'stagnation' (Type 2), in the western half of Bengal. We shall follow with 'high natural increase' (Type 1), in eastern Bengal. The last examples will be taken from 'colonization' (Type 6), as it has been seen among the colonists in north-eastern Assam, most of whom come from eastern Bengal, with mention of the more widely known conditions in the Punjab (from which the district taken as example is drawn). The chief points of physique and morale among peasants and labourers will be described for each example, and wider social and intellectual implications will also receive attention. Finally, it should be said that, while urban communities will be mentioned, the description in the following sections concentrates on rural life.

Examples of the four chief types

'Recurrent crisis' seen in a Deccan 'famine tract' (Type 4)

When first I toured the north-western Deccan (of Bombay and Hyderabad) in 1921–2, the peasants were painfully recovering from the results of repeated droughts which had left them depleted of seed, cows and ploughing cattle, and had plunged them deeper into debt. They themselves were lean in body from inadequate food, and, but for government relief, there would, in fact, have been severe famine and a high death rate from hunger. Three years earlier, too, influenza had struck them down, leaving a corpse in perhaps every second family, or sometimes in every family, in a village. Famines had also occurred in earlier years; and the last great famine to go comparatively unrelieved, that of 1899–1900, had taken many thousands of lives (Type 4). Although I did not witness the passage of this 'pandemic' of influenza in 1918, yet on my first arrival in India it was so fresh in the minds of Indians and Europeans who had worked in some of the worst-hit regions, whether as doctors or missionaries, that their record of the people's terror, grief and despair was unforgettable. Influenza in turn had helped to bring about famine by causing a severe shortage of labour at the time when the autumn-sown crops should have been prepared for and sown, so that there was no reserve of food when the rains failed and crops were lost in the following monsoon. Thus misfortunes had accumulated and led to a major disaster.

A year or so after my first acquaintance with the Deccan peasantry, they had recovered considerably; and though they were still on the edge of want and as deeply indebted as ever, one sensed the difference in their ways. I recall the days spent around a Maratha village in 1922–3 with Maratha friends known and trusted by the villagers, and the nights spent on the *chowdi*, or communal verandah and meeting place, where we slept in the village. By day one saw and spoke with the men individually at work with their plough teams, or saw them strip to plunge for a swim in the cool waters of the tank-well at their midday rest. When night had fallen, there were long talks on harvests and failures, or on sowings with speculation upon the returns for which they hoped or the losses which they feared. The women one hardly saw, and could only guess their states of mind.

One day we had spoken to a peasant at his slow, laborious work of water-lifting with his oxen in order to irrigate his orange grove, his own and his animals' labour not then being required for the primary task of ploughing. That night he spoke of the high interest he had to pay on the loan he had raised to meet the cost of sinking a well in the rock, and the uncertainty of prices in the orange market on which he counted for repayment. Another peasant had decided to do like him, but spoke of the risk that even if a well were dug deep, it might not strike water; and then the land he mortgaged could never pass to his surviving son. With their talk was frankness and common sense, and some recovery of resolution, but not of confidence.

In spite of these troubles, the men gathered one night under a low moon, to dance their vigorous 'Morris' dances, as they might be called. They danced with the gaiety of recovered health, for their own pleasure, for ours, and also (no doubt) for that of their womenfolk, half-hidden in the shadows. By these dances – partly playful, partly martial – the youths learned light-hearted, but disciplined, control of rhythmic group movement, and the older husbandmen, weary from the plough, refreshed their limbs to suppleness and revived their youth. Charades followed, played by boys with some elder as their producer, bringing peals of infectious, side-splitting laughter to us all. These people could once more face life with a sense of purpose, and even rise again to gaiety together. But behind them lay their memory of disaster, and the knowledge that sooner, or later, the rains would fail again, their crops be lost, and they, their children and their elders would face want, in a time of barren ground and famine.

While such impressions – as I believe – are true so far as they go, and are personally valuable to oneself despite their 'imponderability', we must ask how far they compare with the bare facts of the people's existence, vitality and mortality, their varying survival rates as measured by net change and variability. The net increase in this famine tract was generally rather low, having barely reached 30 per cent in fifty years. (For comparison the net increase of England and Wales in the same period, in spite of emigration and a falling birth rate, was 54 per cent.) Clearly, in a region where there is little or no permanent emigration and almost no voluntary check on population, so low an increase is a sign of a high death rate. The variability throughout the famine tract was very great, being 6 or 7 per cent or over, and was extreme in that particular district of this region which is later used to exemplify Type 4. Thus it becomes clear that while there have been periods of rapid increase, testifying to a minimum of fair health, these periods have repeatedly been interrupted by seasons or years of dire loss. Migrations, though appreciable, were a minor factor.

From the years and sign of greatest deviation one can particularize still further. By these we can tell, almost at a glance, whether those belonging to a given age-group at the end of a famine were at least allowed to reach adolescence or youth – although hardly ever their prime – in a period of normal achievement, of fair harvests, of relative sufficiency and advance; or whether, on the contrary, all of them knew fear of death by starvation and all to some extent shared the loss of friends, of at least one of their family, and perhaps of a parent. We can tell whether they passed through the successive stages of life with or without the personal, or communal, experience of loss, as child, as man or wife, as parent or elder. In India such generalizations can be made with relative assurance. Uncertain though we should be over prediction in successive Occidental generations of the proportion of married to unmarried, or the likelihood of parenthood in any age-group or class, in India the important experiences in the cycle of life are almost marked out at birth by the circumstances of the community. That the variability of population is so high, and the security of expectation so low, is the tragedy of an Indian 'famine tract'.

A regional description of peasant morale such as that just given needs to be complemented by some comments on life in the educated class of the same region. In all of the four or five regions to be cited as examples, the intellectuals are drawn mainly from what a medieval European might have called the 'clerkly' castes and classes, and, to a lesser extent, from those he would have recognized as 'gentry' and 'merchants'. In India the keenness of mind and the energy of the Brahmins of the Maratha lands, the 'Marashtra', is outstanding. Of early Nationalist leaders, the names of Tilak and Gokhale will still be remembered by many European readers, as those of upright and vigorous men. In the history of the early nineteenth century, the prolonged resistance to the British forces in the Maratha Wars was due both to the martial qualities of the Maratha peasantry – Sivaji's 'mountain rats', whose sons have fought in both world wars – and to the organizing leadership, civil and military, of the educated class. One may safely say that in spite of poverty, the *Chitpavin* or 'Poona' Brahmins continue to make their mark. Much the same is true of the mercantile castes and classes of the semi-arid western plateau. Gandhi himself, the son of an administrator in the Kathiawar peninsula of western India (20°N, 70°E), is of much the same Jain stock as the dominant broking caste of northern India, the Marwaris. Marwar (or Udaipur state, 24–28°N, 70–74°E), together with the rest of the unirrigated Rajputana, furnishes an extreme example of Type 4, 'recurrent crisis'.

'Stagnation' in Western Bengal (Type 2)

In contrast to the high variability with rather low net increase in a 'famine tract', we noted the minimal variability with equally low (or still lower) increase – that is, stagnation or actual decline – in the area of 'dead' or 'dying' rivers in the west of the Bengal delta. This condition was particularly characteristic of the two deltaic districts of Jessore and Nadia which lie a little east of Calcutta and of the Hooghly and its uppermost reaches.

Rather similar conditions prevailed throughout the crowded alluvial rice-lands extending westwards to and beyond Patna (P on the map) – although this district itself, owing to the visitation of the plague, had a great variability and proves an exception among its neighbours. In the Bengal tract the physical ruin of the larger houses, built nearly a century ago, the growth of 'jungle' about the villages, and the weedy, ill-kept tanks, green with slime, prepare one for the condition of the people. The folk are haggard and lethargic; taught by experience, during the rains they stop work in a passing shower to hasten for shelter lest a chill should bring on fever and leave them trembling with ague; and although the grown folk are lean, the children are pot-bellied with the enlarged spleen of chronic malaria. In the absence of adequate medical statistics, one has to depend chiefly upon those of the Census. There is no doubt that in general, in this region, the high mortality reflects the incidence of malaria. The people's physical condition is paralleled all too closely by their morale. They are almost helpless in the grip of what has been called Bengal's 'malaria mentality' in which not the body alone but the very soul seems moribund.

What concerns us here is not simply the state of the individual in himself, or even the infection passed from the more to the less sick by the deadly mosquitoes in their faintly droning clouds. Invisible, but perhaps as infectious and as deadly as the mosquito or malarial parasite, there move the nebulae of mutual discouragement. Failures in mutual aid are reciprocated, as neighbours fall ill by turns; and chronically high death rates from infancy to age tell of bereavements that are almost habitual. When last I left Bengal, an attempt had begun to renew this western tract by calling in healthier peasants from the now crowded eastern tracts of the delta. It remains to be seen whether their labour will overcome the physical and morale problem of this situation, or whether they themselves will be overcome before the physical environment is improved. Be that as it may, here again the measure (of decline) and index (of minimal variability), plumbing these stagnant depths of mere existence, could have prepared one for the psychological atmosphere we felt about us.

'High natural increase' in Eastern Bengal (Type 1)

It was after prolonged residence in parts of western Bengal – stricken and almost as desolate as those described, but to which, for all their sadness, I had become attached – that I first visited the eastern Delta. It was late in the rains – a period which in the western tracts is the peak of the malaria season. The floods were at their height, and the great rivers streamed like seas over the land, leaving the villages dotted like winding archipelagos among the waters. I shall never forget the sense of activity and vigour given by many of the riverside peasants and fishers. They moved freely in pouring rain, their dark, glistening limbs and torso stout and firm, ready with a ringing hail or even a shout of laughter. When the swinging rivers undermine a whole river-bank or sweep away an island sandbank in the estuaries and mouths of the Ganges–Brahmaputra, these peasants dismantle their neat huts, pack the sections on a little boat and, landing on a new sandbank, stake a new claim. There, they are ready to band together to work it, or to fight for it.

Poverty weighs heavily here too, and I would not wish to sketch a paradise, for the pressure of population had become extreme, although not to the point of suppressing effort. In a few years a plague of water weed, the 'lilac devil', had spread over the whole tract, clogging waterways and spoiling rice fields; but the people responded to guidance in fighting it, and they keep up the fight. As pressure has increased, peasants have flocked into the distant plains of upper Assam; and some, as has just been said, have even moved to the districts adjacent to the west, which were formerly the more densely crowded.

A sharper contrast between brothers in race and religion it would be hard to find than between the western and eastern Delta, between these peoples of almost neighbouring districts separated only by a narrow belt of transitional character. Once more a measure of the vitality of the people is offered by the dual indices of the net change in the eastern Delta (an increase of almost 100 per cent, doubling the population) and of the variability (its minimal percentage marking here the steadiness of increase). From the high vitality there follows the high frequency of unbroken circles of family and neighbourhood; while at the same time the index proves highly suggestive of the general outlook. It is all the sadder that during the last decade or two, local epidemics of malaria have continued to spread eastward, settling down as severe endemic malaria; and sadder still that famine struck the entire province in 1943.

Consider next the contrast in intellectual phase now existing between these last two types (Nos. 2 and 1), belonging to two tracts of one great cultural region, Bengal. Since the twelfth century, the intellect of Hinduism, and later of Islam also, has clustered along two principal zones: 1. on the west, the banks of the upper Hooghly (properly the Bhagirathi) and the red-soiled land to the west of it, forming the Rarh; and 2. on the east, the banks of the lower Ganges or Padma, round Dacca. By far the greater historic contributions to literature and learning came to birth in the western of these two zones, that which leads out to India's eastern coastlands; and the smaller, not unnaturally, arose in the more outlying eastern zone. This regional predominance of the west continued through the British period almost up to 1870, when malaria broke out as a terrible epidemic, and then settled down in endemic form. I have described the effects upon the ordinary village folk of endemic malaria, seen at its worst, in parts of this zone, which were once a home of culture, arts and government. In matters of the mind the result of severe malaria was that culture wilted.

At this time those of the upper classes who could afford to do so fled to Calcutta, where their descendants have led in the professions; but few members of the upper castes born and reared in any village of the western zone have risen to eminence in this century. In the last century the eastern zone was slower in sending its sons afield to find new lustre, partly because it was more distant from Calcutta, and hence from opportunities in the modern world. Even so, in this century the eclipse of the westerners by the easterners from villages round Dacca was only possible owing to the ruin of health and morale in the west, and to the growing numbers, the relatively good health and the high morale found in the east of Bengal.

The general ability of the middle class or gentlefolk from the Dacca or Bikrampur area is well known in Bengal and eastern India; but in pursuing the matter I have been struck by the change, in the last two generations, in the personnel of the professions – of science, literature and art, as of administration and politics – which has followed the fading of the ancient west, the Rarh. As the earliest example of this historic western supremacy the name of Jayadeva, author of the 'Indian Song of Songs', may be cited to the Occidental reader; no such medieval classic was created in the Dacca region. At the end of the eighteenth century, Ram Mohan Ray was recognized in the Occident for his personality, as he is revered in Bengal for his insight. For the nineteenth century a list of other names could be supplied which, like Ray's, were all from the west, with one exception. Of the Tagore family, both branches are landed proprietors in the north of the Delta, and not strictly from either of these zones. In the twentieth century, however, although many men – like the distinguished Vice-Chancellor of Calcutta University, the late Sir Asutosh Mukerjee – might be of the western stock, they were rarely born in this old culture zone. In particular it is the region of Dacca which has sent forth the great majority of the staff of the Universities of Calcutta and Dacca alike, of the *swamis* of the Brotherhood of Ramakrishna (himself a native of Hooghly-side), of Rabindranath Tagore's 'University Group' at Santiniketan (on the Western Bengal uplands), or of the Bose Institute, Calcutta. A large number both of the officials of the provincial and indeed of the central government, and also of the Bengali leaders of Congress, are natives of eastern Bengal.

Now to turn back to our example of 'recurrent crisis' (Type 4), the Brahmins of Marashtra have held their own, in spite of poverty, where those of Western Bengal have lost their lead. By itself, the depressing effect of poverty on the literates in the last two generations might have been no more severe – perhaps less so – in the western half of Bengal than in the Maratha 'famine tracts'. But while famine is tragic at the time, only the poor suffer from its direst effects. With malaria it is otherwise. Such bodily infection cannot wholly be escaped by any class, even by those relatively protected by better food and absence of fatigue, and, for the last few years at least, by medicine and other preventive measures. Thus the morale of the whole community is directly sapped by malaria as it is not by famine. Such facts of causation and their effects cannot be clearly indicated by any one index of mere survival. Yet since no condition other than endemic malaria (or similar 'fevers') gives the combination of net arrest of population increase combined with minimal variability, this index gives at least a clue to the complex of physical and psychological states of a community over some two generations.

'Colonization' in Assam and the Punjab (Type 6)

In this, the last regional type, 'colonization', by introducing a new factor, has revolutionized change and brought high increase with high variability. We have noted the vigorous type of emigrant who leaves eastern Bengal for Assam. And the Punjabi is sufficiently outstanding, by his height and presence and – to those personally unfamiliar with him – by his place in literature, to need little description here. In the Canal Colonies of the Punjab the already self-respecting Punjabi holds his own. Brayne adds that the most startling progress in efficiency, honesty and cleanliness among the colonists come from some of the formerly disreputable gypsy cattle thieves of the Thar steppe who have been forced to settle down. This seems natural, in a place and time of well-founded, general hope and reasoned confidence in which, whatever the loss of his gypsy life may mean to a man, a wife and mother has everything to gain by acquiring a home; a home such as those she may well have slunk enviously by as a gypsy beggar, but can now call her children's and her own. Not every class will show so great a revolution in morale as do the gypsies; and we need not be surprised that it is among those who actually belonged to the environment now transformed, the steppe, that the revolution in outlook and social relations is either abortive or complete. Further north in the long-settled northern Punjab, though variability is often great and increase (locally) is low, both are due to the ready outlet of emigration, exceptional in India on so great a scale. This explains the apparent anomaly (for India) of comparatively progressive communities falling (in the statistical sense) into the 'intermediate' type (No. 3). Change in the prevailing ways of life, even in these northern parts, seems to be coming faster than in other tracts with equally long-established customs. Cooperation is relatively progressive, and the re-allotment and consolidation of fragmented holdings is increasingly undertaken by common consent of peasant land-holders.

Culturally, we find very different conditions in Assam and in the Punjab. Assam is a land of ancient Hindu culture which is being 'colonized' by a Muslim peasantry. If these incoming Muslims take to modern instruction, as they ultimately will, it is difficult to see how Assamese culture can remain uninfluenced. Meantime, however, the Bengali peasantry by its vigour is adding to the economic resources of the province, although their presence, and the cultural problem they offer, can hardly be said at the moment to have reached beyond the early stage of arousing defensive attitudes in the intellectual life of Assamese Hinduism.

In the Punjab, the actual Canal Colonies do not straightway attract the professions, though merchants flock thither as brokers of the cash crops grown there, and as money-lenders. The professional classes are to a great extent enriched at a distance; from 1921 to 1931 Lahore grew faster than any other Indian city and has maintained this rapid growth up to 1941. Lahore's University is an active centre, the city's trade and its administration are busy; Amritsar and other old centres have their colleges too. It is the progressive outlook of the Canal Colonies which quickens the life of the province as a whole, and invigorates that of the educated classes.

Postscript

Since this paper was drafted, the Census Report of India for 1941 has appeared (albeit in abbreviated form), and shortly after, the official reports upon the famine of 1943 in Bengal. These have been followed in turn by brief statements of severe crop scarcity and food shortage in many regions, many of them regions in which famine has long been a recurrent scourge. Scrutiny of the district statistics to 1941 makes it clear that had the change and variability figures been recalculated for the sixty-year period, (1) the rate of increase per cent would have been greater almost everywhere, so that the values of change to be given would have risen; while (2) the curve

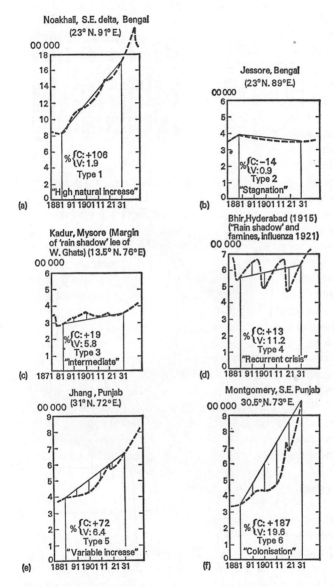

Fig. 1 Population change and variability, six types. (In the internal legends of these figures, C=net change and V=variability. The vertical ordinate of the graphs is population.)

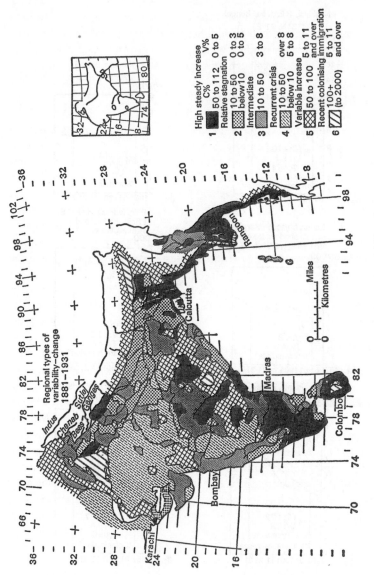

High steady increase
    C%   V%
1 ■ 50 to 112   0 to 5
Relative stagnation
2 ▦ 10 to 50   0 to 3
      below10   0 to 5
Intermediate
3 ▨ 10 to 50   3 to 8
Recurrent crisis
4 ▧ 10 to 50   over 8
      below 10   5 to 8
Variable increase
5 ▨ 50 to 100   5 to 11
      and over
Recent colonising immigration
6 ▨ 100+   5 to 11
      (to 2000) and over

Regional types of
variability–change
1881–1931

Indus Chenab Sutlej Beas Ganges

Karachi

Bombay

Madras

Colombo

Calcutta

Rangoon

Miles
Kilometres

Fig. 2   Regional types of variability change.

would have been free of any violent new rise, or certainly free of a sudden fall. The curve of each graph exemplifies these two facts by the dashed line linking the six statistical points, which is carried on to 1941. But the difference of the sixty-year calculations from those shown would only have been a matter of degree: the boundaries of the type-areas would still have stood out in much the same regional distribution.

But when the present decade comes to a close, greater differences will be apparent. Prolongation of the war, when crop failures brought disaster to Bengal, the cessation of the imports of rice from Burma and the loss of exports of jute, brought the long period of high steady increase to a catastrophic end. The area is small, but the provincial population (60 million of India's 400 millions) is large. There were periods of scarcity elsewhere, but in none was the death roll so high. Since then, notably during 1946–7, war and failures of rain have led to crop scarcity such that the increased population now exceeds the available food supply. Inevitably, it seems, the suffering will be severe, the death roll will be heavy, the rate of change will be lowered and the variability heightened once more.

What are the psychological responses to all this cannot be said; but it seems right to ask whether the appalling 'communal' riots and strife can be adequately understood as having merely a 'religious' or 'political' significance. It is too rarely pointed out that in India the worst of the rioting has occurred either in the great modern cities, filled with rival immigrants (preponderatingly males), where the ghastly struggle of merchant-brokers, employers and employees sets the starving, the fevered and the desperate at one another's throats. The first great rural exception has been eastern Bengal, where famine and fever have taken toll among the manly Muslim peasantry who angrily begrudge the mainly Hindu landlord class their rents and the mainly Hindu 'up-country' broker class their unchecked and inordinate famine-profits. Naturally, once fanaticism is let loose, the poorest suffer with the comparatively well-to-do, and the Hindu untouchables are 'beaten up' along with their 'betters' – or rather, being unprotected, it is they who suffer most. In India the world war has left the rich richer, but the poor still poorer than before. The first budget introduced by a Government composed of Indians has brought in a new policy of severe taxation upon excess profits, coupled with a lightened burden upon a universal necessity, salt (Feb.–Mar. 1947). But the most enlightened social and economic guidance and control will be required to fill the gap between food supply and population, without which the areas of 'crisis' or 'stagnation' will inevitably spread – signs that not only the body of the Indian masses but their outlook, mind and very soul are sick.

3   Population – growth or decline?

Eivind Gilje and Terry Gould

We know much more securely than we know almost any other social or economic factor relating to the future that, in the place of the steady and indeed steeply rising level of population which we have experienced for a number of decades, we shall be faced in a very short time with a stationary or declining level.

John Maynard Keynes, 1937

The actual growth of population in England and Wales and predictions for continued growth are presently causing considerable concern both in the government and among the general public, despite the recent downward revisions in the official estimates of future population. The likely consequences for Britain of this growing population were recently reported by the Population Panel (1973). Future population levels are, though, a subject for disagreement; witness the above quotation. There has been a continued fall in fertility since 1964 and, as death rates have decreased only marginally, one could, instead of the predicted continued growth, envisage a decreasing population in the future, or at least a population that is not growing.

The government's population projections are made by the Government Actuary's Department, which projects the population of England and Wales, and by the Office of Population Censuses and Surveys, which produces the Registrar General's estimates of future levels of population in Greater London, within the framework of the projections for England and Wales. Population projections for Greater London are also produced by the GLC Intelligence Unit.

The Registrar General's projections and those of the GLC both reflect a falling trend for Greater London but give dissimilar future population levels due to different assumptions about fertility. The Registrar General's projections for Greater London use the fertility assumptions of the Government Actuary's projections for England and Wales, adjusted for regional differences. The GLC's fertility assumptions, however, are based on quite different premises about future fertility patterns; and, in order to highlight the effects of employing these differing fertility assumptions, the GLC has

GILJE, EIVIND and GOULD, TERRY (1973) 'Population – growth or decline?', in *GLC Intelligence Unit Quarterly Bulletin*, no. 24, September 1973, 29–35.

produced projections for England and Wales using its own fertility assumptions and methodology.

Projections for England and Wales

Reviews of the Government Actuary's 1968 and 1969-based population projections appeared in two previous issues of the *Quarterly Bulletin* (Thompson, 1969; 1970). The two most recent official projections for England and Wales are based on the 1971 and 1972 mid-year estimated population (Government Actuary 1972, 1973).

The Government Actuary's projections and the GLC's two alternative projections presented in this article use the same death and migration assumptions. The initial death rates are based on the average rates for 1967–9. Over the 40-year projection period the rates for males aged under 40 and females aged under 50 are assumed to decline to one-half of the initial rates; for ages above these, the decline is progressively smaller. The projections assume there will be net outward migration of 16,000 persons in 1971, rising to 30,000 persons per year from 1981 onwards. The fertility assumptions and the method used for calculating future births are different, however, for the two sets of projections. The Government Actuary estimates mean completed family sizes and applies these to the projected population of married women. The GLC's method uses projected age-specific birth rates and applies them to the projected total female population in the relevant age groups. Although the two methods differ somewhat, the end results are comparable when the gross reproduction rates [1] implied in each projection are examined.

The gross reproduction rates for selected years over the last fifty years are shown in Table 1. The rates implied by the Government Actuary's and GLC's projections for England and Wales for the next forty years can be compared in Table 2.

The actual gross reproduction rate fell from a peak of 1·40 daughters per woman in 1964 to 1·13 in 1972. Replacement-level fertility (i.e. the level at which a population just replaces itself) is currently equal to a gross

1 The gross reproduction rate is simply the average number of daughters who would be born to a woman if the current age-specific fertility rates remained constant for the rest of her child-bearing life. The mean completed family size, or the average number of children per family, is then an estimate of the number of female and male children combined and is approximately double the gross reproduction rate. (As there are 1.06 boys born for every girl, the mean completed family size will be somewhat more than twice the gross reproduction rate.)

Table 1   Gross reproduction rates for England and Wales

Year	Gross reproduction rate
1922–4	1·15
1932–4	0·86
1939–49	1·03
1950–4	1·06
1956–60	1·22
1964	1·40
1966	1·33
1970	1·16
1971	1·15
1972	1·13*

* Estimate.
Sources: General Register Office (1967). Personal communication from O P C S.

Table 2   Estimated gross reproduction rates for England and Wales

Year	Gross reproduction rate			
	Government Actuary's projections		GLC projections	
	Mid-1971-based	Mid-1972-based	Low	High
1972	1·11	—	1·14	1·14
1973	1·15	1·03	1·11	1·11
1976	1·16	1·06	1·03	1·03
1981	1·13	1·13	0·92	1·02
1986	1·14	1·13	0·86	1·02
1991	1·12	1·13	0·86	1·02
2001	1·12	1·13	0·86	1·02
2011	1·11	1·13	0·86	1·02

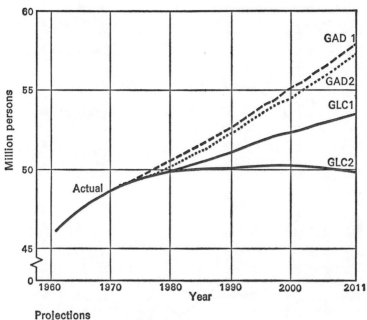

Projections
GAD 1 −GAD mid 1971 based
GAD 2 −GAD mid 1972 based
GLC 1 −Age specific fertility rates falling to 1977 then constant
GLC 2 −Age specific fertility rates falling to 1984 then constant

Fig. 1   England and Wales: total population 1961–71 and projections to 2011.

reproduction rate of 1·02 daughters per woman. Neither of the Government's Actuary's projections (1971-based or 1972-based) assume that the gross reproduction rate will fall below replacement level in the next forty years. The GLC's projections, however, assume a falling rate which reaches replacement level in 1977. The population levels resulting from the various projections are shown in figure 1.

Fertility patterns in recent years

Fertility patterns (legitimate fertility) are the product of several factors:

(a) the number of married women in the fertile age group (15–49)
(b) the family size goal (the desired or 'ideal' family size)

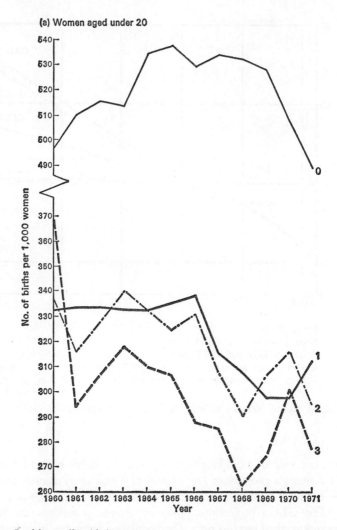

Fig. 2 Legitimate live birth rates to women married only once according to age and marriage duration 1960–71. *Note:* The numbers on the right of these diagrams show completed years of marriage. *Source:* Office of Population Censuses and Surveys (1973c).

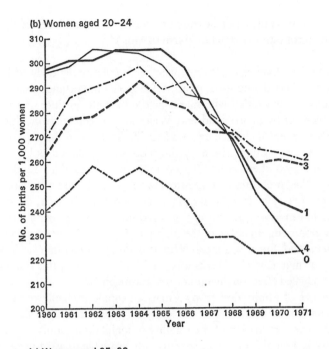

(b) Women aged 20–24

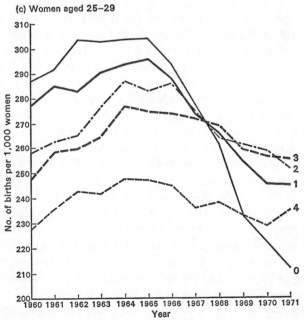

(c) Women aged 25–29

(c) the actual family size (the extent to which the 'ideal' is realized)
(d) the rate of family formation (birth spacing)

Changes in marriage patterns, whether people marry early or late, will indirectly affect the number of births. Of special importance are changes in the numbers of women who marry before they are 30 since 97 per cent of legitimate births in England and Wales are to women from this group. The most recent major change has been the increase in the supply of marriage eligibles brought about by the post-war population bulge. Between 1966 and 1970 there were 214,000 more marriages than in the period 1961–5. The proportion of spinsters who marry before they are 30 rose from 913 per 1,000 in 1961 to 949 per 1,000 in 1970. In 1971, however, the proportion marrying in this age group decreased to 943 per 1,000, the decrease occurring mainly in the 20–24 age group (Office of Population Censuses and Surveys 1973a). Will this decrease continue as this extra supply of marriage eligibles is used up? The answer to this question will have a marked effect on the numbers of future births.

The size of family desired by a married couple probably results from a combination of prevailing social attitudes towards family size and the couple's own estimation of their ability to maintain a family. Two sample surveys of desired family size are currently available to assist in forecasting mean completed family size figures. The first of these (Woolf 1971) was done in 1967 and gives the average desired family size as approximately 2·5 children for women who married in the 1960s. In a review of the survey, however, Langford (1972) disagrees with the conclusion that the average intended family size is a good indicator of actual future child-bearing. The second survey which asked questions about intended family size was the General Household Survey (Office of Population Censuses and Surveys 1973b). This survey, carried out in 1971, gives a somewhat reduced desired family size of 2·3 children. A criticism of both surveys is that they may reflect particular feelings at the time of the interview rather than realistic family size plans (Hawthorn 1973).

An indication of the degree to which the 'ideal' family size is being achieved can be obtained from mean family size figures (Office of Population Censuses and Surveys 1973c). During the past 50 years the mean family size has declined from 2·32 for women marrying in the early 1920s to 2·00 for women marrying in the early 1940s. When the families of women marrying in the 1950s and the early 1960s are complete, their mean size is likely to exceed the 2·32 figure of the 1920s. For women marrying in the late 1960s and early 1970s, family building has just begun, and we can therefore only base our estimates of completed family size on observed fertility in the first years of marriage. The mean family size of this latter group, when analysed by marriage duration, seems to have dropped somewhat. Whether this small decline is an indication that when current families are completed their size will be below the 2·32–2·33 level used by the Government Actuary in the 1971 and 1972-based projections, is still a matter for conjecture. The continued decline in the number of births since 1964, however, may be an indication that mean completed family size could be smaller than the currently predicted level.

Part of the change in fertility patterns is due to changes in the rates of family formation, i.e. the spacing of births. Changes in birth spacing are noticeable when age-specific legitimate birth rates by calendar year are examined. Figure 2 shows the changes during the 1960–70 period for those aged under 30 at marriage who have been married for 0–4 years. The marked decline after 1964 in the birth rate for women married less than two years has virtually reversed the pre-1964 pattern of having the first child early in marriage. It is now more probable that the first birth will occur after two or three years of marriage.

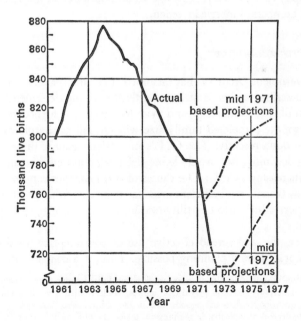

Fig. 3   England and Wales: live births in 1961–72 and recent GAD projections to 1976.

Government Actuary's birth and family size assumptions

The 1971 and 1972-based projections both show an increase in the number of births over the 40-year projection periods, 1971–2011 and 1972–2012. The increase in the number of births is, however, only about half as large as that assumed in the 1970-based projection. Although the implied fertility rates for the 1971-based projection do not change markedly during the projection period, increases in the number of women of child-bearing age from previous years of high birth rates, combined with the assumption that fertility will remain considerably above the replacement level, result in a steady increase in the number of births over the projection period. In the 1972-based projection, the fertility levels are assumed to be slightly above replacement level from 1972 until 1974, then to increase gradually until 1982 and finally to remain constant for the rest of the projection period. The number of births resulting from these fertility assumptions are shown in figure 3.

The projected number of live births is calculated, as noted previously, by applying sets of fertility rates, consistent with the assumed mean completed family size and varying by age at, and duration of, marriage, to the projected numbers of married women.

GLC's birth assumptions

The Government Actuary has assumed that the pattern of fertility changes described earlier is at least partly due to the deferment of child-bearing until later in marriage and to an increased spacing between births; if this is so, the completed family size will not fall as sharply as fertility rates have done recently. The GLC's projections assume that legitimate fertility is declining, not merely being deferred, and that spacing between births is increasing as well. The causes of these changes can only be conjectured, as there is not sufficient evidence to be able to pinpoint the effect of the factors which affect fertility (see Hawthorn 1970, 1973, Population Panel 1973).[2]

However, the widespread effective use of contraceptive methods now makes accurate family planning possible. Thus, if a couple want to post-

---

2 There is an obvious difficulty in drawing firm conclusions about fertility patterns; such an analysis of necessity relies on period-type indices, while women have their families over time spans much longer than the periods used in the indices. Also, behaviour in one time period is interdependent with that in the previous period. Fertility analysis since 1900 is based upon a period of transition in which the obvious fluctuations may well conceal basic influences on fertility.

pone parenthood for any number of reasons – for instance, so that a wife can continue her career, gaining satisfaction from an activity other than motherhood and at the same time enabling the couple to enjoy a higher standard of living – they can do so.

The authors' supposition is, therefore, that more and more couples will decide to limit the size of their family to a level they can support while still enjoying a fairly high level of material well-being. Also, any postponement of parenthood in a social climate which defines an appropriate age range for bearing children will result in some couples passing beyond this age range and becoming socially too old for a family, or at least a large family, even though biologically the woman is still fertile.

Alternative fertility assumptions for England and Wales

The birth rates used in the GLC projections are based on GLC estimates of the mid-1971–72 age-specific fertility rates. These rates have been adjusted by applying 'improvement' factors [3] over time to produce two alternative projections. These projections are exploratory rather than predictive, the purpose being to investigate likely patterns of population change up to the year 2011 that would result from varied fertility assumptions. Figures 1 and 4 show the populations and the births resulting from these projections.

The first GLC projection results from reducing the fertility rates until replacement level is reached (in 1977) and then keeping the rates constant at this level until the end of the projection period. The second GLC projection is based on the assumption that fertility falls at a rate of 2 per cent per year until 1984 resulting in a facsimile of zero population growth from 1997 to 2011.

Projections for Greater London

The Registrar General's 1969 projection for Greater London was reviewed in *Quarterly Bulletin* No. 13 (Thompson, 1970). The Registrar General's 1971-based projection (Office of Population Censuses and Surveys 1973d) and the GLC's 1971-based projections are shown in Table 3. From this table the effect of differing assumptions about fertility and migration can easily be seen.

3 The 'improvement' factors are the geometric mean of changes in the age-specific fertility rates over the period 1964–71.

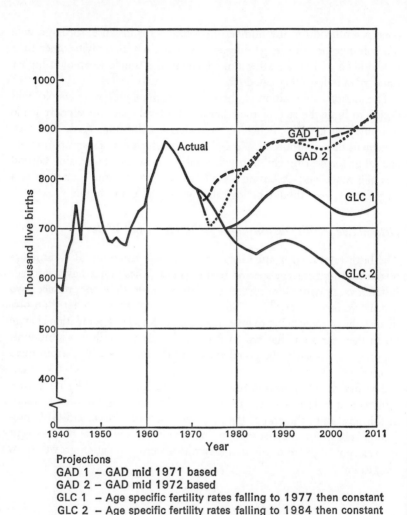

Fig. 4   England and Wales: live births 1940–72 and projections to 2011.

For the Registrar General's 1971-based projections, migration assumptions are those used for the 1969 projections adjusted for recent trends in international migration and incorporating recent information about increased population outflow from the South East. The lower GLC projection assumes the maintenance of current (1971) net out-migration levels

Table 3 Mid-1971-based population projections for Greater London

Thousand persons

Year	Registrar General's projection*			GLC low projection			GLC high projection		
	Population	Average annual natural increase	Average annual net migration	Population	Average annual natural increase	Average annual net migration	Population	Average annual natural increase	Average annual net migration
1971	7,418	+40	−100	7,431	+15	−116	7,431	+14	−109
1976	7,120	+37	−100	6,945	+2	−115	6,977	+1	−90
1981	6,803	+27	−90	6,379	+2	−106	6,533	+3	−76
1986	6,487	+18	−90	5,863	+4	−89	6,168	+7	−65
1991	6,129			5,440			5,874		

Source: Office of Population Censuses and Surveys (1973d).

*

until 1981 and then the level is allowed to decrease proportional to the decrease in population until 1991. The higher GLC projection allows net out-migration to decrease in proportion to the decrease in population over the entire period.

The fertility assumptions used by the Registrar General are those used in the Government Actuary's projections adjusted for recent information on regional fertility differentials. The fertility rates used in the GLC's projections are based on the experience in the Greater London area from 1964 to 1970. Both GLC projections assume that fertility will continue to fall by about 3·5 per cent per year until 1977, and then remain constant. The effect on the age structure of making these assumptions is shown in Table 4; the greatest change is the loss in the 0–14 age group, brought about by the out-migration of couples with young children.

Table 4   Comparison of 1971-based projections for Greater London

	Change 1971–1981					
	Registrar General's projection‡		*GLC low projection*		*GLC high projection*	
Age group	'000	%	'000	%	'000	%
Children 0–14	−216	−14	−371	−24	−321	−21
Working ages*	−450	−10	−590	−13	−501	−11
Reitrement ages†	+51	+4	−91	−8	−76	−7

* Males 15–64, females 15–59.
† Males 65+, females 60+.
‡ *Source:* Office of Population Censuses and Surveys (1973d).

Conclusions

The GLC's projections for England and Wales give lower future population levels than those of the Government Actuary. Figure 1 shows that, although fertility is at the replacement level from 1976 onwards for the first GLC projection, the population continues to grow. This of course is

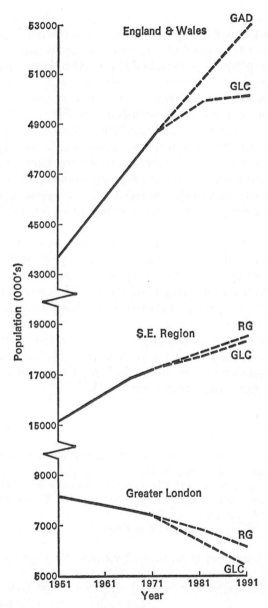

Fig. 5 A comparison of 1971-based projections for England and Wales, the South East, and Greater London.

Sources: Government Actuary (1972). Office of Population Censuses and Surveys (1973). Thompson (1973).

due to the large number of persons already born (from the post-war baby boom and the recent period of high birth rates up to 1964) at the start of the projection period. The second GLC projection shows what would result if fertility levels continued to decline until 1984 – namely that the population of England and Wales would cease to grow. This situation arises when the number of births equals the number of deaths and would occur about the year 2004 according to this projection. The population is then at a zero growth level and afterwards begins to fall slightly. Although this projection is markedly different from the Government Actuary's, the fall in fertility that is currently being experienced and the changes in family formation patterns discussed above indicate that it is possible that England and Wales could experience a decreasing population pattern after the year 2000.[4]

For Greater London also, the GLC's projections show lower future population levels than the Registrar General's projections. The lower fertility assumptions used in the GLC projections result in an age structure different from that of the official projections. This is most noticeable (see Table 4) in the 0–14 age group which in the lower GLC projection decreases about twice as much as in the official projection.

Finally, the Greater London projections, when examined in the context of projections for the South East and England and Wales (Figure 5) shows the likely continued decrease in London's population and a lessened increase for the region and the country as a whole.

References

FREJKA, T. (1973) 'The Prospects for a Stationary World Population', *Scientific American*, vol. 228, no. 3, 15–23.

General Register Office (1967) *The Registrar General's Statistical Review of England and Wales for the Year 1964: Part III: Commentary* London, H M S O, table C56, 70.

Government Actuary (1972) *Population Projections No 2 1971–2011* London, H M S O.

Government Actuary (1973) *Population Projections No 3 1972–2012* London, H M S O.

HAWTHORN, G. (1970) *The Sociology of Fertility* New York, Collier-Macmillan.

HAWTHORN, G. (1973) *Population Policy: A Modern Delusion* London, Fabian Society. [Fabian Tract 418.]

4 For a further discussion of the fertility levels necessary to achieve zero population growth see Thomas Frejka's article 'The Propects for a Stationary World Population'. (Frejka 1973)

LANGFORD, C. (1972) Review of *Family Intentions* by Woolf, Myra, *Population Studies*, vol 26, no 2, 333–5.

Office of Population Censuses and Surveys (1973a) *The Registrar General's Statistical Review of England and Wales for the Year 1971: Part II: Tables, Population* London, H M S O, Table QQ(b), 184.

Office of Population Censuses and Surveys (1973b) *The General Household Survey: Introductory Report* London, H M S O, 73.

Office of Population Censuses and Surveys (1973c) *The Registrar General's Statistical Review of England and Wales for the Year 1971: Part II: Tables, Population* London, H M S O, Table K, 60.

Office of Population Censuses and Surveys (1973d) *The Registrar General's Quarterly Return for England and Wales: Quarter Ended 30 September 1972* London, H M S O, no 495, 44–51.

Population Panel (1973) *Report of the Population Panel* London, H M S O, Cmnd 5258.

THOMPSON, E. J. (1969) 'Aspects of Some Recent Official Population Projections', *GLC Research and Intelligence Unit Quarterly Bulletin*, no 8, September 1969, 42–52.

THOMPSON, E. J. (1970) 'Aspects of Some Recent Official Population Projections – II', *GLC Intelligence Unit Quarterly Bulletin*, no 13, December 1970, 23–34.

THOMPSON, E. J. (1973) 'Some Implications of Recent Population Trends for South-East England', *GLC Intelligence Unit Quarterly Bulletin*, no 22, March 1973, 37–43.

WOOLF, MYRA (1971) *Family Intentions* London, H M S O, X [Office of Population Censuses and Surveys, Social Survey Division.]

Part II Communication

Introduction

In this Part *communication* is taken as one of the significant aspects of society, to be studied both as a constant feature of human interaction and as something which has changed in its detailed realization over the course of human history. 'Communication' is clearly a very wide term and, unlike, say, 'politics' or 'economics', is not a facet of social life which has usually been recognized as comprising a single discipline or established field of study. Nevertheless, it is an area of human society that has received attention from specialists in a number of different disciplines – for example linguistics, psychology, sociology, geography and technology – with each taking a different perspective on the field. As such, communication is beginning to prove an increasingly attractive area for study and, though only certain aspects of this vast subject can be pursued in this Reader, to provide a useful focus for cooperation between a number of disciplines.

The present selection begins with two extracts which consider communication at the *interpersonal* level as, for example, when two people engage in conversation. They offer, however, very contrasting kinds of analysis. The first by Michael Argyle is about eye contact and the direction of gaze. It is taken from his interesting little book *The Psychology of Interpersonal Behaviour*. Argyle explains how eye contact can be investigated experimentally and collects together the results of various studies, mostly of an experimental kind, to show the variety of functions eye contact serves in social interaction. The second extract is by R. D. Laing, H. Phillipson and A. R. Lee and comes from their book *Interpersonal Perception*. It is based on clinical and human experience rather than experimental data. It emphasizes that our only access to the behaviour of others when we are interacting is through the filter of our experience. A person will often perceive himself and what he does and says very differently from the way in which these are experienced by the person he is communicating with. The authors discuss the vicious circle of misinterpretation and conflict often generated in social interaction situations by such 'disjunctions' of experience. The model involved here is primarily the simplest one of communication between *two* people, speaker and listener – in other words, a *dyadic* model. But it becomes clear from both these extracts that this kind of analysis can be extended to involve additional people and wider groupings – the kinds of social contexts in which most of our lives take place.

Besides these continuing patterns of interpersonal communication the subject can also be approached by asking the question of how communication has *differed* at different periods of human history or in different forms of society. This applies both to the actual media used and to the way the communication system is socially organized and controlled. Some scholars have argued persuasively that the dominance of one particular medium in a society – say writing as against oral communication, or telecommunications as opposed to print – has a whole series of consequences for the nature of that society. This position is discussed at some length in the course material and is alluded to here in the brief but carefully stated comment by Ong 'Is literacy passé?'. It is also treated in the longer extract by Colin Cherry, one of the leading international authorities on communication. He explains some of the implications and characteristics of the various media of communications (summarized in the table on p. 119) and in this sense might seem to lend some support to the general notion of the crucial importance of the *technology* of communication. But he also balances this by his insistence on *socially* rather than *technologically* conditioned choices: any one medium can be used, he points out, in a variety of ways and 'serves many, quite different purposes'. Human rather than technical requirements are seen as the crucial ones.

Communication can involve not just the transmission of symbolic messages through media like speech, writing or telecommunications, but also the physical transport of people and things. In his extract Cherry pays attention both to the postal system, with its increasingly rapid transport of mail, and to the questions of air and sea traffic and the number of passengers actually involved in physical mobility in this way – another angle to communication [1] which may seem far from the types of communication more often considered by psychologists or sociologists, but which is nevertheless an essential complement to them in the overall communication system of any society.

Communication can also be brought into the arena of political sociology. Among the questions which have concerned political sociologists have been what it is that makes up a community or, at another level, a nation: in his discussion of 'Peoples, nations, and communication' Deutsch looks for the answer to these questions in the notion of *communication*. As he puts it: 'The community which permits a common history to be experienced as common, is a community of complementary habits and facilities of communication'.

One common theme which emerges from the selection of otherwise

---

[1] One discussed at some length in the course material in the context of transport geography, but not represented by a separate extract here.

somewhat disparate readings here is the way communication is always *structured*. It is tempting to begin from a model of free and unconstrained communication in which every individual communicates (or should ideally communicate) in a free and untrammelled and, as it were, transparent context. But it becomes clear that the reality is, and has to be, very different. This is so even at the simplest and most personal level. In interpersonal communication, Argyle demonstrates the structured patterns of eye-contact that can be detected, related to both personality and situation; and Laing *et al.* emphasize the process of *interpretation* in communication and the expectations that are inevitably involved, even when neither party recognizes their existence consciously. Similarly the communication patterns in a society are generally structured by a range of factors: for example the nature of the particular media most developed in that society, the way the institutions surrounding the various communication media are socially organized or politically and economically controlled, or the human choices as to which of many potential uses are exploited. The transport systems too, on which much communication depends, result from a complex inter-action of geographical, economic and political factors, and cannot be under-stood in isolation from these. In Deutsch's analysis, finally, the existence of communities and of nations rests on shared patterns of communication: and this social communication is 'bound up indissolubly with the ends and means of life, with men's values and the patterns of their teamwork . . . with all the psychological, political, social and economic relationships that influence the security and happiness of individuals'.

Man as a communicator, in short, cannot be seen in a void but as essentially communicating within the structured patterns of society. Communication in this sense is structured through the psychological, social, economic, political and technological forms and spatial constraints of the society and groups in which it takes place.

Ruth Finnegan

4   Eye-contact and the direction of gaze

Michael Argyle

The movements of the eyes perform a number of important functions in social interaction. During interaction A looks at B in the region of the eyes, intermittently and for short periods – this will be referred to as 'Looking' or 'gaze'. For some of this time B is Looking back at A in the region of the eyes – this will be called 'eye-contact' (EC). Figure 1 shows how these phenomena can be studied.

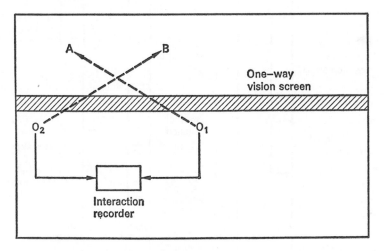

Fig. 1   Laboratory arrangements for studying gaze-direction.

Two subjects A and B are seated, perhaps at a table, and are asked to discuss some topic. A's gaze is recorded by observer 1, B's gaze by observer 2; the observers press buttons which activate some kind of interaction recorder. The observers may also record periods of speaking. One kind of interaction recorder marks periods of looking or speaking as deflections of inked lines on a paper tape, as shown in figure 2. It is also possible to record

ARGYLE, MICHAEL (1972) 'Eye-contact and the Direction of Gaze', in *The Psychology of Interpersonal Behaviour* Harmondsworth, Penguin, 80–93.

electronically, on equipment that summates periods of button-pressing (needed for EC) and number of presses.

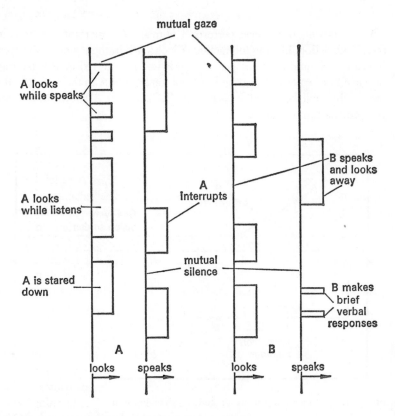

Fig. 2   Record of looking and speaking (Argyle 1969).

Experiments by Von Cranach (1972) and his colleagues at the Max Planck Institute for Psychiatry in Munich have shown that subjects and observers cannot discriminate between gazes directed towards the eyes and to other parts of the face, and that accuracy is less at greater distances. What is being recorded as eye-directed gaze should perhaps be described as face-directed gaze. On the other hand there are special reasons for looking at the eyes – there is probably an innate interest in eyes, eyes provide crucial information about where the other is looking, and the area round the eyes is extremely expressive. For these reasons it is probable that most face gaze is in fact directed to the immediate region of the eyes. The main exception to this is that deaf people focus on another person's mouth while he is speaking. When not looking at the face most people look right away – either at objects under discussion, or blankly into space.

The normal pattern of gaze

When two people are engaged in conversation they Look each other in the eye intermittently. The percentage of the time each Looks is usually between 25 per cent and 75 per cent of the time, though the full range from nought to a hundred per cent has been seen in our laboratory. The glances vary in length from about three to seven seconds, which is much longer than the fixations of 0·25–0·35 seconds common for visual scanning. While A is Looking at B, B will Look back part of the time, producing EC, typically for 15 per cent to 50 per cent of the total interaction time, in periods of about 1–3 seconds on average.

The direction of gaze is closely related to the pattern of speech. People Look nearly twice as much while listening as while speaking, their glances are longer, and their away-glances are shorter. We shall distinguish between Looking while listening and Looking while talking. If A breaks EC before B, this is not necessarily because he has been 'stared down'; it may be because he is starting to speak, and is avoiding distraction. When A is just about to start speaking he looks away from B; at the ends of sentences or phrases he Looks up briefly, and at the end of his utterance he gives B a more prolonged gaze. He does not Look at hesitations or pauses in the middle of sentences, but only at natural breaks. B, who is listening, will at the same time be giving rather longer glances, and may respond to A's short glances by signals of various kinds. Part of this general pattern can be seen in figure 3, which is based on data collected by Dr Adam Kendon from conversations between pairs of students who were asked 'to get acquainted'.

The importance of gaze signals for synchronizing has been shown in two other experiments. It was found that if one subject wore dark glasses there were more pauses and interruptions (Argyle, Lalljee and Cook 1968). When subjects were asked to deliver monologues preliminary to conversation proper they looked 45 per cent of the time, compared with 65 per cent for conversation, where the synchronizing signals were needed. (These

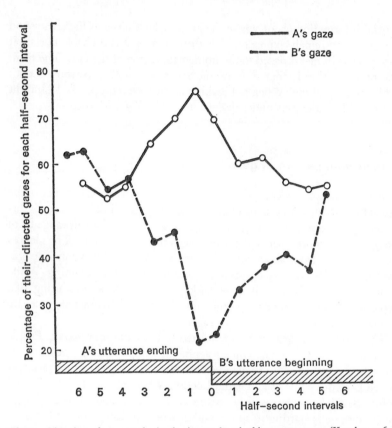

Fig. 3　Direction of gaze at the beginning and end of long utterances (Kendon 1967).

percentages are rather higher than usual because the subjects were looking through a one-way screen, and could not be seen themselves; the experiment is described below.)

Looking as information seeking

An experiment was carried out at Oxford in which two subjects were separated by a one-way screen (Argyle, Ingham 1972). A could see but not be seen, while B could be seen but not see. The person who could see looked 65 per cent of the time, compared with 23 per cent for the other. This demonstrated that Looking is primarily for obtaining information. People Look while listening in order to obtain visual information to supplement the auditory information – facial expression and gestures provide commentary and illustrations on what is being said. They Look while talking to get feedback on the person's reactions, since one of the most important sources of feedback is facial expression. The upper half of the face shows more than the bottom, and once one looks in this area it is difficult not to focus on the other's eyes; the reason for this is probably the innate attraction of eyes. The main reason why people Look at the end of their utterances is that they need feedback on the other's response. This may be of various kinds. A wants to know whether B is still attending – his direction of gaze shows if he is asleep, or looking at someone else. A also wants to know how his last message was received – whether B understood, agreed, thought it was funny. At pauses in the middle of long speeches, A will Look for continued permission to carry on speaking, and B will nod or grunt if he is agreeable to this.

In another experiment strong support was obtained for the hypothesis that Looking is used to gain information on the other's response. Vision between A and B was interfered with in various ways, e.g. B wore 1) dark glasses, 2) a mask with only eyes showing, 3) both mask and dark glasses. In these conditions A was increasingly uncomfortable, was increasingly less clear about how B was reacting, and expressed a desire for more information about B's responses. The experiment shows that it is more useful to see the face than the eyes, though it was necessary to see the eyes themselves for signals about synchronizing (Argyle, Lalljee and Cook 1968).

However too much information is distracting, and interferes with the production of utterances. In the one-way screen experiment subjects who could see without being seen Looked more than under normal conditions but on average only 67 per cent. While talking they Look only 55 per cent. The reason is probably that people do not want to be distracted by too much incoming information, especially at the beginning of an utterance while it is being planned and organized.

Similarly, Kendon found that A looks away during hesitating and unfluent passages; if A Looks while speaking he speaks faster – these are the fluent, well-rehearsed parts of his utterance. When the material itself is more complex and difficult, there is less EC for the same reason, as Exline has found.

Looking as a signal or social technique

When A Looks at B, this conveys information of various sorts to B, and can therefore be regarded as a kind of signal. A may or may not consciously intend to send B such a signal, but nevertheless B is likely to act upon it. In the one-way screen experiment described above it was found that the subjects who could see nothing at all still looked in the immediate direction of the other about 23 per cent of the time, presumably to send signals of some kind. What precisely those signals are depends on A's facial expression, the sequence of interaction, and the situation they are in. The main alternatives are as follows:

1   A wants to initiate interaction with B, for example at a party, or in a situation where a number of other people are present. If B Looks back it means that he is willing to engage in interaction. In some cases, if B lets A catch his eye, he is under some obligation to enter the relationship, as is the case with waiters and chairmen. It is interesting that these people are rather good at not letting their eye be caught, presumably by skilful peripheral vision. Conversely, if B Looks away while A is speaking, A realizes that B is no longer attending to what he has to say.

2   A shows B the attitude or emotions which he feels towards B. The most common is that of friendliness; there is more EC towards people that are liked. If B is an attractive member of the opposite sex, Looking combined with a friendly expression conveys A's sexual attraction to B – he is 'making eyes' at B – especially if EC is prolonged. Looking combined with a hostile expression means that A dislikes B, or wishes to dominate him.

3   If, after A has Looked at him in one of these ways, B wishes to show that he accepts this kind of relationship, he will Look back in the appropriate way. If he wishes to reject A's definition of the situation he will first Look angrily at A and then look away entirely. Exline has found that if B is arbitrarily given more power than A, then A will look away – he is rejecting the relationship which he is being offered.

4   At the end of each speech A is likely to Look at B. This is taken as a signal that A has finished and that B may speak. Kendon (1967) found that if A does not Look, B either does not answer at all, or delays longer before doing so. This happened in 71 per cent of cases, compared with 29 per cent when A did look up.

5   If A accompanies his speech with Looking, B will feel that A is more believable, more confident, and more favourable in his attitude to B. As

we shall see, these impressions are to some extent justified, since people Look more when they like the person they are talking to, and when they are telling the truth.

6 Much interaction is accompanied by a series of fairly short glances on both sides. If A gives B rather longer glances than are normal, B will interpret this as meaning that A is concerned primarily with B as a person, or with the relationship between A and B, rather than with whatever it is they are talking about. This can be seen in the case of young lovers who are ostensibly talking about politics, religion or mathematics. It can also be seen in the rather impassive gaze used by some psychiatrists – which signals an interest in the patient as a patient as opposed to what he is saying.

The motivational basis of looking

We have seen that people Look to obtain information and to send signals, and that they restrain their Looking while talking to avoid distraction. This is all concerned with the flow of information needed to perform the social skills of interacting. In addition Looking is affected by more basic motivations. Infants are attracted towards eyes at a very early age. Looking may be rewarded, if a child finds that he is usually responded to by a smiling face, which in turn is associated with rewards of other kinds, such as food or bodily contact. It is probably for this reason that being Looked at is experienced as rewarding. It is also emotionally arousing – it has been found that electrical activity in the brain-stem of rhesus monkeys increases when humans Look at them.

While short periods of Looking may simply be part of the signalling and information-gathering processes, longer periods signify a heightened interest in the other person – either in an affiliative, sexual, or aggressive-competitive sense. When under the sway of one of these motivations, if the situation is appropriate, there will be more Looking. For example, if A is high in affiliative motivation, and likes B, he will engage in more Looking (Exline and Winters 1965).

Although EC is satisfying, it is unpleasant and embarrassing if there is too much of it, and if mutual glances are too long. This may be because unpleasantly high levels of physiological arousal are generated. Or it may be because long glances carry a special meaning, as suggested above. Or it may be because there are also avoidance components connected with EC. We have mentioned one of these already – the avoidance of distraction at certain points of the conversation. However, there is no doubt that it is more comfortable watching others from behind a one-way vision screen than watching others who can Look back. This suggests that being aware of being observed by another is disturbing. We shall discuss experiments on the effects of being observed later.

If there are forces both to engage in EC and also to avoid it, there will be a state of conflict. It follows that there is an equilibrium level of Looking for each person and of EC for any two people, and that when the approach forces are relatively strong there will be more EC. We will now consider some implications of this equilibrium when the positive forces for EC are mainly affiliative or sexual, as opposed to dominative or aggressive. EC is one of several components of 'intimacy', along with physical proximity, intimacy of topic, smiling and tone of voice. If we suppose that there is an overall equilibrium for intimacy, it follows that when one of the component elements is disturbed there will be some complementary change among the others to restore the equilibrium. Several examples of this have been observed.

Argyle and Dean (1965) tested the hypothesis that greater proximity would result in less EC. Subjects took part in three three-minute discussions with stooges trained to stare, at distances of two, six and ten feet. The amount of EC was recorded by observers in the usual way (fig. 4). In later experiments it was found that the same results were obtained with pairs of genuine subjects; most of the distance effect was due to changes in Looking while listening, though for male-female pairs Looking while talking was also affected; the change of EC was mainly due to changes in the amount of individual gaze, rather than to changes in the timing of gazes (Argyle and Ingham 1972). The one-way screen experiment shows how much gaze is reduced by the occurrence of EC: a person who can see without being seen looks 65 per cent of the time, compared with 50 per cent under normal conditions.

Other experiments provide further evidence for the equilibrium model, by showing inverse relationships between affiliative signals. Exline, Gray and Schuette (1965) found that if subjects are interviewed by a continuously gazing interviewer there is less E C when more personal questions are asked. Kendon found an inverse relationship between smiling and EC when different points in conversations were compared. If A smiles, B is also likely to smile, and thus the level of intimacy is raised. At these points in the conversation EC is reduced – which is what would be expected from the equilibrium model. In another experiment the author asked subjects to stand 'as close as it is comfortable to see well' to a series of objects in what was disguised as an experiment on vision. The objects included the

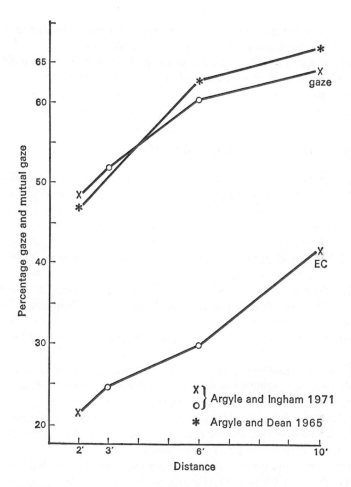

Fig. 4   Relation between eye-contact and distance apart of subjects.

author with eyes shut, and the author with eyes open. In each case a neutral-to-pleasant expression was adopted. Subjects came eight inches less close when the author's eyes were open than when they were shut. EC caused less proximity.

There are some amendments that need to be made to the equilibrium model. The degree of intimacy between two persons is not necessarily fixed, but may change. And if A emits smiles or other reinforcements, B is likely to act similarly through imitation. There is no evidence that this operates for gaze, but it does work for smiles, and other affiliative signals, which may affect the position of the equilibrium for intimacy.

There appears to be a certain amount of support for the equilibrium hypothesis, though it is clearly only one process among several operating in 2-person relationships.

The experience of being looked at

Being looked at for short periods is experienced as rewarding and enjoyable, but being looked at for long periods produces discomfort and anxiety, as we have seen. Some people want to avoid being seen ('audience anxiety') and also want to be seen ('exhibitionism'). These two traits are independent, so that the same person can experience both, and be in a state of conflict.

The origins of audience anxiety are not known – it may derive from the child's experience of being watched over and supervised by parents. When A is talking to B, A can both observe B, and be observed by B. A number of experiments at Oxford were carried out to find when people felt observed. It was found that subjects felt observed when being interviewed and when the other person was older; young females felt observed by young males.

When a person feels observed, he feels that he is being assessed or evaluated, that he must put on a good performance. People often want to present an improved version of themselves or to conceal things.

Exline found that if subjects are induced to cheat in an experiment, and later interviewed, they showed less eye-contact (1961). This suggests that the intimacy produced by E C is incompatible with deception, and acts as a source of pressure towards making embarrassing disclosures. It follows that social situations are probably a source of stress for people who are concealing large areas of their self-images. In some mental patients, the experience of being looked at is particularly disturbing.

1 A may expect to see rejecting, negative facial expressions on B's face, as a result of past experiences A has had with parents or others. Laing (1960a) reports on a number of patients who suffered from aversion of gaze for this reason – they were 'overwhelmed by a feeling of rejection'.

2 Another possibility is that people are disturbed by becoming an object for another's perception. Laing (1960b) reports on other patients who felt that they were turned to stone by being gazed at by another, that they lost their spontaneity, or were under the other's control.

However we still do not fully understand this phenomenon. In a number of experiments we have found that people feel more comfortable in social encounters if they wear dark glasses – though the other people feel less comfortable. This could be because people are made anxious by their eyes being seen, or it could be that wearing dark glasses puts someone in the role of observer, because he can see better.

Individual differences in looking

There are great variations between individuals in the amount of Looking they habitually engage in and how they do it. Experiments were carried out in which a number of subjects each interacted with a series of other subjects. It was found that subjects who looked a lot also used longer gazes, looked less often and had more EC. Subjects produced similar patterns of gaze with different partners, although they also varied their pattern of Looking to some extent between different partners (Kendon and Cook 1969).

A number of studies have been carried out to find whether gaze varies with personality traits. Extraverts are found to look more than introverts, and with longer glances. People high in the need for affiliation Look more, but only when the situation is a friendly or cooperative one. If the situation is competitive, these subjects Look less, and subjects high in dominative needs Look more. The effect is particularly marked in women. This finding can be used to explain the greater Looking by women: females are higher in affiliative motivation and lower in dominative, so that in the friendly setting of most of these experiments they should Look more (Exline 1963).

Exline has also found that people who think in an abstract way Look more than people who think in a concrete way. Abstract thinkers have greater powers of integrating incoming data, and are probably less affected by the distracting aspects of EC. A very low rate, or a total absence of Looking is found in autistic children and some schizophrenics. The cause is probably a failure of early attachment to the mother, or a long experience of rejection. 'Machiavellians' have a different pattern of EC from normals. They are people who are motivated to control others with cynical disregard for their welfare. Where others will reduce EC when they have a guilty secret to conceal, Machiavellians contrive to stare unabashed, as Exline has found.

Women engage in more gaze than men, especially when talking to other women. In addition, same-sex pairs Look more than opposite-sex pairs.

The reason for this is probably that Looking is a signal for sexual attraction, and this is something that has to be kept in check under laboratory conditions. In other situations, of course, there is a great deal of EC between opposite-sex pairs. Women also differ from men in their pattern of Looking. Exline and Winters (1965) found that women will Look at the other more while speaking, if they like her, while men look more when listening, if the other is liked. The explanation of this result is so far obscure.

References

ARGYLE, M. and DEAN, J. (1965) 'Eye Contact, Distance and Affiliation', *Sociometry*, 28, 289–304.

ARGYLE, M., LALLJEE, M. and COOK, M. (1968) 'The Effects of Visibility on Interaction in a Dyad', *Human Relations*, 21, 3–17.

ARGYLE, M. (1969) 'Observer or Observed? A Reversible Perspective in Person Perception', *Sociometry*, 32, 396–412.

ARGYLE, M. and INGHAM, R. (1972) 'Gaze, Mutual Gaze and Distance', *Semiotica*, 84.

EXLINE, R. V. (1961) 'Visual Interaction in Relation to Machiavellianism and an Unethical Act', *American Psychologist*, 16, 396.

EXLINE, R. V. (1963) 'Explorations in the Process of Person Perception : Visual Interaction in Relation to Competition, Sex and Need for Affiliation', *Journal of Personality*, 31, 1–20.

EXLINE, R. V., GRAY, D. and SCHUETTE, D. (1965) 'Visual Behaviour in a Dyad as Affected by Interview Content, and Sex of Respondent', *Journal of Personality and Social Psychology*, 1, 201–9.

EXLINE, R. V. and WINTERS, L. C. (1965) 'Affective Relations and Mutual Glances in Dyads', in Tomkins, S. and Igard, C. (eds) *Affect, Cognition and Personality* New York, Springer.

KENDON, A. (1967) 'Some Functions of Gaze Direction in Social Interaction', *Acta Psychologica*, 28 (1), 1–47.

KENDON, A. and COOK, M. (1969) 'The Consistency of Group Patterns in Social Interaction', *British Journal of Psychology*, 60, 481–94.

LAING, R. D. (1960a) *Self and Others* London, Tavistock Press.

LAING, R. D. (1960b) *The Divided Self* London, Tavistock Press.

CRANACH, M. VON (1972) 'The Role of Orienting Behavior in Human Interaction', in Esser, A. H. (ed.) *The Use of Space by Animals and Men*, University of Indiana Press.

5   Interaction and interexperience in dyads

R. D. Laing, H. Phillipson and A. R. Lee

In a science of persons, we state as axiomatic that:

1 behaviour is a function of experience
2 both experience and behaviour are always in relation to some one or something other than self

The very simplest schema for the understanding of the behaviour of one person has to include at least two persons and a common situation. And this schema must include not only the interaction of the two, but their interexperience.

Thus:

In terms of this schema, Peter's behaviour towards Paul is in part a function of Peter's experiences of Paul. Peter's experience of Paul is in part a function of Paul's behaviour towards Peter. Paul's behaviour towards Peter is in turn partly a function of his experience of Peter, which in turn is in part a function of Paul's behaviour towards him. Thus, the behaviour of Peter towards Paul, and of Paul towards Peter, cannot be subsumed under an exclusively inter*behavioural* schema . . . For, if Peter and Paul are persons, the behaviour of each towards the other is mediated by the *experience* by each of the other, just as the experience of each is mediated by the behaviour of each.

The transformation of Paul's behaviour into Peter's experience entails

---

LAING, R. D., PHILLIPSON, H. and LEE, A. R. (1966) 'Interaction and Interexperience in Dyads', in *Interpersonal Perception* London, Tavistock Publications, 9–18.

all the constitutional and culturally-conditioned learned structures of perception that contribute to the ways Peter construes his world. Much of this learning has never been open to reflective awareness. To a much greater extent than most of us realize, and any of us wish to believe, we have been 'programmed' like computing machines to handle incoming data according to prescribed instructions. Often this has been accompanied by meta-instructions against being aware that we are being thus instructed. This is an additional factor in the frequently great difficulty that many people have in opening their own 'programming' to their own conscious reflection.

If each of us carries around a set of criteria by which we judge certain acts as loving and tender or hating and brutal, what may be a loving act to one person may be a hating act to another. For example, one woman may be delighted if her suitor uses a 'caveman approach' with her; another woman may think of him as repugnant for just the same behaviour. The woman who sees the caveman approach as loving may in turn interpret a more subtle approach as 'weak', whereas the woman who is repelled by a caveman approach may see the more subtle approach as 'sensitive'. Thus behaviour even of itself does not directly lead to experience. It must be perceived and interpreted according to some set of criteria. [. . .]

In order for the other's behaviour to become part of self's experience, self must perceive it. The very act of perception entails interpretation. The human being learns how to structure his perceptions, particularly within his family, as a subsystem interplaying with its own contextual subculture, related institutions and overall larger culture. Let us take, for example, a situation in which a husband begins to cry. The behaviour is crying. This behaviour must now be experienced by his wife. It cannot be experienced without being interpreted. The interpretation will vary greatly from person to person, from culture to culture. For Jill, a man crying is inevitably to be interpreted as a sign of weakness. For Jane, a man crying will be interpreted as a sign of sensitivity. Each will react to a greater or lesser extent according to a preconceived interpretive model which she may or not be aware of. At its simplest level, Jill may have been taught by her father that a man never cries, that only a sissy does. Jane may have been taught by her father that a man can show emotion and that he is a better man for having done so. Frequently such intermediary steps (regulative schemata) that contribute to the determination of the experience are lost to awareness. Jill simply experiences her husband as weak; Jane simply experiences hers as sensitive. Neither is clear why. They might even find it difficult to describe the kinds of behaviour which have led them to their conclusion. [. . .]

Our experience of another entails a particular interpretation of his behaviour. To feel loved is to perceive and interpret, that is, to experience, the actions of the other as loving. The alteration of my experience of my behaviour to your experience of my behaviour – there's the rub.

I act in a way that is *cautious* to me, but *cowardly* to you.
You act in a way that is *courageous* to you, but *foolhardy* to me.
She sees herself as *vivacious*, but he sees her as *superficial*.
He sees himself as *friendly*, she sees him as *seductive*.
She sees herself as *reserved*, he sees her as *haughty and aloof*.
He sees himself as *gallant*, she sees him as *phoney*.
She sees herself as *feminine*, he sees her as *helpless and dependent*.
He sees himself as *masculine*, she sees him as *overbearing and dominating*.

Experience in all cases entails the perception of the act *and* the interpretation of it. Within the issue of perception is the issue of selection and reception. From the many things that we see and hear of the other we select a few to remember. Acts highly significant to us may be trivial to others. We happen not to have been paying attention at that moment; we missed what to the other was his most significant gesture or statement. But, even if the acts selected for interpretation are the same, even if each individual perceives these acts as the same act, the interpretation of the identical act may be very different. She winks at him in friendly complicity, and he sees it as seductive. The act is the same, the interpretation and hence the experience of it disjunctive. She refuses to kiss him goodnight out of 'self-respect', but he sees it as rejection of him, and so on.

A child who is told by his mother to wear a sweater may resent her as coddling him, but to her it may seem to be simply a mark of natural concern.

In one society to burp after a good meal is good manners; in another it is uncouth. Thus, even though the piece of behaviour under consideration may be agreed upon, the interpretation of this behaviour may be diametrically disagreed upon.

What leads to diametrically opposed interpretations? In general, we can say interpretations are based on our past learning, particularly within our family (i.e. with our parents, siblings and relatives) but also in the larger society in which we travel.

Secondly, the act itself is interpreted according to the context in which it is found. Thus, for example, the refusal of a goodnight kiss after one date may seem to be perfectly normal for both parties, but after six months' dating a refusal would seem more significant to each of them. Also a refusal after a previous acceptance will seem more significant.

What happens when two people do not agree on the meaning to be assigned a particular act? A very complicated process ensues. If communication is optimum, they *understand* that they differ on the interpretation of the act, and also *realize that they both understand* that they differ in its interpretation. Once this is established they may get into a struggle over whether or not to change the act under consideration in the future. This struggle may take various forms:

Threat – Do this or else.
Coaxing – Please do this.
Bribery – If you do this I will do that in return.
Persuasion – I believe it is a good idea for you to do this because, etc.

However, often in human affairs where there is a disagreement there is also a *misunderstanding* and *failure of realization of misunderstanding*. This may be deliberate, i.e. a simple attempt to ignore the other person's point of view, or it may be an unwitting overlooking of the opposing viewpoint. In either case a disruption of communication occurs. [...]

Now, we know that to different extents in different people and circumstances Peter's view of himself is related to what Peter thinks Paul thinks of him; that is, to Peter's metaperspective and meta-identity. If what Peter thinks Paul thinks of him is not what Peter wants to have thought of him, Peter has, in principle, as a means of controlling the condition that controls him, the option of acting upon Paul to change Paul, or of acting upon his own experience of Paul to change his experience of Paul. By acting on Paul, Peter may intend to act upon Paul's experience of Peter, or he may intend merely to act on Paul's action. If, for instance, he says 'Shut up', this injunction may say in effect: 'I don't care what you feel about me, just keep it to yourself.' [...]

I may so act as to induce the other to experience me in a particular way. A great deal of human action has as its goal the induction of particular experiences in the other of oneself. I wish to be seen by the other as generous, or tough, or fair-minded. However, I may or may not know what it is that I have to do to induce the other to interpret my action and experience me as I desire, whether generous or tough or fair-minded. His criteria for making these evaluations may be diametrically opposed to my criteria, and this I may or may not be aware of. Thus a passively resistant person (e.g. a Gandhi) may seem to one person to be tough, whereas to another he may seem to be weak.

Further, the other may wittingly or unwittingly be set to interpret every possible action of mine as indicating a preconceived hypothesis (e.g. that I am hurtful). For example, at a conjoint therapy session a wife interpreted her husband's absence as proof that 'he wished to hurt her'. When he showed up late she quite calmly assumed that he had finally decided to *come* 'in order to hurt her'. [...]

I therefore tend to select others for whom I can be the other that I wish to be, so that I may then reappropriate the sort of meta-identity I want. This requires that I find another who agrees with my criteria. But such stratagems may entail a remarkable alienation. My centre of gravity may become *the other I am to the other*. In such circumstances, in order to achieve the identity that I wish, through being the desired other for the other, the other must be malleable by me, or pervious to me. I must select carefully those others with whom I shall have to interact, acting towards them in such a way that I will be able to be to them what I want to be. I shall be in a serious dilemma, however, if I cannot make the other person regard me as that other that I wish to be for him. I may wish to be a mother to someone who is also wanting to be a mother, or to be generous to some-one who insists on seeing me as mean, and so on. Alternatively, under those circumstances I may in desperation adopt the strategy of acting upon my *own* experience of the other, so that in a sense I render my meta-identity independent of the other.

Let us consider this latter strategy in more detail. We see it in one form of self's action on self, namely, Peter's action on his own experience of Paul, under the name of projection. Projection is a form of action directed at one's own experience of the other. [...]

Projection is clearly a most important stratagem and may function in different ways in an interpersonal system, but in every case it is one of a class of *actions whose primary object is not the other's experience of me, but my experience of the other.* Secondarily, of course, it must also affect the other's experience of me. For example, when the paranoid individual 'projects', he may experience the other as hurting him and not helping him. This in turn forces the other to experience the paranoid as a person who sees him as a hurtful person. [...]

We have already suggested that projection is one way of acting on the other by, paradoxically, not acting directly on him as a real person, but on one's experience of him. But if I convey to the other how I experience him I am certainly influencing him. Indeed, one of the most effective ways to affect the other's experience of me is to tell him how I experience him. Every flatterer knows that, all things being equal, one tends to like someone by whom one is liked. If I am ugly, I am not ugly only in my eyes, I see myself in the looking-glass of your eyes as ugly too. You are the witness of my ugliness. In fact, insofar as ugliness is relative, if you and everyone else saw me as beautiful, I might be ugly no more. If I cannot induce you to see me as I wish, I may act on my experience of you rather than your experience of me. I can invent your experience of me. Many projections, of course, are the apparently compulsive inventions of persons who see themselves as ugly, and wish to extrude this perception from their own self-self relation. [...]

In Zarathustra, the ugliest man abolishes God because he cannot stand an eternal witness to his ugliness, and replaces him with nothing.

Projection refers to a mode of experiencing the other in which one experiences one's outer world in terms of one's inner world. Another way of putting this is that one experiences the perceptual world in terms of one's phantasy system, without realizing that one is doing this. [...]

Pure projection tells us nothing about the other. Projection refers only to one area of the dyadic interaction, namely, the way you act on your own experience of me, or the way I act on my own experience of you, although it will, we know, be influenced by, and will influence, the other areas, since your way of experiencing me interrelates with the way I act towards you, and so on. The way Peter acts towards Paul will have something to do with the way Paul experiences Peter, and with the way Paul, for his part, now acts towards Peter. Unfortunately, there is no systematic theory to guide us here, and a paucity of empirical data. We have no language even to describe various things that can happen in other parts of the dyadic circuit when projection occurs in one section. For instance, how does Paul react to his realization that Peter's experience of Paul is largely projection, and to his realization that Peter's actions are not addressed to the Paul that Paul takes himself to be, but to a Paul who is largely Peter's invention? One way to ease the situation is for Paul systematically to discover the data upon which Peter is constructing him into a person he does not recognize. This is more exacting than to assume that Peter is purely inventing his view of Paul. By this tactic, it becomes Paul's job to discover the criteria by which Peter is coming to his discordant conclusions. These are inevitably there, but they may be hidden or so strange, even to Peter, let alone to Paul, that they are neglected, ignored, or considered insignificant; that is, invalidated in one way or another.

For example, a husband and wife, after eight years of marriage, described one of their first fights. This occurred on the second night of their honeymoon. They were both sitting at a bar in a hotel when the wife struck up a conversation with a couple sitting next to them. To her dismay her husband refused to join the conversation, remained aloof, gloomy and antagonistic both to her and the other couple. Perceiving his mood, she became angry at him for producing an awkward social situation and making her feel 'out on a limb'. Tempers rose, and they ended in a bitter fight in which each accused the other of being inconsiderate. This was the extent of their report of the incident. Eight years later, however, we were able to tease out some of the additional factors involved. When asked why she had struck up the conversation with the other couple, the wife replied: 'Well, I had never had a conversation with another couple as a wife before. Previous to this I had always been a "girl friend" or "fiancée" or "daughter" or "sister". I thought of the honeymoon as a fine time to try out my new role as a wife, to have a conversation as a wife with my husband at my side. I had never had a husband before, either'. She thus carried into the situation her expectancy that the honeymoon would be an opportunity to begin to socialize as a couple with other couples. She looked forward to this eagerly and joyfully. By contrast, her husband had a completely differing view of the honeymoon. When questioned about his aloofness during the conversation he said: 'Of course I was aloof. The honeymoon to me was a time to get away from everyone – a time when two people could learn to take advantage of a golden opportunity to ignore the rest of the world and simply explore each other. I wanted us to be sufficient unto ourselves. To me, everyone else in the world was a complication, a burden and an interference. When my wife struck up that conversation with the other couple I felt it as a direct insult. She was telling me in effect that I was not man enough for her, that I was insufficient to fill her demands. She made me feel inadequate and angry.'

Eight years later they were able to laugh at the situation. He could say, 'If I had only known how you felt it would have made a great difference'. The crucial point is that each interpreted the other's action as inconsiderate and even deliberately insulting. These attributions of inconsiderateness and insult and maliciousness were based on hidden discrepant value systems and discrepant expectations based on these value systems.

6   Is literacy passé?

Walter J. Ong SJ

It may be that we have come to the end of the Gutenberg era. The electronic age may not yet have made printing obsolete, but it certainly has ended the monopoly rule of published matter over our habits of thinking.

Our 'typographical culture' began about five hundred years ago with the invention of the printing press, which enabled handwritten documents to be duplicated rapidly, thus facilitating the swift diffusion of ideas; but more importantly, the press changed our sense of what thinking itself is. To gauge the extent of that change we need only reflect on the communications systems used by preliterate and pre-typographical man.

Preliterate man knew no history in our sense of the term. His knowledge of the past was limited pretty much to what his parents and grandparents or great-grandparents could tell him. He lived in a voice-and-ear culture. His knowledge was stored in the mind, and when verbalized was communicated primarily by the voice and by other sounds. But sound, the ground of all verbal communication, is time-bound and evanescent. It exists only while it is passing out of existence. I cannot pronounce the last part of a word until the first part no longer exists. The alphabet – which appeared quite late in history, around 2000 B.C. – reduces the evanescence of sound in time to relative permanence in space. Pictures also do this, in a way. They enable us to recall an image or a concept, and thereby the word. But the alphabet turns the picture process inside out and upside down. It breaks the sound itself up into little spatial parts, which it reassembles on a surface in countless configurations. The alphabet thus had a revolutionary effect on our thinking processes.

However, the tug of habit is a strong one: the oral-and-aural tradition persisted long after the adoption and eventual spread of the alphabet. When, a few decades before Christ, Marcus Tullius Cicero wanted to bring Greek knowledge to the somewhat backward Romans of his day, he did not read scrolls in order to master that knowledge, but rather went to Greece to listen to the lecturers and orators of that country. Significantly, Cicero used to speak his orations aloud, then write them down as a kind of afterthought.

ONG, WALTER J. SJ (1959) 'Is Literacy Passé?', in *The Saturday Review*, 28 November 1959.

With the dawn of the European Middle Ages, Western man developed a 'manuscript culture'. Medieval scholars could not listen to Rome's learned men as Cicero had 'audited' those of Greece. So they pored through handwritten manuscripts: medieval culture produced the bookworm. However, it also retained massive oral–aural commitments. We know from Saint Augustine that men of his time continued to read aloud even when they were reading to themselves. Words were worth little unless they could be vocalized. In the medieval universities written exercises beyond the level of elementary instruction were absolutely unknown. Written texts abounded, but they were used as take-off points for speeches, for lectures, or for 'disputations', highly organized verbal tilts in which the students proved their mastery of logic, physics, and other subjects. Yet despite the persistence of this oral–aural cast of mind, medieval culture was preeminently a manuscript culture, a fact which prepared the way for printing and which perhaps made printing inevitable. For printing was and is a cheap way of producing what a manuscript culture wanted – something to read.

After the invention of the printing press, man's whole way of thinking about his own intellectual processes changes subtly. The 'spatial parts' embodied in the alphabet are made even more manoeuvrable by the press's movable type, and are given greater permanence by its fonts. Thinking processes are now taken to be concerned with getting things into an order comparable with that observed in a printed book. Thought begins to have 'content' just as books have tables of contents – a concept quite foreign to medieval and ancient man, for whom truth was not commonly associated with some kind of containment or boxing process, but rather with communications or teaching ('doctrine').

In our time a new drift, away from the 'typographical' and towards the 'oral-and-aural' culture, towards the world of sound, has definitely set in. As human society, despite its swelling size, becomes more closely knit around the globe, sound asserts itself more and more, supplemented and augmented by such marvels as the telephone, TV, rapid transportation systems, and earth satellites which speak to us in tiny, beep-beeping voices.

As corollary of this deep-rooted transformation, language itself is undergoing a profound overhauling. Grammar, which is based upon the written word, is giving way to linguistics, a discipline rooted in the spoken word, i.e. the word at first hand instead of at one remove.

In philosophical circles interest is veering away from logic to dialogue, from thinking conceived of as a private, silent affair, to thinking seen in its full social and public setting. There is a growing awareness that science itself at any moment is only arrested dialogue, and that the difference between what we know and what men five hundred years ago knew, or between what we know and what men a hundred thousand years from now will know, can be charted not in terms of men's private thoughts but in terms of what they have said to one another.

The new world will not forget the old. It never does. Printing is here to stay. But now, more than ever, it is only one part of a constellation of activities. Its monopoly is broken.

7   On communication, ancient and modern

Colin Cherry

Television? The word is half Latin and half Greek.
No good can come of it.

Attributed to C. P. Scott of The Manchester Guardian

We previously examined, to some extent, the nature of human language
and of its significance to individuals and to society, in an attempt to
destroy the over-simple idea that communication consists only of our sending messages one to another, and to replace it by the concept of human
involvements of many kinds. Our present day systems of communication,
such as radio, films, television, newspapers and others, have introduced the
possibility of extending human relationships, and involvements, over
larger areas of the globe, thereby giving rise to many completely new social
questions. I have said 'possibility', for how we adapt to and use these
systems now and in the future are totally different matters. In order to
discuss such questions rationally and to avoid only too common emotional
judgements heard about 'mass-communication', it is well to consider not
only the way in which our modern communication systems spread their
tentacles over the globe, but also how this has come about; that is, something of the dynamics, the history, of the change. So many of the questions
raised today, concerning mass-communication, are meaningful only on a
comparative basis; judgements are better made, not so much as to whether
today's mass-communication systems are good or bad, but rather whether
they are better or worse, and how our personal and national relationships
have been changed by them and changed so rapidly within one generation. . . .

Communication in antiquity

When modern mass-communication systems and their influence upon us
are discussed, it is most usual that their speed is mentioned, together with

CHERRY, COLIN (1971) 'On Communication, Ancient and Modern', in *World
    Communications: Threat or Promise?* New York, Wiley Interscience,
    28–53, 185–9.

Table 1   List of main applications of radio

1. Land based	(a) *Public services*	Inland microwave telephone links Sound broadcasting Television broadcasting Overseas radio-telephone (Mobile) radio-telephone (Mobile) radio-telegraphs
	(b) *Government, Industrial*	Aeronautical, fixed services (navigation, safety) Radio telemetering Police radio Radio and telephone-line data transmission Military, Naval, Air Force communication Closed circuit television
	(c) *Private*	Amateur radio stations Amateur services (training)
2. Maritime		(Mobile) ship stations (ship/ship/air; ship/shore) Port operations service Coast stations Ship emergency transmissions Survival craft (e.g. lifeboat) stations Distress calling systems Radio navigation (land and mobile) Radar Radio-telephones and telegraphs
3. Air		Aircraft stations (air/air; air/ground) Blind landing systems Radio altimeters Radio direction finders Radio beacon Radar Radio navigation Defence early warning Air traffic control
4. General		Radio astronomy Meteorological aids Radiosonde Standard frequency transmissions Time Signal Service Medical (diathermy, etc.) Industrial processings Experimental (research) work

such things as 'the stress of modern life' (whatever that ridiculous phrase may mean). Speed certainly is very important indeed, but *not* only because it enables affairs to proceed faster. Two other important social aspects of modern communications derive first from their great reliability and second, from their universal availability: meaning that their use is no longer confined to authorities.

In earlier historic times long-distance communication certainly existed (Neal 1960), linking whole empires, but its use was confined to military, diplomatic and governmental purposes, by generals, governors, emperors and other privileged élite: those in control. This has been true from the days of the Persian Empire to the coming of the railways and it is only comparatively recently that common man has had personal access to long-distance communication aids. But the structures of our advanced societies today (our institutions and how we regard our relationships with one another) are very much determined by our personal use of such things as telephones, telegraphs, data links and the postal service, T V, together with 'official usage' of these and other facilities on our behalf for such things as aircraft navigation, weather bulletins, by the police, fire brigades, industry, government and many other institutions. (Table I lists a number of uses of radio alone.) And it is their *reliability* and *universal access* to 'the common people' or their agents which makes our modern industrial society possible.

The widespread use of radio, telegraphs, T V, data links etc., is at present largely concentrated in areas of the world having high literacy rates (although radio is fast spreading elsewhere). Literacy is an essential prerequisite for the *active* adoption of technology on any scale not only because of the need to read technical instructions but because of mental attitudes. I say 'active' meaning technology in the sense of productive industries: the mere *possession* of transistor sets is another matter. We should perhaps remind ourselves that today some 40 per cent of the world's adults are illiterate (UNESCO 1970).

Indeed I would go so far as to say that *societies can develop and advance only as far and fast as they can acquire, use and maintain systems of communication: systems of acquiring, recording, assimilating and disseminating information.*

'Recording' is particularly important, whether this be on parchment, on paper, or in the magnetic store of a modern computer.

Man's progress from the earliest communities of the East and Middle East, through the great empires of antiquity, up to the highly complex industrial societies of today has been one long story of extended and improved means of communication. As these have developed so have people's effective interrelations, i.e. their organizations, bringing all the advantages of the division of labour and production of wealth, of broadened cultural horizons, of law and order, and especially the possibility of increased personal *trust* and *security* over far wider circles than a family or a village. I stress the word *possibility* here. At the same time, military development also has come from the same sources of improved communication. As communication within a country improves, social advancement is made theoretically more possible, because institutions may be organized more flexibly, though there is no reason to assume that it is certain to happen. (To take a modern example, it may be argued that crime can be reduced if the police are provided with more and better means of communication; this is true, but this will not attack the primary *sources* of crime increase.)

The importance of *recording* has been emphasized, as the first artefact or technology of communication. The earliest Mediterranean scripts were in pictograph, ideographs and hieroglyphic, giving direct picture-representation of objects and, by associations, of names, actions and ideas of all sorts. But it was the evolution of phonetic writing, during the Coptic Period, which was the great step; speech and writing became closely linked. The civilizations which did not adopt this technique (e.g. China) have been handicapped in certain ways throughout their history.

This simplification of script did not stop there, however. For example, ancient Hebrew was written without vowels. Deliberate condensation is not confined to present day newspaper advertisements (Dsrbl f'hd rsdnc; all mod cons; gs, elec . . .)[1] but was tried in numerous ancient writings: Church Slavonic abbreviated common words in much the same way. Shorthand too is not modern, but is said to have been used by the Greek slave Tyro for recording the lengthy speeches of Cicero. This looks not unlike modern shorthand, but was based on spelling; it continued to be used in Europe until the Middle Ages.

Together with other invented systems of recording messages, other remarkably early methods were found for transmitting them. Polybius, for example, is well known for his description of telecommunication using torches and other visual means, as well as for his coding of the alphabet. The classical historians Herodotus, Xenophon and Polybius each stress the need for communication services for the control of scattered empires and for waging wars.

How were the great empires of antiquity, such as that of Rome, held together? How did Caesar know what his generals were doing, when they

1 In full : Desirable freehold residence; all modern conveniences; gas, electricity.

were spread over half of Europe, from the North African coast to the borders of Scotland? It was done by a postal service, the forerunner of our modern services.

The postal service of the Romans was preceded by that of the Persians, by which official letters were carried on horseback in relays between established postal stations, a system which was later introduced into Imperial Rome by Augustus. The Roman Empire was 'held together' by an elaborate network of couriers, on horseback or in carriages (similar in form to the old Romany gypsy caravans) with relay posting stations at regular intervals along all main roads. Each posting station kept 40 horses and grooms and the speed would have been about 50 miles per day (Pflaum 1950, Ramsay 1925), with accurate fixed times for collection and delivery. A similar system was used by the Great Khan Kublai, as described by Marco Polo. (The earliest known postal service was probably that of semitic Babylonia, about 3800 b.c.)

I have referred to the Roman Empire as being 'held together'. Considering the great continental scale of that Empire and the extent of its activity in warfare, roadbuilding and governing, the bonds must have been very loose indeed, by our present day standards of national and civic integration, first because of the limited number of messages that could be sent per day and second, because of the great *time delay* between sending and receiving them. Time delay is very important. It means that in any day's interval between sending some order and its receipt, events may have taken place which rendered that order useless, or wrong, or even dangerous. Similarly with the time delay between sending a return message to headquarters, asking for instructions. This situation, with long time delays between the two ends, is well known to control engineers today as being a situation which can become 'unstable', that is to say, out of hand. It can only be concluded that the Roman Empire consisted of many strong *local* governments, dealing with all day-to-day affairs, and associated with Rome only for matters of general policy and important decisions. One of the characteristics of today's industrial societies is the high *speed* of connexion between Authorities and the Public, for governmental and social purposes of all kinds; when we use the phrase 'by return of post' we literally mean the next day, or day after, whilst the telephone is virtually instantaneous.

The coming of mass-communication

The great importance of *reliability* of communication has already been stressed. Various accounts of the ancient postal services all emphasize these points: precision of timing and certainty of delivery. Caesar, no less than any present day authority, had to know that messages were received and when he could expect a reply. Truly, the speed of communication has been increased many-fold in modern times, to be virtually instantaneous, but of first importance is the fact that we have also increased its reliability. People may now travel about with a greater sense of security, *knowing* that they will be able to telephone or telegraph home if necessary. In fact, if someone does find difficulty in getting swift contact on the telephone with the right person, he may get righteously angry about it. It has become an assumed right, taken for granted, as much a part of Nature as the air he breathes.

The Roman postal service was carried into Europe by the Roman occupation forces, and stayed there in various centres long after their withdrawal, at the collapse of their Empire (Pflaum 1950, Ramsay 1925). Indeed the system remained substantially unchanged until the late Medieval period. At that time several postal establishments in various States of Europe were run by the universities! The University of Paris, for instance, ran a postal service from the early thirteenth century until the eighteenth (Pflaum 1950).

From the earliest days, postal services seem to have been organized under government control and used for carrying the King's messages. Even today, in Britain, we speak of 'Her Majesty's Mail' [2] and all our stamps must bear an effigy of the monarch's head, symbolic of the security or protection offered.

It was not until the seventeenth century that the full *social* needs were recognized, for the postal service to be used by government officials, merchants, all but 'the common people'. In 1633 a regular weekly mail was set up between London, Antwerp and Brussels which took four to five days. By the time of Oliver Cromwell (1599–1658) regular services were running on all main roads of England, under licence from that remarkable new Institution, the English Parliament. It was during the same century that the Press developed, the original purpose being for *advertising*, which then was not distinguished from news.

Surprisingly, for those times, several attempts were made by private persons to set up postal services. John Hill, for example, organized a

2 The word *mail* comes from Old French *male*, meaning a bag for travellers.

'penny post' throughout England, but it was regularly attacked by Cromwell's soldiers. As early as 1680 a private London and suburban postal service was established (by William Dockwra), with hourly collections, sorting offices and postboxes, which was later incorporated into the state system. Similar developments took place in America, at much the same date.

We may read of constant efforts being made, throughout this early history of postal communication, to improve the reliability of the mails, and of growing public confidence. By the time of Queen Anne (1665–1714) regular mails were reaching England's scattered colonies and security was, officially, ensured. Whereas under Cromwell's regime, foreign mails were read by a Board of Examiners, now only Secretaries of State had the authority to do this!

Attack and robbery on the highways were steadily defeated, by higher speeds of travel and by arming the coach guards, so that public confidence further increased. But it was the coming of the railways which finally established the postal service as part of the life of every man, woman and child, as something utterly reliable and always available: that which we today accept as our due.

To quote my own country, Britain, by the time of Sir Rowland Hill's Post Office Reform Bill (1837), letters in the mails totalled 88 million per annum (whilst today there are over 11,000 million packages of all kinds per annum) (HMSO 1970). The *postage stamp* was invented in Britain, in acknowledgment of which it is the only country in the world whose stamps do not bear the name of the country (although the Monarch's head must always appear). Britain is also the main printer of stamps for the world, for no less than 125 foreign countries (e.g. see *Guardian* for 29 November 1966).

The railways were dominant, not only in the development of the mails, but also in the early history of telegraphy. It was the railways which were first to adopt the new electric 'telegraph', as an alternative to the post: the first invented 'electronic' system of communication. Although the suggestion that messages might be sent over a wire (by discharging a Leyden jar) was made as early as 1753, the first really practical trials were made by the railway companies (starting in 1837) and for a long time telegraphs were used only by the railways (International Telecommunication Union 1965). Even today we still have the familiar sight of telegraph poles and wires through our railway carriage windows.

Soon companies were formed. In 1851, the year of the Great Exhibition, the Stock Exchanges of London and Paris were connected by telegraph so that prices could be rapidly compared for the first time. The Atlantic was crossed by telegraph successfully in 1866 whilst by 1871 there was a connexion to India. Public confidence grew further and people were prepared to pay high prices for telegrams but for some period during the middle of last century the service was still confined to those towns and cities which were connected by the railways.

Of the story of the coming of the telephone little will be told here, for it is widely documented and it brings us into relatively modern times anyway. It is worth remembering that there are people alive today who can recall living in a world without the telephone; also it may be worth observing here that the telephone came into truly widespread use only after the Second World War.

Technically speaking, the telephone is an extension of the telegraph. Indeed, the first microphone made, by the German Philip Reis in 1861, operated rather in the manner of a very high-speed telegraph, the sound-waves of the voice 'making' and 'breaking' an electric current (popularly called today the bang–bang principle (Harder 1960, Neal 1960). Credit is usually given to Graham Bell for the first practical telephone, though others were working upon the same idea independently, including Elisha Gray and the lesser known Daniel Drawbaugh (Harder 1960, International Telecommunication Union 1965). Early experiments upon electric voice transmission had already been carried out by Page in Massachusetts (in 1837) and by Bourseul in Paris (in 1854). Thus the telephone was conceived very shortly after the telegraph, and that had developed alongside the railways.

It is these three modes of communication (rail, telegraph, telephone) introduced within such a short period of time, that ensured the coming of the kind of industrial world which we know today, with its huge and complex industrial organizations.

Something quite new in the history of communication was called for when telephones came into use, that is, some kind of *subscriber organization*. Every telephone in a country cannot be connected to every other telephone, so a *telephone exchange* is required. Telephone books, and a regular system of central accounting, etc., are needed. The first patent for a 'central station' to which houses could be connected had already been taken out in 1851.

The coming of radio at the turn of the century introduced something new again: simultaneous communication between some *central* (broadcasting) Authority and a large number of receivers. Other users of radio today (e.g. naval, military, police, etc.) operate similarly, see Table 1: that is, *broadcast*. Radio is somewhat analogous to the Press as a medium of communication, if only in this respect. It is to be expected that radio, and T V later, have come to serve some of the functions of the Press: entertainment, news and advertising, though in essentially different ways. The various natures and functions of the different modes of communication will be examined in [the next] Section.

It was the coming of broadcasting, as a supplement to an already established Press, into our society, by then highly literate, though of widely varied standards of education, that has created in many people's minds the symbol of *mass-communication*, which is certainly one of the most important characteristics of our advanced societies today. It is a phenomenon, no less. But the name mass-communication is a very misleading one, and it will be discussed later.

The coming of electrical communication, starting with the telegraph, enforced two great breaks from the traditional modes, such as horse and railway. The first was due to the immense increase in speed with which messages could be sent; in one step, *the speed was increased some* 10 *million times,* so that virtually no time delay occurred. The second was due to their availability for use by the common man.

'Use by the common man' is a phrase which may be taken too literally. Certainly the older modes, the post and the *inland* telephone, are widely used today, but the intercontinental routes (e.g. the transatlantic telephone to the U.S.A.) are mainly used by authorities, for very few people out of our population have as yet any reason to make private intercontinental calls. The 'common man' does not much *use* these world-systems, any more than he would have used the *cursus publicus* in Roman times, though the systems are now *available* to him, not withheld. The difference between *use* and *availability for use* may seem a quibble, but in my opinion it is not.

In all industrial countries the use of telephones, telegraphs and radio increased steadily, but slowly, until the Second World War; then afterwards, starting in the late 1940s, their usage within all advanced countries increased suddenly, in a way which can only be described as 'explosive'.

Mass-communication media

The term 'mass-communication' is of fairly recent origin, being taken over, by analogy, from the earlier expression 'mass-production'. It is a false analogy and carries with itself the unfortunate suggestion that mass-communication means the mass-production of minds: the very word 'mass' comes from the Greek maza, meaning barley-meal! It can then be used as an emotional term, being convenient to use in argument as a broad generality and to avoid specificity. Thomas Carlyle was one of the first to use the expression in a way suggesting contempt and fear, when he spoke of 'the masses' as: 'Swarmery, Sons of the Devil, blockheadism, gullibility, bribeability, amenability to beer and balderdash.' Barley-meal, porridge, is a poor epithet for people.

It might well be asked first: who are 'the masses'? Are you and I two of such people? Do you and I ever think of ourselves as such, or do we think of a grey amorphous lump, millions of others, 'out there'? What have the masses got in common that makes them a social group, to be referred to in this way?: reading the same newspaper? watching the same TV programme? voting for the same Party? having the same occupation? Clearly, such different groups would not comprise the same people. The term the masses is meaningless, unless it is qualified: 'the mass of people who do so-and-so'. It has degenerated into an emotional term which may conveniently be used in a contemptuous or pejorative way.

As S. Maclean Jr (1967) has put it: 'There are some implications in the term "mass-communication" that there are scheming powers of evil that will influence and change many of us, and that somehow they are going to harm us – like evil gods or something.' I agree. 'The Masses' form almost an existentialist idea, like 'The One' of Heidegger (*One ought to* . . .), an abstract 'They' ('*They say that it's going to rain*'). The Masses are never you nor me, only 'the others'.

The very words, the masses, convey a sense of contempt. Even today for us there still lingers around these words a feeling of fear, as there did for John Stuart Mill, a hundred years ago: fear of 'the mob'. But, strictly speaking, you cannot communicate with the masses; a better wording would be: you communicate with individual human beings, in massive numbers – a very different matter. . . .

So much for the masses; now let us look at the word *communication*. There are so very many different media of communication and transport, newspapers, books, radio, aeroplanes, railways, TV . . . and they each have quite different characters and have enabled societies to change in different ways. Each has contributed what I shall call a different *quality*. It is incorrect to regard any one mode as wholly supplanting an earlier one, which thereby becomes 'old-fashioned'. Thus TV has not supplanted radio, nor has it totally replaced the cinema and film (fig. 1), nor has the telephone supplanted the telegraph, nor have cars replaced railways (figs. 2 and 3).

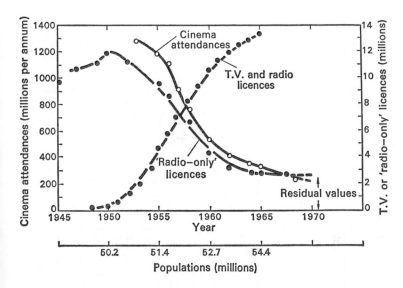

Fig. 1   Television has not entirely replaced the cinema and sound radio.
(Example relates to the U.K.)
(From the *U.K. Annual Abstract of Statistics*, by kind permission of H M S O)

Another prognostication so often made today is that newspapers will soon
be replaced by data links, in homes and offices, showing news printed on a
TV screen. Such new techniques may indeed come (and our present TV news
bulletins are a small step towards this), but, if they do, newspapers will
continue to be published; though their form and functions will change,
as they have been doing for 350 years past. It is often said that books will
soon be replaced by texts stored in computers, or by rolls of microfilm, but
don't you believe it! Books can be used in so many different ways, not only
read for factual information. They can be scribbled on in their margins,
read outdoors or in the train, fondled. The demand for books and libraries
is rising fast today, in countries rich and poor. The 'electronic media' do
not replace them, quite the contrary. Nevertheless, the introduction of any
new mode of communication certainly changes the values and uses of
earlier ones.

   Each mode has contributed something quite new, some additional
quality, to the growing structure of communication. The way in which we
regard one another in our various groups (families, social classes, nation-

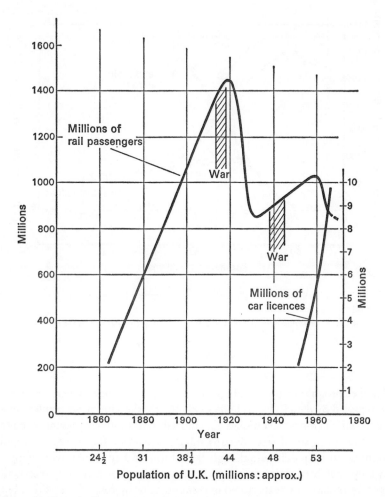

Fig. 2 Decline of rail passenger traffic in the United Kingdom.

alities . . .) and so, in turn, the way in which we each think about ourselves, depend upon which of these various modes of communication we possess. In the advanced countries we possess the lot; 30-odd years ago we did not have television, and we were changed by its coming; a hundred years ago we didn't have the telephone, and people had no conception of being free to do many things which they can do today.

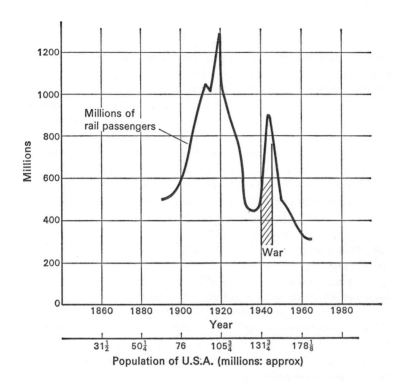

Fig. 3   Decline of rail passenger traffic in the United States of America.

The fact that any one new-introduced mode of communication does not wholly replace, or supplant, an earlier one is evidenced by a host of statistics (Escarpit 1968, HMSO 1970, UNESCO 1970). A number of typical examples may be shown here, drawn from British and U.S.A.[3] sources. We see from the historical curves of figures 2 and 3 that the motor car did not destroy the railways, though passengers rapidly *reduced* drastically, following the end of the First World War in 1918, to a level which has changed more slowly during later years, as cars have increased in numbers.

The futility of trying to predict future demands solely by projecting

3   When U.S.A. growth statistics are referred to, due note should be taken of their very rapid population increase.

D.O.S.—7

curves of statistics skywards is well illustrated here. Thus the boosted rise, and subsequent reduction, of rail traffic (see figs. 2 and 3) is coincident with the First World War and its immense demands for transport. Major changes of demand are as likely to be the result of changing social circumstances as they are of technical innovation.

To take another instance, television has not destroyed the cinema (fig. 1) but has only taken over some of its values (and introduced its own).

Again, the very rapid growth of overseas air traffic has not stopped the increase in sea passengers, though certain routes have grown to favour one or the other (Alexandersson and Nordström 1963). Thus transatlantic air routes are relatively short, inexpensive and under very high demand,[4] whereas countries like Australia or New Zealand, being very remote places, favour sea travel. The traditional maritime countries, Britain, Scandinavia and Holland, also maintain a heavy sea-traffic. (Their combined sea passengers in 1965 were five times as many as air passengers; for South Africa too, the ratio was three to one.)

The postal service too is very old, but this also has not been made old-fashioned by electronic communication, and continues in increased and more varied use, in countries both rich and poor.

The lessons from statistics of this kind are clear. New methods of communication do not supplant old ones in all respects. They may improve certain social values, or introduce wholly new ones, but some values of the older modes still remain.

In the manufacturing industries many new machines do actually supplant older ones, which fall out of use. But it seems that in the field of human communication, this does not happen. We may ask : why?

The only answer can be that there is a continual demand for the old modes so that, as emphasized before, *these various modes, old and new, are essentially not of the same nature.* The telephone is not just a better telegraph; television is not just a better cinema or radio; they are categorically different, though each brings its own 'quality' to the whole structure of human communication. It is most deceptive and confusing to lump all together as mass-communication.

The various modes of comunication which have been evolved or invented at different times in history have very varied significances and it is important to distinguish them. Thus a telephone call is quite different in its nature from a letter and both are different from telegrams; again, a radio broadcast differs in function from a newspaper report or a TV news bulletin, and so on. All are methods of communication, but quite distinct in

4 Nevertheless, sea passage demand also still rises.

character and in the ways they serve to change us. Only too frequently do we hear the expression mass-communication used to refer to all modern methods, both print and electronic, lumped together. Not only does confusion sometimes arise for this reason, but also because most members of the public think only of their use in the home, their *domestic* use, whereas so many of their uses are not private; these *public* uses remain so often unobtrusive or even out of sight. For example, their uses by the Police, by the Army, for aircraft navigation, and by Banks, businesses and other

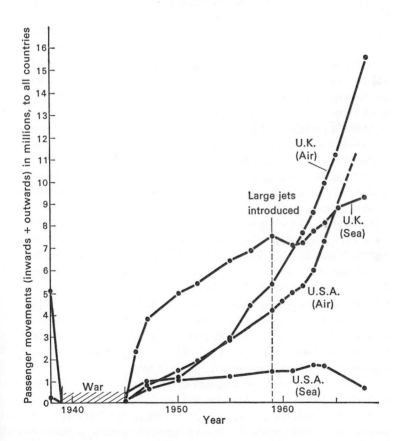

Fig. 4   Postwar growths of both sea and air passenger traffic between (a) United Kingdom (b) United States of America and all other countries.
Figures from (a) *U.K. Annual Abstracts of Statistics* and (b) *Statistical Abstracts of the U.S.A.*, with grateful acknowledgments.

public authorities. It is worth considering their different social functions and characters, in turn and in historical order.

First, speech itself; this is what primarily distinguishes man from the animals; it is part of human nature (Langer 1957). Speech is always *between* people (even 'we' with 'ourselves' when soliloquizing) giving us a sense of individuality and of sociability at one and the same time. Speech does many things to us and to our relationships; it signifies our cultural beliefs, our moods, our attitudes: many things. It essentially reveals our personal states and natures, both as unconscious and as thinking creatures.

Next, writing and all forms of scribing. These, from the earliest cave drawings onwards, are all deliberate, conscious, *intellectual* acts. I can babble nonsense with no effort whatever, even in my sleep; but I cannot write or draw by virtue of similar muscular habit; I must *think*, however little. Secondly, though related, writing connects past, present and future and enforces the concept of historic *time* upon us. Thus I wrote these words in this book in the past, for the purpose of your reading them in the future; we write *for* the future, but read *about* the past. Such connexion enables comparisons to be made, records, differences noted, and so *questionings* to be forced upon us: deliberate, intellectualized questionings, the raising of doubts and their resolutions.

Next, the invention of printing enabled these various questionings to be spread among large literate populations, thereby providing more sources of *group questionings*. New philosophies could be formed, discussed and widely criticized. Among these, the field of thought called *science* emerged. Science is possible only where records are made, and compared. Leonardo da Vinci achieved his remarkable results not only by virtue of being a remarkable thinker, but because he kept careful records, writings and drawings. Another well-known example is John Locke. Yet another is Jules Verne, whose remarkable predictions rested upon his file of 25,000 items. On a longer time scale, it is true to say that the whole historic movement called the Renaissance arose from a new examination of old Islamic, Hebrew and Greek scientific records when translated into Latin; the old theories could then be questioned and their *recorded* facts doubted (Hall 1954), new theories evolved and tested, whole cultural or national philosophies attacked.

Next, the postal service. As a means of communication this serves both private and public needs. In Roman times the *cursus publicus* would primarily have been of public service, in the sense of use by the military or governing officials and, later, in Europe, of the ruling courts. Its private use emerged only in recent centuries, especially the seventeenth. As a mode of communication letters, of course, provide a person-to-person service, or else an authority-to-person service.

Broadly speaking, the postal service carries out both of these two distinct functions; either private and confidential, between friends, acquaintances (or would-be acquaintances), or else impersonal: orders, instructions, information, demands and acknowledgments. Such multiple use, or *diversity*, is found in all modern modes of communication: radio, T V, telegraphs and even road and railways. The reasons are economic.

Therefore, since the post facilitates both person-to-person and authority-to-person communication, the specific quality which postal services have contributed to civilization is their power to *organize*, whether personally or publicly; patterns of relationships could be set up, more complex business, industrial and national organizations created, operating over larger areas.

Historically, the next step in the evolution of communication has been the coming of electrical methods, the invention of the telegraph, closely followed by that of the telephone. Technically speaking, the two are closely alike, but socially they are utterly different.

The chief quality newly introduced by the telegraph was that of speed. At one stroke, the speed of messages was raised some *ten million times* by the telegraph, from that of the horse to that of electricity. The implications of this vast increase of speed have been several-fold. Basically it implied that an institution or organization, say a business (the 'pattern of relationships'), could send far more messages and receive more replies per day than before; that is to say, more instructions, advices, decisions, etc., could be made per day. *Ceteris paribus* this would mean far higher costs per day. However, such increased message traffic and correspondingly increased costs mean only that these institutions were enabled *to grow in size*; larger economic organizations could exist, with the message traffic dispersed among more people and over greater areas of the world. If mesages are faster, then more 'elements' of an organization can be related per day or per week. In particular, world news services have developed; news agencies have followed wherever the telegraph has gone.

The function of the telephone is different. It is not only personal, in the sense that private letters are, but it has far greater significance, for the simple reason that human *conversations* are possible. Conversation is an essential human relationship. When you speak to someone on the 'phone, even a stranger, you hear far more than factual premeditated messages; you respond to tones of voice, to moods; you may interject a remark; it is a person you are involved with, not a machine. Though unseen, you continue to gesture, to smile or frown, and move your hands; you are *conversing*, linked, 'involved' and 'committed'. You can discuss, persuade, enquire, argue and perhaps reach agreement in a few minutes, in a personal way. Rapid converse, enquiry, resolution are the powers offered by telephones to organizations.

In private homes the telephone has added other qualities. It has enabled members of the family to travel, or even to emigrate, not only with increased security, but with less personal distress. It is the *availability* of the international telephone service which is of such significance to the common man today. He may not use it personally very often; but it is there. A telephone conversation means far more to, say, a mother, than any letter arriving after three days' delay or even a telegram; a call can resolve uncertainties, doubts, or anxieties and give greater *assurance;* even if the news told is bad, the truth can be made known. The telephone has contributed to personal *mobility* in a way no other medium has because the traveller does not have to stay in one place, waiting for an answer, but may continue his journey and telephone later from a callbox or hotel.

All these various communication techniques so far referred to are seen to contribute quite distinct and various qualities to society : writing, printing, the post, telegraphs and telephones. No one technique has supplanted an earlier one, but rather changed the nature of communication and the structure and size of our organizations.

The story continues. The coming of radio at the turn of the century has been dramatic in its eventual social effects. Its immediate value was for ships at sea which could, for the first time, keep in contact with one another or with shore bases, when out of sight. But, further still, it meant that they could all be contacted simultaneously. Radio changed the whole nature of warfare, during the Russo-Japanese War of 1904–5. *Broadcast* communication had come, though public 'broadcasting' was delayed by the First World War. In a sense, radio today is most closely analogous to printing, which also is a broadcast system, but it has the speed of the telegraph, allied to some of the values of the human voice.

What other particular new quality can be said then to have been contributed by radio? I would say without hesitation that of *sociability*. Now I am aware that such belief will be furiously contradicted by many readers, so please bear with me a moment, whilst I explain.

By sociability I do not mean that, because we have radio and TV, we shall all come to love one another more. I mean only that radio has the power to affect our sociability, both for better and for worse because it is the first medium we have found for simultaneously speaking to virtually all the citizens of our already vast national populations. In the Greek city-states a single speaker could do this by oratory, but we cannot in the modern world, without radio. But whether or not radio is actually used wisely is another matter. It merely has this potential. . . .

Perhaps it may be better to illustrate by example the great power that radio has for affecting our sociability, for better or worse. First, every American will remember his experience on the early afternoon of 22 November, 1963, whichever town or city he was in, when President Kennedy was assassinated (Greenberg and Parker, 1965). The spread of the news and its social consequences that day have been fully recorded (Barton 1963, Schramm 1965, Sheatsley and Feldman 1964). Within half an hour of the shooting *two out of every three people* in the U.S.A. knew. Within less than two hours, over 90 per cent knew.

The consequences of this rapid spread of the news showed sociability *in extremis*, comparable only to that experienced by civilians during or after air bombardment during the Second World War. They also illustrate the possible *stabilizing* effect of rapid news spread, mentioned earlier. Rumour and counter-rumour were prevented, for all knew the main events, virtually at the same time. About half the American population heard or saw the news on radio and T V, whilst the other half learned by telephone calls from acquaintances and relatives, or by word of mouth (Schramm 1965).

Similarly, during the Second World War the values of broadcasting for maintaining and raising civilian morale were clear to everybody. Radio could be used to combat the demoralizing effects of rumour and counter-rumour. It did much to maintain our sense of community. . . .

So much for radio, for the moment. Now what specific qualities did television introduce?

Before deciding upon this, we should perhaps remind ourselves of one or two points. First, that the coming of television and its very rapid spread have occurred almost entirely since the end of the Second World War. It has spread in two ways: geographically, inasmuch as there is some television broadcasting done, or being planned, in almost every country of the world, and socially, because television has spread in depth, within the major industrial countries, and has entered nearly every home. It is also important that within these countries television has come upon a public already inured to the cinema, radio and the Press.

During this 'era of television', there has also been an educational revolution; many standards have greatly improved and, at least in industrial countries, universities have greatly expanded in proportion to population, young people travel more and class mobility has increased.

Television came during the postwar period of great social change. During this same period private wealth has increased[5] so that a great section of our population can now afford to possess, or rent, a T V set who, before the War, would not have conceived of having other comparable possessions of the time, such as a refrigerator or small car.

It is easy to explain this rapid and universal adoption of T V in the sort of terms so often heard: that people like it because it is a 'drug', or that it obviates the need to think or to *do* anything, or that it is forced upon people by commercial pressures or advertising, etc., etc. These are not real explanations, but only vague and emotional generalizations. The fact is that T V *has* come into nearly every home in the wealthier countries: and these homes are as varied as the winds, containing families of all kinds, all economic and educational levels, all interests.

At first sight television may seem to be nothing more than a cinema in the home, which may be switched on and off at will, so that we can get our entertainment without taking the bother to go out of the house and walk or drive to the cinema. But in some ways the two do not compare. The cinema is basically an extension of the live theatre, which itself developed from the mystery plays and masques of the seventeenth century (performed before audiences in church or in special tents outside). Both the theatre and the cinema give presentations before collective audiences. The cinema took over some of the traditions of the theatre, especially developing the cult of 'stars'. It could reach larger audiences, because the same film, with identical actors of star repute, could be shown concurrently in many towns. Children could afford to go to the cinema and the triviality of many of the plots and themes which satisfied them showed the great need for *sheer visual display*. Film themes did not need to be original or particularly deep; it was visual display, exotic, romantic, and *active* above all, that was so needed in the drab grey industrial cities of our advanced countries. . . .

Television has brought visual displays into the home, but the showing of films by television may give no better, or even less, satisfaction than at the cinema. It is a medium which can be used for so many other different purposes and has at least two qualities which the cinema lacks: *immediacy* and *domesticity*. Television can show events whilst they are happening, though you may not deeply sense that fact; you are not really 'there', and it shows these to you privately, with only your family or friends around you, totally unconscious of millions of others outside. Again, going to the cinema or the theatre is an *occasion*; looking at a T V programme at home, is not.

In Table 2 an attempt has been made to distinguish some of the charac-

5   Not in all sections, e.g. the elderly.

teristic 'qualities' of the various media (or modes) of communication, as they have been discussed here, shown in historic order of their coming. No suggestion is made that this list is complete, or widely accepted. It shows the opinions of the writer only, purely as a tentative schema. Before closing this Section, perhaps mention should be made of another source of confusion. This is overgeneralization. Not only are the various modes quite different, telephones, radio, newspapers, etc., but any one of these serves many, quite different purposes. Thus the existence of the Press enables other and varied journals to be published also, from scientific papers to comics, whilst the whole printing industry also supports a very wide range of different kinds of book.

It is confusing then to speak of *the* Press, or *the* television or *the* telephone, just as confusing as to speak about *the* wheel (for push-chairs? automobiles? clocks and watches?). . . .

Table 2   Modes of communication, in historical order, and qualities contributed

Mode	Qualities or values
Speech	Thinking, knowing. Self-consciousness within society.
Writing and scribing	Intellectualization. Deepened sense of 'historic time' and of social change. Personal questionings.
Printing	Comparisons across time intervals. Group questionings.
Postal service	Organization of groups. Personal mobility with security.
Telegraph	Speed of organization. Larger groups in stable operation; aid to industrial activity.
Telephone	Speech; human personality. Conversation. Personal mobility, with security. Resolving and decision-making.
Cinema	Broadcast communication (i.e. in groups). Cult of stars. High emotional involvement. Education potential.
The modern Press	Broadcast communication. Increased political awareness. Advertising; enhanced industrial activity. The slogan.
Radio (sound only)	Broadcast communication over very wide areas; sociability. Immediacy. Domesticity. Education potential at higher levels.
Television	Cult of stars. Education potential. Wide social penetration. Social unity potential. Visual display in homes. News and public affairs *as* entertainment.
Data links, computers	Growth of industrial and other economic groups. Larger social enterprises. Improved planning (national and international).

On books in the 'Age of Television'

Whereas radio, films and TV can be directed to all people, whether literate or not, with various degrees of effectiveness, and newspapers too may spread their news to illiterate populations by being read aloud, books are far more confined, for several reasons.

One obvious reason is economic. Most books, even paperbacks, are very expensive in relation to the incomes of most people in this world. (UNESCO defines a *book* as 'a non-periodical printed publication of at least 49 pages, excluding the cover pages'.) Another reason is that most of them are written in one of a few languages only. Yet another is that libraries are most readily established in towns and cities, making it difficult and expensive to serve scattered rural populations who, in some countries, are a majority. In many poorer areas of the world illiteracy and cost are the obvious major restrictions. Though public lending libraries do exist in many poor countries, in Colleges, Schools, Embassies (or their Information Bureaux), Social centres, and other institutions, e.g. The British Council, they are often relatively small, little used, contain mostly European and often unsuitable stocks, and many have been established only recently.

Even within the industrial countries, the familiar free Municipal Public Library, used by citizens of all interests, classes and conditions, is not a very ancient institution (although by the 18th century, the habit of reading was already established in Britain among an educated class) (Irwin 1964). After all, Public Municipal Lending Libraries did not start in Britain or the U.S.A. until the early 1850s. That is to say, Public Libraries in the modern sense of Municipal, rate-supported, free lending libraries for the man in the street. There have been many 'non-private' libraries in Britain since the fifteenth century, especially including those at Oxford and Cambridge Universities. (Prior to 1850 there had of course been Subscription Libraries, Mechanics Institutes and libraries in many institutions, but the First Public Libraries Act was passed in the U.K. in 1850; in the U.S.A. in 1849.) Even then, for many years few people had any idea of their purpose; there was no demand for them. It was not until after such Libraries had been started that people realized their purposes and values, and demand began slowly to rise. Books are a medium of communication and, just as with all the other media, it is supply which creates demand. As McColvin (1956) has said about public libraries: '. . . here is, definitely, a case when supply created demand, not where demand created supply. And the same, let us never forget, is true today in every country in the world, be it Indonesia or Italy,

Pakistan or Peru'. The same thing can be said about book writing and publishing in general; they are not done as a result of public demand. The extent to which libraries exist and are used in any country, and also sales of books, do not depend solely upon literacy, but upon other social conditions too, including a certain level of education, an arousal of curiosity, interest and motives for enquiry, aspirations, spare mental energy, free time, proximity to urban centres and other characteristics of people of the more 'advanced' societies, possessing a substantial 'middle class'. But literacy alone is not enough. Furthermore, the mere *size* of the community in which a person lives may determine the size of the library that it can support, and hence the range of titles and subjects. Scattered, rural populations cannot be so well or easily served; travelling libraries, organized arrangements for book exchanges between libraries on a nationwide basis, etc., require the conditions of rapid transport and communication that exist only in the more advanced countries. Even within those countries, these conditions can vary much. Thus a greater proportion of the British population lives in large conurbations than does that of the U.S.A., where towns and cities are also much farther apart and there is a far greater number of small and widely dispersed communities. At the 1960 census, for example, about 30 per cent of the population of the U.S.A. were living in communities of less than 1000 people. The corresponding figure for Britain cannot be stated exactly because many communities are so close together as to merge and often form suburbs of adjoining urban areas (e.g. one sixth of the whole population of Britain lives within the single conurbation of Greater London). If parishes be taken as the unit then only 7 per cent of the population of England and Wales lives in parishes having less than 100 population. (*Census 1961, England and Wales, Age, Marital Condition and General Tables,* HMSO, 1964. With kind permission.) These geographical and demographic differences between the U.K. and the U.S.A. may partly account for the great difference in the usage made of public lending libraries in these two countries; thus, in 1962, the public library circulation in the U.S.A. was nearly 4½ books per head of population, whilst in Britain it was 9½. This difference certainly has nothing whatever to do with the quality and services of American libraries, many of which are unmatched anywhere in the world. Their problem of *distribution* is far greater than ours in Britain, especially among rural, small town populations. At the same time, one cannot refrain from commenting again upon the extraordinary addiction to the printed word shown by the British, which has origins going back centuries; as was noted before, the British buy more newspapers than any other people and produce far more books (by titles), for their population size, than do Americans. By the eighteenth century Britain was the most literate country in the world. Her early industrialization and urban conditions favoured the introduction of public libraries. In other countries, where libraries and literature of religious or political types were dominant, as in Holland, Belgium and Eastern Europe, public libraries 'made little and difficult progress'. This has also been true where sharp distinction has been traditional between 'scholarly' and 'popular' libraries, as in Italy, Austria and Germany. The social origins and patterns of development of public libraries have been closely similar in Britain, the U.S.A. and Scandinavia, where they started, from very different backgrounds, under the inspiration of private people of great social insight, including clergymen and teachers.

Within the industrial countries, with their abundance of media claiming the attention – books, cinemas, newspapers, magazines, and many and varied forms of entertainment – that hoary question is so often heard asked: 'Since television, does anybody read any more?' Indeed, I have heard the opinion widely expressed that, 'now that we are all glued to the goggle-box, libraries are falling out of use.' This belief is, of course, the reverse of the truth; library usage and book buying are both on the increase. It is cinema attendance which has declined in the industrial countries, but not, I am led to believe, in the U.S.S.R. (see Fig. 1). If anything, television acts as a stimulus to reading; as a medium, it replaces, not reading, but rather many of the functions of the cinema. Very little research has been published yet concerning the effect of *particular* TV and radio programmes (e.g. plays, documentaries, educational progammes, serialized books, etc.) upon the subsequent sales of 'the book' or lendings from public libraries (see fig. 1). This seems to the author to be a matter of major sociological importance to educators, broadcasters, librarians, sociologists and others.

Figure 5 shows the increase of book lendings from the Municipal Public Libraries in the United Kingdom, since the introduction of universal primary education in 1870, from figures supplied by the Library Association, London; later figures are published annually, by library authority, in the *Municipal Yearbook*. The dates of various Education Acts, Library Acts, and of the start of broadcasting and TV are also marked.

The coming of broadcasting in 1922, and the restarting of the BBC Television Service after the War, both preceded spurts in book lendings. This curve shows that, far from declining, library books circulated in ever increasing numbers during the period when TV sets came to enter into virtually every home in Britain. Population increase does not account for this.

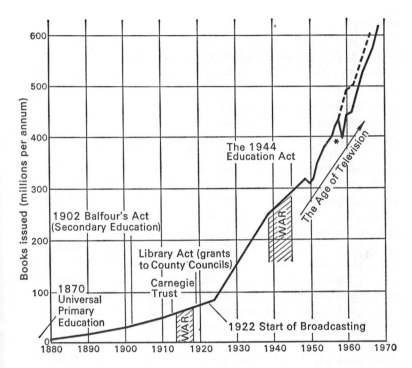

Fig. 5   The number of books issued from Municipal Libraries in Britain, over the past century. Figures kindly supplied by the Library Association, London.

* After 1958, issues from school libraries run by Public Libraries were not listed. This accounts for the sudden drop. The dotted line is estimated, but not over-generously. Figures are published annually in the *Municipal Yearbook*, but there is a slight uncertainty introduced because it is not always possible to distinguish clearly between issues from Public Libraries and school libraries.

It must be admitted that great precision cannot be attached to this curve; for one thing, the basis of calculation of book lendings differs from one Local Authority to another and, in addition, the coverage for the various years is incomplete in different ways and an estimate has been made for most of these years to cover those Authorities that did not report. Nevertheless, the general trend is undeniable; book circulation continues to increase, rapidly.

It would be wrong to jump to the conclusion that radio and television were the sole immediate *causes* of this increase in book reading, for other pressures have been at work. Perhaps none are more important than the rising standards and spread of education (in Britain, for example, the 1944 Education Act introduced secondary education for all). Nor should we discount the effects of the Second World War upon people's interests in world and home affairs; for example, we shall note later the very great increase in newspaper reading during the Second World War, especially by women. Rising standards of education and increased wealth for increasing numbers of the population have played their part; so has the so-called 'paper-back revolution', in drawing the attention of new readers, by display in bookshop windows, and otherwise. Nor should we discount the far greater attractiveness of modern library architecture, exterior and interior, and the improved stocks. Far more money has been made available since the last War, not only for libraries but for education in general in the public sector. In Britain, as elsewhere, educational standards for very many people have greatly risen, and radio and television are a part of that process. As further evidence of rising standards we might note that, since the War, the total enrolment at all major (adult education) evening Institutes has increased steadily. Yet again, evidence is offered by the great increase in buying of 'quality' newspapers since before the War. (The Press itself recognizes the two classes, 'quality' and 'popular'.)

We are here speaking of *averages* which, of course, completely conceal all knowledge of who it is that is borrowing or buying more books nowadays. There is no reason to believe that the people who are heavy viewers of T V are necessarily the same ones who are reading more. The habits of doing either, or both, may depend upon a host of other social factors. For this, and other reasons, the effects of television upon people's reading habits cannot reliably be studied by direct comparison of two communities, a) one which had television early and b) another which had no television until some years later; more subtle means of research must be used.

The curve in figure 5 holds another trap of misinterpretation, if we are not careful, which is this: although library circulations have undoubtedly increased rapidly since the coming of television, we do not know whether the increase might not have been even greater if T V had not been invented. One study, made in Illinois, indicates that it would have been; the predicted increase being about one book a year per person, with a likelihood for this to have come from the Fiction shelves of the libraries.

Mere increase in the volume of circulations is one thing, equally important is the *quality* of reading: how has this changed since the coming of T V?

First, let us note that Public, rate-supported Lending Libraries are normally administered by committees of Local Authorities (the adminstering authorities and organizations vary between countries) and City Fathers, who are ultimately responsible, are not, on the whole, inclined towards pornography.

To be serious, a number of major studies of changes in public reading tastes during the coming of television arrive at rather similar conclusions, namely, that television tends to widen children's tastes, introducing them to literature other than fiction; further, they have noted the increase in reading of more serious papers and magazines, with corresponding reduction in circulation of comics and 'low brow' magazines and books. This has been reported in Britain, in the U.S.A. and Japan and, no doubt, elsewhere.

Unfortunately no detailed statistics are available, to the writer's knowledge, to show how reading interests have waxed and waned among different subjects. But it is known that, generally speaking, non-fiction has become somewhat more popular at the expense of fiction; non-fiction means not only technical subjects, but includes history, travel, hobbies of all kinds, accountancy, affairs, and many other fields.

With regard to book *production*, more details are known for, among other sources, the *U.N. Statistical Yearbook* for 1966 publishes the figures for each country, listed under classes of subject: General, Philosophy, Religion, Social Sciences, etc. These relate only to the various national productions; it is not known how many are actually written within those countries, nor in what languages. The figures show that the proportion of non-fictional books has been rising since the Second World War.

This tendency is not confined to countries having many T V or radio sets, but is a general one throughout the world.

References

ALEXANDERSSON, G. and NORDSTRÖM, G. (1963) *World Shipping* New York, Wiley.

BARTON, A. H. et al. (1963) 'Social Organization Under Stress: A Sociological Review of Disaster Studies' Washington, D C, *National Acad. Sci., Nat. Res. Council.*

ESCARPIT, R. (1968) *The Book Revolution* London, Harrap, with UNESCO.

GREENBERG, B. S. and PARKER, E. B. (eds) (1965) *The Kennedy Assassination and the American Public: Social Communication in Crisis* Stanford, California, Stanford University Press (detailed analysis according to age, sex, social class, etc.).

HALL, A. R. (1954) *The Scientific Revolution, 1500–1800* London, Longmans.

HARDER, W. J. (1960) *Daniel Drawbaugh* Philadelphia, University of Philadelphia Press.

HMSO (1970) *Abstracts of Statistics* London, HMSO (Central Statistical Office).

INTERNATIONAL TELECOMMUNICATION UNION (1965) *From Semaphore to Satellite* Geneva. Also serialized during 1965 in *Telecomm. Jour.*

IRWIN, R. (1964) *The Heritage of the English Library* London, Allen and Unwin.

LANGER, SUSANNE K. (1957) *Philosophy in a New Key - A Study in the Symbolism or Reason, Rite and Art,* 3rd ed. Cambridge, Massachusetts, Harvard University Press.

MACLEAN, S. JR (1967) 'Systems of News Communication', from Thayer, Lee (ed) *Communication: Theory and Research* C. C. Thomas, Springfield, Illinois.

MCCOLVIN, L. R. (1956) *The Chance to Read: Public Libraries in the World Today* London, Phoenix House.

NEAL, H. E. (1960) *Communication from Stone Age to Space Age* London, Phoenix House.

PFLAUM, H. G. (1950) *Essai sur la 'Cursus Publicus' sous le Haut-Empire Romain* Paris, Imprimerie Nationale.

RAMSAY, A. M. (1925) 'The Speed of the Roman Imperial Post', *Journal of Roman Studies,* **15,** 60.

SCHRAMM, W. (1965) 'Communication in Crisis', in *The Kennedy Assassination and the American Public: Social Communication in Crisis* Stanford, California, Stanford University Press.

SHEATSLEY, P. B. and FELDMAN, J. J. (1964) 'The assassination of President Kennedy', *Pub. Opinion Quart.,* **28,** 2.

UNESCO (1970) *Statistical Yearbook* Paris.

8   Peoples, nations and communication

Karl W. Deutsch

Social scientists have collected a vast number of facts on the changing
alignment of individuals in peoples, national cultures, and national political movements. We know that these problems are important, that even
experienced statesmen have often seriously misjudged them, and that we
need to understand them better. But what is meant by understanding?

To seek understanding means to seek a conceptual model of the processes
of nationalism and nationality. We seek a model which will fit the known
facts, and facilitate some prediction and control of events. More than that,
we want it to suggest new questions and new fact-finding techniques,
which in turn may some day lead to further ideas. Altogether, we are looking for a set of concepts which should meet as closely as practicable the
following conditions:

1 Each concept should be operational. It should be clearly specified in
terms of possible observations or measurements, from which it is derived
and by which it can be tested. In this it should go beyond a mere explanation which uses familiar images but which cannot be so tested.
2 Each concept should be fruitful. It should suggest some further observations or experiments.
3 Each concept should be 'critical'. It should permit statements specific
enough to exclude the possibility of certain observational data or results,
so that, if these results are found, the concept clearly will have to be revised.
The concept must not be so vague and elastic as to fit all conceivable
empirical results.

Several concepts will have to be used together in a description of the
processes of nationalism and nationality. Such a description should meet
as nearly as possible the following conditions:

1 It should apply to the behaviour of individuals as well as to groups.
2 It should apply to rational as well as to so-called 'irrational' behaviour
of groups or individuals.

DEUTSCH, KARL W. (1966) 'Peoples, Nations and Communication', in *Nationalism and Social Communication* Cambridge, Massachusetts, MIT Press,
2nd ed., 86–106.

3   It should utilize data observable by strictly external methods, as well as subjective data available from introspection, and indirectly from literature.
4   The description should generally utilize the power of specialized disciplines and fit their findings within each field.
5   It should link the specialities so as to permit the transfer and recombination of their knowledge between different fields; and
6   It should, therefore, permit group attack on data too voluminous for one investigator.

Looking for such concepts, we may perhaps find them in the notion of communication. Processes of communication are the basis of the coherence of societies, cultures, and even of the personalities of individuals; and it may be worth while to see whether concepts of communication may not help us to understand the nature of peoples and of nations.

Society, culture, and communication

One set of facts about nationality deals with it in terms of society. By *society* is meant here a group of individuals made interdependent by the division of labour, the production and distribution of goods and services: 'A "society" refers to a group of people who have learned to work together' (Linton 1945, p. 79).

To the extent that there are marked differences in the degree of such interdependence, not just in respect to a few particular goods and services, but in regard to many services, we may consider one society as separate from others. A few special commodities may be carried over long distances from one society to another, just as jade in the Stone Age or cotton and rubber in the first half of the twentieth century. But exchange of a few special goods does not make a society; it takes the exchange or combination of many goods and services to accomplish that. A society in this sense is a group of individuals connected by an intense division of labour, and separated from other societies by a marked drop in this intensity.

In the past, any more elaborate division of labour has implied a division of society into *occupational groups* (such as 'town' and 'country') as well as into *social strata, castes, or classes* (which cut across some of these special occupations). Several societies may be connected with each other by a larger interchange of goods and services than with any other societies. In this case we might say that together they form a sort of *great society*, something parallel in some respects to what is sometimes called a civilization, but not identical with it.

It is essential to distinguish this concept of society sharply from that of *community* or *culture*, as used by anthropologists. Culture at first sight seems to consist of institutions, such as a particular dance, and a marriage ceremony, and of particular things, such as a particular kind of axe or spear, or food, or clothing. On looking more closely, we then find that these things somehow hang together: the same people are used to certain kinds of axes and clothes and food and marriages; they have similar accepted ideas about beauty in ornaments, and of 'good' behaviour in children and adults. All these things, it appears, somehow hang together in their minds. They form, as the technical term has it, a culture *configuration*.

If we look still more deeply into each configuration of culture, an Indian *pueblo*, a German *Gesangverein*, or the basketball team of Middletown High School, we find in each of these, behind the visible configuration of accepted things and accepted behaviour, an invisible *configuration of values*, of dos and don'ts, of rules for discriminating between actions as good or bad, beautiful or ugly, familiar or strange, safe or dangerous, interesting or indifferent. The positive elements in culture, the acts we see, the words we hear, the things we touch, are set, as it were, in the background which consists in each culture in the particular behaviour which we do *not* see, because there it is regarded as unseemly, the words we do not hear because they may be *tabu*, the things which are not there because they are not used. Silences are eloquent. Without silences there is no speech, and it is their culture which teaches men when to speak and when to be silent. Culture in this sense is a screen or sieve, a configuration of 'historically created selective processes which channel men's reactions both to internal and external stimuli' (Kluckhohn and Murray 1948, p. 10).

A common culture, then, is a common set of stable, habitual preferences and priorities in men's attention, and behaviour, as well as in their thoughts and feelings. Many of these preferences may involve communication; it is usually easier for men to communicate within the same culture than across its boundaries. In so far as a common culture facilitates communication, it forms a *community*.

But this is not always so. A particular culture may form a pattern of *interlocking roles*, such as man and woman, father and child, master and slave. If this is carried far, communication between the interlocking groups may be throttled down to the narrow range of conventionalized words, subjects, and sentiments permitted by established etiquette. Such an etiquette restricts communications between Whites and Negroes in some parts of the South: they may meet for years, always making the customary gestures and phrases, and yet know very little of each other. Despite this wide rift in communications, some writers still speak of one 'culture' comprising Whites *and* Negroes in such situations; other writers have compromised by speaking of separate 'subcultures' of Whites and of Negroes within this framework. On any showing, in such extreme situations, the common culture – common, that is, to both groups – is relatively poor. It is a restricted culture, restricted by its own inner barriers, which make it at the same time a restricted community.

No terminology should try to be more accurate than life. 'Culture' and 'community' can be used interchangeably because they describe a single complex of processes. When we say 'culture', we stress the configuration of preferences or values; when we say 'community' we stress the aspects of communication; just as, when speaking about traffic flow in a city, we may sometimes speak of the network of streets, and sometimes of the sets of traffic lights. But without the city streets, the 'stop' and 'go' lights would be meaningless. Similarly, we must never forget that it is the channels of culture which give to the values of culture their meaning.

There is another side to this description. When we say 'culture', we stress the habits, preferences and institutions as such, as if they were a configuration of disembodied ghosts. When we say 'community' we stress the collection of living individuals in whose minds and memories the habits and channels of culture are carried.

Both terms, then, have their distinct usefulness. In much of the rest of this paper, nationality will be discussed in terms of community, as here defined. But a great deal of valuable literature on peoples and nations has been written in terms of the culture concept. The overlapping relationship between community and culture should be remembered in order to maintain the connection between these different approaches, and to prevent any rift in this field of knowledge that could only work to the detriment of both.

The channels of culture, like those of society, consist of material facilities. Like those of society they originated through processes of history, are changed by history, and may be destroyed by it. But they are utterly unlike the channels of society in the kind of thing that passes through them.

The kind of thing that is transmitted through the channels of culture is exceedingly hard to describe. Our everyday language has no single word for it. Some parts of it we call knowledge, others we call values, still others, customs, mores, or traditions. Still other parts of it are mere gossip or just news, and still others are orders or commands. We have a qualitative understanding of these things. We can recognize them when we see or hear them, and we also know that they are interrelated, that they often shade over into each other. Yet, there is no everyday word that expresses their unity or the connections between them, and there is no long-established concept familiar to social scientists that would permit accurate analysis or quantitative measurement of them.

Perhaps the most effective way to overcome this difficulty would be for us to borrow a concept from another group of sciences and adapt it to our purpose. At best, such a concept will yield us only a simplified model of an inexhaustibly rich reality, yet we may hope that it will make at least some significant aspects of that reality stand out more clearly.

The concept of information

A concept for that which knowledge, values, traditions, news, gossip, and commands all have in common has been developed by communications engineers. They have called it information. In building a telegraph line or a telephone network, the main problem of communications engineers has not been the content of the messages that were to be transmitted. They might be true or untrue, profane or sacred, facetious or profound. They might contain descriptions of physical matter or of human affairs. They might be messages about other messages; or they might be orders intended to redirect men's attention or to change their behaviour. The communications engineer had to care for what was common to all these messages: the need to get them transmitted quickly, with least effort and with least distortion.

Communications engineers therefore developed methods of analysing messages into small, discrete units – letters in an alphabet, dots and dashes in a Morse code, black and white points on a television screen – and they learned to measure how many of these elements of a message, how many of these units of information, were transmitted through a channel and how many were lost. In so doing they found an accurate way of measuring the loss or distortion of messages, and of measuring the capacities of a system of communication.

In the beginning, this involved ignoring the content of the messages and concentrating on the mere fact of their complexity. A very crude line screen might take the same number of image points to transmit a picture from a comic strip or a crude likeness of Leonardo's 'Mona Lisa'. A good reproduction of the Mona Lisa however, would require a much richer system of communication, a much larger number and greater variety of image points. Although communications engineers therefore could not predict what kind of messages a communications system would carry, they could predict the potential performance of which it would be capable.

It is these concepts of *information*, of the *capacity* of a communications system, and of the *complementarity* of its parts, which would be helpful in the field of social science. For all cooperation among human beings requires at least some degree of communication. The richer their cooperation in producing tangible goods and services, in developing highly organized societies, and in developing and sharing intangible treasures of knowledge, art, and values, the greater their need for rich, varied, quick, and accurate communication. We cannot measure directly the piety, beauty, courage, or steadfastness of human beings, but we can measure to a significant extent the ranges and kinds of messages which they can transmit to each other, the speed and accuracy with which they can do so, and the price in effort and in lost information which they have to pay.

What we are interested in here is the observable ability of certain groups of men and women to share with each other a wide range of whatever might be in their minds, and their observable inability to share these things nearly as widely with outsiders. We all know that men can share with each other much more easily what is in their hands than what is in their minds, and yet the difference between the community that arises from the one kind of sharing and the community that arises from the other has rarely been seen in its full significance.

In what follows, therefore, I shall accept the view of anthropologists that both society and community are developed by social learning, and that a community consists of people who have learned to communicate with each other and to understand each other well beyond the mere interchange of goods and services.

I cannot use for this analysis the concept of community which a group of eminent social scientists have introduced from the field of biology where a 'community' of plants and animals is sometimes decribed as a collection of plants and animals which happen to exist next to each other in some particular locality (Wirth 1948, pp. 11–17). 'Society' for this group of scientists is, then, a group of persons who have become conscious of 'belonging' together in some sense. The distinction which is proposed here for an analysis of nationality differs from both these poles. Rarely shall we be interested in mere coexistence, and, on the other hand, before analysing or discussing consciousness, we shall try to understand what are the objective facts of which man can become conscious, even though these facts should exist as habits, mores, or preferences inside our own minds.

For this discussion I shall have to borrow terms from the study of communications, and I must apologize for the barbarous and quasi-mechanical sound which they may have in the ears of readers unfamiliar with them. I have three grounds for my apology: first, that the scientific study of processes of communication does not in fact lead to a mechanistic philosophy, but rather to its opposite; second, that I am using the simplified terms merely in order to make easier the tracing of certain infinitely larger and more complex social processes (much as a simple bell may facilitate the tracing of the movements of a far more complex cat); and third, that this approach in the end might be justified by its results.

Societies produce, select, and channel goods and services. *Cultures produce, select, and channel information.* A railroad or a printing press is a matter of society. A traffic code or an alphabet is a matter of culture. Society can build walls; culture can impose tabus. Society communicates tangible goods or inputs of energy called work; culture communicates patterns. These may be patterns of the arrangement of objects in space, from pottery and ornaments to tools and buildings. They may be patterns of action, such as games, dances, or models of graceful behaviour. Or they may be patterns of preference, of dos and don'ts, such as standards of morality or taste. Or, finally, they may be codes and symbols, that is, patterns so arranged as to convey information about other patterns, up to the vast extent of what the biologist Huxley (1947) called 'man's unique biological characteristic of tradition', and of what Edmund Burke (1790, p. 106) identified with the state when he called it a 'partnership in all art . . . and all perfection'.

If we knew how to compare and measure the ability of groups and cultures to transmit information, we might gain a better understanding of their behaviour and their capacities. But how can information be measured?

Possible measurements of information

The distinction between society and culture, or society and community, corresponds in a sense to the distinction in modern technology between power engineering and communications engineering. Power engineering transfers amounts of electric energy; *communications engineering transfers information.* It does not transfer events; *it transfers a patterned relationship between events.*

When a spoken message is transmitted through a sequence of mechanical vibrations of the air and of a membrane, thence through electric impulses in a wire, thence through electric processes in a broadcasting station and through radio waves, thence through electric and mechanical processes in a receiver and recorder to a set of grooves on the surface of a disc, and is finally played and made audible to a listener – what has been transferred through this chain of processes, or channel of communication, is something that has remained unchanged, invariant, over this whole sequence of processes. It is not matter, nor any one of the particular processes, nor any major amount of energy, since relays and electronic tubes make the qualities of the signal independent from a considerable range of energy inputs.

The same principle applies to the sequence of processes from the distribution of light reflected from a rock to the distribution of chemical changes on a photographic film, and further, to the distribution of black and white dots on a printing surface, or the distribution of electric 'yes' or 'no' impulses in picture telegraphy or television. What is transmitted here is neither light rays nor shadows, but information, the patterns of relationships between them.

In the second group of examples, we could describe the *state* of the rock in terms of the distribution of light and dark points on its surface. This would be a *state description* of the rock at a particular time. If we then describe the state of the film after exposure in terms of the distribution of the dark grains of silver deposited on it and of the remaining clear spaces, we should get another state description. Each of the two state descriptions would have been taken from a quite different physical object – a rock and a film – but a large part of these two state descriptions would be identical, whether we compared them point by point or in mathematical terms.

There would again be a great deal of identity between these two descriptions and several others, such as the description of the distribution of black and white dots on the printing surface, or of the electric yes or no impulses in the television circuits, or of the light and dark points on the television screen. The extent of the physical possibility of transferring and reproducing these patterns corresponds to the extent that there is something unchanging in all the relevant state descriptions of the physical processes by which this transmission is carried on. That something is *information – those aspects of the state descriptions of each physical process which all these processes had in common.*

To the extent that the last state description in such a sequence differs from the first, information has been lost or distorted during its passage through the channel. This amount of lost information can be measured. We can measure it in very refined ways, as in telephone or television engineering, where a message is broken up into very many electric impulses, sound frequencies, or image points. The percentage of the impulses or image points arriving at the other end is measured on a statistical basis, and their significance is evaluated in terms of the change each of them makes in the probability distribution of the picture which is already there. Or, we can measure it in simpler terms, by breaking up a message into a few simple parts, and asking how many of these parts were transmitted within a given minimum standard of accuracy, and how drastically the probability of the picture at the other end was changed by the absence of the pieces which were lost.

Refined or crude, more accurate or less, each of these methods would give us some quantitative measure of the *fidelity* of a communications channel in comparison with other channels. By either technique, we may derive a measure for the *efficiency* of a channel, as well as of the relative efficiency or *complementarity* of any parts or stages of the channel in relation to the others.

Other measures for the performance of a communications system, or for the complementarity of its parts, would be the speed at which information could be transmitted, or the range of different kinds of information that could be carried. Common to all of these approaches would be the fact that patterns of information can be measured in quantitative terms. They can be described in mathematical language, analysed by science, and transmitted or processed on a practical industrial scale.

Some implications for social science

This development is significant for wide fields of natural and social science. Information is indeed the 'stuff as dreams are made on'. Yet it can be transmitted, recorded, analysed, and measured. Whatever we may call it, information, pattern, form, *Gestalt*, state description, distribution function, or negative entropy, it has become accessible to the treatment of science.

Information differs from the 'matter' and 'energy' of nineteenth-century mechanical materialism in that it cannot be described adequately by their conservation laws. But it also differs, perhaps more so, from the 'idea' of 'idealistic' or metaphysical philosophies in that it is based on physical processes during every single moment of its existence, and that it can and must be dealt with by physical methods. It has material reality. It exists and interacts with other processes in the world, regardless of the whims of any particular human observer, so that its reception, transmission, reproduction, and in certain cases its recognition, can be mechanized.

As spaced dots of animal footprints, patterns of information were the basis of primitive hunting and tracking. As varied electric impulses, patterns of information are today the basis of modern telegraphy, electronics, and automatic equipment. As patterns of sound, sight, or action, they have always been the basis of signalling, of language, of society, and of culture. There is no communication without physical processes, without work. But the information transmitted is separable from any one process by which it is carried. There is no community nor culture without society. And there can be no society, no division of labour, without a minimum of transfer of information, without communication. Yet the difference between society and community is crucial, for it is the complex interplay between society and community which is at the root of many of the baffling problems of nationality.

Individuals of different cultures often live in one society, such as Czechs and Germans in Bohemia, or Moslems and Hindus in Bengal. For many years they may exchange goods and services but relatively little information. They may have very few complementary channels of communication. Many of their experiences in their common society may be similar, as were those of Czech and German miners in the same mining town, but they are not necessarily shared. On the other hand, within each community of communication many experiences of certain individuals may be quite dissimilar, such as those of German miners and German mine owners, but they can be shared; in particular, information about some of the German mine owners' experiences may be shared vicariously by the German miners. Here are the baffling cases cited by Professor Chadwick (1945): members of different peoples may live through the same events for generations and yet emerge from this supposed 'community of fate' quite dissimilar in behaviour, or even bitterly opposed.

Communication and the concept of a people

The community which permits a common history to be experienced as common, is a community of complementary habits and facilities of communication. It requires, so to speak, equipment for a job. This job consists in the storage, recall, transmission, recombination, and reapplication of relatively wide ranges of information; and the 'equipment' consists in such learned memories, symbols, habits, operating preferences, and facilities as will in fact be sufficiently complementary to permit the performance of these functions. *A larger group of persons linked by such complementary habits and facilities of communication* we may call a *people.*

The test of *complementarity* of any set of communications equipment is communicative effectiveness. How fast and how accurately do messages get through? How complex and voluminous is the information that can be so transmitted? How effectively are operations on one part of the net transmitted to another? The extent of complementarity for any set of facilities, or any community, will be indicated by the answers to these questions.

Complementarity or communicative efficiency is a function, an overall result. The same or a closely similar result may be reached by several different combinations of elements, or even by the entire replacement of some elements by others. This is obvious in the simple examples from communications engineering which were cited earlier, but it also applies to social communication. The communicative facilities of a society include a socially standardized system of symbols which is a language, and any number of auxiliary codes, such as alphabets, systems of writing, painting, calculating, etc. They include information stored in the living memories, associations, habits, and preferences of its members, and in its material facilities for the storage of information, such as libraries, statues, signposts, and the like; and a good deal more. Some of these facilities, individual and social, also deal with the treatment of information, its recall from storage or memory, its transmission and recombination to new patterns. Taken all together, they include, therefore, in particular the elements of that which anthropologists call culture. If these elements are in fact sufficiently complementary, they will add up to an integrated pattern or configuration of communicating, remembering, and acting, that is, to a culture in the sense of the citations quoted earlier in our discussion; and the individuals who have these complementary habits, vocabularies, and facilities are what we call a people.

It is now clear why all the usual descriptions of a people in terms of a community of languages, or character, or memories, or past history, are open to exception. For what counts is not the presence or absence of any single factor, but merely the presence of sufficient communication facilities with enough complementarity to produce the overall result. The Swiss may speak four different languages and still act as one people, for each of them has enough learned habits, preferences, symbols, memories, patterns of landholding and social stratification, events in history, and personal associations, all of which together permit him to communicate more effectively with other Swiss than with the speakers of his own language who belong to other peoples. 'I found that my German was more closely akin to the French of my [French-Swiss] friend than to the likewise German (*Ebenfallsdeutsch*) of the foreigner,' says the editor of a prominent German-Swiss paper in his reminiscences. 'The French-Swiss and I were using different words for the same concepts, but we understood each other. The man from Vienna and I were using the same words for different concepts, and thus we did not understand each other in the least.' (Schuerch 1943, pp. 36–7).

What is proposed here, in short, is a functional definition of nationality. Membership in a people essentially consists in wide complementarity of social communication. It consists in the ability to communicate more effectively, and over a wider range of subjects, with members of one large group than with outsiders. This overall result can be achieved by a variety of functionally equivalent arrangements.

This function of nationality differs from the old attempts to specify nationality in terms of some particular ingredient, somewhat as modern technological trends towards evaluating materials in terms of their performance differ from the older practice of evaluating materials in terms of their composition. In both cases, 'composition specifications' are replaced by 'performance tests', based on more detailed analysis of the functions carried out.

Peoples are held together 'from within' by this communicative efficiency, the complementarity of the communicative facilities acquired by their members. Such 'ethnic complementarity' is not merely subjective. At any moment, it exists as an objective fact, measurable by performance tests. Similar to a person's knowledge of a language, it is relatively independent of the whim of individuals. Only slowly can it be learned or forgotten. It is a characteristic of each individual, but it can only be exercised within the context of a group.

Ethnic complementarity, the complementarity that makes a people, can be readily distinguished by its relatively wide range from the narrow vocational complementarity which exists among members of the same profession, such as doctors or mathematicians, or members of the same vocational group, such as farmers or intellectuals. Efficient communication among engineers, artists, or stamp collectors is limited to a relatively narrow segment of their total range of activities. In most other things they do, in their childhood memories, in courtship, marriage, and parenthood, in their standards of beauty, their habits of food and drink, in games and recreation, they are far closer to mutual communication and understanding with their countrymen than with their fellow specialists in other countries.

The facts of social class may change this picture. But if and where they change it, they will do so not because of anything in the theory but because they are facts, and to the extent that they are facts. Where workers in industry are cut off from the rest of the community, from better housing on the 'right side' of the railroad tracks, from conviviality and intercourse, from education and careers, from comforts and income, from security and prestige – there Disraeli's word (1913, pp. 76–7) of the 'two nations . . . the rich and the poor' may express a real state of affairs. Under such conditions, men may discover more similar experiences and greater mutual understanding with their fellow workers in other countries than with their 'own' well-to-do countrymen who will see them only at the servant's entrance.

At certain times and places the barriers of class may thus outweigh the ties of language, culture, and tradition. Wage earners may then deliberately seek to advance their fortunes in a competitive society by seeking international class alignments; or they may choose to press for improvement of their lot along national lines, trying to keep out cheaper foreign labour, and to secure for themselves some share in the national prosperity of their employers.

Where, on the other hand, wage earners have more ample ties with the rest of the community, and fuller opportunities, not merely in words but in substance; if they find not merely factories and slums but schools, parks, hospitals, and better housing; where they have a political and economic 'stake in the country' and are accorded security and prestige, there the ties to their own people, to its folkways and living standards, education and tradition, will be strong in fact. There will be a greater stock of common experiences, a greater flow of social communication across class lines, more conviviality and informal social association, more vertical mobility and intermarriage, and, as a result of all these, probably far more effective complementarity of social communication within the people than across its borders. Social reforms, as Bismarck knew, may knit a people more closely (Eyck 1943, p. 36); high wages, as Lenin (1939, pp. 105–8) observed, may tend to assimilate the outlook of workers to that of their middle-class compatriots; and periods of democracy and social progress, as Otto Bauer (1923, p. 135) predicted, may leave different peoples more unified internally, but more sharply marked off from each other.

The critical facts of social communication and intercourse can be surveyed, tested, and to some extent measured, before political decisions must be taken. 'To the blind, all things are sudden' (Leighton 1946, p. 258). But for enlightened statesmanship it should be possible to do systematically what some men, like Disraeli himself, did in a rough and ready way; to appraise the many specific channels of communication within a people, and between its different classes, so as to be able to estimate how such a group will respond to a strain. Will India's Hindus and Moslems form in the long run one nation or two, and what are the chances for an eventual reunion between India herself and Pakistan? Will French workers turn right or left in politics? With careful investigation of the elements which go into the making of these social decisions, their outcome could at least be guessed at more intelligently before policy finds itself overtaken by events.

Even where we have one people, the range and effectiveness of social communication within it may tell us how effectively it has become integrated, and how far it has advanced, in this respect, toward becoming a nation. 'That universal circulation of intelligence,' Arthur Young (1792, pp. 146–7) noted on the eve of the French Revolution, 'which in England transmits the least vibration of feeling or alarm, with electric sensibility, from one end of the kingdom to another, and which unites in bands of connection men of similar interests and situations, has no existence in France.'

The notion of complementarity might be extended so as to include the actual or probable communicative efficiency of individuals over a range of different social arrangements. In this sense complementarity would be lower if it permitted efficient communication between individuals only in a very few relationships, such as, perhaps, only in the context of their familiar native village, or of their familiar economic institutions. Burke and Disraeli assumed such a limited type of complementarity when they prophesied that Frenchmen or Englishmen would cease to be a people if they should lose their traditional aristocratic social institutions, and that in such an event they would have to take 'many a weary step' before they could regain 'a true political personality.'

Complementarity is greater if it permits individuals to communicate efficiently no matter how often they change their residence or their occupations. In this sense complementarity may be that elusive property of individuals which, in the words of Dr Hermann Finer (1950, p. 108), 'makes society cohere', or which in our teminology makes it a community, perhaps even despite considerable variations in external circumstances. This, on the whole, has been the experience of the American nation. Men could move from the theocracy of Massachusetts Bay to the freedom of Rhode Island, or from the established institutions of the tidewater regions to the new conditions of the frontier, and yet retain their capacity to cooperate and form a nation. 'A nation well regulated,' Benjamin Franklin (1751, par. 23) wrote, 'is like a polypus: take away a limb, its place is soon supplied, cut it in two, and each deficient part shall speedily grow out of the part remaining. Thus, if you have room and subsistence enough . . . you may, of one, make ten nations, equally populous and powerful; or, rather, increase the nation tenfold in strength.'

Peoples are marked off from each other by communicative barriers, by 'marked gaps' in the efficiency of communication. Such gaps are relative. In geography, divides between river basins are effective, not by their absolute heights or steepness, but by the difference between their opposite slopes. Similarly barriers to communication are more or less effective not only according to the difficulty of communication across them but also according to the relative ease and attractiveness of alternative channels of communication available to the individual.

What are the effects of these cultural channels and barriers in a modern society, divided by its peculiar economic institutions and divisions of labour into metropolitan centres and less developed areas, and into different social strata and classes?

Nationalism and the position of peoples in a stratified society

Here we find that a *people* forms a social, economic, and political alignment of individuals from different social classes and occupations, around a centre and a leading group. Its members are united by more intensive social communication, and are linked to these centres and leading groups by an unbroken chain of connections in communications, and often also in economic life, with no sharp break in the possibilities of communication and substitution at any link, and hence with a somewhat better probability of social rise from rank to rank.

The primary basis of this alignment is the complementarity of communication habits. Its secondary basis is the complementarity of acquired social and economic preferences which involve the mobility of goods or persons. These are the widespread preferences for things or persons of 'one's own kind' (that is, associated with one's particular communication group) in such matters as buying and selling, work, food and recreation, courtship and marriage. A third factor has made all such alignments more important: the rise of industrialism and the modern market economy which offer economic and psychological rewards for successful group alignments to tense and insecure individuals – to men and women uprooted by social and technological change, exposed to the risks of economic competition, and taught to hunger for success. For almost any limited group within a competitive market, both security and success can be promoted by effective organization, alignment of preferences, and coordination of behaviour. Vast numbers have felt a need for such a group and have answered it by putting their trust in their nation.

In the political and social struggles of the modern age, *nationality*, then, means an alignment of large numbers of individuals from the middle and lower classes linked to regional centres and leading social groups by channels of social communication and economic intercourse, both indirectly from link to link and directly with the centre.

A 'leading social group' in this sense may be, but need not be, the established 'upper class' of the moment. The upper class – such as the aristocracy – may function as such a leading group if it promotes nationalism or accepts the leadership thrust upon it by a national or regional movement. If its main interests and ties, however, lie elsewhere, perhaps outside the country, or if it has accepted alien speech, habits, or religion, or if, finally, it has come to care only for its own group interests in a quite narrow manner, then the national and social leadership may devolve upon the next class below it, or still farther down to whichever class is sufficiently strong, respected, and locally accessible to become in fact the 'leading group of the national movement'. Thus the English Crown and aristocracy were assigned the function of national leadership in Bolingbroke's concept of the 'patriot King', and again by the 'Tory democracy' of Disraeli. The German aristocrats received a similar mandate from the German middle class in the Bismarckian era. On the other hand, José Ortega y Gasset (1937, p. 39) has said of Spain since the seventeenth century that 'beginning with the Monarchy and continuing with the Church, no national power in all that time has thought of anything outside itself. When did the heart – in the last analysis, a foreign heart – of Spanish monarch or Spanish church ever beat for ends that were profoundly Spanish? Never.' Similarly, important spokesmen of the French nobility before 1789 refused to accept membership in the French nation; and in 1941 the French socialist ex-Premier Leon Blum (1946, pp. 92–3) drew up a long and specific denial of the ability or willingness of the French middle class henceforth to lead the nation. Just who the 'leading social group' is going to be, therefore, may well change from period to period, but there is usually some such group at any given time, and its character will in turn have its influence on the character of the national movement.

At all times, however, it will be necessary for the 'leading social group' to be 'above' some of the main groups to be led, at least in terms of current prestige, and usually in the long run in terms of economic, political, and social opportunities, skills, wealth, organization, and the like, so that a member of another social group, on joining this 'leading group' would have in some sense a real experience of 'rising in the world', or, as some sociologists have termed it, of 'moving vertically in society' (Sorokin 1927). As an alignment with a centre and a leading group, nationality offers to its members the possibility of vertical substitutions unbroken from any one link to the next. In a competitive economy or culture, nationality is an implied claim to privilege. It emphasizes group preference and group peculiarities, and so tends to keep out all outside competitors. It promises opportunity, for it promises to eliminate or lessen linguistic, racial, class, or caste barriers to the social rise of individuals within it. And it promises security, for it promises to reduce the probability of outside competition for all sorts of opportunities, from business deals to marriages and jobs.

To the extent that the division of labour in a particular society is competitive and stratified, nationality can thus be used to hamper 'horizontal' substitution from individuals outside the group, and to facilitate 'vertical' substitution within it. To the extent of these conditions, the barriers and patterns of communication gain added significance and power from the barriers and patterns of society. Once the pressures of uprooting and insecurity are then added to these horizontal and vertical barriers, the stage is set for the rise of the political movement of modern nationalism – that is, for the vast effort to convert the channels of culture into stormladders for masses of individuals to social advancement and economic privilege.

There are significant variations in this process among different peoples and in different areas. Nationalism may indeed appear simply as a rapid process of Westernization, as it did, at least on the surface, in the Turkey of Kemal Ataturk, in the 1920s, and perhaps in Indonesia in the 1930s and 1940s. Or it may, on the contrary, assert its allegiance to the old ways and the old traditions; it may continue to acknowledge the prestige and leadership of the old social classes, symbols, and institutions, with little drive towards serious modernization, as in the case of much of Arab nationalism between 1917 and 1952. Sometimes, again, the appearance may be conservative, as in the Japanese Meiji 'Restoration' of 1868 with its battle cry 'Revere the Emperor!' although the substance of the process may be one of drastic and far-reaching change. Thus the Meiji Restoration replaced the power of the Shogun's court by that of the 'outer clans'; it offered new opportunities to the impoverished lower nobility, the 'Ronin', and to the merchants of the cities; it dispossessed through the pressure of taxation a sizable portion of peasants; and it created a modern Japanese industry, a modern labour market, modern metropolitan centres, and a modern army and navy.

Yet perhaps the common elements prevail. Either the 'prenationalistic' ruling class could accept the new movement and promote it for reasons of its own, as did some rulers, nobles, or landowners in Germany, Austria, England, and Japan, all of whom promoted manufactures, or improvements in agriculture, education, or military efficiency, and reaped as a byproduct an increase in nationalistic or patriotic sentiment. Or the rulers may cling to the substance of the social *status quo*. If they fail, they may be swept away, as were the Bourbons of France, the Sultan of Turkey, and the Emperor of China. If they succeed, and if the river of social change is not yet running fast in their territory, their position may remain secure for the time being, and nationalism among their people may be impressive in rhetoric, but feeble in power or performance.

In any case, the strength of the nationalist or patriotic process – the two may not yet be distinguishable at this stage – may then depend on two major elements. First, it may depend on the extent to which the ruling class itself promotes this process, not merely in its outward trappings, but in its social substance; the extent, therefore, also to which the ruling class remains accessible to the members of other classes for communication, entry, alliance, or alignment. Second, it may depend on the extent to which the masses of the people have become mobilized, with or without the cooperation of their rulers, for realignment with the new nationalist movement and the new changes in their old ways of life.

Both of these elements involve the problem of coercion. What are the means of social compulsion in a given area, and in the service of which groups, which policies, and which patterns of behaviour will they continue to be used? As nationalism gains ground within a people, it comes to approach this inevitable question of power. In trying to gain and exercise power for its ends, the efforts of nationalists may transform a people into a nationality.

Nationalities and nation-states

In the age of nationalism, *a nationality* is a people pressing to acquire a measure of effective control over the behaviour of its members. It is a people striving to equip itself with power, with some machinery of compulsion strong enough to make the enforcement of its commands sufficiently probable to aid in the spread of habits of voluntary compliance with them. As the interplay of compliance habits with enforcement probabilities, such power can be exercised through informal social arrangements, pressure of group opinion, and the prestige of national symbols. It can be exercised even more strongly through formal social or political organizations, through the administration of educational or economic institutions, or through the machinery of government. Whatever the instruments of power, they are used to strengthen and elaborate those social channels of communication, the preferences of behaviour, the political (and sometimes economic) alignments which, all together, make up the social fabric of the nationality.

All group power thus acquired by members of the nationality leads them to ask for more. Formally or informally, dissenters find themselves pressed into line, while a significant part of the members of the nationality begin to demand control of the state or part of it.

Once a nationality has added this power to compel to its earlier cohesiveness and attachment to group symbols, it often considers itself a *nation* and is so considered by others. In this sense, men have spoken of a Polish, Czech, or Irish nation, even after these groups had lost their earlier political states, or before they had yet acquired control of any state at all.

In all these cases, nationalities turn into nations when they acquire power to back up their aspirations. Finally, if their nationalistic members are successful, and a new or old state organization is put into their service, then at last the nation has become sovereign, and a *nation-state* has come into being. At this moment, if not earlier, the successful nation may face a new immediate problem: how to use its new panoply of power against the claims of other nationalities. The more successful it has been in promoting its own members into privileged or controlling positions in society, the more it will now have to fear the rise of other peoples and other nationalist movements.

At the end of this road a successful career of nationalism might turn a nation into a class. All its members in that event would become members of the privileged strata of society, and none would have to stoop to humbler occupations, for other peoples would be made to furnish the drawers of water and the hewers of wood. The national channels of communication would no longer even in part cut across the barriers of society; on the contrary, the barriers of class would become reinforced by the barriers of nationality, language, and culture. Something of this was implied in the vision of some British empire builders towards the end of the nineteenth century, and it found its extreme expression in the Nazi idea of a German *Herrenvolk*. But every step towards this goal has to be paid for with an increase in danger. Ever more remote from fundamental economic production, ever more cut off morally and politically from the majority of mankind, the would-be 'master race' would of necessity become the obvious target for all social and national processes of revolt and of destruction. Nationalism, which set out to make the nation strong, may at this point begin to make it potentially weaker and more vulnerable. Whether men and women will follow nationalist leaders to the end of this path, or whether they will be able to break the fatal cycle may well depend on the availability of alternative leadership, and perhaps even more on the nature of their own experiences and aspirations drawn from their everyday life.

Nationalism and 'cultural autonomy'

One suggestion may emerge already at this stage from our discussion of nationality, culture, and communication. Culture and complementarity of communication are not things apart from the rest of life, as the Sunday supplements of some newspapers are apart from the serious business of carrying the day's news. At every step we find social communication bound up indissolubly with the ends and means of life, with men's values and the patterns of their teamwork, with employment and promotion, with marriage and inheritance, with the preferences of buyers and sellers, and with economic security or distress – with all the psychological, political, social, and economic relationships that influence the security and happiness of individuals. Nationality, culture, and communication are not the only factors that affect all these, but they are always present to affect them.

It seems therefore utopian to imagine a blissful state of 'cultural autonomy' where 'culture' will be carried on detached from real life, where schools will be detached from taxes and students from the need for jobs, where families and businessmen need not worry about tariffs or government controls, nor office workers about employment or promotion. All these problems can be dealt with and are being dealt with in many countries; but they cannot be dealt with completely apart from the problems of culture and nationality on the one hand, and of political and economic life on the other.

Culture itself is of interest to men and women only to the extent that it does go into the daily texture of their lives. 'Cultural autonomy' cannot be divorced from the personal, local, regional, or occupational autonomy of human beings. Every step in the tragic rise of nationalistic violence during our century has shown us individuals struggling not merely for an abstract 'cultural autonomy' but for something that involved the very fabric of their lives and the places and regions where these lives are lived;

and every wave of nationalism has reasserted even more stridently this claim to its 'integral', 'total', ever more inclusive character.

References

BAUER, O. (1923) *Die Nationalitaetenfrage und die Sozialdemokratie*, 2nd ed. Vienna, Brand.

BLUM, L. (1946) *For All Mankind* New York, Viking Press.

BURKE, E. (1790) 'Reflections on the Revolution in France', *Works*, vol. IV London, World's Classics ed.

CHADWICK, H. M. (1945) *The Nationalities of Europe* Cambridge, Cambridge University Press.

DISRAELI, B. (Earl of Beaconsfield) (1913) *Sybil, or Two Nations* London, Longmans.

EYCK, E. (1943) *Bismarck*, Vol II Zurich, Eugen Rentsch Verlag.

FINER, E. (1950) in Bryson, L. et al. (eds) *Goals for American Education* New York, Harper.

FRANKLIN, B. (1751) 'Observations Concerning the Increase of Mankind', in Hacker, L. M. (1947) *The Shaping of the American Tradition* New York, Columbia University Press.

HUXLEY, J. S. (1947) *Man in the Modern World* New York, Pelican-Mentor.

KLUCKHOHN, C. and MURRAY, H. A. (1948) *Personality in Nature, Society and Culture* New York, Knopf.

LEIGHTON, A. H. (1946) *The Governing of Men: General Principles and Recommendations based on Experience at a Japanese Relocation Camp* Princeton, New Jersey, Princeton University Press.

LENIN, V. I. (1939) *Imperialism, the Highest State of Capitalism* New York, International Publishers.

LINTON, R. (ed.) (1945) *The Science of Man in the World Crisis* New York, Columbia University Press.

ORTEGA Y GASSET, J. (1937) *Invertebrate Spain* New York, Norton.

SCHUERCH, E. (1943) *Sprachpolitische Erinnerungen* Bern, Paul Halpt Verlag.

SOROKIN, P. (1927) *Social Mobility* New York, Harper.

WIRTH, L. (1948) in Wright, Q. (ed.) *The World Community* Chicago, University of Chicago Press.

YOUNG, A. (1792) *Travels during the Years 1787, 1788 and 1789* London, and cited in Innis, H. A. (1950) *Empire and Communication* Oxford, Clarendon Press.

Part III Production and allocation

Introduction

How people get their living, and what kind of a living they get, are central concerns in every kind of society. Nature does not furnish such an abundance of everything that the means of life can be had for the taking. They have to be worked for. Fields must be ploughed, iron must be smelted, trees must be felled, and a host of other activities must be carried on, in order to produce what is needed for survival in a world where resources are scarce in relation to the demands made on them. The kinds of things that are produced, and the methods of production that are used, differ greatly from one society to another, but one thing is true for almost all of them: the majority of people spend the greater part of their working lives engaged directly or indirectly in the production process. Even when all a society's resources are being used to the full, the volume of output is never enough to satisfy everyone's wants and needs completely, and sometimes it is hardly sufficient even to keep everyone alive; so the question of how it is shared out within the society is a vital one. In the study of societies, therefore, two of the key questions that have to be asked are, first, how is the process of production organized? and second, how is the product allocated among the people who make up the society?

These are not only important questions in themselves. The answers also throw light on many other aspects of social life. The character of a society's economy goes a long way to shape its political and social structure as well, so that it is hardly possible to explain the latter without reference to the system of production and allocation. Moreover, economies do not stand still. Populations grow; resources increase through the creation of new means of production; the advance of knowledge provides new technologies which change the methods of production. These developments affect not only the volume and composition of output, but also exert effects, often profound ones, on the pattern of social relationships and the distribution of political power.

The main aim in that section of the course which is related to this part of the book is to analyse the system of production and allocation in our own industrial economy. To set this in perspective, and to emphasize the fact of continuing change, the first week's work (out of the four in the section) examines the characteristics of 'pre-industrial' societies. It is for this reason that the first extract in this part of the book is a description of the medieval economy – part of a chapter from Marc Bloch's classic *Feudal Society*, in which the author traces the development of European society through the 'two ages of feudalism'. This is followed by a chapter from *The First Industrial Nation*, by Peter Mathias, in which the origins of the 'industrial revolution' are described and discussed, and it is argued that no simple, single-cause theory of industrialization will serve to explain it. Between them, these pieces cover a good deal of historical ground; but it is not necessary to go into the past to study pre-industrial economies. A contemporary example is provided in the third extract – Scarlett Epstein's article on 'Productive Efficiency and Customary Systems of Rewards in Rural South India', in which she describes the pattern of production and allocation in a society which is still ruled by traditional practices.

In the next two weeks the characteristics and functioning of industrial capitalist economies are described and analysed in detail; in the fourth week a comparison is made between 'market' and 'planning' systems, and some current trends in the development of the modern economy are examined. To summarize the main characteristics of planned and market economies, a chapter from *Benham's Economics*, by F. W. Paish, is reprinted here. It does not attempt to compare the two systems in terms of the performance of countries actually practising them, but it gives a clear and concise account of the principles involved from what might be called the 'orthodox' point of view. It is followed by a less orthodox discussion of the question – a chapter from J. K. Galbraith's *The New Industrial State,* in which he argues that modern industrial development has created production possibilities with which the 'market mechanism' cannot deal. Lastly, the concept of 'post-industrial' society is introduced in an article by Robert L. Heilbroner in his article 'Economic problems of a post-industrial society' in which he explains why it is worth introducing a special term for the type of economy that can be expected to follow 'industrialism'.

F. S. Brooman

9   Material conditions and economic characteristics of feudal society

Marc Bloch

The two ages of feudalism

The framework of institutions which governs a society can in the last resort be understood only through a knowledge of the whole human environment. For though the artificial conception of man's activities which prompts us to carve up the creature of flesh and blood into the phantoms *homo oeconomicus, philosophicus, juridicus* is doubtless necessary, it is tolerable only if we refuse to be deceived by it. That is why, despite the existence of other works on the various aspects of medieval civilization, the descriptions thus attempted from points of view different from ours did not seem to us to obviate the necessity of recalling at this stage the fundamental characteristics of the historical climate in which European feudalism flourished. Need I add that in placing this account near the beginning of the book there was no thought of claiming any sort of illusory primacy for facts of this kind? When it is a question of comparing two particular phenomena belonging to separate series – a certain distribution of population, for example, with certain forms of legal groups – the delicate problem of cause and effect undoubtedly arises. On the other hand, to contrast two sets of dissimilar phenomena over a period of several centuries, and then say: 'Here on this side are all the causes; there on that are all the effects', would be to construct the most pointless of dichotomies. A society, like a mind, is woven of perpetual interaction. For other researches, differently oriented, the analysis of the economy or the mental climate are culminating points; for the historian of the social structure they are a starting-point.

In this preliminary picture, designedly limited in scope, it will be necessary to retain only what is essential and least open to doubt. One deliberate omission, in particular, deserves a word of explanation. The wonderful flowering of art in the feudal era, at least from the eleventh century on, is not merely the most lasting glory of that epoch in the eyes of posterity. It served in those times as a vehicle for the most exalted forms of religious

BLOCH, MARC (1962) 'Material Conditions and Economic Characteristics', in *Feudal Society* London, Routledge and Kegan Paul, 59–71.

sensibility as well as for that interpenetration of the sacred and profane so characteristic of the age, which has left no more spontaneous witness than the friezes and capitals of certain churches. It was also very often the refuge, as it were, of certain values which could not find expression elsewhere. The restraint of which the medieval epic was incapable must be sought in Romanesque architecture. The precision of mind which the notaries were unable to attain in their charters presided over the works of the builders of vaults. But the links that unite plastic expression to the other features of a civilization are still insufficiently understood; from the little that we know of them they appear so complex, so subject to delays and divergences that it has been necessary in this work to leave aside the problems posed by connections so delicate and contradictions that to us seem so astonishing.

It would, moreover, be a grave mistake to treat 'feudal civilization' as being all of one piece chronologically. Engendered no doubt or made possible by the cessation of the last invasions, but first manifesting themselves some generations later, a series of very profound and very widespread changes occurred towards the middle of the eleventh century. No definite break with the past occurred, but the change of direction which, despite inevitable variations in time according to the countries or the phenomena considered, affected in turn all the graphs of social activity. There were, in a word, two successive 'feudal' ages, very different from one another in their essential character. We shall endeavour in the following pages to do justice as much to the contrasts between these two phases as to the characteristics they shared.

The first feudal age: density of population

It is and always will be impossible for us to calculate, even approximately, the population of Western countries during the first feudal age. Moreover, there undoubtedly existed marked regional variations, constantly intensified by the spasms of social disorder. Compared with the veritable desert of the Iberian plateaux, which gave the frontier regions of Christendom and Islam the desolate appearance of a vast 'no man's land' – desolate even in comparison with early Germany, where the destruction wrought by the migrations of the previous age was being slowly made good – the country districts of Flanders and Lombardy seemed relatively favoured regions. But whatever the importance of these contrasts and whatever their effect on all the aspects of civilization, the fundamental characteristic remains the great and universal decline in population. Over the whole of Europe, the population was immeasurably smaller than it has been since the eighteenth century or even since the twelfth. Even in the provinces formerly under Roman rule, human beings were much scarcer than they had been in the heyday of the Empire. The most important towns had no more than a few thousand inhabitants, and waste land, gardens, even fields and pastures encroached on all side amongst the houses.

This lack of density was further aggravated by very unequal distribution. Doubtless physical conditions, as well as social habits, conspired to maintain in the country districts profound differences between systems of settlement. In some districts the families, or at least some of them, took up their residence a considerable distance apart, each in the middle of its own farmland, as was the case, for example, in Limousin. In others on the contrary, like the Île-de-France, they mostly crowded together in villages. On the whole, however, both the pressure of the chiefs and, above all, the concern for security militated against too wide dispersal. The disorders of the early Middle Ages had in many cases induced men to draw nearer to each other, but these aggregations in which people lived cheek by jowl were separated by empty spaces. The arable land from which the village derived its sustenance was necessarily much larger in proportion to the number of inhabitants than it is today. For agriculture was a great devourer of space. In the tilled fields, incompletely ploughed and almost always inadequately manured, the ears of corn grew neither very heavy nor very dense. Above all, the harvests never covered the whole area of cultivation at once. The most advanced systems of crop-rotation known to the age required that every year half or a third of the cultivated soil should lie fallow. Often indeed, fallow and crops followed each other in irregular alternation, which always allowed more time for the growth of weeds than for that of the cultivated produce; the fields, in such cases, represented hardly more than a provisional and short-lived conquest of the waste land, and even in the heart of the agricultural regions nature tended constantly to regain the upper hand. Beyond them, enveloping them, thrusting into them, spread forests, scrub and dunes – immense wildernesses, seldom entirely uninhabited by man, though whoever dwelt there as charcoal-burner, shepherd, hermit or outlaw did so only at the cost of a long separation from his fellow men.

The first feudal age: intercommunication

Among these sparsely scattered human groups the obstacles to communication were many. The collapse of the Carolingian empire had destroyed the last power sufficiently intelligent to concern itself with public works, sufficiently strong to get some of them carried out. Even the old Roman roads, less solidly constructed than has sometimes been imagined, went to rack and ruin for want of maintenance. Worse still, bridges were no longer kept in repair and were lacking at a great number of river-crossings. Added to this was the general state of insecurity, increased by the depopulation to which it had itself in part contributed. Great was the surprise and relief at the court of Charles the Bald, when in the year 841 that prince witnessed the arrival at Troyes of the messengers bringing him the crown jewels from Aquitaine: how wonderful that such a small number of men, entrusted with such precious baggage, should traverse without accident those vast areas infested on all sides by robbers. The Anglo-Saxon Chronicle shows much less surprise when relating how, in 1061, one of the greatest nobles of England, Earl Tostig, was captured and held to ransom by a handful of bandits at the gates of Rome.

Compared with what the world offers us today, the speed of travel in that age seems extremely slow. It was not, however, appreciably slower than it was at the end of the Middle Ages, or even the beginning of the eighteenth century. By contrast with today, travel was much faster by sea than by land. From 60 to 90 miles a day was not an exceptional record for a ship: provided (it goes without saying) that the winds were not too unfavourable. On land, the normal distance covered in one day amounted, it seems, to between nineteen and twenty-five miles – for travellers who were in no hurry, that is: say a caravan of merchants, a great nobleman moving round from castle to castle or from abbey to abbey, or an army with its baggage. A courier or a handful of resolute men could by making a special effort travel at least twice as fast. A letter written by Gregory VII at Rome on 8 December 1075 arrived at Goslar, at the foot of Harz, on 1 January following; its bearer had covered 29 miles a day as the crow flies – in reality, of course, much more. To travel without too much fatigue and not too slowly it was necessary to be mounted or in a carriage. Horses and mules not only go faster than men; they adapt themselves better to boggy ground. This explains the seasonal interruption of many communications; it was due less to bad weather than to lack of forage. The Carolingian *missi* had earlier made a point of not beginning their tours till the grass had grown. However, as at present in Africa, an experienced foot-traveller could cover astoundingly long distances in a few days and he could doubt-less overcome certain obstacles more quickly than a horseman. When Charles the Bald organized his second Italian expedition he arranged to keep in touch with Gaul across the Alps partly by means of runners.

Though poor and unsafe, the roads or tracks were in constant use. Where transport is difficult, man goes to something he wants more easily than he makes it come to him. In particular, no institution or method could take the place of personal contact between human beings. It would have been impossible to govern the state from inside a palace: to control a country, there was no other means than to ride through it incessantly in all directions. The kings of the first feudal age positively killed themselves by travel. For example, in the course of a year which was in no way excep-tional, the emperor Conrad II in 1033 is known to have journeyed in turn from Burgundy to the Polish frontier and thence to Champagne, to return eventually to Lusatia. The nobleman with his entourage moved round constantly from one of his estates to another; and not only in order to supervise them more effectively. It was necessary for him to consume the produce on the spot, for to transport it to a common centre would have been both inconvenient and expensive. Similarly with the merchant. Without representatives to whom he could delegate the task of buying and selling, fairly certain in any case of never finding enough customers assembled in one place to assure him a profit, every merchant was a pedlar, a 'dusty foot' (*pied poudreux*), plying his trade up hill and down dale. The cleric, eager for learning or the ascetic life, was obliged to wander over Europe in search of the master of his choice: Gerbert of Aurillac studied mathematics in Spain and philosophy at Rheims; the Englishman Stephen Harding, the ideal monachism in the Burgundian abbey of Molesmes. Before him, St Odo, the future abbot of Cluny, had travelled through France in the hope of finding a monastery whose members lived strictly according to the rule.

Moreover, in spite of the old hostility of the Benedictine rule to the *gyrovagi*, the bad monks who ceaselessly 'vagabonded about', everything in contemporary clerical life favoured this nomadism: the international character of the Church; the use of Latin as a common language among educated priests and monks; the affiliations between monasteries; the wide dispersal of their territorial patrimonies; and finally the 'reforms' which periodically convulsed this great ecclesiastical body and made the places first affected by the new spirit at once courts of appeal (to which people came from all parts to seek the good rule) and mission centres whence the zealots were despatched for the conquest of the Catholic world. How many foreign visitors came to Cluny in this way! How many Cluniacs journeyed forth to foreign lands! Under William the Conqueror almost all the dioceses and great abbeys of Normandy, which the first waves of the 'Gregorian' revival were beginning to reach, had at their head Italians or Lorrainers; the archbishop of Rouen, Maurille, was a man from Rheims who, before occupying his Neustrian see, had studied at Liège, taught in Saxony and lived as a hermit in Tuscany.

Humble folk, too, passed along the highways of the West: refugees, driven by war or famine; adventurers, half-soldiers, half-bandits; peasants seeking a more prosperous life and hoping to find, far from their native land, a few fields to cultivate. Finally, there were pilgrims. For religious devotion itself fostered travel and more than one good Christian, rich or poor, cleric or layman, believed that he could purchase salvation of body and soul only at the price of a long journey.

As has often been remarked, it is in the nature of good roads to create a vacuum around them – to their own profit. In the feudal age, when all roads were bad, scarcely any of them was capable of monopolizing the traffic in this way. Undoubtedly such factors as the restrictions of the terrain, tradition, the presence of a market here or a sanctuary there, worked to the advantage of certain routes, although far less decisively than the historians of literary or artistic influences have sometimes believed. A fortuitous event – a physical accident, the exactions of a lord in need of money – sufficed to divert the flow, sometimes permanently. The building of a castle on the old Roman road, occupied by a race of robber knights – the lords of Méréville – and the establishment some distance away of the St Denis priory of Toury, where merchants and pilgrims found by contrast a pleasant reception, were sufficient to divert traffic from the Beauce section of the road from Paris to Orleans permanently westward, so that the ancient roadway was abandoned from that time on. Moreover from the beginning of his journey to the end, the traveller had almost always the choice of several itineraries, of which none was absolutely obligatory. Traffic, in short, was not canalized in a few great arteries; it spread capriciously through a multitude of little blood-vessels. There was no castle, burg, or monastery, however far from the beaten track, that could not expect to be visited occasionally by wanderers, living links with the outer world, although the places where such visits were of regular occurrence were few.

Thus the obstacles and dangers of the road in no way prevented travel. But they made each journey an expedition, almost an adventure. If men, under pressure of need, did not fear to undertake fairly long journeys (they feared it less, perhaps, than in centuries nearer to our own) they shrank from those repeated comings and goings within a narrow radius which in other civilizations form the texture of daily life; and this was especially so in the case of humble folk of settled occupations. The result was an ordering of the scheme of human relations quite different from anything we know today. There was scarcely any remote little place which had not some contacts intermittently through that sort of continuous yet irregular 'Brownian movement' which affected the whole of society. On the other hand, between two inhabited centres quite close to each other the connections were much rarer, the isolation of their inhabitants infinitely greater than would be the case in our own day. If, according to the angle from which it is viewed, the civilization of feudal Europe appears sometimes remarkably universalist, sometimes particularist in the extreme, the principal source of this contradiction lay in the conditions of communication: conditions which favoured the distant propagation of very general currents of influence as much as they discouraged, in any particular place, the standardizing effects of neighbourly intercourse.

The only more or less regular letter-mail service which functioned during the whole of the feudal era was that which linked Venice to Constantinople. Such a thing was practically unknown in the West. The last attempts to maintain a royal posting-service, on the model left by the Roman government, had disappeared with the Carolingian empire. It is significant of the general disorganization that the German monarchs themselves, the true heirs of that empire and its ambitions, should have lacked either the authority or the intelligence necessary to secure the revival of an institution clearly so indispensable to the control of vast territories. Sovereigns, nobles, prelates were obliged to entrust their correspondence to special couriers, otherwise – as was usual among persons of lesser rank – the transport of letters was simply left to the kindness of passing travellers; as, for instance, the pilgrims on their way to St James of Galicia. The relative slowness of the messengers, the mishaps that at every stage threatened their progress, meant that the only effective authority was the one on the spot. Forced constantly to take the gravest steps – the history of the papal legates is in this respect very instructive – every local representative of a great potentate tended only too naturally to act for his personal advantage and thus finally to transform himself into an independent ruler.

As for knowledge of distant events, everyone, whatever his rank, was obliged to rely on chance encounters. The picture of the contemporary world which the best-informed men carried in their minds presented many lacunae; we can form an idea of them from the unavoidable omissions even from the best of those monastic annals which are as it were the written reports of medieval news-hawks. Moreover, it was seldom exact as to time. It is, for example, remarkable to find a person so well placed for acquiring information as Bishop Fulbert of Chartres showing astonishment on receiving gifts for his church from Cnut the Great: for he admits that he believed this prince to be still a heathen, although in fact he had been baptized in infancy. The monk Lambert of Hersfeld is quite well-informed about German affairs, but when he goes on to describe the grave events which occurred in his time in Flanders (a region bordering on the Empire and in part an imperial fief), he soon makes a series of the strangest blunders. Such an imperfect state of knowledge was a poor foundation for any large political designs.

The first feudal age: trade and currency

The life of the Europe of the first feudal age was not entirely self-contained. There was more than one current of exchange between it and the neighbouring civilizations, and probably the most active was that which linked it to Moslem Spain, as witnessed by the numerous Arab gold pieces which, by this route, penetrated north of the Pyrenees and were there sufficiently sought after to become the object of frequent imitations. In the western Mediterranean, on the other hand, long-distance navigation was now practically unknown. The principal lines of communication with the East were elsewhere. One of them, a sea-route, passed through the Adriatic, at the head of which lay Venice, to all appearance a fragment of Byzantium, set in a world apart. On land the Danube route, for a long time severed by the Hungarians, was almost deserted. But farther north, on the trails which joined Bavaria to the great market of Prague and thence, by the terraces on the northern flank of the Carpathians, continued to the Dnieper, caravans passed back and forth, laden on the return journey with products of Constantinople or of Asia. At Kiev they met the great transversal which, running across the plains and from river to river, linked the riparian countries of the Baltic with the Black Sea, the Caspian or the oases of Turkestan. For the West had missed its chance of being the intermediary between the north or north-east of the continent and the eastern Mediterranean, and had nothing to offer on its own soil to compare with the mighty comings and goings of merchandise which made the prosperity of Kievian Russia.

Not only was this trade restricted to very few routes; it was also extremely small in volume. What is worse, the balance of trade seems to have been distinctly unfavourable – at any rate with the East. From the eastern countries the West received almost nothing except a few luxury articles whose value – very high in relation to their weight – was such as to take no account of the expense and risks of transport. In exchange it had scarcely anything to offer except slaves. Moreover, it seems that most of the human cattle rounded up on the Slav and Lettish territories beyond the Elbe or acquired from the slave-traders of Britain took the road to Islamic Spain; the eastern Mediterranean was too abundantly provided with this commodity from its own sources to have any need to import it on a large scale. The profits of the slave-trade, in general fairly small, were not sufficient to pay for the purchase of precious goods and spices in the markets of the Byzantine world, of Egypt or of nearer Asia. The result was a slow drain of silver and above all of gold. If a few merchants unquestionably owed their prosperity to these remote transactions, society as a whole owed scarcely anything to them except one more reason for being short of specie.

However, money was never wholly absent from business transactions in feudal Europe, even among the peasant classes, and it never ceased to be employed as a standard of exchange. Payments were often made in produce; but the produce was normally valued item by item in such a way that the total of these reckonings corresponded with a stipulated price in pounds, shillings and pence. Let us therefore avoid the expression 'natural economy', which is too summary and too vague. It is better to speak simply of shortage of currency. This shortage was further aggravated by the anarchic state of minting, another result of the subdivision of political authority and the difficulty of communication : for each important market, faced with the threat of shortage, had to have its local mint. Except for the imitation of exotic coinages and apart from certain insignificant little pieces, the only coins now produced were *denarii*, which were rather debased silver pieces. Gold circulated only in the shape of Arab and Byzantine coins or imitations of them. The *libra* and the *solidus* were only arithmetical multiples of the *denarius*, without a material basis of their own. But the various coins called *denarii* had a different metallic value according to their origin. Worse still, even in one and the same area almost every issue involved variations in the weight or the alloy. Not only was money generally scarce, and inconvenient on account of its unreliability, but it circulated too slowly and too irregularly for people ever to feel certain of being able to procure it in case of need. That was the situation, in the absence of a sufficiently active commerce.

But here again, let us beware of too facile a formula – the 'closed economy'. It would not even apply exactly to the small farming operations of the peasants. We know that markets existed where the rustics certainly sold some of the produce of their fields or their farmyards to the towns-folk, to the clergy, to the men-at-arms. It was thus that they procured the *denarii* to pay their dues. And poor indeed was the man who never bought a few ounces of salt or a bit of iron. As to the 'autarky' of the great manors, this would have meant that their masters had gone without arms or jewels, had never drunk wine (unless their estates produced it), and for clothes had been content with crude materials woven by the wives of tenants. Moreover, even the inadequacies of agricultural technique, the disturbed state of society, and finally the inclemency of the weather contributed to maintain a certain amount of internal commerce: for when the harvest failed, although many people literally died of starvation, the whole popula-tion was not reduced to this extremity, and we know that there was a traffic in corn from the more favoured districts to those afflicted by dearth, which lent itself readily to speculation. Trade, therefore, was not non-existent, but it was irregular in the extreme. The society of this age was certainly not unacquainted with either buying or selling. But it did not, like our own, live by buying and selling.

Moreover, commerce, even in the form of barter, was not the only or perhaps even the most important channel by which at that time goods circulated through the various classes of society. A great number of pro-ducts passed from hand to hand as dues paid to a chief in return for his protection or simply in recognition of his power. It was the same in the case of that other commodity, human labour: the *corvée* furnished more labourers than hire. In short, exchange, in the strict sense, certainly played a smaller part in economic life than payment in kind; and because ex-change was thus a rare thing, while at the same time only the poorest could resign themselves to living wholly on their own produce, wealth and well-being seemed inseparable from authority.

Nevertheless, in an economy so constituted the means of acquisition at the disposal even of the powerful were, on the whole, singularly restricted. When we speak of money we mean the possibility of laying by reserves, the ability to wait, the 'anticipation of future values' – everything that, con-versely, the shortage of money particularly impedes. It is true that people tried to hoard wealth in other forms. The nobles and kings accumulated in their coffers gold or silver vessels and precious stones; the churches amassed liturgical plate. Should the need arise for an unexpected disburse-ment, you sold or pawned the crown, the goblet or the crucifix; or you even sent them to be melted down at the local mint. But such liquidation of assets, from the very fact of the slowing down of exchange which made it necessary, was never easy nor was it always profitable; and the hoarded treasure itself did not after all constitute a very large amount. The great as well as the humble lived from hand to mouth, obliged to be content with the resources of the moment and mostly compelled to spend them at once.

The weakness of trade and of monetary circulation had a further consequence of the gravest kind. It reduced to insignificance the social function of wages. The latter requires that the employer should have at his disposal an adequate currency, the source of which is not in danger of drying up at any moment; on the side of the wage-earner it requires the certainty of being able to employ the money thus received in procuring for himself the necessities of life. Both these conditions were absent in the first feudal age. In all grades of the hierarchy, whether it was a question of the king's making sure of the services of a great official, or of the small landlord's retaining those of an armed follower or a farm-hand, it was necessary to have recourse to a method of remuneration which was not based on the periodic payment of a sum of money. Two alternatives offered: one was to take the man into one's household, to feed and clothe him, to provide him with 'prebend', as the phrase went; the other was to grant him in return for his services an estate which, if exploited directly or in the form of dues levied on the cultivators of the soil, would enable him to provide for himself.

Now both these methods tended, though in opposite ways, to create human ties very different from those based on wages. Between the prebend-holder and the master under whose roof he lived the bond must surely have been much more intimate than that between an employer and a wage-earner, who is free, once his job is finished, to go off with his money in his pocket. On the other hand, the bond was almost inevitably loosened as soon as the subordinate was settled on a piece of land, which by a natural process he tended increasingly to regard as his own, while trying to reduce the burden of service. Moreover, in a time when the inadequacy of communications and the insufficiency of trade rendered it difficult to maintain large households in relative abundance, the 'prebend' system was on the whole capable of a much smaller extension than the system of remuneration based on land. If feudal society perpetually oscillated between these two poles, the narrow relationship of man and man and the looser tie of land tenure, the responsibility for this belongs in large part to the economic regime which, to begin with at least, made wage-earning impracticable.

The economic revolution of the second feudal age

We shall endeavour, in another work, to describe the intensive movement of repopulation which, from approximately 1050 to 1250, transformed the face of Europe: on the confines of the Western world, the colonization of the Iberian plateaux and of the great plain beyond the Elbe; in the heart of the old territories, the incessant gnawing of the plough at forest and wasteland; in the glades opened amidst the trees or the brushwood, completely new villages clutching at the virgin soil; elsewhere, round sites inhabited for centuries, the extension of the agricultural lands through the exertions of the assarters. It will be advisable then to distinguish between the stages of the process and to describe the regional variations. For the moment, we are concerned only with the phenomenon itself and its principal effects.

The most immediately apparent of these was undoubtedly the closer association of the human groups. Between the different settlements, except in some particularly neglected regions, the vast empty spaces thenceforth disappeared. Such distances as still separated the settlements became, in any case, easier to traverse. For powers now arose or were consolidated – their rise being favoured by current demographic trends – whose enlarged horizons brought them new responsibilities. Such were the urban middle classes, which owed everything to trade. Such also were the kings and princes; they too were interested in the prosperity of commerce because they derived large sums of money from it in the form of duties and tolls; moreover they were aware – much more so than in the past – of the vital importance to them of the free transmission of orders and the free movement of armies. The activity of the Capetians towards that decisive turning-point marked by the reign of Louis VI, their aggressions, their domanial policy, their part in the organization of the movement of repopulation, were in large measure the reflection of considerations of this kind – the need to retain control of communications between the two capitals, Paris and Orleans, and beyond the Loire or the Seine to maintain contact with Berry or with the valleys of the Oise and the Aisne. It would seem that while the security of the roads had increased, there was no very notable improvement in their condition; but at least the provision of bridges had been carried much farther. In the course of the twelfth century, how many were thrown over all the rivers of Europe! Finally, a fortunate advance in harnessing methods had the effect, about the same time, of increasing very substantially the efficiency of horse-transport.

The links with neighbouring civilizations underwent a similar transformation. Ships in ever greater numbers ploughed the Tyrrhenian Sea,
and its ports, from the rock of Amalfi to Catalonia, rose to the rank of great
commercial centres; the sphere of Venetian trade continually expanded;
the heavy wagons of the merchant caravans now followed the route of
the Danubian plains. These advances were important enough. But relations
with the East had not only become easier and more intimate. The most
important fact is that they had changed their character. Formerly almost
exclusively an importer, the West had become a great supplier of manufactured goods. The merchandise which it thus shipped in quantity to the
Byzantine world, to the Latin or Islamic Levant and even – though in
smaller amounts – to the Maghreb, belonged to very diverse categories.
One commodity, however, easily dominated all the rest. In the expansion
of the European economy in the Middle Ages, cloth played the same vital
role as did metal and cotton goods in that of nineteenth-century England.
If in Flanders, in Picardy, at Bourges, in Languedoc, in Lombardy, and
yet other places – for the cloth centres were to be found almost everywhere – the noise of the looms and the throbbing of the fullers' mills
resounded, it was at least as much for the sake of foreign markets as for
local requirements. And undoubtedly this revolution, which saw our
Western countries embarking on the economic conquest of the world by
way of the East, is to be explained by a multiplicity of causes and by
looking – as far as possible – towards the East as well as towards the West.
It is none the less true that it could not have occurred without the demographic changes mentioned above. If the population had not been more
numerous than before and the cultivated area more extensive; if the fields
– their quality improved by augmented manpower and in particular by
more intensive ploughing – had not become capable of yielding bigger and
more frequent harvests, how could so many weavers, dyers or cloth-
shearers have been brought together in the towns and provided with a
livelihood?

The North was conquered, like the East. From the end of the eleventh
century Flemish cloth was sold at Novgorod. Little by little, the route of
the Russian plains became hazardous and was finally closed. Thencefor-
ward Scandinavia and the Baltic countries turned towards the West. The
process of change which was thus set in motion was completed when, in
the course of the twelfth century, German merchants took over the Baltic.
From that time onwards the ports of the Low Countries, especially Bruges,
became the centres where northern products were exchanged not only for
those of the West itself but also for merchandise from the East. Strong

international links united the two frontiers of feudal Europe by way of Germany and especially through the fairs of Champagne.

Such a well-balanced external trade could not fail to bring a flow of coin and precious metals into Europe and so add substantially to its monetary resources. This relative easing of the currency situation was reinforced – and its effects multiplied – by the accelerated rhythm of circulation. For in the very heart of the West the progress of repopulation, the greater ease of communications, the cessation of the invasions which had spread such an atmosphere of confusion and panic over the Western world, and still other causes which it would take too long to examine here, had led to a revival of commerce.

Let us avoid exaggeration, however. The picture would have to be carefully shaded – by regions and by classes. To live on their own resources remained for long centuries the ideal – though one that was rarely attained – of many peasants and most villages. Moreover, the profound transformations of the economy took place only very gradually. It is significant that of the two essential developments in the sphere of currency, one, the minting of larger pieces of silver much heavier than the *denarius*, appeared only at the beginning of the thirteenth century (and even at that date in Italy alone) and the other, the resumption of the minting of gold coins of an indigenous type, was delayed till the second half of the same century. In many respects, what the second feudal age witnessed was less the disappearance of earlier conditions than their modification. This observation applies to the part played by distance as well as to commerce. But the fact that the kings, the great nobles, and the manorial lords should have been able to begin once more to amass substantial wealth, that wage-earning, sometimes under legal forms clumsily adapted from ancient practices, should have increasingly supplanted other methods of remunerating services – these signs of an economy in process of revival affected in their turn, from the twelfth century onwards, the whole fabric of human relations.

Furthermore, the evolution of the economy involved a genuine revision of social values. There had always been artisans and merchants; individuals belonging to the latter class had even been able, here and there, to play an important role, though collectively neither group counted for much. But from the end of the eleventh century the artisan class and the merchant class, having become much more numerous and much more indispensable to the life of the community, made themselves felt more and more vigorously in the urban setting. This applies especially to the merchant class, for the medieval economy, after the great revival of these decisive years, was always dominated, not by the producer, but by the trader. It was not for the latter class that the legal machinery of the previous age – founded on an economic system in which they occupied only an inferior place – had been set up. But now their practical needs and their mental attitude were bound to imbue it with a new spirit. Born in the midst of a very loosely-knit society, in which commerce was insignificant and money a rarity, European feudalism underwent a fundamental change as soon as the meshes of the human network had been drawn closer together and the circulation of goods and coin intensified.

10 The industrial revolution – identity and beginning

Peter Mathias

The term industrial revolution, which is now used so widely in all manner of publications, needs defining. More particularly, the problem is to limit its definition. Emphatically, the expression should not be used just to denote industrial or mechanical innovation, an advance in a technique of production or the mechanization of a process in a single industry, or even the conversion of a single industry onto a mass-production basis with large plants driven by more than human power. If the concept is to mean only this, then the search for its origin would be lost in the remote past. Did it begin with the gig-mill, or the blast-furnace in the fifteenth and sixteenth centuries, the fulling-mill in the thirteenth century or the water- and wind-mill in more remote classical and medieval times? Professor Nef has claimed an industrial revolution in the years 1540–1640. Professor Carus Wilson has attached the term to the fulling-mill. Professor Gordon Child once spoke of 'the industrial revolution of the late Bronze Age'. A typical industrial transformation occurred to urban brewing in London during the seventeenth century, when the structure of the industry was translated from being a handicraft affair where individual families and publicans brewed their own beer to where commercial brewers, producing possibly 10,000 barrels a year in specialized places of manufacture, supplied dependent publicans whose economic function had been reduced to simple retailing. Yet other industries retained their medieval form of production and structure of organization until the later nineteenth century – such as flour-milling, glove-making, shoe-making. The ready-made suit industry was a development of the twentieth century. The present decade is seeing much traditional food-processing leaving the family kitchen and entering the factory and shop. Where can the line be drawn? Clearly, to define the industrial revolution in this way is to universalize the term, to rob it of all limitations as to time and space. A similar semantic problem bedevils the concept of the Renaissance. Innovations in techniques of production, in technical change, although differing as to the pace and scale of change, form a continuum in history.

MATHIAS, PETER (1969) 'I Prologue: the industrial revolution – identity and beginning', in *The First Industrial Nation* London, Methuen, 1–18.

To be given identity, the concept implies the onset of a fundamental change in the structure of an economy; a fundamental redeployment of resources away from agriculture, becoming self-evident over time. This does not necessarily mean that investment in agriculture, output in agriculture or the labour force in agriculture go down. Indeed all these things may need to increase in absolute terms. But growth in production, investment and the labour force grows more rapidly in other sectors of the economy, which therefore becomes more differentiated. The British economy in 1850 had become structurally more different compared with 1750 than 1750 was with 1650 or compared with structural changes coming in any previous century. One can only see how important this trend is by trying to relate each main sector of the economy, and their relative rates of change, to the whole.

The concept involves also the assumption that industrial production begins to expand at a higher and sustained rate – speaking of output as a whole. The popular phrase is that coined by Professor W. W. Rostow, 'the take-off into self-sustained growth' – in other words the onset of industrialization. Essentially this presumes the idea of measuring the rate of growth of the whole economy (the gross national product or the national income, as the total value of goods and services produced in the economy) or industrial output as a whole. One speaks of a *rate* of growth of production. This has to be so conceptually, even though evidence may be desperately short for certain sectors of the economy, to work out national income and industrial growth rates statistically until after 1800. But if gross national product is to increase by up to 2 per cent per annum – and this is broadly what self-sustained growth meant in Britain – it will have been increasing much faster than in any pre-industrialized economy, which would be growing at less than 1 per cent per annum. And such a rate of growth would involve changes, sooner or later, in every aspect of a country's history and its institutions. Economic 'growth' in this sense of differentiation – structural change, 'deepening' of investment, technical change involving a change in 'production functions' – has to be distinguished from economic 'expansion' – extending a traditional pattern of economic activity without such qualitative changes.

When one asks these questions about the beginning of rapid, cumulative, structural change, with the onset of rates of growth of up to 2 per cent per annum, with all the implications this involved, the industrial revolution can be located in time and place. Britain saw the beginning of such a process between the 1740s and the 1780s. Here came a break with a tradition of economic life, and a pace of change, which had lasted for centuries and which, in certain essential characteristics, had been universal across all countries of the globe up to that time. The actual term industrial revolution was coined in the early nineteenth century in France, in conscious parallel to the French Revolution, but it had also been expressed in other words by contemporaries in Britain like Robert Owen. In 1837 a French economist, Blanqui, explicitly claimed that since the late eighteenth century (he mentioned Watt and Arkwright by name) deep-seated economic changes of this nature were affecting Britain, as fundamental in their effects on the national life, although operating in a less dramatic way, as the political upheavals which had changed the traditional face of France in 1789. The metaphor 'revolution' has one disadvantage: the assumption of very rapid change in a short space of time. In Britain the pace of change has been proved slower than in many subsequent case-histories (for example, the rate of growth of industrial production in Russia in the 1890s), and slower also than literary metaphors like 'revolution' or 'take-off' suggest whenever people have tried to measure that rate of change statistically and to pin-point the take-off point. The metaphor is over-dramatic and implies over-precision in dating. However, judged against the long perspectives of history, the eighteenth century did see pivotal changes of this nature and the development of new trends which may be claimed in retrospect to have changed the entire nature of the economy and to have established the watershed between an essentially medieval and an essentially modernized context in the economic sense.

Britain's was the first industrialization of any national economy in the world. Even more remarkable, it occurred spontaneously, not being the result of conscious government policy sponsoring industrial progress. Although inevitably the results of state policy were significant in legal processes, taxation policies and the like, it derived virtually no momentum directly from public taxation, or public effort, or state-guaranteed loans to raise capital for productive investment. Nor was there imported capital on any scale. Considerable Dutch investment in British government funds during the earlier part of the eighteenth century (which would be releasing indigenous capital for other things) was being repatriated after 1780, exactly when the need for capital investment in Britain was rising. It is worth stressing from the outset that the state had its back turned to the economy, as far as *directly* promoting industrial growth or new industrial skills on any scale were concerned. All later industrializations have been much more involved with public initiative and imported capital, while in the eighteenth century, on the other side of the Channel, much greater efforts were being made to promote new industrial skills by state decree and favour. Even in the United States in the early nineteenth century much of the capital raised for canals, like the famous Erie Canal from the Great Lakes to the Hudson River, was obtained from the sale of state bonds in London, with interest being guaranteed from local tax revenues, if need be; and American railways often prospered, like many of their colleges, on land grants from state governments. In the twentieth century most governments whose countries are not already industrialized have decided that an industrial revolution is something no country can afford to be without, and have set about creating one by state decree. Britain saw an industrial revolution by consent. It owed nothing to planners and nothing to policemen – a phenomenon, as Professor Chambers has remarked, which grows the more remarkable as it recedes in time.

Increasing interest is now being shown in the British experience by economists and planners wrestling with the problems of generating economic growth in developing societies in our own day. In turn, much light has been thrown on the British experience by the work of scholars with a practical and contemporary orientation to their research. In many senses, all nations concerned with economic growth at the present time are treading the path Britain first set foot on in the eighteenth century. Even though many of the solutions available today are very different, as are so many aspects of the contexts in which they are placed, many of the problems are basically the same, even though differing in scale.

The elemental truth must be stressed that the characteristic of any country before its industrial revolution and modernization is poverty. Life on the margin of subsistence is an inevitable condition for the masses of any nation. Doubtless there will be a ruling class, based on the economic surplus produced from the land or trade and office, often living in extreme luxury. There may well be magnificent cultural monuments and very wealthy religious institutions. But with low productivity, low output per head, in traditional agriculture, any economy which has agriculture as the main constituent of its national income and its working force does not produce much of a surplus above the immediate requirements of consumption from its economic system as a whole. Most of what is produced beyond these elemental consumption needs flows into various forms of conspicuous expenditure and construction rather than into productive investment. The population as a whole, whether of medieval or seventeenth-century England, or nineteenth-century India, lives close to the tyranny of nature under the threat of harvest failure or disease, which can bring the death rate up to seventy to one hundred per thousand in a 'dismal peak' and average it between thirty and forty per thousand. Increasing numbers in these circumstances, if there is a shortage of fertile land cultivable by traditional methods, without changes in the economic system will eventually bring checks: diminishing returns in traditional agriculture and a higher incidence of emigration, famine or disease. Even if population establishes an equilibrium with resources through various types of social control, influencing the number of marriages and the number of children per marriage, thus avoiding Malthusian checks in their direct form, that equilibrium will be at a very low level of real income. The graphs which show high real wages and good purchasing power of wages in some periods tend to reflect conditions in the aftermath of plague and endemic disease, as in the fifteenth century. If one looks to late fourteenth- and fifteenth-century England as the golden age of labour as Thorold Rogers did, it is really the equivalent of advocating the solution of India's difficulties now by famine and disease – of counting it a success to raise *per capita* national income by lessening the number of people rather than by expanding the economy.

These problems of poverty, of the threat of mass-starvation, have been unknown in Britain since the industrial revolution, and it is well to emphasize such a generalization in advance of more detailed discussion about movements in the standard of living during the first century of industrialization after 1750. Gregory King's evidence of mass poverty reveals a situation which cannot be solved by the redistribution of income, only by enlarging the flow of resources being produced by the economy. And to increase the national income as a whole, and productivity per head, means changing the nature of the economic system. This is why the industrial revolution, the start of this rapid transformation in Britain, becomes the fundamental watershed in the economic development of this country when seen in the time-scale of centuries. The last paragraph of Professor Ashton's book on the industrial revolution, one of the most influential paragraphs in the writing of economic history in the present generation, deserves quoting here in full.

. . . The central problem of the age was how to feed and clothe and employ generations of children outnumbering by far those of any earlier time. Ireland was faced by the same problem. Failing to solve it, she lost in the 'forties about a fifth of her people by emigration or starvation or disease. If England had remained a nation of cultivators and craftsmen she could hardly have escaped the same fate, and, at best, the weight of a growing population must have pressed down the spring of her spirit. She was delivered, not by her rulers, but by those who, seeking no doubt their own narrow ends, had the wit and resource to devise new methods of production and new methods of administering industry. There are today on the plains of India and China men and women, plague-ridden and hungry, living lives little better, to outward appearance, than those of the cattle that toil with them by day and share their places of sleep by night. Such Asiatic standards, and such unmechanized horrors, are the lot of those who increase their numbers without passing through an industrial revolution (Ashton 1954, p. 161).

To pose the question of what needs to happen before self-sustained economic growth can develop is to search for a Holy Grail of explanation for the secrets of economic growth being hunted so assiduously in our own day. No single equation, no single mode of combinations of factors, can provide the answer. There is no single, general theory of economic growth to which all case-histories conform. Relationships between factors, the relative importance of individual factors, have changed dramatically according to their context in time or place. A very deep-seated instinct exists to look for a pervasive single-cause explanation for historical phenomena (preferably one which no one else has yet thought of) in terms of which to seek to explain everything. In most cases, this tidy assumption is surely misguided in principle and impossible to employ operationally, at least when one is dealing with such a deep-seated and widespread historical phenomenon like the industrial revolution or the Renaissance. To search for a single-cause explanation for the industrial revolution is to pose a false analogy with a simple equation governing chemical change. It is less tidy, less satisfying, less simple, but nevertheless more accurate to suppose that there was no one secret key which undid the lock, no single operative variable, no one prime relationship which had to be positive and in terms of which all other aspects of change may be regarded as dependent variables.

To create some confusion, which is always a stimulus to thought, it is worth challenging each factor which has been put forward as a single cause explanation in its own right. The favourable natural resources position existing in Britain had been existing for a very long time before the mid-eighteenth century. Other countries had been equally bountifully endowed by nature. By itself, therefore, a favourable resource position was not a sufficient, though it may have been a necessary, condition for the industrial revolution. The Protestant Nonconformists have also been heralded as the secret weapon of European economic growth, the Calvinist and other sects who became active economic agents of change, the carrier of capitalism. But even though Protestant Nonconformist sects became important activists in the process of growth in Britain, identical basic religiou theologies flourished in countries innocent of dramatic industrial change, in Denmark, Sweden, Northern Scotland and other primitive agricultural areas of Europe. A rising population is also said to have created the unique context for growth by expanding the internal market and the labour-force. But Ireland, and subsequently Norway and Sweden and many other non-European countries, have also experienced rapid population growth without concomitant economic development. In turn, such factors as a bourgeois social structure with attitudes orientated towards trade and economic gain, the extent of trade itself or the plentifulness of capital have each been championed as the great unique advantages which put Britain in a class by herself. But were any of these things true by themselves? The rate of interest was consistently lower in Holland and capital more abundant there – seeking investment opportunities abroad which were lacking in industry at home. And wealth from foreign trade, the extent of markets in foreign trade, was greater in Holland than in Britain, relative to the size of her economy. The Dutch social structure was also equally fluid; the 'middling orders' in her society were as important as in England. The economic ethic in that bourgeois, merchant society was equally favourable in this sense as social values in England. Wealth and enterprise, particularly trading enterprise, gave status in Holland equally as in England. Holland was also a constitutional state with political power reflecting new wealth there as in England. No one could say that in Holland the extravagances of a lavish court robbed the nation of productive resilience, investment resources or the motivations toward business success, which some have posited in the case of France or Prussia. Yet the Dutch economy did not progress from mercantile and shipping supremacy to industrial strength. But Holland had no coal or iron, while high taxation to sustain her world-wide colonial and naval commitments did put a strain on her economy in the eighteenth century.

Nor can industrialization be explained by any sudden outburst of mechanical ingenuity or inventive genius. France had as impressive a record of scientific advance, of high standards of mechanical contrivance in luxury-market industries like watch-making and automata (performing toys) as England. Much greater positive, deliberate help was given by government to acquiring new industrial skills in France and other continental states than in England. The period of main advance in precision skills such as scientific instrument making was in the late seventeenth century, not the mid-eighteenth. Some key inventions, known for many decades, were not actively diffused in the economy until the later eighteenth century, time-lags which suggest that the acquisition of new technical knowledge was not a prime determinant of timing in the development of many new techniques. And if it was just the natural genius of the British people to do these things, there is an onus of proof on explaining just why that genius saw fit to wait until the mid-eighteenth century to throw aside its disguise, and why that natural genius faded in relation to that of other countries a brief century later on. If the natural genius of Protestants, or Anglo-Saxons, or Scotsmen, or any other theologically or racially determined category was so responsive to other criteria in this way, it suggests that those other criteria are the operationally important ones to examine when seeking the explanation for the source and timing of the momentum for economic change, however much that process may have been influenced by these particular groups.

It is much easier methodologically to defend the proposition that, if any *one* prime factor had not been present in eighteenth-century England, if there had developed in any one of half a dozen relationships in the economy absolute resistance, absolute unresponsiveness to change, the whole process of economic growth leading into industrialization might have been held back or slowed down. Setting up the issue in this way sidesteps the precise relationship between variables in the British case, but it is a useful initial analytical tool. What prime relationships can be identified? Causation must be divided into factors which operated on a long time scale and those generating change in the shorter run: slowly generating forces and 'trigger-mechanisms'. This division is useful provided the analogy does not mislead by exaggerating the stability before the changes which came during the eighteenth century and implying too sudden a change thereafter. Compared with the experience of later case-histories of industrialization, such as Japan, and twentieth-century growth rates of leading industrial nations, the main characteristic of growth in eighteenth-century and early nineteenth-century Britain was moderation.

Arthur Lewis, when referring to the contemporary world, gave top priority to what he called 'the will to industrialize'. He meant that there must be a social system and a government which has not got its face turned against economic change, or at least has not got effective power and influence to prevent spontaneous forces for change from acting. Where the momentum for change is mainly spontaneous and the mechanisms and institutions promoting economic growth mainly private, rather than state-inspired or organized, the social context, its structure and attitudes, becomes strategic. The values of the whole society are not necessarily orientated to economic growth (although momentum will be maximized if these are permissive, responsive to change) but certainly the values of activist minorities must be positive. Social prejudice against enterprise or status won by new wealth, may not prove very significant unless it is institutionalized in law and given sanctions by the state and the judicial system. This generalization may be more applicable to the 'supply side' of the process of growth, looking at inputs of factors of production such as entrepreneurship, capital and so forth. The social structure and prevailing social attitudes were probably of greater generalized significance on the 'demand side', affecting market structures and the patterns of demand. In many of these relationships, Britain proved to be fortunately endowed by the early eighteenth century. Government, in terms of aggressive economic nationalism, actively underwrote the development of trade, bound up with imperial expansion and naval potential. The revenue demands of war, even more than deliberate protectionism, created high tariff walls round the economy in the late seventeenth century, which gave considerable shelter to domestic industry. The social structure in England had become more flexible (particularly considering mobility over one or two generations) than any in Europe except, perhaps, Holland. An economy already much differentiated with trade and commerce had become associated with a much differentiated social structure, known throughout Europe for the importance of its 'middling orders', and a political structure giving much influence to commercial and professional interests. The social differentiation was also marked by an increasing religious heterodoxy with the various groupings, particularly of the Protestant Nonconformists, associating their different theological bases with differing social ethics and economic roles. The peerage was 'open-ended' with noble status confined to the eldest son (unlike many continental parallels), and strong pressures existed to create a flow of new recruits and capital to land ownership and a complementary flow away from land. For all these reasons, Britain possessed one of the most active land markets in Europe, and associated with this, a most commercially orientated attitude to land and agriculture.

A second prerequisite for economic growth was sufficient economic resources to develop new sides to the economy. When a country has become industrialized, in the circumstances of the late nineteenth or twentieth centuries, with modern methods of ocean and inland transport and modern energy resources, it is extraordinary to consider how much of its vital raw materials and energy requirements can be imported rather than being indigenous. Incalculable natural advantages still remain, such as an equable climate and sufficient water (the most important raw material of all), but coal is now the only major natural resource Britain possesses in abundance, with low-grade iron ore. However, at the beginning of the process a favourable resource position was vital, particularly in energy resources and particularly in relation to existing methods of transport. Favourable local mineral fuel supplies close to navigable water was, in fact, a key locational advantage for developing a mass-output, low-cost heavy industry. The logistics of energy inputs based upon coal, translated against available transport in a pre-railway age, precluded any major industrial complex in heavy industry from developing *except* where coal and ore were plentiful and adjacent to one another and to water carriage. Here Britain enjoyed very considerable advantages when her natural resource position was matched to the technology upon which the early stages of industrialization were based. Plentiful coal and iron ore were conveniently placed with regard to water carriage in many regions of the island; a strategic river system, in particular the Trent and the Severn, stretched into the heart of industrial England. These natural advantages cannot be related to the precise timing of the industrial revolution, having existed long before the mid-eighteenth century. But technological change and extending river navigation was gradually making more of these potential advantages, a geological and climatic endowment, into active economic assets.

To economic resources must be added inventiveness, applied science or, from some source or other (even if it means importing other people's ideas and skills), a flow of technical innovations through which production and productivity can be increased. Applied science does not seem to have been particularly prominent in this process during the eighteenth century, save in a minority of strategic points in its latter decades. But of the general energetic questing for experiment, innovation, trying new ways of doing things, there is no doubt. It was expressed, however, largely in an empirical tradition of shrewd heads and clever fingers, the emerging scientific experimental tradition being one aspect of this general context. Certainly the flow of innovations from applied science was in no wise comparable to that which came after 1850. Technical innovation and business development also have a human dimension. Economic growth, on the land as well as at sea, in the factory or the mine, meant the appearance and growth of an entrepreneurial group, the men under whose charge new sectors of the economy could be developed and innovations brought into productive use. Such men were the shock troops of economic change.

A collateral requirement to effect technical change is always the demand for capital embodied in such investment. Innovation in industry or agriculture meant, in the circumstances of eighteenth-century England or any underdeveloped country today, investing capital in the productive process, whether for enclosure, drainage and improvement in agriculture, expensive fixed capitals in industry or in new methods of transport – roads, canals and then railways – to cope with the new flows of materials. The largest investments of all were probably outside the direct context of industry, in transport and then in increasing investment in social capital (not directly productive in the same way as factories or machines) to meet the social implications of the new changes in production. For example, urbanization, changes in the local distribution of population and increases in total numbers multiplied severalfold the impact of demand for new housing. When economic growth involved the agglomeration of population into industrial towns – urbanization as well as industrialization – new forms of capital investment in social overheads appeared – sanitation, water supplies, paving, lighting, hospitals – all virtually unknown in village England. Increasing output per head meant directly more capital equipment per man of the labour force in industry and agriculture, as well as greater capital investment in the necessary services to sustain these sectors, such as transport.

The industrial revolution implied an increase in the rate of growth of industrial production, which meant in turn increasing the rate of investment to sustain it. This increase in the aggregate national rates of investment is now not thought to have been as high or as rapid as Professor Rostow once suggested (taking his figure from Professor Arthur Lewis), from below 5 per cent to above 10 per cent of G N P. But sectionally, in those areas of the economy which were expanding rapidly, rates of investment had to be greatly increased. Few people would now think that England was short of aggregate savings for this necessary increase in investment, which rose gradually, it seems, from about 5 per cent G N P in the mid-eighteenth century to 7 per cent by 1800 and to 10 per cent of G N P only in the 1840s, under the impact of railway construction. War was very much more expensive than the demands of the economy in its claims on loanable funds, and massive sums were raised for war. Government loans totalled £500 million from 1793 to 1815, whereas only £20 million was invested in the canal system between 1750 and 1815. The capital problem remained much more an institutional one of creating legal procedures, instruments and channels along which savings could flow from those groups receiving them in society to those other groups who needed credit and capital. The problems involved in raising the rate of investment, the process by which this was done and the purposes for which savings were invested provide one key to industrial progress in eighteenth-century England. 'It is the habit of productive investment that distinguishes rich from poor nations,' Arthur Lewis has written, 'rather than differences in equality of income or

differences in the respect accorded to wealthy men . . . The really significant turning point in the life of a society is not when it begins to respect
wealth, as such, but when it places in the forefront productive investment
and the wealth associated therewith.' Possibly this will not be an attitude
typical of the entire society, but it will certainly be characteristic of those
social enclaves which provide the active agencies of economic change.

The responsiveness of two sectors in the economy in generations before
the decades of the eighteenth century, with which the term industrial revolution is usually associated, also proved vital conditioning factors to industrialization in Britain: agriculture and foreign trade. Agricultural progress
needs to match industrial development or problems will intensify. This is
potentially vital for food supplies, conditions of demand, the supply of
savings and the creation of an industrial labour force. Agriculture was not
a leading sector in England's industrialization destined for the same
strategic role as in the case of Denmark. But even without being a main
source of momentum, agricultural development proved a crucial enabling
condition – perhaps a precondition – for industrialization. The critical
innovations, new crops and rotation techniques, antedated the mid-
eighteenth century – one even speaks of an agricultural revolution of the
seventeenth century (Kerridge 1968) – and agricultural output was growing markedly in the first half of the eighteenth century, if the movement
of prices and agricultural exports are a guide. But the main pace of development in enclosure and drainage came after 1750, with rising population and
prices. That is to say, agriculture continued to respond when industrialization got under way and did not become a source of constraint. It gave rising
production, to cope with rising population, and rising productivity, to
cope with changes in the structure of the labour force in the country as a
whole, as a declining proportion of the population remained involved in
growing food.

Foreign trade also proved a vital sector which did see dramatic changes
and expansion coming in the century before industrialization. One can
also speak of a commercial revolution from 1650 to 1750 (Davis 1967).
Foreign trade proved an important generating source for economic momentum in different ways long before the mid-eighteenth century, affecting
levels of wealth, the size of markets available to the industry of a relatively
small country, sources of savings, the differentiation of the economy and
society (that is to say, the higher percentage of GNP and occupational
groups associated with trade and services, compared with agriculture) in
England in relation to other countries. When new production techniques
enabled British industrialists to undercut the handicraft industries of the

rest of the world in price and quality, very great opportunities resulted.

In a sense, the roots of many of these changes go back into the remote past, long before the eighteenth century. Obviously there was no sudden appearance in the mid-decades of the eighteenth century of such things as a favourable natural resource endowment or a social structure favourable to economic growth or new Protestant sects, such as Quakers and Unitarians, to provide the enterprise groups in industrialization or new social attitudes to provide a catalyst for change. The same is probably true for the existence of capital; there does not seem to have been evidence of great capital scarcity in Restoration England. The development of these long-run relationships is on a longer time-scale and certainly not responsive just to economic relationships. Developments in Europe between 1500 and 1700 (including foreign trade and agricultural change) were, in many ways, the crucial differentiating themes when considering the mysteries of why industrialization should spring from the British or European context in the eighteenth century, and not from the Asian. However, change in most sectors of the economy (apart from agriculture and foreign trade) up to the mid-eighteenth century occurred slowly, piecemeal, and in aggregate – relative to the total national income – did not develop much spontaneous momentum to drag other sectors of the economy forward in harness with them. Population as a whole, it seems, rose very slowly, if at all, in the preceding century. Certainly no violent redeployment of numbers took place from countryside to town, from agriculture to non-agriculture, from south-east to north-west in population density, before the mid-eighteenth century, to compare with the sustained movement after the mid-eighteenth century. London and some west-coast towns, such as Bristol, grew in response to growing foreign trade, and some important regional increases in the first part of the eighteenth century may be disguised under a national average of stable numbers.

Nor did any major break-through in industrial productivity occur before the mid-eighteenth century, at least in strategic industries like metals and textiles. This awaited massive machinery, made of iron, and the massive water-powered textile mills of the 1770s; then Watt's rotary steam engine of the 1780s. Technical progress had been proceeding in various branches of industry before this, but as significant is the fact that some major technical innovations, such as smelting iron with mineral fuel and steam power, had been pioneered, but not brought into general use or adopted by entrepreneurs in the industries as a whole. Invention did not produce cumulative innovation on the same scale as it did after the mid-eighteenth century.

Greater differentiation also came to the economy, developing at about the same time. Before the mid-eighteenth century no major changes had come to the economic range of traditional methods of transport for shifting bulk goods, to sustain the deployment of the increased flows of material coming with industrialization and rising population. Turnpikes had been improving the road approaches to London, and some river navigations were being extended, but the canal age began in the 1750s, with improvements before that time being piecemeal with no great capital investment taking place in transport. The major development of financial institutions on a national scale needed to service the vastly increased transactions and credit involved with industrialization, again came after 1750, with the rise of a linked national network of country banks, London bankers, bill brokers and other specialized intermediaries handling the transfer of credit between different regions of the country. Although great wealth from land and foreign trade was available, potentially, for mobilization long before 1750, the institutional development which accompanied the changes in economic structure came primarily after the mid-century.

These new beginnings sprang in necessary response to the more rapid rate of industrial change and rise in population, and may be summarized under the definition of structural change and differentiation in the economy. If one defines the industrial revolution by a break in the rate of change in series measured quantitatively, there are reasons for putting the 'take-off' at the end of the American War in 1783 when foreign trade values began to rise very steeply. Certainly the 1780s saw a sharply increased rate of growth in many new developments, such as transport investment and the spread of banking, and crucial technical innovations in cotton, iron and steam power. The 1750s and 1760s saw the onset of many structural changes and important trends in industrial innovation in key industries. Apart from the longer-run conditions which favoured economic growth in eighteenth-century England, which have sometimes been given the name of 'pre-conditions', shorter-run influences conditioned the timing of new growth during the eighteenth century. Low farm and food prices in the agricultural depression 1730–50 probably gave a boost to internal consumer demand. Foreign trade values showed a great leap, particularly in the 1740s, which was strategic for the expansion of markets in certain industries, even though the total level of internal trade was several times greater than that of external commerce. The maintenance of money wages, and a rise in money wages in some areas, then gave a strong boost to internal markets with rising population after 1750. During the generation from 1750 to 1780, foreign trade does not appear to have been as important a trigger-mechanism relative at least to the internal market. Rising demand, high wages, the shortage and inflexibility of skilled labour then created a great stimulus in the mid-decades of the century to innovation, mechanical advance and an eventual break-through to new forms of power, materials, machines and factory production. After 1783 foreign trade once again provided a strong boost to industrial expansion on the demand side. Once innovations had allowed cost-reducing techniques and rising productivity to become established, then the circle became a self-reinforcing process with strong forces built in to diffuse and institutionalize further innovation.

References

ASHTON, T. S. (1954) *The Industrial Revolution* London, Oxford University Press.

DAVIS, R. (1967) *A Commercial Revolution* London, Historical Association, General Series, no. 64.

KERRIDGE, E. (1968) *The Agricultural Revolution* London, Allen and Unwin.

11 Productive efficiency and customary systems of rewards in rural South India

Scarlett Epstein

Introduction

Economics is concerned with the phenomena of production and distribution. Market and non-market economies alike have to meet the same problems: goods have to be produced and distributed among the population. It is on the former that economists have concentrated their attention. At the same time they have tended to neglect the interactions and conflicts between the market and other social institutions. However, in the study of societies which are changing over from non-market to market economies such factors cannot be so easily ignored. Since the majority of the world's population lives in societies where this transition is now occurring, the development of underdeveloped areas has become a central problem in world affairs, and a central concern of economists and others. Ways and means have to be devised to increase output so as to allow for a surplus to be sold, by which the economy is incorporated in the market system. Economic development involves here not only the use of new and more productive methods, it also depends on the presence of appropriate incentives which will induce the population to adopt the new techniques. In these circumstances, therefore, the recognition of the interplay of all social institutions becomes particularly important. This probably explains why economists have developed so few models to show the working of traditional non-market economies. They have concentrated their attention rather on the emerging and growing capitalist sector (Lewis 1954, pp. 139–91, and 1958, pp. 1–32). Yet in order to establish the conditions for the emergence and growth of a capitalist sector in underdeveloped countries an understanding of the principles underlying the customary non-market economies is essential. Apart from its purely theoretical interest, this is necessary to explain why some development schemes are successful and others fail; why the indigenous population of underdeveloped areas is

---

EPSTEIN, SCARLETT (1967) 'Productive Efficiency and Customary Systems of Rewards in Rural South India', in Firth, Raymond (ed.) *Themes in Economic Anthropology*, London, Tavistock Publications, 229–52.

prepared to react positively to some new economic opportunities and not to others.

Here I seek to explore some of these issues by focusing on hereditary labour relationships as they operate in India. My analysis is concerned to examine the implications of this system for productive efficiency, for the principles that underlie it and the way in which these differ from forms of capitalist economic organization. I shall show the importance of average productivity in underdeveloped Indian villages as opposed to the emphasis placed on marginal productivity in industrial economies.

The *jajmani* system

Economists sometimes assume that all farming economies are composed of self-sufficient owner–occupier households (e.g. Lewis 1954, p. 148). However, there are many rural societies in which members perform specialized functions: Indian farming communities with their complex division of labour provide a good example. The character of economic relationships in Indian villages is largely determined by the high degree of specialization that exists and by the particular sets of beliefs and observances that underlie and perpetuate this division of labour. It is in fact the caste system that throws into relief the complex division of labour in Indian society. A major feature of the caste system is that labour relationships between the land-owning castes and their dependent servicing castes are usually hereditary and rewards are paid annually in the form of fixed quantities of farming produce.

In the past, villages were largely self-sufficient; goods and services were mutually exchanged by the different specialist castes within small rural communities. Services and duties which the various castes performed for one another and the rewards associated with these were regulated by a socio-economic system known as the *jajmani* system. According to Sanscritic Indian usage, '*jajmani*' refers to a client who receives religious services and gives gifts in return for them. But, following Wiser, the term *jajmani* has come to be accepted for the system as a whole. He defined *jajmani* as follows: 'These service relationships reveal that the priest, bard, accountant, goldsmith, florist, vegetable grower, etc., etc., are served by all the other castes. They are the *jajmans* of these other castes. In turn each of these castes has a form of service to perform for the others. Each in turn is master. Each in turn is servant. Each has his own clientele comprising members of different castes which is his "*jajmani*" or "*birt*". This system of interrelatedness in service within the Hindu community is called the Hindu "*jajmani* system"' (Wiser 1958, p. xxi). Beidelman has criticized Wiser for describing a Hindu caste village as a system of idyllic mutuality, whereas in reality castes are linked in unequal relationships based upon power (1959, p. 6). This asymmetrical dimension of the *jajmani* system had its roots in land tenure, numerical predominance, political influence, and ritual differentiation in the caste hierarchy. From this point of view, Gould has described *jajmani* as 'a matter of landowning, wealth and power controlling castes providing a structurally fixed share of their agricultural produce along with numerous "considerations", in exchange for craft and menial services rendered by the mainly landless impoverished, politically weak lower castes' (1958, p. 431). Similarly, Beidelman speaks of *jajmani* as 'a feudalistic system of prescribed hereditary obligations of payment and of occupational and ceremonial duties between two or more specific families of different castes in the same locality' (1959, p. 6). In short, where Wiser talks of mutual rights and obligations, Beidelman and Gould emphasize the high degree of economic and political differentiation characteristic of India's customary system of labour relations. On the face of it, these views of the *jajmani* system are plainly inconsistent. I shall try to show later, however, that both are in a sense correct; the inconsistency arises from the fact that each stresses only one aspect of the total system.

All writers on the *jajmani* system stress the point that rewards and duties were strictly defined. The interdependence between the different caste occupations was based on hereditary ties. Rewards were in terms of agricultural produce, and quantities were fixed. As a result, methods of work were handed down from generation to generation and a certain rhythm of productive activities became a fixed aspect of the Indian villager's life.

Types of traditional labour relations

In order to understand the traditional economic relationships which have been described as falling within the *jajmani* system, their component parts and variations in different places and under different conditions must be made clear. The extreme form of *jajmani*, that is the prescribed hereditary relationship involving all castes in any one rural settlement, appears to have been largely limited to certain areas in North India. Yet the division of labour supported by the caste system, and expressed in the hereditary ties between different caste households, occurred to some extent in most Indian villages. Thus in Mysore in South India I found two types of hereditary link in the villages: one between Peasant [1] masters and their Untouchable labourers, the other between Peasants and certain functionary castes, such as Washerman, Barber, and Blacksmith, whose services were continually required. Village craftsmen, such as the Goldsmith and Potter, whose services were not in regular demand, had no hereditary relationship with Peasant caste households; they were not rewarded annually, but rather on the occasions when their services were required. In these Mysore villages landholding was vested in Peasants, who possessed what Srinivas has called 'decisive dominance' (1959, pp. 1–16), that is they dominated numerically, economically, politically, and also largely ritually. (There were no Brahmins in this village.) Though most of the servicing caste households had some land of their own, their holdings were too small to suffice for their subsistence. Therefore the castes with little land contributed their labour and/or skills to the life of the community and in return received a fixed share of the total agricultural output produced. These economic relations were, however, only one aspect of the multiple relations which linked the different caste households in the Indian village. For instance, the hereditary relationship between a Peasant master and his Untouchable labourer operated not only in the economic but also in the political and ritual spheres. If an Untouchable was involved in a dispute with another, whether Untouchable or not, his Peasant master had to come to his support. Similarly, the Untouchable allied himself with his Peasant master in disputes. He was expected to be prepared to fight for the latter, even against Untouchables aligned with other Peasants in conflict with his own master. Perhaps even more important, the Untouchable had to perform a number of ritual services for his Peasant master, such as carrying a torch ahead of a funeral procession from his master's household. These different types of relations – political, economic, and ritual – reinforced each other and in turn helped to ensure the stability of Indian peasant economies. Furthermore, the Hindu concepts of Karma (destiny) and Dharma (innate endowment), as well as beliefs in ritual pollution, stressed the maintenance of the *status quo*. Caste indeed pervaded the total complex of Indian society. There are, therefore, many aspects to caste relations. For the purpose of the present argument, however, we need concern ourselves only with the way in which the different aspects of the hereditary ties affected the purely economic part of the relationship. The more general social and political advantages, which, as we have seen, are part of the system of customary labour relationships, acted as additional incentive to landowners to meet their econo-

1 Caste names are written with capital initials: thus a Peasant is a member of the Peasant caste, whereas a peasant is a farmer.

mic liabilities in good and bad harvest years alike. The non-economic aspects of labour relations are probably even more important from the workers' point of view. Not only are Untouchable labourers assured of a minimum subsistence level in bad harvests, but the hereditary relationship provides them with a benevolent master who is expected to look after them as a father provides for his children. In fact, the customary relationship between Peasant masters and Untouchable labourers is couched in kinship terms; a Peasant calls his Untouchable labourer his 'Old Son' (*Hale maga*). Moreover, by leading the good life of an Untouchable, a labourer can hope to be reborn into a higher caste in his next existence.

The caste system incorporated two types of economic relationship. There were strictly hereditary ties between landowners and their servicing castes; these were highly prescribed. There were also the less prescribed but more personally contractual relationships between landowners and certain artisan castes, such as Basketmaker and Potter, whose services were not in regular demand. The establishment of links with outside markets brought new economic opportunities to Indian villages. The possibility of selling crops and labour offered incentives to enterprising men to improve their productive efficiency. We can investigate, therefore, whether these different types of socio–economic relationship produced reactions to the new opportunities. I shall illustrate my discussion mainly with material from two villages: Wangala, with its strictly prescribed hereditary system of rewards; and Dalena, where the diversification of economic activities had already largely undermined the traditional relationships (Epstein 1962).

Customary systems of rewards and improved production techniques

Following irrigation, Wangala lands required more and deeper ploughing. Farmers, therefore, had to replace their customary wooden ploughs with iron ones. Not only did these need more maintenance than wooden ploughs, but repairs also demanded greater skill. Wangala's Blacksmith, who had hereditary relations with Peasant farmers in the village, found that he had to learn how to repair the new iron ploughs. He also found that he was kept busier by his Peasant clients than he had been prior to irrigation. Yet his annual reward in kind remained the same. When he approached Peasant elders about an increase in the customary reward, they flatly refused it. They argued that it had been fixed by elders in the distant past and they saw no reason to increase the quantity of agricultural produce given annually to the Blacksmith, since it was still adequate to feed him.

The Blacksmith then carefully considered his position and came to the conclusion that it would be in his best interest to discontinue his hereditary relations with Peasant households altogether and work instead for cash. However, when he proposed this to Wangala's Peasant elders, who composed the village *panchayat*, they opposed his suggestion most strongly. They pointed out to him that relations which had lasted through generations could not be broken off at one stroke. It was, of course, in their own interest that the traditional arrangement should be maintained. They threatened that if the Blacksmith refused to perform his customary duties they would make his life in the village pretty much impossible. Since he had a small landholding in Wangala he was reluctant to move to another village. Nevertheless, being a very enterprising man, he was determined to be rid of his customary obligations, which he regarded as obstacles in his way to success. He wanted to be able to branch out into other activities, not directly connected with his craft, such as making doors and window-frames. He continued to argue with the Peasant elders until they finally offered a compromise. They suggested that if he could find some other Blacksmith prepared to carry on the traditional relations on customary terms, he himself would then be free to work as he liked. Wangala's Blacksmith managed to find a classificatory brother from another village who, as the youngest of a large family, was pleased to be able to take over the position which Wangala's Blacksmith had come to find so burdensome. Thereafter the new Blacksmith repaired wooden ploughs and other traditional tools belonging to the Peasants for which he received his annual reward of a fixed quantity of agricultural produce; the indigenous Blacksmith repaired their more recently acquired iron ploughs, for which he was paid in cash. Whereas Peasant farmers had at first not been prepared to grant even a small increase in the quantity of annual reward in kind the blacksmith received, they were now quite ready to pay extra cash for the services, which they had previously expected from him as part of their customary arrangements. Though this behaviour may appear strange, I shall show that the rationale and the principles on which it was based are quite clear.

Admittedly irrigation had increased the productivity of land. However, Peasants tended to regard the greater yield as part of the normal windfall profits which had been associated with the system of prescribed hereditary rewards. They rationalized their argument in terms of subsistence requirements and told the Blacksmith that the customary reward was still sufficient to feed him and his family. But the expansion of a cash sector induced the Blacksmith to hold out for higher rewards; this meant that he was no longer prepared to work for a minimum of subsistence. After the Blacksmith had managed to disentangle himself from his customary obligations and had provided a substitute for himself, Peasants were quite prepared to pay different amounts of cash for the various jobs he performed for them and which his substitute was not able to do. As soon as the hereditary ties between Wangala's indigenous Blacksmith and his Peasant clients had been broken as a result of the contact with the wider cash economy, Wangala Peasants acted as typical entrepreneurs in advanced economies. They were prepared to pay extra for the blacksmith's work because it could be associated with a considerable increase in total output.

In the case of Wangala's Blacksmith we are dealing with an extremely enterprising man: he designed a new and improved iron plough and started making it himself; he branched out into house-building and other activities for which the growing prosperity in the area produced a demand. However, before he could take advantage of the new economic opportunities he had to disentangle himself from his hereditary relationship with his Peasant clients. Peasant elders, village *panchayat* members, had used their political influence and power to force the indigenous Blacksmith to provide a substitute for himself to carry out his traditional duties. Thus the customary system of rights and duties continued to exist and exert pressures to ensure conformity. Customary ties are obligatory not only for workers but also and equally, for employers. 'Workers were entitled to their rights from every villager, according to the rules of the village communities; and if the villagers declined to employ their services to which they were entitled, they must still pay the *bullcottee hucks* (reward in kind)' (Wiser 1958, p. xxvi). What is also worth noting, incidentally, is how this system of relationships is modified to operate in India's large and rapidly growing cities. I became aware of this when I stayed with one of my English friends in Bombay. It appears that individual Washermen managed to establish a system of 'customary' relationships with tenants in particular blocks of flats. The Washerman washes all the clothes for the resident families and in turn receives a fixed monthly reward from each of them. When my hosts' Washerman decided to return to his natal village for a few months a year, he arranged for one of his kin to carry on his duties during his absence. Though my hosts were satisfied with their 'own' Washerman, they found the services of his substitute highly unsatisfactory; they therefore wanted to find a different Washerman. However, none of the many underemployed Washermen in Bombay was prepared to take on the job. They all regarded it as the prerogative of the 'customary' Washerman, who in turn had the right and duty to provide a substitute in his stead, if he went absent. In fact my hosts were boycotted by Bombay's Washermen, because they had attempted to change their 'customary' Washerman. The system of customary relationships in this way gives labour relations great stability and tends to eliminate competition, even in a highly competitive urban environment.

Similarly, Wangala's new Blacksmith continued to work according to long-established rules and was completely unaffected by the new economic opportunities in his environment. The existence of hereditary labour relations and fixed annual rewards, therefore, acted as a force to maintain the *status quo* and accordingly as an obstacle to economic growth and expansion. Wiser reports that 'there is very little stimulus for better work. The Washerman has no desire to buy a flat iron to iron his *jajmani's* clothes. If he were to get one, he would simply increase his own labour and get very little, if any more, pay for it' (1958, p. 142).

Craftsmen who have no such prescribed and highly formalized relations with their clients can much more easily branch out into new activities than those who, like Wangala's Blacksmith, are subject to traditional labour relations. For example, in Dalena there were a number of immigrant craftsmen caste households, such as the Basketmaker, whose enterprise was not in any way hampered by traditional agreements. When the growing urban demand for more colourful and nicely shaped mats and baskets became effective, Dalena's Basketmaker changed his products and methods of production. (There was no Basketmaker in Wangala with which to compare him but a comparable craftsman there, a Jeweller, preferred to cultivate his own small plot of land instead of seeking the advantage of the new urban market). Moreover, the Basketmaker's close links with the nearby urban centre made him realize there was a big demand for pork – which may be eaten by lower-caste Hindus. Accordingly, he started rearing pigs in Dalena itself and sold them with considerable profit at the nearest urban market. His enterprise proved so successful that he even sent word to his brother to join him. The latter came and they continued to expand their business. A comparison of the case of Wangala's indigenous Blacksmith with that of Dalena's Basketmaker clearly indicates the drawback of a prescribed system of rewards and obligations when it comes to economic expansion. This point can be further illustrated by the reaction of Wangala Peasants to the introduction of improved production techniques.

Wangala had had some tank-irrigated lands even before canal irrigation reached the village. Thus some of Wangala's peasants were already accustomed to growing paddy (rice) long before canal irrigation made the growing of wet crops a practical proposition. Traditionally, a *gumpu* group of ten or twelve women was employed as a team to transplant the paddy seedlings from the nursery to the paddy fields. Each *gumpu* had a leader, whose responsibility it was to see that her co-workers turned up on the day arranged between her and the Peasant: the leader also received a certain fixed amount of crops per acre of paddy her group transplanted. She gave equal shares of this agricultural produce to each member of her *gumpu* while she kept a slightly larger proportion for herself. Each Peasant always employed the *gumpu* of the wife of the Untouchable with whom he had hereditary relations. Accordingly, there was a traditional relationship between a Peasant farmer and his *gumpu*, involving fixed customary rewards. About 20 years after canal irrigation reached Wangala, the Agricultural Department tried to introduce the Japanese method of paddy cultivation to Wangala farmers. The officials stressed the considerable increase in yield which would result from the new method. Though farmers were quite prepared to believe this, only a few were ready to experiment with the new method, which involved a more laborious way of spacing plants properly. First of all, farmers were not prepared to pay the *gumpu* more for transplanting the new way, because there was pressure from the more conservative farmers against raising the fixed reward for the services of a group of women. Secondly, the few more enterprising men who were prepared to offer a higher reward to the *gumpu* found that the women had developed a certain rhythm of work and were reluctant to change it; besides no one was prepared to pay them for re-training. Similarly, when officials from the Agricultural Department tried to introduce a cheap and most efficient weeding hook, the use of which would have considerably reduced the cultivation labour required, Wangala farmers were not prepared to employ the new tool. At first sight their reaction appears difficult to understand, but it becomes more readily explicable when viewed in the context of hereditary relationships. These make them responsible for providing a minimum of subsistence for their Untouchable labourers. If they substituted tools for labour and therefore saved some agricultural produce in terms of rewards, they might then have to give in charity what they had initially saved. They would therefore have no net gain. Besides, they would be criticized for being mean and selfish.

   In these instances we see the Peasants of Wangala rejecting new techniques which would have increased output. But their response cannot be attributed simply to conservatism – which in any case often indicates a recognition of diffuse benefits not seen on the surface. For in other spheres, which were not covered by the hereditary system of rewards, Wangala Peasant farmers displayed a considerable degree of enterprise. They were, for example, extremely progressive in their attitude towards sugar-cane cultivation, an entirely new venture to them. Since sugar-cane had not been one of the traditionally cultivated crops, there were no customary production techniques or traditional rewards associated with it. Thus farmers felt free to experiment with the new techniques and methods and adopted those that proved most productive and efficient. They paid their labourers in cash on a daily basis. The number of labourers any one farmer employed was largely determined by the interaction between the wage-rate and marginal productivity, as is the case in any capitalist system. Since the problem of the subsistence for the village population was taken care of by the system of hereditary labour relations, a Wangala farmer could operate in spheres outside the customary system like any 'rational' employer in an industrial society: he attempted to maximize his returns by equating marginal returns with marginal costs. A Peasant's hereditary obligation to provide a minimum of subsistence for his dependent households provides an obstacle to improving productive efficiency and maximizing returns. Wherever this obligation is not in existence or has been abandoned, we can expect a more positive reaction to new economic opportunities. This becomes clear when we examine Dalena's economic activities.

Dalena lands had remained dry even after irrigation had reached the area. Dalena farmers therefore sought to participate in the growing prosperity of the region by diversifying their economic activities and by purchasing wet lands in neighbouring villages. This resulted in the breakdown of hereditary ties between Peasant farmers and their Untouchable labourers. In turn, this meant that farmers were left free to employ labourers with whom they had no customary arrangements. Nor were they bound by customary rewards in the form of a fixed quantity of agricultural produce. Unlike his Wangala counterpart, a Dalena Peasant farmer was thus able to select his labourers, who worked for him according to his instructions and under his supervision. His relationship with his labourers was mainly contractual; he paid them in cash on a daily basis. The better worker received a higher daily wage. Moreover, since his hereditary obligation to provide a minimum of subsistence for his dependent Untouchable households had already disappeared, he was keen to employ the new weeding hook, which Wangala farmers were reluctant to accept. This resulted in a considerable saving of labour and therefore in a sizeable gain. Paddy was a new crop to Dalena farmers. But, unlike Wangala landowners, Dalena Peasants were not tied to any customary techniques and arrangements for paddy cultivation, and they showed themselves eager to experiment with the Japanese method of paddy cultivation, which promised them greater returns. In fact, the adoption of the new method of paddy cultivation enabled Dalena farmers to get considerably higher output per acre of paddy than Wangala farmers with their customary method. According to a stratified random sample, which I compiled in the same way in both villages in 1955 and 1956, the average output per acre of paddy cultivation by Dalena farmers was as much as Rs 362 (1962, p. 218), while it amounted to only Rs 281 in Wangala (1962, p. 47). Thus the average yield per acre of paddy was about 30 per cent higher for Dalena than for Wangala farmers. As a matter of fact, Dalena's village headman won the prize in 1953 for the best yield per acre of paddy in the whole district. Although Dalena farmers have less wet land and have to walk longer distances to their fields than Wangala Peasant farmers, yet the disappearance of the prescribed hereditary system of labour relations enabled them to adopt more efficient and productive methods of paddy cultivation and therefore ensured them a considerably higher yield.

Average product and customary rewards

Having discussed the operation of customary systems of reward and shown that they provide serious obstacles to increasing productivity and economic growth in general I want now to attempt an analysis of the principles underlying these labour relations in stagnant village economies. Here I seek to suggest answers to such questions as : What determined the number of masters any one craftsman or agricultural labourer sought? What determined the number of customary labour relationships any one farmer was prepared to continue? And, again, what determined the amount of the fixed annual reward?

Since hereditary labour relationships still operate in Wangala, I shall utilize the numerical data I collected there as the basis for this discussion. Prior to irrigation, *ragi* (*Eleusine corocana*, a millet) used to be the major crop in Wangala; it also provided the staple diet for the villagers. The population was composed of 128 Peasant, 28 Untouchable, 2 Washerman, and 1 Blacksmith households. The total area of dry land cultivated by Wangala villagers was about 540 acres. Output of *ragi* varied from year to year according to climatic conditions. Bad years were those when rainfall was insufficient or fell at the wrong time; famine years were those when most crops failed and a considerable proportion of the population had to go hungry and many even died. Informants told me that bad years used to occur with a frequency of about one in every five or six years; this is borne out by Mysore rainfall statistics. Accordingly, we find that the output per acre of *ragi* varied from a minimum of just over two *pallas* (one *palla* of *ragi* equals 208 lb) in bad seasons to a maximum of about eight or nine *pallas* in good ones. The average daily subsistence requirement of *ragi* per household is just under two *seers* (one *seer* is one-hundredth of one *palla*, or 2 lb); this makes the annual *ragi* requirements for each household about seven *pallas* and for the whole village composed of 159 households, 1,113 *pallas*. In bad years Wangala's total *ragi* output of approximately 1,300 *pallas* was thus slightly more than sufficient to keep all the households fed, provided it was distributed equally among all of them. The average output per household in bad seasons was, therefore, an important factor in determining the size of any one settlement. I shall subsequently return to the importance of the average in stagnant economies. At this stage in the argument it is sufficient to note that in bad years the total product of the village had to be distributed equally among all households in order to keep the population alive. Yet the discrepancy in the landholding by Peasants and their dependent Untouchable labouring households was, and still is, considerable. The average landholding per Untouchable household was about 1½ acres, while that of Peasants was about 4 acres. This meant that in bad years Wangala Untouchable households managed to produce only approximately 3½ *pallas* of *ragi*, while each needed at least 7 *pallas* to survive. By contrast, the average Peasant household produced over 9 *pallas* of *ragi*. Average labour requirements per acre of *ragi* amount to about 35 labour days in bad years. The average Peasant household thus needed a minimum of about 120 labour days to cultivate its *ragi* fields. As cultivation of *ragi* is concentrated into a short period in the year – *ragi* is a two to four months crop – each Peasant farmer needed at least one or two helpers. It is extremely difficult for the Indian farmer to know the marginal product of his labour, i.e. the addition to total output produced by the last unit of labour employed: sometimes two men produce as much as three do, at other times there are differences in return. For the Peasant farmer it is much easier and more reliable to calculate the average product per labourer: this can readily be done by sharing the output equally among all cultivators. In bad years Wangala villagers, Peasants and their dependent households alike, all received an equal share of the total quantity of *ragi* produced. This meant that each Peasant had to give 50 *seers* of *ragi* to each of his two dependent Untouchable households. Fifty *seers* of *ragi* is in fact the quantity of fixed annual reward given by

Wangala Peasant masters to their Untouchable servants. Each Untouchable household had to have hereditary relationships with about eight or nine Peasant masters in order to make up the deficiency in bad years between his family's food requirement and his own output of *ragi*.

Clearly, in bad years Peasants had no more *ragi* supplies than their dependent Untouchables. However, masters were prepared to accept this egalitarian distribution always in the hope of better seasons. In years of bumper crops the average Peasant farmer could produce a surplus of about 25 *pallas* of *ragi* over and above his subsistence needs including the fixed rewards to his Untouchable labourers. This surplus enabled him to throw large feasts, arrange for elaborate weddings, invest in better bullocks or houses, etc. (cash saving was very rare). Good harvests, therefore, provided Peasants with the means with which to conduct their struggle for prestige. Economic differentiation was clearly taking place in good years, whereas in bad seasons the emphasis was on egalitarianism. In order to maximize his total product the Peasant farmer needed helpers; he needed them even more in good years than in bad. To make certain that his helpers were on the spot when required, he in turn was prepared to maintain hereditary relationships with them and give them fixed annual rewards. Other considerations besides the purely economic, such as ritual and political, reinforced the Peasant's preparedness to maintain his customary relationships.

Good years meant better yields also for Untouchables. However, since their landholdings were so much smaller than those of Peasants and their masters had prior claim on their work performance, their own output never reached the village maximum. Labour requirements per acre of *ragi* were higher in good than in bad years: bumper crops needed more weeding and more harvesting. Therefore, in good years Untouchables had even less time for their own fields than in bad seasons. The major part of their food requirements was always provided by their Peasant masters in the form of fixed quantities of annual rewards. Untouchables were prepared to accept the system of fixed rewards because it provided them with security even in bad years. Though no dependent Untouchable ever managed to have a surplus even approaching that of Peasant households in good seasons, the servicing castes did also benefit indirectly from good harvests: they watched the Peasants' lavish weddings and collected food at feasts. They could also get loans from their masters to help purchase cattle. Moreover, the hereditary relationships offered to the dependent Untouchables a number of advantages of more diverse economic and social nature: each Untouchable could count on his Peasant masters to help him in arranging and conducting weddings and in settling disputes and to give him some degree of social security in general.

In our Wangala example we have seen how the small landholdings of the Untouchables buttressed the system of fixed customary rewards. On the basis of this, we may postulate that the quantity of fixed annual rewards will vary according to the total village produce in bad years, the size of the labourers' landholdings, and the number of labour relations any one of them can maintain. This statement may be verified in different ways: first, by examining the fixed annual rewards of landless dependent households; second, by finding out whether there is any correlation between the quantity of fixed rewards and the size of the dependent household's acreage; and, third, by establishing whether or not there are differences in the quantity of fixed rewards in different villages in the same area.

We can satisfy the first point by examining the hereditary relationships in which Wangala's two Washerman households were involved. Prior to irrigation they were completely landless. Each had hereditary relationships with 64 Peasant masters. In turn each Peasant gave his Washerman 15 *seers* of *ragi* per year. This meant that the Washerman households' annual income in terms of *ragi* amounted to 9½ *pallas*, which in bad years was probably more than the *ragi* intake in Peasant households. However, since these Washerman households were completely dependent for their own requirements on their annual rewards, which did not vary at all according to bad or good seasons, Peasants as a group were prepared to let them have slightly more than the average *ragi* output of a bad year. By contrast, the Blacksmith, who owned one acre of dry land and had hereditary relationships with all 128 Peasant households, received only 5 *seers* of *ragi* annually from each of them. Since one Blacksmith could quite easily meet the work requirements of 128 Peasant households and since he owned some land himself, his annual reward from each of his masters was only one-third of that of the Washerman. This clearly indicates that annual rewards were fixed regardless of the service involved.

Furthermore, neighbouring villages in the Wangala area, where the landholding pattern as well as the caste composition of the population is different, also had different quantities of *ragi* making up the annual rewards given by Peasant masters to their dependent households.

The importance of the average product in underdeveloped economies has already been emphasized by Lewis, when he referred to it as setting an objective standard for wages in the capitalist sector; 'men will not leave the family farm to seek employment if the wage is worth less than they would be able to consume if they remained at home' (1954, pp. 148–9).

However, this is not entirely true, because other incentives besides wages may attract men to cities and often they do not understand how much subsistence costs in money terms. In any case, since Lewis's main concern at the time was to show how a newly emerging capitalist sector operates, rather than to analyse the subsistence sector, he did not pursue the point further.

In order to throw into relief the importance of the average product in Indian village economies I shall now describe the operation of a customary system of rewards by a composite picture of a traditional large settlement made up of one Peasant farmer, controlling 50 acres of dry land, and 14 dependent Untouchable households. The output of approximately 120 *pallas* of *ragi* in bad seasons was slightly more than sufficient to keep the small community alive – 7 *pallas* of *ragi* being the annual subsistence minimum per household. The Peasant master, who always hoped for better harvests, wanted to retain his labour force and, therefore, in bad years distributed his total product equally; his own as well as each of his 14 dependent households received 8 *pallas* each.

If, owing to the improvement in climatic conditions, a number of good harvests were experienced in succession, more labour was required to cope with cultivation and, in particular, with harvesting so as to maximize the total product. Thus one or more servicing households may have been attracted to join the 14 Untouchables' households. However, it probably took quite some time before the news of the more favourable harvests spread to less fortunate areas. Furthermore, time had to elapse before putative kinship ties – since hereditary labour relations are couched in kinship terms – could be manipulated so as to arrange for a grafting on to the system of hereditary labour relationships, as in the case of the Blacksmith cited earlier. Conversely, if after an increase in the number of dependent households once more some bad harvests occurred which reduced the output again to 120 *pallas* per year, pressures will have begun to operate on the last accepted member of the group to migrate and lighten the burden of the Peasant's obligation to provide subsistence for his labourers. The time-lag between the variations in harvests and the appropriate adjustment in the size of the labour force helps to explain cases of zero or even negative marginal productivity, as well as incidents of strains and stress in the political and social system of Indian villages.

The share of the Peasant landholder, who himself participated in cultivating, was in bad sessions no larger than the annual reward he had to give to each of his dependent Untouchable households. By contrast, good harvests gave him a surplus of as much as 300 *pallas* of *ragi* over and above the rewards he had to pay to his labourers. He could utilize this surplus to throw large feasts and establish status and prestige for himself. Labourers, on the other hand, were prepared to accept the system of fixed annual rewards, because it assured them of their subsistence requirements, even in bad seasons. Thus, it was the expectation of good harvests which induced the Peasant master to accept in bad years a share equal to the annual rewards his labourers received, whereas the continued threat of bad harvests induced Untouchable labourers to accept a reward which did not vary according to labour performed or according to harvest. The system was, therefore, maintained by the chance occurrences of good and bad harvests. Its essence was chance of profit for the Peasant and assurance of security for the Untouchable. It broke down only in extremely bad harvests, when the total product was not sufficiently large to provide a minimum of subsistence for all the members of the society. Such years were famine periods, during which the customary system of rewards had to be completely suspended. But in normal times, when bad and good harvests occurred fairly regularly, the fixed rewards for customary services were based on the average product produced in bad seasons.

Indian villagers, rich and poor alike, used to be largely at the mercy of climatic conditions. In bad seasons 'share and share alike' was their motto, whereas good harvests facilitated large feasting and economic differentiation with its concomitant struggle for prestige. This may help to explain the contradictory views of the *jajmani* system expressed by Wiser, on the one hand, and by Gould and Beidelman, on the other. Wiser may have examined the *jajmani* system as it operated in bad seasons with its emphasis on equal distribution of output, while Gould and Beidelman may have concentrated their attention on good harvests when extreme economic differentiation occurred and when masters appeared to exploit their dependent helpers as capitalists are supposed to exploit their workers. But the difference may also be due to different philosophical approaches. However, while the success of a capitalist enterprise is largely due to the foresight and organizing ability of its managers, traditional Indian landowners and landless alike relied completely on favourable climatic conditions to provide them with good harvests. No one, of Wiser, Gould, or Beidelman, seems to appreciate that Indian villagers, rich and poor alike, were all subject to the hazards of their environment, over which they had very little control. Mere survival was therefore of the utmost importance to the population of these underdeveloped economies. Indian villagers did not have the technological know-how nor did they have any incentives to initiate growth in these economies, which were geared to stability.

In traditional Indian village economies with hereditary systems of reward, landowners were chiefly concerned with the quantity of the average product in bad years – or to put it in time-perspective: they were interested in the long-term average product, rather than in the marginal addition to total output which any one worker might contribute. This emphasis on the average is noticeable not only in economic relations; it pervades many other aspects of the culture. Beliefs in sorcery and witchcraft sanction 'average' behaviour. For instance, when a Wangala Peasant builds a new house with the surplus he produced in good years, he always hangs a broken pot on to the outside. This is done to protect the new house from evil and jealous spirits. The broken mudpot is supposed to give the impression that the house is not new but really old like all the other houses in the vicinity.

As soon as external forces break down the isolation of Indian villages and new economic opportunities are introduced, innovations and changes at the margin tend to become important. This is precisely what happened in Wangala after irrigation had facilitated cash cropping. As we have seen, Wangala Peasant farmers were not prepared to grant the Blacksmith even a small increase in his customary fixed reward of five *seers* per household. This had been based on the average product in bad years and was regarded as more than sufficient for subsistence. However, as soon as the Blacksmith managed to disentangle himself from his hereditary obligations, Peasants started to think of his work in terms of the contribution it made to the cultivation of their lands. The Blacksmith was obviously an innovator: he designed an improved plough and became a housing contractor. Peasants then began to appreciate their Blacksmith and his contribution to their output, i.e. wet crops, the cultivation of which necessitated iron ploughs in place of the customary wooden ones. Thus the transition from a non-market to a market economy involves a change from emphasis on average productivity to one on marginal productivity. However, before such change in emphasis can take place customary labour relations must be eliminated. Planners would be well advised to bear in mind that it may be easier to improve productive efficiency by introducing entirely new crops or products, rather than by attempting to change the traditional methods and techniques of production. For example, in Saurashtra 'attempts were made to introduce improved methods of cultivation like the Russian method of *bajri* cultivation and the Japanese method of paddy cultivation. Only 34 acres were brought under the Russian method of *bajri* cultivation against the overall target of about 2,600 acres and for the Japanese method, the respective figures were 52 acres and 865 acres' (Government of India

1954, p. 247). If the agricultural officials responsible for this programme had appreciated the principles underlying the traditional organization of labour, they would never have attempted to introduce improved methods for cultivating customary crops, but would have tried to introduce entirely new crops, which could then have been cultivated outside the system of traditional labour relations.

This change-over from emphasis on the average product to stress on the marginal product is not only a symbol of important changes in the economic organization of previously isolated economies, but is also marked by radical changes in the social and political systems. In non-market economies nonconformity is usually penalized. By contrast, economic growth necessitates innovation and needs men who are prepared to take risks. These new entrepreneurs who try to take advantage of the new economic opportunities then want to translate their wealth into social status. They want to replace the system of ascribed social status with one in which status can be achieved. This has been happening in Dalena (Epstein 1962, pp. 276–93) and is evidenced in a great number of societies which are in the process of being integrated into the wider economy and polity. The strains and stresses associated with these changes provide a fascinating field for study and analysis.

Conclusion

A prescribed hereditary system of rights and duties of the kind I have been describing is a mark of a stagnant rather than a developing economy. India's customary systems of rewards and obligations placed great emphasis on stability. In a country such as India, with low soil fertility and little and/or irregular rainfall, there are usually great fluctuations in harvests occurring side by side with small margins of agricultural profits. Accordingly, the security value offered by the stable system of prescribed rights and duties was of great importance. Landowners knew in advance the exact quantity of agricultural produce they had to give as a reward for services rendered them throughout the year. A good harvest brought them windfall profits. However, making allowances for differences of individual skill – and some were very adept in getting the best yield out of a poor soil – the greater yield was due primarily not to any positive efforts of their own, but to more favourable climatic conditions. On the other hand, a good harvest also meant more work for labourers, as well as for certain functionaries, for which they received no extra rewards, though they did get greater fringe benefits. Yet a poor harvest still provided the dependent castes with a minimum of subsistence. Since Indian villagers, landowners and landless alike, were all subject to the hazards of their climate and environment, they were all prepared to participate in a system which offered all of them at least the minimum necessities of life, except in times of extreme crop failure and general famine. There were, therefore, no incentives to initiate growth in these stagnant economies. The relative isolation of traditional Indian villages and the absence of outside markets helped to perpetuate the system of hereditary relationships, which defined most obligations and rewards.

The equal distribution of the total output in bad seasons may help to explain migration whenever population increased to such an extent that the average product in bad years became insufficient to provide a minimum standard for subsistence for villagers. There may be also some correlation with infanticide and the frequency of abortion though this is much more difficult to measure. Moreover, the appreciation of fixed annual rewards, i.e. fixed labour costs, associated with variations in output may clarify the fact of economic differentiation in traditional non-market peasant economies as well as the forms such differentiation has taken.

If my analysis of traditional Indian peasant economies is valid – and I hope I have shown that it is – it may also be relevant to other pre-industrial societies. For instance, we may find that many societies with a low level of technological knowledge and constant inability to control their environment tend to distribute produce in a standard pattern equally in bad as in good seasons. What good seasons do is to facilitate economic differentiation. This tentative suggestion gains support from a study of African farming practices. Allan, an agriculturalist, reckons that before the introduction of cash crops to Africa, men cultivated enough land to bring them in a small surplus in normal years – he calls this a normal surplus. However, in good seasons, when there were favourable climatic conditions, they had bumper harvests with a large surplus; in bad years they went on short commons. Allan worked this out in trying to explain the considerable annual variations in the crops that African tribes now sell on the open market. Before the creation of this external European market, the bumper seasons presumably produced large-scale feasting, while bad harvests involved mutual assistance in terms of the same relations (Allan 1965, pp. 38–49). Though African landholding patterns and labour relations differ from those in India, there seems to be a general similarity. The emphasis on average productivity in bad seasons may also help to throw light on witchcraft beliefs and sorcery in many primitive societies. These are but a few of the many interesting problems raised by the preceding analysis of Indian village economies.

References

A L L A N, W. (1965) *The African Husbandman* London, Oliver and Boyd.
B E I D E L M A N, T. O. (1959) *A Comparative Analysis of the Jajmani System* New York, J. J. Augustin.
E P S T E I N, T. S. (1962) *Economic Development and Social Change in South India* Manchester, Manchester University Press.
G O U L D, H. A. (1958) The Hindu Jajmani system, *Southwestern Journal of Anthropology*, 14, 428–37.
G O V E R N M E N T O F I N D I A (1954) *Evaluation Report* Delhi, Planning Commission.
L E W I S, W. A. (1954) Economic Development with Unlimited Supplies of Labour, *The Manchester School of Economic and Social Studies*, 22, 139–91.
L E W I S, W. A. (1958) Unlimited Labour: Further Notes, *The Manchester School of Economic and Social Studies*, 26, 1–32.
S R I N I V A S, M. N. (1959) The Dominant Caste in Rampura, *American Anthropologist*, 61, 1–16.
W I S E R, W. H. (1958) *The Hindu Jajmani System* Lucknow, Lucknow Publishing House.

12 The social framework

F. C. Benham

Introduction

The unit of government in the modern world is the country, the territorial nation-state. How can a country organize itself to carry out its objectives?

Some kind of organization there must be. No doubt it is attractive to think of a group of people without any formal government, settling their problems by general discussion, sharing their possessions and possibly their children, and following the maxim of 'from each according to his ability, to each according to his need.' This would be communism – true communism, quite unlike the system of state ownership and state control which exists in Soviet Russia. But it would work, if it would work at all, only with a small group. A modern country is far too large to be run on these lines.

The problem is how to control the activities of millions of people, how to determine for what purposes the land and other means of production shall be used. The popular view is that the solution should lie somewhere between the two opposite poles of complete laissez-faire and complete central planning.

There has never been, nor could there be, a complete laissez-faire in a country of any size. A country is not just a collection of individuals, each doing exactly what he likes. It is a community, with a government which makes and enforces laws, and with social customs and social institutions which considerably restrict the freedom of the individual to do whatever he thinks fit. A small group like the Cocos Islanders (among whom crime is unknown) can live without police, but a country such as ours must have rules – laws against murder and theft, traffic regulations, and so forth – and the means to enforce them. The question is how much or how little the Government should restrict the freedom of the individual for the general good.

Central planning, on the other hand, must be fairly complete in order to be effective. Suppose, for example, that the plan calls for a certain output of coal. If workers are free to take whatever jobs they please, and too few of them are willing to work in the coal-mines, the coal required is not pro-

BENHAM, F. C. (1967) 'The Social Framework', in Paish, F. W. (ed.) *Economics: A General Introduction* London, Pitman, 8th ed., 42–56.

duced. The central planning authority must have power to 'direct' labour, in this case to order workers to go to the coal mines, or the plan will break down.

The debate on whether or not complete central planning is desirable is often confused by considerations which are really irrelevant. For example, many people who love liberty and toleration are revolted by the suppression of freedom in Soviet Russia. The citizen of Soviet Russia cannot listen to foreign broadcasts; the university professor cannot teach the scientific views which he believes to be true, unless the authorities favour them; the newspaper cannot say what it likes. But all this is not inevitably associated with central planning. It is true that any form of dictatorship tends to support itself by such devices: control of all organs of propaganda, and a big force of secret police to nip any possible revolt in the bud. Nevertheless complete central planning is quite possible without any such measures.

Our own system of social organization, in Great Britain, is still fundamentally *capitalism*. In this preliminary general survey, I shall point out its chief features – private property, freedom of enterprise, and freedom of choice for consumers. We take these features so much for granted that it seems necessary to draw special attention to them. It will be useful, it will bring out their significance, if I first outline the economic organization of a central-planning community, by way of contrast. This will help us to grasp the two opposite ways of tackling economic problems: the way of making decisions at the centre, and the 'capitalist' way of letting individuals, within limits, make their own.

First, however, I should mention one or two institutions which may exist under either system. One of these is the family. This plays a very important part in our social life. If parents did not take care of their children until they were old enough to earn their own livelihood, some other means of providing for children would have to be found. We have already noted that, under capitalism, the desire to provide for one's family after one dies is a powerful incentive to work and saving, and that it is an advantage (although much less of an advantage today than it was in the past) to be born of well-to-do rather than of poor parents. The family exercises a considerable influence on demand – for example, the size of the family affects the type of house or flat which people want – and children to some extent tend to enter the same occupations as their parents.

Another institution is money, about which I shall have a good deal to say later. I discuss also trade unions. These normally have more power under capitalism than under central planning, for the planners must be able to control and direct labour in order to carry out their plans, and cannot allow themselves to be thwarted by the views of trade unions. Institutions such as the joint-stock company and limited liability belong to capitalism, and are discussed below.

Central planning

Under a system of complete central planning, one person or committee would act as economic dictator, surveying all the labour and other resources of the community and deciding how they should be used and what should be done with their products.

The magnitude of such a task is enormous. In order to carry it out, the dictator must make a vast multitude of decisions; and in order to carry it out at all well, he must somehow obtain and digest a very large amount of information. He must decide how each worker and each piece of land are to be employed. He must decide where each works is to be located and what methods of production it must use. He must decide what plants are to get the various materials, fuel, and items of equipment that are produced, how many houses are to be built and where, how many buses and lorries are to be run and along what routes, and a host of similar questions. Clearly no single person or committee could do all this unaided. In practice, the task of suggesting decisions on whole groups of problems would be delegated to various subordinate committees, who in turn would rely largely on the advice of local sub-committees. But it would be very difficult for the dictator (or central planning committee) to coordinate successfully the suggestions of the various subordinate committees. For example, each industry might demand so many workers, or so much coal, and there might not be nearly enough workers or coal to give every industry all it requested. In the last resort, therefore, the dictator could not split up his economic problems and delegate the solution of one set of problems to one body and of another set to another body. He himself would be compelled to make the final decisions. Only a superman could avoid making many mistakes; that is to say, taking many decisions which he afterwards regretted or found to be impracticable. And it is very unlikely that the political processes that led to the establishment of such a system would throw up to the top the best executive ability available, let alone supermen. Those who are best at mob oratory and political intrigue are not necessarily those best qualified to plan and control the economic life of a country.

Both the advantages and the disadvantages of such a system are often exaggerated. For example, it is usually claimed as an advantage that it abolishes profit and replaces production for profit by production for use. But if the owners of means of production are bought out by the state, and given interest-bearing government bonds, they will get nearly the same income as before, and it will be more secure.[1] Under private enterprise there are losses, heavy and numerous losses, as well as profits, and on balance the profit-receivers as a whole get little more, taking one year with another, than if they had invested instead in Government bonds. Nor is the contrast between 'production for profit' and 'production for use' necessarily an argument for central planning. Production 'for profit' means producing what buyers want, and producing it as efficiently as possible. Production 'for use' means in practice producing what the dictator thinks ought to be produced. Many people may not agree; they would prefer something else. But they have no means of saying so, whereas under private enterprise they can buy what they prefer – every shilling they spend is a vote in favour of what they want. The argument that the rich have more votes than the poor can be met, and is met, by measures which reduce inequality of incomes in so far as this can be done without unduly weakening incentives to work and invest.

On the other hand, the argument that under central planning there can be no proper economic calculations, in order to determine which methods of production are most efficient, is not valid. Money can be used, accounts can be kept, the performances of different factories or other production units can be compared with one another, one method can be tried out in one factory and another method in another factory. Nor is it true that adequate incentives cannot be provided. Soviet Russia pays piece-rates, and gives high salaries and various privileges to managers and others in key posts.

It is true that the planning organization as a whole, including all those engaged in obtaining information, would absorb a considerable proportion of the personnel and other resources of the community. On the other hand, in so far as consumers had to take what they were given, there would be no need for persons to be engaged in advertising and otherwise promoting the sale of particular brands; they could be employed in assisting production more directly.

One important advantage of such a system is that it would abolish unemployment. As we shall see later, a major point made by Keynes is that under free enterprise decisions to save and decisions to invest are made by different people and may not coincide; insufficient private investment may lead to large-scale unemployment. There is no such conflict under central planning. Decisions to save and decisions to invest are one and the same

1 Apart from the risk of inflation.

decisions, made at the same time by the same person, the economic dictator. Nor will workers be unemployed because they want higher wages than private employers are prepared to pay; they will be ordered to work for whatever the dictator decides they should get. If they must move to their jobs, they will be ordered to move, whereas under private enterprise they can stay where they are and draw unemployment benefit.

A central planning system, however, is inevitably a bureaucratic system, with all its disadvantages. Government officers tend to be unwilling to take decisions to do something new, lest they should be blamed and lose their secure positions if their decisions turn out badly; they prefer to follow their orders. Hence a central planning system is likely to be rather wooden, to lack flexibility and initiative. There are also the dangers of graft and bribery, and of undue officiousness by some of the civil servants who control the economic lives of the population.

This brief discussion of central planning is, of course, by no means exhaustive or conclusive. Whether or not capitalism is a better system is a matter of opinion. It certainly leaves far more scope for personal freedom and initiative in economic affairs. On the other hand, it may lead, unless properly controlled, to abuses and evils, such as private monopoly and large-scale unemployment. My purpose in outlining a central-planning system was to bring out, by way of contrast, the basic institutions of capitalism, which we tend to take for granted as 'natural'. But they would not be present, except to a very limited extent, under central planning. They are private property, freedom of enterprise, and freedom of choice by consumers.

Private property

If anybody could have whatever he was powerful enough to seize, output would be very limited. A man would hesitate to sow for somebody else to reap, or to build a house which might be taken from him. Hence it is generally agreed that law and order are desirable, rather than the law of the jungle. Moreover, nobody wants to deprive a person of the exclusive right to the use of his purely personal possessions, such as his clothes or his furniture, although many think that the amount owned by one person should be strictly limited. The real issue is whether means of production, such as land, mines, factories, ships, and railways, should be owned by the State or by private persons.

In Great Britain, the state has 'nationalized' certain industries, including the railways and the coal-mines. But over most of the economic field, means of production are still privately owned. The state paid full compensation to the owners of property which it nationalized, and they were free to invest the proceeds elsewhere. Our system is still essentially one of private property.

The institution of private property means that the owner of any kind of property may use it, or may hire it to somebody else, provided he complies with the law of the state, as he pleases. Thus, if a man owns some land, he may turn it into a private park, or build upon it, or use it for growing, say, wheat, or lease it to somebody else, or leave it idle. His choice is restricted, of course, to the realm of what is possible. His land may be too small in area to make a full-size golf course, and it may not get enough sunshine to produce bananas. But within this realm he is free [2] to do whatever he pleases with the land – and to keep or exchange whatever it yields him. The land is his private property.

Under a system of private property, the simplest form of business organization is individual proprietorship, the 'one-man concern', owned and controlled by a single person. This was the dominant form in the period of small-scale industry, and it is still predominant in agriculture and in retail trade; in Great Britain there are about 300,000 farmers and 500,000 shop-keepers who are individual proprietors.

We can see the advantage of individual proprietorship. The owner has a direct incentive to take care of his property and to make the best use of it, for it is he who takes all the profit from it – and bears all the losses. Moreover, many people take a positive pride and pleasure in owning their own farm or shop or factory. It certainly gives them independence; an owner is his own boss and can run his business as he pleases and take time off when he wishes.

But in some fields – for example, heavy industry, railways, ocean liners, banking, insurance – a firm must be large to be efficient. It must be so large that few individuals have enough capital to be the sole owner. Therefore such firms are companies, the assets of the company being owned jointly by a number of persons, each of whom has provided a part of the capital and gets a corresponding share of the profits. Another reason for the company form of organization is that there is no close correlation between owning capital and possessing business ability. The device of the company enables men of business talent and managerial ability, but with relatively

---

2 Subject, in Great Britain, to the approval of various authorities under the legislation controlling the development of land in the interests of town and country planning.

little capital of their own, to manage businesses on behalf of shareholders who could not manage them so well.

'The magic of property', wrote Arthur Young, 'turns sand into gold.' He was writing of individual proprietorship in farms, towards the close of the eighteenth century in England. Under the old system, large open fields had been farmed in common by a local group. The enclosure movement resulted in individual farms enclosed by a hedge or fence or stone wall. Each farmer himself reaped all the benefit from the hard work and good farming he put into his land. He was free – at his own risk – to try out new crops and improved methods, whereas before he had been compelled to follow the traditional methods under which land was farmed in common. The result was a great improvement in productivity. More care was given to the land, more efficient work was done, more up-to-date methods were applied.

A company is managed by a board of directors elected by the shareholders. A managing director controls the day-to-day affairs of the company; he may have managers of departments or branches under him. The managing director and managers are usually paid salaries. The 'magic of property' is not so potent with them as with an individual proprietor. But they may be paid partly in the form of a bonus which varies with the profits of the company. A majority of the shareholders can turn out their directors, if they are not satisfied with them, and appoint new ones. The managing director can dismiss a manager if he is not efficient enough. Hence there is some 'profit incentive' combined with the desire to keep a well-paid job.

The company form of organization has two advantages which may be mentioned here. In the first place, most companies write 'limited' after their name; they are limited liability companies. Limited liability was introduced in Great Britain by an Act of 1855. It means that a shareholder is liable for the debts of the company only up to the value of his shares in it. An individual proprietor, on the other hand, is liable for the debts of the business to the whole extent of his private fortune. The device of limited liability has given a great stimulus to investment in companies.

In the second place, the shares of a public (but not private) company can be transferred by sale, through the Stock Exchange or otherwise. This is a great advantage to the shareholder. His capital is not permanently tied up. He can sell out his shares if he needs the money for some other purpose or if he thinks he can make a better investment elsewhere.

The company and the individual proprietorship are the two chief forms of business organization (apart from state enterprises). But there are several other forms. For example, there is the partnership. A man with an established business that needs more capital for expansion may take a suitable man, who can provide the extra capital, as his partner. A number of solicitors or doctors, each specializing in some particular branch of his profession, may enter into partnership. But it would be tedious to discuss all the different forms of business organization in any detail. Their general purpose is to bring together ability and capital in the most suitable way.

The state restricts the right and powers of private property-owners. The owner of property must not use it in ways harmful to his neighbours or to the community as a whole. For example, he must not deliberately burn down his house or pollute a river or produce noxious fumes; he may be forbidden to manufacture or trade in dangerous drugs, to run a public gambling place, to publish or distribute obscene books or photographs; he may be compelled to slaughter his cattle if they suffer from certain contagious diseases; he must obey laws requiring him to keep his premises in good sanitary condition and to take precautions to safeguard his workers against accident.

The modern tendency is to control more strictly the rights of owners of property. Building may be prohibited in certain areas, for example in the 'green belt' around London; as part of town and country planning, factories are forbidden in some places and shops in others; land required for public purposes may be bought (whether the owner wants to sell or not) at a 'fair price'. Until 1953, in order to try to surmount Great Britain's economic difficulties, the use of materials such as steel was restricted to approved purposes, and a firm wishing to put up a new works may still be allowed to do so only in certain parts of the country – for example, in South Wales but not near London.

Nevertheless, the basic features of the institution of private property still survive. The owner of property can decide for himself, subject to the laws of the state, what he will do with his property. Hence the great contrast with central planning is that the taking of such decisions is decentralized. They are left to all the millions of property-owners, each using his own judgement and his own knowledge of relevant local facts, under the stimulus of the 'profit motive'. Under central planning, all means of production are owned by the state, and all such decisions are taken by officials and are subject to approval or otherwise by the central planning committee.

Freedom of enterprise

Freedom of enterprise means that everybody is free to engage in whatever economic activity he pleases. No industry or trade or occupation is barred to him. He can choose for himself whatever line he prefers or in which he thinks he will do best. True, he may not have enough capital to set up in business, and he may lack the ability or training to follow certain occupations. But subject to these limitations, and to the laws imposed by the state in the public interest, he is perfectly free to follow his inclinations and to use his judgments and initiative at his own risk. He can decide for himself what part he will play on the economic stage.

This means that the gates are wide open for experiment and innovation. If somebody thinks that a new type of product will appeal to consumers, he is free to risk his own capital (and to try to persuade others to risk theirs) on the venture. Should he succeed, the public benefits as well as he; should he fail, the loss is his. Similarly with methods of production. Anybody is free to try out a new invention (unless it is patented) or a new idea. If he can get the same output at less cost (which means by using less labour and other resources), both he and the community benefit; if he is wrong, the loss is his.[3]

Some people claim that consumers would gain, under central planning, by standardization of products. Instead of countless varieties, just a few standard varieties would be produced and, being produced on a large scale, they would be cheap. But under private enterprise it is open to anybody to take the risk, as Henry Ford took the risk, of embarking on large-scale production in the belief that he could sell large quantities at a lower price.

A wage-earner can choose his industry and occupation and employer. If he does not like his job, he has the right to give notice and move to another, or to remain idle. If it is clear that a group of workers can demand and obtain higher wages, they can choose for themselves, (or through their trade union) whether they will take their gains entirely in higher wages or partly in shorter hours.

A man who has saved money (whether to provide for his old age or for his children, or just as a general reserve against possible bad times) can invest it exactly as he pleases. The more adventurous can choose risky securities which may yield a large return, or, on the contrary, may fall heavily in value; the cautious may choose government bonds or keep their money in a bank or under a mattress. The owner of assets is free to sell them whenever he wishes and to do what he likes with the proceeds.

All this may seem perfectly natural and right to the reader brought up

3 He must pay the market prices for his factors of production, and the excess of his expenses over his receipts comes out of his own pocket. Nevertheless, the community also may lose in so far as he diverts factors from other fields where they would have been used in ways of more advantage to the community. On the other hand, the community may gain in so far as he employs workers who would otherwise have remained unemployed.

in the tradition and atmosphere of freedom of enterprise. Of course, he will say, a person should be allowed to make whatever use he pleases of his own abilities, his own property, his own money. But comprehensive central planning would be impossible under these conditions. The advocates of planning believe that if the whole economy is directed from the centre, the wealth and productivity of the country will increase more than if economic progress is left to the decisions and whims of individuals, each acting as he thinks best, instead of being fitted into a general scheme.

Freedom of choice by consumers

The third basic feature of capitalism is freedom of choice by consumers. We are free to do as much or as little saving as we please, and we can spend our money as we like. In normal times of peace, we are not rationed and we can give full scope to our tastes and preferences. We are limited only by the size of our incomes.

This is clearly incompatible with central planning, under which consumers can have only the goods which the central planning authority decides to produce. For example, under Russia's five-year plans most of her labour and resources have been diverted into developmental projects and heavy industries. Russia embarked upon a gigantic public-works programme designed to increase her future productivity. Consequently, her people had to go short for the time being of housing, clothing, food, and other consumers' goods; it was they who performed the saving and investment as directed by the plan. Within the field of consumers' goods, they could indeed choose freely among those which were unrationed and available, but only those kinds and varieties were available that had been produced in accordance with plans decided upon in advance.

Some people are in favour of consumers being compelled to take what is good for them, instead of being allowed to have what they please. They say that most people are ignorant or foolish, or misled by advertisements. They spend their money unwisely. For example, they get less nutritional value than they should out of their expenditure on food because they buy the wrong kinds of food; or they spend too little on food in order to buy drink or nylon stockings or to go to the cinema.

The same contention is applied to the realm of art. Left to themselves, it is said, most people tend to buy ugly things rather than beautiful ones, and show a poor taste in music, literature, and architecture. They should be made to follow the dictates of persons of good taste – for example, housing plans should be censored by an arts committee, and trashy or vulgar books or films should be forbidden.

Others reply that they would rather eat what they like than what experts say is best for them, that opinions on art change from one generation to another and in no event should be used as an instrument of dictatorship, and that they want to be free to live their own lives. Doubtless the state should help consumers to choose by forbidding advertisers to make false statements, by publishing analyses of the composition and qualities of various branded products, by prohibiting adulterated foodstuffs, by letting the public know the views of expert dieticians, and in similar ways. It should help them to choose, wisely, but it should not choose for them.

I shall not discuss this issue further. It is one which arouses strong feelings – witness the fierce debates on Prohibition. My present point is that freedom of choice is one of the basic institutions of capitalism. The whole system depends on sales; the struggle for profits is a struggle to satisfy as efficiently as possible the wants of the buying public.

The working of the price mechanism

The surprising thing about capitalism is that it literally produces the goods – and distributes them. No central plan, everybody doing more or less what he pleases, and yet every morning there is the milk, there is the paper, there are your means of transport, and the shops and restaurants and theatres are ready to supply you with whatever you want if you can pay for it. What is it that makes the wheels go round?

The dominant motive behind all the decisions of businessmen, farmers, and others is the desire to make money. This is sometimes called the profit motive, but it applies to all kinds of producers, including wage-earners. A wage-earner will choose the job which pays him best, taking into account the hours and working conditions, just as a businessman will choose whatever course pays him best.

This does not imply that everybody is selfish. A man's character shows itself in the way he lives and in what he does with his money; a keen businessman may be a great philanthropist. But, other things being equal, it is only common sense to choose the course which pays best, provided that it is honourable and within the law.

People want money in order to satisfy their wants (which may include helping others). Let us now think of them as consumers. Each has his own tastes, his own preferences, and tries to satisfy them as fully as possible from his limited means. If he would rather spend a shilling more a week on one thing and a shilling less on something else, he does so. He therefore tends to distribute his expenditure so that he would not prefer to transfer a little from one line to another. And under capitalism he is free to spend his money as he pleases, to decide for himself (perhaps acting on behalf of his family) what assortment of goods and services he prefers out of the many possible assortments that he could buy with a given sum, at the prices ruling in the market.

How can consumers make their wants known to producers? Simply by spending, by buying what they want most. If all goods were produced to order, it would be quite clear that the consumer calls the tune, determines what goods shall be produced and in what proportions, and therefore decides for what products means of production shall be used. Most goods are not produced to order; they are ready and waiting for the purchaser. But this comes to much the same thing. All concerned are alert to anticipate the wants of the buying public; that is how they make their living. The whole system depends upon sales. If people buy less of one line, the shops order less of it next time, and less of it is produced; if they buy more of another line, the shops increase their orders, and more of it is produced. If they want something which is not there – for example, a hairdressing saloon or a restaurant in a particular district, a book on a certain subject, a particular type of clothing – it pays somebody (if the potential demand is large enough) to meet their wishes. True, many of the goods produced are not consumers' goods but intermediate products bought by other businesses, yet the same applies to them. If the public demand for canned goods increases the manufacturers need more cans and therefore more tin-plate; the increased demand for tin-plate (and therefore for tin and steel) has its origins in the anticipated or actual demand of consumers.

If it happens that changes in the demands of the buying public are not anticipated, or met promptly (sometimes they cannot be, because some things take time to produce), what happens? The prices of the goods more in demand go up, for more people want them and so they become relatively more scarce. The prices of the goods less in demand go down, for fewer people want them, and so they become relatively more plentiful. Clearly, then, it pays to produce more of the former and less of the latter. The price mechanism registers the changing demands of consumers, and serves as a guide to producers. The purpose of economic activity is to satisfy people's wants; the dominant motive behind economic activity is the desire for gain and the two are harmonized by the price system. It pays to produce what people want.

It pays, moreover, to produce in the most efficient way – efficient in the economic sense of keeping the costs of a given output as low as possible by good organization and by using the most suitable methods. The lower the costs of a given output, the greater the net return to the producer.

Changes may occur on the side of supply as well as on the side of demand. A large crop will bring down the price and stimulate consumption; a small crop will do the opposite. Nobody compels consumers to change the amounts they buy, but the rise or fall of prices induces some of them to do so. Again, an invention (when it comes into general use) may reduce costs of production and bring down the price of the product; less labour and resources are now needed to make the product; this good news is passed on to consumers in the form of a lower price for the product. If one producer does not lower his price, another will (in the absence of monopolistic agreements between them) because he can now increase his profit by selling more, even at the reduced price.

In the absence of monopoly – about which I shall have a good deal to say later – the price system is a marvellous mechanism for regulating economic activity. Some labour, some land, some buildings, and some materials can be used for any of several purposes. How shall they be used? The consumers decide. The means of production which can be transferred to other uses will be transferred if, and only if, consumers would prefer them to be transferred. The consumers indicate their preferences by being willing to pay more for their products in the other lines. If it is possible (assuming full employment) to produce X more of one product at the cost of producing Y less of another – by transferring means of production from the latter industry to the former – this will be done if consumers would rather have the extra X and give up the Y; that is, if they are prepared to pay more for the X than they were for the Y. In this way, the price system *is* a system. Prices reflect alternatives. The public can have £1,000 worth more of one thing by giving up £1,000 worth of something else. Do they want this? If they do, it will pay the owners of the means of production to meet their wishes. Some wage-earners will find they can earn more by moving into the former industry, or some landowners will find they can get a higher net return by growing the former product. That is the way the wheels go round. Every producer, including wage-earners, does what pays him best; and it pays him best to use the means of production under his control for whatever purposes consumers will pay most for, relative to the costs of production. Hence, out of the multitude of different assortments of goods and services that could be produced from the labour and other resources available, the tendency is to produce that assortment which the buying public prefers, which satisfies its wants most fully. And this comes about because producers adjust their behaviour to the preferences of consumers, as indicated by the way they spend their money.

The state

The state, that is to say central and local governments and other public authorities acting on behalf of the community as a whole, plays a large part in modern economic life. In Great Britain, the state does considerably more today than it did before the war. The coal-mines and the railways have been nationalized; so have the Bank of England, Cable and Wireless, and the electricity and gas industries. The Post Office (including the telephone system), Broadcasting, and Civil Aviation were already nationalized before the war. The state controls a comprehensive nation-wide system of social insurance. Until May 1954 it rationed certain foodstuffs. It closely controls economic development, in particular the siting of houses and factories, foreign exchange transactions, and the quantities of imports which are permitted.

Whether we should be better off with less state control is a very controversial question which cannot be discussed adequately in a few sentences or paragraphs. At this stage, I shall merely try to set out the main general principles governing state action.

The dominant economic purpose of the community is to satisfy its wants as fully as possible from the labour and other resources available. To quite a considerable extent the economic self-interest of individuals tends to make them act in harmony with this purpose. But this harmony is not always present or complete. It is the economic function of the state to try to make it complete.

It is agreed by all that the state should maintain law and order. People must be prevented from killing or injuring one another, and from stealing or damaging the property of others. Contracts must be enforced; business would be impossible if people could refuse with impunity to provide the goods or services which they had promised to provide or to pay money which they had promised to pay. And in general, although here there is less agreement on exactly what the law should be on various points, the state should prevent people from behaving, or using their own property, in ways that are harmful to others. As the old gentleman said to the youth twirling his cane in the air : 'Your freedom ends where my nose begins.'

However highly they may value their liberty of action, most people are quite willing to be forced to conform to some general rule which is in the interest of all. A simple illustration is the general rule that traffic should keep on the left. Maybe some individuals would prefer to drive as they please, provided that everybody else had to keep to the left, but clearly that is not possible, and therefore they, too, are prepared to conform to the general rule.

The price system cannot do everything. However smoothly it may work, there will always be some services which cannot or should not be left to private enterprise. Private enterprise provides goods and services which are divisible into units. If a loaf of bread costs 1s 6d you buy two loaves for 3s or three loaves for 4s 6d; the more you pay, the more you get, and if you pay nothing, you get nothing. So bakeries can be run by private enterprise for profit. But an army, for example, guards the whole area; it affords the same protection to any given citizen whether he has paid much or little or nothing towards the cost of it. The benefit which it provides is *indivisible*; it cannot be divided like bread, into units, each person buying as much or as little of it as he pleases. Hence Defence is provided by the state. It might be paid for by public subscription, but this would be unsatisfactory. Public subscription would probably provide far too little money for armed forces of a size which people thought necessary; each might give little or nothing in the hope that others would give more. The fairest method is to pay out of taxation, levied on some system generally approved as being 'fair'. The same applies to other services that are generally desired and that yield an indivisible benefit – for example, public health measures to prevent diseases from arising or spreading.

Again, the state provides some services which could be brought into the price system but are better provided free. For example, if cars or lorries were charged each time they used a road this would mean frequent stoppages to pay tolls; it is simpler to have 'free' roads and to tax motor vehicles and petrol. When fuller use of a public park or a bridge or a museum would add very little to the costs of maintenance, it is usually better to charge nothing and to let it be used by people as much as they wish.

The state provides education, making it compulsory and free. It is generally thought desirable that children should receive a good general education, and specialized training in the professions and in technical subjects is needed to provide enough experts and technicians. But this form of investment, investment in 'human capital' as against investment in physical assets, would not be carried far enough if it were left entirely to private enterprise. Children usually have no means of paying for their own education; their parents are often unable, and sometimes unwilling, to pay the whole cost; and it is not legally possible, nor would it be desirable, for speculators to invest in financing the education of boys and girls, obtaining in return a percentage of their future earnings. Hence education is, in the main, provided and paid for by the state.

Another of the state's major tasks is to prevent monopoly. Monopoly distorts the price system. Output is restricted in order to keep up prices. Hence prices do not properly reflect the alternatives available. If more of a monopolized product could be supplied to consumers at a price of 6d a unit, and the actual price is kept at 1s, the influence of consumers on economic activity is, to that extent, thwarted. They would like a good deal more of the product at 6p, but not at 1s. Hence output and employment are lower than consumers wish in industries where monopoly prevails. The labour and resources of the community do not satisfy wants as fully as they should, for too few of them are in the monopolized industries and too many in other industries, or unemployed. The remedy is for the state to do away with monopolies and monopolistic practices, itself owning or controlling those monopolies which are inevitable.

The above paragraphs are intended only to illustrate how the state endeavours to harness self-interest to the service of the community as a whole, and to supplement the price system, as well as ensuring that it works efficiently.

13   The planning lacunae

J. K. Galbraith

The genius of the industrial system lies in its organized use of capital and technology. This is made possible by extensively replacing the market with planning. The notable accomplishments of the industrial system are all the result of such planning: there would be no flights to the moon and not many to Los Angeles were market incentives relied upon to bring into existence the required vehicles. The same is true of other services, amenities and artifacts of the industrial system from telephone communications to Chevrolets to dentrifices. In all cases there are careful projections of output; careful control of prices; careful steps to see that the projections of output are validated in the greatest possible measure by consumer response; and careful steps to see that the things needed for production – labour, components, machinery – are available in the requisite amounts at the anticipated prices at the right time. To leave these matters to the market would be regarded, by those principally involved, as the equivalent of leaving them to chance.

Yet the myth of the system is quite different. That holds, and a large, expensive though not universally successful educational effort teaches, that all credit belongs to the market which is a force of transcendent power. It alone motivates and regulates performance. There are agnostics who do not place their trust in God. But a deeper faith reposes trust in the market. The community that does so cannot go wrong.

There is an inherent implausibility about this faith – apart from the impossibility of reconciling it with the practice of the industrial system. In all other aspects of business organization, profoundly rational and determinist attitudes are held to rule. As little as possible is left to faith and hope. But then at the ultimate and decisive point, where the great and important decisions are made on what and how much and at what price things are to be produced, there is assumed to be abdication to the impersonal magic of the market. This is improbable as well as wrong. But it still solicits belief.

One consequence is a great deal of physical discomfort. The industrial system performs its tasks with technical competence. That is why it seeks

GALBRAITH, J. K. (1972) 'The Planning Lacunae', in *The New Industrial State* Harmondsworth, Penguin, 2nd ed., 349–56.

to make the competent production of goods the only social purpose and the sole test of social performance. But for a variety of reasons the industrial system does not perform all necessary tasks. Since there is a presumption that the industrial system functions in response to the market, rather than through its instruments for planning supply and demand, it is naturally assumed that the market will also work its unplanned wonders where the writ of the industrial system does not run.

In quite a large area outside the industrial system – the world of the small retail entrepreneur, repairman, independent craftsman, barber, market gardener, bookmaker – the market does work adequately or well. The inferior performance of such services or their absence is one of the notable features of the fully planned economies of Eastern Europe. However there are also products and services, some of them of the highest convenience or necessity, which cannot be called into being by the market. The society recognizes the failure of the market in these areas. But since the market is assumed generally to be a success, the planning in these areas of failure is conceived to be abnormal. It is approached halfheartedly and with a sense of being unfaithful to principle. Nor are all of the requisites of effective planning identified and provided. In consequence, these tasks are badly performed to the general public's discomfort or worse. Were it recognized that they require planning, and in the context of a largely planned economy have been left unplanned, there would be no hesitation or apology in the use of all the necessary instruments for planning. Performance would be much better.

These abstractions may now be fleshed out with specific examples.

The clearest case is urban and inter-urban surface transportation of people. This, it is clear in retrospect, required that there be one corporation, that is to say one planning instrument, covering the cities of an entire region including the lines between. The local systems would then have been developed in relation to the inter-city and inter-regional system with joint use of rights-of-way, terminals and other facilities as appropriate. The prospective growth of the entire system would have been projected in a systematic and orderly way together with the investment requirements in the various parts and at various stages. A planning unit of such scope and power would have been largely independent of local influences and pressures in setting fares. Prices, in other words, would have been wholly or largely under its planning control. It could have held its own with the automobile industry and the airlines in managing, i.e. promoting, the demand for its services. It could have held its own with the automobile industry and the highway users in getting requisite public underwriting of its facilities – were costs and risks too great for it to carry, it could have pleaded military necessity as did the automobile industry and highways users in the case of the interstate highway system. Pleading further the doctrine of military necessity, it could have sought state underwriting of technical development. This would have placed it more nearly on a parity with the airlines which, in the last thirty years, have had many billions of dollars of subsidy in the form of military development of aircraft (ultimately usable as passenger vehicles) and in the development and installation of navigational facilities. The planning unit, assuming success, would have had internal sources of capital from earnings. This would have exempted it from petty interference by local governments or other sources of funds. It would have been able to make its own decisions on growth and technical innovation and would have tended to measure its success by its virtuosity in this regard. Its size and capacity for technical change, including automation, would have given it leverage in dealing with unions. Not least important, such a unit would have had a developed technostructure in which group decision would have replaced the vagaries of individual competence.

None of this has happened. Local transit systems developed under public and private auspices and subject to local political influences and regulation. The railroads, under a different system of regulations, followed their own rather special pattern of development.[1] Each part provided a fraction of the total services of moving people locally and regionally; none, in consequence, could plan the entire service. None had appreciable authority over prices, use of service, capital supply or labour supply. None had a developed technostructure. In an industry which required planning, none of the requisites of planned performance were available. It is not surprising that the results have been singularly bad.

Although no parallels are exact, it is interesting to contemplate the different development of telephone service. This makes use of an old form of elec-

---

1 Most American railroads have had a pattern of development different from that of the firms of similar size in the industrial system. There is no similarly developed technostructure; for most of their history there has been no similar technical dynamic; there has been no similar capacity for taking control of prices, demand for the services, labour and capital supply and the other requisites of successful planning. Regulation, prohibitions on mergers and diversification of activities and a tradition of routine, highly ritualized management of low technical aspiration and competence have all been factors. In Japan, France, Canada and other countries where there has been one national system or one or two dominant systems, the industry has had greater control over the requisites of its planning and its comparative performance and survival value have been much better.

tronic communication. As in the case of the railroads and urban transit, alternative technology has been massively subsidized by the federal government for military purposes. But in the telephone industry one giant corporation had planning authority coordinate with the whole task. It embraced both local and long-distance service. It had resources for competitive technical development and also for seeking government underwriting of such development where, as is usually the case, this could be justified by military application. The scale of A. T. & T. accorded it substantial authority over rates; it could enter actively on the management of the demand for its services; it had control over its capital supply; size combined with technological advance have enabled it to plan its labour requirements, keep them within the prospective supply and maintain authority over its labour force.

Had local telephone service been provided by one or more companies in each city, town and hamlet; had all these rates been subject to local regulation and influence; had long-distance service been supplied by numerous separate companies, only loosely coordinated with the local service; had there been little or no research or technical development anywhere in the system; had the local units been strongly dependent on external authority – municipal government or local banks – for capital; and had there been no planned provision for labour supply or substitute technology, it seems unlikely that telephonic communications could have survived in any very useful form.[2] That they flourished, none can doubt, is owing not to a mindless response to a free market but to the subordination of the market at all points to comprehensive planning.

In recent years, by support to technical development in inter-urban transit and diverse subsidies to local transit systems, steps have been taken to offset the patent incompetence of past performance in the field of surface transportation. This action has been typical of the halfhearted planning which assumes that such action is the exception rather than the rule. The plausible courses, reflecting the rule, would be to constitute one autonomous company with ample capital to take over all mass surface movement of people in the United States (say) east of the Appalachians. This would have running rights over the railroads and full control over other facilities. It would have a wide latitude in setting rates and promoting use. Massive technological innovation would be encouraged and subsidized and urgent defence need would of course be invoked. It is entirely possible, by

2 As a partial demonstration of the point, it has been suggested that, in the absence of automatic transmission of calls, it would require approximately the entire female working force of the country to handle current traffic.

such a step, that urban and inter-urban movement of people might continue to be possible.

Urban and inter-urban transit is one of the most visible and dramatic of the planning lacunae. It is not the most important. The most painful consequences from assuming the competence ot the market are in urban and suburban houses, commercial and other real property development.

In the slums, it has long been recognized, there is no socially useful market response. Rents, because of demand for space, tend to be at the highest level the traffic will bear. Being at the maximum, they will be no higher if the property is replaced, improved or even decently maintained. The most profitable course is to minimize outlay and, where possible, to pack more people in.

Commercial urban development is responsive to the market. But it is also responsive to the greatest opportunity for gain for the individual owner. This will frequently be inconsistent with the best economic opportunity for the community – a profitable slaughterhouse will have more than offsetting effect on the earnings of an adjacent shopping centre or the rents of an adjacent housing development. And the best commercial opportunity, in the manner of the vertical greenhouses on modern Manhattan, will often be either aesthetically inferior or offensive. Only as an act of charity will space be left for pedestrians.

The suburban residential market response is also frequently perverse. Nothing can be sold so cheaply as a house that is unprovided with sewerage, trash collection, police protection and schools. An isolated house without such amenities transgresses only upon itself. A community of such houses is incestuously offensive. The contemporary classic is the strip town which is by way of connecting all urban centres in the United States. This is the pattern of development which the market encourages.

These shortcomings are recognized. Again, however, they are assumed to be isolated failures of the market. In consequence, the corrective is the patchwork planning provided by weakly financed housing authorities of limited power and autonomy; housing and building codes which seek to enforce less profitable, but socially more desirable, behaviour; zoning regulations which seek to deny to the owners of land what seems to them their normal right to the best return; and subsidies to offset the financial advantages of bad use and promote redevelopment. Or, as also happens, nothing is done and the adverse consequences are suffered in the belief or hope that market responses, however bad in the present, will eventually become benign.

The remedy is a twofold one. The first step is to minimize or neutralize the adverse market influences. The second is to develop a planning authority of adequate power. Only strong and comprehensive planning will redeem and make liveable the modern city and its surroundings.

Since the focus of market forces is the return to, and capital gains from, land, this solution means that there must be public land acquisition wherever market influences are palpably adverse. Planning, which under urban and metropolitan administration will never be strong, will not then have to contend in each decision with the resistances of the market. Those with a vested interest in bad land use are unlikely to welcome such a remedy. But, in the end, there will prove to be no other.

The proper instrument for urban and related land acquisition and administration is a strong planning, housing and development authority. And, no less than for the manufacture of automobiles or the colonization of the moon, it will require the scale, financial autonomy, control over prices, and opportunity to develop a technostructure which are the requisites of effective planning.

The remedy also carries a price. Only youthful liberal politicians on first coming to office imagine that there can be social gain with no cost. Although money is important, as elsewhere in the industrial system, power and organization are almost equally important. And, as elsewhere, individuals will have to surrender to the goals of organization. It is thus that planning, like the industrial system in general, accomplishes its tasks. The horse-breeder and the buggy-maker were far less subject to organization than the General Motors man. They were also far less successful in imposing their values on their customers. But they were less efficient in moving people about. The wretched freedoms of the slums are the counterpart of the individualism of the buggy-maker.

Viewing the whole economy in purely technical terms, no natural superiority can be assumed either for the market or for planning. In some places market responses still serve. Over a very large area such responses cannot be relied upon; the market must give way to more or less comprehensive planning of demand and supply. Here, if the industrial system does not plan, performance will be poor and perhaps appalling. The conservation of natural resources, the development of outdoor recreation, forestry in the eastern United States are all further examples. The error is in basing action on generalization. There is no natural presumption in favour of the market; given the growth of the industrial system the presumption is, if anything, the reverse. To rely on the market where planning is in fact required is to invite serious trouble.

To see these problems as they are requires a sharp break with the established economies. This and consumer sovereignty give high sanction to whatever the system produces. If the mix of goods at any given time seems unsatisfactory, consumer sovereignty holds, very simply, that this reflects the dominant consumer will. The tendency of the economy is to an equilibrium of maximized consumer satisfactions. The person who disapproves of this outcome is seeking, in undemocratic, élitist fashion, to substitute his taste for that of a majority. But if the revised sequence is assumed, the mix of goods being produced will be the expression of comparative producer competence and power. If there appear to be too many automobiles and insufficient inter-city or commuter rail service or urban rapid transit, this will be a plausible consequence of the superior power of the automobile industry to plan and persuade. Consumer sovereignty by making questions about too many automobiles, too few houses, an élitist and undemocratic interference with consumer choice, excludes questions about the power of the automobile industry to impose its preference on the public. This, in effect, is the result of existing economic theory. It gives high moral and scientific sanction to social indifference.

14   Economic problems of a 'postindustrial' society

Robert L. Heilbroner

I think I should begin by expressing a certain caution with respect to the premise of my paper, a caution indicated by the quotation marks I have placed around the critical word *postindustrial* in my title. The premise is that we are moving rapidly into a new framework of socioeconomic relationships, a framework sufficiently different from that of the recent past to warrant designation as a new 'stage' of our historical development. As this paper will make clear, I do not quarrel with the argument that deep-seated changes in structure, institutions, and behaviour are indeed surfacing within the economic sphere, whence they spread out to affect social and political life,[1] but unfortunately a certain voguish quality has come to surround the word 'postindustrial' by which we describe this phenomenon.[2] Accordingly, it may be helpful to commence by specifying as clearly as possible what we mean by the 'postindustrial' transformation, both to clarify its relationship to the 'industrial' era now presumably on the wane, and to highlight those aspects of the coming era that are genuinely new.

Let me therefore start by exploring rather sceptically three different means that are commonly advanced with regard to the idea of a 'postindustrial' society :

1   *A postindustrial society is one in which a preponderance of economic activity is located in the 'tertiary' sector of the economy.*

    This definition of postindustrialism calls attention to the shift in occupational locus whose beginnings can be discerned far back in the nineteenth century.[3] As the history of every industrialized country indicates, the pro-

---

1 This statement implies a certain economic determinism. I will deal specifically with this issue at the end of this essay.
2 A great amount of literature – too long for a footnote – now deals with 'postindustrial society'. The most sophisticated version of the concept is to be found in Bell (1971).
3 In England in 1811 less than a third of the work force was employed in agriculture, and over a third was in services throughout the first half of the nineteenth century (Mitchell 1962, p. 60).

HEILBRONER, ROBERT L. (1973) 'Economic Problems of a "Postindustrial" Society,' in *Dissent*, 1 April 1973, 163–76.

portion of the labour force employed in agriculture shrinks to a very small fraction of the total work force: in the United States only 4 per cent of the civilian labour force is to be found on the farm and this includes a considerable residue of subsistence farmers. Meanwhile, the industrial 'core', comprising manufacturing, mining, transportation, construction, and utilities, has stabilized at roughly a third of the work force. The remainder of the population – over 60 per cent of the work force in the United States today – is employed in the congeries of occupations that produce 'final' services.

From one industrial nation to another, the magnitude of these proportions varies, but the 'drift' is visible in all, as the table below clearly indicates:

PERCENTAGE DISTRIBUTION OF EMPLOYED WORKERS

	Agriculture	Industry	Service
U.S., 1900	38	38	24
1970	4	35	61
France, 1950	35	45	20
1970	17	39	44
West Germany, 1950	24	48	28
1968	10	48	42
U.K., 1950	6	56	39
1970	4	45	50

Source: *U.S. Historical Statistics*, p. 74; *Economic Indicators* (1972), European countries: O E C D, *Basic Statistics of the Community* (1970).

Thus the definition of a postindustrial society that rests on a marked shift in the locus of employments can be amply demonstrated by statistical data. Nonetheless, a few cautionary remarks are in order. First, let us note that the industrial sector has not been the source of the main change in the profile of sectoral employment. Although it has declined slightly in France and England during the last 20 years, in Germany the percentage is unchanged; and in the United States *over a period of 70 years* the decline has been minuscule. The great sectoral transformation of our times, in other words, has not been so much a shift from 'industry' to 'service' as a shift from agricultural to service tasks.[4]

In addition, we must note that some part of the rise in service employment represents the transfer of certain kinds of work from the non-monetized household sector to the monetized commercial world. The well-known rise in female labour participation (from 18 per cent of all females of working age to 37 per cent, in the years 1890 to 1969 in the United States) has brought as a consequence the illusion of a rise in service 'employment', as tasks that were formerly carried out within the home, where they remained invisible to the eye of the statistician, emerged on to the marketplace. The growth of the laundry industry, the restaurant industry, the professional care of the aged, even 'welfare', represent instances of this semispurious inflation of the growth of 'employment' in service occupations.

These caveats and distinctions are important to bear in mind when we use the shift in employment locus as the basis for speculations about the implications of the postindustrial era. Let me briefly summarize what these cautionary thoughts might be.

Presumably the importance of the employment shift for a postindustrial system is that a change in occupational habitat brings new social experiences and needs. Without in any way challenging that supposition, let me warn against the misconception of that change as a massive emigration from industrial work. Nothing of that kind is visible. Instead, the primary 'experiential' fact of the employment shift has been the decisive decline of agricultural (farm) employment and a corresponding growth of market-located, service-connected tasks. The industrial 'core' remains roughly constant. Put differently, the industrial factory worker – the key dramatis persona of the Marxian drama – continues to account for approximately the same proportion of the total work experience of the community: unskilled, semi-skilled, and skilled workers – the blue-collar group – constituted 25.5 per cent of the labour force in 1900 and 34.9 per cent in 1968, the main shift taking place *within* this group as most unskilled labour rose to semi-skilled levels. Thus, if postindustrial society in fact represents a new

---

4 The reader should be warned that these statistics must be interpreted with care. For example, some of the decline in employment in the agricultural sector represents a shift of agriculture-related employment into the industrial and service sectors – e.g. the rise of farm machinery manufacture, of chemical fertilizers, and of a government service sector and a private trade sector occupied with agricultural problems and products. Thus the employment *functionally* related to agriculture is larger, perhaps by a considerable degree, than that 'formally' related to it. Nevertheless, the basic shift is unquestionably out of rural pursuits through industry into service tasks.

stage of socio-economic relationships, the cause must be sought elsewhere than in the disappearance of the industrial sector as a milieu for work.

2   *A postindustrial society may refer to a change in the nature of growth-producing inputs from quantitative to qualitative factors.*

Here the primary meaning of 'postindustrial' calls our attention to numerous studies of growth within industrial countries, and to the more or less common conclusions that 'knowledge' has played a steadily rising role in promoting growth, compared with increases in the size of the labour force or the quantity of (unchanged) capital.[5] Drawing on Denison's work we may generalize for the United States that for the two decades prior to 1929 increases in the stock of capital goods and in labour supply together accounted for about two-thirds of our increase in output, whereas in the decades 1929–59 increases in these quantitative factors accounted for only 44 per cent of growth. Conversely, improved education and training, which were credited with only 13 per cent of growth in the earlier period, were presumed to be the source of more than twice that proportion of growth in the later period. Finally, improved technology – which is, after all, only the concrete application of knowledge – rose from 12 per cent of the causes of growth to 20 per cent in the same two periods.

These proportions also differ from nation to nation, as Denison has shown in a study of the sources of growth in Western European nations, but the direction of change – as in the case of the migration of labour – is the same throughout. In sum, there is little doubt that statistical examination of growth patterns among industrialized nations shows a steadily increasing importance of 'knowledge-related' inputs, and a corresponding decline in increases in brute 'labour power' or sheer quantities of unchanged capital (for example, the addition of more railroad tracks).

As in the case of the definition of postindustrialism that emphasizes the shift in the locus of employment, I do not want to denigrate the importance that has been attached to human 'capital'.[6] Nonetheless it is important, as before, that we scrutinize this characterization of postindustrialism with a certain reserve. For when we do so, we encounter some disconcerting considerations.

5 The literature again is too large to be reviewed. Key statements are those of Abramovitz (1956); Solow (1957), and Denison (1962).
6 Janossy (1971), has a dramatic imaginative illustration of the respective importance of knowledge versus 'labour power' or 'capital'. He asks us to imagine the instantaneous transfer of the populations of two nations, one developed and one underdeveloped – say, England and Pakistan (before its civil war). Is there any doubt, he asks, that the growth curve of 'Pakistan' would rapidly turn upward, while that of 'England' would soon turn sharply down?

First, as we have all come to realize, the meaning of growth is both ill-specified and elusive. Between that collection of often arbitrarily defined outputs called 'Gross National Product' and any operational concept of 'welfare' is a wide and perhaps unbridgeable chasm. Hence much of the 'growth' to which modern knowledge seems to contribute so strikingly may be of little or no welfare significance: armaments, space exploration, and pollution-generating production at one extreme; frivolous gadgetry, style changes, and pollution-absorbing technology at the other – the one extreme producing deleterious or dangerous growth, the other illusory or 'defensive' growth. In a word, the *quality* of the growth of a 'postindustrial' society must be compared with that of an 'industrial' society, before we can discuss the rise of knowledge-inputs as a cause for celebration, as well as a simple fact.

Second, before looking for the implications of the shift towards a knowledge-input economy, it behooves us to inquire further into the 'fact' of the increase in knowledge input itself. This brings us to the ways in which knowledge input is *measured*. One of these ways – research and development (R & D) – is certainly grossly inflated. Government statistics show a rise in R & D expenditures from roughly $1 billion at the end of World War I to a level of $28 billion in the early 1970s. This enormous increase has led many observers to conclude that we have now 'institutionalized' the process of scientific discovery and application, thereby radically changing the nature of the propulsive forces within the economy. More sceptical observers have noted that (inflation aside) the R & D figures in the later years are swollen by the growing tendency to include routine testing or marketing procedures within the category of 'research'. The actual amount going for basic research in new industrial products for 1966 was estimated to be not $20 billion, but $1 billion (Blair 1972, p. 15).

In addition, a study by Jewkes, Sawers, and Stillerman (1970) throws considerable doubt on the effectiveness of 'institutional' invention, citing evidence that the preponderance of the important inventions or innovations of the last third of a century have been made by individuals or small firms. Thus there is some reason to regard the institutionalized knowledge-input of the postindustrial society as much less sharply differentiated from that of 'industrial' society than might at first appear.

A further caveat with respect to the supposed information revolution applies to the rise in the 'stock' of education embodied in the work force. Measured by the conventional criteria of man-years of schooling, there is no doubt that this stock has increased markedly: whereas only 6 per cent of the population aged 17 were high school graduates in 1900, nearly 80 per cent had completed high school in 1970. Equally dramatic, whereas those enrolled in college in 1900 constituted only 4 per cent of the population aged 18–21, today well over half of this age group is in college.

No one can gainsay this change which, like the change in the sectoral location of labour, surely augurs new outlooks, experiences, and expectations for the labour force. To this matter we will return. But it would be hasty to jump from the fact of a higher stock of embodied education to the conclusion that the stock of 'knowledge' of the society has increased *pari passu*. For along with the increased training undergone by the labour force has come an increase in the compartmentalization and specialization of its skills, best exemplified by comparing the wide-ranging capabilities of the farmer with the much more narrowly defined work capabilities of the office clerk. To put the matter differently, we cannot assume that a postindustrial society is one in which the general level of 'know-how' is raised along with the general level of formal education. Insofar as formal education is devoted to exposing the student to the broadest vistas of history, the social and natural sciences, etc., one kind of 'knowledge' is undoubtedly increased. In that sense, the average citizen of the postindustrial society is not only 'better educated' but really knows more, with regard to the natural sciences, human behaviour, etc., *considered as abstractions*, than did his counterpart in industrial or preindustrial society. At a less abstract level, however, the gain is much less. And within that very important branch of social knowledge concerned with the operation of the socio–economic mechanism, what seems to mark the education-intensive postindustrial society is a marked *decrease* in the ability of the individual to perform work outside his trained speciality – witness our helplessness in the face of a broken utensil, vehicle, electrical system, or plumbing fixture, compared with the versatility of the farmer (or industrial artisan), proverbially jack of all trades, even if master of none.

To raise these cautions against a simplistic view of the postindustrial society as one characterized by a 'knowledge explosion' is not to deny that profound alterations are visible within contemporary society as a result of greater educational inputs – alterations that are likely to become even more pronounced in the society of the future.

The first, whose implications we will examine again subsequently, is a change in the expected life-styles of a postindustrial population. Whatever else its effects may be, the exposure to prolonged schooling seems to encourage an expectation of careers in white-collar, as opposed to blue-collar, tasks; and this may indeed militate against the willingness of the 'educated' population to consider many manual tasks as appropriate ways of making a livelihood, regardless of the relative incomes to be had from goods-handling, rather than paper-handling, work. Needless to say, this change in expectations accords very well with the actual displacement of labour from agricultural tasks and from the unskilled categories of industrial work, and its increasing deployment in service occupations.

Second and perhaps more important – although necessarily more conjectural – is the educationally based evolution of a 'sub-class' of highly skilled technicians, scientists, and experts who seem to be moving gradually towards a position of greater influence within the socio–economic system as a whole. The rise of this 'knowledge elite' has been remarked by many.[7] The actual power possessed by the new elite, as well as its degree of sub- or superordination to older elites, is as yet unclear. Nonetheless, there seems little doubt that a new education-based stratification has been created at the apex of the system, and that a new mystique surrounds 'the scientist', symbol of the knowledge-oriented postindustrial system, comparable to that which formerly adhered to the 'captain of industry'. Thus the emphasis on 'knowledge' as the *differentia specifica* of a postindustrial system is not misplaced, although the precise nature of this difference requires to be spelled out a good deal more carefully than is often the case.

3 *A postindustrial society can be regarded as a 'postcapitalist' society – that is, as a socio–economic formation in which the traditional problems of capitalism will give way before the new organizational modes of a postindustrial system.*

As with the previous 'visions' of a postindustrial system, I think there is a core of truth in this view. The bitter class divisions endemic to capitalism in the late nineteenth and early twentieth centuries seem to be yielding to a society of much greater economic (if not necessarily social or political) consensus. The 'welfare' state, however inadequate in actuality, is now a generally accepted model for all industrial societies, and brings with it a considerable degree of 'socialism' in the form of guaranteed incomes, family allowances, public health assurance, educational subsidization of lower income groups, and the like. The extreme vulnerability of the system to failures of aggregate demand has been tempered by the growth of a public sector. As a result of these and still other changes, the 'revolutionary' proletariat has failed to materialize; moreover, as we have seen above, the size of the industrial proletariat has remained approximately constant.

Thus there *are* cogent reasons for thinking of the postindustrial society as one that differs in significant ways from the economic performance of

7 See among others, Galbraith (1967), and Heilbroner (1966).

the industrial capitalism to which it is a successor. Nonetheless, as before, it is wise to look for continuities as well as differences in seeking to delineate the nature of the new socio–economic environment.

The first of these is the continuance of a trend whose origins can be traced back at least to the third quarter of the nineteenth century. This is the slow, irregular, but apparently irreversible trend towards the concentration of capital. The figures are well known: in manufacturing, the assets of the top 100 firms in 1968 were as large a share (roughly 49 per cent) of all corporate manufacturing assets as the share of the 200 largest industrial firms in 1950. Similarly the top 200 firms in 1968 controlled as large a fraction of total assets as the top 1,000 firms in 1941 (Blair 1972, chap. 4). Economic society today is strikingly characterized by what Robert Averitt (1968) has called a Centre – a small number of very large and powerful industrial units – and a Periphery – a very large number of generally small and weak firms.

It should be noted that we are far from understanding the dynamics of this two-sector division with regard to the performance of the system as a whole. The oligopolistic Centre has been shown to be the source of much economic inefficiency and perhaps of inflationary pressures (Blair 1972, p. 152), the sprawling Periphery has been identified by at least one student as the main source of business instability (Sherman 1972, pp. 110, 113–14). More important, but even less well understood, are the extent and nature of the linkages that bind the Centre and political power structure. That linkages exist has been amply demonstrated, but the direction in which power flows (*from* the economic *to* the political structure, or vice versa) is unclear or perhaps unstable.[8] That is not a problem for this paper. What I rather wish to stress is the existence of an economic concentrate allied somehow with a political concentrate – a state of affairs that is not basically different from that which existed under 'industrial' society, and which can, incidentally, be seen as well in the economic–political ententes of Japan, France, Germany, and other candidates for entry into the postindustrial realm.

The development of a 'postindustrial' configuration of employment or education does not seem likely to undo this characteristic of economic concentration. Rather, it seems probable that the concentration process will now proceed rapidly in the burgeoning service sector, where significant inroads have already been made (as is also the case in agriculture, still by far the least concentrated sector). We tend to picture the service sector as comprised of large numbers of independent proprietorships (lawyers, self-employed, one-man enterprises); but in fact a considerable proportion of

8 For a few studies of these linkages see Engler (1971), Kolko (1963), Kariel (1961).

employment in this sector is already provided by monopolistic or oligo-polistic units. Of roughly 44 million employed in the service sector in 1970 (not including utilities or transportation), 13 million were in government, 15 million in trade, 4 million in finance (banking, insurance, brokerage, real estate). By comparison with the manufacturing sector, these are all relatively unconcentrated industries, but in terms of *absolute size of units*, the large firm, with its bureaucratic organization, is increasingly evident. A mere 29 retail chains, for instance, control a fifth of all assets in trade; the predominance and growth of large banks and insurance companies is well-known (the top 50 banks account for a third of all banking employ-ment; the top 50 insurance companies for almost half of all employment in that field). *Thus the organizational character of industrial capitalism, with its hierarchies, bureaucracies, and above all its trend towards concentra-tion, seems likely to continue in the postindustrial society.*

Next, we find the distribution of wealth and income little if at all dis-turbed by the types of changes we have discussed. Many studies have shown the extraordinary stability of income-shares accruing to the top and bottom deciles in the United States (Kolko 1962); the top 10 per cent of family units receiving about 30 per cent of income, the bottom 30 per cent less than one-tenth of income. These shares have remained roughly constant, or have inclined slightly towards inequality during the late decade, in which the effects of the postindustrial changes might have been expected to reveal their influence.

More significant is the stubborn continuation and defence of the extreme concentration of wealth in the top 1 or 2 per cent of family units who collectively own about a third of *all* wealth. Control of corporate wealth – by far the most strategic item of wealth – is much more tightly centred, with about two-thirds of such wealth in the hands of 0.2 per cent of all families (Lampman 1962). In passing, it might be remarked that this extreme concentration of control is not peculiar to capitalism – it could no doubt be found under feudalism and (insofar as power can be used as a proxy for wealth) under existing forms of socialism. What is specifically capitalist about the phenomenon is the focus of control on corporate enter-prise; and there is no sign that this concentration or its focus will diminish appreciably in a postindustrial setting, although the wealth-holding elites may recruit newcomers from the scientific–technological community.

Finally, we pass from structure to function. We have already noted that the more extreme destabilizing tendencies of capitalism now seem to be faced with rough-and-ready remedies. Let us only add that the specific features of postindustrialism that we have heretofore discussed – the sectoral shift and the increased education input – are not in themselves the source of any stabilizing tendencies (although one might claim that the defensive weaponry of macro–economics is itself in part a product of the knowledge input of our time). However successfully we may have obviated the threat of mass unemployment and catastrophic income decline, there is scant evidence as yet that postindustrial society has solved problems that reflect the capitalist *modus operandi*. Inflation has replaced deflation, but the one, like the other, is surely a market phenomenon. A massive misallocation of resources, visible especially in the decay of the cities, has taken public priority over mass unemployment; but once again the fault lies with the failure of the market mechanism and the special constraints of private ownership. Specifically 'capitalist' relations with the underdeveloped world seem to have worsened in the most recent period, or perhaps we should simply say that the capitalist problem of 'imperialism' has reemerged to a central position.

All these elements suggest that whatever else we may say about the postindustrial future, *we should consider it as a stage of capitalism and not as a step 'beyond' capitalism*. The stage may display new endemic characteristics and problems – indeed, I shall next turn to an exploration of what these may be – but it must also be expected to manifest many of the structural attributes of industrial capitalism, including concentrated economic power and wealth, a highly unequal distribution of pre (and probably post) tax income, and micro-malfunctions and misallocations of resources that arise from the predominance of the market as the principal allocatory mechanism.

Shall we then dismiss the idea of a 'postindustrial' society as a chimera? That is not my intention. Just as late industrial capitalism differs in striking and significant ways from the small-scale capitalism of Adam Smith's day, so it is probable that the 'postindustrial' trends within contemporary capitalism are pushing in directions that also portend substantial change.

Let me therefore turn the coin over and review the evidence I have just marshalled in order to factor out those elements that seem to me particularly freighted with change. The first of these, we will remember, had to do with the sectoral relocation of the work force away from the farm through the factory and into the office. Is it possible to generalize about the effects of such a massive relocation, particularly when one takes into account the extraordinary heterogeneity of tasks contained within the service sector?

One such generalization is self-evident, but none the easier to interpret.

It is a far-reaching change in the character of what we call, or think of, as 'work'. Like industrial man, postindustrial man is divorced from knowledge of the most fundamental provisioning activities of society: the seasons affect him only insofar as they determine his vacation time, the weather only as it upsets his travel plans or conditions his choice of clothing. Unlike industrial man, however, who also shares in this complete ignorance of the fundamental provisioning tasks, postindustrial man is no longer even familiar with the environment in which the great bulk of our industrial products originate. The bleak expanse of the factory wasteland, surrounded with its high, electrified fence; the clangour of the industrial shed, the dirty work clothes, the lunch pail, the grease, the grime, the dust that we find in most places of industrial work are missing from the store and the office. Changed, too, is the character of work supervision, away from factory whistles, check-ins, foremen. Service work, in all (or most) of its varieties is characterized by trim surroundings, neat dress or a prestigious uniform, constant exposure to a 'clientele', coffee breaks, telephone calls. This is by no means all gain, although some of it is. The physical dangers of work are less; the psychological strains may be greater. The expenditure of physical effort is greatly reduced; that of psychic energies may be greatly increased.

It is difficult to know what conclusions follow from this impressionistically drawn change in work milieu. For example, whether 'alienation' is exacerbated or alleviated is a matter about which we cannot even make informed guesses, not least because of the variety of tasks embraced within the service sector. Yet, in full awareness of the frailty of such 'sociologizing', let me hazard one conjecture that combines the changed work experience mentioned above with a second characteristic of the postindustrial world – namely, the lengthened and broadened exposure of its work force to formal education. The conjecture (it is perhaps too untestable to be dignified with the name of 'hypothesis') is that the lengthened exposure to the 'white-collar' atmosphere of the classroom tends to identify the expected characteristics of 'work'. That is, college prepares one not only intellectually, but experientially, for the store and the office rather than for the factory or the farm. I am aware, of course, of exceptions: agronomists, engineers, and a few similar professions. But in the main I think I am on firm ground in holding that education nurtures the association of 'work' with reading, writing, and calculation, rather than with handling things. Thus the postindustrial society encourages what Veblen called a 'trained incapacity' for 'dirty work' among that ever-growing fraction of the population that pursues formal education through the college level. In passing, I should note that the smooth running of postindustrial society may hinge, even more than that of industrial society, on the presence of that 'secondary' labour force (the drop-outs, casual labour-market participants, or exploited minorities) who continue to be available for the picking of fruit, the digging of ditches, the sweeping of floors, the washing of dishes.

Along with the new sense of what 'work' means there comes, I think, a growing expectation of security in the world of work. A man or woman who has been relieved of virtually all economic necessity until the age of 21 or even 25 is reared in an environment in which some sort of economic provision, even if at a frugal level, is taken for granted. It would not be surprising if the graduates of the postindustrial educational institutions bring with them strong expectations that 'work' is not a scarce privilege to be competed for, but a basic right – the normal reward for having completed the long training that society has enjoined. Guarantees of employment, security of tenure in work, the 'right' to expect an uninterrupted flow of income are thus plausible consequences of the transition to a postindustrial occupational and educational framework. Perhaps this is nothing more than the diffusion among the great bulk of the population of attitudes that were formerly evident mainly among the upper decile.

Let me turn finally to another new attribute of the postindustrial world which also follows from the characteristics we have examined in our previous section. This concerns the problems of economic function and malfunction that a postindustrial society can expect to inherit from its precursor.

Here one major trend seems likely to be reinforced by the postindustrial system. This is the growth of business–state coordination at an overt rather than covert level. Business-state cooperation is, of course, as old as capitalism itself; it is the mythology rather than the reality of laissez-faire, which has dominated the past century. Many forces within the postindustrial framework seem likely to diminish the strength of that mythology, and to strengthen the tendencies toward open coordination. The importance of maintaining an adequate level of aggregate demand in the face of widespread expectations of 'guaranteed white-collar work', of remedying the disruptive effects of the misallocation of resources, and of dealing with the problems of an economic system increasingly polarized between a Centre and a Periphery all seem likely to increase the need for, and the political acceptability of, some kind of 'planning'. No doubt the form and functions of this planning will display differing reaches and effectiveness in various societies with their particular ideological, tradtional, and structural differences. But in all postindustrial systems I would anticipate something that might be described as a 'corporate state' – that is, a state in which the activities of the Centre and the state are brought into compatible paths, in which the risks and instabilities of the Periphery are offset, or at least partially underwritten, and in which acceptable resource allocation is attacked by coordinated action between the public and private sectors.

In suggesting that the changeful elements of the postindustrial trend will encourage overt planning, I do not mean to imply that the politicoeconomic problems of this stage of capitalism will necessarily be easier to solve than those of industrial capitalism. The difficulties of controlling inflation may well be greater than those of overcoming depression, both to diagnose and to cope with politically. The power of the moderately affluent middle classes, and of the service-sector located work force may prove more troublesome for a viable 'incomes policy' than the wage-determination in an industrial setting. No less of a difficult problem for the macromanagement of the postindustrial system may be that of persuading the majority of income recipients, whose incomes lie in the fourth income decile and up, to relinquish substantial sums for the benefit of the poor who are to be found in the bottom three deciles. All these problems seem likely to add further impetus to the overall drift towards business–state planning to which we have already pointed.

Heretofore I have been discussing the postindustrial society from two points of view: first, analysing the inadequacies of certain views concerning the term; second, suggesting the kernel of truth that resides in these views. Now I wish to proceed in a somewhat different direction. First, I wish to inquire into two structural or transformational stresses to which postindustrial society will be subject, beyond those that we have already identified. Finally, I will ask the much more difficult question as to the social consequences we can anticipate as following from these changes.

What further *economic* changes can be expected from the trajectory out of agrarian, through industrial, into the service-centred, education-intensive system we call 'postindustrial'? Two such changes appear integrally connected with this trajectory, although as we shall see, the connections are not the same in each case.

The first change has to do with the progressive mechanization of work – that is, with the further development of the very force that lies behind the trajectory of economic transformation itself. There is no doubt that technology is the major element in bringing about the sectoral migration of the labour force, for it has been the widening 'technicization' of rural and then factory work that has released the manpower that has flowed into the tertiary areas of the economy.[9] We do not fully understand the reason for the particular sequence of technology that has given us this shift and cannot therefore make firm predictions with respect to the future. But every indication is that invention and innovation will be proportionately more concentrated on the tasks performed in the service sector. This seems likely for three reasons: 1. we are reaching the limits of labour displacement in agriculture (although there remains a small group that can still be dispossessed from their jobs in that sector); 2. almost three-quarters of a century of invention and innovation within the industrial core has left the proportion of the labour force relatively unchanged, as we have seen, and we can therefore assume that if the same general forces of technology and demand continue, there will not be significant labour displacement from this sector; and 3. the most 'attractive' sector for the introduction of machinery lies in the heretofore technically 'neglected' service area.[10] In this sector labour costs are high, productivity low, and a new level of technological capability begins to bring many heretofore 'unmechanizable' tasks within the reach of machinery; as a result we have the vending machine for the counter man; the self-service store for the clerk; the programmed lathe, the automatic check-reader, the omnipresent computer.

What will be the effect of this further mechanization? The answer hinges entirely on the elasticity of demand for the services produced in this sector. If demand swells *pari passu* with the increased productivity per service worker that will result from 'automation', then the service sector may continue to absorb its present 60–65 per cent of the labour force. If demand swells more rapidly, or if technology enters more slowly, employment in this sector may rise still further in both absolute and percentage terms. It is also possible that the demand for 'services', like that for 'manufactures', will ultimately reach 'satiety'. In more concrete terms, there may be a limit as to the amount of government services, retail-trade services, education, recreation, financial advice, etc., that a man wants at a given income level; and that the 'amount' of services (measured in the dollars we spend for them) may not rise as rapidly as income rises.

9   A brief technical footnote seems necessary here. Technology releases the manpower, but its migration into another sector thereafter depends on the demand for commodities originating in the various sectors. Had the demand for agricultural output been extremely elastic, the release of labour through mechanization would have resulted only in a much vaster increase in total farm output than we have in fact experienced. The same applies to manufacturing. It is not only technology, but the inelasticity of demand for 'food' (Engels's Law) and the approximately unitary elasticity for manufactured goods that have resulted in the precipitous fall in rural employment and the secular steadiness of manufacturing employment.

10   See Schmookler (1966) for evidence of the role of demand in directing the course of technological discovery and application.

In that case, where will the displaced labour go? Several possibilities for adjustment are available. One is the creation of a public employment sector designed to create employment for those displaced from the service area. This sector need not itself be within the tertiary sector, but might embrace subsidized small farming, labour-intensive subsidized handicraft, labour-intensive public construction, etc. A second possibility is the deliberate steady reduction in the work force, achieved partly by further extending the compulsory years of schooling, partly by reducing retirement ages, partly by shortening the work week. A third possibility is the extension of the transfer mechanism to permit a certain proportion of the young working-age population to live without work, at socially determined subsistence levels, if it so chooses.

All these adjustments – the need for which hinges, let me repeat, on the unpredictable rate of technological displacement and the shift in the demand for various services – portend considerable strains on the 'traditional' capitalist mechanism. They imply a high degree of that over-all plannification of which I spoke earlier. They imply as well new strains on the macroprocesses of a system in which the historic underpinning identified by both Marx and Weber – a propertyless class of workers – has been replaced by a class of workers which, however 'propertyless', are not *forced* to sell their labour power at the prevailing market rate. It would be foolhardy to assert that an economic system operating under the constraints of 'capitalist' ideologies and institutions cannot make these adjustments – one has but to consider the very great degree of social adaptation displayed by the capitalist nations of Scandinavia. But the basic nature of the challenge of mechanization is nonetheless clear. The postindustrial society is likely to be faced with a 'redundancy' of labour owing to the progressive incursion of mechanization into the service sector; and this redundancy – if it is not absorbed by a spontaneous growth of private demand for 'services' – will require intervention into the market process on a far-reaching scale.

A second dimension of the mechanization problem has already engaged our attention. This is the effect of 'automation', on the psychophysical process of 'work' itself. We have already seen that the displacement of 'muscular' by 'intellectual' labour is one of the main attributes of post-industrialization. Even at the simplest level – the man behind the tractor wheel instead of behind the hoe, behind the adding machine instead of behind the ledger, behind the computerized lathe instead of behind the chuck lathe – the nature of human effort in postindustrial society is given a supervisory, rather than directly 'active', aspect. This change in the existential and experiential character of labour offers rich ground for speculation, but little substantial basis for extraeconomic prediction. We return at the conclusion to this problem of social forecasting.

A second structural challenge to be faced by the postindustrial world is the problem of ecological adjustment that must be faced over the coming decades – a problem that will steadily grow in intensity as population densities rise, pollution accumulates, and resources become depleted.

The dimensions of the ecological problem are ultimately very great and its restrictive implications severe. What is at question is the time scale during which adjustment can be made and the degree of technological adaptation that can be achieved. At stake is the level of qualitative well-being, the rate of tolerable growth, and in the end the viability of the planet itself as a human habitat. It need hardly be said that the ecological threat affects not just the 'postindustrial' world, but all nations, albeit in different fashions and at varying time schedules. In terms of the immediate impact on the quality of life, it may well be the most developed nations, with their high rate of pollution and their voracious consumption of resources, that stand to be the first affected.

When the ecological problem arrives 'in earnest', it will pose an acute problem for postindustrial societies. We have already called attention to the presence and the undoubted continuing importance of the industrial core which, together with the agricultural sector, supports the tertiary activities of the postindustrial world. The problem, then, is the extent to which the expansive drive of a capitalist mechanism, expressed through the acquisitive and accumulatory behaviour of its corporations, can be given an appropriate area in which to manifest itself, if unrestricted growth within the industrial sector becomes impermissible for environmental reasons.

Of the many new sources of tension and malfunction within the postindustrial world, this looming constriction of the expansive drive within the industrial sector seems among the most difficult of solution. The export of capital, a major means of venting the expansive drive in the past, becomes less open, owing to environmental problems of pollution in the other developed countries (which are currently most attractive to capital), and to political problems in the underdeveloped world. To what extent the expansive international momentum of capitalism can be diverted to the areas of services is an uncertain question, but not one that seems especially promising, as the various 'service' occupations are now defined.

There is no point in attempting to guess to what degree industrial companies will be able to move into such fields as entertainment, travel, personal services and the like. What is important to bear in mind is that some form of 'growth', with all its money illusions and its mixture of 'goods' and 'bads', is an indispensable means of lessening the tensions generated by the need to divide the total product between wages and property income. In a postindustrial society in which industrial expansion were necessarily constrained because of ecological hazards, and in which the large corporation had not found a satisfactory means of penetrating the service occupations, we could expect serious stresses to manifest themselves – a fall in profit rates and/or a much more acrimonious struggle over the division of the social product. Whether 'capitalism' could adjust to such a situation is moot – in the opinion of economists as different in orientation as Marx and Keynes it could not – but in all likelihood such a trend would accelerate the tendency towards the 'managerialization' of the public–private corporate state to which other tendencies, discussed above, now point.

We have already indulged in sufficient speculation with regard to the socio-economic characteristics of the postindustrial world, and the temptation is to conclude on a note of solid empiricism. Yet I shall resist this temptation in order to explore one last highly conjectural area that seems inescapable in any consideration of what the future may be like.

This is the classic problem of the economic 'base' and the noneconomic 'superstructure' – a problem that finds its starkest expression in Marx, but that can be traced back to the Scottish Historical School. For a fact that must be admitted in all our conjecturings about the shape of things to come is that we reveal ourselves, wittingly or otherwise, to be economic determinists – indeed, even technological determinists. To put it differently, all speculation about postindustrialism assumes that the causal line of inference runs *from* the economic changes *to* the political and social changes, and although feedbacks may be discussed (such as the drive towards plannification) the *primum mobile* of 'prediction' is the economic dynamic of social evolution.

This primacy of economic dynamics has nothing to do with ideology. It arises because we can discern 'lawlike' motions within the economic sphere that have no counterparts in the political and social realms. However indistinct and blurred, these motions can nonetheless be described and, moreover, within broad limits their interactions can be deduced. One of these lawlike motions is the drive for profits characteristic of a capitalist system. Although this drive does not produce the determinate 'equilibrium' solutions of neoclassical economics, it nonetheless permits us to anticipate with a fair degree of certainty such types of behaviour as the search for cost-reducing technology, the concentration of business enterprise (whether for reasons of efficiency or profitable financial manipulation), the probable advent of economies of scale in industries that have not yet been 'invaded' by technology, the crucial role to be played by autonomous public and private expenditures magnified by a 'multiplier' of reasonably known dimensions, and still other regularities.

I hasten to stress the extreme tenuousness of our knowledge in all these fields. Short-run economic prediction, based on presumptively 'known' behavioural functions and technical constraints, has been shown to be egregiously faulty. But this constraint does not apply with quite the same force to the longer run, when the persistent trends of economic life assert themselves over their short-term vagaries. Hence to whatever extent we dare to predict the contours of postindustrial society, it is perforce on the basis of these economic projections. For what 'lawlike' statements can we apply to the organization of political affairs, to social organization, to changes in cultural life-style, and the like? Apart from a few descriptive generalizations – Michels's 'iron law' of oligarchy, Weber's description of bureaucratic organization, Freud's or Erikson's outline of the topography of the psyche and its developmental stages – what do the other social sciences have to offer by way of predictive theory? The answer I fear is, discouragingly little. Thus, however inaccurate or inadequate the economic determinist view may be, it is foisted upon us as an initial mode of viewing the future for lack of any alternative 'positive' approach.

This raises very grave problems for social scientists. Not only are the 'laws of motion' of economics extremely imprecise, but the linkages between any given economic structure and its interlocked political and social accoutrements are even more difficult to describe with any degree of assurance. I must confess to a suspicion that if postindustrial society follows the general economic trajectory I have described, it will be accompanied by a more authoritarian political structure, by more anomic groups in the undereducated, by increasing restlessness and boredom among the educated 'middle classes' still subject to the stimuli of a competitive, acquisitive culture. But this is only conjecture; perhaps one can draw equally or more convincing scenarios of greater stability, communal morale, individual fulfilment.

In this situation of extreme indeterminacy a key may be provided by what Adolph Lowe (1971) has identified as the mood of the times – certainly of the postindustrial age. He calls this 'the end of social fatalism'. By this he means the end of an age in which not only the events of nature but the events of society are taken as 'givens', to be mutely accepted by the uncomplaining masses or explained away in terms of a theological or a political religion.

If this identification of a profound change in mood is true – and I believe that it is – perhaps our view of the future as something to be 'predicted' is fundamentally at variance with the realities of the age. In an era that has rejected social fatalism, the future will no longer 'arrive', but it will be *made*, however crudely, cruelly, or well by the harnessing of political wills and their focusing on deliberately chosen goals. It may therefore be quite mistaken to search, within economics or in its sister disciplines, for 'positive' perspectives on a future that will not come into being by the workings of 'lawlike' mechanisms (although it may be influenced by their residual influence), but by the political selection of social goals whose means of attainment then become the subject for social scientific investigation.

This leaves open, of course, the choice of goals. About this all-important question the social scientist has nothing to say, either as counsellor or as expert 'prognosticator'. Perforce he relinquishes his place to the moral philosopher – his historical godfather – whose task it is to raise the consciousness of men to the alternatives open to them. The goals once chosen, the social scientist again comes into his own in the more modest, but nonetheless important, role of social 'engineer'. If there is one ultimate definition for postindustrial society, then, I would suggest, it is that stage of socioeconomic organization in which men gradually escape from the thraldom of blind mechanisms to enter the perilous, but potentially liberating, terrain in which human beings finally assert themselves, for better or worse, as the masters of their fate.

References

ABRAMOVITZ, M. (1956) *Resource and Output Trends in the United States since 1870* New York, National Bureau of Economic Research.

AVERITT, R. T. (1968) *The Dual Economy* New York, Norton.

BELL, D. (1971) *Survey*, Winter.

BLAIR, J. M. (1972) *Economic Concentration* New York, Harcourt, Brace, Jovanovich.

DENNISON, E. (1962) *Sources of Economic Growth in the United States* New York, Committee for Economic Development.

ENGLER, R. (1971) *The Politics of Oil* New York, Macmillan.

GALBRAITH, J. K. (1967) *The New Industrial State* Boston, Houghton, Mifflin.

HEILBRONER, R. (1966) *The Limits of American Capitalism* New York, Harper and Row.

JANOSSY, F. (1971) *The End of the Economic Miracle* White Plains, New York, International Arts and Sciences Press.

JEWKES, SAWYERS and STILLERMAN (1970) *The Sources of Invention,* 2nd ed., New York, Norton.

KARIEL, H. (1961) *The Decline of American Pluralism* Stanford, California, Stanford University Press.

KOLKO, G. (1962) *Wealth and Power in America* New York, Praeger.

KOLKO, G. (1963) *The Triumph of Conservatism* Glencoe, Illinois, Free Press.

LAMPMAN, R. (1962) *The Share of Top Wealth Holders in National Wealth 1922–56* Princeton, New Jersey, Princeton University Press.

LOWE, A. (1971) 'Is Present Day Higher Education "Relevant"?', *Social Research* Fall.

MITCHELL, B. R. (1962) *Abstract of British Historical Statistics* Cambridge, Cambridge University Press.

SCHMOOKLER, I. (1966) *Invention and Economic Growth* Cambridge, Mass., Harvard University Press.

SHERMAN, H. (1972) *Radical Political Economy* New York, Basic Books.

SOLOW, R. (1957) 'Technical Change and Aggregate Production Function', *Review of Economics and Statistics*, August.

Part IV Work

Introduction

Work is the activity whereby men make the world – and the society – they live in. The products of work are necessary to satisfy those needs upon which our continuing existence is based. That much is clear. But work is also the activity whereby men make – or break – themselves; not simply in the sense that work serves as an avenue of social mobility, but in the more serious sense that work is a crucial *determinant* (and resultant) of a man's identity, culture, social relations, and mental and physical health, and of his opportunity and capacity to develop, in the fullest possible way, his potential as an autonomous and creative human being.

More than this, work is also the means whereby society is made and is revealed. The social and economic organization of work serves to create attitudes and resources which are crucial to the continuation of society. For example, the profits produced by manufacturing a product are reinvested to finance the production of additional products, or different ones, and the wages people are paid in exchange for their labour are used to buy the results of others' labours. Similarly the attitudes that are evident in people's conformity with industrial, factory or organizational discipline (regular attendance, punctuality, commitment to, or at least acquiescence in, the enterprise) and that lie behind our interest in and enthusiasm for, raising the level of our financial rewards, are part and parcel of an interest in constantly improving our standard of living which, in turn, entails the consumption of ever more and ever 'improved' goods and services. And so it goes.

Society is revealed in work in that the nature of work experiences and the differential way in which work is variously evaluated, esteemed and rewarded, can only be understood in terms of the structure and distribution of interests and values in society. People are not paid what they are worth – they are paid what they and others have learnt (or been taught) to accept as appropriate for that-sort-of-work and that-sort-of-person. No satisfactory explanation of the differences between, say, the rewards of coalminers and of stockbrokers can fail to consider the class positions, interests and backgrounds of the two groups, their relative capacities to influence political opinion and events, and the extent to which their interests converge with, or diverge from, those of the dominant political groups in the society.

But it is clear that, if the nature, rewards and organization of work *reveals* to social scientists a great deal about the society within which it occurs, and serves to re-create it, it also reveals it to those concerned, and so serves to generate (and reveal) dissension and conflict. Through work experiences and through the concentration of large numbers of people who share these experiences is often born both an awareness of disadvantage and deprivation, *and* a determination to improve matters. This, of course, only follows from union organization and activity, for it is through unionization that the employee can begin to increase his bargaining strength vis à vis the employer.

Because of its importance work is a topic on which all the social science disciplines have a great deal to say. This part of the reader contains three articles: the first considers the relationship between the temporal organization of modern work and man's physical and psychological capacities, Wilkinson argues that simply in terms of obvious and measurable physical factors, aspects of the organization of work can have serious deleterious consequences, as well as being inefficient.

This article is interesting not because it makes any attempt (or claims) to describe and assess the multitude of consequences that stem from the nature and organization of work – for that would be an enormous venture – but because, in a systematic and compelling way the author shows how one particular aspect of modern work and technology is out of tune with man's physical – indeed biological – capacity and nature. As he puts it: 'the root of many of the problems of the modern industrial state is that machines evolve much faster than men'. This article is also valuable because it derives from a psychological perspective on work, and thus affords us an opportunity to learn and evaluate about this approach to the study of work. More than any other discipline psychology has been used by employers, and those concerned with efficiency and work satisfaction, in their attempts to fit 'jobs to men and men to jobs'. But the success of such a venture depends upon one's assumptions about, and conceptualizations of, the nature and determinants of work, and man. It will be clear from a consideration of the three articles in this part that the three disciplines represented vary importantly in this respect.

The excerpt from Phelps-Brown considers, in a historical context, the nature of the employer–employee relationship and how unionization and conflict arises out of features of this relationship. Phelps-Brown notes that one distinctive feature of the contract of employment, before unionization, is that, because of the differences in resources – in bargaining capacity – the employee is likely to suffer. Another characteristic of the contract is that it involves the control and supervision of the employees. Phelps-Brown also considers the divisive potentials of profit – and interestingly he does not restrict his analysis merely to a formal statement of the nature and origins of profits, but also discusses *the meaning* of profit for those who create it and who, occasionally, feel opposed to those who receive it.

The excerpts from Beynon's book *Working for Ford* have been chosen because they – and the book as a whole – admirably document the nature of assembly-line work – the noise, the tension, the never-ending track moving inexorably, perpetually; dominating every action, every man.

But the excerpts are much more than a description of work on an assembly line, they are also an analysis of the factors that determine the workers' experiences – and hence their attitudes and behaviour. Beynon, like Phelps-Brown, is concerned with analysing the nature of the employer-employee relationship and with delineating those aspects that give rise to conflict and dissension. His analysis proceeds from a different theoretical (and political) perspective from that held by Phelps-Brown, that is evident, but the subject is the same. Beynon is concerned to investigate how such abstractions as 'profit', the 'market', 'economic fluctuations', and so on, are *experienced* by those concerned – how they are felt, and what follows from the experience. In particular, he is interested in their implications for individual conflict, either official or unofficial. In his interest to uncover the relationship between work experiences and industrial or class conflict he has to concentrate on the way in which these experiences are mediated, transformed and interpreted by the systems of meaning employed by workers.

Graeme Salaman

15 Hours of work and the twenty-four-hour cycle of rest and activity

Robert Wilkinson

The National Board for Prices and Incomes has recently brought out a report on 'Hours of work, overtime, and shift working' (1970). One of the conclusions is that overtime and shiftwork are, on the whole, viewed with favour by both men and management. The men get the chance to augment their pay packet. Management can make greater use of existing manpower through overtime, while shiftworking allows fuller implementation of plant. Nevertheless the report calls for a more searching and less intuitive assessment of whether prevailing levels of overtime and shiftwork in fact represent the most efficient or even productive use of our resources. It also questions whether a satisfactory balance has been struck between the economic advantages and the social costs of shiftworking. These questions come opportunely for the nation, and for this chapter. If national interests of health, happiness and stability are to prevail over parochial ones of profit it is necessary that an objective and unbiased authority should exert some influence on these matters, as, of course, the Prices and Incomes Board is trying to do. Its influence, however, can only be as powerful as the evidence it can bring to bear. Producing this is largely the job of the research scientist, and particularly in this context, of the applied psychologist. His role is twofold: first to unearth the facts about how well people work and live under various systems of working hours, and second, on the basis of this to seek explanatory laws which can be applied generally.

The root of many of the problems of the modern industrial state is that machines evolve much faster than men: they do not have to go back to square one as we do at the start of each new generation. In our present context the dilemma takes this form: the human adult is an animal whose body is tuned by evolution and training to go about its business during the hours of daylight and sleep during those of darkness. Ask it to work at night and sleep during the day and it does both rather badly. Yet this is what modern technological progress demands, first when machines are so complex that they must work day and night to repay their cost, and second

WILKINSON, ROBERT (1971) 'Hours of Work and the Twenty-Four-Hour Cycle of Rest and Activity', in Warr, Peter Brian (ed.) *Psychology at Work* Harmondsworth, Penguin, 31–54.

when jet planes are so fast they can move people across several time zones in a few hours. The end result of both of these is that people have to work when they would normally be sleeping and either not sleep at all or sleep when their bodies are expecting to be up and about. This chapter is concerned with how much both performance and sleep are impaired by this, how swiftly the body can adapt to the change, and how best to arrange things so that as little harm as possible comes to people's health, happiness and ability to do the job.

Let us look more closely at the cause of the trouble, man's twenty-four-hour or 'circadian' cycle of rest and activity.

The circadian rhythm of rest and activity in man

According to Kleitman (1963) there is a fifty to sixty-minute rest/activity cycle in the human newborn infant, which soon couples with a three to four-hour gastric cycle. By about four months these have for the most part given way to the normal twenty-four-hour cycle which is reflected in the child's sleeping and waking behaviour and in the levels of various physiological and biochemical measures including body temperature and a number of other cardiovascular variables: activity of the adrenal cortex, urine flow, excretion of phosphate, sodium and potassium, blood constituents, and so on. What concerns us most at present is man's ability to adapt the phase of this circadian cycle; that is, to move his sleep/wakefulness cycle round the clock as he moves from one working shift to another, or from one country to another. First let us examine the twenty-four-hour cycle itself in terms of the two measures which will concern us most: a psychological one, working efficiency, and a physiological one, deep body temperature taken by a normal clinical thermometer.

Body temperature and performance

The circadian variation of body temperature has been studied since at least the middle of the nineteenth century. Recent data by Colquhoun, Blake and Edwards (1968a) are based on two-point rolling means and provide one of the clearest impressions of the shape of the curve (fig. 1). This function was derived from fifty-nine young men whose oral body temperatures were taken at two-hour intervals throughout twenty-four hours on two separate occasions. The important points to note are the deep trough of temperature during the small hours of the morning and the

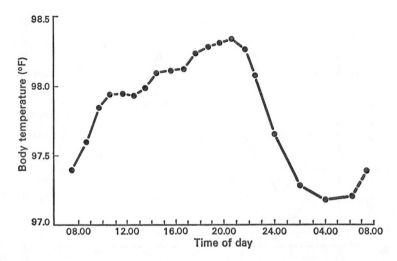

Fig. 1 Oral body temperature of fifty-nine subjects at twenty points of the twenty-four-hour cycle. Note that the curve has been smoothed by taking 'rolling means', that is, each point of the curve is the average of two measurement points, 06.00 and 08.00, then 08.00 and 10.00, and so on. (From Colquhoun *et al.* 1968a)

gradual rise during the day to a peak which is in the mid-evening in these records but which can occur anywhere between noon and late evening as a function, among other things, of the individual's personality and social habits (Blake 1967).

The circadian function of performance is more difficult to record on a twenty-four hour basis. People rarely work for twenty-four hours at a stretch, and if they did mounting fatigue would confuse the picture. What is needed is performance for shorter periods over a numbers of days and at different times of the day and night on successive days. This in fact is achieved, in the interests of a fair distribution of the unpleasant early morning watches, by a conventional naval three watch system of duties. (This system is described later on p. 255 under the name of Three Man System.) Thus when the U.S. Navy asked for this watch system to be compared with others it provided an excellent opportunity for Kleitman and Jackson (1950) to record a composite performance curve with sections from all days, thus covering the whole twenty-four hours. Figure 2 shows this curve for one of the performance tests, choice serial reaction (colour naming) which was administered for about five minutes at roughly two-hour intervals when

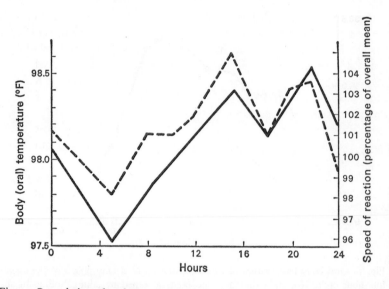

Fig. 2 Co-variation of oral temperature and serial reaction time during the twenty-four hours. Speed of reaction is expressed as a percentage of the average over all subjects in all conditions. The solid line is oral temperature, the broken one reaction time score. (Data adapted from Kleitman 1963, p. 157)

the men were on duty. The points are the average of nine subjects. Oral body temperature was recorded at the same time and is shown also. Clearly the two curves are very similar, and in fact the correlation between body temperature and speed of reaction was + 0·89. This, together with earlier results covering a wider range of tests but during the hours of daylight only, persuaded Kleitman (1963) that 'most of the curves of performance can be brought into line with the known circadian body temperature curve, allowing for individual skewing of the curve towards an earlier or later, rather than mid-afternoon peak'. More recently further studies, particularly the exhaustive ones of Colquhoun, Blake and Edwards (1968a; 1968b; 1969) have supported the existence of a body temperature/performance relationship. Others, however, force us to make some comments and qualifications.

There is no doubt that under normal conditions performance, in some respects at least, is impaired at about the same point in the circadian cycle as body temperature is depressed. The obvious question, raised but rather clouded by Kleitman himself, is that of the causal relationship, if any, between the two measures. Kleitman and Jackson (1950) were at pains to refute the idea that it was the level of the body temperature which directly caused that of performance to vary during the circadian cycle. Yet in his review (1963, p. 163) Kleitman considers the possibility of a direct effect of body temperature upon thought processes by influencing the level of metabolic activity in the cells of the cerebral cortex. Rutenfranz, Aschoff and Mann (1970) discount this in a recent study, similar to that of Kleitman and Jackson, in which they controlled for the effect of time of day by examining the temperature/performance correlation separately at each measurement point of the day or night. The correlation fell almost to zero. This indicates that it is not body temperature which is determining performance but some unknown factor, which varies in circadian fashion and carries body temperature and some aspects of performance along with it. Thus we can still measure body temperature in an attempt to determine working efficiency where this latter cannot easily be assessed but we cannot expect to change the circadian pattern of performance by artificially influencing the level of body temperature.

It should be remembered in this discussion that we are speaking of the body temperature/performance relationship in the context of circadian variations only. It is easy to forget that there are many other non-circadian influences which may enter to disrupt the measurement of the relationship especially when this is attempted outside the laboratory. One of these may be fatigue when tests are presented repeatedly during the day. This fatigue may produce lower levels of performance than would be expected on the basis of body temperature alone. Blake (1967) avoided this difficulty by presenting tests only once a day for five days, a different time being chosen each day. In most of his tests he found that peak performance occurred at 9 p.m., much later than Kleitman found. Would Kleitman's curves have shown this pattern if he had tested only once a day? If so, his body temperature/performance relationship would probably have been less satisfactory. Unfortunately no records of body temperatures are available for Blake's one-test-a-day study.

In his experiment Blake presented eight performance tests, the duration of which ranged from five to sixty minutes. He noted that on the whole the usual time of day effects were most marked in those tests which were long and repetitive; and a quick calculation from his data reveals a correlation of about $+0.7$ between the duration of the task and the degree to which its scores followed the usual rise in body temperature during the course of the day. This influence of task duration, plus the fact that incentive will reduce circadian performance variations (Chiles, Alluisi and Adams 1968) especially in extraverts (Blake and Corcoran 1970) makes the influence of low points of the circadian cycle look very similar to that of sleep deprivation (see Wilkinson 1965). In support of this correspondence is the finding (Wilkinson 1970) that the two interact; effects of loss of sleep are greater in the morning than later in the day, and are usually very marked during the night (Chiles, *et al.* 1968). Now, although the term may lack as precise a scientific foundation as we would like, it may prove useful at this point to think in terms of the level of arousal of the body. Sleep deprivation may be regarded as lowering arousal both physiologically (Ax and Luby 1961) and psychologically (Wilkinson 1965). The correspondence between the behavioural picture of loss of sleep and of that prevailing at the low points of the circadian cycle suggest that the latter too may be reflecting a state of low arousal. To the extent that we understand the effects of loss of sleep on performance (Wilkinson 1965; 1970) this approach may have heuristic value in indicating those working situations in which we can expect body temperature to provide a reasonably accurate guide to the level of working efficiency.

The role of body temperature

We are concerned ultimately with the effects of the circadian cycle on performance, but of course there are many irrelevant factors which may influence working efficiency especially in the less controlled situations of real life. Also in the factory or other field settings it is often impractical to take measures of performance. In the light of this, our interest in the closeness and generality of the body temperature/performance relationship is obvious. To the extent that body temperature can reflect the circadian component of performance its adaptation to abnormal routines may be taken as an indication of the adaptation of working efficiency where the latter cannot be assessed directly in the field. With this in mind let us see what variations in the normal body temperature pattern are to be observed as people adapt or fail to adapt to abnormal patterns of work and rest.

Adaptation of the circadian rhythm of body temperature and performance

This question can be examined both in the laboratory and in the field. We will take the laboratory first, and pay particular attention to those studies in which performance as well as body temperature was measured, thus allowing the two to be correlated.

Adaptation in the laboratory

Perhaps the most comprehensive group of studies of this kind are those undertaken between 1960 and 1967 by a group of workers at the M.R.C. Applied Psychology Unit in Cambridge. These were designed to examine various patterns of shift working in the laboratory and assess their relative efficiency.

The first of these (Wilkinson and Edwards 1968) compared the traditional Naval System of rotating four-hour watches requiring three men per station with a proposed one in which two men worked stabilized five or seven-hour shifts. Figure 3 shows the hours of work involved. In the rotat-

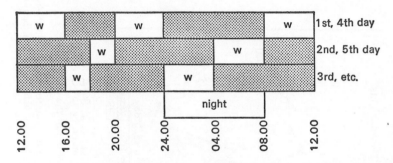

Fig. 3   Plan of work (w) and rest periods (hatched area) in Naval rotating three watch system. (From Wilkinson and Edwards 1968)

ing system the hours move round the clock usually by four hours each day in order to share the unpopular night watches fairly among the three men. As a result no man works the same hours on successive days. In the stabilized system they retain the same hours throughout, one man handling predominantly day and the other the night watches. The stabilized two-man system yielded a level of performance rather *better* than the rotating one requiring three men. This was due partly to the stabilization of the hours of work and partly to the fact that in the two-man system the men alternated work on three tasks throughout a shift, whereas with the three-man system a given job was continued throughout a given shift. Our particular concern here however is with the adaptation of body temperature and performance in the group of men who carried out the 'night' version of the two-man stabilized system, which called for work between the hours of noon and 5 p.m. and midnight and 7 a.m. This programme was carried

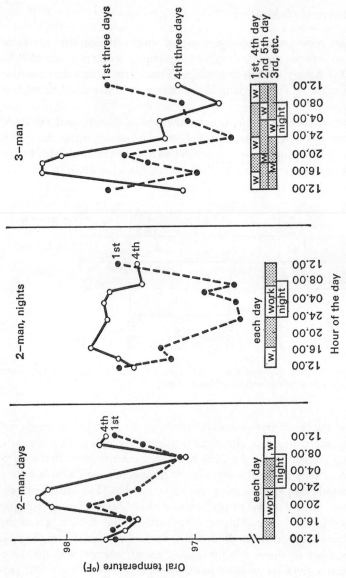

Fig. 4 Adaptation of body temperature from first (dotted line) to fourth (full line) three-day period in a twelve-day programme of work on a stabilized two-man Naval watch system or a rotating three-man one. (From Wilkinson and Edwards 1968)

out for twelve days, sleep being taken between 8 a.m. and noon and in the
early evening. Figure 4 shows the adaptation of body temperature and
performance from first to fourth three-day period. A complete inversion
of body temperature was not obtained. The change is better described as a
flattening of the normal curve involving a definite raising of the level
during the hours of night work. Performance of the three tasks, vigilance,
adding and complex decision-making, also adapted only partially to the
reversal routine. In terms of the speed of adaptation, changes in the relative
levels of day and night performance were becoming apparent by the sixth
day but even after twelve days nothing like a complete inversion of the
circadian cycle of either body temperature or performance could be claimed.

Further experiments were carried out by Colquhoun, Blake and Edwards (1968a; 1968b; 1969) which studied the body temperature/perform-
ance relationship as people adapted over twelve days to two four-hour shifts
(12.30 to 16.30 and 04.00 to 08.00), one eight-hour shift (either 08.00 to
16.00, 16.00 to 00.00, or 00.00 to 08.00), or one twelve-hour shift (either
08.00 to 20.00 or 20.00 to 08.00) a day. Of particular importance in these
studies is the fact that a good relationship was again observed between body

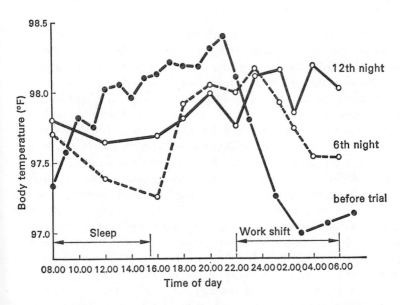

Fig. 5 Progressive but incomplete adaptation to night shift working: twelve days
of working from 22.00 to 06.00 hours every day. (From Colquhoun *et al.* 1968b)

temperature and performance, and this persisted following partial adaptation to the unusual hours. It is worth noting that the tasks involved – vigilance and adding – were of long duration and relatively uninteresting. In the 'night shifts' in these experiments the adaptation of both body temperature and performance was again incomplete, but changes occurred after about five days. Figure 5 provides a good illustration of this in the experiment involving eight-hour shifts.

The failure to produce a complete circadian reversal was, presumably, because the men were surrounded by life going on as usual to the normal routine, as indeed most shift workers are. Would isolation from the world have allowed complete inversion, and if so, how soon would it have been achieved? Answers to these questions have been provided by Aschoff and his colleagues (1969) using sound-proof, light-proof underground shelters to confine their subjects. From a wide range of studies, including free-running rhythms entrained to 26·7 or 22·7-hour days, what concerns us here is that Aschoff was able to achieve a complete phase shift of the normal circadian body temperature and sleep/wakefulness cycles 'immediately or after a very few days' under these conditions.

Time zone transition

Essentially the same situation occurs when people are transported rapidly from one part of the world to another, changing to a life up to twelve hours out of phase with the one they have just left. Here, conditions for adaptation are ideal, the surroundings being completely and naturally at one with the new rhythm that has to be adopted. How rapid is adaptation under these circumstances? There have been a number of scientific studies of this situation; a good example is that of Klein *et al.* (1970). Twelve experienced pilots carried out twelve-minute flights on a flight simulator at two hour intervals throughout the day and night from 9 a.m. to 9 a.m. the following day. These twenty-four hour test periods were repeated on two days in Germany and then, following a flight to U.S.A. on days 1, 3, 5, and 8 in the new time zone eight hours behind the one they had left. After seventeen days they returned to Germany and carried out the same routine. Figure 6 shows deviation from average flying performance on the simulator (+ ve equals impaired) during the various points of the experiment. The first point to note is the clarity of the normal circadian cycle of performance. The test was one of moderate duration but it was operated many times during the course of the study so that it qualifies as a long duration exercise, which the pilots would find complex but also repetitive and rela-

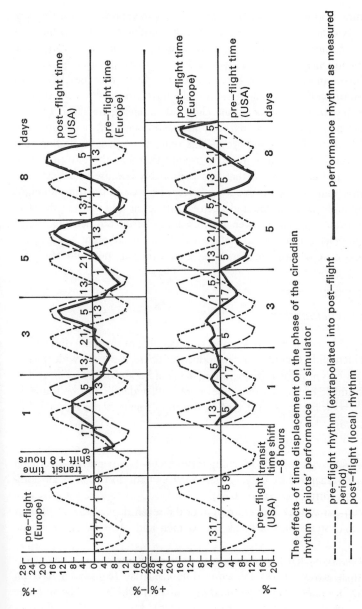

The effects of time displacement on the phase of the circadian rhythm of pilots' performance in a simulator

Fig. 6   Adaptation of pilots' simulator performance to phase shift following a flight from Germany to U.S.A. (top half) and back (bottom half). The heavy line represents true measurements: the dotted line shows where the normal (pre-flight) rhythm would have fallen had it continued during the post-flight days. (from Klein *et al.* 1970)

tively uninteresting. With such curves it is easy to see how at first the new external cycle battles with the old internal one producing a curve which is a resultant of the two influences. This continues until the performance pattern finally snaps almost totally into the new rhythm, although vestiges of the European cycle were still present after eight days in the U.S.A. On the return much the same happened and the now entrained U.S.A. rhythm had to revert to the European one eight hours ahead; however, the disorganization cycle was more marked and lasted longer before performance snapped back to the original cycle. This reflects the general finding that West to East flights produce more disorganization than those from East to West. Klein *et al.* point out that this is probably because the West–East trips, being night ones, involve loss of sleep, because in catching up eight hours the night is truncated and sleep is difficult as one lands at the start of a European day. The answer would seem to lie in commencing West–East flights early in the day so that even with the loss of eight hours it will be sleeping time when passengers land, even if they are not quite ready for sleep.

Adaptation in industry

As a preamble to this section we must consider at least the main dimensions along which shift systems vary in industry. There is a very wide variety of shift systems at present in operation; we could not possibly go into all or even a number of the common ones here. Fuller details can be found in Murrell's book (1965, ch. 19), and in the supplement to the recent P.I.B. report (1970).

There are four main dimensions of shift systems:

1 *Two Shift* systems use a Morning (often 06.00–14.00) and an Afternoon (often 14.00–22.00) shift only. *Three Shift* systems incorporate an additional Night shift (often 22.00–06.00).

2 *Continuous* systems work throughout the seven days of the week. *Discontinuous* systems have a break for all men and plant usually over the weekend.

3 Continuous systems, as a rule, may have *stabilized* shifts, when a particular shift always works the same time each day (e.g. seven days on 'Mornings'), or they may have *rotating* shifts (of which the Naval Three Man System is an example, see pp. 255–257). Here the times of work 'rotate' around the clock each day or at intervals of very few days, so that each day or each few days a man works different hours.

4 Discontinuous systems, as a rule, may have *alternating* shifts where people change at regular intervals, often of one week, from one stabilized shift (say 'Mornings') to another (say 'Nights') the weekend break intervening. *Permanent* shifts involve people remaining permanently on one of the two or three stabilized shifts, either, for example, 'Mornings', 'Afternoons', or 'Nights'.

In the previous section I described the work of Colquhoun and his associates in the laboratory. Let us now follow them into the field to see whether the body temperatures of miners adapt to their particular system of shifts. At Linby Colliery in Nottinghamshire, they found a standard Discontinuous, Stabilized, Weekly Alternating, Three Shift system in operation. In other words, the men worked from Monday to Friday, had the weekend off, and changed shifts each week. The question was whether body temperature, taken orally, would reveal adaptation to the abnormal hours of work within the five weekdays that each shift was worked. In the two shifts calling for abnormal sleeping times, the Morning and the Night, some evidence for adaptation appeared and was more pronounced for the older workers. On the Night shift the modification, as in the laboratory, took the form of a flattening of the normal curve rather than an inversion. Colquhoun and Edwards were careful to point out the inadequacies of measurement in this setting due to unpredictable changes in the manning of particular shifts selected for measurement and unavoidable variation in the times of measurement. They rightly call for more studies of the same kind involving larger numbers of men and different shift systems. Would men on permanent nights, for example, spend so much of their working hours with body temperatures lower than normal, or would some degree of permanent adaptation have occurred? An answer to this question has been provided, in a different setting, by van Loon (1963). He recorded body temperatures of three young men producing parts for typewriters. Normally they worked a day shift from 8.00 a.m. to 5.15 p.m., but were asked to work a night shift for thirteen weeks to clear arrears. The hours were 10.30 p.m. to 7.30 a.m. on the five weekdays. The three men all showed short-term adaptation to the night routine during the week, only to lose it when they returned to normal life during their weekend off. There was thus little evidence of long-term adaptation to the 'permanent' night routine simply because it was not permanent.

Under certain conditions, however, it appears that truly permanent night work can exist. Lobban (1965) was able to examine the potassium excretion level of permanent night shift workers in the mines of Longyearbyen,

Spitzbergen, North Norway. Here there is continual darkness during the months of November, December and January, and continuous daylight during the summer months. Potassium excretion, which shows a normal circadian fluctuation similar to that of body temperature, was 'perfectly entrained to the activity pattern, being reversed in relation to normal working time, throughout the year'. Presumably this adaptation was achieved because the inverted pattern of life penetrated into the leisure hours and activities of the night shift, due to the lack of any light/dark cycle for much of the year.

Comment

Laboratory, time zone and field studies combine to show that within a week or less people can adapt almost completely to a phase shift in the circadian cycle, if the external surroundings change in step, as happens when we travel across time zone boundaries. If surroundings remain locked in the old rhythm, however, as in shift working, the adaptation even over two weeks is only partial. Whether this adaptation would become more complete with time is an important but as yet unanswered question.

The foregoing analysis of laboratory and field studies suggests that under present shift systems, most, if not all, night work is being carried out by people whose psychological levels are ill-adapted to an inverted routine and who are therefore working well below their normal levels of efficiency. Laboratory work also predicts that their sleep cannot be very good either. Webb and Agnew (1967) have shown that sleep during the day is physiologically different from that taken at night. It is shorter and contains fewer of the EEG patterns which normally characterize sleep which is remembered as good (Rechtschaffen, Hauri and Zeitlin 1966). Thus sleep may be inadequate in both quality and quantity. Loss of sleep is another factor which can impair working efficiency even when sleep is reduced by as little as one third on two nights (Wilkinson 1969). More important, the impact of loss of sleep is particularly marked when work is repetitive (Wilkinson 1965), is carried on for prolonged periods (Wilkinson 1958), is lacking in incentive (Wilkinson 1961), and takes place during the low points of the circadian cycle (Wilkinson 1970). Shift working with high overtime in heavily automated production lines appears to present a coalescence of much that can be unfortunate for working efficiency. Both the soil and the seed of fatigue are there. On scientific evidence, limited though it is then, most of today's shift systems should be thoroughly bad for the health of the worker and his output.

Let us see if it really is as bad as this in practice when we ask the people concerned and examine records of health and output.

Shift systems in practice

Non-permanent shift systems

As a result of a questionnaire-based study of nearly 1800 workers embracing a number of industrial units in the Netherlands, Dirken (1966) concluded that 'for subjective well-being in both its somatic and psychological aspects shift work can in general probably hardly be called a problem'. The questionnaire consisted of fifty-eight questions of a Yes/No type about complaints, the items resembling those of the Cornell Medical Health Questionnaire and of neuroticism inventories. It was filled out by 614 shift and 1168 non-shift workers. Whether the former term included all kinds or simply those on alternating shifts is not clear. Nevertheless, the result is surprising in light of what laboratory findings predict. Dirken offers the explanation that some of the adverse effects of shift work may be veiled by self-selection: those who are unable to stand it will have returned to day work so that to some extent shift workers may represent an élite in terms both of their health and of their efficiency on the job. Wedderburn (1967) asked 174 manual workers in a steel works the direct question, 'On the whole, how do you feel about working shifts?' 54 per cent liked them mainly because they provided more time off, but also possibly because they earned more money. 33 per cent had no preference. 13 per cent did not like working shifts. The main reason for their dislike was the interference with their social activities particularly at the weekend. The shifts they preferred were the ones which offended least in this respect, namely discontinuous rather than continuous ones, rapidly rather than slowly alternating ones, and the morning and night rather than the afternoon shift (which prevented going out in the evening). These preferences constitute almost a conspiracy against the adaptation to night work, so necessary on biological grounds if inefficiency at night is to be avoided. However, it might be argued that, since adaptation can only be achieved by a permanently inverted routine permeating both work and leisure activities, and since this only seems obtainable in the northern reaches of Norway, perhaps it is best biologically as well as in terms of the workers' preference to adopt the other extreme, namely a rapid alternation of shifts with weekends free where possible. As this system does not give people time to adapt to night work it spares them the trouble of losing their adaptation when they return to days!

There have been a number of studies of sickness records among shift workers. A typical finding is that of Taylor (1967) who found that continuous weekly alternating three shift workers had a significantly *lower* rate of sickness than day workers doing similar jobs. This may possibly be due to a form of medical selection following the drop-out rate of those shift workers who found the routine too much for them. Taylor, however, places more emphasis on another explanation: he found that shift workers regard themselves as a rather special group of people more involved in their work than day workers, and operating in smaller well-knit social groups providing both a sense of security and high level of morale. While this is probably true, it makes it very difficult to make valid comparisons of the health of shift and non-shift workers.

The problem may be approached obliquely by studying the sleep of shift workers; fortunately most questionnaires contain items on this point and are surprisingly unanimous to the effect that the sleep of shift workers is frequently reported as inferior in both quality and quantity to that of people working during the day, although a negative report by Tune (1969) provides a striking exception to this. A clue may be provided by a particularly important report by Thiis-Evensen (1967) who compared the housing conditions of the people he approached. Those who owned their own houses supported Tune's finding of no important differences, but among those in poor housing 73 per cent of shift workers as compared with 18 per cent of day workers reported insomnia as a problem. On the basis of this finding Thiis-Evensen labels noise during the day as one of the root problems of shift working and calls for sympathetic design of accommodation to ensure that the sleep of shift workers during the day shall be protected from interruption as far as possible.

Working efficiency is difficult to assess under factory conditions. Full records of output are difficult to obtain, and when they are available it is difficult to distinguish the influence of shift systems from the many other factors which can cause production to vary. What information we have, however, supports the laboratory prediction of reduced efficiency when work is being carried out at night. Bjerner, Holm and Swenssen (1955) have carried out the most comprehensive study. They gained access to the logging records in a gas works covering the years 1912 to 1931. The shift system was the conventional Discontinuous, Weekly Alternating, Three Shift one. Figure 7 shows the number of errors made in logging during the course of the three eight-hour shifts, Morning, Afternoon and Night, in

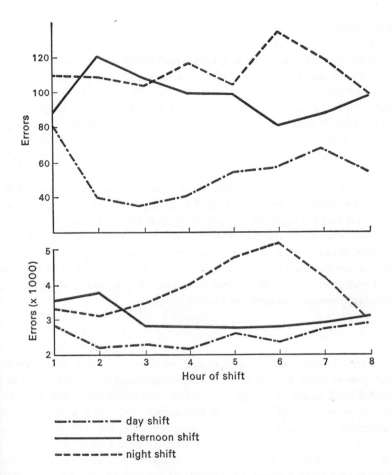

Fig. 7 Total logging errors made in each hour on three shifts in a paper mill (above) and gas works (below). (Data adapted from Murrell 1965)

three separate establishments. Efficiency during the night shift was reduced by between about 10 per cent and 40 per cent. In a shorter but basically similar study by Browne (1950) the delay in answering calls on the part of the teleprinter switchboard operators was about 50 per cent greater during the night shift. Lastly, in a study of rapidly alternating (two-day) shift workers Gavrilescu *et al.* (1966) administered performance tests before, during and after each shift. Again people were less efficient during the night and, to a lesser extent, the afternoon shifts.

Unfortunately none of these studies allows direct comparison of the output of shift and day workers: they merely provide comparisons of night and day shifts within shift workers. The superiority of the day shifts in the comparison, however, may perhaps be regarded as the best indication that, were it possible to keep other things equal, working conditions, health, ability, and so on, a comparison of day with alternating shift workers would favour the non-shift men as regards their ability to work efficiently.

On the other hand, the study of attitudes towards alternating shift systems reveals surprisingly, that on the whole people like them, providing evenings and weekends are not interfered with too much. This is not what the laboratory forebodings of low efficiency, lost sleep and ill health would predict, unless, of course, these considerations are not uppermost in the minds of either workers or management when they contemplate the undoubted short-term advantages of shift working: higher earnings, more free time, and for management lower fixed costs.

Stabilized (permanent) shift systems

The scientist condemns alternating shift systems because they do not allow the body to adapt a stable sleep/work/play cycle either of a normal or inverted kind. Grant this adaptation and biological objections disappear. In theory permanent shift systems should achieve this, since whatever shift is worked, the morning, the afternoon or the night, the body will eventually adapt to the changed routine. As we have seen, there is no guarantee of this when the surrounding stimuli remain synchronized to the normal twenty-four hour rhythm. In practice, as we saw in van Loon's (1963) study, a return to the normal cycle during days off will restrict even partial adaptation on the part of permanent night shift workers. There are further difficulties of a social and domestic nature, well summarized by Mott (1965). These problems are associated with afternoon and night shifts wherever they occur, but they are more pronounced when a permanent routine perpetuates them. From an extensive range of investigation Mott found, broadly speaking, that afternoon shifts restricted people's roles as parents, while night shifts restricted marital roles. Little imagination is needed to picture the day of a family in which father returns home from work at 7 a.m., the children go to school at 8 a.m. Father has a meal at 8.30 and gets to bed about 9.30, while mother starts the housework, which cannot always be a silent process. At 4 p.m. the children return from school, waking their father prematurely. The evening is reasonably normal except that it has to end early when father leaves for work at 9 p.m. and mother goes to bed. On permanent afternoon shifts father may never see his children on weekdays during school term. He is asleep before they go to school in the morning and at work when they return and for the whole evening. Clearly for many people these difficulties and frustrations will outweigh any biological advantages of permanent afternoon or night shifts.

But equally there may be other people for whom these social and domestic difficulties may be less, say a married pair without children and both on nights. Some time ago Vernon (1940) described the life of some permanent night shift workers in a Welsh steelworks; surprisingly they showed no undue signs of ill health. As regards output, both Bonjer (1960) and Bjerner, Holm and Swensson (1955) report that permanent night shift workers do rather better than those on other shifts. All these suggestions, however, are vulnerable to attack on the grounds that night workers may be a self-selected and superior group, the less robust and the less efficient having dropped out. This argument is difficult to counter without records from the same individuals before, during and after a period of permanent night work, and such records appear difficult to find. Questionnaire studies of social and domestic life are less subject to these weaknesses, and two good examples are those of Brown (1957) and Mott (1965). Both suggest that neither the social integration nor the sleeping ability are as disturbed on permanent night work as on alternating shifts.

One of the most convincing indications of people's attitudes is what they do when left free to make a choice. De la Mare and Walker (1968) found this situation among a group of telegraph operators who had a considerable degree of choice as to which shift (in a discontinuous weekly alternating, three shift system) they wished to work each week. This degree of choice was achieved by allowing the workers to exchange shifts so that, for example, if a man wished to work all nights he could trade his afternoon and his morning shifts with other people's 'nights'. The histogram in figure 8 shows the numbers of men electing to spend various percentages of their time on night work. Many people rejected the alternating system in favour of a stabilized one, working either all days or all nights. The important point here is that there does seem to be a considerable proportion of the workers who are quite prepared to work nights on a permanent basis. Given enough to man the whole night shift, the problems of twenty-four-hour working might be greatly reduced. As de la Mare and Walker point out, if the night work is manned by a permanent night shift, then the two day

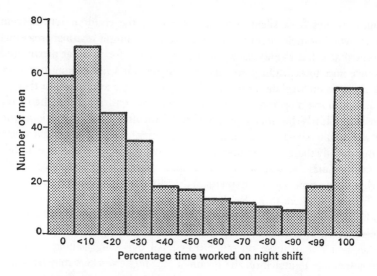

Fig. 8 The effect of allowing men to exchange shifts in an alternating three shift system: distribution of the population in terms of the percentage time spent working nights (which equalled 35 per cent for everyone before any exchanges). (From de la Mare and Walker 1968)

shifts can be handled by an alternating system so that no one has to work the unpopular afternoon shift, with its loss of evening activity, for more than, say, two days at a time. This compromise samples from both extremes of the range of alternation: rapid alternation during the day shifts where problems of adaptation are at a minimum, and no alternation at all during the night shifts, where adaptation to the inverted routine is all-important. This system, the Permanent Night, Double Day System, which Walker (1970) describes as 'uncommon', is the one most likely to win approval from both workers and scientists, and would seem to be greatly superior to many of those in operation at present. The main problem in implementing it may be that of recruiting enough permanent night workers. Higher pay and more relaxed conditions of work can certainly help to encourage more of the population to join this group, but more important in the long term may be the willingness of public authorities to regard permanent night workers as an important growing section of the community who must be catered for as such. Probably the greatest need is for sympathetic design of accommodation. If they are to sleep adequately by day, it is important that these people should be insulated from the noises of the day, especially in crowded urban environments. Second, the marked group consciousness of permanent night workers should be encouraged by the provision of appropriate social clubs, and community facilities, which would of course be open (including the weekend) at the times most convenient for them.

To remain competitive a modern technological state may have to accept an increasing degree of twenty-four hour working of men and machines. If this is to be done efficiently it seems very likely that there will be increasing dependence upon the permanent night shift workers. It behoves government and local authorities to recognize the growing importance of these people and provide appropriately for them.

Summary

The problem is that man has evolved and been trained to a twenty-four-hour cycle of work during the day and sleep during the night, whereas modern technological systems increasingly demand that machines be manned throughout the twenty-four hours. Are the current ways of organizing this round-the-clock working the best from the point of view of the health, happiness and stability of the population, as well as its working efficiency? The twenty-four-hour rhythm of body temperature and performance are described with reference to both laboratory and field studies, and the degree and speed with which both of them adapt to night work or other abnormal routines is assessed. Much depends upon the world around and whether it is geared to the new time routine (as when one crosses a time zone, flying from Europe to U.S.A.) or not (as in night shift work). As regards performance, the kind of work and its duration are also important, suggesting that loss of sleep may be at least as influential as body rhythms in causing ill effects through abnormal working hours. The correlation between performance and body temperature is assessed with a view to using the latter as a guide to working efficiency in the field where the effects of different shift systems cannot be assessed directly by measuring output.

On the whole the message from the biological studies is that many of the shift systems currently in use are bad for output and for health, particularly in terms of the amount of sleep lost. Examining the attitudes of workers and such records as can be obtained the impression is that these shifts are not so bad in practice. However, this may be because shift workers comprise a self-selected élite, thus distorting comparisons between them and non-shiftworkers based on records of output, sickness, absenteeism and accidents. Overall the view is taken that, although alternating shift systems are accepted (probably because they provide more pay and more free time), the effects of these routines upon health and efficiency may still be harmful. Stabilized shift systems, where people remain permanently on one shift, are more satisfactory, particularly the permanent night shift. A system of rapidly alternating morning and afternoon shifts combined with a permanent night shift is supported. The problem of obtaining sufficient permanent night-shift workers could be eased by two moves: first, and most important, reduce the ill-effects of disturbed sleep during the day by providing housing with better sound insulation in the bedroom. Second, provide appropriate round-the-clock community and entertainment facilities for permanent night workers to encourage them to follow their inverted routine even during their days off.

References

ASCHOFF, J. (1969) 'Desynchronisation and Resynchronisation of Human Circadian Rhythm', *Aerospace Medicine*, **40**, 844–9.

AX, A. and LUBY, F. D. (1961) 'Autonomic Responses to Sleep Deprivation', *Archives of General Psychiatry*, **4**, 55–9.

BJERNER, B., HOLM, A. and SWENSSON, A. (1955) 'Diurnal Variation in Mental Performance', *British Journal of Industrial Medicine*, **12**, 103–10.

BLAKE, M. J. F. (1967) 'Relationship between Circadian Rhythm of Body Temperature and Intraversion and Extraversion', *Nature*, **215**, 896–7.

BLAKE, M. J. F. and CORCORAN, D. W. J. (1970) 'Introversion–Extraversion and Circadian Rhythm' in Colquhoun (ed.) *Proceedings of the NATO symposium on the effects of diurnal rhythm and loss of sleep on human performance* London, English Universities Press.

BONJER, F. H. (1960) 'Physiological Aspects of Shiftwork', *Proceedings of the 13th International Congress of Occupational Health*.

BROWN, H. (1957) 'Day and Night and Three-shift Working', *Personnel Management*, **39**, 150–6.

BROWNE, G. (1950) *Patterns of British Life: a Study of Certain Aspects of the British People at Home, at Work and a Compilation of some Relevant Statistics* London, Hulton.

CHILES, W. D., ALLUISI, E. A. and ADAMS, O. S. (1968) 'Work Schedules and Performance during Confinement', *Human Factors*, **10**, 143–95.

COLQUHOUN, W. P., BLAKE, M. J. F. and EDWARDS, R. S. (1968a) 'Experimental Studies of Shiftwork I', *Ergonomics*, **11**, 437–53.

COLQUHOUN, W. P., BLAKE, M. J. F. and EDWARDS, R. S. (1968b) 'Experimental Studies of Shiftwork II', *Ergonomics*, **11**, 527–46.

COLQUHOUN, W. P., BLAKE, M. J. F. and EDWARDS, R. S. (1969) 'Experimental Studies of Shiftwork III', *Ergonomics*, **12**, 865–82.

DIRKEN, J. M. (1966) 'Industrial Shift Work: Decrease in Well-being and Specific Effects', *Ergonomics*, **9**, 115–24.

GAVRILESCU, N. et al. (1966) 'Control-board Shift Work Turning Every Two Days', *Proceedings of the XV International Congress of Occupational Medicine*, **4**, 103–6.

KLEIN, N. K. et al. (1970) 'Circadian Rhythms of Pilot's Efficiency and Effects of Multiple Time Zone Travel', *Aerospace Medicine*, **41**, 125–32.

KLEITMAN, N. (1963) *Sleep and Wakefulness* (2nd ed.) Chicago, University of Chicago Press.

KLEITMAN, N. and JACKSON, D. P. (1950) 'Body Temperature and Performance under Different Routines, *Journal of Applied Physiology*, **3**, 309–28.

LOBBAN, M. C. (1965) 'Time, Light and Diurnal Rhythm' in Edholm, O. E. and Bacharach, A. L. (eds) *The Physiology of Human Survival* London, Academic Press.

DE LA MARE, G. and WALKER, J. (1968) 'Factors Influencing the Choice of Shift Rotation', *Occupational Psychology*, **42**, 1–21.

MOTT, P. E. (1965) *Shiftwork – the Social, Psychological and Physical Consequences* Ann Arbor, Michigan, University of Michigan Press.

MURRELL, K. F. H. (1965) *Ergonomics: Man in his Working Environment* London, Chapman and Hall.

NATIONAL BOARD FOR PRICES AND INCOMES (1970) *Hours of Work, Overtime and Shift Working*, Report no. 161, HMSO.

RECHTSCHAFFEN, J., HAURI, P. and ZEITLIN, M. (1966) 'Auditory Awakening Thresholds in REM and NREM Sleep Stages', *Perceptual and Motor Skills*, **22**, 927–42.

RUTENFRANZ, J., ASCHOFF, J. and MANN, H. (1970) 'The Influence of a Cumulative Sleep Deficit and Length of Preceding Sleep Period on Multiple-choice Reaction Time at Different Times of the Night' in Colquhoun, W. P. (ed.) *Proceedings of the NATO symposium on the effects of diurnal rhythm and loss of sleep on human performance* London, English Universities Press.

TAYLOR, P. J. (1967) 'Shift and Day Work', *British Journal of Industrial Medicine*, **24**, 93–102.

THIIS-EVENSEN, E. (1967) 'Shift Work and Health', *Industrial Medicine*, **23**, 493–7.

TUNE, G. S. (1969) 'Sleep and Wakefulness in a Group of Shift Workers', *British Journal of Industrial Medicine*, **26**, 54–8.

VAN LOON, J. H. (1963), 'The Diurnal Rhythm of Body Temperatures in Night Workers', *Ergonomics*, **6**, 267–73.

VERNON, P. E. (1940), *The Measurement of Abilities* London, University of London Press.

WALKER, K. F. (1970) 'Workers' Participation in Management: Concepts and Reality', delivered to the Second World Congress of the International Industrial Relations Association.

WEBB, W. B. and AGNEW, H. W. (1967) 'Sleep Cycling within Twenty-four-hour Periods', *Journal of Experimental Psychology*, 74, 158–60.

WEDDERBURN, A. A. I. (1967) 'Social Factors in Satisfaction with Rapidly Rotating Shifts', *Occupational Psychology*, 41, 85–107.

WILKINSON, R. T. (1958) *The Effects of Sleep Loss on Performance*, M.R.C. Applied Psychology Research Unit 1, Report no. 323/58.

WILKINSON, R. T. (1961) 'Interaction of Lack of Sleep with Knowledge of Results, Repeated Testing and Individual Differences', *Journal of Experimental Psychology*, 62, 263–71.

WILKINSON, R. T. (1965) 'Sleep Deprivation' in Edholm, O. G. and Bacharach, A. L. (eds.) *The Physiology of Human Survival* London, Academic Press.

WILKINSON, R. T. (1969) 'Sleep Deprivation Tests for Partial and Selective Sleep Deprivation' in Abt, L. A. and Reiss (eds.) *Progress in Clinical Psychology*, vol. 7, Grune.

WILKINSON, R. T. (1970) 'Sleep Deprivation – A Review' in Colquhoun, W. P. (ed) *Proceedings of the NATO Symposium on the Effects of Diurnal Rhythm and Loss of Sleep on Human Performance* London, English Universities Press.

WILKINSON, R. T. and EDWARDS, R. S. (1968) 'Stable Hours and Varied Work as Aids to Efficiency', *Psychonomic Science*, 13, 205–6.

16   The conditions of work

E. H. Phelps-Brown

The conditions of work are central to the problem of industrial relations. That problem arises from the wage-earner's discontent, and this is not created by particular grievances nor assuageable by particular benefits, but pervasive and persistent, drawn in by him with the very air he breathes. In several ways intelligible to us all his working life is inherently unsatisfying or irritating to him.

For one thing, 'master and servant' was long the plain English for 'employer and employed', and the usage shows how the relation between the two parties to a contract of employment was felt to be inherently different from that in a contract of sale, even in the days when employment was on the small and simple scale, when the wheelwright or blacksmith just took on a man to help him in his shop, or the master mason who had undertaken to build a house got his team together. The distinctive marks of the contract of employment were that it was usually made between men of unequal resources, and that the workman put himself under the direction of the employer.

The inequality of resources makes the workman liable to get the worst of the bargain. The trouble is not, as is sometimes said, that his labour is perishable, so that every sale of labour is a forced sale: for the use of the employer's equipment is equally perishable, and the day it stands idle for lack of labour is lost as much as the day the workman is unemployed. What puts him at a disadvantage is rather that, in practice if not in principle, the employer has more in hand to live on while he bargains, so that he is not under such pressure to come to terms. As Adam Smith said, 'A landlord, a farmer, a master manufacturer, or merchant, though they did not employ a single workman, could generally live a year or two upon the stocks which they had already acquired. Many workmen could not subsist a week, few could subsist a month, and scarce any a year without employment. In the long run the workman may be as necessary to his master as his master is to him; but the necessity is not so immediate.'

But this brings no disadvantage to the workman if he is selling his labour in a wide market , or if, whatever the extent of the market, business

P H E L P S - B R O W N, E. H. (1959) from 'The Conditions of Work', in *The Growth of British Industrial Relations* London, Macmillan, 98–113.

is profitable and the demand for labour brisk. A unit of War Loan sold on the Stock Exchange will command the price of the day like any other, even though its own seller is distressed: it is only in the narrow market that the forced sale is liable to have to take the lower price. Even the workman who would be starving within the week if unemployed could get not a job only but a rise, if his labour at the going rate would be highly profitable to employers, and several were competing for it. But the workman has not been able to rely on either of these saving conditions. Because at any one time he wanted to find work within reach of his home, and work moreover in his own trade, he might well have only one or two employers to deal with; he could offer himself to more if he could go farther afield or take up another sort of work, and many a man did this, but it had its costs and limitations. Trade was sometimes brisk, but not always, and when it was not, instead of two employers after one man, there were two men, and more than two, after one employer. The risks to which a way of life is subject colour even its sheltered reaches, and the workman who is for the time being in a wide and rising labour market still sees himself as inherently a suppliant not able to argue about the terms of an engagement if he is offered one at all.

From the middle of the eighteenth century onwards he was the more likely to form that image of his position, because the competition for jobs was continually sustained by the increase of population. Decade after decade the working population rose by not less than ten per cent, sometimes as much as fourteen, even after the emigrants had gone. Let the labour market reach equilibrium, with supply equal to demand at the going rate of wages: within the year there would be jobless men trying to get places. At times of boom, it is true, the demand for labour rose faster even than that ever-rising supply; but the other side of that medal was the depression, when the demand fell absolutely, and there would have been unemployment even if the number seeking work had not risen meanwhile: but it had. Often there were men literally waiting at the gate for the employer to take on at the going rate of wages the moment he wanted them. That was the labour market as the wage-earner saw it. It was once pointed out that a difference of sixpence either way in the balance of income and outlay makes all the difference between serenity and misery. The labour market is like that. Whether there is one more vacancy than there are applicants or one more applicant than there are vacancies decides which of two worlds the wage-earner shall live in, and makes all the difference between two industrial systems. It was in the system of excess applicants that the British wage-earner saw his own life set.

He therefore thought of the employer as inherently having the whip hand over him, so long as he stood alone. Not always by any means, yet more often than not, that was so in fact. Only in a broad market could he reckon on a wage that would be independent of his own power to hold out in the bargaining. Only in the rising phase of the trade cycle was the demand for labour brisk enough to remove the continual overspill of rising population. Where the market was not broad and the demand was not brisk, he needed his job more urgently than the employer needed him.

Though it was in the wage bargain that he dreaded the employer's whip hand most, he might also feel it as work went on day by day. The second distinctive feature of the contract of employment is that the workman puts himself under the employer's direction. It is this that distinguishes the employee from the sub-contractor. The difficulty is only partly that the employee has to do without the independence, spontaneity, and agreeable irregularity, that a man can enjoy who is working on his own. True, herein lay one of the reasons why, when factories were first set up, country people were loath to go into them. They were accustomed to great exertions, but only at times and seasons, or as they chose themselves; to rising at four in the morning often enough, but not early every morning when the hooter blew. Yet this sort of regularity and discipline becomes accustomed in time. Though a few people never can accept it, most men can, and without resentment, because they see it as a requirement that arises out of the situation and not out of any one man's love of power: tasks have to be carried out systematically and orders have to be given wherever men work together. What wage-earners generally resent is not having to work under another man's direction but working for his purpose and his profit. The end for which they have to work is his and he has chosen it without consulting them. They are taken on solely to serve it, and will be laid off as soon as they cease to. It is a short step from this to the conviction that the relationship is inherently one-sided, that the employer is getting something out of them that has no counterpart in what they get from him, in a word that they are being exploited.

But is not this only a peevish illusion? is not the relation essentially reciprocal, a partnership between two men neither of whom can get on without the other? What jobs would the wage-earners have now if the business had not been built up? and so long as they want to stay in those jobs, what prospects of betterment have they save as the business thrives? Each party can prosper only as the other does. That is profoundly true, and yet the conditions of the wage-earner's working life can easily persuade him of the opposite. He can seriously believe that he can prosper only in so far as he can keep the bosses on the run.

One simple reason for this is that at any one time, the product of an industry being what it is, the employees' receipts can be increased only if the proprietors' is diminished: indeed, if we think of proportionate shares, it is always and for ever true that the only way to raise the one is to reduce the other. The now familiar instance of the cake reminds us of the pitfall there, but in all the vast threshing out of social problems before 1914 there was an extraordinary absence of the notion that the cake could be made bigger. In any case, at any one time of bargaining its size is limited and future increases are uncertain: what one party gains here and now seems simply to be taken from the other. It is an easy inference that the employer would like to reduce wages in order to increase his profit. We are all of us apt to project into others impulses that we dare not acknowledge in ourselves, and see those impulses as attacking us from without through those others' agency. For any wage-earner who has acquisitive and aggressive impulses to project, the employer at the bargaining table provides a natural lodgement and bearer.

The sense of a head-on collision of interests is heightened by the very nature of profit. Wages connote deserts, but all down the ages profits have attracted the critical attention of the moralist, because somehow they obstinately appear to be unearned and undeserved. This is so at the most superficial level, simply because they arise as a surplus and there is no contract stating the service for which they are rendered: but a surplus is inherently suspect of being unnecessary. It is fair to reply that profits are the return to factors of capital and enterprise that are no less necessary to the creation of the product than is labour itself. But when one penetrates that much deeper, the difficulty still remains. For the services of putting up money and getting the business going were provided in the past, and yet are found to be levying a perpetual rent-charge on the annual product. It is clear that the buildings and machinery contribute to that product, but were not they in their day the product of labour, and do they not have to be continually renewed by labour? That management plays a necessary present part is no less clear, but managers receive salaries. What is not clear is why those who provided the original funds should go on receiving a return, they and their heirs and assigns in perpetuity.

Once again, it is fair to point out that since savings cost an effort, they have to be paid for, as certainly wage-earners themselves allow when they are asked to contribute to War Savings; and that since it is savings alone that make the construction of equipment possible, their use is unproductive and commands a return in that right. Such a return takes the form, let us say, of an agreement to repay £110 in one year's time for £100 lent now; and if at the end of the year the capital sum is still required in the business, it may be convenient to both parties for the lender to receive £10 and allow the £100 to remain for a further year in return for a further £10; and so on. And this does make sense: there can be no objection to the annually renewed dividends to shareholders, unless one objects to the giving and taking of any interest at all. But still the argument seems contrived; what is written on the face of things is all against it. The profit-taker (not to write profiteer) is like the actually innocent man who happens to be found with a gory knife in his hand not far from a bleeding corpse: given a calm attention and a measure of credence he will be able to establish his innocence, but appearances are against him.

If readiness to believe the worst of profits needed any fostering, moreover, it would get it from the inequality of hazard between employer and employed. The employer has his capital at risk, or some of it; the wage-earner commonly has his whole livelihood. We have already seen one instance and advertisement of that, conspicuous and frequently renewed: the workman was exposed to injury, and sometimes death, as the employer was not, yet until 1897 he or his dependents were commonly unable to enforce the payment of any compensation by the employer. But the same inequality shows itself in the human cost of the rise and fall of industrial fortunes. Shipyards are built where there was once only a fishing harbour; workers come in, street after street extends, the migrant makes a home there and puts down roots. Now the trade is depressed; very likely this is not the employers' fault, but it is they who decide to close the yards down; and the men whom they drew in and who made their homes there say, 'for all they care we can rot'. What would the morale of a battalion be, if the men knew that in any tight corner the officers would take the unit transport and clear out, leaving them on their flat feet? It was the quest for profit that built the town, it is the drying up of profit that has ruined it. So it has come to seem to the wage-earner that the very destinies of his life may be decided for him by the profit-taker. What is more, he has no power to reciprocate. From time to time management calls on him to accept some change, to make some effort, and why? always in order that higher profits may be earned; but he can put no pressure on management in order that higher wages may be earned. So long as his work adds something to profit, he is used; let it cease to, and he will be thrown out. Profit-seeking and the right to hire and fire seem to be bound up together: the boss can sack you and you cannot sack the boss.

There is an answer to this, and a substantial one: the contract of employment can be terminated by either side; in practice, if a workman sees a chance of bettering himself, he will leave, sometimes without even the formality of notice; a business can be carried on only if it pays its employees sufficient to retain them in the presence of alternative opportunities. But that is not how things commonly appear to the wage-earner. Between his employer and himself he sees an inherent difference in power and status. The employer can discard him as he cannot discard the employer. He has that in mind when he considers how the employer makes his profit. Profit looks like the return to the whip hand.

The workman resents his subordination at the place of work more keenly when he is no longer one of a politically subordinate class, but has become a voter in a democracy. One of the unions' positivist sympathizers, Henry Crompton, put the point well in the 1870s. 'When the Radical manufacturers preached political change to the working classes,' he wrote, 'and set up before them political independence as a goal to strive for, they ought not to have been surprised to find that the ideas they had taught with reference to the outer civic actions were at once applied to the inner industrial life. . . . If the right aspiration for every citizen is to be independent and free, that is, not subject to arbitrary power but dependent only upon just laws, the same aspiration must inevitably appear right to him in his capacity as a workman' (Compton 1876, pp. 2–3).

The anxieties and resentments we have been considering are inherent in the very position of the wage-earner, but they are felt with very different intensity at different times and places, and they were less active so long as the average firm was still small. We can understand why. In the small firm, the master commonly worked, if not alongside the men as their leader in a common task, at least near by them, in daily contact with them, well known to them as a human being. He was not set apart from them by differences in manners and class, nor was his capital invested widely so as to insulate him from the misfortunes of the establishment where they worked for him: the slump that cost them their jobs laid him low too. The difference between them was in function more than in class. But the mere quantitative growth of scale brought a qualitative change in human relations. True, that growth was a necessary condition of higher productivity and so of higher real wages, and it brought with it other potentialities of benefit to the wage-earner; but in several ways its immediate effects on him were adverse.

One adverse effect arose simply from the numerical change in the ratio of employers to employed. The proportion of applicants to vacancies as a whole might not be changed, and the growth of industrial centres meanwhile would have brought more firms within the reach of any one workman there; but so far as a given number of jobs came to be administered by a smaller number of employers, each workman would know fewer employers personally. That would decrease a factor of security in his working life. The workman who knows a number of alternative employers personally will always have in mind whom he would turn to if he were in need of a job or found himself unfairly treated where he is now. By the same token, he will be personally known to a number of employers, and the man who has a local reputation as a good workman has little reason to fear unemployment or oppression. Relations of this kind add much to the security of workpeople in trades where the unit of employment is small, and may help to explain the little headway that trade unionism has ever made among shop assistants, domestic servants, and farm labourers. But as the representative unit grew in size, these links of personal knowledge were broken, and the wage-earner became more insecure.

At the same time he came to have less chance of becoming a master himself. Marshall remarked in the 1870s that in some districts more than half the employers had begun as workmen; but the economic forces that were raising the average size of the firm were also making it harder for the small man to get a start. That took away a source of hope, and hope is a vitamin without which most of us cannot live in health of mind. It is true that the workman had a new sort of advance open to him, namely working his way up inside the firm, but he had much less chance of achieving independence. It was natural that he should turn upon the employer he could not escape, and demand more from him. Gambling was said to be a growing evil: it meets a need of those who see no chance of bettering themselves by their own efforts.

As firms got bigger there was also bound to be less personal contact between master and man. Certainly where that contact existed in the small firm it was not always peaceful. There were masters who were renowned for their hot tempers and rough tongues; the angry workman could and did let the boss have it now and then. But all these rows were rows between one man and another, face to face, and the possibility of having them, far from causing anxiety, must have relieved and prevented it. We can see how this will have worked if we contrast what happens when the employer is remote, little seen around, hardly known as a man. At once the workman feels a sense of powerlessness and insecurity. He may have some minor difficulty that he could clear up readily enough if he could speak to the boss in person, but he finds himself confronted instead with a procedure, a channel. What he claims may be refused him by someone who expresses no personal opinion and can enter into no argument, because it conflicts with a ruling that has been laid down by a head office he has never seen; or he may just be told that his claim will be duly reported and the answer will be communicated to him in due course. In a South Wales valley the difference was noticed when the miner who had had a dispute with the deputy or under-manager could no longer walk across the fields and see the owner at the door of his house, but must deal with a manager who was tied down by instructions from the head office of the combine in Cardiff. This having to deal with a poker-faced man whose relation with you was dehumanized and straitjacketed was as infuriating as not being able to deal with the ultimate boss himself. But the fact that this boss was himself remote made for a special anxiety. Here was a source of power that could reach out and change all the workman's life, but that the workman himself could not get to know, understand and depend on, argue with. The position of the wage-earner in the big business might have been specially designed for the projection of paranoid anxieties. That the remote power is malevolent seems infinitely more probable than that it is kind. Let its intentions be of the best, it will be a miracle if they are understood.

Perhaps this is why the term 'absentee landlord' is practically a term of abuse. One could argue that if a man who lives in the village can fairly charge a rent for the use of his land, his removing to a distance cannot make the payment iniquitous; but the tenant is apt to distinguish. It is related that there was a landlord in Ireland who was not an absentee, but in the troubles two men were told off none the less to shoot him; they waited behind a wall to catch him on his way back from market, and when he did not come by at his usual time one said to the other 'Sure an' I hope nothin's happened to the dear old gentleman'. We find it much easier to expect the worst from people we do not meet than from those we do, especially when they have some power over us; and hate them accordingly. The value of the meeting does not lie in any cordiality it may generate but in its discharging the static anxiety that will otherwise be building up. In business the amount of personal contact varies inversely with the size of the firm; and the amount of anxiety directly. The source of the trouble does not lie in ill will, but simply in scale. As firms grow bigger, human relations in them become more difficult, simply because of size.

This growth as it went on in Britain before the First World War was accompanied by some changes in the type of the employer. One such became apparent, and opened a divide between him and his men, as soon as he ceased to take his own jacket off and labour alongside them. The work that was specially his to do as the firm grew was done in a different place, in different dress, and in different hours. The silk hat that he wears in the cartoons of the time he wore in common with some of his clerks, but still it marked him off from the men, and he commonly came to work later in the morning than they, and went in by a different and cleaner entrance. As he grew richer, moreover, there was a traditional upper class for him to enter, that was not so much in conflict with the industrial workmen, as cut off from them by differences in residence, speech, and sport. The sons and grandsons of the self-made man were even more likely than he to 'go county'. It was noticed how the motor-car increased the social distance between the employer and his workman by enabling him to move out into the country; the factory became the place where he made the money to support the life of a country gentleman. He and his family no longer worshipped on Sunday in the same church or chapel as his workmen. To them it was clearer than ever that he was not 'one of us' but 'one of them'.

This increase in social distance was accompanied by an increased disparity in training and ability. The masters in the small firms, taking them as a whole, will have had some superior qualities of character and mind to account for their having set themselves up and taken the lead as their men had not, but they had much the same start in life, and as long as they worked on the same scale their superior capacity could not be made manifest by any great difference of function or scope. As firms grew, however, the function of the employer became more distinctive, and the impact of his abilities wider. A profession of management arose. Its own requirements were ill-defined, but men entered it who had qualified in an established profession, law, engineering, accountancy. Technical training apart, the employer was increasingly likely to have had more general education than the wage-earner. There would still be incapable men among the employers, and men of high innate ability among the employed; but the growth in the size of the firm made it more likely everywhere that the posts of direction and management would be filled by men with more education and brains than their workpeople. Thereby it created a basic and obstinate problem of industrial relations. It is hard not to be jealous, and suspicious, of those who are visibly abler than oneself. In one way, equality was the conscience of the age in Church and state – the equality of all men before God, before the law, and in 'the verdict of democracy'; but how could there be equality in the dealings between bright men and dull men? The clear mind confronted with the stupidity that cannot even recognize its own interests can hardly express goodwill except by a self-imposed fairness and artificial patience that are felt, and resented, as condescension. The slow mind confronted with the quick one expects to be out-smarted, searches simple statements for hidden meanings, fears that to agree will reveal its own helplessness, and keeps its end up by being difficult. If you cooperate you may be taken for a ride. The way to hide your perplexity, uphold your interests, and protect your self-respect, is to be awkward.

But as the scale of business grew the personal employer sometimes disappeared altogether, and his place was taken by a board of directors. This brought its own difficulties. Often where the structure was formally that of a public company there was some one man, the chairman or managing director or general manager it might be, who figured for good reason in the workman's eye as the boss. But this was not necessarily so, and the decisions on which so much might depend for the workmen were taken in practice as well as principle by a board many of whose members were not working directors known in the shops, but representatives of this or that financial interest. It might even be hard for anyone in the business to know where the ultimate control really lay, for the immediately visible board might be only part of some system of interlocking or superimposed interests. Interests they were called, and as they became more remote from the workman he saw ever more clearly what they were an interest in: the sense of community of purpose was gone, and it seemed plain now that those who controlled the business were concerned only with what money they could make out of it. As management became separated from ownership, profits seemed more like rent, 'God's gift to sleeping man'. Put together the two notions there – that the workman is being used as a means to another man's end, and that this end is to take as much as possible out of the product – and what appears is the definition of exploitation and the bedrock of Marxism.

As the employer receded from the workshop, his place there was taken by managers of various levels, from the general manager or works manager down to the foreman. These were themselves employees, under instructions, under pressure. There was always the need for results to make them spur the workman on. They had their own jobs to keep, and had been told what showing was expected; they looked for promotion, and would be judged by their success in keeping output up and costs down. It is usually easier to be hard with other men when one does not deal with them directly but issues orders for others to enforce on them, and the remote employer was to that extent more likely to be hard. The manager or foreman who was himself disposed to press, or who feared he would miss promotion or even lose his job if he did not, could always put the blame on those above him. Remote and indirect control is biased towards inhumanity.

But it was not only the general increase in the size of the firm that was putting more strain on the manager: the changes in equipment and methods that had been coming with it were also asking more of him. Especially was this true of the foreman. So long as he was in charge of craftsmen he had had relatively little to do. The craftsman carried his methods in his own head, and had to be left to solve his problems in his own way and time; the foreman did not have to set work up for him nor provide him with aids, and he could no more usefully stand over him to urge him on than he could over a doctor making his diagnosis at the bedside. But as the craftsman's work was broken down into components that were entrusted to handymen or machinists, their work needed to be co-ordinated and assisted. The new machines they ran could perform automatically what had once depended on the trained hand, but only after they had been set up properly, a new and sometimes exacting task. As operations became repetitive the rate of output came to depend as never before on the sheer pace of the operator's application, and the foreman was expected to see that this was fast. He would hardly have been made a foreman unless he was able to learn his way quickly about the new machines, but what he needed to know about his new tasks of administration and man-management he could not pick up like that, and he was given no training to help him with it. His was a hard job: put in charge of men much like himself, given no training in administration, at once technician, rate-setter, and ganger, a shock absorber between the drive of management and the obsinacy of the men – no wonder if he was sometimes fearful of his authority, artful, harsh or unfair. For many men he was effectively the boss. 'In most works, in the engineering trade at least', one employer wrote in 1917 (quoted in Webb 1917, pp. 27–8), 'the whole industrial life of a workman is in the hands of his foreman. The foreman chooses him from among the applicants at the works gate; often he settles what wages he shall get; no advance of wage or promotion is possible except on his initiative; he often sets the piece-price and has power to cut it when he wishes; and, lastly, he almost always has unrestricted power of discharge. These great powers are exercised by men chosen generally for their energy and driving power. They are usually promoted workmen, with no very marked superiority in education, outlook, or sympathy over those whom they command. It is not surprising, therefore, that these powers are often abused; and a tyranny, both in matters of detail and principle, established, which the higher management, even if it has the desire, has very little power to soften or control.'

The other side of this medal was a harder life for the men. Some of them had lost the independence that craftsmanship gives, and with it the status that set them apart from mere hands. The more intelligent when reduced to repetitive operations lost the satisfaction that problem-solving, planning and building had given. All had more sense of being driven. The changes of the day had not yet brought in the moving belt or assembly line, but it was in these years that the spirit and method of workshop organization came in that were to be satirized in the nightmare factories of *À nous la liberté* and *Modern Times*. Alfred Williams, a poet and rural philosopher by bent, condemned himself to work for twenty years and more in the Great Western Railway engineering shops at Swindon. Writing of them in 1915, an embittered but observant witness (Williams 1915, p. 304), he said: 'A decade and a half ago one could come to the shed fearlessly, and with perfect complacence; work was a pleasure in comparison with what it is now. It was not that the toil was easy, though, as a matter of fact, it was not so exhausting as it is at present, but there was an entirely different feeling prevalent. The workman was not watched and timed at every little operation, and he knew that as the job had been one day so it would be the next. Now, however, every day brings fresh troubles from some quarter or other. The supervisory staff has been doubled or trebled, and they must do something to justify their existence. Before the workman can recover from one shock he is visited with another; he is kept in a state of continual agitation and suspense which, in time, operate on his mind and temper and transform his whole character.

'At one time old and experienced hands were trusted and respected, both by reason of their great knowledge of the work, acquired through many years, and as a kind of tacit recognition of their long connection with the firm, but now, when a man has been in the shed for twenty years, however young he may be, he is no longer wanted. There is now a very real desire to be rid of him. For one thing, his wages are high. In addition to this, he knows too much; he is not pliable. It is time he was shifted to make room for someone lower paid, more plastic and more ignorant of the inner workings of things.'

The belief that there were good old days that came to an end shortly before one reached man's estate oneself is recurrent in many ages, and is less likely to arise from any actual changes of the times than from those within the observer, and particularly from his own disappointment as the hopes of youth give way to the drag and plod of middle age. But what we know independently of the changes that were going on in size and management, machinery and methods in the quarter century before 1914 suggests that there was more than this common projection of inward disenchantment in the statement several men have made who worked in mine or factory then that the work which once had given pride and satisfaction had become a burden. In the interwar years Peter Donnelly was in the steelworks at Barrow-in-Furness. 'From what I was told by the old hands,' he has written (Donnelly 1950), 'I reached the conclusion that workmen in the early days of the steelworks had a better understanding of the nature of work and the nature and use of machines than is common now. . . . Work was not then considered as a necessary evil to be escaped from or whittled away and finally abolished. Men came to the steelworks to make something and making was a pleasure. Although the processes of industry had been broken down even then, the specialization of work was no more than an elementary study. No one had yet attempted to change the human notion that a man can do more work with the help of a machine, for the inhuman notion that a machine can produce more if the man can be integrated with it. . . . It was only by the men of my own age and younger ones, that work in the steelworks was strongly denounced as a vocation, or denied to be an integral part of life which could enrich life in any way, except by providing the money to pay for living.'

The stress that has been laid here on the effects of changes in the size of firms and in their management, equipment, and workshop practice, is a stress, and not an evenly weighted balance. Such a balance would find a place for all the workshops that remained small and all the trades that followed their traditional ways, as well as for all that was being done by good will and common sense in every walk of life to make new ways more tolerable and leaven industrial relations with mutual respect. But strong effects suggest strong causes. We have to explain why those who can prosper only as partners have so often been at daggers drawn, and why the wage-earner has so often chosen as his leaders men who were combative or obstinate by temperament. The stress laid here on what was galling to him in his working life is no more than commensurate with the resentment he has shown.

References

CROMPTON, H. (1876) *Industrial Conciliation* London, H. S. King.
DONNELLY, P. (1950) *The Yellow Rock: An Autobiography* London, Eyre and Spottiswoode.
WEBB, S. (1917) *The Works Manager Today* London, Longman.
WILLIAMS, A. (1915) *Life in a Railway Factory* London, Duckworth.

17   On the line

Huw Beynon

Working in a car plant involves coming to terms with the assembly line. 'The line never stops', you are told. Why not? '. . . don't ask. It *never* stops'. The assembly plant itself is huge and on two levels, with the paint shop on the one floor and the trim and final assembly departments below. The car shell is painted in the paint shop and passed by lift and conveyor to the first station of the trim assembly department. From this point the body shell is carried up and down the 500-yard length of the plant until it is finally driven off, tested, and stored in the car park.

Few men see the cars being driven off the line. While an assembly worker is always dealing with a moving car it is never moving under its own steam. The line – or 'the track' as some managers who have been 'stateside' refer to it – stands two feet above floor level and moves the cars monotonously, easily along. Walking along the floor of the plant as a stranger you are deafened by the whine of the compressed air spanners, you step gingerly between and upon the knots of connecting air pipes which writhe like snakes in your path, and you stare at the moving cars on either side. This is the world of the operator. In and out of the cars, up and over the line, check the line speed and the model mix. Your mind restlessly alert, because there's no guarantee that the next car will be the same as the last, that a Thames van won't suddenly appear. But still a blank – you keep trying to blot out what's happening. 'When I'm here my mind's a blank. I *make* it go blank.' They all say that. They all tell the story about the man who left Ford to work in a sweet-factory where he had to divide up the reds from the blues, but left because he couldn't take the decision-making. Or the country lad who couldn't believe that he had to work on *every* car: 'Oh no. I've done my car. That one down there. A green one it was.' If you stand on the catwalk at the end of the plant you can look down over the whole assembly floor. Few people do, for to stand there and look at the endless, perpetual, tedium of it all is to be threatened by the overwhelming insanity of it. The sheer audacious madness of a system based upon men like those wishing

BEYNON, HUW (1973) from 'On the Line', 'Insecurity and Struggle' and 'The Roots of Activism' in *Working for Ford* Harmondsworth, Penguin, 109–14, 155–9, 185–7.

their lives away. I was never able, even remotely, to come to terms with the line. Mind you, I never worked on it. But that's another story.

In 1970 I talked with a Ford worker in Swansea. His son had recently bought a Capri – the Company's latest model. 'I wouldn't touch them,' he said and pointed repeatedly towards his own car, a Morris Oxford, 'that's my "Ford" there. I wouldn't touch the bloody things: not with what I see going on in that plant.' This denial of any identity with the Ford product is, and always has been, a general phenomenon amongst workers in the motor industry. Continually Ford workers tell you 'never buy a Ford'. Neither is this peculiar to Ford. In the early days of the motor industry in the United States, General Motors workers are reputed to have bought Fords instead of Chevrolets because they 'knew how Chevrolets were built and would not advise anybody to buy one' (see Fine 1969, p. 38).

Living in a society ruled by the tyranny of the market place men frequently find themselves attracted yet at the same time repelled by features of that society. Nothing better demonstrates this state amongst Ford workers than their relationship with the motor car. Most workers would like a car and Ford workers are not exceptions. They want a car because it allows you to leave for work that much later, to go away for day trips with the wife and kids. In short it gives you some freedom. There is also something attractive about the automobile itself, the intricacies of its internal combustion engine, and its glamour. Many of the men I talked to in fact mentioned that they were first attracted to the car plant in some sense by the very fact that cars were produced there and that they might 'find out' about how cars are made. They found out as they put hub caps on, stretched rubber around windscreens or struggled with the dashboard wiring. In our society the motor car has an attraction which makes people endure all sorts of deprivation in order to possess one. Some men talk of little other than cars and the roads are thick with them. The position of the motor car worker, though, is doubly complicated, for the deprivations he endures in order to possess a car are actually defined in the very production of the desired object. . . .

One of the ways that I thought I could explore the way these men came to understand their work was through the notion of an 'ideal job'. This, however, ran into difficulties, as many stewards in particular reacted to this as they had done to the idea of an 'ideal firm'. Bert was very explicit. 'What are you on about now. You work for money. That's what it's all about. I've told you before. I'd shovel shit for money.' Bert was the Wet Deck steward. He'd go out with you for a night, buy lots of beer, give you fags, beat you at darts and tell you stories about his family. When you met him next day he'd say 'here he comes, the man with no hands. You want to watch out for him. Don't go out with him for a night unless you've a spare fiver and a pocket full of ciggies.' He only worked for money – 'he'd shovel shit for it', he said – yet he'd refuse overtime and spent hours at the weekend organizing football matches for the P.T.A. teams. He finally resigned as a steward because he was 'fed up with representing a bunch of selfish bastards'.

Now although few of the stewards were like Bert Owen, if one were to attempt to typify the 'life style' of the stewards this peculiar mixture of a brash, uncompromisingly hard exterior with an almost naïve sentimentality and warmth would be an important element within it. I discussed this at length with several of the stewards, not least because they often laughed at my own 'romanticism' and 'sentimentalism'. To paraphrase the comments of one of them:

> Yes: we're all sentimentalists to some extent. We laugh at each other, criticize each other by calling one another a sentimentalist but I think we're all a bit that way inclined. Believe in the 'brotherhood of man', a better society and shit like that. But you've got to keep it in check or you've had it. You've got to keep your feet on the ground. If you go around the world with rosy ideas about things, about the members, they'll pretty soon come unstuck because the members can be bastards. . . .
>
> A steward will come up to me and say 'I'm not representing that shower of shit any more', or he'll say 'You call this a shop steward committee . . . half of them aren't worth a candle.' I say this see 'You can't pick your team. You've got to make do with what you've got.' It's all very well having your high ideals but we've got to deal with that company in that plant and we can't pick and choose and um and ah.

This particular principle had become incorporated into the ideology of the shop stewards committee, and in its emphasis upon the need to tackle day to day problems it can be seen as a 'direct' reflection of working-class experience. People, living their lives, develop a pretty accurate idea of their own life chances, of the odds they face and the hopes that they can realistically entertain. One of the more obvious criticisms of much that passes for social science is that it drastically underestimates people's intelligence. Working-class people are faced with a limited number of employment prospects all of which are pretty dreary. If you're young, with family responsibilities and want to move out of the house you know to be a slum you attempt to get as much money as you can by selling to the highest bidder. In a hard world you become a hard man. This doesn't mean that you are not aware of alternative things, better ways of living, but merely that these are unlikely to be open to you. If you work at Ford's, on the line, you let your mind go blank and look forward to pay day and the weekend. As one man put it:

> I just adapt to it. I suppose you could adapt to anything really. It depends upon your circumstances. I'm married and I've taken out a mortgage. This affects your attitude to your work. I just close my eyes and stick it out. I think about the kids and the next premium being paid. That's about all there is with this job. It gets frustrating but that's it. What can you do?

I had previously talked to him about the notion of an 'ideal job'. As I have said this involved problems but he did say this:

> Oh. You're talking about in my dreams, like. The sort of thing I'd *really* like to do if I had the chance. Oh yes . . . I'd like to work on a newspaper. I'd like to meet people. To do something like you're doing yourself. Find out the facts about people's problems. You know about social problems. I've a reasonable knowledge of English. I used to write in the school magazine. I've always had it in the back of my mind. My school teachers said I should do it. I often think about it. There's no possibility now, like.

Another man made the relationship between the real and the ideal more explicitly:

> Your choice of job is governed too much by money. You've got to be a realist. What I'd like to do though would be a sports teacher – teach physical education to lads. That's my ideal job, it's important, it would give me a better outlook on life.
>
> You don't achieve anything here. A robot could do it. The line here is made for morons. It doesn't need any thought. They tell you that. 'We don't pay you for thinking' they say. Everyone comes to realize that they're not doing a worthwhile job. They're just on the line. For the money. Nobody likes to think that they're a failure. Its bad when you *know* that you're just a little cog. You just look at your pay packet – you look at what it does for your wife and kids. That's the only answer.

Most of the Ford workers that I talked to expressed sentiments broadly similar to those quoted above. There was a tendency for men working on sub-assembly operations, which involved them in preparing a batch of components for the line operator and enabled them to 'make their own time', to find the work less frustrating than the men who were actually on the line. The differences weren't all that great, all the men I talked to felt that their job was either 'completely dull and monotonous' or 'dull most of the time'. Similarly most of them had some idea of the sort of job that they would like to do if they had or had had the opportunity. The two quotations are unrepresentative in one sense however. While all the 'ideal jobs' mentioned were chosen for their intrinsic qualities, a majority of the sample of members opted for jobs which took them 'outside the system' where they were 'their own boss'. They talked of being back in the services or at sea or driving a lorry again. . . .

Insecurity and struggle

In spite of publicity to the contrary, and talk of easy times on the dole, the life of a working man without work is often desperate. What most working men want of a job is that it offers them some security. Married men with children value a regular wage above all else in their work. Such men dominated the labour force at Halewood, and their stewards, we remember, consistently mentioned security as the most important aspect of a job.

The significance attached to job security becomes all the more important when placed alongside the fact that the production of motor cars has been characterized, almost above all else, by instability. The interdependence of the car plants, the proliferation of small, independent suppliers and market fluctuations have synthesized in the lay-off and short-time working. All of the Halewood workers I talked to had experienced a period of lay-off in the time that they had been employed in the P.T.A., and eight of the stewards and fifteen of the members mentioned instability of wages as a major drawback to working in a car plant. The Ford Motor Company in its move to Halewood attempted to handle fluctuations in the demand for cars through regulating the hours worked by a stable labour force, rather than by seasonal recruitment and lay-off. As a personnel officer put it: 'this has been a hire and fire industry for too long. What we have tried to do in this plant is to keep a stable labour force. Not to kick them out at the drop of a hat, but to try to give continuous production. That's the way to build up a loyalty to the Company.' Ford's operation of this policy made overtime for the workers on the line almost obligatory during periods of peak demand. The shop steward organization grudgingly accepted this, provided that 'proper notice' was given. However, the policy was no safeguard against the market. Market recession brought with it short-time working.

In the summer of 1965 for example, the Company introduced a period of short-time working in which the hourly paid employees in all its British plants were put on a four-day week. . . .

The market affects relationships in the plant. Economic fluctuations reveal themselves in the balance of power on the sections. Given this the actual decision to shut the plant becomes one of a number of strategies in the power game, and the game isn't over once the decision has been made. The men's biggest complaint was that they weren't given more than half an hour's notice of the lay-off.

> They take a terrible attitude to the men on the shop floor here. I don't know how they behave as they do. They tell you nothing. Look, we've been laid off this afternoon and we haven't even been told that officially. They tell you nothing. All your pay can be stopped and they tell you nothing. That's typical of this firm.

Members of the Personnel Department explained the shortness of the notice by the fact that the decision didn't become inevitable until after the dinner break, and that right up to that time it was hoped that a lay-off could be avoided. Even if there is some truth in this explanation – even if the Halewood management were hoping for a reprieve from Warley – it doesn't adequately explain why the possibility of the lay-off was kept as such a closely guarded secret. The reason given for this secrecy by the stewards and several of the members I talked to, was simply that management was afraid of the consequences.

> They see it like this see: they're going to shut the plant down at 2.30 and by that time they'll have produced so many cars. Then they'll know how many cars they'll have to get rid of, they'll be able to work their numbers out. So what they're afraid of is what the blokes will do once they know that the plant is stopping. Nobody trusts anybody in this place. What they're afraid of is the lads saying 'sod you' and either going home or doing bad jobs. It happens you know. When there's trouble like this you often get lads going down the lines with pennies or knives, scraping the paint off the cars.

In a situation ridden with latent conflicts, the decision to lay men off can be likened to a declaration of war, and it is not only the workers who attempt to exact reprisals against the other side in this situation. Often a depressed demand for cars encourages a supervisor to settle some old scores with his steward or with men on his section who have given him trouble. On the material handling section, for example, a skeleton crew was to remain in the plant during the shut down. The decision on the manning of the crew was left in the hands of the supervisor who announced that he intended to 'draw up a list'. The shop steward and several of the men on the section opposed this violently. One of them remarked that 'that bastard wants to fill the place with his "blue eyes" '. A group of the men wanted to crowd into the supervisor's office and 'have it out with him'. Jeff the steward persuaded them against this, arguing that it would be playing straight into his hands. Instead he went to see the supervisor and after a long furious argument it was agreed that the names of the skeleton crew would be picked out of a hat. Jeff said:

> That's what we've got to put up with here see. Big Joe wants to run this section his way all the time. He'd have us saluting if he could. We've managed to get it through to him that we're not having it, that we want some say in what goes on here, by standing up to him. But it only takes something like this for him to think he can start waving the whip again.

The men objected strongly to being laid off; they had children, hire purchase debts and mortgage repayments to make, and to lay them off with half an hour's notice wasn't right. The lay-off can be seen to produce a heightening of the critical attitudes that these men held toward the company. Turner (Turner, Clark and Roberts 1967, p. 331) in fact attributes the industry's strike record and the militant demands of its workers to the fact that men who possess a low moral commitment to their employer and who tend to be more like 'economic men' than other workers experience a very considerable instability of earnings. This example clearly reveals how the lay off is structured into the world of the assembler, how the elements of instability, monotony and conflict over the wage-work bargain all cohere to produce situations of heightening conflict.

There seems to be some evidence that members of management in the motor industry are aware of the significance of insecurity of earnings. To quote Bob Ramsey, The Ford Motor Company's Director of Labour Relations:

> Men have been too easily bounced out of this industry in the past. We have been much too inclined to lay people off. We don't lay people off now unless it's absolutely necessary. You've got to draw the line at some point. But we don't do it if we can help it. We feel that the track shouldn't be stopped by either side. If we keep laying people off they are quite right to say 'why should I worry about production?' We want to get away from all that.

It seems likely that statements such as these, if carried into practice, would have a considerable effect upon work relationships. Nevertheless, it is important to remember that it is not so much the lay-off *in itself* that has given rise to conflict in car plants, but the coherence of other elements in the work situation around the insecurity of employment. Furthermore it should also be remembered, as Ramsey indicates, that the market sets very definite limits upon the extent to which any motor car company in Britain can guarantee security of employment to its workers. Given the instability of motor car production and the severe dependency of the assembly plants upon the supply of components, it seems likely that even where fall-back rates have been negotiated, the assembly line worker will continue to experience insecurity of earnings during the seventies.

This leads to a second, more general point. Apart from administering the selection of skeleton crews on sections where such crews are required the shop steward is virtually helpless in the face of a lay-off. Job insecurity brings home very clearly the fact that while a degree of job control may be established by workers through the shop stewards committee, to work in a factory means to work, to a very large extent, on management's terms. While a shop steward may well find himself in a situation where he has to challenge management's authority on the shop floor, he is more often in situations where he is forced to play the game management's way. Another senior executive of the company saw it like this:

> It's difficult to say what type of steward does best for his members. A militant may well force a new concessions, but we'll always be waiting to get them back or to make life a bit difficult for him. While a quiet, more reasonable bloke may be less dramatic he'll probably get more for his members because if he's in any trouble we'll help him out. We make concessions to him that we wouldn't make to the other bloke.

In the face of a powerful, prestigious adversary, the soft-sell is often the best form of attack and self-defence. This is particularly the case if you're meeting him on his home ground. It takes a lot of courage, conviction and confidence to stick out a confrontation with a manager in a posh office, desk, carpet, good suit. And you in your overalls. It's even more difficult if he flatters you and appears reasonable. Many stewards rarely get over this. For most of the time they play negotiations management's way. They learn the limits of the game and in the routine of their lives in the plant tend not to step outside them : 'You can't fight a battle every day.'

But sometimes they've got to. And this is what makes nonsense of most public debate on industrial relations. Too often it is assumed that if only the shop steward and his members had the 'right attitude', strikes and industrial conflict generally would be tremendously reduced. The only attitude that would ensure this is one of subservience and stupidity. For what the pundits fail to recognize, or choose to ignore, is that we live in a world dominated by capital and a capitalist rationality. In this world decisions are understood as 'investments', what makes a thing good or bad is the 'return' on it. Not it in itself. A good becomes a commodity valued not for what it can do, so much as the price it can be exchanged for. People too become commodities for the commodity world has men's labour at its centre. Spun round by capital and transformed into charts on office walls.

'Labour costs' – that sums it up. Production based upon the sale of labour power. By men, putting themselves at the disposal of other men for over half their lives. In order to live they preserve capital and their bondage. It is not perversity that makes assembly line workers claim that they are treated like numbers. In the production of motor cars they *are* numbers. Numbers to be manipulated by people who are trained and paid to do just that. To cut costs, increase output. And lay men off. As a commodity, so is their power to labour treated. This is not to say that managers are necessarily inhumane people. Many managers, and employers, deeply regret the need to lay men off, to make them redundant. But they recognize that it is a need, a necessity dictated by market forces, for this necessity applies to them as well.

There are real lines of conflict within a car plant. A conflict that will be more obvious at one time than another. But it can never be assumed away, for it runs deeper than the 'cooperativeness' or otherwise of the assembly-line workers and their union representatives. It is underpinned by the very existence of wage labour and the market. While a shop steward may well attempt to play the game management's way, in many circumstances this attempt will be fraught with severe tensions. . . .

The roots of activism

The public school idea of the 'ringleader' takes a long time to die. It still infects the writings of many commentators on industry and it informed a great deal of the thinking behind the Industrial Relations Act. Yet recourse to the idea of a 'ringleader', a 'trouble maker', focuses attention away from an examination of the *position* of the shop floor leader within the factory and in particular the nature of his *relationship* with his members. To understand the shop steward is to understand this relationship. The steward acts and lives through his members. They are in him and he in them. The relationship is not the same in all factories or at all times. It is the living product of circumstances.

The unionism of skilled men for example is quite different from the unionism of the car assembler. The men who printed this book control their place of work through their skill. The skill controls the job and is solidified in the union. Their 'branch' is termed a 'chapel' and the leading figure in the chapel is the 'father', who is a highly skilled man. Nor are his skills solely physical ones. The union as the collective controller of these skills creates within the union leader other skills. In his negotiations with the employer he is able to call upon as great a variety of subtle arguments as his members have control of the job. Printers can refuse to print parts of a newspaper if they find it offensive. To suggest that an assembly line operator might want, let alone try, to affect the colour or the shape of the automobiles he works on brings home the differences between their worlds. The skilled worker already has a freedom. A freedom which finds its expression in the dignity which printers and other skilled men derive from the superiority of their work. A freedom which, however inadequate, has characterized the unionism of skilled workers for a century and which found its political expression in syndicalism. Assembly line workers are not dignified. There is no dignity to be gained from screwing on wheels so they don't think about dignity. The leaders of skilled men have many cards to play, both in their hands and up their sleeves. By contrast the steward on the assembly line deals only in the physical presence of his members on the line. They may be able to affect the quality slightly here and there, but basically they either do the job or they don't. Unlike the father of the chapel, the convenor of an assembly plant has few stopping points this side of a strike. One of the most significant consequences of mass production for the working class has been the increasing use made by workers of the mass strike, the sit-down strike and the picket line.

The steward in the car plant operates within the continuous world of the assembly line. The content of the work creates no relationship between him and them. They don't want his advice on how to attach the petrol tank to the car body; all they want from him is the regulation of the quantity of work that's demanded of them. The Halewood Estate is dominated by a large mushroom-shaped cooling tower. On one of my first vists to the plant I pointed it out to one of the senior stewards and asked him what it was. 'I don't know,' he replied, 'it never gives us any trouble so we leave it alone.' I didn't know if he was joking or not. You walk around a tool-room with a skilled craftsman and you know the difference.

The steward on the trim-line will represent between seventy and 140 operatives depending on the speed of the line. Fluctuating line speeds, absenteeism and labour turnover all work against the development of a stable relationship between the steward and his members. On top of this the men he represents see themselves as small cogs, numbers; they hate their jobs and their life in the factory. One of the trim line stewards put it like this.

> The point about this place is that the work destroys you. It destroys you physically and mentally. The biggest problem for people is getting to accept it, to accept being here day in and day out. So you've got low morale from every

point of view. You're inflicted with a place of work and you've got to adapt because it won't adapt to you. So morale is terribly low. But you can build on this you see. You can't get much lower than hell and so you can increase morale through the union. Pull together sort of thing rather than dog eat dog. That's how I've found it on the trim. We're all in hell and you can get a bond out of that. We're all in it together like. That's where the union comes in.

This after all is what trade unionism is basically about. It is rooted historically in a working class collectivism; not necessarily a class-conscious brotherhood, but certainly an awareness of a clear identity of interest between yourself and the next man. In an assembly plant this mutual identity is fostered by the fact that the next man could be you, for on the line you are nothing – interchangeable numbers. What sort of collectivism do men create in this situation? What is the character of the trade unionism of assembly line workers? In trying to answer these questions it is obviously necessary to consider the nature of the relationship between the activists and the lay membership – the masses. How do these activists emerge, as leaders from the mass, in a work situation where the machine age has done most to reduce all men to a common denominator?

The same steward describes his election:

Three years ago this place was in a very bad way. Ford's controlled everything. We had no steward on the line at the time. The lad who had taken it on broke down. The frustrations and the pressures were too much for him. I knew Eddie, I'd met him at some of the meetings and he told me to have a go. So I stood. Somebody had to do it. I didn't want to be a shop steward. That's the last thing I wanted when I came to this place first. I wanted to get on a bit. But I could see all the injustices being done every day so I thought I had to have a go. It wasn't right that they were having to take all the shit that Ford's were throwing.

Frank Banton also became active in the early days of the P.T.A. plant:

When I came here first we had no representative. The odd steward was recognized as a spokesman but all the negotiations were done through the convenor. I knew that the lads were being brainwashed and kidded. The T & G was trying to organize the place and they were asking for volunteers – to work behind the scenes as it were. I volunteered and took up a job as a collecting steward. Eventually they persuaded me to take on the shop steward's job. I was pretty well known by that time and I was elected. I wanted to do it to look after the interests of my fellow workmen on the shop floor and to fight against these bastards here.

These two accounts summarize a wealth of experience. They contain the crucial elements of the emergent shop floor organization – conflict, sponsorship and a commitment to a humanistic collectivism, a strong desire to 'help your fellow man'. The structure of the shop stewards' committee in the P.T.A. was created during a period of severe, continuous conflict, by a few activists who couldn't stand back and watch 'injustices being done every day'. This is not an uncommon pattern, but rather one which characterizes the entire history of the motor industry. Plants are unionized by men who stick their necks out and survive because of their mates' support. Eighteen of the thirty-six stewards that I talked to were elected in 1963 or 1964, and each of these mentioned conflict with supervision or management as an important contributing factor in his election. These men had come to Halewood to get some more money, perhaps even to get on a bit. They quickly realized that they didn't particularly want to 'get on' in the Ford world and that as workers the Ford Motor Company was a force they had to reckon with. The lads were unorganized – 'it was like Fred Carno's Army, you wouldn't believe half, if I told you' – and they were taking a beating. People like Jimmy Black who had been a steward at Dunlops, and Bob Costello with a life on the building sites behind him, expected to get involved. It had always been Bob's ambition to take out a steward's card, but men like him were exceptional. The vast majority of stewards had no intention of becoming active when they walked through the gates at the start of their first day of work for the Ford Motor Company. The Ford Motor Company made them active.

References

F I N E, S. (1969) *Sit Down: the G.M. Strike of 1936–37* Ann Arbor, Michigan, Michigan University Press.

T U R N E R, H. A., C L A C K, G. and R O B E R T S, T. G. (1967) *Labour Relations in the Motor Industry* London, Allen and Unwin.

Part V Social relations

Introduction

Social relations happen all the time. Whenever an individual ceases to be alone he or she becomes part of a relationship and inevitably begins to interact with another person or group of people, even though the only observable behaviour may be to take no notice of the others. Indeed, it is not quite as simple as that, for whatever we do, even when alone, we do in a social and cultural context. We cannot divest ourselves of the groups to which we belong – family, work group, friends – for we may still be affected by their standards and values even when we are not physically interacting with them. Similarly, an individual may influence others or be a point of reference for them without personal contact.

Relationships both form and change us. An infant's first contacts with its mother are social as well as personal and physical, and the process known as primary socialization begins with these contacts. Early social relationships are the means whereby the infant growing into childhood learns to structure his behaviour and begins to come to terms with the environment in which he is being brought up. Later, as he becomes aware of the social processes and can articulate his wants and ideals, he is capable of changing and even manipulating his environment, very often by means of social relationships.

The complexities of the process of socialization, and some of the controversies which surround theories about it, are explored in the texts of the Open University course which this reader accompanies. Social relations have been taken for granted throughout the course up to this point. Many assumptions about the nature and effects of relationships between individuals or among groups and communities have had to be made in earlier sections of the course, particularly in the section about social problems, for example. The purpose in focusing now on social interaction is to make explicit some of these assumptions and to show how social scientists have tried to explain human development and the processes of social change. This means at this point a concentration on psychological and sociological theories and methods.

The first two articles look at social processes in childhood, from a researcher's point of view. The extract from Margaret Mead comes from her introduction to a collection of articles on patterns of child-rearing. Essays in cultural anthropology often contain fascinating descriptions of the customs and behaviour of people in other societies, and it is sometimes easy to read them merely as fascinating descriptions. Mead is conerned to correct this tendency by outlining the theoretical background to such research; she wishes to persuade the ever-present naïve reader to look beyond the anecdotes to find their anthropological significance. Thus she is describing an essential skill of the trained social scientist – that of ridding oneself of the accepted frame of reference and of making the apparently commonplace a matter for conjecture. She is also aware, however, of the danger of substituting simply another frame of reference and emphasizes the need for constant scepticism and open-mindedness.

The second article, by psychologist Eleanor Maccoby, examines the kinds of variables investigated in studies of socialization – here within a much narrower cultural field. Most of the article is devoted to the idea of socialization in a Western setting. Maccoby reviews some of the issues in the socialization process, such as reward and punishment, identification and warmth of parental attitude. The article has value in giving readers some idea of the varieties and methods of psychological research, together with some of the difficulties of extending laboratory findings to the far more complex social situations that exist in the 'real world'.

Discussion of the anthropological and psychological aspects of social relations is followed by a sociological look at the field. The text of the Open University course at this point centres on the crucial concept of 'role' in the explanation of social phenomena, and cites the work of Erving Goffman, among others, on the theory of roles. The extract from Goffman reprinted here is an outline of some of his ideas, which emphasize the point that roles, like social relationships, are with us all the time. While for most people most of the time roles are taken for granted, the role theorist is constantly watching his own performance, as well as that of others, an unabated attention to self that must prove rather uncomfortable.

Goffman defines social role as the 'enactment of rights and duties attached to a given status'. But for the taxi-driver, whose work-setting is depicted by Davis in the fourth extract, the expectations he can hold out towards his clients' tipping practices are unpredictable, in spite of the labels and categories with which he attempts to typify them and thereby to anticipate behaviour. Besides sensitizing us to features of more sustained interaction, especially in work relationships, the extract provides a good example of the impersonal, transitory encounters that characterize much of modern urban life.

Kay Pole

18   Cultural approaches to childhood

Margaret Mead

In the study of personality in culture we start with a recognition of the biologically given, of what all human beings have in common. In every human society, human infants are born helpless and relatively undeveloped, dependent upon adult nurture and adult transmission of the great body of culture – beliefs, practices, skills – which make it possible for any human group, and for this human group in particular, to function as human beings. Humanity as we know it is not merely a matter of our human physique, of our prehensile thumbs, upright posture, and highly developed brains, but of our capacity to accumulate and build upon the inventions and experience of previous generations. A child who does not participate in this great body of tradition, whether because of defect, neglect, injury, a disease, never becomes fully human.

As every child must learn to accept food, to trust those who care for him, to make his wants known, to walk and talk and assume control of his own body and actions, to identify with own sex and age and develop appropriate behaviour towards individuals of the opposite sex and other ages, we may expect that in the course of this long maturation and learning there will be a great deal in common between childhood among the unclothed, nomadic Australian aborigines and childhood on Park Avenue, or in rural Alabama, in Paris or Bali, Devon or Provence. Whether children are breast-fed, bottle-fed, cup-fed, or spoon-fed, they must eat with their mouths, learn to suck or drink, chew their food, swallow, and discriminate between that which is and that which is not food. They may learn to walk by being hand-led, by being given a walking rail, put in a harness, kept in a play pen, but they all learn to walk within relatively close age limits. Whether they learn to swim, climb, roller skate, or dance will depend on their own culture; minor sequences like standing, then squatting, or squatting, then standing, may be altered by culture. Whether their movements will be rigidly stylized and resistant to new learning or flexibly adjustable to new requirements will again depend on their culture. But walk they must and do, walk in a world where adults are taller, much taller

MEAD, MARGARET (1955) 'Cultural Approaches to Childhood', in Mead, Margaret and Wolfenstein, M., *Childhood in Contemporary Culture* Chicago, University of Chicago Press, 6–14.

than they, pygmies among giants, ignorant among the knowledgeable, wordless among the articulate, with incomprehensible urgencies and desires and fears among adults who appear to have such matters reduced to a system – a system which must be mastered. And to the adults, children everywhere represent something weak and helpless, in need of protection, supervision, training, models, skills, beliefs, 'character'. Children cling and grab and scream, children are periodically inaccessible to any appeal, children in their lack of control represent the impulses which the adults in their childhood laboriously learned to discipline and control. The double threat of fearing to behave like a child and of yearning to behave like a child runs through all adult lives, just as the fear and hope of some day becoming an adult inform the play and fantasies of children.

Because of these recurrent biological similarities – of growth, of parent-child relationships, of needs and fears, and resonances – it is possible to compare childhood in one society with childhood in another. The common elements, the uniformities, are the basis of the comparisons. In some primitive tribes infants born with teeth will be killed as unnatural; Russian children were terrified by the image of the witch baby born with iron teeth, but most babies continue to be born without teeth and to cut their teeth within narrow chronological limits.

Furthermore, men everywhere have to solve certain problems if they are to live in societies – problems of food supply, shelter and protection from sun, rain and cold; of sexual jealousy and permanence of mating for the care of children; of social order, protection against enemies, disease, and catastrophe of a relationship to the world around them and to the conceived universe which gives them spiritual balance, patterns their fantasies, stylizes their aspirations, and releases their capacity to invent, create, and change. The solution to these problems provides a second set of uniformities. Children will have to learn to live in houses, to use tools, to observe social rules, to respect the person and property of others, to see the stars – as the lights of heaven, the frozen residue of celestial mischief, miraculous embodiments of the animals which they must hunt to live, or as future husbands for young girls who wish hard enough. Houses have to have entrances and vents for smoke; clothing has to be put on and taken off; with growing complexity, people have special places to sit, to sleep, to eat. Furthermore, culture grows by borrowing; people incorporate traits of their neighbours, learn their myths, sing their songs, or copy their clothes. People of areas which are in touch with one another – contiguous in space or because of political or religious ties – share the same solutions, and such institutions as currency or law courts, libraries, hospitals, schools, purification offerings or confession, armies and navies and embassies, become characteristic, and characteristic in their particular forms, over large sections of the world.

If the naïve reader encounters a statement on child-rearing practice in modern society, nine-tenths or more of it will seem very familiar. The reader who is not trained in noting small details as significant and who is unaccustomed to thinking in patterns will say, 'Why practically everything those people do to their children is just like what we do – babies are breast- or bottle-fed, trained to be clean, learn to talk, go to school, join the church, pass examinations, etc.'. Often the next step is to seize on the one or two things which do sound a little peculiar – such as the use of wet nurses or swaddling or being constantly carried on the back – and to treat these unfamiliar details as if they had unique importance in producing any differences in adult character which may be admitted.

But while striking differences in behaviour may give rapid clues to important differences in the whole pattern, it is important to realize that it is not any single item of child-rearing practice or of culturally patterned child behaviour – not the presence or absence of feeding bottles or slates, skates or hoops or balls, prayers or homilies or bribes – which is significant in isolation. It is the way in which all these thousands of items, most of which are shared with other cultures, some of which are shared with all other cultures, are patterned or fitted together to make a whole. Within these patterns children grow up, young people learn to be parents, people age and die in terms of the complex learning which has been provided for them and which they have evoked from others, from birth until death.

When we look at behaviour culturally, it means that we look at it comparatively. If there were only one human culture, it would be much harder to identify what behaviour was cultural, what idiosyncratic but learned, and what instinctive. If human beings spoke only one language and we had no records of former versions of that language, the task of identifying which aspects of the language were biologically given, which one alternative among many, which purely fortuitous, which so redundant that they made no contribution, would be very difficult indeed. So when the anthropologist says, 'Children take their father's surname', the culturally naïve will answer, 'Of course, who else's name would they take?' But the culturally sophisticated, whether their sophistication comes from reading, travel, or study, from the knowledge of other periods of history or from a knowledge of other cultures, will realize that in many societies there are no surnames, while in others children take their mother's surname or take the surnames of both parents, and that taking the father's surname is a particular type of cultural behaviour, neither natural to the human race nor a predictable occurrence even for a given part of the world. Every single statement that an anthropologist makes is a comparative statement. 'These people cook their food in pots' implies a comparison with other peoples who cook in bamboo, in earth ovens, or with food wrapped in leaves, on skewers, or in wooden boxes. 'The baby is weaned at a year' compares this people to others who wean at six months, nine months, two years, at walking, when the mother is pregnant again, or who attempt never to wean the youngest child at all. The context of comparison may change – sometimes, for example, American behaviour will be discussed as part of modern Euro-American culture, or as part of the Christian world, or as an inheritor of the Judeo–Christian tradition, or as Protestant in emphasis, or as part of the free world. But, however the context may shift, it is always a comparative context.

Furthermore, anthropological statements refer to identified materials or observations in which class, locality, occupation, age, sex, and religion have been taken into account when the background observations were made. In the statement 'The American flag has forty-eight stars and thirteen stripes', there is explicit recognition that there is no need to qualify this statement by remarks about class, race, or religion. But if a statement has to be made about saluting the flag, then qualifications would have to be introduced about the date at which the salute came in, situations in which the salute has become compulsory, about religious groups like Jehovah's Witnesses who refuse to salute the flag. In the absence of such specific knowledge, an anthropologist could still describe a group of children standing at attention, hands to hearts, facing a banner with specified designs upon it. Provided that place and date were specified, this remains valid cultural information. . . .

The term *cultural regularities* includes the way in which the versions of the culture found in different classes, regions, or occupations are systematically related to one another. So a member of the French bourgeoisie who is also a Protestant will manifest behaviour which is French, which has certain peculiarities in common with the behaviour of French Protestants, which has other peculiarities in common with the French bourgeois, and still others in common with his province, and others in common with his generation, etc. Any single item of his behaviour – that he saves money, drinks wine with his dinner, has a house with a garden gate – will be shared outside France as well as inside, and the circumstance that he walks upright, uses tools and speaks an organized language will be shared with the entire human race. But when we are making a cultural analysis, we are interested in identifying those characteristics – including, if not speci-fying, the possibilities of variation by class, region, religion, period, etc. – which can be attributed to sharing in the tradition of the larger group, whether that group be nation, tribe, province, or some even larger unit with a common tradition, such as the culture of an area like Southeast Asia.

The regularities of behaviour of all those who share a common culture may be attributed to the uniformities in their biological endowments, that all are human beings with bodies and brains which have much in common. The peculiarities of any culture, as compared with any other culture, and the peculiarities of the versions of the culture which one class or region displays are to be referred to different historical conditions, including the whole ecological situation – so that lake dwellers, plains dwellers, and mountain dwellers will have different versions of a common tradition – and to the differences between human beings, whether these differences are regarded as hereditary, congenital, or as resulting from an individual life-history. So at any given period in history, French or American or German culture is an expression of what the predecessors – whether the biological and cultural or cultural only – of the present population have developed, including the particular stamp that has been given by outstand-ing individuals or members of a particular class.

The regularizing features, which make it possible to abstract from the behaviour of all Frenchmen or all Americans certain systematic statements, are their shared humanity and their shared tradition. Each individual who must live out a series of roles – as husband, father, church member, em-ployer or employee, member of a political party, member of an audience, taxpayer, member of the armed forces, sometimes spectator, sometimes actor in the social scene – relates these various aspects of the culture, these various roles, within his own personality. They may be related directly, as when the father role and the employer role and the citizen role are felt to call for the same kind of behaviour; or they may be related tangentially or contrapuntally that is, a man may treat his children differently from his employees, he may perform quite differently for spectators of his own class as compared to those of another class, but he is the same person performing the different roles, and they become in time systematically related to one another within the framework of the historical culture within which he acts.

In changing societies like our own, especially in societies like the United States in which immigration has been such an important factor, these various relationships between roles, between classes, between age groups, will not be so perfectly related, and the regularities will be of a different order. So we may say that it is a regularity of American culture that children expect to behave differently from their parents and will treat their children differently from the way they were treated. Even in those cases where a young mother does treat her baby as her mother treated her, she is conscious of doing so, in contrast to her friends, to people in books, who are behaving differently from their parents. In a homogeneous, very slowly changing culture, a young mother will repeat, without being conscious of any other course, the 'right' way of doing things – of feeding or lulling or scolding a child – and will regard her successes and failures as being as good as, better than, or worse than her mother's. But in a culture like America, the occasional mother who does repeat her mother's practices systematically relates this repetition to an expected nonrepeating pattern.

Similarly, in the United States, where adult immigrants have consciously learned to adjust to American culture after knowing what it means to speak a language and relate themselves in habits and manners to other people, people are regularly conscious of the degree to which they conform to the behaviour of the people with whom they associate. They may choose to conform, they may choose to deviate, but they cannot choose to be unconscious of the problem. So children whose parents have no servants will feel different and inferior among children whose parents have servants, and children whose parents have servants, when no other associated household does, also will feel different and potentially inferior. Here again, this contrast between American culture and other cultures is not absolute. The Balinese girl who reaches puberty later than the girls who are her age mates is shy and embarrassed; Balinese parents will worry about a little son who delays longer than his age mates 'daring the rice fields' alone with an ox or water buffalo. But whereas the Balinese refer to a common chronological age and an expected speed of maturation, people in the United States include also an expected attentiveness to the standards of the group around one.

Some students are helped in identifying the cultural factor in behaviour by the idea of 'style' that intangible configuration of widely shared items which makes it possible to distinguish one 'style' from another or the literature or art of one period from another. Other principles of organizing observation are all abstractions of something that has been observed to be common to a group. Learning to see the regularities of behaviour that are 'American' or 'English' requires the same kind of disciplined familiarity that makes it possible to make statements about the expected play behaviour of children of a given age or sex or class, all of which involves having compared the behaviour of different ages, both sexes, and different classes, so that the differences come into focus.

Students and commentators on human behaviour in the twentieth century vary between the extremes of a high sensitivity to style – style appropriate to age, sex, constitution, class, culture, period, and experience – and a low sensitivity to style, in which differences in detail are never perceived as anything but variations of one over-all pattern. These possibly innate temperamental preferences for working with or without a sense of style and pattern have been accentuated by the traditions of different professions. Social and experimental psychologists and sociologists tend to work with such units as attitudes and traits, where the more-or-less of one trait is correlated with the more-or-less of another ('more people with incomes between three and four thousand tend to own their own homes if they are in a white-collar group than . . .'), in which the integration provided either by identified human beings or by identified groups of human beings is lost. Clinical psychologists, psycho-analysts, and cultural anthropologists, who work with a large number of observations on a small number of individuals, the validity of whose work comes from the number and kinds of *items* of behaviour sampled rather than from the number of *individuals* sampled, have been trained to work with pattern. . . .

The cultural student, like the psychoanalytically trained clinician or the student of the art and literature of a period, works with the expectation of there being a pattern; failures to identify it are attributed to the type of information or to one's own individual inadequacies, but not to the material. Furthermore, an adequate knowledge of the pattern – of the culture, the period, or the particular individual who is being intensively studied – should make it possible to explain all past events by relating them to this knowledge and to predict the style, but *not the detail*, of future events. Prediction as a test of adequacy of a theory – in studies of human behaviour, as in geology – must be retrospective. When we examine the life-histories of delinquents, we find that a very large proportion come from broken homes; but, when we compare a large sample of children from broken and unbroken homes, we can predict neither *which* children nor *how many* of the children from broken homes will become delinquent. Once the sequence of events has occurred – though the events themselves were subject to a large number of historical accidents outside the realm of our present scientific equipment – we should be able to relate them to our understanding of the other behaviour of the members of a culture, or a period, or the previous behaviour of an individual.

19 The choice of variables in the study of socialization

Eleanor E. Maccoby

Perhaps the greatest change that has occurred in the field of child development in the past 15 years has been the increasing emphasis on socialization. . . . What are the important variables in parental behaviour that ought to make a difference in the development of the child? The process of selecting and defining variables is, of course, the very heart of theory-making. There are as many possible variables as there are ideas about what causes what in human development. I cannot attempt here to give any sort of roster of variables; the task would be too great and might not prove very useful. I simply want to point out some of the major classes of variables that have been used and give a little of the history of the reasons why we have chosen to measure these things and not others and perhaps point to a few ways in which we could clarify the meaning of the dimension we are using.

Let us start with the traditional child psychologist, with his interests in motor development, emotional development, intelligence, concept formation, and personality development, all grounded in traditional principles of learning and maturation. He may look upon the current work in socialization with a jaundiced eye and inquire what the excitement is all about. He may feel that he has actually been studying socialization for years without calling it by this name. He might put his question this way: If it is true that socialization is the process of transmitting culture from one generation to another, and that the child acquires the modes of behaviour prescribed by his culture through the process of learning, then how is the study of socialization any different from the study of learning itself? One might reply that in socialization studies, we study not only the child as learner but the parent as teacher. But a sceptic might still wonder how much difference this actually makes. For example, laboratory studies of learning have demonstrated that behaviour which is followed by reward will be strengthened, and its probability of recurrence will be increased. Now, if a student of socialization does a study of dependency, and discovers that parents who reward their children for dependency have more dependent children, has he really found out anything that we didn't know already?

MACCOBY, ELEANOR E. (1961) 'The Choice of Variables in the Study of Socialization', in *Sociometry*, 24, 357-71.

In my opinion, it *is* valuable to carry out at the human level studies which attempt to employ the standard variables that have grown out of laboratory study on learning, where most of the work has been done on sub-human species. But, in the process of applying such variables to socialization studies, the variables almost perforce undergo certain modifications and elaborations, with the result that translating traditional behaviour theory variables into the socialization setting sometimes results in the addition of something new, and the possibility of getting new kinds of principles.

Let me give an example. Suppose we wanted to study the effects of a particular schedule of reward. What do we mean by reward? The traditional approach to reward has been to produce a physiological drive, such as hunger or thirst, through deprivation; and then to reinforce the desired behaviour by presenting a drive-relevant reinforcing stimulus. But even in fairly young children, a rapid development of complex motivation occurs, and this changes the nature of the reinforcements to which children will be responsive. B. F. Skinner encountered this fact when he was developing his teaching machines. The early models were devised so as to emit little pieces of chocolate candy whenever a child made the correct response. But it was soon evident that a child progressed through a series of arithmetic or spelling problems just as readily without the candy; in fact, the giving of candy sometimes disrupted the learning process. Skinner, therefore, abandoned the candy rewards, and the current models of his machine rely upon no other reward than the child's interest in doing his work correctly – buttressed, no doubt, by a certain amount of pressure from the teacher and parents. This incident illustrates a major question about the definition of variable: what happens to the variable 'amount of reward' when it is translated into situations of teacher–child, or parent–child, interaction? In modern societies, children's physiological drives are regularly and quite fully satisfied and are seldom used as a basis for training. That is, most parents do not let the child get hungry, thirsty, wet, or overtired, and then make the satisfaction of these needs conditional on good behaviour. Rather, the rewards used are money, a trip to the zoo, being allowed to stay up for a special T V programme, etc. A gift of candy for some children becomes symbolic of affection instead of vice versa. Very commonly, behaviour is reinforced simply through the giving of approval, affection, or attention. So the concept 'reward', when it refers to the rewards which parents use in socializing their children is not directly comparable to the concept as it was originally developed in studies of animal learning. Of course, it is not really a new idea to point out that different kinds of organisms are capable of being rewarded by different kinds of things. It is clear enough that there are as many kinds of rewards as there are distinguishable motives, and that both motives and rewards vary between species and within species. But the new idea that has been added in socialization studies is that there may be distinguishable *classes* of rewards which may have different effects. The primary distinction made in studies so far has been between material reward and praise. Material reward covers all instances of giving the child some object or privilege that he wants, conditional upon good behaviour. Praise depends to some degree upon the previous establishment of a relationship between the socializing agent and the child, such that the approval of this particular adult is something the child wants. That is, the effectiveness of praise ought to depend upon the identity of the person doing the praising and upon this person's being someone the child loves, fears, or must depend upon for the satisfaction of needs.

The same kind of differentiation of a variable has occurred with respect to punishment. Students of the socialization process have been working under the assumption that not all kinds of aversive events following a child's act will have the same effect. The distinction most commonly made is that between physical punishment and so-called love-oriented discipline, or withdrawal of love. There are other categories of punishment, too, such as withdrawal of privileges and ridicule, which are less interesting than the first two because there are fewer hypotheses about their probable effects. Let us concentrate for a moment on the distinction between physical punishment and withdrawal of love. Physical punishment is easy enough to define, although in rating its frequency and severity, the researcher is always troubled about the problem of how to weigh slaps and shakings in relation to formal spankings. More tricky by far is the matter of defining withdrawal of love. Sears and his associates (1957) have defined it as any act or statement on the part of the parent that threatens the affectional bond between the parent and child. This would include the mother's turning her back on the child, refusing to speak to him or smile at him or be in the same room with him, saying she doesn't like him when he does disapproved things, etc. The system of classification of techniques of discipline presented by Beverly Allinsmith in her chapter in Miller and Swanson's book, *Inner Conflict and Defense* (1960), similarly emphasizes the distinction between 'psychological' and corporal' punishment, but defines psychological discipline somewhat differently. This classification for Allinsmith includes manipulating the child by shaming the child, appealing to his pride or guilt, and expressing disappointment over his misdeeds. But there is another dimension considered in the rating: namely, the amount of emotional control the mother displays in administering her discipline. Thus, if a mother shouts angrily at the child, 'I hate you for doing that', Allinsmith would *not* classify this as psychological discipline, while Sears *et al.* would. But the mother who says calmly and perhaps coldly, 'Now, dear, you know I don't like little boys who do that', would be classified as using psychological discipline in both systems. The difference in these two classification systems stems in part from two different views of the nature of the process which gives psychological discipline its effect. Sears *et al.* view it as a technique which arouses the child's anxiety over whether he is loved and approved of, and thereby elicits efforts on the child's part to regain his parents' approval by conforming, apologizing, or making amends. Allinsmith, on the other hand, emphasizes two things: a) the *modelling* function of discipline, pointing out that a mother who loses her temper at the same time she is trying to teach the child to control his, will have a child who will do as the mother *does* rather than as she *says*; and b) the target the child chooses for the aggressive impulses aroused in him as a consequence of punishment. The reasoning here is that the openly angry mother becomes a more legitimate target for the child's counter-aggression. The distinction between the two definitions of the dimension is further brought out when we consider the kinds of findings reported in the studies using them: Sears *et al.* found that withdrawal of love was associated with high development of conscience, physical punishment with low; Allinsmith found that psychological discipline, as she defined it, was associated with *indirect* fantasy expressions of aggression in the children they studied, corporal punishment with *direct* expression of aggression. All this illustrates the fact that fairly subtle differences in the definition of a dimension can affect the nature of child behaviour that can be predicted from it. But more importantly, both these studies illustrate the fact that when we attempted to take over the variable 'punishment' from the learning laboratories, we found it necessary to subdivide and differentiate the variable and gained predictive power by doing so.

I have been attempting to cite ways in which I think that socialization studies have improved upon some of the standard variables employed in laboratory studies. There are instances, alas, in which we have not taken note of the differences which exist between the laboratory and the standard socialization settings, and thus have failed to identify and make use of some potentially promising variables. For example, in laboratory studies, we can take it for granted that the experimenter is there during training sessions, administering either reinforcements or aversive stimuli in some orderly relationship to the subject's responses. In the parent–child relationship, the parent is by no means always functioning as a trainer, and parents differ greatly in the degree to which they do so. Some parents keep track quite continuously of what the child is doing, and engage in a constant flow of interaction, both verbal and non-verbal, with the child. Other parents, for a substantial portion of the time they are with their children, are bored, busy, withdrawn, intoxicated, watching television, or subject to some other state of activity which precludes their responding to the child unless he becomes very insistent. In such a household the children are, of course, in a very different learning situation than children growing up with more wholly attentive parents. I think the sheer amount of interaction may in some cases be a more important variable for predicting characteristics of the child than the nature of the interaction that does occur. The variable 'amount of interaction' emerged in our factor analysis of the scales in the *Patterns of Child Rearing* study (Sears *et al.* 1957) – we titled this variable 'responsible child-rearing orientation' for lack of a better name, but we never made much use of the variable because it did not fit in with the theoretical formulation of our study. But I suspect that for any future work in which we are trying to predict such things as the child's cognitive maturity level or his achievement motivation, we may find that this variable is a better predictor than the less global variables (such as amount of praise) that we have been relying on up till now.

So far, I have been discussing the process of translating variable from laboratory studies of learning to the socialization setting, and have pointed out that we have been successful in employing such variables as reward and punishment, but that in the process of using these variables, we have found useful ways of subdividing them. Let us consider the theoretical meaning of the elaborations of these variables that have occurred.

When we make the distinction between material reward and praise, and the distinction between love-oriented punishment and punishment that depends for its effect upon producing direct physical pain, we are really taking note of the fact that the effect of discipline, and in fact the very nature of the discipline that is possible to use with a child, depends upon the history of the relationship that has been developed between the child and the person who is training him. And here is a new class of variables that socialization studies have added to the list of variables derived from classical studies of learning. In laboratory studies of learning, it has not been found necessary (at least until very recently) to ask whether the experimental subject loved or hated the machine that was emitting pellets of food and drops of water, or whether the characteristics of the machine or person presenting the rewards made any difference in the effectiveness of the reinforcement. Socialization studies, on the other hand, have found the identity of the socializing agent, and certain of his personality characteristics, to be important.

The emphasis on the importance of the relationship between trainer and learner came, of course, out of psycho-dynamic theories of personality development. Learning theory and psycho-analytic theory differ, I think, with respect to what they believe the basic nature of the socialization process is. This is an oversimplification, but I believe it would be reasonably accurate to say that a learning theorist would regard socialization as a learning process in which certain actions of the child's are selected out by virtue of reinforcement, others tried and dropped because they are in some way punished or non-reinforced. The parents have a primary role in administering the rewards and punishments for the child's actions, although they do not necessarily do this deliberately and consciously as a teaching effort. And, of course, there are other sources of reward and punishment than the parents' reactions which will help to determine what behaviour the child retains.

The psycho-analytic approach, on the other hand, would emphasize not the detailed learning of specific actions on the basis of their outcome, but the providing of conditions which will motivate the child to take on spontaneously the socialized behaviour the parent wants him to have. The terms introjection, internalization, learning through role-playing, and identification have been used in this connection; they all refer to the child's tendency to copy, to take on as his own, the behaviour, attitudes, and values of the significant people in his life, even when the socializing agents have not said 'that's a good boy' or given him a piece of candy for performing these acts or holding these values. I will not go into the controversy concerning which so much has been written as to whether the child is more likely to identify with the person who is powerful and feared or with the person who is loved; nor will I discuss the several thoughtful efforts by personality theorists to reconcile the two points of view. The only important point for our consideration here is that the pyscho-analytic view of socialization has led to an exploration of such variables as the warmth or hostility of the socializing agent toward the child.

There can be no doubt that measures of the warmth of the parent–child relationship have turned out to be enormously useful in socialization studies, in a number of ways. In some studies, warmth has been found to have a direct relationship to some dependent variable. For example, McCord and McCord (1959) have found that warmth in fathers was associated with low crime rate in sons. In other studies, warmth has turned out to be a useful cross-cutting variable which interacts with other variables in such a way that other variables only begin to show their effects when the sample is first subdivided into groups differing in parental warmth. For example, in the *Patterns of Child Rearing* study, Sears *et al.* (1957) found that withdrawal of love is associated with rapid development of conscience, but only if this technique is employed by a warm mother; also that punishment for toilet accidents disrupts the toilet-training process, but that the greatest disruption occurs if punishment is administered by a cold mother.

Warmth also occupies a central role in socialization studies in its relationship to other measures of child-training variables. . . . It is clear that both in terms of its predictive value for the child's behaviour and its central place among the other interrelated child-training variables, warmth is a variable to be taken seriously. Why is it so important? I have already pointed out why the psycho-dynamic theorists believe it to be so – because of its role in producing identification. But the laboratory learning theorists can acknowledge its importance for another very simple reason. Before a parent can socialize a child, he must have established a relationship with the child such that the child will stay in the vicinity of the parent and orient himself toward the parent. A warm parent keeps the child responsive to his directions by providing an atmosphere in which the child has continuous expectations that good things will happen to him if he stays near his parent and responds to his parent's wishes. Fear of punishment can also make the child attentive to the parent, of course, but it establishes as well the conflicting motivation to escape out of reach of the punisher.

I'm sure I needn't belabour any further the notion that warmth is an important variable. But to say this is not enough. We are still faced with considerable difficulty in definition. It has been the experience of a number of people working with child-training data that they find themselves able to make reliable distinctions between mothers they call warm and mothers they call cold, and they find it possible to train others to make similar distinctions, but find it difficult indeed to define exactly what cues they are using to make the rating.

I suspect one source of difficulty is that the behaviour we look for as indicating warmth varies with the age of the child the mother is dealing with. When the child is an infant, we are likely to label a mother as warm if she gives a good deal of the contact comfort that Harlow (1958) has described. As the child grows older, the part played by the giving of contact comfort in the total constellation of warmth undoubtedly declines. When a child is ten, a mother seldom expresses her warm feelings for him by holding him on her lap. Rather, they are more likely to be expressed by the mother showing interest in the child and what he is doing, by helping unconditionally when help is needed, by being cordial and relaxed. Now warmth as expressed this way is not the same thing as giving contact comfort, and it is not to be expected that the same individuals would necessarily be good at both. . . . We would therefore not be surprised if there are low correlations between a mother's warmth toward her infant and her warmth toward the same child when it is older. If a primary ingredient of warmth is being able to gratify the child's needs unconditionally, and if the child's needs change from the infantile needs for being fed and being given contact comfort to the more mature needs for various kinds of ego support, then it is necessary for a mother to change considerably as her child changes, in order to be warm towards him at all ages. Some mothers make this change more easily than others. It is true that Schaeffer and Bayley (1960), in their longitudinal study of a group of mothers, did find a substantial degree of continuity in the degree of warmth displayed by a given mother toward a given child as the child grew older. There were undoubtedly individual differences in the ways warmth was manifested, and in the appropriateness of a mother's particular style of warmth-giving to the needs of her child at each developmental stage.

From the standpoint of making use of the variable in research, it appears that we should recognize that measuring the mother's current warmth at the time the child is, say, in nursery school or in the primary grades may not be an especially good index of how warm she was to the child as an infant. Furthermore, her warmth in infancy might predict quite different characteristics of the child than her warmth in middle childhood. If there is any relation at all between nurturance to an infant and its later personality traits, infant nurturance ought to relate only to those aspects of personality that presumably have their foundation in infancy – such as Erikson's dimension of trust (1950), or various aspects of orality. Achievement motivation, on the other hand, if it is related to the mother's warmth at all, ought to be related to measures of this variable taken when the child is older. A finding of Bronfenbrenner's (1959) seems to support this point about the importance of warmth-giving being appropriate to the developmental level of the child. He was studying high-school-aged children and employed several variables relating to the kind and amount of affectionate interchange between these adolescents and their parents. He measured the parents' affection-giving (in the sense of direct demonstrativeness), use of affective rewards, nurturance, and affiliative companionship. Among these variables, it was only the last one, affiliative companionship, that correlated with the child's current level of responsibility taking. We can speculate that this particular aspect of warmth is the one that fits in much better with an adolescent's needs than either giving him kisses or peanut butter sandwiches. All this means that warmth has to be defined in terms of parental responsiveness to the changing needs of the child.

I have referred to socialization variables that came originally from laboratory studies of learning, and that have been adapted for use in studying the socialization process. I have also referred to variables that originated in psycho-dynamic thinking. There is a set of variables that is difficult to classify in terms of these two theoretical systems; I am referring to the dimension 'permissiveness v. restrictiveness', and to the related dimension of 'control v. laissez-faire'. The theoretical status of these variables is confusing because they relate to both psycho-analytic and learning theory, but the predictions from the two theories as to the probable effects of 'permissiveness' or 'control' are sometimes quite different. To cite a familiar example, there is the issue of what ought to be the effects of permissive treatment of the infant's sucking responses. The question is complex, but a simplified version of the opposing positions would be this: the learning theorist would argue that if an infant is permitted extensive sucking, his sucking habit will be strengthened, and he will be more likely to suck his thumb, pencils, etc., at a later age. The psycho-dynamic theorist would argue that permitting extensive infantile sucking satisfies oral needs and reduces the likelihood of excessive oral behaviour at a later age. The same kind of difference of opinion can be found concerning whether permissive treatment of a child's aggressive or dependent responses should increase or decrease those responses. Now, of course, the fact that different theories produce different predictions concerning the effects of a variable is no reason for abandoning the variable. On the contrary, it is cause for rejoicing, and we should by all means continue to use the variable so that we can get data which will bear upon the validity of the theories. The trouble is that when we arrive at the point of trying to get agreement on the interpretation of findings, it sometimes turns out that the two schools of thought did not mean the same thing by 'permissiveness'. If a study shows that the more permissive parents are toward their children's aggression the more aggressive the children become, the psycho-dynamic theorist may say, 'Well, by permissiveness I didn't mean *licence*; the child must have limits set for him but he must also be allowed to express his feelings.' If, on the other hand, a study shows that children heavily punished for aggression are more aggressive on the playground, or prefer aggressive TV programmes, the learning theorist may say, 'Well, of course, if the parents' methods of stopping aggression are such as to provide additional instigation to aggression, then their non-permissiveness won't eliminate the behaviour.' We begin to see that there are some hidden meanings in such a term as 'permissiveness' and that we are dealing with several dimensions. Continuing with the example of aggression, we can see that permissiveness for aggression could mean the following things:

1   The mother holds the attitude that aggression is an acceptable, even desirable, form of behaviour.
2   The mother does not like aggressive behaviour and expects to limit it in her children, but feels that it is natural and inevitable at certain ages and so does not react strongly when her young child displays anger. A related definition of permissiveness would be pacing the demands for self-control placed upon the child to correspond with his developmental level.
3   The mother is not especially interested in the child or is otherwise occupied, and does not act to stop or prevent his aggression because she does not notice what he is doing.
4   The mother does not act early in a sequence of her child's aggressive behaviour, but waits till the behaviour has become fairly intense.

At the other end of the scale, the effect of *non*-permissiveness ought to depend upon how the non-permitting is done – whether by punishment, by reinforcing alternative behaviour, by environmental control that removes the instigations to undesired behaviour, or some other means. The basic point I wish to emphasize is that I believe 'permissiveness' is not a unitary variable, and that we need to work more directly with its components.

So far I have discussed several classes of variables: the ones translated as directly as possible from laboratory studies of learning (e.g. amount and kind of reward and punishment), and variables such as warmth and permissiveness of the socializing agent, which have their origins more in psycho-dynamic theories. There is another class of variables which has been emerging as more and more important, namely the 'social structure' variables. These variables have their origin largely in sociological thinking. I do not have time to give them more than the most cursory attention, but I do not believe they can be omitted if we are to do any sort of justice to the scope of significant variables employed in current socialization studies. One has only to list a few findings which have come out of the investigation of social structure factors to see how essential it has become to take them into account. Here is a brief sampling of such findings:

1   With adolescents, parents are most strict with children who are of the same sex as the dominant parent (Papanek 1954).

2   A mother's use of strongly dominant child-rearing techniques (called 'unqualified power assertion' in this study) is related to her husband's F score (authoritarian personality score), but not to her own (Hoffman 1960).

3   A mother's behaviour toward her children is more closely related to her husband's education than her own, and her behaviour is more closely related to her husband's education than is *his* behaviour to his own education. Thus it appears that it is the family's social status, as indicated by the husband's education, that influences the mother's socialization practices Bronfenbrenner 1959).

4   Sons are more intra-punitive if their mothers are primarily responsible for discipline than they are if their fathers are the primary disciplinarians (Henry 1956).

5   Aspects of social organization such as whether residence is patrilocal, matrilocal, or neolocal, and whether marriage is polygamous or mono-gamous, determine such aspects of culture as the length of the postpartum sex taboo, the duration of exclusive mother–child sleeping arrangements, and the amount of authority the father has over the child; these factors in turn influence such socialization practices as the age of weaning, the severity of the socialization pressures which are directed toward breaking up the child's dependency upon the mother, and the existence and nature of puberty rites at adolescence. These socialization practices then in their turn influence certain aspects of personality, including certain culturally established defence systems (Whiting, 1959, Whiting *et al.* 1958).

6   When offered a choice between a small piece of candy now v. a large one later, children from father-present homes can postpone gratification more easily than children from father-absent homes (Mischel 1958).

These findings all represent efforts to put socialization practices into a cultural or social–structural context. In each case, socialization practices are regarded as a link in a several-step chain, and consideration is given to the factors which determine the socialization practices themselves, as well as to the effects these practices in their turn have upon the child. It is clear that the way parents treat their children will be a function of their relation-ship to each other (especially of the distribution of authority between them), of the place the family has in the status system of the society in which the family resides, of the society's kinship system, etc. Of course, not every student of socialization need concern himself with all the steps in the complex sequence; he may, and often does, select a set of socialization practices and relate them to the child's behaviour without going back to the conditions which led to these practices. But he needs to be aware of the degree to which socialization practices are embedded in a cultural context, and even needs to be alert to the possibility that the 'same' socialization practice may have different effects when it is part of different cultural settings. So far, few studies have been planned or analysed with this possibility in mind, but it might be worth some empirical examination.

It is time to make explicit an assumption that has been implicit so far about the constancy of personality from one situation to another and from one time to another. When we select aspects of parental behaviour to study, and try to relate these to measured characteristics of the child, we usually measure what we believe to be reasonably pervasive, reasonably enduring 'traits' of the parent and child. Orville Brim (1960) has levelled a direct attack at the notion of trait constancy. He has asserted that there is no such thing as a 'warm' person, nor an 'aggressive' person, nor a 'dependent' person, but that behaviour is specific to roles. This would mean that the same individual may be aggressive with his subordinates and dependent toward his boss; that a child may be emotionally expressive with his same-sexed age mates, but not with his teachers or his parents. The question of exactly how general personality traits are, is of course, a matter that personality theorists have struggled with for many years. But our view of this matter will have some bearing upon our selection and definition of socialization variables. For if a child's behaviour is going to be entirely specific to roles, then there is no point in trying to predict any generalized traits in the child; rather, we should be looking for those aspects of the socialization situation that will determine what behaviour will be adopted by the child in each different role relationship in which he will find himself. If we wanted to find what socialization practices were associated with the child's becoming dominant or submissive, for example, we would have to study how his dominant behaviour had been reacted to when he was playing with same-sexed siblings, and study this separately from the socialization of the same behaviour when he was playing with opposite-sexed siblings. Only thus could we predict, according to Brim, how dominant he would be with other boys in the classroom; and we would have to make a separate prediction of his dominance with girls in the classroom. We have already been following Brim's advice, in essence, when we do studies in which we test how the child's behaviour varies with the role characteristics of the person with whom he is interacting. A good example is Gewirtz's and Baer's study on the interaction between the sex of the experimenter and the effects of interrupted nurturance (1956). But to follow Brim's point further, we would have to investigate the ways in which the child's behaviour toward specific categories of 'others' was conditioned by differential socialization in these role relationships.

I do not believe that either socialization or the child's reaction tendencies are as role-specific as Brim claims; but obviously role differentiation does occur, and he is quite right in calling our attention to the fact that, for some variables at least, we should be studying socialization separately within roles. Actually, role is only one aspect of situational variability; we have known ever since the days of Hartshorne and May (1928) that trait behaviour like 'honesty' is situation-specific. They found, for example, that the child who will cheat on the playground is not necessarily the same child who will cheat in the classroom, and that cheating is a function of the specific task presented to the child. This means that, in studying the effects of socialization we either have to abandon efforts to predict characteristics like 'honesty' and attempt to study only those characteristics of the child that are at least somewhat constant across situations, or we have to choose socialization variables that are themselves much more situation-specific, and make much more detailed predictions. An example of the utility of making socialization variables more specific to the situations they are intended to predict is provided in a study by Levy (1959), in which it was found that a child's adjustment to a hospital experience was *not* a function of the parents having trained the child generally to meet many different kinds of stress situations; rather, the child's response to hospitalization was predicted only from the amount of training the parent gave in advance for the meeting of this *particular* stress situation.

The same sort of situation prevails with respect to trait constancy over time. In their article on dependency, Kagan and Moss (1960) were able to present repeated measurements of dependency in the same group of individuals – measurements which began at the age of three and continued into the late twenties. The most notable feature of their findings was the absence of continuity in this trait. The children who were dependent at age three and four were not the same individuals who emerged as dependent in adulthood. There was simply no continuity at all for boys, while there was some, but not a great deal, for girls. Let us consider Kagan's findings from the standpoint of efforts to study the socialization practices that are related to dependency. The first and obvious point is that we cannot expect to find any characteristic of the parent's behaviour that will correlate with dependency in the young child and also correlate with dependency when the child is an adolescent or adult. This is not to say that the only correlations we can hope for are those between socialization practices and child characteristics measured at the same point in time. It is of course most likely that we shall be able to find aspects of a parent's current behaviour that correlate with characteristics his child is displaying at the same time. But it is also possible that we could find aspects of the parent's current behaviour whose effects will not show up until later. That is, perhaps there were things the parents of Kagan's sample of children were doing when these children were three and four that had some bearing upon how dependent the children became at the age of ten or eleven. But it is clear enough that whatever these delayed-action variables are they could hardly be the same variables as the ones which determined how dependent the children were at age three, since it was not the same children who were displaying large amounts of dependency behaviour at the two ages.

I have pointed to the way in which different theoretical systems, and different social-science disciplines, have converged to define and elaborate some of the variables which have been used in studies of socialization. In some cases this convergence has produced useful new knowledge; in others it has produced confusion over the meaning of variables. More importantly, it has produced a startling range of findings which have not yet been integrated into a theory of socialization. This is a major task that remains to be done.

References

ALLINSMITH, B. (1960) 'Directness with which Anger is Expressed', in Miller, D. R. and Swanson, G. E. (eds) *Inner Conflict and Defense* New York, Holt-Dryden.

BRIM, O. G. (1960) 'Personality Development as Role Learning', in Iscoe, I. and Stevenson, H. (eds) *Personality Development in Children* Austin, Texas, University of Texas Press.

BRONFENBRENNER, U. (1959) 'Some Familial Antecedents of Responsibility and Leadership in Adolescents' Cornell University.

ERIKSON, E. H. (1950) *Childhood and Society* New York, Norton.

GEWIRTZ, J. L. and BAER, D. M. (1956) 'Does Brief Social "Deprivation" Enhance the Effectiveness of a Social Reinforcer ("Approval")?' *American Psychologist*, 11, 428-9.

HARLOW, H. F. (1958) 'On the Nature of Love', *American Psychologist*, 13, 673-85.

HARTSHORNE, H. and MAY, M. A. (1928) *Studies in Deceit* New York, Macmillan.

HENRY, A. F. (1956) 'Family Role Structure and Self-Blame', *Social Forces*, 35, 34-8.

HOFFMAN, M. L. (1960) 'Power Assertion by Parents and Its Impact on the Child', *Child Development*, 31, 129-44.

KAGAN, J. and MOSS, H. A. (1960) 'The Stability of Passive and Dependent Behavior from Childhood through Adulthood', *Child Development*, 31, 577–91.

LEVY, E. (1959) 'Children's Behavior Under Stress and Its Relation to Training by Parents to Respond to Stress Situation', *Child Development*, 30, 307–24.

MCCORD, W. and MCCORD, J. (1959) *The Origins of Crime* New York, Columbia University Press.

MISCHEL, W. (1958) 'Preference for Delayed Reinforcement: An Experimental Study of Cultural Observation', *Journal of Abnormal and Social Psychology*, 56, 57–61.

PAPANEK, M. L. (1954) 'Family Structure and Child-Training Practices', Ph.D. dissertation (unpublished), Radcliffe College.

SCHAEFFER, E. S. and BAYLEY, N. (1960) 'Consistency of Maternal Behavior from Infancy to Pre-Adolescence', *Journal of Abnormal and Social Psychology*, 61, 1–6.

SEARS, R. R., MACCOBY, E. E. and LEVIN, H. (1957) *Patterns of Child Rearing* Evaston, Illinois, Row-Peterson.

WHITING, J. W. M. (1959) 'Sin, Sorcery and the Superego', in Jones M. R. (ed.) *Nebraska Symposium on Motivation* Lincoln, Nebraska, University of Nebraska Press.

WHITING, J. W. M., KLUCKHOHN, R. and ANTHONY, A. (1958) 'The Function of Male Initiation Rites at Puberty', in Maccoby E. E., Newcombe, T. M. and Hartley, E. L. (eds) *Readings in Social Psychology* New York, Holt.

20   Presentation of self to others

Erving Goffman

When an individual enters the presence of others, they commonly seek to acquire information about him or to bring into play information about him already possessed. They will be interested in his general socio–economic status, his conception of self, his attitude toward them, his competence, his trustworthiness, etc. Although some of this information seems to be sought almost as an end in itself, there are usually quite practical reasons for acquiring it. Information about the individual helps to define the situation, enabling others to know in advance what he will expect of them and what they may expect of him. Informed in these ways, the others will know how best to act in order to call forth a desired response from him.

For those present, many sources of information become accessible and many carriers (or 'sign-vehicles') become available for conveying this information. If unacquainted with the individual, observers can glean clues from his conduct and appearance which allow them to apply their previous experience with individuals roughly similar to the one before them or, more important, to apply untested stereotypes to him. They can also assume from past experience that only individuals of a particular kind are likely to be found in a given social setting. They can rely on what the individual says about himself or on documentary evidence he provides as to who and what he is. If they know, or know of, the individual by virtue of experience prior to the interaction, they can reply on assumptions as to the persistence and generality of psychological traits as a means of predicting his present and future behaviour.

However, during the period in which the individual is in the immediate presence of the others, few events may occur which directly provide the others with the conclusive information they will need if they are to direct wisely their own activity. Many crucial facts lie beyond the time and place of interaction or lie concealed within it. For example, the 'true' or 'real' attitudes, beliefs, and emotions of the individual can be ascertained only indirectly, through his avowals or through what appears to be involuntary expressive behaviour. Similarly, if the individual offers the others a product

GOFFMAN, ERVING (1959) 'Presentation of Self to Others', in *The Presentation of Self in Everyday Life* Edinburgh, University of Edinburgh Social Science Research Centre.

or service, they will often find that during the interaction there will be no time and place immediately available for eating the pudding that the proof can be found in. They will be forced to accept some events as conventional or natural signs of something not directly available to the senses. In Ichheiser's terms (1949, pp. 6–7), the individual will have to act so that he intentionally or unintentionally *expresses* himself, and the others will in turn have to be *impressed* in some way by him.

The expressiveness of the individual (and therefore his capacity to give impressions) appears to involve two radically different kinds of sign activity: the expression that he *gives*, and the expression that he *gives off*. The first involves verbal symbols or their substitutes which he uses admittedly and solely to convey the information that he and the others are known to attach to these symbols. This is communication in the traditional and narrow sense. The second involves a wide range of action that others can treat as symptomatic of the actor, the expectation being that the action was performed for reasons other than the information conveyed in this way. As we shall have to see, this distinction has an only initial validity. The individual does of course intentionally convey misinformation by means of both of these types of communication, the first involving deceit, the second feigning.

Taking communication in both its narrow and broad sense, one finds that when the individual is in the immediate presence of others, his activity will have a promissory character. The others are likely to find that they must accept the individual on faith, offering him a just return while he is present before them in exchange for something whose true value will not be established until after he has left their presence. (Of course, the others also live by inference in their dealings with the physical world, but it is only in the world of social interaction that the objects about which they make inferences will purposely facilitate and hinder this inferential process.) The security that they justifiably feel in making inferences about the individual will vary, of course, depending on such factors as the amount of information they already possess about him, but no amount of such past evidence can entirely obviate the necessity of acting on the basis of inferences. As William I. Thomas suggested:

> It is also highly important for us to realize that we do not as a matter of fact lead our lives, make our decisions, and reach our goals in everyday life either statistically or scientifically. We live by inference. I am, let us say, your guest. You do not know, you cannot determine scientifically, that I will not steal your money or your spoons. But inferentially I will not, and inferentially you have me as your guest. (Volkart 1951, p. 5)

Let us now turn from the others to the point of view of the individual who presents himself before them. He may wish them to think highly of him, or to think that he thinks highly of them, or to perceive how in fact he feels toward them, or to obtain no clear-cut impression; he may wish to ensure sufficient harmony so that the interaction can be sustained, or to defraud, get rid of, confuse, mislead, antagonize, or insult them. Regardless of the particular objective which the individual has in mind and of his motive for having this objective, it will be in his interests to control the conduct of the others, especially their responsive treatment of him.[1] This control is achieved largely by influencing the definition of the situation which the others come to formulate, and he can influence this definition by expressing himself in such a way as to give them the kind of impression that will lead them to act voluntarily in accordance with his own plan. Thus, when an individual appears in the presence of others, there will usually be some reason for him to mobilize his activity so that it will convey an impression to others which it is in his interests to convey. Since a girl's dormitory mates will glean evidence of her popularity from the calls she receives on the phone, we can suspect that some girls will arrange for calls to be made, and Willard Waller's finding can be anticipated:

> It has been reported by many observers that a girl who is called to the telephone in the dormitories will often allow herself to be called several times, in order to give all the other girls ample opportunity to hear her paged (Waller 1936).

Of the two kinds of communication – expressions given and expressions given off – this report will be primarily concerned with the latter, with the more theatrical and contextual kind, the non-verbal, presumably unintentional kind, whether this communication be purposely engineered or not. As an example of what we must try to examine, I would like to cite at length a novelistic incident in which Preedy, a vacationing Englishman, makes his first appearance on the beach of his summer hotel in Spain:

> But in any case he took care to avoid catching anyone's eye. First of all, he had to make it clear to those potential companions of his holiday that they were of no concern to him whatsoever. He stared through them, round them, over them – eyes lost in space. The beach might have been empty.

---

1   Here I owe much to an unpublished paper by Tom Burns of the University of Edinburgh. He presents the argument that in all interaction a basic underlying theme is the desire of each participant to guide and control the responses made by the others present. A similar argument has been advanced by Jay Haley in a recent unpublished paper, but in regard to a special kind of control, that having to do with defining the nature of the relationship of those involved in the interaction.

If by chance a ball was thrown his way, he looked surprised; then let a smile of amusement lighten his face (Kindly Preedy), looked round dazed to see that there *were* people on the beach, tossed it back with a smile to himself and not a smile *at* the people, and then resumed carelessly his nonchalant survey of space.

But it was time to institute a little parade, the parade of the Ideal Preedy. By devious handlings he gave any who wanted to look a chance to see the title of his book – a Spanish translation of Homer, classic thus, but not daring, cosmopolitan too – and then gathered together his beach-wrap and bag into a neat sand-resistant pile (Methodical and Sensible Preedy), rose slowly to stretch at ease his huge frame (Big-Cat Preedy), and tossed aside his sandals (Carefree Preedy, after all).

The marriage of Preedy and the sea! There were alternative rituals. The first involved the stroll that turns into a run and a dive straight into the water, thereafter smoothing into a strong splashless crawl towards the horizon. But of course not really to the horizon. Quite suddenly he would turn on to his back and thrash great white splashes with his legs, somehow thus showing that he could have swum further had he wanted to, and then would stand up a quarter out of water for all to see who it was.

The alternative course was simpler, it avoided the cold-water shock and it avoided the risk of appearing too high-spirited. The point was to appear to be so used to the sea, the Mediterranean, and this particular beach, that one might as well be in the sea as out of it. It involved a slow stroll down and into the edge of the water – not even noticing his toes were wet, land and water all the same to *him*! – with his eyes up at the sky gravely surveying portents, invisible to others, of the weather (Local Fisherman Preedy). (Sansom 1956)

The novelist means us to see that Preedy is improperly concerned with the extensive impressions he feels his sheer bodily action is giving off to those around him. We can malign Preedy further by assuming that he has acted merely in order to give a particular impression, that this is a false impression, and that the others present receive either no impression at all, or worse still, the impression that Preedy is affectedly trying to cause them to receive this particular impression. But the important point for us here is that the kind of impression Preedy thinks he is making is in fact the kind of impression that others correctly and incorrectly glean from someone in their midst.

I have said that when an individual appears before others his actions will influence the definition of the situation which they come to have. Sometimes the individual will act in a thoroughly calculating manner, expressing himself in a given way solely in order to give the kind of impression to others that is likely to evoke from them a specific response he is concerned to obtain. Sometimes the individual will be calculating in his activity but be relatively unaware that this is the case. Sometimes he will intentionally and consciously express himself in a particular way, but chiefly because the tradition of his group or social status require this kind of expression and not because of any particular response (other than vague acceptance or approval) that is likely to be evoked from those impressed by the expression. Sometimes the traditions of an individual's role will lead him to give a well-designed impression of a particular kind and yet he may be neither consciously or unconsciously disposed to create such an impression. The others, in their turn, may be suitably impressed by the individual's efforts to convey something, or may misunderstand the situation and come to conclusions that are warranted neither by the individual's intent nor by the facts. In any case, in so far as the others act *as if* the individual had conveyed a particular impression, we may take a functional or pragmatic view and say that the individual has 'effectively' projected a given definition of the situation and 'effectively' fostered the understanding that a given state of affairs obtains.

There is one aspect of the others' response that bears special comment here. Knowing that the individual is likely to present himself in a light that is favourable to him, the others may divide what they witness into two parts; a part that is relatively easy for the individual to manipulate at will, being chiefly his verbal assertions, and a part in regard to which he seems to have little concern or control, being chiefly derived from the expressions he gives off. The others may then use what are considered to be the ungovernable aspects of his expressive behaviour as a check upon the validity of what is conveyed by the governable aspects. In this a fundamental asymmetry is demonstrated in the communication process, the individual presumably being aware of only one stream of his communication, the witnesses of this stream and one other. For example, in Shetland Isle one crofter's wife, in serving native dishes to a visitor from the mainland of Britain, would listen with a polite smile to his polite claims of liking what he was eating; at the same time she would take note of the rapidity with which the visitor lifted his fork or spoon to his mouth, the eagerness with which he passed food into his mouth, and the gusto expressed in chewing the food, using these signs as a check on the stated feelings of the eater. The same woman, in order to discover what one acquaintance (A) 'actually' thought of another acquaintance (B), would wait until B was in the presence of A but engaged in conversation with still another person (C). She would then covertly examine the facial expresions of A as he regarded B in conversation with C. Not being in conversation with B, and not being directly observed by him, A would sometimes relax usual constraints and tactful deceptions, and freely express what he was 'actually' feeling about B. This Shetlander, in short, would observe the unobserved observer.

Now given the fact that others are likely to check up on the more controllable aspects of behaviour by means of the less controllable, one can expect that sometimes the individual will try to exploit this very possibility, guiding the impression he makes through behaviour felt to be reliably informing.[2] For example, in gaining admission to a tight social circle, the participant observer may not only wear an accepting look while listening to an informant, but may also be careful to wear the same look when observing the informant talking to others, observers of the observer will then not as easily discover where he actually stands. A specific illustration may be cited from Shetland Isle. When a neighbour dropped in to have a cup of tea, he would ordinarily wear at least a hint of an expectant warm smile as he passed through the door into the cottage. Since lack of physical obstructions outside the cottage and lack of light within it usually made it possible to observe the visitor unobserved as he approached the house, islanders sometimes took pleasure in watching the visitor drop whatever expression he was manifesting and replace it with a sociable one just before reaching the door. However, some visitors, in appreciating that this examination was occurring, would blindly adopt a social face a long distance from the house, thus ensuring the projection of a constant image.

This kind of control upon the part of the individual reinstates the symmetry of the communication process, and sets the stage for a kind of information game – a potentially infinite cycle of concealment, discovery, false revelation, and rediscovery. It should be added that since the others are likely to be relatively unsuspicious of the presumably unguided aspect of the individual's conduct, he can gain much by controlling it. The others of course may sense that the individual is manipulating the presumably spontaneous aspects of his behaviour, and seek in this very act of manipulation some shading of conduct that the individual has not managed to control. This again provides a check upon the individual's behaviour, this time his presumably uncalculated behaviour, thus re-establishing the assymmetry of the communication process. Here I would like only to add the suggestion that the arts of piercing an individual's effort at calculated unintentionality seem better developed than our capacity to manipulate our own behaviour, so that regardless of how many steps have occurred in the

---

2 The widely read and rather sound writings of Stephen Potter are concerned in part with signs that can be engineered to give a shrewd observer the apparently incidental cues he needs to discover concealed virtues the gamesman does not in fact possess.

information game, the witness is likely to have the advantage over the actor, and the initial asymmetry of the communication process is likely to be retained.

When we allow that the individual projects a definition of the situation when he appears before others, we must also see that the others, however passive their role may seem to be, will themselves effectively project a definition of the situation by virtue of their response to the individual and by virtue of any lines of action they initiate to him. Ordinarily the definitions of the situation projected by the several different participants are sufficiently attuned to one another so that open contradiction will not occur. I do not mean that there will be the kind of consensus that arises when each individual present candidly expresses what he really feels and honestly agrees with the expressed feelings of the others present. This kind of harmony is an optimistic ideal and in any case not necessary for the smooth working of society. Rather, each participant is expected to suppress his immediate heartfelt feelings, conveying a view of the situation which he feels the others will be able to find at least temporarily acceptable. The maintenance of this surface of agreement, this veneer of consensus, is facilitated by each participant concealing his own wants behind statements which assert values to which everyone present feels obliged to give lip service. Further, there is usually a kind of division of definitional labour. Each participant is allowed to establish the tentative official ruling regarding matters which are vital to him but not immediately important to others, e.g. the rationalizations and justifications by which he accounts for his past activity. In exchange for this courtesy he remains silent or non-committal on matters important to others but not immediately important to him. We have then a kind of interactional *modus vivendi*. Together the participants contribute to a single over-all definition of the situation which involves not so much a real agreement as to what exists but rather a real agreement as to whose claims concerning what issues will be temporarily honoured. Real agreement will also exist concerning the desirability of avoiding an open conflict of definitions of the situation.[3] I will refer to this level of agreement as a 'working consensus'. It is to be understood that the working consensus established in one interaction

3 An interaction can be purposely set up as a time and place for voicing differences in opinion, but in such cases participants must be careful to agree not to disagree on the proper tone of voice, vocabulary, and degree of seriousness in which all arguments are to be phrased, and upon the mutual respect which disagreeing participants must carefully continue to express toward one another. This debaters' or academic definition of the situation may also be invoked suddenly and judiciously as a way of translating a serious conflict of views into one that can be handled within a framework acceptable to all present.

setting will be quite different in content from the working consensus established in a different type of setting. Thus, between two friends at lunch, a reciprocal show of affection, respect, and concern for the other is maintained. In service occupations, on the other hand, the specialist often maintains an image of disinterested involvement in the problem of the client, while the client responds with a show of respect for the competence and integrity of the specialist. Regardless of such differences in content, however, the general form of these working arrangements is the same.

In noting the tendency for a participant to accept the definitional claims made by the others present, we can appreciate the crucial importance of the information that the individual *initially* possesses or acquires concerning his fellow participants, for it is on the basis of this initial information that the individual starts to define the situation and starts to build up lines of responsive action. The individual's initial projection commits him to what he is proposing to be and requires him to drop all pretences of being other things. As the interaction among the participants progresses, additions and modifications in this initial informational state will of course occur, but it is essential that these later developments be related without contradiction to, and even built up from, the initial positions taken by the several participants. It would seem that an individual can more easily make a choice as to what line of treatment to demand from and extend to the others present at the beginning of an encounter than he can alter the line of treatment that is being pursued once the interaction is underway.

In everyday life, of course, there is a clear understanding that first impressions are important. Thus, the work adjustment of those in service occupations will often hinge upon a capacity to seize and hold the initiative in the service relation, a capacity that will require subtle aggressiveness on the part of the server when he is of lower socio–economic status than his client. W. F. Whyte (1949, pp. 132–3) suggests the waitress as an example:

> The first point that stands out is that the waitress who bears up under pressure does not simply respond to her customers. She acts with some skill to control their behaviour. The first question to ask when we look at the customer relationship is, 'Does the waitress get the jump on the customer, or does the customer get the jump on the waitress?' The skilled waitress realizes the crucial nature of this question . . .
>
> The skilled waitress tackles the customer with confidence and without hesitation. For example, she may find that a new customer has seated himself before she could clear off the dirty dishes and change the cloth. He is now leaning on the table studying the menu. She greets him, says, 'May I change the cover, please?' and, without waiting for an answer, takes his menu away

from him so that he moves back from the table, and she goes about her work. The relationship is handled politely but firmly, and there is never any question as to who is in charge.

When the interaction that is initiated by 'first impressions' is itself merely the initial interaction in an extended series of interactions involving the same participants, we speak of 'getting off on the right foot' and feel that it is crucial that we do so. Thus, one learns that some teachers take the following view:

> You can't ever let them get the upper hand on you or you're through. So I start out tough. The first day I get a new class in, I let them know who's boss . . . You've got to start off tough, then you can ease up as you go along. If you start out easy-going, when you try to get tough, they'll just look at you and laugh. (Becker 1951)

Similarly, attendants in mental institutions may feel that if the new patient is sharply put in his place the first day on the ward and made to see who is boss, much future difficulty will be prevented (Taxel 1953).

Given the fact that the individual effectively projects a definition of the situation when he enters the presence of others, we can assume that events may occur within the interaction which contradict, discredit, or otherwise throw doubt upon this projection. When these disruptive events occur, the interaction itself may come to a confused and embarrassed halt. Some of the assumptions upon which the responses of the participants had been predicated become untenable, and the participants find themselves lodged in an interaction for which the situation has been wrongly defined and is now no longer defined. At such moments the individual whose presentation has been discredited may feel ashamed while the others present may feel hostile, and all the participants may come to feel ill at ease, nonplussed, out of countenance, embarrassed, experiencing the kind of anomy that is generated when the minute social system of face-to-face interaction breaks down.

In stressing the fact that the initial definition of the situation projected by an individual tends to provide a plan for the cooperative activity that follows – in stressing this action point of view – we must not overlook the crucial fact that any projected definition of the situation also has a distinctive moral character. Society is organized on the principle that any individual who possesses certain social characteristics has a moral right to expect that others will value and treat him in an appropriate way. Connected with this principle is a second, namely that an individual who implicitly or explicitly signifies that he has certain social characteristics ought in fact to be what he claims he is. In consequence, when an individual projects a definition of the situation and thereby makes an implicit or explicit claim to be a person of a particular kind, he automatically exerts a moral demand upon the others, obliging them to value and treat him in the manner that persons of his kind have a right to expect. He also implicitly forgoes all claims to be things he does not appear to be [4] and hence forgoes the treatment that would be appropriate for such individuals. The others find, then, that the individual has informed them as to what is and as to what they *ought* to see as the 'is'.

One cannot judge the importance of definitional disruptions by the frequency with which they occur, for apparently they would occur more frequently were not constant precautions taken. We find that preventive practices are constantly employed to avoid these embarrassments and that corrective practices are constantly employed to compensate for discrediting occurrences that have not been successfully avoided. When the individual employs these strategies and tactics to protect his own projections, we may refer to them as 'defensive practices'; when a participant employs them to save the definition of the situation projected by another, we speak of 'projective practices' or 'tact'. Together, defensive and protective practices comprise the techniques employed to safeguard the impression fostered by an individual during his presence before others. It should be added that while we may be ready to see that no fostered impression would survive if defensive practices were not employed, we are less ready perhaps to see that few impressions could survive if those who received the impression did not exert tact in their reception of it.

In addition to the fact that precautions are taken to prevent disruption of projected definitions, we may also note that an intense interest in these disruptions comes to play a significant role in the social life of the group. Practical jokes and social games are played in which embarrassments which are to be taken unseriously are purposely engineered (Goffman 1959). Fantasies are created in which devastating exposures occur. Anecdotes from the past – real, embroidered, or fictitious – are told and retold, detailing disruptions which occurred, almost occurred, or occurred and were admirably resolved. There seems to be no grouping which does not have a ready supply of these games, reveries, and cautionary tales, to be used as a source of humour, a catharsis for anxieties, and a sanction for inducing individuals to be modest in their claims and reasonable in their projected expectations. The individual may tell himself through dreams of getting

4 This role of the witness in limiting what it is the individual can be has been stressed by Existentialists, who see it as a basic threat to individual freedom. (See Jean-Paul Sartre 1956).

into impossible positions. Families tell of the time a guest got his dates mixed and arrived when neither the house nor anyone in it was ready for him. Journalists tell of times when an all-too-meaningful misprint occurred, and the paper's assumption of objectivity or decorum was humorously discredited. Public servants tell of times a client ridiculously misunderstood form instructions, giving answers which implied an unanticipated and bizarre definition of the situation (Blau 1955). Seamen, whose home away from home is rigorously he-man, tell stories of coming back home and inadvertently asking mother to 'pass the fucking butter' (Beattie 1950). Diplomats tell of the time a near-sighted queen asked a republican ambassador about the health of his king (Ponsonby 1952) . . .

It will be convenient to end this introduction with some definitions that are implied in what has gone before. Interaction (that is, face-to-face interaction) may be roughly defined as the reciprocal influence of individuals upon one another's actions when in one another's immediate physical presence. *An* interaction may be defined as all the interaction which occurs throughout any one occasion when a given set of individuals are in one another's continuous presence; the term 'an encounter' would do as well. A 'performance' may be defined as all the activity of a given participant on a given occasion which serves to influence in any way any of the other participants. Taking a particular participant and his performance as a basic point of reference, we may refer to those who contribute the other performances as the audience, observers, or co-participants. The pre-established pattern of action which is unfolded during a performance and which may be presented or played through on other occasions may be called a 'part' or 'routine'.[5] These situational terms can easily be related to conventional structural ones. When an individual or performer plays the same part to the same audience on different occasions, a social relationship is likely to arise. Defining social role as the enactment of rights and duties attached to a given status, we can say that a social role will involve one or more parts and that each of these different parts may be presented by the performer on a series of occasions to the same kinds of audience or to an audience of the same persons.

5 For comments on the importance of distinguishing between a routine of interaction and any particular instance when this routine is played through, see von Neumann and Morgenstern (1947).

References

BEATTIE, W. M. JR (1950) 'The Merchant Seaman', unpublished M.A. report, Department of Sociology, University of Chicago.

BECKER, H. S. (1951) 'Social Class Variations in the Teacher Pupil Relationship', *Journal of Educational Sociology*, XXV.

BLAU, P. (1955) *Dynamics of Bureaucracy* Chicago, University of Chicago Press.

GOFFMAN, E. (1959) *The Presentation of Self in Everyday Life* New York, Doubleday.

ICHHEISER, G. (1949) 'Misunderstandings in Human Relations', supplement to *American Journal of Sociology*, LV.

VON NEUMANN, J. and MORGENSTERN, O. (1947) *The Theory of Games and Economic Behavior* (2nd ed.) Princeton, New Jersey, Princeton University Press.

PONSONBY, F. (1952) *Recollections of Three Reigns* New York, Dutton.

SANSOM, W. (1956) *A Contest of Ladies* London, Hogarth Press.

SARTRE, J.-P. (1956) *Being and Nothingness*, trans. Barnes H. E., New York, Philosophical Library.

TAXEL, H. (1953) 'Authority Structure in a Mental Hospital Ward', unpublished master's thesis, Department of Sociology, University of Chicago.

VOLKART, E. H. (ed.) (1951) *Social Behavior and Personality*, contributions of Thomas W. I. to theory and social research, Social Research Council.

WALLER, W. (1936) 'The Rating and Dating Complex', *American Sociological Review*, II.

WHYTE, W. F. (1946) 'When Workers and Customers Meet', in *Industry and Society*, Whyte W. F. (ed.) New York, McGraw-Hill.

21   The cabdriver and his fare: facets of a fleeting relationship

Fred Davis

Even in an urban and highly secularized society such as ours, most service relationships, be they between a professional and his client or a menial and his patron, are characterized by certain constraints on too crass a rendering and consuming of the service (Parsons 1951). That is to say, in the transaction, numerous interests besides that of simply effecting an economic exchange are customarily attended to and dealt with. The moral reputation of the parties (Goffman 1956), their respective social standing, and the skill and art with which the service is performed (Hughes 1958) are but a few of the non-instrumental values which are usually incorporated into the whole act.

Tenuous though such constraints may become at times, particularly in large cities where anonymous roles only, segmentally related, occur in great profusion, it is at once evident that for them to exist at all something approximating a community must be present. Practitioners and clients must be sufficiently in communication for any untoward behaviour to stand a reasonable chance of becoming known, remarked upon, remembered, and, in extreme cases, made public. And, whereas the exercise of sanctions does not necessarily depend on a community network (Bott 1957) that is closely integrated (or one in which there is a total identity of values and interests), it does depend on there being some continuity and stability in the relationships that make up the network, so that, at minimum, participants may in the natural course of events be able to identify actions and actors to one another (Merton 1957).

It is mainly, though not wholly, from this vantage point that big-city cabdriving as an occupation is here discussed, particularly the relationship between cabdriver and fare and its consequences for the occupational culture. Approximating in certain respects a provincial's caricature of the broad arc of social relations in the metropolis, this relationship affords an extreme instance of the weakening and attenuation of many of the constraints in other client-and-patron-oriented services in our society. As such, its analysis can perhaps point up by implication certain of the rarely con-

DAVIS, FRED (1965) 'The Cabdriver and His Fare: Facets of a Fleeting Relationship', in *The American Journal of Sociology*, 158–65.

sidered preconditions for practitioner–client relations found in other, more firmly structured, services and professions.

In a large city like Chicago the hiring of a cab by a passenger may be conceived of in much the same way as the random collision of particles in an atomic field. True, there are some sectors of the field in which particles come into more frequent collisions than others, for example, downtown, at rail-road depots, and at the larger neighbourhood shopping centres. But this kind of differential activity within the field as a whole provides little basis for predicting the coupling of any two specific particles.

To a much more pronounced degree than is the case in other client-and-patron-oriented services, the occupation of cabdriver provides its practitioners with few, if any, regularities by which to come upon, build up, and maintain a steady clientele. The doctor has his patients, the schoolteacher her pupils, the janitor his tenants, the waitress her regular diners; and in each case server and served remain generally in some continuing or renewable relationship. By contrast, the cabdriver's day consists of a long series of brief contacts with unrelated persons of whom he has no foreknowledge, just as they have none of him, and whom he is not likely to encounter again.

Furthermore, by virtue of the differential spatial, social, and organizational arrangements of the community, it is also likely that the clients of these other practitioners will, in some manner at least, know one another and be related to one another in ways that often transcend the simple circumstances of sharing the same services: they may also be friends, kin, neighbours, or colleagues. For this reason the clientele of most practitioners is something more than an aggregate of discrete individuals; it is, as well, a rudimentary social universe and forum to which the practitioner must address himself in other than purely individual terms (Merton 1957).

The cabdriver, by comparison, has no such clientele. He has no fixed business address, and his contacts with passengers are highly random and singular. To a striking degree he is a practitioner without reputation because those who ride in his cab do not comprise, except perhaps in the most abstract sense, anything approximating a social group. They neither know nor come into contact with one another in other walks of life, and, even if by chance some do, they are unaware of their ever having shared the services of the same anonymous cabdriver. Even were the driver deliberately to set out to build up a small nucleus of steady and favoured passengers, the time–space logistics of his job would quickly bring such a scheme to nought. Unable to plot his location in advance or to distribute time according to a schedule, he depends on remaining open to all comers wherever he finds himself. Much more so than other classes of service personnel, cabdrivers are both the fortuitous victims and the beneficiaries of random and highly impersonal market contingencies.

This set of circumstances – fleeting, one-time contact with a heterogeneous aggregate of clients, unknown to one another – exerts an interesting influence on the role of cabdriver.

Unable, either directly through choice or indirectly through location, to select clients, the cabdriver is deprived of even minimal controls. His trade therefore exposes him to a variety of hazards and exigencies which few others, excepting policemen, encounter as frequently; for example: stickups, belligerent drunks, women in labour, psychopaths, counterfeiters, and fare-jumpers. Unlike the policeman's, however, his control over them is more fragile.

Nor, incidentally, is the cabdriver's social status or level of occupational skill of much help in inducing constraint in fares. Patently, his status is low, in large part precisely because, unlike the professional and other practitioners commanding prestige, he can hardly be distinguished from his clients in task-relevant competence. Not only is the operation of a motor car a widely possessed skill, but a large proportion of fares have, for example, a very good idea of the best routes to their destination, the rules and practices of the road, and the charges for a trip. Though they are rarely as adept or sophisticated in these matters as the cabdriver, the discrepancy is so small that many think they know the driver's job as well as he does. Periodically, a cabdriver will boldly challenge a difficult and critical passenger to take over the wheel himself. Others, wishing to impress on the fare that theirs is a real service requiring special talent and skill, will resort to darting nimbly in and out of traffic, making neatly executed U-turns and leaping smartly ahead of other cars when the traffic light changes.

Goffman (1956) speaks of a category of persons who in some social encounters are treated as if they were not present, whereas in fact they may be indispensable for sustaining the performance. He terms these 'nonpersons' and gives as an example a servant at a social gathering. Although cabdrivers are not consistently approached in this way by fares, it happens often enough for it to become a significant theme of their work. Examples are legion. Maresca (1945) tells of the chorus girl who made a complete change from street clothing into stage costume as he drove her to her theatre. More prosaic instances include the man and wife who, managing to suppress their anger while on the street, launch into a bitter quarrel the moment they are inside the cab; or the well-groomed young couple who after a few minutes roll over on the back seat to begin petting; or the businessman who loudly discusses details of a questionable business deal. Here the driver is expected to, and usually does, act as if he were merely an extension of the automobile he operates. In actuality, of course, he is acutely aware of what goes on in his cab, and, although his being treated as a non-person implies a degraded status, it also affords him a splendid vantage point from which to witness a rich variety of human schemes and entanglements.

The fleeting nature of the cabdriver's contact with the passenger at the same time also makes for his being approached as someone to whom intimacies can be revealed and opinions forthrightly expressed with little fear of rebuttal, retaliation, or disparagement. And though this status as an accessible person is the product of little more than the turning inside-out of his non-person status – which situation implies neither equality nor respect for his opinion – it nevertheless does afford him glimpses of the private lives of individuals which few in our society, apart from psychiatrists and clergy, are privileged to note as often or in such great variety. It is probably not a mistaken everyday generalization that big-city cabdrivers, on their part, feel less compunction about discussing their own private lives, asking probing questions, and 'sounding off' on a great many topics and issues than do others who regularly meet the public, but less fleetingly.

In cabdriving, therefore, propriety, deference, and 'face' are, in the nature of the case, weaker than is the case in most other service relationships. This absence contributes to a heightened preoccupation with and focusing on the purely instrumental aspect of the relationship which for the driver is the payment he receives for his services. This perhaps would be less blatantly the case were it not for the gratuity or tip. For the non-cab-owning company driver, the sum collected in tips amounts roughly to 40 per cent of his earnings. Considering, for example, that in Chicago in the late forties a hard-working cabdriver, who worked for ten hours a day, six days a week, would on the average take home approximately seventy-five dollars a week including tips, the importance of tipping can readily be appreciated. For the family man who drives, tips usually represent the difference between a subsistence and a living wage. Also, tips are, apart from taxes, money 'in the clear', in that the driver does not have to divide them with the company as he does his metered collections. Sum for sum, therefore, tips represent greater gain for him than do metered charges.

It would probably be incorrect to hold that pecuniary considerations are the sole ones involved in the cabdriver's attitude towards the tip. Yet in such tip-sensitive occupations as cabdriving, waitering, and bellhopping to suggest that the tip's primary significance is its symbolic value as a token of affection or appreciation for a service well performed would be even wider of the mark. Vindictive caricatures abound among cabdrivers, as they do among waiters, waitresses, and bellhops, of the 'polite gentleman' or 'kind lady' who with profuse thanks and flawless grace departs from the scene having 'stiffed' (failed to tip) them. In occupations where the tip constitutes so large a fraction of the person's earnings, the cash nexus, while admittedly not the only basis upon which patrons are judged, is so important as to relegate other considerations to a secondary place. Will the fare tip or will he 'stiff'? How much will he tip? The answers remain in nearly every instance problematic to the end. Not only is there no sure way of predicting the outcome, but in a culture where the practice of tipping is neither as widespread nor as standardized as in many Continental countries, for example, the driver cannot in many cases even make a guess.

No regular scheme of work can easily tolerate so high a degree of ambiguity and uncertainty in a key contingency. Invariably, attempts are made to fashion ways and means of greater predictability and control; or, failing that, of devising formulas and imagery to bring order and reason in otherwise inscrutable and capricious events. In the course of a long history a rich body of stereotypes, beliefs, and practices has grown up whose function is that of reducing uncertainty, increasing calculability, and providing coherent explanations.

A basic dichotomy running through the cabdriver's concept of his client world is of regular cab users and of non-cab users, the latter referred to as 'jerks', 'slobs', yokels', 'public transportation types', and a host of other derogatory terms. The former class, though viewed as quite heterogeneous within itself, includes all who customarily choose cabs in preference to other forms of local transportation, are conversant with the cab–passenger role, and, most of all, accept, if only begrudgingly, the practice of tipping. By comparison, the class of non-cab users includes that vast aggregate of persons who resort to cabs only in emergencies or on special occasions, and are prone too often to view the hiring of a cab as simply a more expensive mode of transportation.

Take, for example, the familiar street scene following a sudden downpour or unexpected breakdown in bus service, when a group of individuals cluster about a bus stop, several of whom dart from the kerb now and then in hope of hailing a cab. Such persons are almost by definition non-cab users or they would not be found at a bus stop in the rain; nor would they be keeping an eye out for a possible bus. A potential fare in this predicament is to the cabdriver a foul-weather friend, and drivers are on occasion known to hurtle by in spiteful glee, leaving the supplicant standing.

He who hires a cab only on special occasions, frequently to impress others or, perhaps, himself alone, is another familiar kind of non-cab user. Writing of his experiences as a London cabdriver, Hodge relates a by no means uncommon encounter:

> But tonight is different. Perhaps the Pools have come up for once. Anyhow, he's got money. He signals me with exaggerated casualness from the cinema entrance. . . . She steps in daintily, the perfect lady, particular where she puts her feet. As soon as she's safely inside, he whispers the address . . . and adds, as one man of the world to another, 'No hurry, driver.' Then he dives in with such utter *savoire faire, comme il faut,* and what not, that he trips over the mat and lands face first on the back seat. (Hodge 1939)

Perhaps the most obvious kind of non-user is the person who, after hailing a cab, will ask the driver some such question as, 'How much will it cost to take me to 500 Elm Street?' By this simple inquiry this person stands revealed as one who takes a narrow view of cab travel and from whom not much, if anything, can be expected by way of tip. On the other hand, regular cab users demonstrate in a variety of ways that for them this is a customary and familiar mode of travel. The manner in which they hail a cab, when and how they announce their destination, the ease with which they enter and exit, how they sit – these, and more, though difficult to describe in precise detail, comprise the Gestalt.

There exists among drivers an extensive typology of cab users, the attributes imputed to each type having a certain predictive value, particularly as regards tipping. Some of the more common and sharply delineated types are:

The Sport. The cabdriver's image of this type combines in one person those attributes of character which he views as ideal. While the Sport's vocation may be any one of many, his status derives more from his extra-vocational activities, e.g. at the race track, prize fights, ball games, popular restaurants, and bars. He is the perennial 'young man on the town'. Gentlemanly without being aloof, interested without becoming familiar, he also is, of course, never petty. Most of all, his tips are generous, and even on very short rides he will seldom tip less than a quarter. A favourite success story among cabdrivers describes at length and in fine detail the handsome treatment accorded the driver on an all-night tour with a Sport.

The Blowhard. The Blowhard is a false Sport. While often wearing the outer mantle of the Sport, he lacks the real Sport's casualness, assured manners, and comfortable style. Given to loquaciousness, he boasts and indiscriminately fabricates tales of track winnings, sexual exploits, and the important people he knows. Often holding out the promise of much by way of tip, he seldom lives up to his words.

The Businessman. These are the staple of the cab trade, particularly for drivers who work by day. Not only are they the most frequently encountered; their habits and preferences are more uniform than those of any other type: the brisk efficiency with which they engage a cab, their purposefulness and disinclination to partake of small talk. Though not often big tippers, they are thought fair. Thus they serve as something of a standard by which the generosity or stinginess of others is judged.

The Lady Shopper. Although almost as numerous as businessmen, Lady Shoppers are not nearly as well thought of by cabdrivers. The stereotype is a middle-aged woman, fashionably though unattractively dressed, sitting somewhat stiffly at the edge of her seat and wearing a fixed glare which bespeaks her conviction that she is being 'taken for a ride'. Her major delinquency, however, is undertipping; her preferred coin is a dime, no more or less, regardless of how long or arduous the trip. A forever repeated story is of the annoyed driver, who, after a gruelling trip with a Lady Shopper, hands the coin back, telling her, 'Lady, keep your lousy dime. You need it more than I do.'   •

Live Ones. Live Ones are a special category of fare usually encountered by the cabdriver who works by night. They are, as a rule, out-of-town conventioneers or other revellers who tour about in small groups in search of licentious forms of entertainment: cabarets, burlesques, strip-tease bars, pick-up joints, etc. As often as not, they have already had a good deal to drink when the cabdriver meets them, and, being out-of-towners they frequently turn to him for recommendations on where to go. In the late forties an arrangement existed in Chicago whereby some of the more popular Near North Side and West Madison Street 'clip joints' rewarded cabdrivers for 'steering' Live Ones to their establishments. Some places paid fifty cents 'a head'; others a dollar 'for the load'. As do the many others who regularly cater to Live Ones – e.g. waitresses, bartenders, female bar companions (B-girls), night-club hosts and hostesses, entertainers, prostitutes – cabdrivers often view them as fair game. And while their opportunities for pecuniary exploitation are fewer and more limited than those open, for example, to B-girls and night-club proprietors, many drivers feel less inhibited about padding charges and finagling extras from Live Ones than they do from other fares. Often extravagant in their tips because of high spirits and drink, Live Ones are also frequently careless and forget to tip altogether. Knowing that Live Ones are out to 'blow their money' anyway, many drivers believe they are justified in seeing to it that they are not deprived of a small portion.

Although the cab culture's typology of fares stems in a large part from the attempt to order experience, reduce uncertainty, and further calculability of the tip, it is questionable of course as to how accurate or efficient it is. For, as has often been remarked, stereotypes and typologies have a way of imparting a symmetry and regularity to behaviour which are, at best, only crudely approximated in reality. Too often it happens, for example, that a fare tabbed as a Sport turns out to be a Stiff (non-tipper), that a Blowhard matches his words with a generous tip, or that a Lady Shopper will give fifteen or even twenty cents. The persistence of the typology therefore has perhaps as much to do with the cabdriver's a posteriori reconstructions and rationalizations of fare behaviour as it does with the typology's predictive efficiency.

To protect and insure themselves against an unfavourable outcome of tipping, many drivers will, depending upon circumstances, employ diverse tactics and stratagems (some more premeditated than others) to increase the amount of tip or to compensate for its loss should it not be forthcoming. Certain of these are listed below. It should be understood however, that in the ordinary instance the driver makes no attempt to manipulate the fare, believing resignedly that in the long run such means bear too little fruit for the effort and risk.

Making change. Depending on the tariff and the amount handed him, the driver can fumble about in his pockets for change, or make change in such denominations as often to embarrass a fare into giving a larger tip than he had intended. The efficacy of this tactic depends naturally on the determination and staying power of the fare, qualities which many fares are averse to demonstrate, particularly when it comes to small change.

The hard-luck story. This is usually reserved for young persons and others who, for whatever reason, evidence an insecure posture vis-à-vis the driver. Typically, the hard-luck story consists of a catalogue of economic woes, e.g. long and hard hours of work, poor pay, insulting and unappreciative passengers, etc. In 'confiding' these to the fare, the driver pretends to esteem him as an exceptionally sympathetic and intelligent person who, unlike 'the others', can appreciate his circumstances and act accordingly. Most drivers, however, view the hard-luck story as an unsavoury form of extortion, beneath their dignity. Furthermore, while it may work in some cases, its potential for alienating tips is probably as great as its success at extracting them.

Fictitious charges. The resort to fictitious and fraudulent charges occurs most commonly in those cases in which the driver feels that he has good reason to believe that the fare will, either through malice or ignorance, not tip and when the fare impresses him as being enough of a non-cab user as not to know when improper charges are being levied. Once, when I complained to a veteran cabdriver about having been 'stiffed' by a young couple, newly arrived in Chicago, to whom I had extended such extra services as carrying luggage and opening doors, I was told: 'Wise up kid! When you pick up one of these yokels at the Dearborn Station carrying a lot of cheap straw luggage on him, you can bet ninety-nine times out of a hundred that he isn't going to tip you. Not that he's a mean guy or anything, but where he comes from, they never heard of tipping. What I do with a yokel like that is to take him to where he's going, show him what the fare is on the meter, and tell him that it costs fifteen cents extra for each piece of luggage. Now, he doesn't know that there's no charge for hand luggage, but that way I'm sure of getting my tip out of him.'

The psychological approach. Possibly attributing more art to their trade than is the case, some drivers are of the opinion that a cab ride can be tailored to fit a passenger in much the same way as can a suit of clothes. One cab-driver, boasting of his success at getting tips, explained: 'In this business you've got to use psychology. You've got to make the ride fit the person. Now, take a businessman. He's in a hurry to get someplace and he doesn't want a lot of bullshit and crapping around. With him you've got to keep moving. Do some fancy cutting in and out, give the cab a bit of a jerk when you take off from a light. Not reckless, mind you, but plenty of zip. He likes that. With old people, it's just the opposite. They're more afraid than anyone of getting hurt or killed in a cab. Take it easy with them. Creep along, open doors for them, help them in and out, be real folksy. Call them "Sir" and "Ma'am" and they'll soon be calling you "young man". They're suckers for this stuff, and they'll loosen up their pocketbooks a little bit.'

In the last analysis, neither the driver's typology of fares nor his stratagems further to any marked degree his control of the tip. Paradoxically, were these routinely successful in achieving predictability and control, they would at the same time divest the act of tipping of its most distinguishing characteristics – of its uncertainty, variability, and of the element of revelation in its consummation. It is these – essentially the problematic in human intercourse – which distinguish the tip from the fixed service charge. And though another form of remuneration might in the end provide the cabdriver with a better wage and a more secure livelihood, the abrogation of tipping would also lessen the intellectual play which uncertainty stimulates and without which cabdriving would be for many nothing more than unrelieved drudgery.

That the practice of tipping, however, expressively befits only certain kinds of service relationships and may under slightly altered circumtances easily degenerate into corruption or extortion is demonstrated, ironically enough, by the predicament of some cabdrivers themselves. To give an example: In the garage out of which I worked, nearly everyone connected with maintenance and assignment of cabs expected tips from drivers for performing many of the routine tasks associated with their jobs, such as filling a tank with gas, changing a tyre, or adjusting a carburettor. Although they resented it, drivers had little recourse but to tip. Otherwise, they would acquire reputations as 'stiffs' and 'cheapskates' be kept waiting interminably for repairs, and find that faulty and careless work had been done on their vehicles. Particularly with the dispatcher did the perversion of the tipping system reach extortionate proportions. His power derived from the assignment of cabs; to protect themselves from being assigned 'pots' (cabs that would break down in the middle of the day), drivers tipped him fifty cents at the beginning of every week. Since nearly every driver tipped the dispatcher and since there were more drivers than good cabs, a certain number of drivers would still be assigned 'pots'. Some, wishing to insure doubly against this would then raise the bribe to a dollar and a half a week, causing the others to follow suit in a vicious spiral. If little else, this shows how the tip – as distinguished from the gift, honorarium, inducement, or bribe – depends for its expressive validity on there not being a too close, long sustained, or consequential relationship between the parties to a service transaction.

Among service relationships in our society, that between the big city cabdriver and his fare is, due to the way in which they come into contact with each other, especially subject to structural weakness. The relationship is random, fleeting, unrenewable, and largely devoid of socially integrative features which in other client and patron orientated services help sustain a wider range of constraints and controls between the parties to the transaction. (Much the same might be said of such service occupations as waitress, bellhop and hotel doorman, the chief difference being, however, that these operate from a spatially fixed establishment, which in itself permits of greater identifiability, renewability, and hence constraint in one's relationship to them.) As a result, the tendency of the relationship is to gravitate sharply and in relatively overt fashion towards those few issues having to do with the basic instrumental terms of the exchange. The very fact of tipping, its economic centrality and the cab culture's preoccupation with mastering its many vagaries reflect in large part the regulative imbalance inherent in the relationship.

By inference, this analysis raises anew questions of how to account for the many more formidable and apparently more binding practitioner–client constraints found in other personal service fields, in particular the professions. To such matters as career socialization, colleague groups, socially legitimated skill monopolies, and professional secrecy there might be added a certain safe modicum of continuity, stability, and homogeneity of clientele. For, given too great and random a circulation of clients among practitioners, as might occur for example under certain bureaucratic schemes for providing universal and comprehensive medical service, the danger is that informal social control networks would not come into being in the community, and, as in big-city cabdriving, relations between servers and served would become reputationless, anonymous, and narrowly calculative.

References

BOTT, E. (1957) *Family and Social Network* London, Tavistock.

FREIDSON, E. (1959) 'Varieties of Professional Practice', unpublished paper.

GOFFMAN, E. (1956) *The Presentation of Self in Everyday Life* Edinburgh, University of Edinburgh Social Science Research Centre.

GOODE, W. (1957) 'Community Within a Community: The Professions', *American Sociological Review*, XXII.

HODGE, H. (1939) 'I Drive a Taxi', *Fact,* no. 22.

HUGHES, E. C. (1958) *Men and Their Work* Glencoe, Illinois, The Free Press.

MARESCA, J. (1945) *My Flag Is Down* New York, Dutton.

MERTON, R. (1957) 'The Role Set: Problems in Sociological Theory', *British Journal of Sociology*, VIII.

PARSONS, T. (1951) *The Social System* Glencoe, Illinois, The Free Press.

Part VI Attitudes and beliefs

Introduction

Each of the readings for this dimension of the course demonstrates the diversity of approaches to an understanding of society available in the social sciences. The part itself divides between two main perspectives on beliefs and attitudes. In the first we are concerned with the formation and nature of beliefs and attitudes in the individual, whereas in the second we are analysing the social and societal context of beliefs, attitudes and belief systems. In discipline terms the first perspective is devoted to the contributions of psychology and social psychology whilst the second develops the sociological understanding of beliefs, attitudes and belief systems as characteristics of the interests and action of social groups.

People conventionally treat beliefs and attitudes as matters of individual concern, as idiosyncratic characteristics of specific personalities. Both the psychologist and the sociologist are interested in going beyond the commonsense view, to explore the typical nature of beliefs, values, attitudes and ideas, and the sorts of generalizations and understandings that can be constructed from them. Clearly, if we want to understand why people act in certain ways, we have to investigate the relationship of their reasons and motivations to their actions. There are two levels on which we can do this: we can examine those mechanisms which are internal to the individual and which are responsible for individual variations in beliefs, attitudes, values and ideas; or we can look at the way beliefs, attitudes, etc., are expressions of expectations, orientations and obligations imposed and made available by the society in which the individual lives. The types of beliefs and attitudes that people hold are indications of the values, norms and knowledge in terms of which their actions and interactions are orientated. In exploring beliefs and attitudes we are investigating how people make their subjective and objective worlds meaningful.

We are not simply concerned with the social or psychological construction of meaning: we are at the same time interested in explaining processes of change, of both attitude change in the individual and the sources of societal change. In one sense the questions posed by individual and society appear to be similar. Some people would argue that if we knew why individuals change their attitudes and their behaviour we would have the material on which to construct an explanation of social change. Others would argue that such knowledge is insufficient, that in order to understand social change we must have information about the dynamics of interaction between social groups and that these dynamics are not simply aggregate of individual characteristics but processes irreducibly social or *super-individual*.

The six readings in this part explore some elements of these questions. The first reading is an extract from the book *Man for Himself* by Erich Fromm. He argues that man's needs are not only those of biological survival and satisfaction but stem also from his capacity for awareness, conceptualization and imagination. Man strives to make sense of the world and to give 'meaning' to his life. This quest for meaning is generated by existential conflicts arising from the fact that, unlike other species, the pattern of his living is not sufficiently determined by specific instinctual patterns, but also has to respond to social and historical contexts. Fromm's argument is somewhat speculative, more philosophical and humanistic than some of the other readings. This does not mean that his work is only of philosophical significance; the processes of theory construction in the social sciences may often begin with such global arguments, which may suggest problems and topics of research that can be refined into testable propositions.

The Katz reading is pitched at a more concrete level. Whilst opening up the idea that attitudes express cognitive or evaluative orientations, it presents a classificatory scheme for definitions of the concepts of attitude and belief; and discusses their relationship to values and to knowledge by reference to the concept of *function* : that is, Katz is proposing that we can differentiate between types of attitudes in terms of their *consequences* for individual psychological adjustment and motivation.

The next four readings operate at a quite different level, involved with the dynamics of social change. They are essentially sociological in scope and intention, and each reading demonstrates a facet of the sociological method of conceptualizing beliefs and attitudes. Those by Zilsel and Merton are related to a case study in the course on the rise of science, and are addressed to the problem of explaining the role of beliefs and ideas in social change. The reading by Zilsel begins to suggest a view of science based on a 'sociology of knowledge' which implies a determinate relation between social structure and the structure and form of knowledge. Zilsel explains the rise of science as a consequence of changes in social structure and in the development of capitalist economic institutions in the period 1300-1600. Zilsel is opposed to treating the development of science as a problem in the 'history of ideas', and he argues that sociological and economic factors are primary features of an adequate understanding of the rise of science in the West.

In the reading extracted from Robert Merton's important book *Science, Technology and Society in Seventeenth-Century England*, we find a qualification of Zilsel's materialist view. First published in 1938, Merton's book was the first to propose a sophisticated sociological analysis of the institutionalization of science in England during the seventeenth century. Rather than making social and economic organization (material factors) the basic causes of scientific development, Merton elaborates a view taken from the great German sociologist Max Weber. Weber, in a classic study of the relationship between Calvinism and capitalism, had argued for an explanation of that relationship in terms of what he called an 'elective affinity' between material interests and religious values of certain social groups. What he meant was that beliefs and attitudes employed in a religious context could be interpreted as motives to economic action in another context. Merton applied this notion of 'elective affinity' to the relationship between Puritanism and the emergent scientific community, and the reading illustrates his treatment of the dimensions of this relationship.

In the two final readings, by Hill and Talmon, we are more concerned with general connections between beliefs, social groups, group interests and actions. The Hill reading, taken from his recent book on the sociology of religion, is a discussion of the Halévy thesis on religion as a counter-revolutionary ideology. Hill's reading thus presents another aspect of the social change argument: it explores how beliefs can restrain certain sorts of change by redefining the meaning of the world for certain social groups.

The reading from Yonina Talmon's article on millenarian movements provides a description and analysis of types of social groups characterized by their revolutionary religious beliefs. Usually such groups are formed from the deprived strata of a society, or may form (as with the 'cargo cults') a whole society placed in a context of meaningless social change by external factors such as colonization and economic exploitation. Talmon's article is valuable because it attempts to analyse the power of such movements to inaugurate radical social change as part of their attempt to make their social condition meaningful. Millenarianism puts social conflict into a cosmic symbolic frame capable of liberating hitherto untapped energies in those it recruits. Its typological similarity with political revolutionism makes the study of millenarianism a useful way of comprehending apparently 'irrational' motives towards radical social change.

Peter Hamilton

22   The human situation

Erich Fromm

The first element which differentiates human from animal existence is a negative one: the relative absence in man of instinctive regulation in the process of adaptation to the surrounding world. The mode of adaptation of the animal to its world remains the same throughout; if its instinctual equipment is no longer fit to cope successfully with a changing environment, the species will die out. The animal can adapt itself to changing conditions by changing itself – autoplastically; not by changing its environment – alloplastically. In this fashion it lives harmoniously, not in the sense of absence of struggle but in the sense that its inherited equipment makes it a fixed and unchanging part of its world; it either fits in or dies out.

The less complete and fixed the instinctual equipment of animals, the more developed is the brain and therefore the ability to learn. The emergence of man can be defined as occurring at the point in the process of evolution where instinctive adaptation has reached its minimum. But he emerges with new qualities which differentiate him from the animal: his awareness of himself as a separate entity, his ability to remember the past, to visualize the future, and to denote objects and acts by symbols; his reason to conceive and understand the world; and his imagination through which he reaches far beyond the range of his senses. Man is the most helpless of all animals; but this very biological weakness is the basis for his strength, the prime cause for the development of his specifically human qualities.

The existential and the historical dichotomies in man

Self-awareness, reason, and imagination have disrupted the 'harmony' which characterizes animal existence. Their emergence has made man into an anomaly, into the freak of the universe. He is part of nature, subject to her physical laws and unable to change them, yet he transcends the rest of nature. He is set apart while being a part; he is homeless, yet chained to the home he shares with all creatures. Cast into this world at an accidental

F R O M M, E R I C H (1949) from 'Human Nature and Character', in *Man for Himself* London, Routledge and Kegan Paul, 39–50.

place and time, he is forced out of it, again accidentally. Being aware of himself, he realizes his powerlessness and the limitations of his existence. He visualizes his own end: death. Never is he free from the dichotomy of his existence: he cannot rid himself of his mind, even if he should want to; he cannot rid himself of his body as long as he is alive – and his body makes him want to be alive.

Reason, man's blessing, is also his curse; it forces him to cope everlastingly with the task of solving an insoluble dichotomy. Human existence is different in this respect from that of all other organisms; it is in a state of constant and unavoidable disequilibrium. Man's life cannot 'be lived' by repeating the pattern of his species; *he* must live. Man is the only animal that can be *bored*, that can be *discontented*, that can feel evicted from paradise. Man is the only animal for whom his own existence is a problem which he has to solve and from which he cannot escape. He cannot go back to the prehuman state of harmony with nature; he must proceed to develop his reason until he becomes the master of nature, and of himself.

The emergence of reason has created a dichotomy within man which forces him to strive everlastingly for new solutions. The dynamism of his history is intrinsic to the existence of reason which causes him to develop and, through it, to create a world of his own in which he can feel at home with himself and his fellow men. Every stage he reaches leaves him discontented and perplexed, and this very perplexity urges him to move towards new solutions. There is no innate 'drive for progress' in man; it is the contradiction in his existence that makes him proceed on the way he set out. Having lost paradise, the unity with nature, he has become the eternal wanderer (Odysseus, Oedipus, Abraham, Faust); he is impelled to go forward and with everlasting effort to make the unknown known by filling in with answers the blank spaces of his knowledge. He must give account to himself of himself, and of the meaning of his existence. He is driven to overcome this inner split, tormented by a craving for 'absoluteness', for another kind of harmony which can lift the curse by which he was separated from nature, from his fellow men, and from himself.

The emergence of reason has created a dichotomy within man which forces him to strive everlastingly for new solutions. The dynamism of his history is intrinsic to the existence of reason which causes him to develop and, through it, to create a world of his own in which he can feel at home with himself and his fellow men. Every stage he reaches leaves him discontented and perplexed, and this very perplexity urges him to move toward new solutions. There is no innate 'drive for progress' in man; it is the contradiction in his existence that makes him proceed on the way he set out.

Having lost paradise, the unity with nature, he has become the eternal wanderer (Odysseus, Oedipus, Abraham, Faust); he is impelled to go forward and with everlasting effort to make the unknown known by filling in with answers the blank spaces of his knowledge. He must give account to himself of himself, and of the meaning of his existence. He is driven to overcome this inner split, tormented by a craving for 'absoluteness', for another kind of harmony which can lift the curse by which he was separated from nature, from his fellow men, and from himself.

This split in man's nature leads to dichotomies which I call existential [1] because they are rooted in the very existence of man; they are contradictions which man cannot annul but to which he can react in various ways, relative to his character and his culture.

The most fundamental existential dichotomy is that between life and death. The fact that we have to die is unalterable for man. Man is aware of this fact, and this very awareness profoundly influences his life. But death remains the very opposite of life and is extraneous to, and incompatible with, the experience of living. All knowledge *about* death does not alter the fact that death is not a meaningful part of life and that there is nothing for us to do but to accept the fact of death; hence, as far as our life is concerned, defeat. 'All that man has will he give for his life' and 'the wise man', as Spinoza says, 'thinks not of death but of life.' Man has tried to negate this dichotomy by ideologies, e.g. the Christian concept of immortality, which, by postulating an immortal soul, denies the tragic fact that man's life ends with death.

That man is mortal results in another dichotomy: while every human being is the bearer of all human potentialities, the short span of his life does not permit their full realization under even the most favourable circumstances. Only if the life span of the individual were identical with that of mankind could he participate in the human development which occurs in the historical process. Man's life, beginning and ending at one accidental point in the evolutionary process of the race, conflicts tragically with the individual's claim for the realization of all of his potentialities. Of this contradiction between what he *could* realize and what he actually does realize he has, at least, a dim perception. Here, too, ideologies tend to reconcile or deny the contradiction by assuming that the fulfilment of life takes place after death, or that one's own historical period is the final and

1 I have used this term without reference to the terminology of existentialism. During the revision of the manuscript I became acquainted with Jean-Paul Sartre's *Flies* and his *Is Existentialism a Humanism?* I do not feel that any changes or additions are warranted. Although there are certain points in common, I cannot judge the degree of agreement since I have had as yet no access to Sartre's main philosophical opus.

crowning achievement of mankind. Still another maintains that the meaning of life is not to be found in its fullest unfolding but in social service and social duties; that the development, freedom, and happiness of the individual is subordinate to or even irrelevant in comparison with the welfare of the state, the community, or whatever else may symbolize eternal power, transcending the individual.

Man is alone and he is related at the same time. He is alone inasmuch as he is a unique entity, not identical with anyone else, and aware of his self as a separate entity. He must be alone when he has to judge or to make decisions solely by the power of his reason. And yet he cannot bear to be alone, to be unrelated to his fellow men. His happiness depends on the solidarity he feels with his fellow men, with past and future generations.

Radically different from existential dichotomies are the many historical contradictions in individual and social life which are not a necessary part of human existence but are man made and soluble, soluble either at the time they occur or at a later period of human history. The contemporary contradiction between an abundance of technical means for material satisfaction and the incapacity to use them exclusively for peace and the welfare of the people is soluble; it is not a necessary contradiction but one due to man's lack of courage and wisdom. The institution of slavery in ancient Greece may be an example of a relatively insoluble contradiction, the solution of which could be achieved only at a later period of history when the material basis for the equality of man was established. . . .

Man can react to historical contradictions by annulling them through his own action; but he cannot annul existential dichotomies, although he can react to them in different ways. He can appease his mind by soothing and harmonizing ideologies. He can try to escape from his inner restlessness by ceaseless activity in pleasure or business. He can try to abrogate his freedom and to turn himself into an instrument of powers outside himself, submerging his self in them. But he remains dissatisfied, anxious, and restless. There is only one solution to his problem: to face the truth, to acknowledge his fundamental aloneness and solitude in a universe indifferent to his fate, to recognize that there is no power transcending him which can solve his problem for him. Man must accept the responsibility for himself and the fact that only by using his own powers can he give meaning to his life. But meaning does not imply certainty; indeed, the quest for certainty blocks the search for meaning. Uncertainty is the very condition to impel man to unfold his powers. If he faces the truth without panic he will recognize that *there is no meaning to life except the meaning man gives his life by the unfolding of his powers, by living productively*;

and that only constant vigilance, activity, and effort can keep us from failing in the one task that matters – the full development of our powers within the limitations set by the laws of our existence. Man will never cease to be perplexed, to wonder, and to raise new questions. Only if he recognizes the human situation, the dichotomies inherent in his existence and his capacity to unfold his powers, will he be able to succeed in his task : to be himself and for himself and to achieve happiness by the full realization of those faculties which are peculiarly his – of reason, love, and productive work. . . .

The most striking feature in human behaviour is the tremendous intensity of passions and strivings which man displays. Freud more than anyone else recognized this fact and attempted to explain it in terms of the mechanistic-naturalistic thinking of his time. He assumed that those passions which were not the obvious expressions of the instinct of self-preservation and of the sexual instinct (or as he formulated it later of Eros and the Death instinct) were nevertheless only more indirect and complicated manifestations of these instinctual-biological drives. But brilliant as his assumptions were they are not convincing in their denial of the fact that a large part of man's passionate strivings cannot be explained by the force of his instincts. Even if man's hunger and thirst and his sexual strivings are completely satisfied 'he' is not satisfied. In contrast to the animal his most compelling problems are not solved then, they only begin. He strives for power, or for love, or for destruction, he risks his life for religious, for political, for humanistic ideals, and these strivings are what constitutes and characterizes the peculiarity of human life. Indeed, 'man does not live by bread alone'.

In contrast to Freud's mechanistic-naturalistic explanation this statement has been interpreted to mean that man has an intrinsic religious need which cannot be explained by his natural existence but must be explained by something transcending him and which is derived from supernatural powers. However, the latter assumption is unnecessary since the phenomenon can be explained by the full understanding of the human situation.

The disharmony of man's existence generates needs which far transcend those of his animal origin. These needs result in an imperative drive to restore a unity and equilibrium between himself and the rest of nature. He makes the attempt to restore this unity and equilibrium in the first place in thought by constructing an all-inclusive mental picture of the world which serves as a frame of reference from which he can derive an answer to the question of where he stands and what he ought to do. But such thought-systems are not sufficient. If man were only a disembodied intellect his aim would be achieved by a comprehensive thought-system. But since he is an entity endowed with a body as well as a mind he has to react to the dichotomy of his existence not only in thinking but also in the process of living, in his feelings and actions. He has to strive for the experience of unity and oneness in all spheres of his being in order to find a new equilibrium. Hence any satisfying system of orientation implies not only intellectual elements but elements of feeling and sense to be realized in action in all fields of human endeavour. Devotion to an aim, or an idea, or a power transcending man such as God, is an expression of this need for completeness in the process of living.

The answers given to man's need for an orientation and for devotion differ widely both in content and in form. There are primitive systems such as animism and totemism in which natural objects or ancestors represent answers to man's quest for meaning. There are non-theistic systems like Buddhism, which are usually called religious although in their original form there is no concept of God. There are philosophical systems, like Stoicism, and there are the monotheistic religious systems which give an answer to man's quest for meaning in reference to the concept of God. In discussing these various systems, we are hampered by a terminological difficulty. We could call them all religious systems were it not for the fact that for historical reasons the word 'religious' is identified with a theistic system, a system centred around God, and we simply do not have a word in our language to denote that which is common to both theistic and non-theistic systems – that is, to all systems of thought which try to give an answer to the human quest for meaning and to man's attempt to make sense of his own existence. For lack of a better word I therefore call such systems 'frames of orientation and devotion'.

The point, however, I wish to emphasize is that there are many other strivings which are looked upon as entirely secular which are nevertheless rooted in the same need from which religious and philosophical systems spring. Let us consider what we observe in our time: We see in our own culture millions of people devoted to the attainment of success and prestige. We have seen and still see in other cultures fanatical devotion of adherents to dictatorial systems of conquest and domination. We are amazed at the intensity of those passions which is often stronger than even the drive for self-preservation. We are easily deceived by the *secular* contents of these aims and explain them as outcomes of sexual or other quasi-biological strivings. But is it not apparent that the intensity and fanaticism with which these secular aims are pursued is the same as we find in religions; that all these secular systems of orientation and devotion differ in content but not in the basic need to which they attempt to offer answers? In our culture the picture is so particularly deceptive because most people 'believe' in monotheism while their actual devotion belongs to systems which are, indeed, much closer to totemism and worship of idols than to any form of Christianity.

But we must go one step further. The understanding of the 'religious' nature of these culturally patterned secular strivings is the key to the understanding of neuroses and irrational strivings. We have to consider the latter as answers – individual answers – to man's quest for orientation and devotion. A person whose experience is determined by 'his fixation to his family', who is incapable of acting independently is in fact a worshipper of a primitive ancestor cult, and the only difference between him and millions of ancestor worshippers is that his system is private and not culturally patterned. Freud recognized the connection between religion and neurosis and explained religion as a form of neurosis, while we arrive at the conclusion that a neurosis is to be explained as a particular form of religion differing mainly by its individual, non-patterned characteristics. The conclusion to which we are led with regard to the general problem of human motivation is that while the need for a system of orientation and devotion is common to all men, the particular *contents* of the systems which satisfy this need differ. These differences are differences in value; the mature, productive, rational person will choose a system which permits him to be mature, productive and rational. The person who has been blocked in his development must revert to primitive and irrational systems which in turn prolong and increase his dependence and irrationality. He will remain on the level which mankind in its best representatives has already overcome thousands of years ago.

Because the need for a system of orientation and devotion is an intrinsic part of human existence we can understand the intensity of this need. Indeed, there is no other more powerful source of energy in man. Man is not free to choose between having or not having 'ideals', but he is free to choose between different kinds of ideals, between being devoted to the worship of power and destruction and being devoted to reason and love. All men are 'idealists' and are striving for something beyond the attainment of physical satisfaction. They differ in the kinds of ideals they believe in. The very best but also the most satanic manifestations of man's mind are expressions not of his flesh but of this 'idealism', of his spirit. Therefore a relativistic view which claims that to have some ideal or some religious feeling is valuable in itself is dangerous and erroneous. We must understand every ideal including those which appear in secular ideologies as expressions of the same human need and we must judge them with respect to their truth, to the extent to which they are conducive to the unfolding of man's powers and to the degree to which they are a real answer to man's need for equilibrium and harmony in his world. We repeat then that the understanding of human motivation must proceed from the understanding of the human situation.

23 The functional approach to the study of attitudes

Daniel Katz

Nature of attitudes: their dimensions

Attitude is the predisposition of the individual to evaluate some symbol, or object or aspect of his world in a favourable or unfavourable manner. Opinion is the verbal expression of an attitude, but attitudes can also be expressed in nonverbal behaviour. Attitudes include both the affective, or feeling core of liking or disliking, and the cognitive, or belief, elements which describe the object of the attitude, its characteristics, and its relations to other objects. All attitudes thus include beliefs, but not all beliefs are attitudes. When specific attitudes are organized into a hierarchical structure, they comprise *value systems*. Thus a person may not only hold specific attitudes against deficit spending and unbalanced budgets but may also have a systematic organization of such beliefs and attitudes in the form of a value system of economic conservatism.

The dimensions of attitudes can be stated more precisely if the above distinctions between beliefs and feelings and attitudes and value systems are kept in mind. The *intensity* of an attitude refers to the strength of the *affective* component. In fact, rating scales deal primarily with the intensity of feeling of the individual for or against some social object. The cognitive, or belief, component suggests two additional dimensions, the *specificity* or *generality* of the attitude and the *degree of differentiation* of the beliefs. Differentiation refers to the number of beliefs or cognitive items contained in the attitude, and the general assumption is that the simpler the attitude in cognitive structure the easier it is to change (cf. Krech & Crutchfield 1948, pp. 160–3). For simple structures there is no defence in depth, and once a single item of belief has been changed the attitude will change. A rather different dimension of attitude is the *number and strength of its linkages to a related value system*. If an attitude favouring budget balancing by the Federal government is tied in strongly with a value system of economic conservatism, it will be more difficult to change than if it were a fairly isolated attitude of the person. Finally, the relation of the value

KATZ, DANIEL (1960) from 'The Functional Approach to the Study of Attitudes', in *Public Opinion Quarterly*, 24, 163–77.

system to the personality is a consideration of first importance. If an attitude is tied to a value system which is closely related to, or which consists of, the individual's conception of himself, then the appropriate change procedures becomes more complex. The *centrality* of an attitude refers to its role as part of a value system which is closely related to the individual's self-concept.

An additional aspect of attitudes is not clearly described in most theories, namely, their relation to action or overt behaviour. Though behaviour related to the attitude has other determinants than the attitude itself, it is also true that some attitudes in themselves have more of what Cartwright (1949) calls an action structure than do others. Brewster Smith (1947) refers to this dimension as policy orientation and Katz and Stotland (1959) speak of it as the action component. For example, while many people have attitudes of approval towards one or the other of the two political parties, these attitudes will differ in their structure with respect to relevant action. One man may be prepared to vote on election day and will know where and when he should vote and will go to the polls no matter what the weather or how great the inconvenience. Another man will only vote if a party worker calls for him in a car. Himmelstrand's work is concerned with all aspects of the relationship between attitude and behaviour, but he deals with the action structure of the attitude itself by distinguishing between attitudes where the affect is tied to verbal expression and attitudes where the affect is tied to behaviour concerned with more objective referents of the attitude (cf. 1960). In the first case an individual derives satisfaction from talking about a problem; in the second case he derives satisfaction from taking some form of concrete action.

Attempts to change attitudes can be directed primarily at the belief component or at the feeling, or affective, component. Rosenberg theorizes that an effective change in one component will result in changes in the other component and presents experimental evidence to confirm this hypothesis (cf. 1960). For example, a political candidate will often attempt to win people by making them like him and dislike his opponent, and thus communicate affect rather than ideas. If he is successful, people will not only like him but entertain favourable beliefs about him. Another candidate may deal primarily with ideas and hope that, if he can change people's beliefs about an issue, their feelings will also change.

Four functions which attitudes perform for the individual

The major functions which attitudes perform for the personality can be grouped according to their motivational basis as follows:

1 *The instrumental, adjustive, or utilitarian function* upon which Jeremy Bentham and the utilitarians constructed their model of man. A modern expression of this approach can be found in behaviouristic learning theory.

2 *The ego-defensive function* in which the person protects himself from acknowledging the basic truths about himself or the harsh realities in his external world. Freudian psychology and neo-Freudian thinking have been preoccupied with this type of motivation and its outcomes.

3 *The value-expressive function* in which the individual derives satisfactions from expressing attitudes appropriate to his personal values and to his concept of himself. This function is central to doctrines of ego psychology which stress the importance of self-expression, self-development, and self-realization.

4 *The knowledge function* based upon the individual's need to give adequate structure to his universe. The search for meaning, the need to understand, the trend towards better organization of perceptions and beliefs to provide clarity and consistency for the individual, are other descriptions of this function. The development of principles about perceptuals and cognitive structure have been the contribition of Gestalt psychology.

Stated simply, the functional approach is the attempt to understand the reasons people hold the attitudes they do. The reasons, however, are at the level of psychological motivations and not of the accidents of external events and circumstances. Unless we know the psychological need which is met by the holding of an attitude we are in a poor position to predict when and how it will change. Moreover, the same attitude expressed towards a political candidate may not perform the same function for all the people who express it. And while many attitudes are predominantly in the service of a single type of motivational process, as described above, other attitudes may serve more than one purpose for the individual. A fuller discussion of how attitudes serve the above four functions is in order.

1. The adjustment function

Essentially this function is a recognition of the fact that people strive to maximize the rewards in their external environment and to minimize the penalties. The child develops favourable attitudes towards the objects in his world which are associated with the satisfactions of his needs and unfavourable attitudes towards objects which thwart him or punish him. Attitudes acquired in the service of the adjustment function are either the means for reaching the desired goal or avoiding the undesirable one, or are effective associations based upon experiences in attaining motive satisfactions (Katz & Stotland 1959). The attitudes of the worker favouring a political party which will advance his economic lot are an example of the first type of utilitarian attitude. The pleasant image one has of one's favourite food is an example of the second type of utilitarian attitude.

In general, then, the dynamics of attitude formation with respect to the adjustment function are dependent upon present or past perceptions of the utility of the attitudinal object for the individual. The clarity, consistency, and nearness of rewards and punishments, as they relate to the individual's activities and goals, are important factors in the acquisition of such attitudes. Both attitudes and habits are formed towards specific objects, people, and symbols as they satisfy specific needs. The closer these objects are to actual need satisfaction and the more they are clearly perceived as relevant to need satisfaction, the greater are the probabilities of positive attitude formation. These principles of attitude formation are often observed in the breach rather than the compliance. In industry, management frequently expects to create favourable attitudes towards job performance through programmes for making the company more attractive to the worker, such as providing recreational facilities and fringe benefits. Such programmes, however, are much more likely to produce favourable attitudes towards the company as a desirable place to work than towards performance on the job. The company benefits and advantages are applied across the board to all employees and are not specifically relevant to increased effort in task performance by the individual worker.

Consistency of reward and punishment also contributes to the clarity of the instrumental object for goal attainment. If a political party bestows recognition and favours on party workers in an unpredictable and inconsistent fashion, it will destroy the favourable evaluation of the importance of working hard for the party among those whose motivation is of the utilitarian sort. But, curiously, while consistency of reward needs to be observed, 100 per cent consistency is not as effective as a pattern which is usually consistent but in which there are some lapses. When animal or human subjects are invariably rewarded for a correct performance, they do not retain their learned responses as well as when the reward is sometimes skipped (Jenkins & Stanley 1950).

2. *The ego-defensive function*

People not only seek to make the most of their external world and what it offers, but they also expend a great deal of their energy on living with themselves. The mechanisms by which the individual protects his ego from his own unacceptable impulses and from the knowledge of threatening forces from without, and the methods by which he reduces his anxieties created by such problems, are known as mechanisms of ego defence. A more complete account of their origin and nature will be found in Sarnoff (1960). They include the devices by which the individual avoids facing either the inner reality of the kind of person he is, or the outer reality of the dangers the world holds for him. They stem basically from internal conflict with its resulting insecurities. In one sense the mechanisms of the defence are adaptive in temporarily removing the sharp edges of conflict and in saving the individual from complete disaster. In another sense they are not adaptive in that they handicap the individual in his social adjustments and in obtaining the maximum satisfactions available to him from the world in which he lives. The worker who persistently quarrels with his boss and with his fellow workers, because he is acting out some of his own internal conflicts, may in this manner relieve himself of some of the emotional tensions which beset him. He is not, however, solving his problem of adjusting to his work situation and thus may deprive himself of advancement or even of steady employment.

Defence mechanisms, Miller and Swanson (1960) point out, may be classified into two families on the basis of the more or less primitive nature of the devices employed. The first family, more primitive in nature, are more socially handicapping and consist of denial and complete avoidance. The individual in such cases obliterates through withdrawal and denial the realities which confront him. The exaggerated case of such primitive mechanisms is the fantasy world of the paranoiac. The second type of defence is less handicapping and makes for distortion rather than denial. It includes rationalization, projection, and displacement.

Many of our attitudes have the function of defending our self-image. When we cannot admit to ourselves that we have deep feelings of inferiority we may project those feelings on to some convenient minority group and bolster our egos by attitudes of superiority towards this underprivileged group. The formation of such defensive attitudes differs in essential ways from the formation of attitudes which serve the adjustment function. They proceed from within the person, and the objects and situation to which they are attached are merely convenient outlets for their expression. Not all targets are equally satisfactory for a given defence mechanism, but the point is that the attitude is not created by the target but by the individual's emotional conflicts. And when no convenient target exists the individual will create one. Utilitarian attitudes, on the other hand, are formed with specific reference to the nature of the attitudinal object. They are thus appropriate to the nature of the social world to which they are geared. The high school student who values high grades because he wants to be admitted to a good college has a utilitarian attitude appropriate to the situation to which it is related.

All people employ defence mechanisms, but they differ with respect to the extent that they use them and some of their attitudes may be more defensive in function than others. It follows that the techniques and conditions for attitude change will not be the same for ego-defensive as for utilitarian attitudes.

Moreover, though people are ordinarily unaware of their defence mechanisms, especially at the time of employing them, they differ with respect to the amount of insight they may show at some later time about their use of defences. In some cases they recognize that they have been protecting their egos without knowing the reason why. In other cases they may not even be aware of the devices they have been using to delude themselves.

3. The value-expressive function

While many attitudes have the function of preventing the individual from revealing to himself and others his true nature, other attitudes have the function of giving positive expression to his central values and to the type of person he conceives himself to be. A man may consider himself to be an enlightened conservative or an internationalist or a liberal, and will hold attitudes which are the appropriate indication of his central values. Thus we need to take account of the fact that not all behaviour has the negative function of reducing the tensions of biological drives or of internal conflicts. Satisfactions also accrue to the person from the expression of attitudes which reflect his cherished beliefs and his self-image. The reward to the person in these instances is not so much a matter of gaining social recognition or monetary rewards as of establishing his self-identity and confirming his notion of the sort of person he sees himself to be. The gratifications obtained from value expression may go beyond the confirmation of self-identity. Just as we find satisfaction in the exercise of our talents and abilities, so we find reward in the expression of any attibutes associated with our egos.

Value-expressive attitudes not only give clarity to the self-image but also mould that self-image closer to the heart's desire. The teenager who by dress and speech establishes his identity as similar to his own peer group may appear to the outsider a weakling and a craven conformer. To himself he is asserting his independence of the adult world to which he has rendered childlike subservience and conformity all his life. Very early in the development of the personality the need for clarity of self-image is important – the need to know 'who I am'. Later it may be even more important to know that in some measure I am the type of person I want to be. Even as adults, however, the clarity and stability of the self-image is of primary significance. Just as the kind, considerate person will cover over his acts of selfishness, so too will the ruthless individualist become confused and embarrassed by his acts of sympathetic compassion. One reason it is difficult to change the character of the adult is that he is not comfortable with the new 'me'. Group support for such personality change is almost a necessity, as in Alcoholics Anonymous, so that the individual is aware of approval of his new self by people who are like him.

The socialization process during the formative years sets the basic outlines for the individual's self-concept. Parents constantly hold up before the child the model of the good character they want him to be. A good boy eats his spinach, does not hit girls, etc. The candy and the stick are less in evidence in training the child than the constant appeal to his notion of his own character. It is small wonder, then, that children reflect the acceptance of this model by inquiring about the characters of the actors in every drama, whether it be a television play, a political contest, or a war, wanting to know who are the 'good guys' and who are the 'bad guys'. Even as adults we persist in labelling others in the terms of such character images. Joe McCarthy and his cause collapsed in fantastic fashion when the telecast of the Army hearings showed him in the role of the villain attacking the gentle, good man represented by Joseph Welch.

A related but somewhat different process from childhood socialization takes place when individuals enter a new group or organization. The individual will often take over and internalize the values of the group. What accounts, however, for the fact that sometimes this occurs and sometimes it does not? Four factors are probably operative, and some combination of them may be necessary for internalization.   1) The values of the new group may be highly consistent with existing values central to the personality. The girl who enters the nursing profession finds it congenial to consider herself a good nurse because of previous values of the importance of contributing to the welfare of others, 2) the new group may in its ideology have a clear model of what the good group member should be like and may persistently indoctrinate group members in these terms. One of the reasons for the code of conduct for members of the armed forces, devised after the revelations about the conduct of American prisoners in the Korean War, was to attempt to establish a model for what a good soldier does and does not do, 3) the activities of the group in moving towards its goal permit the individual genuine opportunity for participation. To become ego-involved so that he can internalize group values, the new member must find one of two conditions. The group activity open to him must tap his talents and abilities so that his chance to show what he is worth can be tied into the group effort. Or else the activities of the group must give him an active voice in group decisions. His particular talents and abilities may not be tapped but he does have the opportunity to enter into group decisions, and thus his need for self-determination is satisfied. He then identifies with the group in which such opportunities for ego-involvement are available. It is not necessary that opportunities for self-expression and self-determination be of great magnitude in an objective sense, so long as they are important for the psychological economy of the individuals themselves, 4) finally, the individual may come to see himself as a group member if he can share in the rewards of group activity which includes his own efforts. The worker may not play much of a part in building a ship or make any decisions in the process of building it. Nevertheless, if he and his fellow workers are given a share in every boat they build and a return on the proceeds from the earnings of the ship, they may soon come to identify with the ship-building company and see themselves as builders of ships.

4. The knowledge of function

Individuals not only acquire beliefs in the interest of satisfying various specific needs, they also seek knowledge to give meaning to what would otherwise be an unorganized chaotic universe. People need standards or frames of reference for understanding their world, and attitudes help to supply such standards. The problem of understanding, as John Dewey (1910) made clear years ago, is one 'of introducing 1) *definiteness* and *distinction* and 2) *consistency* and *stability* of meaning into what is otherwise vague and wavering'. The definiteness and stability are provided in good measure by the norms of our culture, which give the otherwise perplexed individual ready-made attitudes for comprehending his universe.

Walter Lippmann's classical contribution to the study of opinions and attitudes was his description of stereotypes and the way they provided order and clarity for a bewildering set of complexities (1922). The most interesting finding in Herzog's familiar study of the gratifications obtained by housewives in listening to daytime serials was the unsuspected role of information and advice (1944). The stories were liked 'because they explained things to the inarticulate listener'.

The need to know does not of course imply that people are driven by a thirst for universal knowledge. The American public's appalling lack of political information has been documented many times. In 1956, for example, only 13 per cent of the people in Detroit could correctly name the two United States Senators from the state of Michigan and only 18 per cent knew the name of their own Congressman (Katz & Eldersveld 1961). People are not avid seekers after knowledge as judged by what the educator or social reformer would desire. But they do want to understand the events which impinge directly on their own life. Moreover, many of the attitudes they have already acquired give them sufficient basis for interpreting much of what they perceive to be important for them. Our already existing stereotypes, in Lippmann's language, 'are an ordered, more or less consistent picture of the world, to which our habits, our tastes, our capacities, our comforts and our hopes have adjusted themselves. They may not be a complete picture of the world, but they are a picture of a possible world to which we are adapted' (1922). It follows that new information will not modify old attitudes unless there is some inadequacy or incompleteness or inconsistency in the existing attitudinal structure as it relates to the perceptions of new situations.

Determinants of attitude arousal and attitude change

The problems of attitude arousal and of attitude change are separate problems. The first has to do with the fact that the individual has many predispositions to act and many influences playing upon him. Hence we need a more precise description of the appropriate conditions which will evoke a given attitude. The second problem is that of specifying the factors which will help to predict the modification of different types of attitude.

The most general statement that can be made concerning attitude arousal is that it is dependent upon the excitation of some need in the individual, or some relevant cue in the environment. When a man grows hungry, he talks of food. Even when not hungry he may express favourable attitudes towards a preferred food if an external stimulus cues him. The ego-defensive person who hates foreigners will express such attitudes under conditions of increased anxiety or threat or when a foreigner is perceived to be getting out of place.

The most general statement that can be made about the conditions conducive to attitude change is that the expression of the old attitude or its anticipated expression no longer gives satisfaction to its related need state. In other words, it no longer serves its function and the individual feels blocked or frustrated. Modifying an old attitude or replacing it with a new one is a process of learning, and learning always starts with a problem, or being thwarted in coping with a situation. Being blocked is a necessary, but not a sufficient, condition for attitude change. Other factors must be operative and will vary in effectiveness depending upon the function involved.

References

C A R T W R I G H T, D. (1949) 'Some Principles of Mass Persuasion', *Human Relations*, vol. 2, 253–67.

D E W E Y, J O H N (1910) *How We Think* New York, Macmillan.

H E R T Z O G, H. (1944) 'What Do We Really Know About Daytime Serial Listeners?' in Lazarsfeld, Paul S. and Stanton, F. N. (eds.) *Radio Research*, 1942–3, New York, Dewell, Sloan and Pearce.

H I M M E L S T R A N D, U. (1960) *Public Opinion Quarterly*, vol 24, 224–50.

J E N K I N S, W. O. and S T A N L E Y, G. C. (1950) 'Partial Reinforcement: A Review and Critique', *Psychological Bulletin*, vol. 47, 1950, 193–234.

K A T Z, D. and E L D E R S V E L D, S. (1961) A study of the impact of party organisation on political behaviour in the Detroit area. Katz, D. and Eldersveld, in manuscript.

K A T Z, D. and S T O T L A N D, E. (1959) 'A Preliminary Statement to a Theory of Attitudes Structure and Change' in Koch, Sigmund (ed.) *Psychology: A Study of a Science*, vol. 3, New York, McGraw-Hill, 423–75.

K R E C H, D. and C R U T C H F I E L D, R. S. (1948) *Theory and Problems of Social Psychology* New York, McGraw-Hill, 160–63.

L I P P M A N N, W A L T E R (1922) *Public Opinion* New York, Macmillan.

M I L L E R, D. R. and S W A N S O N, G. (1960) *Inner Conflict and Dissense* New York, Holt, 1960.

R O S E N B E R G, S. (1960) *Public Opinion Quarterly*, vol. 24, 224–50.

S A R N O F F, I. (1960) *Public Opinion Quarterly*, vol. 24, 251–79.

S M I T H, M. B R E W S T E R (1947) 'The Personal Setting of Public Opinion: A Study of Attitudes Toward Russia, *Public Opinion Quarterly*, vol. 11, 507–23.

24   The sociological roots of science

Edgar Zilsel

Were there many separate cultures in which science has developed and others in which it is lacking, the question about the origin of science would generally be recognized as a sociological one and could be answered by singling out the common traits of the scientific in contrast to the nonscientific cultures. Historical reality, unfortunately, is different, for fully developed science appears once only, namely, in modern Western civilization. It is this fact that obscures our problem. We are only too inclined to consider ourselves and our own civilization as the natural peak of human evolution. From this presumption the belief originates that man simply became more and more intelligent until one day a few great investigators and pioneers appeared and produced science as the last stage of a one-line intellectual ascent. Thus it is not realized that human thinking has developed in many and divergent ways – among which one is the scientific. One forgets how amazing it is that science arose at all and especially in a certain period and under special sociological conditions.

It is not impossible, however, to study the emergence of modern science as a sociological process. Since this emergence took place in the period of early European capitalism, we shall have to review that period from the end of the Middle Ages until 1600. Certain stages of the scientific spirit, however, developed in other cultures too, e.g. in classical antiquity and, to a lesser degree, in some oriental civilizations and in the Arabic culture of the Middle Ages. Moreover, the scientific and half-scientific cultures are not independent of each other. In modern Europe the beginnings of science, particularly, have been greatly influenced by the achievements of ancient mathematicians and astronomers and medieval Arabic physicians. We shall, however, discuss not this influence but the sociological conditions which made it possible. We can, necessarily, give but a sketchy and greatly simplified analysis of this topic here. All details and much of the evidence must be left to a more extensive exposition at another place.

Human society has not often changed so fundamentally as it did with the transition from feudalism to early capitalism. These changes are generally

ZILSEL, EDGAR (1942) 'The Sociological Roots of Science', in *The American Journal of Sociology*, XLVII, January, 544–60.

known. Even in a very brief exposition of the problem, however, we must mention some of them, since they form necessary conditions for the rise of science.

1 The emergence of early capitalism is connected with a change in both the setting and the bearers of culture. In the feudal society of the Middle Ages the castles of knights and rural monasteries were the centres of culture. In early capitalism culture was centered in towns. The spirit of science is worldly and not military. Obviously, therefore, it could not develop among clergymen and knights but only among townspeople.

2 The end of the Middle Ages was a period of rapidly progressing technology and technological inventions. Machines began to be used both in production of goods and in warfare. On the one hand, this set tasks for mechanics and chemistry and, on the other, it furthered causal thinking and, in general, weakened magical thinking.

3 In medieval society the individual was bound to the traditions of the group to which he unalterably belonged. In early capitalism economic success depended on the spirit of enterprise of the individual. In early feudalism economic competition was unknown. When it started among the craftsmen and tradesmen of the late medieval towns, their guilds tried to check it. But competition proved stronger than the guilds. It dissolved the organizations and destroyed the collective-mindedness of the Middle Ages. The merchant or craftsman of early capitalism who worked in the same way as his fathers had was outstripped by less conservative competitors. The individualism of the new society is a presupposition of scientific thinking. The scientist too relies, in the last resort, only on his own eyes and his own brain and is supposed to make himself independent of belief in authorities. Without criticism there is no science. The critical scientific spirit (which is entirely unknown to all societies without economic competition) is the most powerful explosive human society ever has produced. If the critical spirit expanded to the whole field of thinking and acting it would lead to anarchism and social distintegration. In ordinary life this is prevented by social instincts and social necessities. In science itself the individualistic tendencies are counterbalanced by scientific cooperation. This, however, will be discussed later.

4 Feudal society was ruled by tradition and custom, whereas early capitalism proceeded rationally. It calculated and measured, introduced bookkeeping, and used machines. The rise of economic rationality furthered development of rational scientific methods. The emergence of the quantitative method, which is virtually non-existent in medieval theories, cannot be separated from the counting and calculating spirit of capitalistic

economy. The first literary exposition of the technique of double-entry bookkeeping is contained in the best textbook on mathematics of the fifteenth century, Luca Pacioli's *Summa de arithmetica* (Venice, 1494); the first application of double-entry bookkeeping to the problems of public finances and administration was made in the collected mathematical works of Simon Stevin, the pioneer of scientific mechanics (*Hypomnemata mathematica* [Leyden, 1608]), and a paper of Copernicus on monetary reform (*Monetae cudendae ratio* [composed in 1552]) is among the earliest investigations of coinage. This cannot be mere coincidence.

The development of the most rational of sciences, mathematics, is particularly closely linked with the advance of rationality in technology and economy. The modern sign of mathematical equality was first used in an arithmetical textbook of Recorde that is dedicated to the 'governors and the reste of the Companio of Venturers into Moscovia' with the wish for 'continualle increase of commoditie by their travell' (*The Wetstone of Witt* [London, 1557]). Decimal fractions were first introduced in a mathematical pamphlet of Stevin that begins with the words: 'To all astronomers, surveyors, measurers of tapestry, barrels and other things, to all mintmasters and merchants good luck!' (*Die thiende* [Leyden, 1585]). Apart from infusions of Pythagorean and Platonic metaphysics, the mathematical writings of the fifteenth and sixteenth centuries first deal in detail with problems of commercial arithmetic and, second, with the technological needs of military engineers, surveyors, architects, and artisans. The geometrical and arithmetical treatises of Piero de' Franceschi, Luca Pacioli, and Tartaglia in Italy, Recorde and Leonard Digges in England, Dürer and Stifel in Germany, are cases in point. Classical mathematical tradition (Euclid, Archimedes, Apollonius, Diophantus) could be revived in the sixteenth century because the new society had grown to demand calculation and measurement.

Even rationalization of public administration and law had its counterpart in scientific ideas. The loose state of feudalism with its vague traditional law was gradually superseded by absolute monarchies with central sovereignty and rational statute law. This political and juridical change promoted the emergence of the idea that all physical processes are governed by rational natural laws established by God. This, however, did not occur before the seventeenth century (Descartes, Huyghens, Boyle) (Zilsel 1942)

We have mentioned a few general characteristics of early capitalistic society which form necessary conditions for the rise of the scientific spirit. In order to understand this development sociologically, we have to distinguish three strata of intellectual activity in the period from 1300 to 1600: the universities, humanism, and labour.

At the universities theology and scholasticism still predominated. The university scholars were trained to think rationally but exercised the methods of scholastic rationalism which differ basically from the rational methods of a developed economy. Tradesmen are interested in reckoning; craftsmen and engineers in rational rules of operation, in rational investigation of causes, in rational physical laws. Schoolteachers, on the other hand, take an interest in rational distinction and classifications. The old sentence, 'bene docet qui bene distinguit', is as correct as it is sociologically significant. Schoolteaching, by its sociological conditions, produces a specific kind of rationality, which appears in similar forms wherever old priests, intrusted with the task of instructing priest candidates, rationalize vague and contradictory mythological traditions of the past. Brahmans in India, Buddhist theologians in Japan, Arabic and Catholic medieval scholastics conform in their methods to an astonishing degree. Jewish Talmudists proceeded in the same way, though, not being priests by profession, they dealt with ritual and canon law rather than with proper theological questions. This school rationality has developed to a monstrous degree in Brahmanic Sankhya-philosophy (sankhya means 'enumeration').

As a rule the specific scholastic methods are preserved when theologians, in the course of social development, apply themselves to secular subject matters. Thus in Indian literature Brahmans who had entered the service of princes discussed politics and erotics by meticulously distinguishing and enumerating the various possibilities of political and sexual life (Kautilya, Vatsyayana). In a somewhat analogous way the medieval scholastics and the European university scholars before 1600 indulged in subtle distinctions, enumerations, and disputations. Bound to authorities, they favoured quotation and uttered their opinions for the most part in the form of commentaries and compilations. After the thirteenth century mundane subject matters were treated by scholars too and, as an exception, even experience was referred to by some of them. But when the Schoolmen were at all concerned with secular events they did not, as a rule, investigate causes and, never, physical laws. They endeavoured rather to explain the ends and meanings of the phenomena. Obviously, the occult qualities and Aristotelian substantial forms of scholasticism are but rationalizations of pre-scientific, magic, and animistic teleology. Thus till the middle of the sixteenth century the universities were scarcely influenced by the development of contemporary technology and by humanism. Their spirit was still substantially medieval. It seems to be a general sociological phenomenon that rigidly organized schools are able to offer considerable resistance to social changes of the external world.[1]

The first representatives of secular learning appeared in the fourteenth century in Italian cities. They were not scientists but secretaries and officials of municipalities, princes, and the pope looking up with envy to the political and cultural achievements of the classical past. These learned officials who chiefly had to conduct the foreign affairs of their employers became the fathers of humanism. Their aims derive from the conditions of their profession. The more erudite and polished their writings, the more eloquent their speeches, the more prestige redounded to their employers and the more fame to themselves. They therefore chiefly strove after perfection of style and accumulation of classical knowledge. In the following centuries the Italian humanists lost in large part their official connections. Many became free literati, dependent on princes, noblemen, and bankers as patrons. Others were engaged as instructors to the sons of princes, and several got academic chairs and taught Latin and Greek at universities. Their aims remained unchanged, and their pride of memory and learning, their passion for fame, even increased. They acknowledged certain ancient writers as patterns of style and were bound to these secular authorities almost as strictly as the theologians were to their religious ones. Though humanism also proceeded rationally, its methods were as different from scholastic as from modern scientific rationality. Humanism developed the methods of scientific philology, but neglected causal research and was ignorant of physical laws and quantitative investigation. Altogether it was considerably more interested in words than in things, more in literary forms than in contents. Humanism spread over all parts of western and central Europe. Though the professional conditions and intellectual aims of the humanists outside Italy were somewhat more complex, on the whole their methods were the same.[2]

1 Pierre Duhem has brought into prominence the fourteenth-century Ockhamists of the university of Paris (Buridan, Oresme, and others) and has attempted to vindicate for them scientific priority to Copernicus and Galileo Though knowledge of late scholasticism has been greatly furthered by Duhem's investigation of the Paris Schoolmen, he has considerably overrated their 'anticipations' of modern physical and astronomical ideas. He singles out the scarce and rather extrinsic conformities with modern natural science and omits the abundance of differences. Duhem's opinion has been uncritically adopted by many followers.
2 It seems to be a rather general sociological phenomenon that, where there are professional public officials, secular learning first appears in the form of humanism. In China also after the dissolution of feudalism in the period of Confucius a group of literati officials developed who were chiefly interested in perfection of style and who acknowledged certain ancient writings as literary models. In the following period admission to civil service was made dependent on examinations regarding literary style and knowledge of antiquity. In China even calligraphy belonged to the formal requirements of higher education, Chinese writing characters

The university scholars and the humanistic literati of the Renaissance were exceedingly proud of their social rank. Both disdained uneducated people. They avoided the vernacular and wrote and spoke Latin only. Further, they were attached to the upper classes, sharing the social prejudices of the nobility and the rich merchants and bankers and despising manual labour. Both, therefore, adopted the ancient distinction between liberal and mechanical arts: only professions which do not require manual work were considered by them, their patrons, and their public to be worthy of well-bred men.

The social antithesis of mechanical and liberal arts, of hands and tongue, influenced all intellectual and professional activity in the Renaissance. The university-trained medical doctors contented themselves more or less with commenting on the medical writings of antiquity; the surgeons who did manual work such as operating and dissecting belonged with the barbers and had a social position similar to that of midwives. Literati were much more highly esteemed than were artists. In the fourteenth century the latter were not separated from whitewashers and stone-dressers and, like all craftsmen, were organized in guilds. They gradually became detached from handicraft, until a separation was effected in Italy about the end of the sixteenth century. In the period of Leonardo da Vinci (about 1500) this had not yet been accomplished. This fact appears rather distinctly in the writings of contemporary artists who over and over again discussed the question as to whether painting and sculpture belong with liberal or mechanical arts. In these discussions the painters usually stressed their relations to learning (painting needs perspective and geometry) in order to gain social esteem. Technological inventors and geographical discoverers, being craftsmen and seamen, were hardly mentioned by the humanistic literati. The great majority of the humanists did not report on them at all. If they mentioned them, they did so in an exceedingly careless and inaccurate way. From the present point of view the culture of the Renaissance owes its more important achievements to the artists, the inventors, and the discoverers. Yet these men entirely recede into the background in the literature of the period.

Beneath both the university scholars and the humanistic literati the arti-

---

being more complicated than European ones. Secular scribes, proud of their profession and learning and bound to ancient models, can be found also in ancient Egypt and the neo-Parthian empire. In classical antiquity there was an abundance of rhetors, grammarians, philologists, and philosophers rather resembling the humanistic literati of the Renaissance. Yet lack of professional civil servants in the republican period prevented development of a perfect correspondence.

sans, the mariners, shipbuilders, carpenters, foundrymen, and miners worked in silence on the advance of technology and modern society. They had invented the mariner's compass and guns; they constructed paper mills, wire mills, and stamping mills; they created blast furnaces and in the sixteenth century introduced machines into mining. Having outgrown the constraints of guild tradition and being stimulated to inventions by economic competition, they were, no doubt, the real pioneers of empirical observation, experimentation, and causal research. They were uneducated, probably often illiterate, and, perhaps for that reason, today we do not even know their names. Among them were a few groups which needed more knowledge for their work than their colleagues did and, therefore, got a better education. Among these superior craftsmen the artists are more important. There were no sharp divisions between painters, sculptors, goldsmiths, and architects; but very often the same artist worked in several fields, since, on the whole, division of labour had developed only slightly in the Renaissance. Following from this a remarkable professional group arose during the fifteenth century. The men we have in mind may be called artist-engineers, for not only did they paint pictures, cast statues, and build cathedrals, but they also constructed lifting engines, canals and sluices, guns and fortresses. They invented new pigments, detected the geometrical laws of perspective, and constructed new measuring tools for engineering and gunnery. The first of them is Brunelleschi (1377–1446), the constructor of the cupola of the cathedral of Florence. Among his followers were Ghiberti (1377–1466), Leone Battista Alberti (1407–72), Leonardo da Vinci (1492–1519), and Vanoccio Biringucci (d. 1538) whose booklet on metallurgy is one of the first chemical treatises free of alchemistic superstition. One of the last of them is Benvenuto Cellini (1500–71), who was a goldsmith and sculptor and also worked as military engineer of Florence. The German painter and engraver Albrecht Dürer, who wrote treatises on descriptive geometry and fortifications (1525 and 1527), belongs to this group. Many of the artist–engineers wrote – in the vernacular and for their colleagues – diaries and papers on their achievements. For the most part these papers circulated as manuscripts only. The artist–engineers got their education as apprentices in the workshops of their masters. Only Alberti had a humanistic education.

The surgeons belonged to a second group of superior artisans. Some Italian surgeons had contacts with artists, resulting from the fact that painting needs anatomical knowledge. The artificers of musical instruments were related to the artist–engineers. Cellini's father, for example, was an instrument-maker, and he himself was appointed as a pope's court musician for a time. In the fifteenth and sixteenth centuries the forerunners of the modern piano were constructed by the representativs of this third group. The makers of nautical and astronomical instruments and of distance meters for surveying and gunnery formed a fourth group. They made compasses and astrolabes, cross-staffs, and quadrants and invented the declinometer and inclinometer in the sixteenth century. Their measuring-instruments are the forerunners of the modern physical apparatus. Some of these men were retired navigators or gunners. The surveyors and the navigators, finally, were also considered as representatives of the mechanical arts. They and the map-makers are more important for the development of measurement and observation than of experimentation.

These superior craftsmen made contacts with learned astronomers, medical doctors, and humanists. They were told by their learned friends of Archimedes, Euclid, and Vitruvius; their inventive spirit, however, originated in their own professional work. The surgeons and some artists dissected, the surveyors and navigators measured, the artist–engineers and instrument-makers were perfectly used to experimentation and measurement, and their quantitative thumb rules are the forerunners of the physical laws of modern science. The occult qualities and substantial forms of the scholastics, the verbosity of the humanists were of no use to them. All these superior artisans had already developed considerable theoretical knowledge in the fields of mechanics, acoustics, chemistry, metallurgy, descriptive geometry, and anatomy. But, since they had not learned how to proceed systematically, their achievements form a collection of isolated discoveries. Leonardo, for example, deals sometimes quite wrongly with mechanical problems which, as his diaries reveal, he himself had solved correctly years before. The superior craftsmen, therefore, cannot be called scientists themselves, but they were the immediate predecessors of science. Of course, they were not regarded as respectable scholars by contemporary public opinion. The two components of scientific method were still separated before 1600 – methodical training of intellect was preserved for upper-class learned people, for university scholars, and for humanists; experimentation and observation were left to more or less plebeian workers.

The separation of liberal and mechanical arts manifested itself clearly in the literature of the period. Before 1550 respectable scholars did not care for the achievements of the nascent new world around them and wrote in Latin. On the other hand, after the end of the fifteenth century, a literature published by 'mechanics' in Spanish, Portuguese, Italian, English, French, Dutch, and German had developed. It included numerous short treatises on navigation, vernacular mathematical textbooks, and dialogues dealing with commercial, technological, and gunnery problems (e.g. Étienne de la Roche, Tartaglia, Dürer, Ympyn), and various vernacular booklets on metallurgy, fortification, bookkeeping, descriptive geometry, compass-making, etc. In addition there were the unprinted but widely circulated papers of the Italian artist–engineers. These books were diligently read by the colleagues of their authors and by merchants. Many of these books, especially those on navigation, were frequently reprinted, but as a rule they were disregarded by respectable scholars. As long as this separation per-sisted, as long as scholars did not think of using the disdained methods of manual workers, science in the modern meaning of the word was impos-sible. About 1550, however, with the advance of technology, a few learned authors began to be interested in the mechanical arts, which had become economically so important, and composed Latin and vernacular works on the geographical discoveries, navigation and cartography, mining and metallurgy, surveying, mechanics, and gunnery.[3] Eventually the social barrier between the two components of the scientific method broke down, and the methods of the superior craftsmen were adopted by academically trained scholars: real science was born. This was achieved about 1600 with William Gilbert (1544–1603), Galileo (1564–1642), and Francis Bacon (1561–1626).

William Gilbert, physician to Queen Elizabeth, published the first printed book composed by an academically trained scholar which was based entirely on laboratory experiment and his own observation (*De magnete* [1600]). Gilbert used and invented physical instruments but neither employed mathematics nor investigated physical laws. Like a modern experimentalist he is critically-minded. Aristotelism, belief in authority, and humanistic verbosity were vehementaly attacked by him. His scientific method derives from foundrymen, miners, and navigators with whom he had personal contacts. His experimental devices and many other details were taken over

3 Peter Martyr (1511, 1530), Peter Apian (1529), Gemma Phrysius (1530), Orontius Finaeus (1532), Nunes (1537, 1546, 1566), George Agricola (1544, 1556), Pedro de Medina (1545). Ramusio (1550), Leonard Digges (1556, 1571, 1579), Mercator (1569, 1578, 1594), Benedetti (1575), Guido Ubaldo (1577), Hakluyt (1589), Thomas Hood (1590, 1592, 1596, 1598), Robert Hues (1594), Edward Wright (1599), and others. The high percentage of English authors is striking. They seem to have been interested in the mechanical arts earlier than Continental writers (cf. Johnson 1937). On the other hand, in the same period a few 'mechanics' rose to a scientific level in their activities and their writings: the Dutch engraver and map-maker Abraham Ortelius (1527–98), who became geographer to Philip II of Spain and a scientific cartographer; the French barber-surgeon Ambroise Paré (1510–90), who became surgeon to Henry II of France and the founder of modern scientific surgery; the cashier and bookkeeper of the municipalities of Antwerp and Bruges, Simon Stevin (1548–1620), who became techno-logical and mathematical instructor and adviser to Maurice of Nassau, quartermaster-general of Holland, and one of the founders of modern scientific mechanics.

from a vernacular booklet of the compass-maker Robert Norman, a retired mariner (1581) (Zilsel 1941, pp. 1-32).

Galileo's relations to technology, military engineering, and the artist–engineers are often underrated. When he studied medicine at the University of Pisa in the eighties of the sixteenth century, mathematics was not taught there. He studied mathematics privately with Ostilio Ricci, who had been a teacher at the Accademia del Disegno in Florence, a school founded about twenty years earlier for young artists and artist-engineers. Its founder was the painter Vasari. Both the foundation of this school (1562) and the origin of Galileo's mathematical education show how engineering and its methods gradually rose from the workshops of craftsmen and eventually penetrated the field of academic instruction. As a young professor at Padua (1592–1610), Galileo lectured at the university on mathematics and astronomy and privately on mechanics and engineering. At this time he established work-rooms in his house, where craftsmen were his assistants. This was the first 'university' laboratory in history. He started his research with studies on pumps, on the regulation of rivers, and on the construction of fortresses. His first printed publication (1606) described a measuring tool for military purposes which he had invented. All his life he liked to visit dockyards and to talk with the workmen. In his chief work of 1638, the *Discorsi*, the setting of the dialogue is the Arsenal of Venice. His greatest achievement – the detection of the law of falling bodies, published in the *Discorsi* – developed from a problem of contemporary gunnery, as he himself declared. The shape of the curve of projection had often been discussed by the gunners of the period. Tartaglia had not been able to answer the question correctly. Galileo, after having dealt with the problem for forty years, found the solution by combining craftsmanlike experimentation and measurement with learned mathematical analysis. The different social origin of the two components of his method – which became the method of modern science – is obvious in the *Discorsi*, since he gives the mathematical deductions in Latin and discusses the experiments in Italian. After 1610 Galileo gave up writing Latin treatises and addressed himself to nonscholars. His greatest works, consequently, are written completely or partially in Italian. A few vernacular poets were among his literary favourites. Even his literary taste reveals his predilection for the plain people. His aversion to the spirit and methods of the contemporary professors and humanists is frequently expressed in his treatises and letters.

The same opposition to both humanism and scholasticism can be found in the works of Francis Bacon. No scholar before him had attacked belief in authority and imitation of antiquity so passionately. Bacon was enthusiastic about the great navigators, the inventors, and the craftsmen of his period; their achievements, and only theirs, are set by him as models for scholars. The common belief that it is 'a kind of dishonour to descend to inquiry upon matters mechanical' seems 'childish' to him. Induction, which is proclaimed by him as the new method of science, obviously is the method of just those manual labourers. He died from a cold which he caught when stuffing a chicken with snow. This incident also reveals how much he defied all customs of contemporary scholarship. An experiment of this kind was in his period considered worthy rather of a cook or knacker than of a former lord chancellor of England. Bacon, however, did not make any important discovery in the field of natural science, and his writings abound with humanistic rhetoric, scholastic survivals, and scientific mistakes. He is the first writer in the history of mankind, however, to realize fully the basic importance of methodical scientific research for the advancement of human civilization.

Bacon's real contribution to the development of science appears when he is confronted with the humanists. The humanists did not live on the returns from their writings but were dependent economically on bankers, noblemen, and princes. There was a kind of symbiosis between them and their patrons. The humanist received his living from his patron and, in return, made his patron famous by his writings. Of course, the more impressive the writings of the humanist, the more famous he became. Individual fame, therefore, was the professional ideal of the humanistic literati. They often called themselves 'dispensers of glory' and quite openly declared fame to be the motive of their own and every intellectual activity. Bacon, on the contrary, was opposed to the ideal of individual glory. He substituted two new aims: 'control of nature' by means of science and 'advancement of learning'. Progress instead of fame means the substitution of a personal ideal by an objective one. In his *Nova Atlantis* Bacon depicted an ideal state in which technological and scientific progress is reached by planned cooperation of scientists, each of whom uses and continues the investigations of his predecessors and fellow-workers. These scientists are the rulers of the New Atlantis. They form a staff of public officials organized in nine groups according to the principle of division of labour. Bacon's ideal of scientific cooperation obviously originated in the ranks of manufacturers and artisans. On the one hand, early capitalistic manual workers were quite accustomed to use the experience of their colleagues and predecessors, as is stressed by Bacon himself and occasionally mentioned by Galileo. On the other hand, division of labour had advanced in contemporary society and in the economy as a whole.

Essential to modern science is the idea that scientists must cooperate in order to bring about the progress of civilization. Neither disputing scholastics nor literati, greedy of glory, are scientists. Bacon's idea is substantially new and occurs neither in antiquity nor in the Renaissance. Somewhat similar ideas were pointed out in the same period by Campanella and, occasionally, by Stevin and Descartes. As is generally known, Bacon's *Nova Atlantis* greatly influenced the foundation of learned societies. In 1654 the Royal Society was founded in London, in 1663 the Académie française in Paris; in 1664 the *Proceedings* of the Royal Society appeared for the first time. Since this period cooperation of scientists in scientific periodicals, societies, institutes, and organizations has steadily advanced.

On the whole, the rise of the methods of the manual workers to the ranks of academically trained scholars at the end of the sixteenth century is the decisive event in the genesis of science. The upper stratum could contribute logical training, learning, and theoretical interest; the lower stratum added causal spirit, experimentation, measurement, quantitative rules of operation, disregard of school authority, and objective cooperation.[4]

The indicated explanation of the development of science obviously is incomplete. Money economy and co-existent strata of skilled artisans and secular scholars are frequent phenomena in history. Why, nevertheless, did science not develop more frequently? A comparison with classical antiquity can fill at least one gap in our explanation.

Classical culture produced achievements in literature, art, and philosophy which are in no way inferior to modern ones. It produced outstanding and numerous historiographers, philologists, and grammarians. Ancient rhetoric is superior to its modern counterpart both in refinement and in the number of representatives. Ancient achievements are considerable in the fields of theoretical astronomy and mathematics, limited in the biological field, and poor in the physical sciences. Only three physical laws were correctly known to the ancient scholars: the principles of the lever and of Archimedes and the optical law of reflection. In the field of technology one difference is most striking: machines were used in antiquity in warfare,

---

4 The development of modern astronomy took place in a somewhat different way. After the days of the Babylonian priests, the links connecting astronomy with priesthood, calendar-arranging, and religious feasts had never been quite interrupted. Astronomy, therefore, was linked with the idea of celestial sublimity and always belonged to the free arts. As a consequence Pythagorean and nonmechanical animistic ideas are conspicuous in Copernicus and Kepler. Practical astronomy, on the other hand, was linked with navigation, which was interested in exact star positions and measuring instruments. In the period of Newton the metaphysical and astrological spirit was definitely overcome in scientific astronomy.

for juggleries, and for toys but were not employed in the production of goods. On the whole, ancient culture was borne by a rather small upper class living on their rents. Earning money by professional labour was always rather looked down upon in the circles determining ancient public opinion. Manual work was even less appreciated. In the same manner as in the Renaissance, painters and sculptors gradually detached from handicraft and slowly rose to social esteem. Yet their prestige never equalled that of writers and rhetors, and even in the period of Plutarch and Lucianus the greatest sculptors of antiquity would be attacked as manual workers and wage-earners. Compared with poets and philosophers, artists were rarely mentioned in literature, and engineers and technological inventors virtually never. The latter presumably (very little is known of them) were superior artisans or emancipated slaves working as foremen. In antiquity rough manual work was done by slaves.

As far as our problem is concerned, this is the decisive difference between classical and early capitalistic society. Machinery and science cannot develop in a civilization based on slave labour. Slaves generally are unskilled and cannot be entrusted with handling complex devices. Moreover, slave labour seems to be cheap enough to make introduction of machines superfluous. On the other hand, slavery makes the social contempt for manual work so strong that it cannot be overcome by the educated. For this reason ancient intellectual development could not overcome the barrier between tongue and hand. In antiquity only the least prejudiced among the scholars ventured to experiment and to dissect. Very few scholars, such as Hippocrates and his followers, Democritus, and Archimedes, investigated in the manner of modern experimental and causal science, and even Archimedes considered it necessary to apologize for constructing battering-machines. All these facts and correlations have already been pointed out several times.

It may be said that science could fully develop in modern Western civilization because European early capitalism was based on free labour. In early capitalistic society there were very few slaves, and they were not used in production but were luxury gifts in the possession of princes. Evidently lack of slave labour is a necessary but not a sufficient condition for the emergence of science. No doubt further necessary conditions would be found if early capitalistic society were compared with Chinese civilization. In China, slave labour was not predominant, and money economy had existed since about 500 B.C. Also there were in China, on the one hand, highly skilled artisans and, on the other, scholar-officials, approximately corresponding to the European humanists. Yet casual, experimental, and quantitative science not bound to authorities did not arise. Why this did not happen is as little explained as why capitalism did not develop in China. The rise of science is usually studied by historians who are primarily interested in the temporal succession of the scientific discoveries. Yet the genesis of science can be studied also as a sociological phenomenon. The occupations of the scientific authors and of their predecessors can be ascertained. The sociological function of these occupations and their professional ideals can be analysed. The temporal succession can be interrupted and relevant sociological groups can be compared to analogous groups in other periods and other civilizations – the medieval scholastics with Indian priest-scholars, the Renaissance humanists with Chinese mandarins, the Renaissance artisans and artists with their colleagues in classical antiquity. Since, in the sociology of culture, experiments are not feasible, comparison of analogous phenomena is virtually the only way of finding and verifying causal explanations. It is strange how rarely investigations of this kind are made. As the complex intellectual constructs are usually studied historically only, so sociological reseach for the most part restricts itself to comparatively elementary phenomena. Yet there is no reason why the most important and interesting intellectual phenomena should not be investigated sociologically and causally.

References

J O H N S O N, F. R. (1937) *Astronomical Thought in Renaissance England* Baltimore.

Z I L S E L, E. (1941) 'The Origin of William Gilbert's Scientific Method', *Journal of the History of Ideas*, II.

Z I L S E L, E. (1942) 'The Genesis of the Concept of Physical Law', *Philosophical Review*, LI.

25   Motive forces of the new science

Robert K. Merton

What we call the Protestant ethic was at once a direct expression of dominant values and an independent source of new motivation. It not only led men into particular paths of activity; it exerted a constant pressure for unswerving devotion to this activity. Its ascetic imperatives established a broad base for scientific inquiry, dignifying, exalting, consecrating such inquiry. If the scientist had hitherto found the search for truth its own reward, he now had further grounds for disinterested zeal in this pursuit. And society, once dubious of the merits of those who devoted themselves to the 'petty, insignificant details of a boundless Nature', largely relinquished its doubts.

The Puritan spur to science

As we have seen, the capital elements of the Puritan ethic were related to the general climate of sentiment and belief. In a sense, these tenets and convictions have been accentuated through a biased selection, but this sort of bias is common to all positive inquiries. Theories which attempt to account for certain phenomena require facts, but not all facts are equally pertinent to the problem in hand. 'Selection', determined by the limits of the problem, is necessary. Among the cultural variables which invariably influence the development of science are the dominant values and sentiments. At least, this is our working hypothesis. In this particular period, religion in large part made articulate much of the prevailing value-complex. For this reason, we must consider the scope and bearing of the contemporary religious convictions, since these may have been related, in one way or another, to the upsurge of science. But not all of these convictions were relevant. A certain degree of selection is therefore necessary for the purpose of abstracting those elements which had such a perceivable relation.

Puritanism attests to the theorem that non-logical notions with a transcendental reference may neverthelesss exercise a considerable influence

MERTON, ROBERT K. (1970) 'Motive Forces of the New Science', in *Science, Technology and Society in Seventeenth-Century England* New York, Harper and Row, 80–110.

upon practical behaviour. If the fancies of an inscrutable deity do not lend themselves to scientific investigation, human action predicated upon a particular conception of this deity does. It was precisely Puritanism which built a new bridge between the transcendental and human action, thus supplying a motive force for the new science. To be sure, Puritan doctrines rested ultimately upon an esoteric theological base but these were translated into the familiar and cogent language of the laity.

Puritan principles undoubtedly represent to some extent an accommodation to the current scientific and intellectual advance. Puritans had to find some meaningful place for these activities within their view of life. But to dismiss the relationship between Puritanism and science with this formula would indeed be superficial. Clearly, the psychological implications of the Puritan system of values independently conduced to an espousal of science, and we would grossly simplify the facts to accord with a preestablished thesis if we failed to note the convergence of these two movements. Moreover, the changing class structure of the time reinforced the Puritan sentiments favouring science since a large proportion of Puritans came from the rising class of bourgeoisie, of merchants (Troeltsch 1931, p. 681). They manifested their increasing power in at least three ways. First, in their positive regard for both science and technology, which reflected and promised to enhance this power. Equally notable was their increasingly fervent belief in progress, a profession of faith which stemmed from their growing social and economic importance. A third manifestation was their hostility towards the existing class structure which limited and hampered their participation in political control; an antagonism which found its climax in the Revolution.

Yet we cannot readily assume that the bourgeoisie were Puritans solely because the Puritan ethic appealed to bourgeois sentiments. The converse was perhaps even more important, as Weber has shown. Puritan sentiments and beliefs prompting rational, tireless industry were such as to aid economic success. The same considerations apply equally to the close connection between Puritanism and science: the religious movement partly 'adapted' itself to the growing prestige of science but it initially involved deep-seated sentiments which inspired its followers to a profound and consistent interest in the pursuit of science.

The Puritan doctrines were nothing if not lucid. If they provided motivation for the contemporary scientists, this should be evident from their words and deeds. Not that scientists, any more than other mortals, are necessarily aware of the sentiments which invest with meaning their way of life. None the less, the observer may often, though not too readily perhaps, uncover these tacit valuations and bring them to light. Such a procedure should enable us to determine whether the putative consequences of the Puritan ethic truly proved effective. Moreover, it will disclose the extent to which all this was perceived by the very persons whom it most concerned. Accordingly, we shall examine the works of the natural philosopher who 'undoubtedly did more than any one of his time to make Science a part of the intellectual equipment of educated men', Robert Boyle (Fulton 1932, pp. 77–102). His investigations in physics, chemistry and physiology, to mention only the chief fields of achievement of this omnifarious experimentalist, were epochal. Add to this the fact that he was one of the individuals who attempted explicitly to establish the place of science in the scale of cultural values and his importance for our particular problem becomes manifest. But Boyle was not alone. Equally significant were John Ray, whom Haller termed, a bit effusively, the greatest botanist in the history of man; Francis Willughby, who was perhaps as eminent in zoology as was Ray in botany; John Wilkins, one of the leading spirits in the 'invisible college' which developed into the Royal Society; Oughtred, Barrow, Grew, Wallis, Newton – but a complete list would comprise a Scientific Register of the time. Further materials for our purpose are provided by the Royal Society which, arising about the middle of the century, provoked and stimulated scientific advance more than any other immediate factor. In this instance we are particularly fortunate in possessing a contemporary account, written under the constant supervision of the members of the Society in order that it might be representative of the motives and aims of that group. This is Thomas Sprat's widely-read *History of the Royal-Society of London*, published in 1667, after it had been examined by Wilkins and other representatives of the Society. From these works, then, and from the writings of other scientists of the period, we may glean the chief motive forces of the new science.

To the 'Glory of the Great Author of Nature'

Once science has become firmly institutionalized, its attractions, quite apart from any economic benefits it may bestow, are those of all elaborated and established social activities. These attractions are essentially twofold: generally prized opportunities of engaging in socially approved patterns of association with one's fellows and the consequent creation of cultural products which are esteemed by the group. Such group-sanctioned conduct usually continues unchallenged, with little questioning of its reason for being. Institutionalized values are conceived as self-evident and require no vindication.

But all this is changed in periods of sharp transition. New patterns of conducts must be justified if they are to take hold and become the foci of social sentiments. A new social order presupposes a new scheme of values. And so it was with the new science. Unaided by forces which had already gripped man's will, science could claim only a bare modicum of attention and loyalty. But in partnership with a powerful social movement which induced an intense devotion to the active exercise of designated functions, science was launched in full career.

A clear manifestation of this process is not wanting. The Protestant ethic had pervaded the realm of science and had left its indelible stamp upon the attitude of scientists toward their work. Expressing his motives, anticipating possible objections, facing actual censure, the scientist found motive, sanction and authority alike in the Puritan teachings. Such a dominant force as religion in those days was not and perhaps could not be compartmentalized and delimited. Thus in Boyle's highly-commended apologia of science, we read:

> . . . it will be no venture to suppose that at least in the Creating of the Sublunary World, and the more conspicuous Stars, two of God's principal ends were, the Manifestation of His own Glory, and the Good of Men. (Boyle 1664, p. 22)
> . . . it will not be perhaps difficult for you [Pyrophilus] : to discern, that those who labour to deter men from sedulous Enquiries into Nature, do (though I grant, designlessly) take a Course which tends to defeat God of both those mention'd Ends. (Boyle 1664, p. 27)

This is the motif which recurs in constant measure in the very writings which often contain considerable scientific contributions: these worldly activities and scientific achievements manifest the Glory of God and enhance the Good of Man. The juxtaposition of the spiritual and the material is characteristic and significant. This culture rested securely on a substratum of utilitarian norms which identified the useful and the true. Puritanism itself had imputed a threefold utility to science. Natural philosophy was instrumental first, in establishing practical proofs of the scientist's state of grace; second, in enlarging control of nature and third, in glorifying God. Science was enlisted in the service of individual, society and deity. That these were adequate grounds could not be denied. They comprised not merely a claim to legitimacy, they afforded incentives which can not be readily overestimated. One need but look through the personal correspondence of seventeenth century scientists to realize this.

John Wilkins (1710, pp. 236ff.) proclaimed the experimental study of Nature to be a most effective means of begetting in men a veneration for God. Francis Willughby, probably the most eminent zoologist of the time, was prevailed upon to publish his works – which, his excessive modesty led him to deem unworthy of publication – only when Ray insisted that it was a means of glorifying God. And Ray's panegyric (1691, pp. 126–9, et passim) of those who honour Him by studying His works so well received that five large editions were issued in some twenty years.

Many 'emancipated souls' of the present day, accustomed to a radical cleavage between religion and science and largely convinced of the relative social unimportance of religion for the modern Western world, are apt to generalize this state of affairs. To them, these recurrent pious phrases signify Machiavellian tactics or calculating hypocrisy or at best merely customary usage, but nothing of deep-rooted motivating convictions. This evidence of extreme piety leads to the charge that *qui nimium probat nihil probat.* But such an interpretation is possible only upon the basis of an unwarranted extension of twentieth century beliefs and attitudes to seventeenth-century society. Though it always serves to inflate the ego of the iconoclast and sometimes to extol the social images of his own day, 'debunking' may often supplant truth with error. As a case in point, it is difficult to believe that Boyle who manifested his piety by expending considerable sums to have the Bible translated into foreign tongues as well as in less material ways, was simply rendering lip service to Protestant beliefs. As Professor G. N. Clark (1929, p. 323) properly notes in this connection:

> There is . . . always a difficulty in estimating the degree to which what we call religion enters into anything which was said in the seventeenth century in religious language. It is not solved by discounting all theological terms and treating them merely as common form. On the contrary, it is more often necessary to remind ourselves that these words were then seldom used without their accompaniment of meaning, and that their use did generally imply a heightened intensity of feeling. This sense of the closeness of God and the Devil to every act and fact of daily life is an integral part of the character of the century.

In various ways, then, general religious ideas were translated into concrete policy. This was no mere intellectual exercise. Puritanism transfused ascetic vigour into activities which, in their own right, could not as yet achieve self-sufficiency. It so redefined the relations between the divine and the mundane as to move science to the front rank of social values. As it happened, this was at the immediate expense of literary, and ultimately, of religious pursuits. For if the Calvinist God is irrational in the sense that

He cannot be directly grasped by the cultivated intellect, He can yet be glorified by a clear-sighted, meticulous study of His natural works. Nor was this simply a compromise with science. Puritanism differed from Catholicism, which had gradually come to tolerate science, in demanding, not merely condoning, its pursuit. An 'elastic concept', the Catholic and Protestant definitions of which differed so fundamentally as to produce entirely opposed consequences, the 'glorification of God', thus came to be, in Puritan hands, the 'fructification of science'.[1]

'Comfort of Mankind'

But Protestantism had afforded further grounds for the cultivation of science. The second dominant tenet in the Puritan ethos, it will be remembered, designated social welfare, the good of the many, as a goal ever to be held in mind. Here again, the contemporary scientists adopted an objective which carried with it, in addition to its own obvious merits, a cluster of religious sentiments. Science was to be fostered and nurtured as leading to the improvement of man's lot on earth by facilitating technologic invention. The Royal Society, we are told by its worthy historian (Sprat 1667, pp. 78–9), 'does not intend to stop at some particular benefit, but goes to the root of all noble inventions'. Further, those experiments which do not bring with them immediate gain are not to be contemned, for as the noble Bacon had declared, experiments of Light ultimately conduce to a whole troop of inventions useful to the life and state of man (Sprat 1667, p. 245). This power of science to better the material condition of man, he continues, is, apart from its purely mundane value, a good in the light of the Evangelical Doctrine of Salvation by Jesus Christ.

Boyle, in his last will and testament, echoes the same attitude, petitioning the Fellows of the Society in this wise: 'Wishing them also a happy success in their laudable Attempts, to discover the true Nature of the Works of God; and praying that they and all other Searchers into Physical Truths, may Cordially refer their Attainments to the Glory of the Great Author of Nature, and to the Comfort of Mankind.' 'Experimental science was to Boyle, as to Bacon, itself a religious task' (Burtt 1927, p. 188).

Earlier in the century, this keynote had been sounded in the resonant, eloquence of that 'veritable apostle of the learned societies', Francis Bacon.

---

1 The changing definitions of nominally identical concepts comprise a fruitful field for sociological research. Such students of the sociology of knowledge as Mannheim and historians of ideas (Lovejoy, Boas, Crane) have contributed significant studies of such developments.

Himself the initiator of no scientific discoveries; unable to appreciate the importance of his great contemporaries, Gilbert, Kepler and Galileo; naively believing in the possibility of a scientific method that 'places all wits and understandings nearly on a level'; a radical empiricist holding mathematics to be of no use in science; he was, nevertheless, highly successful in being one of the principal propagandists in favour of positive social evaluation of science and of the disclaim of sterile scholasticism. As one would expect from the son of a 'learned, eloquent and religious woman, full of puritanic fervour' who was admittedly influenced by his mother's attitudes, he speaks in the *Advancement of Learning* of the true end of scientific activity as the 'glory of the Creator and the relief of man's estate'.[2] Since, as is quite clear from many official and private documents, the Baconian teachings constituted the basic principles on which the Royal Society was patterned, it is not strange that in the charter of the Society, the same sentiment is expressed.[3] Thomas Sydenham, the zealous Puritan, likewise had a profound admiration for Bacon. And, like Bacon, he was prone to exaggerate the importance of empiricism to the very point of excluding theoretical interpretation entirely. 'Pure intellectual curiosity . . . seemed to him, perhaps partly owing to the Puritan strain in his character, of little importance. He valued knowledge only either for its ethical value, as showing forth the glory of the Creator or for its practical value, as promoting the welfare of man' (Payne 1900, p. 234). Empiricism characteristically dominated Sydenham's approach to medicine which set above all the value of clinical observation, the 'repeated, constant observation of particulars'. It is of some interest that the greatest clinical observers of this century, Mayerne and Sydenham, were of Puritan stock.

Throughout there was the same point to point correlation between the principles of Puritanism, and the avowed attributes, goals and results of scientific investigation. Such was the contention of the protagonists of science at that time. If Puritanism demands systematic, methodic labour, constant diligence in one's calling, what, asks Sprat, more active and industrious and systematic than the Art of Experiment, which 'can never be finish'd by the perpetual labours of any one man, nay, scarce by the successive force of the greatest Assembly?' (Payne 1900, pp. 341–2). Here is employment enough for the most indefatigable industry since even those

2 In the *Novum Organum*, Book I, LXXXIX, science is characterized as the handmaid of religion since it serves to display God's power. This is not, of course, a novel contention.
3 In the second Charter, which passed the Great Seal on April 22, 1663, and by which the Society is governed to this day, we read that the studies of its Fellows 'are to be applied to further promoting by the authority of experiments the sciences of natural things and of useful arts, to the glory of God the Creator, and the advantage of the human race'.

hidden treasures of Nature which are farthest from view may be uncovered by pains and patience (Ray 1691, p. 125).

Does the Puritan eschew idleness because it conduces to sinful thoughts (or interferes with the pursuit of one's vocation)? 'What room can there be for low, and little things in a mind so *usefully* and successfully employ'd [as in natural philosophy]?' (Sprat 1667, pp. 344–5). Are plays and play-books pernicious and flesh-pleasing (and subversive of more serious pursuits)?[4] Then it is the 'fittest season for Experiments to arise, to teach us a Wisdom, which springs from the depths of Knowledge, to shake off the shadows, and to scatter the mists [of the spiritual distractions brought on by the Theatre]' (1667, p. 362). And finally, is a life of earnest activity within the world to be preferred to monastic asceticism? Then recognize the fact that the study of natural philosophy 'fits us not so well for the secrecy of a Closet: It makes us serviceable to the World' (1667, pp. 365–6). In short, science embodies patterns of behaviour which are congenial to Puritan tastes. Above all, it embraces two highly prized values: utilitarianiasm and empiricism.

In a sense this explicit coincidence between Puritan tenets and the eminently desirable qualities of science as a calling which was suggested by the historian of the Royal Society is casuistry. No doubt it is partly an express attempt to fit the scientist *qua* pious layman into the framework of the prevailing moral and social values. Since both the constitutional position and the personal authority of the clergy were much more important then than now, it probably constituted a bid for religious and social sanction. Science, no less than literature and politics, was still, to some extent, subject to approval by the clergy.

But this is not the entire explanation. Present-day discussions of 'rationalization' and 'derivations' have been wont to becloud certain fundamental issues. It is true that the 'reasons' adduced to justify one's actions often do not account satisfactorily for this behaviour. It is also an acceptable hypothesis that ideologies seldom *give rise* to action and that both the ideology and action are rather the product of common sentiments and values upon which they in turn react. But these ideas cannot be ignored for two reasons. They provide clues for detecting the basic values which motivate conduct. Such sign posts cannot be profitably neglected. Of even greater importance is the rôle of ideas in directing action into *particular* channels. *It is the dominating system of ideas which determines the choice between alternative modes of action which are equally compatible with the*

---

4 Cf. Barclay, the Quaker apologist, who specifically suggests 'geometrical and mathematical experiments' as innocent divertissements to be sought instead of pernicious plays.

underlying sentiments. Without such guidance and direction, non-logical action would become, within the limits of the value-system, random.

In the seventeenth century, the frequent recourse of scientists to religious vindication suggests first of all that religion was a sufficiently powerful social force to be invoked in support of an activity which was intrinsically less acceptable at the time. It also leads the observer to the peculiarly effective religious orientation which could invest scientific pursuits with all manner of values and could thus serve to direct the interests of believers into the channels of science.

The efforts of Sprat, Wilkins, Boyle or Ray to justify their interest in science do not represent simply opportunistic obsequiousness, but rather an earnest attempt to justify the ways of science to God. The Reformation had transferred the burden of individual salvation from the Church to the individual, and it is this 'overwhelming and crushing sense of the responsibility for his own soul' which accounts in part for both the acute longing for religious justification and the intense pursuit of one's calling. If science were not demonstrably a 'lawful' and desirable calling, it dare not claim the attention of those who felt themselves 'ever in the Great Taskmaster's eye'. It is to this intensity of feeling that such apologias were due.

Rationalism and empiricism

The exaltation of the faculty of reason in the Puritan ethos – based partly on the conception of rationality as a curbing device of the passions – inevitably led to a sympathetic attitude toward those activities which demand the constant application of rigorous reasoning.[5] But again, in contrast to medieval rationalism, reason is deemed subservient and auxiliary to empiricism. Sprat is quick to indicate the preeminent adequacy of science in this respect.[6] It is on this point probably that Puritanism and the scientific

5   It must be remembered that the use of reason was lauded by the Puritans partly because it served to differentiate man from beast. The extent to which this idea seeped into the thought of contemporary scientists may be indicated by a statement made by Boyle. 'So much admirable workmanship as God hath displayed in the universe, was never meant for eyes that wilfully close themselves, and affront it with the not judging it with the speculating, *Beasts inhabit and enjoy the world, man, if he will do more, must study & spiritualize it.*'
6   'Who ought to be esteem'd the most carnally minded? The Enthusiast, that pollutes his Religion, with his Passions? or the Experimenter, that will not use it [reason] to flatter and obey his own desires, but to subdue them.' Baxter, it will be remembered, in a fashion representative of the Puritans, had decried the invasion of 'enthusiasm' into religion. Reason 'must maintain its authority in the command and government of your thoughts'. In like spirit, those who, at Wilkins's lodgings, laid the foundations of the Royal Society 'were invincibly arm'd against all the inchantments of Enthusiasm'. (Sprat 1667, p. 53)

temper are in most salient agreement, for the combination of rationalism and empiricism which is so pronounced in the Puritan ethic forms the essence of the spirit of modern science. Puritanism was suffused with the rationalism of neo-Platonism, derived largely through an appropriate modification of Augustine's teachings. But it did not stop there. Associated with the designated necessity of dealing successfully with the practical affairs of life within this world – a derivation from the peculiar twist afforded largely by the Calvinist doctrine of predestination and *certitudo salutis* through successful worldly activity – was an emphasis upon empiricism. These two currents brought to converge through the ineluctable logic of an internally consistent system of theology were so associated with the other attitudes of the time as to prepare the way for the acceptance of a similar coalescence in natural science.

The Puritan insistence upon empiricism, upon the experimental approach, was ultimately connected with the identification of contemplation with idleness, of the expenditure of physical energy and the handling of material objects with industry. Experiment was the scientific expression of the practical, active and methodical bents of the Puritan. This is not to say, of course, that experiment was derived in any sense from Puritanism. But it serves to account for the ardent support of the new experimental science by those who had their eyes turned toward the other world and their feet firmly planted on this. Moreover, as Troeltsch has suggested, Calvinism which abolished the absolute goodness of the Godhead tended to an emphasis on the individual and the empirical, the practically untrammelled and utilitarian judgment of all things. He finds in the influence of this spirit a most important factor of the empirical and positivist tendencies of Anglo-Saxon thought.

A blunt Puritan, Noah Biggs, evidences this attitude in his sharp attack on the universities of his day.

> . . . wherein do they [universities] contribute to the promotion or discovery of truth? . . . Where have we any thing to do with Mechanicall Chymistrie the hand maid of Nature, that hath outstript the other Sects of Philosophy, by her multiplied real experiences? Where is there an examination and consecution of Experiments? encouragements to a new world of Knowledge, promoting, completing, and actuating some new Inventions? where have we constant reading upon either quick or dead Anatomies, or an ocular demonstration of Herbs? Where a Review of the old Experiments and Traditions, and casting out the rubbish that has pestered the Temple of Knowledge?

It was a common practice for Puritans to couple their intense scorn for a 'jejeune Peripatetick Philosophy' with extravagant admiration for mechanicall knowledge', which substituted fact for fantasy. From every direction, elements of the Puritan ethic converged to reinforce this set of attitudes. Active experimentation embodied all the select virtues and pre-cluded all the baneful vices. It represented a revolt against that Aristo-telianism which was traditionally bound up with Catholicism; it supplanted passive contemplation with active manipulation; it promised practical utilities instead of sterile figments; it established in indubitable fashion the glories of His creation. Small wonder that the Puritan trans-valuation of values carried with it the consistent endorsement of experi-mentalism.

Empiricism and rationalism were canonized, beatified, so to speak. It may well be that the Puritan ethos did not directly influence the method of science and that this was simply a parallel development in the internal history of science, but it becomes evident that, through the psychological sanction of certain modes of thought and conduct, this complex of attitudes made an empirically founded science commendable rather than, as in the medieval period, reprehensible or at best acceptable on sufferance. In short, Puritanism altered social orientations. It led to the setting up of a new voca-tional hierarchy, based on criteria which inevitably bestowed prestige upon the natural philosopher. As Professor Speier (1935, p. 79) has well said, 'There are no activities which are honourable in themselves and are held excellent in all social structures.' And one of the consequences of Puri-tanism was the reshaping of the social structure in such fashion as to bring esteem to science. This could not but have influenced the direction of some talents into scientific fields which otherwise would have been devoted to callings which were, in another social context, more highly honoured.

The shift to science

As the full import of the Puritan ethic manifested itself – even after the political failure of the Revolution which should not be erroneously identi-fied with the collapse of Puritan influence upon social attitudes – the sciences became foci of social interest. Their new fashionableness contrasts with their previous state of comparative obscurity. This was not without its effects. Many, who hitherto might have turned to theology or rhetoric or philology, were directed, through the subtle, largely unperceived and newly-arisen predisposition of society, into scientific channels. Thus, Thomas Willis, whose *Cerebri Anatome* was probably the most complete and accurate account of the nervous system up to that time and whose name is immortalized in the 'circle of Willis', 'was originally destined to theology, but in consequence of the unfavourable conditions of that age for theological science, he turned his attention to medicine'.

No less indicative of a shift of interest is the lament of Isaac Barrow, when he was Professor of Greek at Cambridge: 'I sit lonesome as an Attic owl, who has been thrust out of the companionship of all other birds; while classes in Natural Philosophy are full.' Evidently, Barrow's loneliness proved too much for him, for, as is well known, in 1663, he left this chair to accept the newly-established Lucasian Professorship of Mathematics, in which he was Newton's predecessor.

The science-loving amateur, so prominent a feature of the latter part of the century, is another evidence of the effect of this new attitude. Nobles and wealthy commoners turned to science, not as a means of livelihood, but as an object of devoted interest. Particularly for these individuals were direct utilitarian benefits of an economic nature a wholly negligible consideration. Science afforded them an opportunity of devoting their energies to a highly honoured task; an imperative duty as the comforts of unrelieved idleness vanished from the new scale of values.[7]

In the history of science the most famous of these amateurs is of course Robert Boyle, but perhaps the best index of their importance is to be found in their rôle in the formation of the Royal Society. Of those who, in that 'wonderful pacifick year', 1660, constituted themselves into a definite association, a considerable number – among them Lord Brouncker, Boyle, Lord Bruce, Sir Robert Moray, Dr Wilkins, Dr Petty and Abraham Hill – were amateurs of this type. Hardly less assiduous were the efforts of such virtuosi as Lord Willughby, John Evelyn, Samuel Hartlib, Francis Potter and William Molineux.

This social emphasis on science had a pecularily fruitful effect, probably because of the general state of scientific development. The methods and objects of investigation were frequently not at many removes from daily experience, and could hence be understood not only by the especially equipped but by a large number of persons with comparatively little technical education. To be sure, dilettantish interest in science seldom enriched its fruits directly, but it did serve to establish it more firmly as a socially estimable

7 This is clearly brought out by William Derham's estimate of the virtuoso and zoologist, Willughby '. . . he prosecuted his design with as great application as if he had to get his bread thereby; all of which I mention . . . for an example to persons of great estate and quality that they may be excited to answer the ends for which God gives them estates, leisure, parts and gifts, or a good genius; which was not to exercise themselves in vain or sinful follies, but to be employed for the glory and in the service of the infinite Creator, and in doing good offices in the world.'

pursuit. And this same function was performed no less ably by Puritanism. The fact that science today is largely and probably completely divorced from religious sanctions is itself of interest as an example of the process of secularization. Having grown away from its religious moorings, science has in turn become a dominant social value to which other values are subordinated. Today it is much more common to subject the most diverse beliefs to the sanctions presumably afforded by science than to those yielded by religion; the increasing reference to scientific authority in contemporary advertisements and the eulogistic connotation of the very word 'scientific' are perhaps not too far-fetched illustrations of the enhanced prestige of science.

The process of secularization

The beginnings of such secularization, faintly perceptible in the latter Middle Ages, were, in one sense, emerging more fully in the Puritan ethos. But the Puritan was not simply the last of the medievalists or the first of the moderns. He was both. It was in the system of Puritan values, as we have seen, that reason and experience began to be considered as independent means of ascertaining even religious truth. Faith which is unquestioning and not 'rationally weighed', proclaimed Baxter, is not faith, but a dream or fancy or opinion. In effect this grants to science a power which may ultimately limit that of religion. This unhesitant assignment of a virtual hegemony to science is based on the explicit assumption of the unity of knowledge, experiential and supersensuous, so that the testimony of science must perforce corroborate religious convictions.[8]

This conviction of the mutually confirmatory nature of reason and revelation afforded a further basis for the favourable attitude toward experimental studies, which, it is assumed, will simply reinforce basic theological dogmas. The active pursuit of science, thus freely sanctioned by unsuspecting religionists, however, created a new tone and habit of thought which is the 'supreme arbiter of the opinions of successive periods'. As a consequence of this change, ecclesiastics, no longer able to appeal to commonly accepted teachings of science which seem rather to contravene

---

8 There is so admirable an accord and correspondency between the findings of natural science and supernatural divinity, says Baxter, that the former 'greatly advantageth us' in the belief of the latter. This illustrates the incipient tendency of theology to become in a sense the handmaid of science since religious concepts become dependent upon the type of universe which man can know.

various theological doctrines, are likely once again to substitute authority for reason in an effort to emerge victorious from the conflict.

In one direction, then, Puritanism led inevitably to the elimination of religious restriction on scientific work. This was the distinctly modern element of Puritan beliefs. But this did *not* involve the relaxation of religious discipline over conduct; quite the converse. Compromise with the world was intolerable. It must be conquered and controlled through direct action and this ascetic compulsion was exercised in every area of life. It is, therefore, a grievous error to portray the Puritan espousal of science as simply an 'accommodation' to the intellectual environment of the age. Such secularized elements there were, especially with the passage of time, but these were far less significant than the unyielding constraint for devotion to the thrice-blessed calling of natural philosopher.

Paradoxically but inevitably, then, this religious ethic, based on rigid theological foundations, furthered the development of the very scientific disciplines which later seem to confute orthodox theology.

The articulation of these several ideas, each the focus of strong sentiments, into a system which was all the more forceful precisely because it was psychologically rather than logically coherent, led to a long chain of consequences not least of which was the substantial destruction of this very system itself. Though the corresponding religious *ethic*, as we shall see, does not necessarily lose its effectiveness as a social force immediately upon the undermining of its theological foundations, it tends to do so in time. This sketch of the influence of science in the processes of secularization should serve to make intelligible the diverse, quite opposed rôles which religion and theology may play in their relations to science.

A religion – understood here, as throughout this essay, as those ethical and moral beliefs and practices which constitute a system of faith and worship, that is, as a religious ethic – may indirectly promote the cultivation of science, although specific scientific discoveries are at the same time vehemently attacked by theologians, who suspect their possibly subversive nature. Precisely because this pattern of interlocking and contradictory forces is so often unanalysed, it is imperative that we distinguish clearly between the intentions and aims of religious leaders and the (frequently unforeseen) consequences of their teachings (Tawney 1936, p. 277). Once this pattern is clearly understood, it is not surprising or inconsistent that Luther particularly, and Melanchthon less strongly, execrated the cosmology of Copernicus. Likewise, Calvin frowned upon the acceptance of numerous scientific discoveries of his day, whereas the religious ethic which stemmed from him inevitably inspired the pursuit of natural science.

This failure to foresee some of the most fundamental social effects of their teachings was not solely the result of the Reformers' ignorance. It was rather an outcome of that type of non-logical thought which deals primarily with the motives rather than the probable results of behaviour. Righteousness of motive is the basic concern; other considerations, including that of the probability of attaining the end, are precluded. Action enjoined by a dominant set of values *must* be performed. But, with the complex interaction which society constitutes, the effects of action ramify. They are not restricted to the specific area in which the values were originally centred, occurring in inter-related fields specifically ignored at the outset. Yet it is precisely because these fields are in fact interrelated that the further consequences in adjacent areas react upon the basic system of values. It is this usually unlooked-for reaction which constitutes a most important factor in the process of secularization, of the transformation or breakdown of value-systems. This is the essential paradox of social action – the 'realization' of values may lead to their renunciation.

Insofar as the attitudes of the theologians dominate over the, in effect, subversive religious ethic – as did Calvin's authority largely in Geneva until the first part of the eighteenth century – scientific development may be greatly impeded. For this reason, it is of no small importance to discriminate between the early and late periods of Calvinism. The implications of these dogmas found expression only with the passage of time. But upon the relaxation of this hostile influence and with the influx of an ethic, stemming from it and yet differing significantly, science takes on new life, as indeed was the case in Geneva from about the middle of the eighteenth century. This development was particularly retarded in Geneva because there the authority resting in Calvin himself, rather than in the implications of his religious system, was not soon dissipated.

The integration of religion and science

It is thus to the religious ethos, not the theology, that we must turn if we are to understand the integration of science and religion in seventeenth-century England.

Perhaps the most directly effective belief in this ethos for the sanction of natural science held that the study of nature enables a fuller appreciation of His works and thus leads us to admire and praise the Power, Wisdom and Goodness of God manifested in His creation. Though this conception was not unknown to medieval thinkers, the consequences deduced from it were entirely different. For example, Arnaldus of Villanova, in studying the products of the Divine Workshop, adheres strictly to the medieval scholastic ideal of determining the properties of phenomena from *tables* (in which, according to the canons of logic, all combinations of chance were set forth) (Pagel 1935, p. 112). But in the seventeenth century, the contemporary emphasis upon empiricism led to the investigation of nature primarily through experience.[9] This difference in interpretation of substantially the same doctrine can only be understood in the light of the different values permeating the two cultures. Cloistered contemplation was foresaken; active experimentation was introduced.

The Royal Society was of inestimable importance, both in the propagation of this new point of view and in its actual application. These achievements gain added stature by contrast with the lethargy of the English universities. It is well known that the universities were the seats of conservatism and virtual neglect of science, rather than the nurseries of the new philosophy. It was the learned society which effected the association and social interaction of scientists with such signal results. The *Philosophical Transactions* and similar journals largely did away with the previously prevailing and unsatisfactory mode of communicating new scientific ideas through personal correspondence. Associated with the popularity of science was the new tendency to write even scientific works in the vernacular – so especial a characteristic of Boyle – or, in any case, to have English translations of the esoteric Latin and Greek. It was this type of cumulative interaction between science and society which was destined to mould a climate of opinion in which science stood high in public esteem, long after its religious justification had been forgotten.

But in the seventeenth century, this justification was of sterling importance, not only in preparing the social atmosphere for a welcome acceptance of scientific contributions, but also in providing an ultimate aim for many of the scientists of the period. For a Barrow, Boyle or Wilkins, a Ray or Nehemiah Grew, science found its rationale in the end and all of existence – His glorification and the Good of Man. Thus, from Boyle:

> ... the knowledge of the Works of God proportions our Admiration of them, they participating and disclosing so much of the inexhausted Perfections of their Author, that the further we contemplate them, the more Footsteps and Impressions we discover of the Perfections of their Creator; and our utmost Science can but give us a juster veneration of his Omniscience.[10]

9 It is not maintained, of course, that this empiricist bent derived solely from Puritanism. As we shall see, at least one other source was economic and technological. But Puritanism did contribute an added force to this development which has often been overlooked.

10 Boyle continues in this vein. '. . . God loving, as he deserves, to be honour'd in all our

Ray carries this conception to its logical conclusion, for if Nature is the manifestation of His power, then nothing in Nature is too mean for scientific study. The universe and the insect, the macrocosm and microcosm alike, are indications of 'divine Reason, running like a Golden Vein, through the whole Leaden Mine of Brutal Nature'.

On such bases as these, then, was religion invoked as a sanctioning power of science. But it is necessary to place this and the similar connections previously noted in a proper perspective. This is imperative if we are to correct an unavoidable implication of this discussion, namely, that religion was the independent and science the dependent variable during this period, although as was remarked at the outset, this is not in the least our intention.

The integration of the Puritan ethic with the accelerated development of science seems undeniable, but this is simply to maintain that they were elements of a culture which was largely centred about the values of utilitarianism and empiricism. It is perhaps not too much to say, with Lecky, that the acceptance of every great change of belief depends less upon the intrinsic force of its doctrines or the personal capabilities of its proponents than upon the previous social changes which are seen – *a posteriori*, it is true – to have brought the new doctrines into congruence with the dominant values of the period. The reanimation of ancient learning; the hesitant, but perceptibly defined, instauration of science; the groping, yet persistent, intensification of economic tendencies; the revolt against scholasticism – all helped bring to a focus the social situation in which the Protestant beliefs and scientific interests found acceptance. But to realize this is simply to recognize that both Puritanism and science were components of a vastly complicated system of mutually dependent factors. If some comprehensible order is to be attained, a fraction of this complex situation must be substituted for the whole; a defensible procedure only if this provisional formulation is not confused with a 'complete explanation'.

The integration of religious values and many of those basic to the contemporary scientists' activity is not fully evidenced by the fact that so many

---

Faculties, and consequently to be glorified and acknowledged by the acts of Reason, as well as by those of Faith, there must be sure a great Disparity betwixt that general, confus'd, and lazy Idea we commonly have of his Power and Wisdom, and the distinct, rational and affecting notions of those Attributes which are form'd by an attentive inspection of those Creatures in which they are most legible, and which were made chiefly for that very end.' Sprat (1667, p. 83), speaking for the Royal Society, explicitly defines the place of science in the means–end schema of life. 'It cannot be deny'd, but it lies in the Natural Philosophers hands, best to advance that part of Divinity [knowledge] : which though it fills not the mind, with such tender, and powerful contemplations, as that which shews us Man's Redemption by a Mediator, yet it is by no means to be pass'd by unregarded : *but is an excellent ground to establish the other.'*

of the leading scientists and mathematicians of the day – for example Oughtred, Barrow, Wilkins, Ward, Ray, Grew, etc. – were also clerics. Such service in the church may have been – though other evidence leads us to doubt it in these instances – a matter of economic consideration since the clerical life provided a fairly adequate income and ample leisure for the pursuit of science. Moreover, it must be remembered that every person appointed to a college fellowship had to be in holy orders. Hence such 'external' considerations, are at best suggestive, not convincing. They are clearly less significant than those disclosed by a study of the lives of the outstanding scientists. Boyle, though he never took orders, was deeply religious: not only did he devote large sums for the translation of the Bible and establish the Boyle lectures in theology, but he learned Greek, Hebrew, Syriac and Chaldee that he might read the Scriptures in the original! For a similar reason did Nehemiah Grew, the estimable botanist, study Hebrew, as he states in his *Cosmologia Sacra*. Napier and Newton assiduously pursued theological studies and, for the latter, science was in part highly valued because it revealed the divine power (More 1934, p. 134).

Religion, then, was a prime consideration and as such its teachings were endowed with a power which stands forth with striking emphasis. Moreover, there is no need of entering into the matter of the motivations of individual scientists to trace this influence for such indications are really supererogatory for our study. Irrespective of the possibility of tracing its direct influence upon specific individuals, it is apparent that the religious ethic, considered as a social force, so consecrated science as to make it a highly respected and laudable focus of attention.

It is this *social* animus which facilitated the development of science by removing the incubus of derogatory social attitudes and instilling favourable ones instead. It is precisely this social influence which would seldom be noticed by the individual scientists upon whom it impinged. Yet since religion directly exalted science, since religion was a dominant social force, since science was obviously held in higher social esteem during the latter part of the century, we must infer that religion played an important rôle in this changed attitude, particularly because of so much external corroborative evidence. This minimum of inference is inescapable.

Community of tacit assumptions in science and Puritanism

Up to this point we have been concerned, in the main, with the directly felt sanction of science by the Protestant ethic. Now, while this was of great importance, there was still another relationship which, subtle and difficult of apprehension though it be, was perhaps of equal significance. Puritanism was one element in the preparation of a set of largely implicit assumptions which made for the ready acceptance of the characteristic scientific temper of the seventeenth and subsequent centuries. It is not simply that Protestantism promoted free inquiry, *libre examen*, or decried monastic asceticism. These oft-mentioned characteristics touch only the bare surface of the relationship.

It has become manifest that in each age there is a system of science which rests upon a set of assumptions, usually implicit and seldom, if ever, questioned by most of the scientific workers of the time. The basic assumption in modern science, that is, in the type of scientific work which becoming pronounced in the seventeenth century has since continued, 'is a widespread, instinctive conviction in the existence of an *Order of Things*, and, in particular, of an Order of Nature'. This belief, this faith, for at least since Hume it must be recognized as such, is simply 'impervious to the demand for a consistent rationality'.

In the systems of scientific thought of Galileo, of Newton and of their successors, the testimony of experiment is the ultimate criterion of truth, but as has been suggested, the very notion of experiment is ruled out without the prior *assumption* that Nature constitutes an intelligible order, that when appropriate questions are asked, she will answer, so to speak. Hence this assumption is final and absolute. Now, as Professor Whitehead has so well indicated, this 'faith in the possibility of science, generated antecedently to the development of modern scientific theory, is an unconscious derivative from medieval theology' (Whitehead 1931, p. 19). But this conviction, prerequisite condition of modern science though it is, was not sufficient to induce its development. What was needed was a constant interest in searching for this order of nature in an empirical and rational fashion, i.e. an *active interest* in this world and in its occurrences plus a specifically empirical approach. With Protestantism religion provided this interest – it actually imposed obligations of intense concentration on secular activity with an emphasis on experience and reason as bases for action and belief. The good works which for the sects influenced by Calvinism provided conviction of grace are not to be confused with the Catholic conception of 'good works'. In the Puritan case it involved the notion of a transcendental god and an orientation to the 'other world'. It is true, but it also demanded a mastery over this world through a study of its processes; while in the Catholic instance, it demanded complete absorption, save for an unbanishable minimum, in the supersensuous, in an intuitive love of God.

It is just at this point that the Protestant emphasis upon reason and experience is of prime importance. In the Protestant system of religion, there is the unchallenged axiom, *gloria Dei*, and, as we have seen, the scheme of behaviour which was non-logically linked with this principle tends to assume a utilitarian tinge. Virtually all conceptions other than this are subject to, nay, demand, the examination of reason and experience. Even the Bible as final and complete authority was subject to the interpretation of the individual upon these bases, for though the Bible is infallible, the 'meaning' of its content must be sought, as will be remembered from Baxter's discussion of this point. The similarity between the approach and intellectual attitude implicit in the religious and scientific systems is of more than passing interest. This religious point of view could not but mould an attitude of looking at the world of sensuous phenomena which was highly conducive to the willing acceptance and, indeed, preparation for, the same attitude in science . . .

The willingness of the Protestant leaders to have reason and experience 'test' all religious beliefs, save the basic assumption, which just as in science, is simply accepted as a matter of faith, is in part grounded upon the previously mentioned conviction of the inherent consistency, congruence and mutually confirmatory nature of all knowledge, sensuous and supersensory. It would seem, then, that there is, to some extent, a community of assumptions in Protestantism and science: in both there is the unquestioned basic assumption upon which the entire system is built by the utilization of reason and experience. Within each context there is rationality, though the bases be naive and non-rational. The significance of this fundamental similarity is profound though it could hardly have been consciously recognized by those whom it influenced: religion had, for whatever reasons, adopted a cast of thought which was essentially that of science so that there was a reinforcement of the typically scientific attitudes of the period. This society was permeated with attitudes toward natural phenomena which were derived from both science and religion and which unwittingly enhanced the continued prevalence of conceptions characteristic of the new science.

References

BOYLE, R. (1664) *Some Considerations Touching the Usefulness of Experimental Natural Philosophy* (2nd ed.) Oxford.

BURTT, E. A. (1927) *The Metaphysical Foundations of Modern Physical Science* New York.

C L A R K, G. N. (1929) *The Seventeenth Century* Oxford.

F U L T O N, J. F. (1932) 'Robert Boyle and His Influence on Thought in the Seventeenth Century', *Isis*, **XVIII.**

M E R T O N, R. K. (1936) 'The Unanticipated Consequences of Purposive Social Action', *American Sociological Review*, **I.**

M O R E, L. T. (1934) *Isaac Newton: A Biography* New York.

P A G E L, W. (1935) 'Religious Motives in the Medical Biology of the Seventeenth Century', *Bulletin of the Institute of the History of Medicine*, **III.**

P A Y N E, J. F. (1900) *Thomas Sydenham* New York, Longmans Green.

R A Y, J. (1691) *Wisdom of God* London.

S P E I E R, H. (1935) 'Honor and Social Structure', *Social Research*, **II.**

S P R A T, T. (1667) *The History of the Royal Society of London* London.

T A W N E Y, R. H. (1936) *Religion and the Rise of Capitalism* New York.

T R O E L T S C H, E. (1931) *Social Teachings of the Christian Churches* New York, Macmillan.

W H I T E H E A D, A. N. (1931) *Science and the Modern World* New York.

W I L K I N S, J. (1710) *Principles and Duties of Natural Religion* London.

26   The Halévy thesis

Michael Hill

Closely related to Weber's thesis of a link between Calvinism and the growth of capitalism is the interpretation given by Elie Halévy to the importance of religious ideology in preventing a political revolution in the late eighteenth and early nineteenth centuries in Britain. 'The Halévy thesis is in many respects the political corollary, applied in a more restricted historical and geographical context, of the broader thesis put forward by Weber, and there are some interesting parallels between the two. They were both developed at about the same time (Halévy's first account was published in 1906), and the major premiss of both is that religious ideas may exert an important autonomous influence within a process of social change. A recent assessment of the current status of the Halévy thesis might almost have been taken from one of its more sympathetic accounts of Weber's important study: 'The present status of the Halévy thesis is most curious. Again and again, in current historical literature, one encounters the casual but firm assumption that the thesis has been discredited or at least significantly modified.' (Himmelfarb 1968, p. 292). But the statement that follows indicates the real difference between the two, for of the Halévy thesis it is noted: 'Yet in fact there has been no serious or sustained analysis of it. And the few brief critiques contradict each other more than they do the thesis itself'. (Himmelfarb 1968, p. 292). While Weber's work has generated an almost unparalleled amount of sociological and historical research, the important insight of Halévy has been almost totally ignored.

In this chapter, Halévy's original intepretation will be developed as being potentially a very valuable device for understanding the role of religious ideas in social change. Just as it was earlier suggested that one of the proofs of the Weber thesis lies in the use of *chronology* as a technique for gauging the relative autonomy of religious factors, so it will be found that the historical sequence that can be traced between religious and political movements has become an important issue in the arguments of sociologists and historians over the extent to which religion ever operates as an independent variable.

HILL, MICHAEL (1973) 'The Halévy Thesis', in *A Sociology of Religion* London, Heinemann, 183–204.

In the following chapter, the wealth of material on millennial movements – and especially the studies of cargo cults – will be set in the framework of alternating religious and political solutions to the problems experienced when societies undergo a process of rapid social change.

Halévy was primarily interested in the history of nineteenth-century England, but he drew his background material from as far back as the early eighteenth century. His main preoccupation was with explaining 'the extraordinary stability which English society was destined to enjoy throughout a period of revolutions and crises; what we may truly term the miracle of modern England, anarchist but orderly, practical and business like, but religious, and even pietist' (Halévy 1924, p. 339). And he clearly saw that no simple answer could be given using the evidence of English religious institutions, for he regarded them as intricate and complex and a source of disorder, even anarchy, in the seventeenth century. However, the key to the problem in his view lay with the eighteenth-century Methodist and Evangelical revival: it is crucial to an understanding of his explanation that he was interested not simply in Methodism, nor solely in the influence of this religious movement on the emergent industrial working class, but in the broader permeation of the Methodist revival through the Evangelical movement. Thus he summarized his position: 'We shall witness Methodism bring under its influence, first the dissenting sects, then the establishment, finally secular opinion' (Halévy 1924, p. 339). It is perhaps ironic that the aspect of Halévy's thesis that might have provided the basis for a thoroughgoing Marxist analysis of religious legitimation among members of a ruling class, and for which evidence will later be given, has been so little pursued, as a result of the preoccupation with Methodism and its supposed influence on the working class.

The period in which the Methodist revival began (Halévy dates its origin as 1739, the year in which Wesley began his field-preaching among the Kingswood miners) is seen as one of general disturbance characterized by economic and political crisis and by strikes and riots. 'Similar conditions a half-century later must have given rise to a general movement of political and social revolution,' notes Halévy in an historicist parallel which is intended to convey the significant effect of the religious revival (Halévy 1924, p. 341). But in 1739 the revolt assumed a different form as the discontented workers came under the influence of Wesley and his followers and substituted a new religious fervour in place of their mood of incipient revolt.

In pointing to the fact that John and Charles Wesley and their colleague George Whitfield were all Anglican clergymen with a deep commitment to the defence and regeneration of the established church, Halévy indicate the impeccable social location of the original leaders of the movement. On the other hand, partly owing to the 'radicalization' of the message being preached – which Halévy describes as an 'eccentric style of preaching' and 'doctrinal extravagance' – the Methodists found themselves barred from many Anglican churches and thus became increasingly a marginal group on the frontier of the Church of England, and it was here that the vast organization of Methodism was founded. Halévy obviously regarded as central to his thesis the 'double environment' of Methodism, which it derived from its Anglican origins and its increasingly close identification with nonconformist dissent. Viewed thus, Methodism takes on the role of a movement which filled both a social *and* an ideological vacuum, and in doing so *opened up the channels of social and ideological mobility (for this is what Halévy goes on to argue), which worked against the polarization of English society into rigid social classes, each with a distinct ideology that could be given religious expression.*

The importance of Methodism is thus to be seen in terms of its distinctiveness, both from nonconformist dissent, which Halévy regarded as taking on many of the characteristics of a relaxed and to a large extent inert religious observance in the eighteenth century, and Anglicanism, which became closely identified with the privileges and abuses of the secular establishment. 'An Established Church apathetic, sceptical, lifeless; sects weakened by rationalism, unorganized, their missionary spirit extinct. This was English Protestantism in the eighteenth century (Halévy 1924, p. 359). In this environment the influence of Methodism was more quickly felt among the nonconformist groups than by the Church of England, Halévy argued – though there is evidence to suggest that its impact on the Church of England was being felt by the end of the eighteenth century. In one sense, the effect on nonconformity was an unintended consequence of the Methodist revival, at least as far as John Wesley was concerned, since the original goal had been to revitalize the Church of England, but Halévy thinks it became impossible for the Methodist societies to remain faithful to a church which repudiated them: a separate organization also brought with it certain compensations in the form of enhanced ministerial status and freedom of action. As a result, Methodism 'exported' Anglicanism and adopted an interstitial role in terms of its organization between the Church of England and nonconformity:

> In short, the Methodist connexion adopted a position intermediate between the Establishment and the older Nonconformist bodies. It thus constituted a transition between the former and the latter, which became the more insensible

when new sects arose in turn from Wesleyanism and occupied the space between the Connexion and the original sects. (Halévy, p. 363)

Halévy's model of social mobility through religious mobility is equally interesting, although in the absence of detailed historical research it remains hypothetical. In order to become a member of the establishment, he argues, it was necessary for a wealthy dissenter to join the Church of England: 'If a successful man of business wished to enter the governing class, to entertain at his country seat the clergy or the gentry of the neighbourhood, to obtain a title or a position in the Civil Service, he must not be a Dissenter' (Halévy 1924, p. 370). Here there seems to be an implied equation between dissent and business success, and Halévy elsewhere depicts the social composition of nonconformity as being primarily lower middle class. The argument continues:

> Puritan nonconformity thus tended to become a transitional creed, a stage in the history of an English family. The unskilled labourer becomes in turn a skilled workman, an artisan, the head of a small business, a business man possessed of a modest capital, and as he rises out of the barbarism in which the working class was plunged, he becomes a Nonconformist. If he himself rises still higher on the social ladder, or if his children rise after his death, he or they go over to the Church of England. (Halévy 1924, p. 371)

The significance of Wesleyan Methodism in this process was that it stood in an intermediate position between dissent and established religion and was thus able to ease the transition from one to another:

> The constitution of the Wesleyan body rendered the transition imperceptible. And what is most characteristic of the new spirit in Dissent is its acceptance of this subordinate position. The middle-class Nonconformist was content to be despised by the members of a Church which his own family might some day enter. He compensated himself by indulging an even deeper contempt for the common people of the fields or factories from whom his family had emerged. (Halévy 1924, p. 371)

Halévy's notion of social and religious progress moving in parallel presents an interesting reworking of the idea of religion as a source of 'supernatural blinkers'. The nonconformist bourgeois is seen as possessing much the same pair of blinkers as Comte's Protestant or Gibbons' recluse fanatic, only in this case their purpose is the one which is more normally associated with blinkers, which is to keep the wearer on a forward track. The interpretation of the role of religion in social change which Halévy develops relates also to more recent findings in the sociology of education. Educational movement, like religious movement, may be regarded symbolically as an indicator of social position, and various pieces of research, including an interesting study by Himmelweit on the social background and attitudes of school-teachers, suggests that over-conformity to the prevailing norms of the most prestigious educational institutions may be more typical of individuals who have been upwardly socially mobile than of others (Hollander and Hunt 1967). At all events, there is an explicit hypothesis in Halévy's account which it might be possible to test.

The logic of the next part of his argument is the common stock of many discussions of 'the religious factor', and takes the form of a successive elimination of other factors which might be held responsible for the features observed, leaving religion as the only other variable present which might explain them. The problem for Halévy is: 'why was it that of all the countries of Europe England has been the most free from revolutions, violent crises and sudden changes? We have sought in vain to find the explanation by an analysis of her political institutions and economic organization' (Halévy 1924, p. 371). England's political institutions were such that society might have lapsed into anarchy had there existed in England – and here the emphasis given by Halévy is important to note – a bourgeoisie which was animated by the spirit of revolution. Similarly, the system of economic production was sufficiently disorganized to make revolution possible had there only existed middle-class leaders who could have provided the working class with articulate and effective leadership. 'But the élite of the working class, the hard-working and capable bourgeois, had been imbued by the Evangelical movement with a spirit from which the established order had nothing to fear' (Halévy 1924, p. 371).

Halévy's view of the bourgeoisie as potential providers of revolutionary leadership for the new industrial proletariat might appear almost bizarre unless we bear in mind that Halévy was working with an implied contrast between English and French history at the end of the eighteenth and beginning of the nineteenth centuries. In both societies there existed a powerful *traditional* ruling class against which the aspirations of both the proletariat and the new middle class might be directed. In France the aspirations of the bourgeoisie had been blocked, with radical consequences, but in England there existed sufficiently fluid channels of social mobility, together with an inbuilt mechanism of anticipatory socialization through the 'transitional' creed of Evangelicalism, to allow a more stable accommodation of the newer social groups into the established order. In brief, the Halévy thesis, rather than concerning itself primarily with the question of an 'opiate for the masses', is an early version of the embourgeoisement thesis.

The next stage of Halévy's argument is concerned with the origins of the trade-union leadership after 1815. He remarks that Continental observers have always pointed to the distinctive characteristics of the leaders of the English labour movement, who are

> sometimes blamed for their middle-class morality and want of imagination, at others praised for their solid virtue and capacity for organization. Perhaps these qualities and defects are inseparable; in any case they derive from a common origin. The majority of the leaders of the great trade-union movement that would arise in England within a few years of 1815 will belong to the Nonconformist sects. They will often be local preachers, that is practically speaking ministers. Their spiritual ancestors were the founders of Methodism. In the vast work of social organization which is one of the dominant characteristics of nineteenth-century England, it would be difficult to overestimate the part played by the Wesleyan revival. (Halévy 1924, p. 372)

And it is clear that Halévy regarded the conservative, Tory strain in Wesleyan Methodism – which was strongly embodied in John Wesley's own leadership and ably perpetuated in the nineteenth-century leadership of Jabez Bunting – as one of its most characteristic features. He quotes from the 1792 statutes of the Wesleyan body, which state: 'None of us shall either in writing or in conversation speak lightly or irreverently of the Government. We are to observe that the oracles of God command us to be subject to the higher powers; and that honour to the King is there connected with the fear of God' (Halévy 1924, p. 373).

Finally, having traced the links upwards from dissent through Methodism to the Church of England, Halévy forges an important link down from the Church of England to Methodism: he attributes a decisive influence to the Evangelical movement in the Church of England.

> To be sure John Wesley had been driven from the church of which he was an ordained priest. But he had left a rear-guard behind him which persisted in the attempt to realize his original dream, not the creation of a new sect, but the regeneration of the Church herself. . . . If the Wesleyan sect, with its hierarchic constitution, and frank political conservatism, constituted the High Church of Nonconformity, the new Low Church or evangelical party was a species of Anglican Methodism. (Halévy 1924, p. 373)

Thus a mutual accommodation took place: Wesley exported Anglicanism to the new social strata, which might have been expected to provide radical leadership for the industrial working class; while in turn, the Evangelical movement in the Church of England imported much of the fervour and a few of the techniques, including in some cases itinerant preaching (Balleine 1951), of the Wesleyan revival.

There is little doubt that the evangelizing success of Wesleyanism stimulated a parallel movement in the Church of England, and it is principally through the efforts of this movement that Halévy sees influence being brought to bear on the governing élite, especially in the early years of the nineteenth century. The 'Clapham Sect', one of the most characteristic embodiments of the Evangelical movement in the Church (it was not a 'sect' in any sociological meaning of the term but an informal grouping of like-minded individual members of the Church of England), consisted of wealthy Anglicans who were 'at bottom conservative in their attitude to the social order' (Oxford Dictionary of the Christian Church 1963), but their role in Halévy's view was very much one of upward linkage: 'This was a group of laymen who linked the Evangelical clergy with the world of politics and business to which they belonged (Halévy 1924, p. 380). Nor were the members of the Evangelical movement narrowly committed to the Church of England, for 'they systematically refused to interest themselves in the theological differences which held Protestants apart' (Halévy 1923, p. 382). This was to prove of immense value in the programme which the Evangelicals did so much to propagate and which was subsequently such a marked feature of the Victorian ethos – the programme of individual moral (as against collective social) reform.

This is a fairly comprehensive, though necessarily brief, summary of the Halévy thesis. Its major concern is with the importance of social and religious linkage and mobility, and little space has been devoted in the initial outline to the important secondary theme of religion as an 'opiate', which channelled off secular revolutionary fervour. In part, this is more appropriately considered in the context of criticisms and elaborations of Halévy's interpretation, but it can also be treated in terms of the attention which was given by the governing élite of the late eighteenth and early nineteenth centuries to the issue of the moral regeneration of English society. Wesley may well have exported from within the Church of England a conservative ethic to potentially disaffected social groups, but the Evangelicals in the Church of England reimported much of Methodism's fervour and moral preoccupations, and the final stage of this process can perhaps best be seen as the redirection of religious concern – at a time of serious social and political crisis in England – into the growth of foreign missions. We will shortly return to this topic.

Much as Fischoff has viewed the proponents and opponents of Weber's thesis regarding the rise of capitalism in the West in terms of their attitudes to capitalism, Himmelfarb sees the reactions of historians of Wesleyanism in a similar polemical perspective: either they accept Halévy's thesis for good and bad – 'that is, they accept the fact that a conservative and counter-revolutionary force might have had liberalizing and humanitarian effects' 'Himmelfarb 1968, p. 293) – or they reject it for good and bad by denying that Wesleyanism had the significant influence that has been attributed to it (Kent 1966), or, finally, they accept the large measure of influence that Methodism had, but emphasize its 'progressive' role in the radical Methodist offshoots, the trade union movement and the Labour Party – this is the point that Halévy himself makes in later volumes of his *History*.

Radical historians are seen as mostly following the line of interpretation set out by the Hammonds, and as viewing evangelicalism as an instrument of suppression and reaction in the service of the ruling class: 'Repressive, inhibiting, intolerant, obsessed with spiritual salvation and tormented with the fear of eternal damnation, it distracted men from their economic and social grievances and effectively destroyed any impulse to rebellion' (Himmelfarb 1968, p. 293). However, the Hammonds also acknowledged that some of the 'unintended' consequences of Methodism might have benefited the working class, for they argue: 'The teaching of Methodism was unfavourable to working-class movements; its leaders were hostile and its ideals perhaps increasingly hostile; but by the life and energy and awakening that it brought to this oppressed society it must, in spite of itself, have made many men better citizens, and some even better rebels' (Himmelfarb 1968, p. 294). One brief comment on the intended or unintended effects of Evangelicalism in stifling revolutionary fervour: it is not sufficient to *imply*, from the observation that the Methodist and Evangelical movements appear to have mobilized working-class support in an anti-revolutionary direction, that this was the result of conscious manipulation by the ruling class. To put forward such an argument one would need evidence of the way in which Evangelicalism was legitimated *by* the ruling class, and this is why it is so important to consider groups like the Clapham Sect.

E. P. Thompson is a notable *proponent* of the Halévy thesis, though not of the underlying tone of approval found in Halévy. If anything, he pushes the thesis even further and 'portrays a Methodism that was even more influential than Halévy's and more insidious than Hammonds'' (Himmelfarb 1968, p. 294), Thompson's contribution to the debate is highly significant in the present context because his argument is based throughout on the establishment of a *chronology* in which political activism turns into religious withdrawal. This is certainly one perspective in which to analyse the link between religion and social change: whether it can be seen as the *only* perspective, even using the same historical data as Thompson, is dubious.

The basis of Thompson's argument is the same as Halévy's – that Methodism was closely linked with Toryism and had an ambivalent attitude towards the Church of England, and thus the Wesleyans 'fell ambiguously between Dissent and the Establishment, and did their utmost to make the worst of both worlds, serving as apologists for an authority in whose eyes they were an object of ridicule or condescension, but never of trust' (Thompson 1968, p. 385). One of the results of the Establishment's disparagement of Methodism was, according to Thompson, to make it easier for the movement to engage in 'moral espionage'. During the Napoleonic Wars, the gains of Methodism were – according to this account – greatest among the new industrial working class; and the ministerial bureaucracy which was developing at the same time made it easier for the ministers to impose discipline on their followers. In this they served the establishment well, since the Church of England was too 'distanced' from the poor (another echo of Halévy) to have much effect on them. However, Thompson diverges from Halévy on the question of Methodism's social composition. Halévy, being primarily interested in Wesleyan Methodism, sees it more as a religion of the striving bourgeoisie: Thompson locates its class base lower than this when he argues that 'the Methodists – or many of them – *were* the poor' (Thompson 1968, p. 386). At the same time, he draws on the Weber thesis to suggest that Methodism was a simple extension of the Puritan ethic in a changed environment and was thus exceptionally well adapted 'both to self-made mill-owners and manufacturers and to foremen, overlookers, and sub-managerial groups' (Thompson 1968, pp. 390–1). Therefore, the problem in Thompson's view is one of explaining how, at the beginning of the nineteenth century, Methodism was able to serve simultaneously as the religion of the industrial bourgeoisie and of wide sections of the proletariat.

As far as the bourgeoisie are concerned, Thompson largely accepts the interpretation of Weber and Tawney of the utility of the Puritan work-ethic. He also notes Weber's observation that the capitalist requirement of a disciplined work-force has always encountered 'the immensely stubborn resistance of . . . pre-capitalist labour' (Thompson 1968, p. 392), and that this was especially important in the transition to a system in which labour was exclusively measured in money earnings. The systematization of factory production required that the labour force should be imbued with a disciplined and methodical ethic – a goal that was expressed in the words of a contemporary, 'It is, therefore, excessively the interest of every mill-owner to organize his moral machinery on equally sound principles with his mechanical . . .' (Thompson 1968, p. 397) – and it is in providing such an ethic for the industrial proletariat that Thompson finds an important catalyst in Methodist theology.

If we avoid Thompson's dubious connotation of Methodist theology with 'promiscuous opportunism' (Thompson 1968, p. 348), there are some valid elements of 'elective affinity' between it and the ethic of work-discipline. The Arminian component of Wesleyan Methodism, which emphasized that grace was freely available to all who believed, became conditional on three means of maintaining grace: the first was through service to the church; the second was through religious exercises, especially the reliving of the conversion experience; and the third was through methodical discipline in every aspect of life. Above all, the channelling of spontaneity into 'enthusiastic' religious practices meant that Wesleyan emotionalism was *intermittent* and allowed for the methodical, disciplined and repressed character of everyday life, so that the 'Sabbath orgasms of feeling made more possible the single-minded weekday direction of these energies to the consummation of productive labour' (Thompson 1968, p. 406).

Having thus established the utility of Methodism as a work-discipline, the next step of the argument is to explain 'why so many working people were willing to submit to this form of psychic exploitation' (Thompson 1968, p. 411). During the period 1790–1830 three reasons are given: 1. direct indoctrination; 2. the sense of community that Methodism invoked; and 3. the compensation it provided when revolutionary impulses were stifled. Indoctrination was achieved primarily through the evangelical Sunday schools, with their insistence on morality and discipline – 'religious terrorism' is the epithet that Thompson takes from Lecky (Thompson 1968, p. 415). The notion of Methodist fellowship, represented in class and group meetings, provided a new basis of community to replace those that had been disrupted by the urbanization of the Industrial Revolution: this is a process that has often been noted in the growth of sectarian and other face-to-face religious groups during periods of rapid social change (Roberts 1968).

The third reason given is one that requires close analysis, for Thompson presents a view of Methodism as 'the chiliasm of despair', a form of hysterical reaction to the defeat brought about by counter-revolutionary repression. Himmelfarb notes 'the difficulty presented by Thompson's proposition, which is that England was on the brink of revolution from 1790 to 1832

If Methodism prevailed so widely among the masses and penetrated so deeply into their individual and collective psyche, where did the impulse and perennial threat of revolution come from?' (Himmelfarb 1968, pp. 294–5). In one sense, this criticism is justified. In attributing such immense importance to Methodism as a source of the work-discipline that was demanded by the capitalist system, Thompson gives it greater prominence than Halévy as a stabilizing influence. And yet, when it comes to a question of dating the growth of Methodism he is considerably more careful and precise. He notes that the phenomenon of Methodist conversion appears to run in waves between 1790 and 1832, and states specifically that the most substantial growth in Methodist numbers occurred after the eve of the French Revolution, when counter-revolutionary feeling was strongest. Furthermore, he qualifies his account by referring to his explanation as hypothetical: 'This is not the customary reading of the period; and it is offered as an hypothesis, demanding closer investigation' (Thompson 1968, p. 427).

His interpretation is that the working class was imbued with strong radical hopes before the 1790s, and that they turned only temporarily to religion when these hopes were crushed: 'whenever hope revived, religious revivalism was set aside, only to reappear with renewed fervour upon the ruins of the political messianism which had been overthrown' (Thompson 1968, p. 427). The advance in numbers lends some weight to Thompson's argument. On the eve of the French Revolution, Methodism claimed about 60,000 adherents in Great Britain, which 'indicated little more than footholds in all but a few of the industrial districts' (Thompson 1968, p. 427). In 1800 there were 90,619; in 1810: 137,997; in 1820: 191,217; in 1830: 248,529. Furthermore, years that showed most revivalist activity are seen as being periods of maximum political awareness and activity. At this point in the discussion the idea of chronology is brought in.

Thompson rejects the argument that religious revivalism and political activism ran in parallel. Instead, he finds it possible (and *tentatively* suggests) that 'religious revivalism took over just at the point where "political" or temporal aspirations met with defeat'. (Thompson 1968, p. 427). The only precise general example given of this is the wave of revivalism that began in 1813 in the aftermath of Luddism (1811–12) and then gave way to a political revival in the winter of 1816–17. The particular example given is that of the Pentridge 'rising' of June 1817, *after* which a Primitive Methodist revival is claimed to have taken place in the area. More recent evidence suggests that the chronology in this particular case should be reversed: Primitive Methodist activity preceded the 'rising'. (Peel 1971, p.

42 and 43n.) On empirical grounds, it cannot be claimed that Thompson succeeds in demonstrating the interesting hypothesis that there occurred 'something like an oscillation, with religious revivalism at the negative, and radical politics (tinged with revolutionary millenarialism) at the positive pole'. (Thompson 1968, p. 429)

Eric Hobsbawm's counter-argument to the Halévy thesis asserts basically that Methodism was never as pervasive nor as potent as had been suggested, and that there was no revolution because the ruilng class knew when to make concessions and thus never lost control. Behind his argument, however, is a notion of chronology which differs from that of Thompson and which Thompson explicitly attacks. While maintaining a similar position over the prevalence of revolutionary feeling in large parts of the country between 1790 and the late 1840s, he adopts Lenin's view that a deterioration in the conditions of the masses, together with an increase in their political activity, are not sufficient conditions for the emergence of revolution: also necessary is a crisis in the affairs of the ruling order and a body of revolutionaries who are capable of directing and leading the movement – these, he argues, were absent. While this argument detracts somewhat from the emphasis given by Thompson to the 'chiliasm of despair' that was available in Methodism, it does not fundamentally undermine Halévy's original thesis, which was explicitly concerned with the way in which potential working-class leadership was diverted. Hobsbawm's subsequent statement that 'Methodism was not responsible for the moderation and flexibility of the Parlimentary politicians or the Utilitarian radicals' (Hobsbawm, 1957, p. 116) appears to be a much more serious challenge to Halévy – whose insistence on the upward permeation of the Wesleyan revival involves us in a consideration of Evangelicalism among the governing élite – until Hobsbawm makes it clear that he will not give any attention to this aspect of the problem: 'In order to demonstrate [that Methodism had no such responsibility] . . . it is necessary to discover – in so far as this is possible – what effect it had on the politics of the British *working classes* in our period . . .' (Hobsbawm 1957, p. 116). Thus the discussion gravitates from Wesleyan Methodism, which is generally accepted as a group with conservative leadership and a strong lower middle-class element, to the more radical Methodist seceding groups, the Kilhamites or New Connexion (1797), the Primitive Methodists (1811) – 'the most purely "proletarian" of the major sects' (Hobsbawm 1957, p. 118) – and the Bible Christians (1815).

Using information drawn from the Religious Census of 1851, Hobsbawm concludes that in the new industrial cities and in some mining areas organized religion *as a whole* was weak, and that the different branches of Methodism could be expected to have a major political influence on popular agitations only in the North, Midlands, East Anglia and the extreme South-west (still a sizable area, although Bristol, Birmingham and London – where a great deal of revolutionary unrest was centred – are specifically excluded). *Wesleyan* Methodism is seen to have only one stronghold, in the West Riding of Yorkshire. Projecting back from 1851, Hobsbawm argues that at the beginning of the nineteenth century Methodism was numerically much weaker: 'It does not seem likely that a body of, say, 150,000 out of 10 million English and Welsh in 1811 could have exercised decisive importance.' (Hobsbawm 1957, p. 120) Nor does there appear to be much evidence of the 'moderating influence' of Wesleyans in their early ninteeenth-century strongholds, for Luddism and other radical activities were well evidenced in those areas of the West Riding where Wesleyanism was strongest. In fact, 'The truth is that Methodism developed in this area and so did Radicalism.' (Hobsbawm 1957, p. 121). In Cornwall, on the other hand, Wesleyanism was strongest among the miners, who were also weak in radical political activity but the correlation does not point to the influence of Methodism, since the structure of Cornish industry was responsible for the lack of working-class consciousness. In view of these and similar pieces of evidence, Hobsbawm suggests that although the official leadership of Methodism wished to retain its conservative position, the movement was not strong enough numerically to have much influence, nor were its leaders able to prevent the rank-and-file from forming radical offshoots and from engaging in radical agitation.

The question of chronology is brought up to explain why the effectiveness of official Wesleyan conservatism has often been exaggerated. Hobsbawm challenges the assumption that workers in early industrial Britain turned towards various sects *as an alternative* to revolutionary or radical politics. To some extent they did – though the only examples cited are drawn from continental mystical and quietist sectarianism – but 'there is another kind of religion which might seize the miserable mass of the people at such times. Preachers, prophets and sectarians might issue what the labourers would regard as calls to action rather than to resignation.' (Hobsbawm 1957, pp. 123-4). Instead of adopting Thompson's unitary continuum of activism-quietism, in which religious movements are closely identified with the quietist pole and political ones with the activist, Hobsbawm broadens the scope of his analysis to include both quietist and activist religious movements. In this way, the chronological links between religious and political radicalism run in parallel. Methodism is seen as advancing when radicalism advanced, and religious revivals 'normally did *not* occur when economic conditions were coming to their worst, for instance, at the bottom of trade depressions. The periods when Wesleyanism [a more specific application of the perspective] recruited most rapidly . . . were also, with the exception of the boom-years 1820–4, periods of mounting popular agitation . . .' (Hobsbawm 1957, p. 124). Reversing the Halévy thesis completely, Hobsbawm argues that workers became Methodists and radicals for the same reasons, the logic of this argument is somewhat vague.

Thompson and Hobsbawm maintain quite different interpretations, both of the significance of Methodism and of the chronological links between religious revival and political radicalism, and yet there has never been a direct confrontation between the two views. Thus in two of the most important recent treatments of certain aspects of the Halévy thesis the issues remain unresolved. However, it can be maintained that too much attention has been concentrated on the direct influence of Methodism on its (supposedly) working-class membership, and that the major emphasis of Halévy's construction lies elsewhere. To take up the point made by Hobsbawm, could part of the explanation for the flexibility of the ruling class at the beginning of the nineteenth century be given in terms of the influence of Methodism and Evangelicalism?

An article by Kiernan suggests that it could. (Kiernan 1952) Although not directly intended as an empirical test of the Halévy thesis (Halévy's name appears only twice in footnotes, and then only in connection with points of detail), it comes much closer to an understanding of his argument, because firstly, it concentrates on a wider social and religious context than that of working-class Methodism; and secondly, it draws a contrast between the socio–political situation in England and contemporary developments in France. Kiernan sets out to document the influence of the French Revolution on the Evangelical revival in England, and especially on elements within the upper class, in the late eighteenth and early nineteenth centuries. Some of the implications of his research provide even better grounds for a Marxian analysis than the accounts of Hobsbawm and Thompson.

The Methodist revival, which began in 1739, is seen as being greatly influenced in its first 100 years by the complex socio–economic changes that accompanied its development. But around the year 1800:

> there was a sudden acceleration, a broadening of a sectarian cult into something like a national faith. It may be permissible to say that in general, as in this case, religious impulses begin at the lower social levels, in response to changes to which the mass of people are more sensitive, because more directly

exposed, than those above them; and that the latter move from hostility to acceptance only when an external shock comes to emphasize the dangers of internal discontent. Jacobinism, which abolished the Christian calendar in France, helped to establish the Victorian Sabbath in England. (Kiernan 1952, p. 44)

This identification of all 'religious influences' with lower social origins is untenable as a generalized hypothesis – certain *types* of religious expression may originate in this way, but these, as well as their precise social location, are a subject of immense complexity, (Weber 1965). Nevertheless, in so far as the urban lower-middle class and artisans may be argued to have 'a definite tendency towards congregational religion, towards religion of salvation, and finally towards rational ethical religion', (Weber 1965, p. 96) this may validly be applied to the inception of Methodism: its 'acceptance' by more privileged social groups is a matter for detailed historical enquiry rather than a priori assumption. But it is in establishing this upward permeation that Kiernan's study is most important.

Around 1800, it is suggested, the religious enthusiasm of the Evangelical revival 'was recognized as a possible support of order and stability'. (Kiernan 1952, p. 44). The eighteenth-century upper class had begun by deriding or denouncing much of the enthusiasm of the Wesleyan revival, and this in itself was a positive factor when revivalism came to be enlisted in defence of the established order: 'In religion as in politics, an idea which is to disarm discontents must at some time, in some sense, have seemed both to friend and foe an idea of rebellion'. (Kiernan 1952, p. 45). Since Jacobinism was so closely associated with atheism, Christianity became synonymous with loyalty to the existing social order. However, the Church of England was not as it stood at the time of the French Revolution in a strong position to meet the new needs. Its hierarchy, especially at the top, was closely identified with the governing élite, and its parochial clergy were either pauperized or had plural livings. Its theology too had been much influenced by the idea of 'the reasonableness of Christianity', but 'a public creed only looks "reasonable" . . . so long as the prevailing relations between man and man are accepted as reasonable. And when an upper class appeals to common sense, others follow its example. Reason was now divided against itself. Burke, with tremendous passion, appealed to men's good sense; but so did Thomas Paine'. (Kiernan 1952, p. 46). (In just the same way, Weber argued that natural law had become 'deeply discredited' as a result of its use as an ideological weapon.) There thus appeared side by side two different conceptions of religion: on the one hand, the 'civic religion' of a stable, established society; in contrast to this stood the salvation religion of individual conversion provided by Methodism and the broader Evangelical movement.

In order to regain social stability, some form of common ground was needed between the upper and lower classes, but Kiernan gives evidence of initially substantial opposition from conservatives within the ruling class to the notion of evangelicalism as such a source of common ground: 'To bring the respectable round to this point required both hard experience and able advocacy. The distance they had to travel may be seen by comparison of Burke's *Reflections* (1709) with Wilberforce's *Practical View* (1797) – both addressed to the upper classes, and both immediately applauded by them.' (Kiernan 1952, p. 47). While Burke provided an orthodox conservative defence of the Church of England, the Evangelical William Wilberforce (a member of the 'Clapham Sect') advocated the need for a new religious solution to the perils threatening property and political stability. Thus he stated his political case quite openly: his intention was 'to suggest inferior motives to readers, who might be less disposed to listen to considerations of a higher order'. (Kiernan 1952, p. 48). In other words Wilberforce was concerned to legitimate, in terms that would gain the support of members of the ruling class, the *political* advantages of a set of *religious* beliefs which he quite genuinely held: 'what was emotionally necessary to him, he could recommend to others as politically necessary. He had no novel ideas; his mind fused together Wesley's conviction that man's soul was in danger, and Burke's that society was in danger. His book came out, appropriately, at the crisis of the great naval mutinies.' (Kiernan 1952, p. 48). By combining these two convictions, Wilberforce presented the characteristic Evangelical diagnosis that what lay behind the social crisis of his time was a moral, rather than a political problem: thus it involved all social classes, and Christianity was the only thing that could save the social fabric from falling apart – 'Moderating the insolence of power, [Christianity] . . . renders the inequalities of the social state less galling to the lower orders, whom also she instructs, in their turn, to be diligent, humble, patient.' (Kiernan 1952, p. 48).

Not that Wilberforce argued in favour of some form of simulated religion with which to control the masses. Religion could not merely be set up to serve the State (just as Durkheim later argued that it was no simple practical solution to the incidence of suicide) (Durkheim 1970, pp. 374–6), and thus Burke's prescription was dismissed: 'Whereas Burke had put the religious horse squarely before the political cart, Wilberforce concealed the horse behind the cart. Or, more properly, he transformed the characters of both.' (Kiernan 1952, p. 49). The appeal that Wilberforce made to Evan gelical Christianity was in its own way a radical one, since at the time it was a derided, even a suspect creed. But its theological fluidity, its egalitarian distribution of sin and eternal damnation (without disturbing the existing social structure), and the way in which it channelled the sense of social crisis into a conception of individual guilt, left unchallenged the basic structure of English society. As Kiernan notes of the sweeping denunciations of national vice and calls for contrition on the part of the Evangelicals: 'Implicit in such sweeping judgements was a denial of any peculiar blame attaching to griping landlord or brutal mill-owner.' (Kiernan 1952, p. 50). But if the rich could not be condemned for grinding the faces of the poor, they were certainly accused, along with the poor, of Sabbath-breaking, since Sabbatarianism was an important plank in the Evangelicals' programme of moral reform. Circulation of the Bible (the British and Foreign Bible Society, which was largely an Evangelical enterprise, was founded in 1804) was another form taken by the national reformation of morals, and it is not without significance that the period 1790–1810 saw a very rapid growth in the number of societies devoted to foreign missionary work: in this way, evangelical fervour was 'exported' in a quite literal sense.

It would be too crude to portray the political consequences of the Methodist revival and the Evangelical revival which it stimulated in the Church of England as intended consequences. Kiernan sometimes comes near to this – as, for instance, when it is claimed that there was in the revival after 1800 'a strong admixture of pretence' (Kiernan 1952, p. 54) – although the documentation gives considerable support to most of the arguments. On the other hand, Wilberforce can be credited with having made *manifest*, at an important stage in the history of the Evangelical revival in the Church of England, some of its more politically advantageous *latent* features. Furthermore, Wilberforce was an influential member of the ruling class, and if we are to understand the complex of influences which, in Hobsbawm's view, lay behind the maintenance of sufficient control and flexibility on the part of the ruling class to prevent the development of a revolutionary situation, we must look at the views of legitimators and apologists like Wilberforce *as well as* at detailed statistics of Methodist growth and influence.

The Halévy thesis, we have argued, is not primarily a statement about working-class religiosity (a concept largely disclaimed by Halévy) but about the social and religious linkage and mobility that Methodism made possible, and the resulting influence that Methodism was able to exert, first of all on dissent, *'then the establishment*, finally secular opinion'. (Halévy

1924, p. 339). By concentrating so much attention on the influence (or lack of it) that the different branches of Methodism were able to exert on their (supposed) working-class membership, the effects of the permeation of Methodism via Evangelicalism into the establishment itself, and its propagation by some apologists as a political expedient, have tended to be overlooked. Paradoxically, this same area might provide a valuable empirical test of at least one Marxian hypothesis: that is to say, if religion's function as an opiate for the masses depends in part on its adoption and assiduous inculcation by the ruling class, it is important to find evidence of the latter's perception of this link. Kiernan's variation on Halévy's original thesis provides some valuable evidence for the conclusion that Evangelicals such as Wilberforce managed, from within the ruling class itself, to legitimate the growing but often suspect Evangelical revival in the Church of England on the grounds of its contribution to the maintenance of the status quo as well as on purely religious grounds.

The Halévy thesis contains several interesting insights, both on a particular historical level and on a broader theoretical level, into the relationship between religious beliefs and organization and the process of rapid social change. Because it has been so widely ignored, attention has in the main been devoted to a detailed restatement of the original thesis and an examination of more recent elaborations and criticisms of it. Of particular importance in the study of religion and social change is the means by which religion as an independent variable is isolated from other variables: thus Halévy selects three institutional areas – economic, political and religious – and, by a process of eliminating the economic and political variables successively, puts forward an explanation in which religion is the key variable. One line of criticism has been to reassert the significance of the other variables. Hobsbawm, for instance, argues that greater weight should be given to the political structure – though even here, it has been suggested, there are still important components of the Halévy thesis that remain untouched. Another line of criticism – and of elaboration – has adopted a procedure that has produced valuable results in recent discussions of the place of religion in social change.

References

BALLEINE, G. R. (1951) *A History of the Evangelical Party in the Church of England* London, Church Book Room Press.

DURKHEIM, E. (1970) *Suicide* London, Routledge and Kegan Paul.

HALEVY, E. (1924) *A History of the English People in 1815*, translated by Watkin, E. I. and Barker, D. A., London, T. Fisher Unwin.

HIMMELFARB, G. (1968) *Victorian Minds* London, Weidenfeld and Nicolson.

HOBSBAWM, E. J. (1957) 'Methodism and the Threat of Revolution in Britain', *History Today*, vol. VII, 115–24.

HOLLANDER, E. P. and HUNT, R. G. (eds) (1967) *Current Perspectives in Social Psychology* (2nd ed.) New York, Oxford University Press.

KENT, J. (1966) *The Age of Disunity* London, Epworth Press.

KIERNAN, V. (1952) 'Evangelicalism and the French Revolution', *Past and Present*, vol. 1, no. 1, February.

The Oxford Dictionary of the Christian Church (1963) edited by Cross, F. L., London, Oxford University Press.

PEEL, J. D. Y. (1971) *Herbert Spencer: The Evolution of a Sociologist* London, Heinemann.

ROBERTS, B. R. (1968) 'Protestant Groups and Coping with Urban Life in Guatemala City', *American Journal of Sociology*, vol. 73, no. 6, May.

THOMPSON, E. P. (1968) *The Makings of the English Working Class* Harmondsworth, Penguin.

WEBER, M. (1965) *The Sociology of Religion*, translated by Fischoff, E., London, Methuen.

27   Millenarian movements

Yonina Talmon

The Latin term *millenium* and its Greek equivalent *chilias* literally mean
a period of a thousand years. According to the millenarian tradition, which
is based on Jewish apocalyptic literature and on the Revelations to St John,
Christ will reappear in the guise of a warror, vanquish the devil and hold
him prisoner. He will then build the Kingdom of God and reign in person
for a thousand years. Those saints who remained steadfast and gave their
life for their faith shall be raised from the dead and serve as his royal
priesthood. At the end of this period Satan will be let loose again for a
short while and will be finally destroyed. The victory will be followed by
the general resurrection of the dead, the last judgment and final redemption.

The term 'millenarian' (or chiliastic) movements is now used not in its
specific and limited historical sense but typologically, to designate *religious
movements that expect imminent, total, ultimate, this-worldly collective
salvation*. Employed thus the term applies to a wide range of movements. ...

Conditions of development

What are the conditions which account for the emergence and continuance
of millenarian movements, and in which social groups are they anchored?
By and large the data support the hypothesis that posits that millenarism
is the religion of *deprived* groups: the lower social strata, and oppressed
and persecuted minorities (Mannheim 1952).

Millenarism usually is engendered by severe and protracted suffering. In
many cases we find at its roots *multiple deprivation*, that results from the
combined effect of poverty, low status and lack of power. The effect of
multiple deprivation accounts for the prominence of members of pariah
groups and pariah peoples among the promulgators and followers of millenarism. The low status of such groups derives from their despised ethnic
origin and cultural tradition, and from their limitation to menial and de-
grading occupations imposed upon them. Being at the bottom rung of the

---

TALMON, YONINA (1966) 'Millenarian Movements', in *Archives Européennes
de Sociologie*, VII, 159, 181–200.

social ladder on so many counts, they are attracted to the myth of the elect, and to the fantasy of a reversal of roles which are important elements in the millenarian ideology.

Millenarism often flares up as a reaction to *cumulative deterioration* of life conditions, and as a result of the awareness of prospects for further decline in the future. We note also the precipitating effect of *sudden and dramatic crises* which aggravate endemic deprivation and at the same time symbolize and highlight it. Many of the outbursts of millenarism took place against a background of disaster: plagues, devastating fires, recurrent long droughts that were the dire lot of the peasants, slumps that caused widespread unemployment and poverty, calamitous wars. These catastrophes which bring in their wake hunger, illness, cruel death and degradation, engender a deep sense of doom and a fervent craving for salvation (Barker 1941). Repeated historical experiences of breakdown and disaster lead to a rejection not only of actual history but of history as such. The fantastic hope of total redemption is born out of abysmal despair.

The hypothesis of acute multiple deprivation as the breeding ground for millenarian trends provides an important clue to our understanding of these phenomena, yet taken by itself it is inadequate and cannot fully account for the emergence and the development of millenarism, and requires considerable modification and amplification.

First, it should be noted that the predisposing factor is, in many an instance, not severe hardship but a *markedly uneven relation between expectations and the means of their satisfction* (Firth 1955). Often it is predominantly the inability of those attracted to millenarism to fulfil traditional expectations. In medieval Europe millenarism affected mainly people who were cut off from the traditional order, and were unable to satisfy wants which this order instilled in them. The insidious onslaught of the developing capitalistic order on a backward and isolated peasant economy created the same basic difficulty in Spain and Italy centuries later, although there it affected not only people who were cut off from their rural base but also rural community as a whole. We encounter the same type of frustration in primitive societies, but there it increasingly results not so much from the lack of means to supply traditional wants, but rather from the emergence of a set of new expectations. The encounter with modern societies engenders enormously inflated expectations, without a concomitant and adequate development of institutional means for their fulfilment. This discrepency creates a void which is often bridged by millenarian hope. That such frustration may be much more important than actual hardship becomes evident from the fact that millenarian unrest was caused in certain parts of New Guinea not by any direct contact with the white man. Although there were hardly any changes in the *status quo ante*, indirect contacts and the impact of hearsay brought about a change of expectations and resulting acute frustration. It should be stressed that in many cases millenarian outbursts were caused not by a deterioration of conditions but by *a limited amelioration* which raised new hopes and new expectations but left them largely unfulfilled.

The incongruity between ends and means it not the only source of frustration. Much of the deep dissatisfaction stems from incongruities and difficulties in the realm of the *regulation of ends*. Rapid change and the encounters with radically different systems of values result in more or less severe cultural disintegration and disorientation. The impinging cultural influences penetrate into the traditional setting and undermine the effectiveness of traditional norms as guides of action. Even central traditional values cease to be self-evident and sacred. Inasmuch as these traditional values are internalized, and are an integral part of a personal identity, the disintegration of the traditional system results in a serious self alienation. When the alien culture is that of a more prestigious upper class or that of a colonial ruling class, willingly or unwillingly, consciously or unconsciously it is often acknowledged as superior. This creates a nagging feeling of inferiority and even self-hatred.

The effect of the incongruity between the indigenous and external influences is aggravated by the discrepancies between the values and policies of different external agencies. In most colonial countries there is a constant conflict between the government, the traders and the missions, and open, often bitter rivalry between the different missions. There are in addition inner contradictions and inconsistencies between different elements of religious doctrine and a divergence between religious ideals and religious reality. In most spheres of life contradictory norms and mutually exclusive obligations make themselves felt. Since conflicting claims tend to neutralize and annul each other, the impinging influences weaken and destroy the traditional system without substituting a new set of values. Anomie and disorientation are often more important predisposing factors than deprivation. Millenarism recurrently is born out of the search for a tolerably coherent system of values, a new cultural identity and a regained sense of dignity and self-respect.

Another important factor operative in the emergence of millenarism is *social isolation* brought about by the disruption of traditional group ties. Analysis of the medieval material indicates that millenarism did not appeal much to people who were firmly rooted in well-integrated kinship groupings, and effectively organized in, and protected by cohesive local communities. Most exposed to the new pressures, and therefore more prone to millenarian heresy, were the mal-integrated and the isolated who could find no assured and recognized place in cohesive primary groups. Comparative historical analysis underlines the important contribution of migrant groups and itinerant workers to the development and diffusion of millenarism. The disruption of social ties entailed in inter-county and intra-county migration is one of the major predisposing factors also in modern society. The estrangement and loneliness that result from the breakdown of kinship and local groupings are a major theme in all studies of millenarism.

It is significant that millenarism occurs mainly in *periods of transition*. Millenarian movements in primitive societies provide the clearest proof of this hypothesis. Millenarism usually does not appear in areas largely untouched by modernization, and it appears only rarely in areas in which modernization has reached an advanced stage. It occurs mainly during the intermediate, 'neither here nor there' stages of modernization. This has given rise to the hypothesis that millenarism in primitive societies is a 'halfway' or 'quarter-way' phenomenon (Belshow 1950). While it is difficult to specify exactly at which point along the line millenarism begins or where it ceases to be feasible, the basic hypothesis which views it as a concomitant of transition is corroborated in other settings as well. In modern societies we find that people who have undergone the double transition of inter- and intra-country migration, and are both new immigrants and new urbanites, are particularly prone to millenarism. Millenarian movements have proliferated during the transition between the premodern and the modern way of life in rural Spain and Italy. Millenarian outbursts abounded towards the end of the Middle Ages and the beginning of modern times. The Judaeo–Christian formulation of millenarism developed during the stormy period which preceded and anteceded the destruction of the Second Temple. The frustration, disorientation and disruption engendered by these upheavals are at the very heart of the matter.

Yet even the combination of such factors as deprivation, frustration and isolation does not supply us with an adequate answer to our problem. The most important contribution of recent studies of millenarism to this analysis lies in the insistence that millenarism is essentially a *pre-political, non-political and post-political phenomenon* (Worsley 1957). In primitive societies it appears mainly in so-called stateless segmentary societies which have rudimentary political institutions or lack any specialized political institutions altogether. When it emerges in societies with fairly or well developed political institutions it appeals mainly to strata which are politically passive and have no experience of political organization and no access to political power. Instances of such 'non-political' strata in societies with a more or less developed political structure are the peasants in feudal societies, the peasants in isolated and backward areas in modern societies, marginal and politically passive elements in the working class, recent immigrants and mal-integrated and politically inarticulate minority groups. Sometimes millenarism is 'post-political', appearing after the downfall of a fairly developed political system. The collapse of an entire political system by a crushing defeat and the shattering of tribal or national hopes have sometimes led to widespread millenarism. It is the sense of blockage – the lack of effective organization, the absence of regular institutionalized ways of voicing grievances and pressing claims, that pushes such groups to a millenarian solution. Not being able to cope with their difficulties through concerted political action, they turn to millenarism. Millenarism is born out of great distress coupled with political helplessness.

The effect of the various predisposing economic and social factors is further clarified when we examine more closely the *sources of recruitment*. The hypothesis that millenarism is a religious ideology of lower strata is based on the assumption that it is a concomitant of social and economic differentiation and a manifestation of class society. Examination of the data indicates that this is true in most cases but not in all. Millenarism is not confined to stratified societies. In quite a number of instances it marks the reaction of a largely undifferentiated primitive society to the unsettling impact of social change. Primitive societies undergo only slow and gradual, almost imperceptible social change. The dominant time dimension is the mythical past; life in the present is experienced as repetition of the paradigmatic events of the *urzeit*. The idea of *endzeit* is either non-existent or marginal. Swift and radical change disrupts this repetitive rhythm and transforms life conditions. The cosmic and social orders can no longer be anchored in the mythical beginning, and so the major emphasis shifts to the mythical future. The image of the future age of bliss may be largely an extrapolated replica of the former image of a past golden age. It may, on the other hand, be change-oriented and partly independent of this image of the mythical past. The main predisposition factor in such cases is the loss of anchorage in the life-giving myth of the *urzeit* and this loss affects society as a whole. Millenarism of this type is rooted in the dilemma of stability and disruptive change, and not so much in a polarization of under and over privileged strata. This problem of breakdown of continuity is of central importance also in the emergence of 'post-historical' millenarism.

When we centre our attention on stratified societies, we find that under-privileged groups predominate but they do not have a complete monopoly in millenarism. At one time or another, millenarism has found support in all levels of society. There is, for instance, a distinctly middle-class element in British millenarism. It is true that groups such as those that built their hopes on Mother Ann Lee of Manchester were usually of humbler origin, and that from the days of Wesley, through the initial period of the Salvation Army to the present day frequenters of Kingdom Halls, the poor were in the majority. However, in most movements we find members, and especially leaders of middle-class origin. There is even one distinctly middle-class movement: there were few, if any, underprivileged elements in the affluent 'Irvingite' Catholic Apostolic Church which developed in the middle of the nineteenth century in England (Shaw 1946). The leaders were upper middle-class men of culture and education with some social importance.

To mention another instance – the Skoptsi who in the nineteenth century numbered tens of thousands of adherents, scattered all over Russia, included nobles, officials, rich merchants, as well as peasants. Joining the organization involved castration in the case of men, and the cutting of breasts in the case of women. The movement expected a world-wide millennial Kingdom of sexless beings. The case of the Skoptsi is important because from the point of view of the social origin of members and leaders, as well as from the point of view of the movement's conception of the millennium, it cannot be interpreted in terms of class interests.

It is significant also that adherents to millenarian movements are not always the most underprivileged among the underprivileged. Members of the deprived stratum who are somewhat better off are often more able to take stock of their situation, to react and reorganize. The upper strata of an inferior minority group or the indigenous aristocracy of a colonial country may identify with the dominant group. They may, on the other hand, identify with their own membership group and want to share its destiny. As indiscriminate invidious evaluation of all members of the inferior group, and the existence of an insurmountable barrier between it and the dominant group strengthen the solidarity of the underprivileged group and blur internal status differentiation. The tendency of members of such upper strata to join and lead millenarian protest movements is enhanced if their traditional status is threatened and bypassed.

Many studies underline the prominence of members of a frustrated secondary elite among the leaders of millenarian movements (Kayz 1961). Many leaders of the medieval movements were members of the lower clergy, priests, monks and friars, who, for some reason or another, decided to turn back on the church. Thomas Münzer is the most famous example of such men. Some of the prophets were obscure laymen who somehow contrived to acquire a clerical education. Typical of such men are the heretical Beghards, Konrad Schmidt and John of Leiden. Occasionally we come across eccentric members of the lower nobility, like Eudes de l'Etoile and Enrico of Leiningen. It was these marginal *déclassés* intellectuals and semi-intellectuals who preserved, edited and developed the eschatological lore throughout the Middle Ages. A disproportionately large number of the initiators, leaders and active members of the Sabbatean Movement were itinerant preachers, learned men without any officially recognized position in their community. Among the leaders of primitive movements we encounter minor leaders of traditional society. Knor of Biak, for instance, was a village chief before he proclaimed himself a prophet. More common is the figure of the non-traditional leader who is an alien in both the native and white-colonial social settings. Paliaw of Manus and Kimbangu, and André Matswa of Congo are representatives of this type of semi-modern alienated leader.

In the biography of many of the prophets we encounter precipitating incidents: resented personal failure and acute disappointment. Frustrated aspirations, disillusionments, rebuke and humiliation occur in many life histories. The repeated failure of Hung Hsin Ch'un, the leader of the Taiping rebellion, to pass his civil service examination, is a case in point. Scrutiny of the social origin and of the personal life histories of the leaders indicates that frustration and isolation have had more impact than deprivation.

So far we have dealt mainly with the economic and social factors. That the combination of all the predisposing factors will actually lead to millenarism, and will not result in the development of other types of religious ideology, is conditioned also by the type of prevalent religious beliefs. The yearning for an earthly paradise and for final salvation is very widespread, and millenarian elements appear in most religions. It should be stressed, however, that certain types of religion are more conducive to millenarism than others. Clearly, religions in which history has no meaning whatsoever, and religions which have a cyclical repetitive conception of time are not conducive to millenarism (Eliade 1954). Apocalyptic eschatology is essentially alien to religions of a philosophical and mystical cast which turn the eye of the believer towards eternity where there is no movement and no process. This is certainly the case with some nature and cosmic religions that view the universe in terms of ever-recurring cycles of rise and decline.

Another important factor operative in this sphere is a 'this-worldly' emphasis. Religions with a radical, other-worldly orientation which put all the emphasis on the hereafter or on a purely spiritual and totally non-terrestrial salvation do not give rise to a vision of the Kingdom of God on earth. The myth of Kalki as an incarnation of Vishnu in a period of abundance, and the doctrine of the future Buddha whose advent will bring a Golden Age, prove that even such basically non millenarian religions as Hinduism and Buddhism are not devoid of millenarian conceptions. It should be noted, however, that there is hardly any millenarian tradition in Hinduism, and that it has not occupied an important place in Buddhism.

It is mainly world views that are based on a notion of the divine will working through history towards a preordained end that provide an overall scheme conducive to millenarism. The majority of millenarian movements appeared in countries which had direct or indirect contact with the Judaeo–Christian messianic traditions. The Christian missions were the most important agency for the worldwide diffusion of millenarism. Several fundamentalist sects and millenarian movements played a particularly important role in this process. The Kitawala movement, which is an African offshoot of Jehovah's Witnesses, is a case in point (Cunnison 1958). It should be noted, however, that millenarism appeared also in cases in which the main contact was mediated by less apocalyptic versions of Christianity. In such cases, millenarism is reinstated to its central position by a process of selection and reinterpretation.

We should take into consideration autochthonous religious concepts as well. Some primitive mythologies contain suitable beliefs, such as the expectation of the future return of the culture hero or the idea of the return of the dead as a prelude to a millennial era. It should be stressed, though, that these themes appeared in a rather embryonic form in primitive mythology and did not occupy a particularly important position. They were developed, reinterpreted and elaborated into full-fledged millenarian conceptions only under the impact of new situations, and after contact with Christianity or Islam.

The pre-existing primitive conceptions affected the development of millenarism in yet another way. The prevalence of millenarism in Melanesia, and the importance of expectations of cargo in this view of the millennium are, it would seem, due to the strong and almost exclusive emphasis which the indigenous religion puts on ritual activity oriented towards the acquisition of material goods. Analysis of the withdrawal motif provides another striking instance of continuity between the millenarian movements and indigenous concepts and practices (Van der Kroef

1959). Withdrawal from the constituted authority of the village headman by those who disagreed with him as a well institutionalized response pattern in the Toredja society. The millenarian movement which developed there sought the withdrawal of the true believers so that they could join the ancestors in the upper world. During the later stage the movement incited its followers to withdraw from the area of Dutch authority. There is considerable evidence to show that the prominence of the withdrawal motif in the Brazilian millenarian movements is due, at least in part, to the persistence of the native mythical theme of the Land Without Evil. To cite another example: in many cases a basic similarity between the primitive Shaman and the charismatic prophet may be observed. Legitimation by means of soul journeys, seizures, hallucinations and visions is often a reproduction of the traditional pattern. Legitimacy of self-selections as a mode of recruitment to traditional religious roles facilitates the emergence of non-traditional charismatic leaders.

The most important ideological starting point of millenarism may be a new importation or it may be the native tradition that exists of old. In a number of instances it seems to be predominantly a largely independent reaction to the pressure of circumstances. Availability of pre-existing millenarian precepts and patterns facilitates the development of a full-fledged millenarian ideology and the organization of a millenarian movement. Such millenarian precepts may be dormant for a long time until they are activated by suitable circumstances and by crisis. The readily found millenarian representations are invested with the particularity and immediacy necessary to convert them into an effective ideology which serves as a basis for collective action.

Comparative research underlines the close correspondence and interdependence between millenarism and economic and social conditions. At the same time, it indicates the potency and partial independence of the religious factor. The Sabbatean movement supplies us with clear proof of the inadequacy of a reductionist interpretation, and is a crucial case in this respect. This movement evolved in the wake of two waves of unprecedented massacres and persecutions in Poland. Many thousands of Jews were slaughtered, and many more fled before the sword. Hundreds of communities were completely ruined. Since the messianic movement erupted shortly after the massacres it was viewed as a direct reaction to them. Examination of the differential appeal of messianism in different countries reveals, however, that it was not at its strongest in communities which bore the full brunt of the disaster, and that it was just as powerful, and sometimes even more powerful in countries in which the Jews lived in com parative peace and were unmolested. The calamity indeed contributed to the emergence of the movement by emphasizing the fundamental precariousness of Jewish existence, and by enhancing the consciousness of exile. Yet in and by itself, this cannot account for its development and differential impact. It is further significant that messianism spread in prosperous and expanding communities just as in destitute and declining ones. Intra-community differentiation affected recruitment more than inter-community differentiation. Part of the established elite distrusted and rejected the Messiah, and the secondary elite was more active than the primary one. It should be noted, though, that the majority of the elite and upper strata joined the movement and were as enthusiastic as the mass of the people. We find among the adherents members of all strata of society, ranging from the millionaire merchants, who offered to donate their entire fortune to the Messiah, to the poorest of the poor. The predominant predisposing factor which accounts for the deep and lasting impact and for the almost universal appeal of the movement in all countries of the diaspora, was the very wide spread of Lurianic Kabbala about a generation before the advent of Shabbatai Zevi. This mystic doctrine aimed at the restitution of cosmic harmony through the terrestrial medium of a spiritually elevated Judaism. It laid far greater stress on the inner aspects of redemption than on its external historical and political aspects. Yet since it viewed liberation from the yoke of servitude and exile as a byproduct of spiritual salvation, and since it considered the coming of the Messiah as imminent, it furthered tense messianic expectations. To the large circles of Lurianic devotees the coming of Shabbatai Zevi was an actualization of the promise and prediction of the Kabbala. The antinomian deviations of Sabbateanism were anchored in the non-traditional elements of the mystic conception of redemption. The inner dynamics of the movement, and especially its transformation during its later phases are unintelligible without recourse to a detailed and full analysis of the precepts and symbols of the Lurianic Kabbala.

In concluding this causal analysis it should be emphasized that the various predisposing factors are interrelated (Smelser 1963). There is a low correlation between any one of them and the emergence of millenarism. Only by a close examination of their intricate interplay and their combined effect the results become more satisfactory. Moreover, to suggest that most millenarian movements arise in situations which have certain identifiable features in common is not to suggest that wherever such situations exist millenarian movements must inevitably arise. An inherent openness and indeterminacy remains even after we have considered all the major determinants. Examination of cases of occurrence, near-occurrence and non-occurrence under basically similar conditions as far as degree of strain and structural and cultural conduciveness are concerned indicates the considerable importance of historical incidents. Availability or non-availability of leaders with strong suggestive powers, occurrence or non-occurrence of precipitating crises affect the chances of the movement to emerge and organize itself. The variation in the reaction of the authorities to the movement's efforts of mobilization is another important factor. Persistent and effective repression may prevent the emergence of the movement of defeat and quench it soon after it appears. Increased responsiveness and flexibility may open avenues of reform and thereby deflect it from its purpose. It is mainly when unresponsiveness and inflexibility are combined with a certain ineffectiveness or at least some relaxation of control, that the millenarian movement has a chance to emerge and spread.

Functional analysis

What are the consequences of millenarism? How does it serve the needs of the followers, and what does it contribute to the social strata and societies in which it appears? We find *two main diametrically opposed interpretations* in this sphere. There is first the approach which underlines the negative functions of millenarism and considers it as a dangerous collective madness. According to this viewpoint, millenarism is a paranoid fantasy, an outlet for extreme anxiety and a delusion bred by despair. The megalomaniac view of oneself as wholly good and abominably persecuted, the attribution of demoniac power to the adversary, the inability to accept the inescapable limitations of human existence on the one hand, and the excessive emotionality, the antinomian rituals and the destructive activities on the other hand, are all diagnosed as symptoms of mental illness. The millenarian ideology is considered as disruptive and destructive with regard to the movement itself and to overall society as well. Millenarism is a flight to the world of fantasy. Its goals are unrealizable, and the means of achieving them are impracticable. The sense of magic mastery diverts the followers from attempts to cope with their problems in a more practical and rational way. Millenarian movements cultivate deviant tendencies and encourage resistance to the existing order without being able to bring about actual change. Moreover, millenarism, by its very nature, is abortive. Since it makes false promises, failure is inbuilt and inevitable. The crisis of non-actualization enhances the aggressive and antinomian tendencies inherent in the millenarian world view. Disillusionment and the ensuing inward turning of aggression result in inner strife and constant fission. The millenarian movement can counteract the disintegrating tendencies inherent in its religious ideology for an considerable time, but this is achieved at a great cost of malintegration with respect to the total society. Disappointment often pushes the adherents to extremism. Many former members have become apostles of unbridled political apocalypses such as Fascism, Nazism and Communism.

The second approach rejects this negative evaluation of millenarism and underlines its positive functions. The highly emotional and aggressive behaviour is related to the revolutionary nature of the movement which strives to overthrow the old order and establish a new one. The severing of strong ties, and the rejection of internalized norms demand an enormous effort and engender a deep sense of guilt. Hence much of the hysteria and aggression. Many of the antinomian manifestations are a deliberate negation of the accepted norms, not in order to throw overboard morality altogether, but in order to create a new brotherhood and a new morality. The 'paranoid' manifestations stem from the contradictions inherent in the situation in which such movements appear and from the difficulties inherent in their revolutionary task rather than from the psychological aberrations of individual followers. If we take into consideration the social conditions and the cultural milieux which give rise to them they cease to be bizarre and fantastic and become fully understandable reactions. The promillenarism viewpoint emphasizes its underlying realism and its inherent, though hidden, rationality.

Millenarism is considered to be integrative on all levels. First, the millenarian ideology supplies the believers with invaluable safeguards and supports. The predominant element in millenarism is inner certainty and hope, not despair. Adherents are assured of being in history, of being with history and of being in the fold. They are in the know, and are working on the winning side. The movement fosters a new collective identity and engenders a feeling of belonging and a sense of purpose. The promise that first will be last and last will be first transforms inferiority into superiority and fosters self-confidence and a sense of ethical righteousness. The division of humanity into saints and devils enables the followers to focus and express their aggression and to affirm the solidarity and integrity of their group. Vibrant expectation, pride and hope lift them out of their apathy and bring about inner regeneration and rehabilitation.

The positive functions of millenarism become even more evident on the social level. Millenarism is an emancipating, activating and unifying force in hitherto stagnant, politically passive and segregated groups. In recent and in contemporary history it has served as a precursor of political awakening, and as a forerunner of political organization. Millenarism has played an important role in overcoming divisions and in joining together previously isolated or even hostile groups. Though faced by the same common problems, and sometimes even sharing the same culture, these groups cannot act as a unified force except on a localized and ad hoc basis. When confronted by crisis and by necessity to take concerted action, they are compelled to create a new unity which transcends kinship and local loyalties. This task of unification has been performed by other types of movements as well, but millenarian movements are far more potent in this respect. Millenarism usually evokes exceptionally intense commitment and fervour, and since exaltation eases communication it expands swiftly, as if by contagion. It draws out and organizes large masses of people almost simultaneously, cross-cutting and breaking down local barriers. It widens the horizon of identification and participation and creates wider unities. Millenarism has a strong formative power and germinates a far-reaching reoganization of social life. The millenarian fantasy transcends reality, yet it is essentially realistic. It does not offer its followers a comforting otherworldly hope which assuages discontent and diverts attempts at actual change. Its this-worldly emphasis prevents the displacement and spiritualization of the craving for redemption. Equally important are the emphasis on the collective and the activity orientation. Conversion, which acts as a sudden overpowering awakening, does not lead the followers inwards to repentance and meditation but rather draws them outwards to involvement and participation.

The revolutionary nature of millenarism makes it a very potent agent of change. It demands a fundamental transformation and not just improvement and reform. The radical versions of millenarism incite followers to active anticipation of the advent and even to active revolt. It invests their struggle with the aura of a final cosmic drama and interprets present difficulties as signs of the beginning of the end. Every small success is viewed as proof of invincibility and as a portent of future triumph. Millenarism arouses truly great hopes, and therefore can make equally great demands on its followers. By promising complete salvation, it is able to liberate formerly untapped energies and to generate a supreme effort without which no major break with the existing order can be achieved.

Millenarism helps to bring about a breakthrough to the future. Yet its special efficacy lies also in its power to bridge future and past. We have already noted that even the more traditional versions of millenarism are in fact selective reworkings and reinterpretations of the past, and that also the most anti-traditional version of millenarism is in fact a synthesis between the old and the new. Even when rejecting and transcending the old, millenarism reinstates important aspects of it. It constantly reinterprets such traditional elements and places them in a new context. It invests the old with new meanings while the new elements may often have traditional connotations. Even when it negates the content of tradition it does not invalidate the principles by which truth is traditionally sought and preserved. The continuity between past and future is not broken.

While bridging the gap between future and past, millenarism also connects religion and politics. Operating in societies or in social strata completely dominated by religion, millenarism couches its political message in the familiar and powerful language and images of traditional religion, employing and revitalizing its age-old symbols. In such milieux recruitment to new political goals is often possible only when expressed in religious terms. Frequently it is also the only means of establishing cooperation between leaders and followers. Millenarism provides an important mechanism of recruitment of new leaders. It opens up new avenues of ascent and develops a set of new statuses. Although some of the new leaders derive their authority from their central or marginal position in the traditional order, more often than not their authority stems at least in part from their comparatively superior knowledge and greater experience in non-traditional spheres of activity and has no traditional legitimation. Millenarism helps them to establish their authority. Externalization and sanctification of the source of authority puts the leader above sectional loyalties and enables him to avoid sectional discord. By projecting their authority to the supernatural sphere they objectify and legitimize it. Millenarism closes the gap which often develops between a more 'advanced' and more politically minded leader and the more traditional mass of his followers. In many cases he cannot hope to reach his followers and really communicate with them if he does not express his protest in popular and widely understood religious terms. Sometimes the movement is started by an 'advanced' and politically minded leader, but when its political ideology reaches the masses, it is spontaneously interpreted in religious terms. The best examples of such a process are the development of Amicalism, started by André Matswa in Africa (Benz 1965) and the ensuing transformation of the movement led by Yali in Garia.

The resort to a religious appeal is sincere and non-manipulative in most cases. During the first stages of reorganization most of the leaders have little experience in the political sphere and can express their striving only in a religious form. During later phases of development, the resort to religion may sometimes become a conscious propagandist and organizational device. The leader clothes his political ideology in religious terms because he realizes that this is the only way to mobilize followers. He often emphasizes the religious components of his ideology also for the purpose of hiding his real intentions from the authorities.

Millenarism is, according to this view, a *connecting link* between pre-political and political movements. It facilitates the passage from pre-modern religious revolt to a full-fledged revolutionary movement. The process of transition can be actually traced in both primitive and recent pre-modern movements. There are two main distinct avenues of transition. In some cases the movements gradually change their nature, slowly becoming less ritualized and more secular in emphasis. They start to pay much more attention to purely political and economic goals, attach far more importance to strategy and tactics and organize more effectively. Yet they do not sever their ties with their millenarian tradition and continue to derive much of their revolutionary zeal from its promise of final salvation. Another major direction of development entails the absorption of the millenarian movement within a secular revolutionary movement. When the millenarian movement fails to achieve its goals and disintegrates, its disappointed followers turn to secular revolutionism, embracing an extreme and militant version of either nationalist or socialist ideology. In such cases the millenarian movement serves as a kind of preparatory school for revolutionaries. When they 'graduate' from it they are ready to go over to militant secular movements. Millenarism is not abortive, the failure of its prophecy is not a defeat of its aims, it generates an enormous liberating power and has lasting social consequences.

Assessment of the outcome of millenarism clearly reflects value premises. The two viewpoints on this matter stem, at least in part, from different ideological attitudes. The anti-millenarian stream of research is gradualist and reformist, while the pro-millenarian stream is revolutionary and favours radical change. It should be noted, in addition, that the two viewpoints have emerged out of research in different historical and social settings. The positive evaluation grew mainly out of the study of millenarism developed by *rising groups* at the upsurge of their efforts of emancipation.. It deals mainly with movements which were precursors and concomitants of secular revolutionary action. Such movements engender active change and leave their mark on the whole of society. Millenarism has, in fact, played an important role in all national and social liberation movements in pre-modern and modern Europe. It has preceded and permeated many incipient nationalist and socialist movements in developing countries.

The negative evaluation of millenarism is based mainly on the study of movements developed by *doomed* or *declining groups*. Such movements have served as alternatives rather than precursors or concomitants of secular collective action and had few lasting social consequences. Most medieval millenarian movements were ephemeral outbursts. Since they had little chance to change the massive structure of medieval society, most of these revolutionary revivals 'short-circuited' and disappeared. Material on the American Indians suggests that radical millenarism there has played a limited and largely disruptive role. Any movement with a revolutionary potential was quickly suppressed, leaving an aftermath of disillusion and disorganization. The task of rehabilitation and integrating the Indians was performed mainly by reformist cults oriented towards peaceful accommodation to the white society (Vogt 1956). Most millenarian movements in modern society are radically anti-political. They conduct a violent campaign against secular movements and enjoin on their members to keep away from them. Religious and secular revolutionism are in these cases competing and mutually exclusive, rather than mutually reinforcing, complementary solutions.

The outcome of any millenarian movement depends on the historical circumstances, on the type of society and on the nature of the group in which it occurs, and cannot be dealt with out of context. Of crucial importance are factors such as the degree of differentiation, the religious and political sphere, the position of the millenarian group in the changing balance of power and its chances to promote its goals through political action.

Religious and secular revolutionism

The basic similarities and interconnections between religious and secular revolutionism is a major theme in most recent studies of millenarism, irrespective of their ideological position. First we note the *typological affinity*. Secular revolutionary movements differ greatly from other types of secular political movements and have in a certain sense a semi-religious character. Their world view is total and all-embracing. It purports to solve basic problems of meaning and to trace and interpret the unfolding of world history. The revolutionary ideology is a matter of ultimate concern and utmost seriousness; it demands from its adherents unquestioning faith and unconditional loyalty. It is therefore all-pervasive and defines every aspect of life. Much like the great religious movements of the past, secular revolutionism has deeply stirred a large mass of people, evoking intense fervour and dedication to its cause.

There is an even more marked affinity between these political movements and millenarism. Secular revolutionism shares with millenarism the apocalyptic element. Like millenarism it looks forward to a total and imminent realization of its ideals. Millenarism shares with secular revolutionism its collective and terrestrial emphasis as well as the radical condemnation of the existing social order. Both the religous and secular versions of revolutionism are catastrophic, they reject gradual and peaceful improvement and prepare for a final decisive struggle. Millenarism has a more passive definition of the role of the follower but, by and large, we find in both versions of revolutionism a potent merger of inevitability and freedom which assures the revolutionaries of their final triumph, and endows them with some power to hasten or retard salvation.

Second, we find the *similarity of predisposing factors*. Like millenarism, secular revolutionism is brought about by a combination of deprivation, frustration, disorientation and disintegration of primary groups. Equally important also is the inflexibility, unresponsiveness and ineffectiveness of agencies of social control.

Last but not least are the *dynamic interconnections* between the two types of revolutionism. We have already mentioned that millenarism is often a precursor and concomitant of secular revolutionism. It should be noted that the process of transition from one to the other is not one-way directed. Many of the internal changes which occur in the secular movements cannot be interpreted without taking into consideration the millenarian ingredients in their ideology. The freezing of ideology into dogma, the development of an institutionalized sacred text, and the ritualization of public ceremonial, are prevalent symptoms of the emergence and strengthening of religious components. National independence or victory in the class struggle become millenarian goals when they are expected to usher in a new era and solve all problems. The sanctification of the leader and his transformation into a messianic redeemer is yet another manifestation of latent millenarism. We encounter a process of historization and secularization of religious revolutionism as well as a process of mythologization and sanctification in secular revolutionism (Apter 1963).

To be sure, the analogy between millenarism and secular revolutionism should not be pushed too much, since it highlights similarities and glosses over differences which are as great and as important as the affinities. As noted above, the contention of a direct continuity between religious and secular revolutionism is borne out only by part of the material, and religious and secular revolutionism are often independent of each other. The affinities stem from the similarity of the predisposing factors and from the dynamics of the common revolutionary position rather than from any direct interchange of ideas or transfer of members from one to the other. Yet, notwithstanding these reservations, the basic similarities and the inter-connections are present, and they are unmistakable.

The most important feature of millenarism seems to be its composite 'intermediate' nature. It combines components which are seemingly mutually exclusive: it is historical as well as mythical, religious as well as political, and most significant, it is future-oriented as well as past-oriented. It is precisely this combination of a radical revolutionary position with tradi-tionalism which accounts for the widespread appeal of millenarism and turns it into such a potent agent of change.

References

APTER, D. E. (1963) 'Political Religion in the New Nations', in Geertz, C. (ed.) *Old Societies and New Nations* New York.

BARBER, B. (1941) 'Acculturation and Messianic Movements', *American Socio-logical Review*, VI, 663–9.

BELSHOW, C. S. (1950) 'The Significance of Modern Cults in Melanesian De-velopment', *The Australian Outlook*, V. 116–25.

BENZ, E. (1965) *Messianische Kirchen, Sekten und Bewegungen im Heutigen Africa* Leiden/Koln.

CUNNISON, I. (1958) 'Jehovah's Witnesses at Work: Expansion in Central Africa', *The Times: British Colonies Review*, no. 29, London.

ELIADE, M. (1954) *The Myth of Eternal Return* New York.

FIRTH, R. (1955) 'The Theory of the Cargo-Cults: A Note on Tikopea', *Man*, LV.

KAYZ, J. (1961) *Tradition and Crisis – Jewish Societies at the End of the Middle Ages* New York.

MANNHEIM, K. (1952) *Ideology and Utopia* London.

SHAW, P. E. (1946) *The Catholic Apostolic Church* New York.

SMELSER, N. J. (1963) *Theory of Collective Behavior* New York.

VAN DER KROEF, J. M. (1959) 'Javanese Messianic Expectations', *Comparative Studies in Society and History*, I, 299–323.

VOGT, E. (1956) 'The American Indian; Transition, Reformation and Accom-modation', *American Anthropologist*, LCIII, 249–64.

WORSLEY, P. (1957) *The Trumpet Shall Sound* London, McGibbon and Kee.

Part VII Power

Introduction

Power is like love; it's a word understood intuitively and defined rarely. Many people would probably say that there isn't much point anyway in trying to define such words; they recognize the conventional wisdom that you have power over me when you can get me either to do something I wouldn't otherwise do or not do something I would have done. Such a conventional wisdom is not wrong, but it is, on inspection, very limited for purposes of analysis. Social scientists who have studied and written about the nature of power have had to go a great deal further. This accounts for the very rich and varied literature on relationships of power, which enter into so many areas of social life that they figure in the work of all social science disciplines (although predominantly in political science and sociology). For this reason, it is worthwhile to approach the study of power in an interdisciplinary way. And this is what we have done here.

The shaping of societies through history, the conflicts that occur within and between societies, and the ways in which societies are integrated and held together involve in a very central way the dimension of power. This area of power in relation historically to both social conflict and social integration is the focus of the set book by M. Duverger, *The Study of Politics* (1972), for this dimension of the Open University course. Students devote much of their time in this section of the course to studying Duverger's book. This is why only two selections on the dimension of power are included in this Reader.

The first selection is Dahl's essay on power in the *International Encyclopedia of the Social Sciences* (always a useful place to begin, by the way). As one would expect in an encyclopedia entry, mention is made of a wide range of studies relevant to the concept, the history of it is traced, various aspects of it are discussed, and a number of problems of research are considered. Dahl devotes quite a lot of attention to problems of measurement and empirical analysis, and thereby provides a nice complement to the treatment by Duverger, who has little to say about such problems.

Olsen's short essay on Marx as a power theorist provides a perspective different from Dahl's on the nature and analysis of power in society. Whereas Dahl generally treats power as an approach to the study of politics, Marx sees power as originating primarily in economic production and permeating all aspects of society. For Marx, the main wielders of power in society are not governments but social classes. Marx was the first scholar to treat power in this societal way, and has rightly been called the father of what has now come to be identified as the field of political sociology. Olsen's essay, therefore, not only provides a different approach from Dahl's, but also states succinctly the Marxist position on power which is treated in Duverger but in a more discursive fashion.

The course materials sent to students make use of the two selections in this Reader and the book by Duverger in three ways. One is to provide for students an extended discussion of various conceptions of power, the distinction between coercion and authority, and Max Weber's typology of three main types of authority – charismatic, traditional, rational–legal. The second is to provide an extended discussion for students of power and social stratification, with particular attention given to Marxist, elitist and pluralist models of society. The third feature is to provide for students a specially prepared series of television and radio programmes, accompanied by extended written comment, on the introduction of the Bay Area Rapid Transportation system connecting San Francisco and neighbouring cities. This case is used to illustrate for students in a concrete way some of the rather more abstract discussions on power to be found in this Reader and the course as a whole.

David Potter

28 Power

Robert A. Dahl

In approaching the study of politics through the analysis of power, one assumes, at a minimum, that relations of power are among the significant aspects of a political system. This assumption, and therefore the analysis of power, can be applied to any kind of political system, international, national, or local, to associations and groups of various kinds, such as the family, the hospital, and the business firm, and to historical developments.

At one extreme, an analysis of power may simply postulate that power relations are one feature of politics among a number of others – but nonetheless a sufficiently important feature to need emphasis and description. At the other extreme an analyst may hold that power distinguishes 'politics' from other human activity; to analysts of this view 'political science, as an empirical discipline, is the study of the shaping and sharing of power' (Lasswell & Kaplan 1950, p. xiv).

In either case, the analyst takes it for granted that differences between political systems, or profound changes in the same society, can often be interpreted as differences in the way power is distributed among individuals, groups, or other units. Power may be relatively concentrated or diffused; and the share of power held by different individuals, strata, classes, professional groups, ethnic, racial, or religious groups, etc., may be relatively great or small. The analysis of power is often concerned, therefore, with the identification of elites and leadership, the discovery of the ways in which power is allocated to different strata, relations among leaders and between leaders and non-leaders, and so forth.

Although the approach to politics through the study of power relations is sometimes thought to postulate that everyone seeks power as the highest value, analysts of power generally reject this assumption as psychologically untenable; the analysis of power does not logically imply any particular psychological assumptions. Sometimes critics also regard the analysis of power as implying that the pursuit of power is morally good or at any rate that it should not be condemned. But an analysis of power may be neutral as to values; or the analyst may be concerned with power, not to glorify it, but in order to modify the place it holds in human relations and to increase

DAHL, ROBERT A. (1968) 'Power', in *International Encyclopaedia of the Social Sciences*, vol. 12, New York, Macmillan, 405–15.

the opportunities for dignity, respect, freedom, or other values (Jouvenel 1945; Lasswell & Kaplan 1950; Oppenheim 1961, ch. 8, 9).

Indeed, it would be difficult to explain the extent to which political theorists for the past twenty-five centuries have been concerned with relations of power and authority were it not for the moral and practical significance of power to any person interested in political life, whether as observer or activist. Some understanding of power is usually thought to be indispensable for moral or ethical appraisals of political systems. From a very early time – certainly since Socrates, and probably before – men have been inclined to judge the relative desirability of different types of political systems by, among other characteristics, the relations of power and authority in these systems. In addition, intelligent *action* to bring about a result of some kind in a political system, such as a change in a law or a policy, a revolution, or a settlement of an international dispute, requires knowledge of how to produce or 'cause' these results. In political action, as in other spheres of life, we try to produce the results we want by acting appropriately on the relevant causes. As we shall see, power relations can be viewed as causal relations of a particular kind.

It therefore seems most unlikely that the analysis of power will disappear as an approach to the study of politics. However, the fact that this approach is important and relevant does not shield it from some serious difficulties. These have become particularly manifest as the approach has been more earnestly and systematically employed.

Origins

The attempt to study and explain politics by analysing relations of power is, in a loose sense, ancient. To Aristotle, differences in the location of power, authority, or rule among the citizens of a political society served as one criterion for differentiating among actual constitutions, and it entered into his distinction between good constitutions and bad ones. With few exceptions (most notably Thomas Hobbes) political theorists did not press their investigations very far into certain aspects of power that have seemed important to social scientists in the twentieth century. For example, most political theorists took it for granted, as did Aristotle, that key terms like *power, influence, authority,* and *rule* (let us call them 'power terms') needed no great elaboration, presumably because the meaning of these words was clear to men of common sense. Even Machiavelli, who marks a decisive turning point from classical–normative to modern–empirical theory, did not consider political terms in general as particularly technical. Moreover, he strongly preferred the concrete to the abstract. In his treatment of power relations Machiavelli frequently described a specific event as an example of a general principle; but often the general principle was only implied or barely alluded to; and he used a variety of undefined terms such as *imperio, forza, potente,* and *autorità.*

From Aristotle to Hobbes political theorists were mainly concerned with power relations within a given commuity. But external relations even more than internal ones force attention to questions of relative power. The rise of the modern nation-state therefore compelled political theorists to recognize the saliency of power in politics, and particularly, of course, in international politics (Meinecke 1924).

Thus political 'realists' found it useful to define, distinguish, and interpret the state in terms of its power. Max Weber both reflected this tradition of 'realism' and opened the way for new developments in the analysis of power. 'Power' (*Macht*) is the probability that one actor within a social relationship will be in a position to carry out his own will despite resistance, regardless of the basis on which this probability rests' (Weber [1922] 1957, p. 152). This definition permitted Weber to conclude that 'the concept of power is highly comprehensive from the point of view of sociology. All conceivable . . . combinations of circumstances may put him [the actor] in a position to impose his will in a given situation' (p. 153). It follows that the state is not distinguishable from other associations merely because it employs a special and peculiarly important kind of power – force. In a famous and highly influential definition, Weber characterized the state as follows: 'A compulsory political association with continuous organization (*politischer Anstaltsbetrieb*) will be called a "state" if and in so far as its administrative staff successfully upholds a claim to the *monopoly* of the *legitimate* use of physical force in the enforcement of its order' (p. 154).

In his well-know typologies and his analyses of political systems, however, Weber was less concerned with power in general than with a special kind that he held to be unusually important – legitimate power, or authority.

Later theorists, practically all of whom were directly or indirectly influenced by Weber, expanded their objectives to include a fuller range of power relations. In the United States attempts to suggest or develop systematic and comprehensive theories of politics centring about power relations appeared in books by Catlin (1927; 1930), an important essay by Goldhamer and Shils (1939), and numerous works of the Chicago school – principally Merriam (1934), Lasswell (1936), and, in international politics,

Morgenthau (1948). In the decade after World War II the ideas of the Chicago school were rapidly diffused throughout American political science.

Elements in the analysis of power

Power terms evidently cover a very broad category of human relations. Considerable effort and ingenuity have gone into schemes for classifying these relations into various types, labelled power, influence, authority, persuasion, dissuasion, inducement, coercion, compulsion, force, and so on, all of which we shall subsume under the collective label power terms. The great variety and heterogeneity of these relations may, in fact, make it impossible – or at any rate not very fruitful – to develop general theories of power intended to cover them all.

At the most general level, power terms in modern social science refer to *subsets of relations among social units such that the behaviours of one or more units* (the responsive units, *R*) *depend in some circumstances on the behaviour of other units* (the controlling units, *C*). (In the following discussion, *R* will always symbolize the responsive or dependent unit, *C* the controlling unit. These symbols will be used throughout and will be substituted even in direct quotations where the authors themselves have used different letters.) By this broad definition, then, power terms in the social sciences exclude relations with inanimate or even nonhuman objects; the control of a dog by his master or the power of a scientist over 'nature' provided by a nuclear reactor would fall, by definition, in a different realm of discourse. On the other hand, the definition could include the power of one nation to affect the actions of another by threatening to use a nuclear reactor as a bomb or by offering to transfer it by gift or sale.

If power-terms include *all* relations of the kind just defined, then they spread very widely over the whole domain of human relations. In practice, analysts of power usually confine their attention to smaller subsets. One such subset consists, for example, of relations in which 'severe sanctions . . . are expected to be used or are in fact applied to sustain a policy against opposition' – a subset that Lasswell and Kaplan call power (1950, pp. 74–5). However, there is no agreement on the common characteristics of the various subsets covered by power terms, nor are different labels applied with the same meaning by different analysts.

Despite disagreement on how the general concept is to be defined and limited, the variety of smaller subsets that different writers find interesting or important, and the total lack of a standardized classification scheme and nomenclature, there is nonetheless some underlying unity in the various approaches to the analysis of power. In describing and explaining patterns of power, different writers employ rather similar elements (compare Cartwright 1965). What follows is an attempt to clarify these common elements by ignoring differences in terminology, treatment, and emphasis.

Some descriptive characteristics

For purposes of exposition it is convenient to think of the analysis of power in terms of the familiar distinction between dependent and independent variables. The attempt to understand a political system may then be conceived of as an effort to *describe* certain characteristics of the system: the dependent variables; and to *explain* why the system takes on these particular characteristics, by showing the effects on these characteristics of certain other factors: the independent variables. Some of the characteristics of a political system that analysts seek to explain are the *magnitude* of the power of the Cs with respect to the Rs, how this power is *distributed* in the system, and the *scope*, and *domain*, of control that different individuals or actors have, exercise, or are subject to.

Magnitude. Political systems are often characterized explicitly or implicitly by the differences in the 'amounts' of power (over the actions of the government or state) exercised by different individuals, groups, or strata. The magnitude of C's power with respect to R is thought of as measurable, in some sense, by at least an ordinal scale; frequently, indeed, a literal reading would imply that power is subject to measurement by an interval scale. How to compare and measure different magnitudes of power poses a major unsolved problem; we shall return to it briefly later on. Meanwhile, we shall accept the assumption of practically every political theorist for several thousand years, that it is possible to speak meaningfully of different amounts of power. Thus a typical question in the analysis of a political system would be: Is control over government highly concentrated or relatively diffused?

Distribution. An ancient and conventional way of distinguishing among political systems is according to the way control over the government or the state is distributed to individuals or groups in the systems. Aristotle, for example, stated: 'The proper application of the term "democracy" is to a constitution in which the free-born and poor control the government – being at the same time a majority; and similarly the term "oligarchy" is properly applied to a constitution in which the rich and better-born control

the government – being at the same time a minority' (*Politics*, Barker ed.,
p. 164). Control over government may be conceived as analogous to income,
wealth, or property; and in the same way that income or wealth may be
distributed in different patterns, so too the distribution of power over
government may vary from one society or historical period to another. One
task of analysis, then, is to classify and describe the most common distribu-
tions and to account for the different patterns. Typical questions would be:
What are the characteristics of the *C*s and of the *R*s? How do the *C*s and *R*s
compare in numbers? Do *C*s and *R*s typically come from different classes,
strata, regions, or other groups? What historical changes have occurred in
the characteristics of *C* and *R*?

Scope. What if *C*s are sometimes not *C*s, or *C*s sometimes *R*s, or *R*s
sometimes *C*s? The possibility cannot be ruled out that individuals or
groups who are relatively powerful with respect to one kind of activity
may be relatively weak with respect to other activities. Power need not be
general; it may be specialized. In fact, in the absence of a single world ruler,
some specialization is inevitable; in any case, it is so commonplace that
analysts of power have frequently insisted that a statement about the power
of an individual, group, state, or other actor is practically meaningless
unless it specifies the power of actor *C* with respect to some class of *R*'s
activities. Such a class of activities is sometimes called the range (Cartwright
1965) or the scope of *C*'s power (Lasswell & Kaplan 1950, p. 73). There is
no generally accepted way of defining and classifying different scopes.
However, a typical question about a political system would be: Is power
generalized over many scopes, or is it specialized? If it is specialized, what
are the characteristics of the *C*s, the elites, in the different scopes? Is power
specialized by individuals in the sense that C_a and C_b exercise power over
different scopes, or is it also specialized by classes, social strata, skills,
professions, or other categories?

Domain. *C*'s power will be limited to certain individuals; the *R*s over
whom *C* has or exercises control constitute what is sometimes called the
'domain', or 'extension', of *C*'s power (Lasswell & Kaplan 1950, p. 73;
Harsanyi 1962*a*, p. 67). Typical questions thus might be: Who are the *R*s
over whom *C* has control? What are their characteristics? How numerous
are they? How do they differ in numbers or characteristics from the *R*s not
under *C*'s control?

Given the absence of any standard unit of measure for amounts, distri-
butions, scopes, domains, and other aspects of power, and the variety of
ways of describing these characteristics, it is not at all surprising that there
is an abundance of schemes for classifying political systems according to

some characteristic of power. Most such schemes use, implicitly or explicitly, the idea of a *distribution of power over the behaviour of government*. The oldest, most famous, and most enduring of these is the distinction made by the Greeks between rule by one, the few, and the many (*see* Aristotle, *Politics*, Barker ed., pp. 110 ff.). Some variant of this scheme frequently reappears in modern analyses of power (e.g. Lasswell & Kaplan 1950, p. 218). Often, as with Aristotle himself, the distribution of power is combined with one or more other dimensions (e.g. Dahl 1963, p. 38). Rough dichotomous schemes are common. One based on 'the degree of autonomy and interdependence of the several power holders' distinguishes two polar types, called autocracy and constitutionalism (Loewenstein 1957, p. 29). American community studies have in recent years called attention to differences between 'pluralistic' systems and unified or highly stratified 'power structures'. In one study that compares four communities the authors developed a more complex typology of power structures by combining a dimension of 'distribution of political power among citizens' with the degree of convergence or divergence in the ideology of leaders; the four types of power structures produced by dichotomizing these two dimensions are in turn distinguished from regimes (Agger et al. 1964, pp. 73 ff.).

Some explanatory characteristics

Given the different types of political systems, how are the differences among them to be explained? If, for example, control over government is sometimes distributed to the many, often to the few, and occasionally to one dominant leader, how can we account for the differences? Obviously these are ancient, enduring, and highly complex problems; and there is slight agreement on the answers. However, some factors that are often emphasized in modern analysis can be distinguished.

Resources. Differences in patterns or structures of power may be attributed primarily, mainly, or partly to the way in which 'resources', or 'base values', are distributed among the individuals, strata, classes, and groups in different communities, countries, societies, and historical periods. This is an ancient, distinguished, widespread, and persuasive mode of explanation, used by Aristotle in Greece in the fourth century B.C., by James Harrington in seventeenth-century England, by the fathers of the American constitution in the late eighteenth century, by Marx and Engels in the nineteenth century, and by a great many social scientists in the twentieth century. A central hypothesis in most of these theories is that the greater one's resources, the greater one's power. Although explanations of this kind do not always go beyond tautology (by defining power in terms of resources), logical circularity is certainly not inherent in this mode of explanation. However, there is no accepted way of classifying resources or bases. Harold Lasswell has constructed a comprehensive scheme of eight base values which, although not necessarily exhaustive, are certainly inclusive; these are power (which can serve as a base for more power), respect, rectitude or moral standing, affection, well-being, wealth, skill, and enlightenment (Lasswell & Kaplan 1950, p. 87). Other writers choose more familiar categories to classify resources: for example, in trying to account for the patterns of influence in one community, the author described the patterns of social standing; the distribution of cash, credit, and wealth; access to legality, popularity, and control over jobs; and control over sources of information (Dahl 1961, pp. 229 ff.).

Skill. Two individuals with access to approximately the same resources may not exercise the same degree of power (over, let us say, government decisions). Indeed, it is a common observation that individuals of approximately equal wealth or social status may differ greatly in power. To be sure, this might be accounted for by differences in access to other resources, such as the greater legality, bureaucratic knowledge, and public affection that fall to any individual who is chosen, say, to be prime minister of Britain or president of the United States. Another factor, however, one given particular prominence by Machiavelli, is political skill. Formally, skill could be treated as another resource. Nonetheless, it is generally thought to be of critical importance in explaining differences in the power of different leaders – different presidents, for example, as in Neustadt's comparison of presidents Roosevelt, Truman, and Eisenhower (1960, pp. 152 ff.). However, despite many attempts at analysis, from Machiavelli to the present day, political skill has remained among the more elusive aspects in the analysis of power.

Motivations. Two individuals with access to the same resources may exercise different degrees of power (with respect to some scope) because of different motivations: the one may use his resources to increase his power; the other may not. Moreover, since power is a relationship between Cs and Rs, the motivations not only of the Cs but also of the Rs are important. One person may worship authority, while another may defy it. A number of writers have explored various aspects of motivations involved in power relations (e.g. Lasswell 1930; Rogow & Laswell 1963; Cartwright 1959).

Costs. Motivations can be related to resources by way of the economists' language of cost – a factor introduced into the analysis of power by a mathematical economist (Harsanyi 1962*a*; 1962*b*). In order to control R, C may have to use some of his resources. Thus C's supply of resources is likely to have a bearing on how far he is willing to go in trying to control R. And variations in C's resources are likely to produce variations in C's power. C's *opportunity costs* in controlling R – that is, what C must forgo or give up in other opportunities as a result of using some of his resources to control R – are less (other things being equal) if he is rich in resources than if he is poor in resources. In concrete terms, to a rich man the sacrifice involved in a campaign contribution of \$100 is negligible; to a poor man the sacrifice entailed in a contribution of \$100 is heavy. C's willingness to use his resources to control R will also depend on the value to C of R's response; the value of R's response is, in turn, dependent in part on C's motivations. The relationship may also be examined from R's point of view. R's opportunity costs consist of what he is then unable to do if he complies with C. In R's case, as in C's, his supply of resources and his motivations help determine his opportunity costs. Thus a power relation can be interpreted as a sort of transaction between C and R.

Problems of research

Like all other approaches to an understanding of complex social phenomena, the analysis of power is beset with problems. At a very general level, attempts to analyse power share with many – perhaps most – other strategies of inquiry in the social sciences the familiar dilemma of rigor versus relevance, and the dilemma has led to familiar results. Attempts to meet high standards of logical rigor or empirical verification have produced some intriguing experiments and a good deal of effort to clarify concepts and logical relationships but not rounded and well-verified explanations of complex political systems in the real world. Conversely, attempts to arrive at a better understanding of the more concrete phenomena of political life and institutions often sacrifice a good deal in rigor of logic and verification in order to provide more useful and reliable guides to the real world.

There are, however, a number of more specific problems in the analysis of power, many of which have only been identified in the last few decades. Relevant work is quite recent and seeks 1) to clarify the central concepts, partly by expanding on the analogy between power relations and causal relations, 2) to specify particular subsets that are most interesting for social analysis, 3) to develop methods of measurement, and 4) to undertake empirical investigations of concrete political phenomena.

Power and cause

The closest equivalent to the power relation is the causal relation. For the assertion '*C* has power over *R*', one can substitute the assertion, '*C*'s behaviour causes *R*'s behaviour'. If one can define the causal relation, one can define influence, power, or authority, and vice versa Simon [1947–56] 1957, p. 5).

Since the language of cause is no longer common in the formal theoretical language of the natural sciences, it might be argued that social scientists should also dispense with that language and that insofar as power is merely a term for a causal relation involving human beings, power-terms should simultaneously be dispensed with. But it seems rather unlikely that social scientists will, in fact, reject causal language. For the language of cause, like the language of power, is used to interpret situations in which there is the possibility that some event will intervene to change the order of other events. In medical research it is natural and meaningful to ask, Does cigarette smoking cause lung cancer and heart disease? In social situations the notion of cause is equally or even more appropriate. What makes causal analysis important to us is our desire to act on causes in the real world in order to bring about effects – reducing death rates from lung cancer, passing a civil-rights bill through Congress or preventing the outbreak of war.

To interpret the terms *power, influence, authority*, etc., as instances of causal relations means, however, that the attempt to detect true rather than spurious power relations must run into the same difficulties that have beset efforts to distinguish true from spurious causal relations. Some analysts have confronted the problem; others have noted it only to put it aside; most have ignored it entirely, perhaps on the assumption that if social scientists tried to solve the unsolved problems of philosophy they would never get around to the problems of the social sciences. Yet if power is analogous to cause – or if power relations are logically a subset of causal relations – then recent analyses of causality must have relevance to the analysis of power.

In the first place, properties used to distinguish causation also serve to define power relations: covariation, temporal·sequence, and asymmetry, for example. The appropriateness of these criteria has in fact been debated, not always conclusively, by various students of power (e.g. Simon [1947–56] 1957, pp. 5, 11, 12, 66; Dahl 1957, p. 204; Cartwright 1959, p. 197; Oppenheim 1961, p. 104).

Thus, the problem whether *A* can be said to cause *B* if *A* is a necessary condition for *B*, or a sufficient condition, or *both* necessary *and* sufficient, has also plagued the definition of power-terms. Some writers have explicitly stated or at least implied that relations of power mean that some action by C is a necessary condition for R's response (Simon 1953, p. 504; March 1955, p. 435; Dahl 1957, p. 203). Oppenheim has argued, however, that such definitions permit statements that run flatly counter to common sense; he holds that it would be more appropriate to require only that C's action be sufficient to produce R's response (1961, p. 41). Riker has suggested in turn that 'the customary definition of power be revised . . . to reflect the necessary-and-sufficient condition theory of causality' (1964, p. 348). However, Blalock in his *Causal Inferences in Non-experimental Research* has shown that defining cause in terms of necessary and sufficient conditions leads to great practical difficulties in research. 'In real-life situations we seldom encounter instances where B is present if and only if A is also present' (1964, p. 30); moreover, specifying necessary and sufficient conditions requires the researcher 'to think always in terms of attributes and dichotomies', whereas 'there are most certainly a number of variables which are best conceived as continuously distributed, even though we may find it difficult to measure them operationally in terms of a specified unit of some kind' (p. 32). 'The use of "necessary and sufficient" terminology . . . may work well for the logician but not [for] the social scientist' (p. 34). Blalock's criticism, and indeed his whole effort to explore problems of causal inference in nonexperimental research, are highly relevant to the analysis of power.

Aside from these somewhat rarefied philosophical and definitional questions, which many social scientists are prepared to abandon to metaphysicians or philosophers of science, the analogy between power and cause argues that the problem of distinguishing cause from correlation, or true from spurious causation, is bound to carry over into the analysis of power. And indeed it does. The difficulty of distinguishing true from spurious power relations has proved to be quite formidable.

The most rigorous method of distinguishing true from spurious causation is, of course, experimentation, and this would be the most rigorous method for distinguishing true from spurious power relations, provided the proper experimental conditions were present. Unfortunately, however, as in many areas of the social sciences, so too in the analysis of power, experimental methods have so far been of limited value, and for similar reasons. In non-experimental situations the optimal requirements for identifying causal relations seem to be the existence of satisfactory interval measures, a large supply of good data employing these measures, and an exhaustive analysis of alternative ways of accounting for the observations (Blalock

1964). Unfortunately, in the analysis of power, existing methods of measurement are rather inadequate, the data are often inescapably crude and limited, a variety of simple alternative explanations seem to fit the data about equally well, and in any case the complexity of the relations requires extraordinarily complex models.

The shortage of relevant models of power may disappear in time. In fact, the causal analogue suggests that the development of a great array of carefully described alternative models to compare with observations is probably a prerequisite for further development in the analysis of power. Again, the analogy between power and cause readily reveals why this would seem to be the case. In trying to determine the cause of a phenomenon it is of course impossible to know whether all the relevant factors in the real world are actually controlled during an investigation. Consequently, it is never possible to demonstrate causality.

> It is possible to make causal *inferences* concerning the adequacy of causal models, at least in the sense that we can proceed by eliminating inadequate models that make predictions that are not consistent with the data.... [Such] causal models involve 1) a finite set of explicitly defined variables, 2) certain assumptions about how these variables are interrelated causally, and 3) assumptions to the effect that outside variables, while operating, do not have confounding influences that disturb the causal patterning among the variables explicitly being considered. (*ibid.*, p. 62)

If power relations are a subset of causal relations, these requirements would also be applicable in the analysis of power.

In analysing power, why have analysts so rarely attempted to describe, in rigorous language at any rate, the alternative causal models relevant to their inquiry? There seem to be several reasons. First, students of power have not always been wholly aware that distinguishing true from spurious power relations requires intellectual strategies at a rather high level of sophistication. Second, the crude quality of the observations usually available in studying power may discourage efforts to construct elegant theoretical models. Third, until recent times the whole approach to power analysis was somewhat speculative: there were a good many impressionistic works but few systematic empirical studies of power relations. Of the empirical studies now available most are investigations of power relations in American communities undertaken since 1950. These community studies have provoked a good deal of dispute over what are, in effect, alternative models of causation. So far, however, investigators have usually not described clearly the array of alternative models that might be proposed to explain their data, nor have they clearly specified the criteria they use for rejecting all the alternatives except the one they accept as their preferred explanation.

Theories about power relations in various political systems are of course scattered through the writings of a number of analysts (e.g. Pareta 1916, volume 4; Mosca 1896, passim; Lasswell & Kaplan 1950, chapters 9, 10; Mills 1956; Dahl 1961; Rossi 1960; Polsby 1963; Parsons 1963a; 1963b). But a straightforward presentation of an empirical theory of power relations in political systems is a rarity. A notable exception is offered by March's formulation of six models of social choice that involve, in some sense, relationships of power.

The analogy between cause and power calls attention to one further point: any attempt to develop an empirical theory of power will run headlong into the fact that a causal chain has many links; that the links one specifies depend on what one wishes to explain; and that what one wishes to explain depends, in part, on the theory with which one begins. In causal analysis, it is usually

> . . . possible to insert a very large number of additional variables between any two supposedly directly related factors. We must stop somewhere and consider the theoretical system closed. Practically, we may choose to stop at the point where the additional variables are either difficult or expensive to measure, or where they have not been associated with any operations at all. . . . *A relationship that is direct in one theoretical system may be indirect in another,* or it may even be taken as spurious. (Blalock 1964, p. 18)

Some of the links that a power analyst may take as 'effects' to be explained by searching for causes are the outcomes of specific decisions; the current values, attitudes, and expectations of decision markers; their earlier or more fundamental attitudes and values; the attitudes and values of other participants – or nonparticipants – whose participation is in some way significant; the processes of selection, self-selection, recruitment, or entry by which decision makers arrive at their locations in the political system; the rules of decision making, the structures, the constitutions. No doubt a 'complete' explanation of power relations in a political system would try to account for all of these effects, and others. Yet this is an enormously ambitious task. Meanwhile, it is important to specify which effects are at the focus of an explanatory theory and which are not. A good deal of confusion, and no little controversy, are produced when different analysts focus on different links in the chain of power and causation without specifying clearly what effects they wish to explain; and a good deal of criticism of dubious relevance is produced by critics who hold that an investigator has focused on the 'wrong' links or did not provide a 'complete' explanation.

Classifying types of power

Even though the analysis of power has not produced many rigorous causal models, it has spawned a profusion of schemes for classifying types of power relations (e.g. Parsons 1963*a*; 1963*b*; Oppenheim 1961; French & Raven 1959; Cartwright 1965).

Among the characteristics most often singled out for attention are 1) legitimacy: the extent to which R feels normatively obliged to comply with C; 2) the nature of the sanctions: whether C uses rewards or deprivations, positive or negative sanctions; 3) the magnitude of the sanctions: extending from severe coercion to no sanctions at all; 4) the means or channels employed: whether C controls R only by means of information that changes R's intentions or by actually changing R's situation or his environment of rewards and deprivations. These and other characteristics can be combined to yield many different types of power relations.

As we have already indicated, no single classification system prevails, and the names for the various categories are so completely unstandardized that what is labelled power in one scheme may be called coercion or influence in another. Detached from empirical theories, these schemes are of doubtful value. In the abstract it is impossible to say why one classification system should be preferred over another.

Nonetheless, there are some subsets of power relations – types of power, as they are often called – that call attention to interesting problems of analysis and research. One of these is the distinction between *having* and *exercising* power or influence (Lasswell & Kaplan 1950, p. 71; Oppenheim 1961, chs. 2, 3). This distinction is also involved in the way anticipated reactions function as a basis for influence and power (Friedrich 1963, ch. 11).

To illustrate the problem by example, let us suppose that even in the absence of any previous communication from the president to Senator R, or indeed any previous action of any kind by the president, Senator R regularly votes *now* in a way he thinks will insure the president's favour *later*. The senator calculates that if he loses the next election, he may, as a result of the president's favourable attitude, be in line to receive a presidential appointment to a federal court. Thus, while Senator R's voting behaviour is oriented towards future rewards, expected or hoped for, his votes are not the result of any specific action by the president.

If one holds that C cannot be a cause of R if C follows R in time, then no act of the incumbent president *need* be a cause of Senator R's favourable vote. Obviously this does not mean that Senator R's actions are 'uncaused'. The immediate determinant of his vote is his expectations. If we ask what 'caused' his expectations, there are many possible answers. For example, he might have concluded that in American society if favours are extended to C, this makes it more likely that C will be indulgent later on. Or he may have acquired from political lore the understanding that the general rule applies specifically to relations of senators and presidents. Thus, the causal chain recedes into the senator's previous learning – but not necessarily to any specific *past* act of the incumbent president or any other president.

This kind of phenomenon is commonplace, important, and obviously relevant to the analysis of power. Yet some studies, critics have said, concentrate on the exercise of power and fail to account for individuals or groups in the community who, though they do not exercise power, nonetheless have power, in the sense that many people try assiduously to anticipate their reactions (Bachrach & Baratz 1962). This failure may be a result of certain paradoxical aspects of having power that can make it an exceedingly difficult phenomenon to study.

For in the limiting case of anticipated reactions, it appears, paradoxically, that it is not the president who controls the senator, but the senator who controls the president – i.e. it is the senator who, by his loyal behaviour, induces the president to appoint him to a federal court. Thus, it is not C who controls or even attempts to control R, but R who attempts to control C – and to the extent that R anticipates C's reactions correctly, R does in fact control C. It is, then, not the king who controls the courtier but the courtier who controls the king.

Now if we examine this paradox closely we quickly discover that it arises simply because we have tried to describe the relationship between king and courtier, president and senator, C and R by distinguishing only one aspect, namely, the exercise of power. The courtier does indeed exercise power over the king by successfully anticipating the reactions of the monarch and thereby gaining a duchy. But it was not this that we set out to explain. For it is the king who has, holds, or possesses the capacity to confer that dukedom, and even though he does not *exercise* his power, he gains the willing compliance of the courtier.

What is it, then, that distinguishes having power from exercising power? The distinction could hinge upon the presence or absence of a manifest intention. We could define the *exercise* of power in such a way as to require C to manifest an intention to act in some way in the future, his action to be contingent on R's behaviour. By contrast, C might be said to *have* power when, though he does not manifest an intention, R imputes an intention to him and shapes his behaviour to meet the imputed intention. If one were to accept this distinction, then in studying the *exercise* of power, one would have to examine not only R's perceptions and responses but also C's intentions and actions. In studying relationships in which C is thought to *have* power, even though he does not exercise it, one would in principle need only to study R's perceptions, the intentions R imputes to C, and the bearing of these on R's behaviour. Carried to the extreme, then, this kind of analysis could lead to the discovery of as many different power structures in a political system as there are individuals who impute different intentions to other individuals, groups, or strata in the system.

The distinction between having and exercising power could also turn on the directness involved in the relation between C and R and on the specificity of the actions. In the most direct relationship R's response would be tripped off by a signal directly from C. In this case, C is exercising power. But some relationships are highly indirect; for example, C may modify R's environment in a more or less lasting way, so that R continues to respond as C had intended, even though C makes no effort to control R. In these cases, one might say that although C does not exercise control over R, he does *have* control over R. There are a variety of these indirect, or 'roundabout' controls (Dahl & Lindblom 1953, pp. 110 ff.).

Measuring power

Even more than with power terms themselves, notions of 'more' or 'less' power were in classical theory left to the realm of common sense and intuition. Efforts to develop systematic measures of power date almost wholly from the 1950s. Of those, some are stated partly in mathematical formulas, some entirely in non-mathematical language. Since the essential features can be suggested without mathematics, we shall describe these measures in ordinary language. (The reader should consult the sources cited for the precise formulations. Most of the best-known measures are presented and discussed in Riker 1964.)

In a rough way, the various criteria for measuring power can be classified into three types: game-theoretical, Newtonian, and economic.

Game-theoretical criteria. Shapely, a mathematician, and Shubik, an econometrician, have jointly formulated a 'method for evaluating the distribution of power in a committee system' (1954). This is intended to measure the power accruing to a voter where the outcome of decision is determined exclusively by voting. In these cases the rules prescribe what proportion of votes constitutes a winning proportion (e.g. a simple majority of all committee members). Thus each member has a certain abstract probability of casting the last vote that would be needed to complete a winning coalition, in other words to occupy a pivotal position with respect to the outcome. By adding his vote at this crucial juncture, a voter may be conceived of as having made a particularly decisive contribution to the outcome; thus, gaining his vote might have considerable value to the other members of a coalition that would lose without his vote. Shapely and Shubik proposed measuring the power of a voter by the probability that he would be the pivotal voter in a winning coalition. Because their measure is entirely limited to voting situations and excludes all outcomes other than the act of voting itself, the utility of the measure is limited to cases where most of the other familiar elements of political life – various forms of persuasion, inducement, and coercion – are lacking.

Newtonian criteria. On the analogy of the measurement of force in classical mechanics, a number of analysts propose to measure power by the amount of change in R attributable to C. The greater the change in R, the greater the power of C; thus C_a is said to exert more power than C_b if C_a induces more change in R_a than C_b induces in R_a (or in some other R). Measures of this kind have been more frequently proposed than any other (Simon 1947–56; March 1957; Dahl 1957; 1963, ch. 5; Cartwright 1959; Oppenheim 1961, ch. 8).

'Change in R' is not, however, a single dimension, since many different changes in R may be relevant. Some of the important dimensions of the 'change in R' brought about by C that have been suggested for measuring the amount of C's power are 1) the probability that R will comply; 2) the number of persons in R; 3) the number of distinct items, subjects, or values in R; 4) the amount of change in R's position, attitudes, or psychological state; 5) the speed with which R changes; 6) the reduction in the size of the set of outcomes or behaviours available to R; and 7) the degree of R's threatened or expected deprivation.

Economic criteria. Where the game-theoretical measure focuses on the pivotal position of C, and Newtonian measures on changes in R, a third proposal would include 'costs' to both C and R in measuring C's power. Harsanyi has argued that a complete measure of power should include 1) the opportunity costs of C of attempting to influence R, which Harsanyi calls the *costs* of C's power, and 2) the opportunity costs to R of refusing to comply with C, which Harsanyi calls the *strength* of C's power over R (1962a, pp. 68 ff.). The measure Harsanyi proposes is not inherently limited to the kinds of cost most familiar to economists but could be extended – at least in principle – to include psychological costs of all kinds.

Empirical studies discussed by Cartwright (1965), March (1965), and others, and particularly community studies, have called attention to the neglected problem of designing acceptable operational definitions.

Designing operational definitions

The concepts and measures discussed in this article have not been clothed in operational language. It is not yet clear how many of them can be. Yet the researcher who seeks to observe, report, compare, and analyse power in the real world, in order to test a particular hypothesis or a broader theory, quickly discovers urgent need for operationally defined terms. Research so far has called attention to three kinds of problems. First, the gap between concept and operational definition is generally very great, so great, indeed, that it is not always possible to see what relation there is between the operations and the abstract definition. Thus a critic is likely to conclude that the studies are, no doubt, reporting *something* in the real world, but he might question whether they are reporting the phenomena we mean when we speak of *power*. Second, different operational measures do not seem to correlate with one another (March 1956), which suggests that they may tap different aspects of power relations. Third, almost every measure proposed has engendered controversy over its validity.

None of these results should be altogether surprising or even discouraging. For despite the fact that the attempt to understand political systems by analysing power relations is ancient, the systematic empirical study of power relations is remarkably new.

References

AGGER, R. E., GOLDRICH, D. and SWANSON, B. (1964) *The Rulers and the Ruled: Political Power and Impotence in American Communities* New York, Wiley.

ARISTOTLE (1962) *The Politics of Aristotle*, trans. and ed. by Barker E., New York, Oxford University Press.

BACHRACH, P. and BARATZ, M. (1962) 'Two Faces of Power', *American Political Science Review*, 56, 947–52.

BLALOCK, H. M. JR (1964) *Causal Inferences in Nonexperimental Research* Chapel Hill, University of North Carolina Press.

CARTWRIGHT, D. (ed.) (1959) *Studies in Social Power*, Research Center for Group Dynamics, Publication no. 6. Ann Arbor, University of Michigan, Institute for Social Research.

CARTWRIGHT, D. (1965) 'Influence, Leadership, Control', in March, James G. (ed.) *Handbook of Organizations* Chicago, Rand McNally.

CATLIN, G. E. G. (1927) *The Science and Method of Politics* London, Routledge.

CATLIN, G. E. G. (1930) *A Study of the Principles of Politics, Being an Essay Towards Political Rationalization* New York, Macmillan.

DAHL, R. A. (1957) 'The Concept of Power', *Behavioral Science*, **2**, 201–15.

DAHL, R. A. (1961) 1963, *Who Governs? Democracy and Power in an Ameri-City* New Haven, Yale University Press.

DAHL, R. A. (1963) *Modern Political Analysis* Englewood Cliffs, N.J., Prentice-Hall.

DAHL, R. A. and LINDBLOM, C. E. (1953) *Politics, Economics, and Welfare: Planning and Politico–economic Systems Resolved Into Basic Social Processes* New York, Harper. A paperback edition was published in 1963.

FRENCH, J. R. P. and RAVEN, B. (1959) 'The Basis of Social Power', in Cartwright, D. (ed.) *Studies in Social Power*, Research Center for Group Dynamics, Publication no. 6. Ann Arbor, University of Michigan, Institute for Social Research.

FRIEDRICH, C. J. (1963) *Man and His Government: An Empirical Theory of Politics* New York, McGraw-Hill.

GOLDHAMER, H. and SHILS, E. (1939) 'Types of Power and Status', *American Journal of Sociology*, **45**, 171–82.

HARSANYI, J. C. (1962a) 'Measurement of Social Power, Opportunity Costs, and the Theory of Two-person Bargaining Games', *Behavioral Science*, **7**, 67–80.

HARSANYI, J. C. (1962b) 'Measurement of Social Power in *n*-Person Reciprocal Power Situations', *Behavioral Science*, **7**, 81–91.

JOUVENEL, B. DE (1945) 1952, *Power: The Natural History of Its Growth* (rev. ed.) London, Batchworth.

LASSWELL, H. D. (1930) 1960, *Psychopathology and Politics* (new ed.) with afterthoughts by the author, New York, Viking.

LASSWELL, H. D. (1936) *Politics: Who Gets What, When, How?* New York, McGraw-Hill.

LASSWELL, H. D. and KAPLAN, A. (1950) *Power and Society: A Framework for Political Inquiry* Yale Law School Studies, vol. 2, New Haven, Yale University Press.

LOEWENSTEIN, K. (1957) *Political Power and the Governmental Process* Chicago, University of Chicago Press.

MARCH, J. G. (1955) 'An Introduction to the Theory and Measurement of Influence', *American Political Science Review*, 49, 431–51.

MARCH, J. G. (1956) 'Influence Measurement in Experimental and Semiexperimental Groups', *Sociometry*, 19, 260–71.

MARCH, J. G. (1957) 'Measurement Concepts in the Theory of Influence', *Journal of Politics*, 19, 202–26.

MARCH, J. G. (ed.) (1965) *Handbook of Organizations* Chicago, Rand McNally.

MEINECKE, F. (1924) 1957, *Machiavellism: The Doctrine of Raison d'État and Its Place in Modern History* New Haven, Yale University Press.

MERRIAM, C. E. (1934) *Political Power: Its Composition and Incidence* New York, McGraw-Hill. A paperback edition was published in 1964 by Collier.

MILLS, C. W. (1956) *The Power Elite* New York, Oxford University Press.

MORGENTHAU, H. J. (1948) 1967, *Politics Among Nations: The Struggle for Power and Peace* (4th ed.) New York, Knopf.

MOSCA, G. (1896) 1939, *The Ruling Class (Elementi di scienza politica)* New York, McGraw-Hill.

NEUSTADT, R. E. (1960) *Presidential Power: The Politics of Leadership* New York, Wiley. A paperback edition was published in 1962.

OPPENHEIM, F. E. (1961) *Dimensions of Freedom: An Analysis* London, Macmillan.

PARETO, V. (1916) *The Mind and Society: A Treatise on General Sociology*, 4 vols, New York, Dover.

PARSONS, T. (1963a) 'On the Concept of Influence', *Public Opinion Quarterly*, **27**, 37–62. A comment by Coleman J. S. appears on pages 63–82; a communication by Bauer, R. A. on pages 83–6; and a rejoinder by Parsons, Talcott on pages 87–92.

PARSONS, T. (1963b) 'On the Concept of Political Power', American Philosophical Society, *Proceedings*, **107**, 232–62.

POLSBY, N. W. (1963) *Community Power and Political Theory*, Yale Studies in Political Science, vol. 7, New Haven, Yale University Press.

RIKER, W. H. (1959) (A Test of the Adequacy of the Power Index', *Behavioral Science*, **4**, 120–31.

RIKER, W. H. (1964) 'Some Ambiguities in the Notion of Power, *American Political Science Review*, **58**, 341–9.

ROGOW, A. A. and LASSWELL, H. D. (1963) *Power, Corruption and Rectitude* Englewood Cliffs, N.J., Prentice-Hall.

ROSSI, P. H. (1960) 'Power and Community Structure', *Midwest Journal of Political Science*, **4**, 390–401.

SHAPLEY, L. S. and SHUBIK, M. (1954) 'A Method for Evaluating the Distribution of Power in a Committee System', *American Political Science Review*, **48**, 787–92.

SIMON, H. A. (1947–56) 1957, *Models of Man: Social and Rational; Mathematical Essays on Rational Human Behavior in a Social Setting* New York, Wiley.

SIMON, H. A. (1953) 'Notes on the Observation and Measurement of Political Power', *Journal of Politics*, **15**, 500–16.

WEBER, M. (1922) 1957, *The Theory of Social and Economic Organization*, by Parsons, T. (ed.) Glencoe, Ill., Free Press.

29   Marx as a power theorist

Marvin E. Olsen

Political philosophers from Plato onward have written extensively about the exercise of power, but Karl Marx must be singled out as the principal intellectual father of contemporary political sociology. Whereas most political philosophers prior to him had in one way or another linked their discussions of power to the state, seeing government and related organizations (such as the military) as the main foci of power in society, Marx broke sharply with this tradition. He argued instead that power originates primarily in economic production, that it permeates and influences all aspects of society, that the main wielders of social power are social classes, and that government is essentially a servant of the dominant social class. Marx thus expanded the concept of power from a specifically political phenomenon to a ubiquitous social process and offered a theory of societal development based on the exercise of power.[1]

This essay has two purposes: first, to sketch the highlights of Marx's basic theory; and second, to suggest directions in which his provocative insights might be broadened into a more encompassing power theory of social organization.[2]

Marx's ideas on the nature of society can be divided into three major components: a sociological perspective – primacy of economically generated power; a philosophy of history – dialectic social change; and a connecting thesis – social classes in continual conflict.

Intensive study of Western European societies, in both their feudalistic and industrialized stages, led Marx to adopt the fundamental postulate that *all Western societies rest on a foundation of economic production*. Since men must first produce goods and services if they are to survive or attain

1 The only writer who might seriously challenge Marx as a founder of political sociology was Alexis de Tocqueville. He also treated power as a pervasive social process extending far beyond the political state, but he did not provide a systematic theory of power with the scope or consistency of Marx's ideas, and hence has not had an impact comparable to that of Marx or later writers. Quite belatedly, many political sociologists are today 'rediscovering' Tocqueville and giving much closer attention to his works.
2 This discussion of Marx is drawn from several sources, including: Bottomore and Rubel (1956); Dahrendorf (1959); Marx (1954); Mills (1962); Schumpeter (1962); and Zeitlin (1967).

OLSEN, MARVIN E. (1970) 'Marx as a Power Theorist', in *Power in Societies* New York, Collier-Macmillan, 70–6.

goals, the nature and effectiveness of the productive process will inevitably influence – though never totally determine – all other aspects of social and cultural life. Any real society will contain many diverse 'modes of production', but for analytical purposes, Marx argued, we need examine only the dominant mode of a given era. In feudal societies this is agriculture, whereas in industrialized societies it is manufacturing.

Within a society's dominant mode of production, the 'forces of production', or technological and physical aspects of economic activity, are important in determining how effectively surplus resources (that is, wealth) can be produced. But economic technology does not determine how these resources will be used and distributed in society. Especially crucial for social organization, therefore, is a second aspect of the economy, which Marx called the 'social relations of production'. By this he meant the relationships of various segments of the population to the economy – who owns or controls the major means of production, and who doesn't. Whoever controls the dominant mode of economic production in a society will determine how the existing technology will be utilized and how the resulting resources will be distributed, with the consequence that these persons will exercise power throughout the total society.

This theoretical perspective gave Marx a key to understanding the power dynamics of all societies, but it did not explain long-term trends in human history. For this he turned to the idea of dialectic social change. From the philosopher Hegel he took the dialectic model of a prevailing thesis giving rise to a conflicting antithesis, both of which eventually merge into a new synthesis, which in turn forms the thesis of a new dialectic. But he applied this process to social conditions rather than to philosophical ideas, on the grounds that ideas have meaning only in relation to the social conditions from which they arise. In his words, he 'stood Hegel on his feet'.

The dialectic process was for Marx not an inherent tendency within human society, but rather an analytical tool with which to explain the broad sweep of human history – at least in Western Europe. In other words, *dialectic change is never inevitable, but when major social changes do occur they tend to follow the dialectic process*. Because the component sectors of a society are in continual conflict for control over the means of economic production (and hence for power and wealth), all societies contain within themselves potential 'seeds' of change. Whether or not these 'seeds' actually 'blossom' into radical social changes remains a problematic question for both the participants and scientific observers, however. Theoretically, all societies can be expected to develop from the thesis of feudalism through the antithesis of capitalism to the synthesis of socialism. Empirically, though, this process is contingent on many intervening factors, including the amount of control the ruling elites exercise over the rest of society, the degree of organization existing among the nonelites, and the effectiveness of the leaders advocating social change. For this reason, Marx saw himself first of all as a spokesman for the masses in industrial society, urging them to become aware of their common situation, to organize themselves, and to take action to overthrow the ruling owners of industry. Only in this manner could capitalism be destroyed and the process of dialectic change be carried to fruition.

If Marx had ended his analysis at this point he would have left two major questions unanswered. First, what are the segments of a society which compete for control of the means of production and how do they relate to one another? Second, why won't socialism become the thesis for further dialectic change? He answered both of these questions by bridging the theoretical gap between his sociological perspective and his philosophy of history with the thesis of conflicting social classes. This thesis consists of a definition of classes, an analysis of the nature of capitalism, and an argument for class conflict and revolution. He defined a social class as a population of people within a society who stand in a common relation to the major means of economic production, and who therefore exercise similar amounts of power in society and are in continual conflict with other classes. He analysed the capitalistic economic system in great depth to discover why it produced the extreme exploitation of workers he observed in all industrialized societies. And he concluded that dialectic social change would end only if social classes were completely abolished and radically new types of society were established.

Marx believed that for analytical purposes the industrialized societies of Europe (which at that time were all thoroughly capitalistic) could be seen as consisting of two major social classes: the bourgeoisie who owned the means of production (the factories), and the proletariat who were forced to sell their labour to the industrialists. He clearly recognized the existence of other classes as well, such as agricultural peasants, small merchants, and professionals and intellectuals, but he contended that they were not analytically important because they were either rapidly disappearing or were slowly being driven from their 'middle-class' positions into the proletariat. Using current nineteenth-century economic theory, Marx argued that the dominant bourgeoisie were forced by the intrinsic laws of capitalism to exploit their workers by paying them less than the value of their labour. If capitalists did not exploit their workers they made no profit and soon went out of business. Hence the inherent economic injustice of industria capitalism. Although much of Marx's technical economic analysis has been rejected by contemporary economists, there is abundant historical evidence that early industrialists did in fact severely exploit their workers to increase their profits. We realize today, furthermore, that the exploitation and other conditions Marx witnessed are common problems of the basic process of industrialization, whatever its form.

The proletariat in industrial societies constitutes a 'class-in-itself', as determined by its subordinate relationship to the means of production. But before it can become a 'class-for-itself' and take action to alter its social condition, it must develop class consciousness and class organization. The bourgeoisie make their fatal mistake, Marx contended, when they begin to drive the old middle class, especially intellectuals, into the industrial proletariat by forcing them to sell their services on the labour market. These intellectuals can provide the leadership that the workers have previously lacked, promote class consciousness and organization among the workers, and initiate revolutionary social change of the entire society.

The resulting social change might conceivably be quite gradual, but Marx insisted that in practice this is highly unlikely. From his observations of the historical shift from feudalism to capitalism, he concluded that the dominant class will never voluntarily surrender its control over society, but instead will use all its power – especially that of the government and the military – to resist change. Hence *if the proletariat is ever to gain control of the means of production from the bourgeoisie, it must do so through violent class conflict,* or total revolution.

Following this revolution, the leaders of the proletariat will face the demanding task of completely reordering society by putting all productive activities under public ownership and of teaching the workers to assume the wide responsibilities which are now theirs. In this interim period it will therefore be necessary to create a temporary 'dictatorship of the proletariat' headed by the revolutionary leaders. Marx firmly believed, however, that eventually a truly 'classless society' could be achieved, in which there would be no more economic exploitation, in which the state as an enforcer of social control would no longer be necessary and hence would largely wither away, and in which the full possibilities of creative human life would be enjoyed by all. The final stage of dialectic social change would thus be reached under socialism, when true 'human history' would begin.

His reasoning in support of this belief went as follows: In a fully communistic society control over the means of economic production would be shared by everyone, so that by definition there would be no more social classes. If no social classes, then no more class exploitation and class conflict. Hence no remaining bases for dialectic social change. A morally perfect society will then have been attained on earth, in which all people participate and benefit equally. Individual and collective social responsibility, not power and exploitation, will now form the basis of organized social life.

In sum, by defining social classes in terms of their differing relationships to the means of economic production and by maintaining that public control over the means of production will end class exploitation, conflict, and dialectic change, Marx neatly joined his sociological perspective and his philosophy of history into a unified theory of society as he then knew it.

Putting aside whatever moral evaluations we might want to make about Marx's ideal 'classless society', we are faced with the question of what sociological insights did he suggest that may be useful in understanding social organization? Included in any such inventory of Marx's sociological contributions would be these five ideas:

1 The fundamental importance of economic production in providing resources necessary for all other kinds of social activities within a society. Although the economy may not directly affect numerous spheres of social life, it does provide a foundation on which all other social organization rests. We do not have to be 'economic determinists' to appreciate the extensive indirect influence of economic activities throughout a society.

2 A conception of society as consisting of numerous subparts – whether they be social classes or any other organized entities – which are functionally interrelated but which also possess considerable autonomy to pursue their own goals, and which therefore come into frequent conflict with each other. From this perspective a society is not a completely unified and harmonious whole, nor do requirements and goals of the total society normally take precedence over those of its subparts. Intrasocietal conflict, not integration, is the 'normal' state of human affairs, and the attainment of harmony and unity is at best an imperfectly achieved goal.

3 A broad view of human history as a continual process of social change towards increasingly complex – and demanding – forms of social organization. Whether or not the dialectic model provides the most useful analytical tool with which to examine societal change is an unresolved empirical question, but the fact that human history is a story of constant conflict and change cannot be denied.

4 The crucial significance of powerful elites in shaping and controlling virtually all societies. The size, composition, and power of such elites has of course varied from one society to another and also through time, but all known societies beyond the bare subsistence level have contained elites who

exercised various kinds of power over others. At this point in history we do not know whether power concentration is inherent in all social organization or whether the current slow trend toward increased equality for all can be carried to full realization. But quite clearly neither the historian nor the sociologist can ignore the actions of elites in their studies of all past and present societies.

5 Finally and perhaps most important of all, Marx's writings provide the beginnings of a general power theory of social organization. His stress on relationships to the means of production as the primary determinant of social structure, together with his analyses of the ways in which elites have historically controlled their societies, suggests that we should look to the exercise of power as the principal cause of social ordering in society. Marx did not elaborate a general power theory of social organization in precise detail, but he did convincingly demonstrate the relevance of such a theory for understanding human society. The unfinished task now confronting contemporary social scientists is to expand, refine, and formalize power theory so that it can be adequately tested in empirical research.

A necessary first step in constructing a general power theory of social organization is to extend Marx's ideas along several dimensions. *Three directions in which theoretical extensions might be made are in the types of power considered, the resource bases available for generating power, and the possible patterns of actual power wielding.* First, many sociologists have argued that Marx gave too much attention to force (especially violence), and neglected other kinds of power such as dominance and authority. Indeed, it may be that as societies become 'modernized' and 'civilized' they tend to substitute functional dominance and legitimate authority for at least the more oppressive forms of force as bases of social order.[3] Second, it can also be argued that Marx's concern with ownership of the means of economic production as the major resource base for social power is too limited to fit contemporary developed societies. While not denying the importance of this source of power, we must also consider such resource bases as access to political decision making, information flows through the mass media, scientific research and applied engineering, and police and military organizations. Third, we need not limit our analysis of actual power patterns to 'downward' exertion from a single source. A highly organized society might in fact contain a diverse variety of power patterns with influence and control flowing in all directions. Max Weber's ideal type of

---

3 The thesis of increased reliance on functional dominance in highly developed organizations has been presented by Hawley (1968). The importance of legitimate authority in modern organizations has been stressed by Dahrendorf (1959).

hierarchical bureaucracy further contributed to the assumption that a centralized hierarchy of power is the most efficient and rational form of social organization, so that only recently have many social scientists begun to explore other possible patterns of power. In the past few years, however, numerous writings have examined power decentralization and polyarchy.[4]

By expanding the scope of power theory in these directions our theoretical perspective becomes considerably more inclusive and complex than Marx's scheme. But have we not at the same time lost much of the predictive capability of Marxian theory? Have we sacrificed a limited but useful theory for a broader but much more vague theoretical perspective? This criticism undoubtedly has some validity, so that if we leave our 'power perspective' at this point we may have given up more than we have gained in theoretical insight. Clearly needed now are attempts to formulate a rigorous and precise power theory of social organization that takes into account these necessary extensions. One possible direction which such theory construction might take is suggested by contemporary ecological theory.[5]

A central theorem of social ecology is that the parts of an organization that control the flow of necessary resources from the environment into the organization – its 'key functionaries' – exercise dominance over all other parts with which they are functionally interrelated. In a loosely structured (or relatively 'open') organization many parts are in direct contact with the environment, so that no one part wields much dominance. When an organization becomes more tightly unified (or 'closed'), however, most of these parts are cut off from the environment, leaving only one or a very few key functionaries which mediate all resource procurement. All other parts of the organization then become dependent on the remaining key functionaries for their necessary resources, and at the same time are complexly interrelated with one another. Within such a highly interdependent system each part continues to exercise some dominance, but the strength of its power is inversely related to its functional distance from the key functionaries.

Without too much distortion, Marx's emphasis on control over production – and more generally on the economic foundation of society – can be translated into these ecological terms of key functionaries exercising dominance throughout society. In all past and present human societies, scarcity of economic resources has been a crucial factor imposing limitations on all other social activities. Hence the economy has tended to

---

4   As an example of this literature, see Dahl and Lindblom (1953).
5   The following discussion is drawn largely from Hawley (1968).

dominate all other parts of the society, and those actors who controlled it have been in a position to exercise dominance throughout social life. But what might happen in a society if the economy became so efficient and effective that economic scarcity were no longer a major problem? No society has yet approached such a condition of economic abundance, but recent trends in highly industrialized nations such as the United States indicate that this is not impossible.

The ecological scheme can easily be extended to cover this kind of 'post-industrial society'. Under conditions of total economic abundance the economy and those who operated it would no longer be the key functionaries with dominant power in society – as long as the economy continued to operate without interruption. Other scarce resources might then assume critical importance, giving those who controlled them dominant power. One possible scarce resource could be scientific and technical knowledge and trained manpower, since all segments of society (including the economy) would presumably be highly dependent on educated specialists and the knowledge and skills they possessed. In this case, the crucial sphere of activity for the society would become education, especially higher education. Scientists, professors, and teachers would then become the key functionaries with dominant social power in society. In Marx's terms, there could be a new ruling class, determined by relationships to informational and educational production.

This kind of ecological theorizing suffers from many of the same limitations of Marxian theory and is open to numerous criticisms. It substitutes dominance for force as the principal type of power in society, and completely ignores legitimate authority. It also considers only one major resource base for generating power, although this need not be economic production. And it continues to utilize a single pattern of power exertion, from the 'top' of a functional hierarchy downward. Nevertheless, it does provide stimulating ideas for extending Marxian theory into 'post-industrial societies'. The challenge now facing sociologists is to carry these theoretical explorations even further, towards the formulation and testing of a truly encompassing yet rigorous power theory of social organization.

References

BOTTOMORE, T. B. and RUBEL, M. (1956) *Karl Marx: Selected Writings in Sociology and Social Philosophy* London, C. A. Watts.
DAHL, R. A. and LINDBLOM, C. E. (1953) *Politics, Economics and Welfare* New York, Harper and Row.

DAHRENDORF, R. (1959) *Class and Class Conflict in Industrial Society* Stanford, California, Stanford University Press.

HAWLEY, A. H. (1968) 'Human Ecology', in *International Encyclopedia of the Social Sciences*, vol. 4, New York, Macmillan.

MARX, K. (1954) *Capital* Moscow, Foreign Languages Publishing House.

MILLS, C. W. (1962) *The Marxists* New York, Dell.

SCHUMPETER, J. (1962) *Capitalism, Socialism and Democracy* New York, Harper and Row.

ZEITLIN, I. M. (1967) *Marxism: A Re-Interpretation* Princeton, N.J., Van Nostrand.

Part VIII Social change

Introduction

One of the themes running through the course which this Reader serves is that of change in society, and its causes. In some sections of the course this is treated quite explicitly, as in the discussion connecting Protestantism and the rise of capitalism, or the varying media of communication with a whole range of changes in society. In others, the question is not raised directly, but a particular model of society and its dynamics often in fact underlies the selection and presentation of the material. It obviously makes a difference to one's interpretation of the facts whether one takes the crucial factor to lie in, say, the technological sphere, or in the belief system of a society, or in the attitudes of individuals. Similarly, one's view of both change and stability in society is affected by whether one sees the course of history in terms of a broad evolutionist sweep through set stages or as a much more piecemeal and unpredictable affair. Broad assumptions of this type about the basic nature of society and of social change may not be directly stated, but have often been in play in the course, as in social science writing generally. To some extent different approaches in this respect may coincide with the distinctions between the various social science disciplines but they also cut across these conventional divisions and condition the kinds of analyses that social scientists of all disciplines find themselves making, not only of past and present events and institutions, but even in their predictions of possible futures.

One of the more common emphases in social science writing on social change has been on the significance of economic factors. It is therefore not surprising that there has often been a stress on the concept of 'industrial' as a crucial characteristic for differentiating societies and/or historical stages. This is evident both in this course, with its recurrent mention of the 'pre-industrial', 'industrial' and 'post-industrial' phases, and in the common preoccupation of social scientists with 'industrialization' and their interest, established by the classic nineteenth-century sociologists, in the basic dichotomy between industrial and non-industrial society. The various approaches here are of course complex, but the one common thread running through this can be seen as the assumption that there is something special about 'industrialization' as experienced in Western Europe which makes it a kind of turning point by reference to which we define and study modern society.

Such an emphasis clearly provides one useful framework for approaching the study of society. But, as is evident both in the material for this course, and in the writings of more recent historians and social scientists, it is one that can be questioned.

There are a number of lines that can be followed here. Some, for instance, would query whether the European 'Industrial Revolution' did in fact mark such a revolutionary and unique turning point. Perhaps even more important is the questioning of the whole assumption that economic factors are necessarily the crucial ones in change. It is true that one of the most common directions for social scientists and others to look for their central explanations of change is indeed in the economic and technological sphere and that this has proved a fruitful line of investigation. There are many variations on this general theme (Marx is far from being its only protagonist, even though he is perhaps the most famous one). A number of these approaches occur in the course, and are discussed succinctly here in the extract by W. E. Moore. But that this set of approaches is not the only one comes out clearly in some of the material in the course (that on religion in particular) and in the line taken up by a number of other social scientists. Max Weber is notable here for his refusal to construct a model of change based primarily on *one* variable. We have reprinted here his classic introduction to his study *The Protestant Ethic and the Spirit of Capitalism* (first published in German in 1904/5) in which he discusses the many possible factors that may have been involved in shaping the development of 'modern European civilization' as it then appeared. These, he stresses, include not only economic causes but also religious and spiritual forces, aspects which it is perhaps easy to overlook but which may well play as crucial a part in social change as the more frequently stressed economic factors.

Another query that is increasingly coming to the fore is whether social scientists should now be moving on, from a preoccupation with industrial society as it was following the period of industrialization in Europe, to a concentration on the more recent changes of the twentieth century which may prove to be equally significant. Part of this move to look more closely at present trends, rather than the classic type of 'industrial society' as formulated by earlier writers, has led to the idea of the 'post-industrial' stage which is both incipient now and likely to develop further in the future.

It is only in recent years that serious social scientists have begun to come to terms with the future as an object of study. Previously, those interested in the future were dismissed as utopians or as more concerned with practice than theory. Even today, many social scientists look askance at the practice of 'futurology' and are often justified in their scepticism because the attractions of discussing the future are sufficiently great to attract a proportion of cranks and the difficulties are formidable enough to repel many sound scholars. In spite of all this, the prevalence of acute social problems and the need of policy-makers for more information to guide their decisions are attracting growing numbers of social scientists to future-oriented studies.

Perhaps the greatest difference between this development and previous ventures in the application of social science knowledge is the extent to which serious study of the future casts a new light on the nature of social science. Whereas studies of present and past can focus on the empirical, consideration of the future inevitably involves speculation and value-judgement. The problems of thinking about the future of society centre around methods of forecasting the development of society and the difficulty of accommodating facts, forecasts and value-judgements in the same discourse. A further problem, which is of relevance to the nature of the course, is the fact that forecasting often involves a number of disciplines. For all these reasons a new body of ideas has grown up, under various names and in many countries, among those interested in the future – or, rather, futures, since those involved tend to emphasize the open nature of the futures and the range of alternative possibilities.

The first of our two extracts on the future, by Webber, contrasts this view of the future, which he associates with post-industrial society, with ideas about the future in industrial and pre-industrial societies. Of course, only a minority of the population subscribe to the post-industrial view. Most people in economically developed countries continue in the industrial manner, expecting the future to differ from the present as the present differs from the past, but without radical change. Most people in developing countries perhaps retain a 'pre-industrial view of the future'.[1] This extract is extremely brief, being no more than the introduction to a paper discussing the relevance of future-thinking to city planning.

The second extract is of a different nature, coming as it does from one of the classic books of the futures movement, Bertrand de Jouvenel's *The Art of Conjecture*. Jouvenel is one of those who most strongly emphasize that the future cannot be the subject of scientific knowledge but only of informed conjecture. He makes the useful distinction between primary forecasts, which state what will happen if existing trends continue,

1   Though it should be noted that many social anthropologists would reject Webber's characterization of 'pre-industrial societies' as being far too sweeping and generalized to do justice to the detailed facts.

secondary forecasts, which state what might happen if certain action were taken, and tertiary forecasts, which assess the likelihood of a particular future being brought into being through political action. The excerpt reproduced here deals with various elementary forms of primary forecasting with the twin objectives of demonstrating that scholars have been making forecasts for centuries (although not in any systematic way) and to introduce some of the ideas which still lie behind most forecasts, even when camouflaged by sophisticated terminology. His discussion highlights some of the problems which have confounded forecasters in the past and thus emphasizes the need for rigour if future forecasters are to be more useful to society.

A final point that should be mentioned directly in this section is the question of the role of the social sciences. The controversies on this are manifold and the complex philosophical and moral issues involved clearly cannot be discussed here. But it is pertinent to make the point that where the main concentration of social scientists has been primarily on the past or the-present-as-a-result-of-the-past, there is little opportunity to do more than *analyse* it – or, at most, make moral judgements about it or use it as a tool for making normative statements about the present state of the world (many social scientists indeed would consider even that extra step unjustified anyway, taking their stand with Weber that 'whoever wants a sermon should go to a conventicle'!). But, in any case, the social scientist in this situation has basically to be content with words, not action on his subject matter. But when the future or the-present-as-becoming-the-future becomes accepted as a major part of the field, the situation is perhaps different. There is the possibility not just of analysing and asssessing the course of events, but of actually changing it: of doing something about it. In many 'futurology' studies this element is very marked and – as you may well feel in reading the extracts here – it raises pressingly yet another issue to be considered in the well-worn controversies about the aims and status of social science.

Some social scientists tend to emphasize mainly their role of trying as best they can to establish facts and relationships or to analyse illuminatingly, and see normative judgments or political action as something they can practise *qua* citizens or political activists rather than *qua* social scientists. They emphasize the difficulty of reaching certain or rapid conclusions, our existing ignorance about many aspects of human behaviour, and the importance of resisting the temptation to parade fashionable bandwagons as truths established by social science. Others however consider this approach as ultimately just too easy. They point to the challenge raised by the future and our responsibility for it, as well as to the difficulty (or even impossibility) of disentangling value judgement from forecasts of the future – or even from analyses of the past or present. Others fall somewhere between these two extremes. Though this is of course a continuing controversy that can only be raised, not resolved, in the course, a number of relevant comments on it can be found in the various positions taken up in the excerpts in this section.

Ruth Finnegan
Philip Sarre

W. E. Moore

A great many scholars, impressed by the extreme rapidity of social change, have sought explanations in the dynamic relations between economy and society. The most widely held views, unsupported either by fact or logic, attribute primary causal significance to economic factors in social change. All may be called forms of 'economic determinism'. The varying emphases may be conveniently reduced to four: the primacy of economic (roughly, hedonistic) motives, the inherent dynamics of economic organization and institutions, the independent expansion of industrial technology, and the innovating role of the entrepreneur, which, in one view of economic change, constitutes the essential dynamic element in modern industrial capitalism.

There are two other aspects of socio-economic change. One is the far-reaching and yet little noted significance of changing occupational structures in modern industrial societies. The other is the process of industrialization itself. The historic developments in Western societies are now being repeated, in some form or degree, throughout the world. The breadth of evidence through time and place allows an almost experimental approach to uniform and variable elements in the process of economic change.

Economic determinism

Of the four principal types of economic determinism, the primacy of materialistic motives is least often supported as an explicit cause, but it is implicitly assumed in a vast range of economic literature. Knowledge of extensive cultural variability of values and motives has sufficed to prevent most sociologists from subscribing to the view.

The thesis that the character of the economic organization shapes the main contours of the social order, and provides the initial impetus to societal changes, has received more elaborate development. Perhaps the clearest exposition is still that of Marx and his interpreters. According to Marx,

M O O R E, W. E. (1964) 'The Interpretation of Social Change', in *Economy and Society* New York, Random House, 34–43.

the character of society is fundamentally determined by the 'economic factor', including resources, technology, and productive organization.

The difficulty with this position in general is that the economic factor is poorly identified and indeed upon close examination is found to include elements perfectly capable of variation quite independently of productive or market organization. Such, for example, is the case with property. If the economic factor is defined so as to include most of the institutional features of society, then to attribute primary causal significance to it in the interpretation of social change loses all precision. At the extreme, this becomes a theory that 'everything causes everything', which is not very helpful.

An economic interpretation which has gained wide currency in sociology views social change in terms of resistance and adaptations to expanding technology, the latter regarded as inherently accumulative or dynamic. Veblen's maintenance of this position was largely confined to economic developments in recent times, and did not entirely neglect the independent significance of nontechnological values – which Veblen (1919, 1921), however, is inclined to lump under the heading of 'vested interests'. More recent adaptations of the position, particularly as exemplified in the 'culture lag' hypothesis, have been less restrained in the claims made, and have done considerably more violence to fact and logic.

Perhaps the greatest difficulty in the assessment of the accuracy of the various forms of 'economic interpretations' is the definition and identification of the variables. As previously noted, few sociologists have subscribed to the patently erroneous view that all human behaviour may be reduced to the struggle for existence, the 'acquisitive instinct', or the satisfaction of economic wants expressed in mainly physiological terms. It is rather in the conditions, forms, and organization of productive enterprise that most adherents to the doctrine of economic primacy find their prime mover. Marx and his followers, for example, have emphasized the effect of technology and 'relationships of production' in providing the dynamic factors that lead to the gradual or sudden transition from one productive system to another. Two difficulties are encountered in this interpretation:

1   The economic factor so defined includes a number of distinct elements, at least some of which are independently variable. It thus becomes difficult to assess precisely what dynamic role is to be assigned to each of the elements. The fact of independent variability has an even further significance, for some of the elements are economically relevant, but are far from being determined by other elements. Thus, property arrangements may be modified to give more or less power to an employer, or profits taxed away to provide unemployment relief or to finance an international war. The ex-

ploitative power of the owner of capital may be regulated by law, and the terms of the wage contract limited by legislation designed to protect the health of children. These are changes in the conditions and relationships of production; but the dynamic lies outside the economic organization, in norms and institutions, and not the other way around.

Actually, of course, a functional relationship holds, and its interpretation may be conveniently approached by primary attention to changes in the productive organization. The difficulty lies in claiming that this matter of convenience is something more – that it represents the true basis of societal organization. It is perhaps equally convenient to examine the functional relationships from any other starting point.

2 Above all, however, it is necessary to examine the character of the conditions not included as elements in the economic factor but which are in fact conditions necessary for the supposed course of economic development actually to take place. Notable in this respect is the constancy of ends. The explicit denial by various economic determinists that any assumption is made concerning the primacy of economic motives, and the partially accurate insistence that the behaviour of specific individuals is rather a function of their position in the system, do not eliminate the relevance of ends.

One form of productive enterprise will lead to a more efficient or more highly organized form only so long as and to the extent that the value system remains reasonably favourable to the change. When conflicts of interests, economic and otherwise, arise, as they inevitably must in a dynamic situation, the victory of certain interests depends upon the whole normative and structural situation. There is no *a priori* reason for supposing that economic interests will prevail. Neither is there an *a priori* reason for supposing that the economic structure is any more immanently dynamic than any other.

The role of technology

A current and very popular mode of interpretation of social change places primary or exclusive emphasis on an inherently expanding technology. Its popularity seems to be a function of its simplicity, and partly a fortuitous result of its being superficially correct for some of the data arrayed under its aegis. In its crudest form this interpretation attempts to draw a distinction between accumulative material culture (machines, tools, artifacts), and nonmaterial or adaptive culture (ideas, knowledge, values) (Ogburn 1936.)

This view makes the initial error of failing to see that culture objects are only part of the culture in so far as they embody ideas and values, and that the same objects may have substantially different functional significance in other cultural contexts. The attention to the material culture has left the impression that machines are self-inventing, self-perpetuating, and self-expanding, and that nonmaterial culture tends to lag behind the existing pile of objects.

A more tenable formulation makes of technology (which is a system of ideas, principles, and interests) a segment of culture more subject to change than other aspects of culture, and therefore possibly of causal significance in social change. Under certain conditions this proposition is likely to be correct, precisely because of the *instrumental character* of technology. That is, the elaboration of techniques for the achievement of some societal values is likely to require modification of other practices and possibly of beliefs. Thus, changes in the design and performance of automobiles have certainly 'caused' modification of American recreational customs, and have been relevant to changes in courtship ideals and practices. Likewise, the increased mechanization of industry has increased the competitive advantage of large industries and 'caused' considerable industrial transformations.

The error of attributing sole or primary causal importance to an expanding technology has consisted in the neglect of the important qualification, 'under certain conditions'. These conditions may be briefly stated.

For technological change to be *primary* the end or goal of technological progress must be assumed, and must remain constant. A change of ends makes previous technology wasteful, and creates a temporary lag in the development of a new technology. Thus a nation at war finds its peacetime industrial technology oriented toward ends that are no longer primary (such as refrigerators and automobiles) and its wartime production limited by an inadequate technology. In this case it is obviously the goal that is of causal significance in the change, and not the technology.

The doctrine of technological primacy has had some validity in the interpretation of industrial transformation, precisely because the goal of economic productivity has been more or less correctly assumed, and has remained reasonably constant. Other scientific principles could be applied to other practical (that is, socially approved) ends, and to a considerable degree have been in such fields as medicine, public health, and even propaganda and social control.

As a universally valid principle the technological interpretation of social change is forced to find some source of the ends to be achieved. Thus, there is a marked tendency for this view to become a watered-down version of the doctrine of economic causation, and fall heir to the difficulties of that doctrine as well.

Among the proponents of the primacy of technological change there is evident an unmistakable tone of moral disapproval directed against the lags – that is, resistances to structural and normative adaptations occasioned by innovation. Were there no such counterbalancing of technical changes, the social structure would collapse, or rather, would not have existed in the first place.

Inventions, then, do have social results; they also have social causes, and their acceptance or rejection depends upon the social framework. Some of the results are likely to be unanticipated. If those unanticipated results are changes that the existing structure is poorly designed to accept or incorporate they will result in culture lag.

But culture lag is certainly not the predestined result of the slowness of adaptive culture in catching up with the inevitably changing material culture; the lag is in fact capable of purposive solution. It is possible to adjust to the machine (thus preserving the dominance of the original goal, but modifying others), or it is possible to change, modify, regulate, or abandon the machine in view of other values. Even in the modern industrial world the dictum that 'You cannot fight social (that is, technological) trends' is discounted by the fact that inventions are customarily controlled when their results would be contrary to business interests.

Entrepreneurship

In classical economic doctrine, the factors of production were land, labour, and capital. Their use in the productive process yielded three forms of income: rent, wages, and interest, respectively. Subsequent modifications of economic analysis often added a fourth productive factor: the entrepreneur. As originally conceived the entrepreneur was a manager (and thus, a type of labourer) but also a risk-taker. The risk-taking function yielded a fourth type of income, profits.

This conception of the economic system was not, strictly speaking, static as long as the factors of production were not entirely used, and used in their most favourable proportions. But beyond that point, the conceptual scheme provided for little change in economic structure.

As an essentially new interpretation of economic history, the late Joseph A. Schumpeter (1950) offered a different conception of the entrepreneur. This approach made of the entrepreneur an *innovator*: whether of products, productive techniques, or organizational arrangements.

This reinterpretation raised questions of sociological interest not previously noted in economic history, such as the social conditions for the development and success of economic innovators. In Schumpeter's view, a view which was partially developed on the basis of the work of Marx and Weber, early capitalist development depended upon innovators who broke loose from conventional processes and ideas of economic propriety. Schumpeter does suggest, however, that a social order already undermined was essential to the success of entrepreneurs.

This innovating function of the entrepreneur is not really antithetical to the earlier concept of risk-taking. It puts the latter in a dynamic context. Schumpeter adds that with the organization of the modern corporation, both entrepreneurial functions have become 'obsolescent'. In the modern large corporation the entrepreneur is a possibly useful fiction of economic analysis. Decisions of all sorts, including decisions on new products and processes, are the consequences of interdependent group action, with the pooling and compromising of competences and personal views and influences.

The entrepreneurial interpretation of economic change leads, however, to an important aspect of modern economic organization – *the organization and institutionalization of change*. People are employed, capital invested, and organizational resources are committed to constant change in organization, process, and product. Research is a major component of modern industrial activity, and is by no means confined to research departments.

This commitment to deliberate change, which provides some of the seeming support for types of technological determinism, is not limited to business and industry. Schools and universities, legislatures, and many governmental agencies are committed to advancing knowledge, improving current practice, and rectifying abuses.

It is possible to argue, on somewhat shaky evidence, that the economic innovator has been more highly rewarded than others. On still shakier evidence, it might even be alleged that entrepreneurship in this sense has set the pace for social change generally. The solid fact is that modern industrial societies not only change rapidly, but in large measure deliberately.

Changing occupational structure

Technological change in production, whether of products or processes, has important consequences for the demand for skills in the labour force. Three such consequences can be distinguished: the obsolescence of skills, the dilution of skills, and the demand for new skills.

Skills are made obsolescent by the declining demand for particular products and by mechanization of operations. Dilution of skills is mainly the consequence of specialization of tasks, often in conformity with mechanical processes. This is what is usually meant by *division* of labour, and what is usually commented on adversely with reference to the subservience of labour to the machine.

A correlative development is less often noted as an aspect of changing technology and organization – the demand for new skills, including the design of processes, the coordination of specialized activities, and the supply of information.

The general significance of these concurrent changes in occupational role is rather markedly different from that painted by ardent critics of capitalism and industrialism. The processes of mechanization and large-scale organization have not produced a growing mass of unskilled and routinized workers, supervised by a handful of bosses.

On the contrary, the major changes through time have been the steady reduction of the proportion of unskilled workers, and the growing proportions of semiskilled and skilled workers, and particularly of clerical, technical, managerial, and professional workers. The handicraft worker is often displaced by mechanization, it is true. But at later stages, the servant of the machine is often displaced by the machine designer, the machine builder, and the machine master.

The changing occupational structure of industrial societies may be seen within the business enterprise, and in the economy as a whole. Within the enterprise, the most notable trends are the growing number of distinct occupations, a specialization made possible by the large scale of operations, and the growing proportion of clerical, administrative, and staff positions relative to production workers. In the larger scene the same shifts are manifest. Even if all employees of manufacturing corporations are viewed as 'engaged in manufacturing', which is not true in an occupational sense, this sector of the labour force has diminished rather than grown in the United States over recent decades. Services of all sorts, including finance, transportation, and distribution, but also including repairs, professional practice, and entertainment, represent growing proportions of total occupations and of national income.

These trends in occupational structure have rather far-reaching but largely unnoticed implications for theories of long-term economic change. They suggest, for example, that the Marxian theory of increasing 'polarization' of the economically active population into 'capitalists' and the 'proletariat' is radically false. Indeed, the division between bosses and workers appears sharpest at very early stages of industrialization (when Marx observed and speculated) (Moore 1954, 1951). By extension, the steady diversification of occupations, and the tendency of distinct occupational interests to take priority over collective loyalties to management or labour, undermine the internal solidarity of these categories.

Changes in occupational structure also throw light on some disputed issues with respect to trends in occupational mobility and, in this sense, economic opportunity. A common, and quite factually unsupported, doctrine of our time is that mobility has slowed up and classes have become more rigid since the last century. Had the structure not changed, there is some evidence that upward mobility within single *occupational* careers would have declined, but not necessarily within single lifetimes in view of the growing importance of education as a ladder, and its expanding availability. Advanced education not only allows an individual to start at a higher position (and thus to have been mobile before he enters an occupation) but also improves his chances of mobility later. But the argument that mobility is declining is tendentious indeed when account is taken of the tremendous expansion of jobs to be filled at least in middle positions (as measured by income or prestige).

Industrialization and economic growth

One of the most sweeping movements of modern times is the spread of the industrial system and its products to all parts of the world. In many areas the penetration has been recent and small, but it is significant for its present impact on traditional social structures as well as for its implications for the future.

The industrialization process relates to a general theory of social change in at least three ways indicated by the following questions: 1) Are there relatively standard sequences of changes in the structure of economies through industrial development, valid through time and space? 2) Are there predictable consequences of traditional social structures with the advent and development of industrial modes of production? 3) Are there principles of social change that will account for the form and rate of industrialization in relatively underdeveloped areas?

That these questions are rarely asked and currently scarcely answerable is further evidence of the neglect of theories of long-term change in both economics and sociology.

Available evidence provides some partial answers, and affords the opportunity of some speculations.

To the question about standard sequences, a tentative yes can be hazarded. From the history of Western industrial countries, it appears that the most rapid *rate* of economic growth may have moved through the following stages: [1]

1 Food production and agriculture generally
2 Physical manufacture
  a Physical capital (transportation, power, plant, machines)
  b Consumer nondurables
  c Consumer durables
3 'Industrialization' of agriculture
4 Technical skills and services
  a Experts on the nonhuman environment
  b Experts on human motivation and organization

It should be noted that in a highly industrialized system all of these aspects of production are to some extent concurrent. The hypothesis advanced here relates simply to priorities in the allocation of resources and their changes through time. It is also probable that late-comers to the industrialization process (the underdeveloped countries) will import plant and equipment, and some technical skills, and will start manufacturing with consumer nondurables. The latter tend to be labour-intensive (and labour is generally in abundant numerical supply) rather than capital-intensive (and capital is clearly in short supply).

To the question of the impact of industry on the structure of society, at least partial answers are available. Industrialization involves urbanization in some degree, and is uniformly destructive of extended kinship systems (where binding mutual obligations prevail among many relatives of various degrees), and traditional modes of social stratification. In one way or another, all of these consequences are linked to the industrialization process by the *mobility* required by the latter.

To account for the marked success of industry in penetrating primitive and agrarian societies, and at the same time to account for the highly unequal rates of economic change, requires an extensive analysis that has largely not been undertaken. Why are France and Italy so little industrial-

---

This 'stage theory of economic growth' represents a speculative extension of data and ideas presented by Simon Kuznets in a paper, 'Toward a Theory of Economic Growth', prepared for the Columbia University Bicentennial Conference on 'National Policy for Economic Welfare at Home and Abroad', May 1954.

ized as compared with England and Germany, despite an earlier start? Why did Japan, with limited resources and rigid stratification, industrialize and China, with greater resources and a relatively 'open' class system, not do so? It is obvious, but not precisely helpful, that values and institutional arrangements differ, as do resources, climate, population, and other elements relevant to production. A truly general theory of economic growth cannot be formulated until the complexity and diversity of social experience are better known and better understood.

References

MOORE, W. E. (1951) *Industrialization and Labor* Ithaca, Cornell University Press.

MOORE, W. E. (1954) 'Occupational Structure and Industrial Conflict', in Dubin, R., Kornhauser, A. and Ross, A. (eds) *Industrial Conflict* New York, McGraw-Hill.

OGBURN, W. F. (1936) *Social Change* New York, Viking Press.

SCHUMPETER, J. A. (1950) *Capitalism, Socialism and Democracy* (3rd ed.) New York, Harper and Bros.

VEBLEN, T. (1919) *The Vested Interests and the State of the Industrial Arts* New York, Huebsch.

VEBLEN, T. (1921) *The Engineers and the Price System* New York, Huebsch.

31   The development of modern Western civilization

Max Weber

A product of modern European civilization, studying any problem of universal history, is bound to ask himself to what combination of circumstances the fact should be attributed that in Western civilization, and in Western civilization only, cultural phenomena have appeared which (as we like to think) lie in a line of development having *universal* significance and value.

Only in the West does science exist at a stage of development which we recognize today as valid. Empirical knowledge, reflection on problems of the cosmos and of life, philosophical and theological wisdom of the most profound sort, are not confined to it, though in the case of the last the full development of a systematic theology must be credited to Christianity under the influence of Hellenism, since there were only fragments in Islam and in a few Indian sects. In short, knowledge and observation of great refinement have existed elsewhere, above all in India, China, Babylonia, Egypt. But in Babylonia and elsewhere astronomy lacked – which makes its development all the more astounding – the mathematical foundation which it first received from the Greeks. The Indian geometry had no rational proof; that was another product of the Greek intellect, also the creator of mechanics and physics. The Indian natural sciences, though well developed in observation, lacked the method of experiment, which was, apart from beginnings in antiquity, essentially a product of the Renaissance, as was the modern laboratory. Hence medicine, especially in India, though highly developed in empirical technique, lacked a biological and particularly a biochemical foundation. A rational chemistry has been absent from all areas of culture except the West.

The highly developed historical scholarship of China did not have the method of Thucydides. Machiavelli, it is true, had predecessors in India; but all Indian political thought was lacking in a systematic method comparable to that of Aristotle, and, indeed, in the possession of rational concepts. Not all the anticipations in India (School of Mimamsa), nor the extensive codification especially in the Near East, nor all the Indian and

WEBER, MAX (1962) from the Author's Introduction to *The Protestant Ethic and the Spirit of Capitalism* London, Allen and Unwin, 13–31.

other books of law, had the strictly systematic forms of thought, so essential to a rational jurisprudence, of the Roman law and of the Western law under its influence. A structure like the canon law is known only to the West. . . .

There was printing in China. But a printed literature, designed *only* for print and only possible through it, and, above all, the Press and periodicals, have appeared only in the Occident. Institutions of higher education of all possible types, even some superficially similar to our universities, or at least academies, have existed (China, Islam). But a rational, systematic, and specialized pursuit of science, with trained and specialized personnel, has only existed in the West in a sense at all approaching its present dominant place in our culture. Above all is this true of the trained official, the pillar of both the modern State and of the economic life of the West. He forms a type of which there have heretofore only been suggestions, which have never remotely approached its present importance for the social order. Of course the official, even the specialized official, is a very old constituent of the most various societies. But no country and no age has ever experienced, in the same sense as the modern Occident, the absolute and complete dependence of its whole existence, of the political, technical, and economic conditions of its life, on a highly trained *organization* of officials. The most important functions of the everyday life of society have come to be in the hands of technically, commercially, and above all legally trained government officials.

Organization of political and social groups in feudal classes has been common. But even the feudal state of *rex et regnum* in the Western sense has only been known to our culture. Even more are parliaments of periodically elected representatives, with government by demagogues and party leaders as ministers responsible to the parliaments, peculiar to us, although there have, of course, been parties, in the sense of organizations for exerting influence and gaining control of political power, all over the world. In fact, the State itself, in the sense of a political association with a rational, written constitution, rationally ordained law, and an administration bound to rational rules or laws, administered by trained officials, is known, in this combination of characteristics, only in the Occident, despite all other approaches to it.

And the same is true of the most fateful force in our modern life, capitalism. The impulse to acquisition, pursuit of gain, of money, of the greatest possible amount of money, has in itself nothing to do with capitalism. This impulse exists and has existed among waiters, physicians, coachmen, artists, prostitutes, dishonest officials, soldiers, nobles, crusaders, gamblers, anbeggars. One may say that it has been common to all sorts and conditions of men at all times and in all countries of the earth, wherever the objective possibility of it is or has been given. It should be taught in the kindergarten of cultural history that this naïve idea of capitalism must be given up once and for all. Unlimited greed for gain is not in the least identical with capitalism, and is still less its spirit. Capitalism *may* even be identical with the restraint, or at least a rational tempering, of this irrational impulse. But capitalism is identical with the pursuit of profit, and forever *renewed* profit, by means of continuous, rational, capitalistic enterprise. For it must be so: in a wholly capitalistic order of society, an individual capitalistic enterprise which did not take advantage of its opportunities for profit-making would be doomed to extinction. . . .

For the purpose of this conception all that matters is that an actual adaptation of economic action to a comparison of money income with money expenses takes place, no matter how primitive the form. Now in this sense capitalism and capitalistic enterprises, even with a considerable rationalization of capitalistic calculation, have existed in all civilized countries of the earth, so far as economic documents permit us to judge. In China, India, Babylon, Egypt, Mediterranean antiquity, and the Middle Ages, as well as in modern times. These were not merely isolated ventures, but economic enterprises which were entirely dependent on the continual renewal of capitalistic undertakings, and even continuous operations. However, trade especially was for a long time not continuous, like our own, but consisted essentially in a series of individual undertakings. Only gradually did the activities of even the large merchants acquire an inner cohesion (with branch organizations, etc.). In any case, the capitalistic enterprise and the capitalistic entrepreneur, not only as occasional but as regular entrepreneurs, are very old and were very widespread.

Now, however, the Occident has developed capitalism both to a quantitative extent, and (carrying this quantitative development) in types, forms, and directions which have never existed elsewhere. All over the world there have been merchants, wholesale and retail, local and engaged in foreign trade. Loans of all kinds have been made, and there have been banks with the most various functions, at least comparable to ours of, say, the sixteenth century. Whenever money finances of public bodies have existed, money-lenders have appeared, as in Babylon, Hellas, India, China, Rome. They have financed wars and piracy, contracts and building operations of all sorts. In overseas policy they have functioned as colonial entrepreneurs, as planters with slaves or directly or indirectly forced labour, and have farmed domains, offices, and, above all, taxes. They have financed party leaders in elections and *condottieri* in civil wars. And, finally, they have been speculators in chances for pecuniary gain of all kinds. This kind of entrepreneur, the capitalistic adventurer, has existed everywhere. With the exception of trade and credit and banking transactions, their activities were predominantly of an irrational and speculative character, or directed to acquisition by force, above all the acquisition of booty, whether directly in war or in the form of continuous fiscal booty by exploitation of subjects. . . .

But in modern times the Occident has developed, in addition to this, a very different form of capitalism which has appeared nowhere else: the rational capitalistic organization of (formally) free labour. Only suggestions of it are found elsewhere. Even the organization of unfree labour reached a considerable degree of rationality only on plantations and to a very limited extent in the *Ergasteria* of antiquity. In the manors, manorial workshops, and domestic industries on estates with serf labour it was probably somewhat less developed. Even real domestic industries with free labour have definitely been proved to have existed in only a few isolated cases outside the Occident. The frequent use of day labourers led in a very few cases – especially State monopolies, which are, however, very different from modern industrial organization – to manufacturing organizations, but never to a rational organization of apprenticeship in the handicrafts like that of our Middle Ages.

Rational industrial organization, attuned to a regular market, and neither to political nor irrationally speculative opportunities for profit, is not, however, the only peculiarity of Western capitalism. The modern rational organization of the capitalistic enterprise would not have been possible without two other important factors in its development: the separation of business from the household, which completely dominates modern economic life, and closely connected with it, rational book-keeping. A spatial separation of places of work from those of residence exists elsewhere, as in the Oriental bazaar and in the *ergasteria* of other cultures. The development of capitalistic associations with their own accounts is also found in the Far East, the Near East, and in antiquity. But compared to the modern independence of business enterprises, those are only small beginnings. The reason for this was particularly that the indispensable requisites for this independence, our rational business book-keeping and our legal separation of corporate from personal property, were entirely lacking, or had only begun to develop. The tendency everywhere else was for acquisitive enterprises to arise as parts of a royal or manorial household (of the *oikos*), which is, as Rodbertus has perceived, with all its superficial similarity, a fundamentally different, even opposite, development. However, all these peculiarities of Western capitalism have derived their significance in the last analysis only from their association with the capitalistic organization of labour. Even what is generally called commercialization, the development of negotiable securities and the rationalization of speculation, the exchanges, etc., is connected with it. For without the rational capitalistic organization of labour, all this, so far as it was possible at all, would have nothing like the same significance, above all for the social structure and all the specific problems of the modern Occident connected with it. Exact calculation – the basis of everything else – is only possible on a basis of free labour. . . .

Now the peculiar modern Western form of capitalism has been, at first sight, strongly influenced by the development of technical possibilities. Its rationality is today essentially dependent on the calculability of the most important technical factors. But this means fundamentally that it is dependent on the peculiarities of modern science, especially the natural sciences based on mathematics and exact and rational experiment. On the other hand, the development of these sciences and of the technique resting upon them now receives important stimulation from these capitalistic interests in its practical economic application. It is true that the origin of Western science cannot be attributed to such interests. Calculation, even with decimals, and algebra have been carried on in India, where the decimal system was invented. But it was only made use of by developing capitalism in the West, while in India it led to no modern arithmetic or book-keeping. Neither was the origin of mathematics and mechanics determined by capitalistic interests. But the *technical* utilization of scientific knowledge, so important for the living conditions of the mass of people, was certainly encouraged by economic considerations, which were extremely favourable to it in the Occident. But this encouragement was derived from the peculiarities of the social structure of the Occident. We must hence ask, from *what* parts of that structure was it derived, since not all of them have been of equal importance?

Among those of undoubted importance are the rational structures of law and of administration. For modern rational capitalism has need, not only of the technical means of production, but of a calculable legal system and of administration in terms of formal rules. Without it adventurous and speculative trading capitalism and all sorts of politically determined capitalisms are possible, but no rational enterprise under individual initiative, with fixed capital and certainty of calculations. Such a legal system and such administration have been available for economic activity in a comparative state of legal and formalistic perfection only in the Occident. We must hence inquire where that law came from. Among other circumstances, capitalistic interests have in turn undoubtedly also helped, but by no means alone nor even principally, to prepare the way for the predominance in law and administration of a class of jurists specially trained in rational law. But these interests did not themselves create that law. Quite different forces were at work in this development. And why did not the capitalistic interests do the same in China or India? Why did not the scientific, the artistic, the political, or the economic development there enter upon that path of rationalization which is peculiar to the Occident?

For in all the above cases it is a question of the specific and peculiar rationalism of Western culture. Now by this term very different things may be understood, as the following discussion will repeatedly show. There is, for example, rationalization of mystical contemplation, that is of an attitude which, viewed from other departments of life, is specifically irrational, just as much as there are rationalizations of economic life, of technique, of scientific research, of military training, of law and administration. Furthermore, each one of these fields may be rationalized in terms of very different ultimate values and ends, and what is rational from one point of view may well be irrational from another. Hence rationalizations of the most varied character have existed in various departments of life and in all areas of culture. To characterize their differences from the viewpoint of cultural history it is necessary to know what departments are rationalized, and in what direction. It is hence our first concern to work out and to explain genetically the special peculiarity of Occidental rationalism, and within this field that of the modern Occidental form. Every such attempt at explanation must, recognizing the fundamental importance of the economic factor, above all take account of the economic conditions. But at the same time the opposite correlation must not be left out of consideration. For though the development of economic rationalism is partly dependent on rational technique and law, it is at the same time determined by the ability and disposition of men to adopt certain types of practical rational conduct. When these types have been obstructed by spiritual obstacles, the development of rational economic conduct has also met serious inner resistance. The magical and religious forces, and the ethical ideas of duty based upon them, have in the past always been among the most important formative influences on conduct.

Two older essays have been placed at the beginning[1] which attempt, at one important point, to approach the side of the problem which is general

[1]   Of the series to which this is the introduction [Eds].

most difficult to grasp: the influence of certain religious ideas on the development of an economic spirit, or the *ethos* of an economic system. In this case we are dealing with the connection of the spirit of modern economic life with the rational ethics of ascetic Protestantism. Thus we treat here only one side of the causal chain. The later studies on the Economic Ethics of the World Religions attempt, in the form of a survey of the relations of the most important religions to economic life and to the social stratification of their environment, to follow out both causal relationships. . . .

In another respect the uninitiated at least must be warned against exaggerating the importance of these investigations. The Sinologist, the Indologist, the Semitist, or the Egyptologist, will of course find no facts unknown to him. We only hope that he will find nothing definitely wrong in points that are essential. How far it has been possible to come as near this ideal as a non-specialist is able to do, the author cannot know. It is quite evident that anyone who is forced to rely on translations, and furthermore on the use and evaluation of monumental, documentary, or literary sources, has to rely himself on a specialist literature which is often highly controversial, and the merits of which he is unable to judge accurately. Such a writer must make modest claims for the value of his work. All the more so since the number of available translations of real sources (that is, inscriptions and documents) is, especially for China, still very small in comparison with what exists and is important. From all this follows the definitely provisional character of these studies, and especially of the parts dealing with Asia. Only the specialist is entitled to a final judgment. And, naturally, it is only because expert studies with this special purpose and from this particular viewpoint have not hitherto been made, that the present ones have been written at all. They are destined to be superseded in a much more important sense than this can be said, as it can be, of all scientific work. But however objectionable it may be, such trespassing on other special fields cannot be avoided in comparative work. But one must take the consequences by resigning oneself to considerable doubts regarding the degree of one's success.

Fashion and the zeal of the *literati* would have us think that the specialist can today be spared, or degraded to a position subordinate to that of the seer. Almost all sciences owe something to dilettantes, often very valuable viewpoints. But dilettantism as a leading principle would be the end of science. He who yearns for seeing should go to the cinema, though it will be offered to him copiously today in literary form in the present field of investigation also. Nothing is farther from the intent of these thoroughly serious studies than such an attitude. And, I might add, whoever wants a sermon should go to a conventicle. The question of the relative value of the cultures which are compared here will not receive a single word. It is true that the path of human destiny cannot but appal him who surveys a section of it. But he will do well to keep his small personal commentaries to himself, as one does at the sight of the sea or of majestic mountains, unless he knows himself to be called and gifted to give them expression in artistic or prophetic form. In most other cases the voluminous talk about intuition does nothing but conceal a lack of perspective toward the object, which merits the same judgment as a similar lack of persepective toward men. . . .

Finally, we may make a reference to the *anthropological* side of the problem. When we find again and again that, even in departments of life apparently mutually independent, certain types of rationalization have developed in the Occident, and only there, it would be natural to suspect that the most important reason lay in differences of heredity. The author admits that he is inclined to think the importance of biological heredity very great. But in spite of the notable achievements of anthropological research, I see up to the present no way of exactly or even approximately measuring either the extent or, above all, the form of its influence on the development investigated here. It must be one of the tasks of sociological and historical investigation first to analyse all the influences and causal relationships which can satisfactorily be explained in terms of reactions to environmental conditions. Only then, and when comparative racial neurology and psychology shall have progressed beyond their present and in many ways very promising beginnings, can we hope for even the probability of a satisfactory answer to that problem. In the meantime that condition seems to me not to exist, and an appeal to heredity would therefore involve a premature renunciation of the possibility of knowledge attainable now, and would shift the problem to factors (at present) still unknown.

32   A new concept of the future

Melvin M. Webber

We are constantly amazed at the speed with which our images and attitudes absorb new ideas and new technologies. Novelty appears to have a rapid decay rate in the modern western world. Once television was made cheap enough for mass distribution, it quickly became part of people's everyday lives. Within a year after Sputnik was launched, space shots scarcely seemed remarkable any more, even though the recent satellites' experiment packages are surely far more sophisticated achievements than the vehicles that orbit them. Then, when satellite transmission of television broadcasts became work-a-day, we readily accepted simultaneous worldwide visual communication as just another clever technological novelty. By next year, heart-transplants will scarcely warrant notice by the news media. And so it has gone, step by step, each dramatic achievement – even the unanticipated big leap – has a way of becoming commonplace after the fact.

Because we have lacked adequate predictive theory of technological or social change, we have tended to confront each incremental development as it occurs, regarding it as a unitary, independent event. Few people have tried to trace the waves of repercussions that those events might in turn generate through the larger systems of which they become new component parts. Fewer still have tried to predict the chains of consequences that numerous and *cumulative* changes would then induce within the larger systems. And so we have calmly accepted each new accretion, telling ourselves that 'the more things change, the more they remain the same'.

Virtually everyone now knows that the rate of discovery and invention has been explosive during these past two decades; and yet we in the developed world seem to have accepted even that fact as a stable condition and take rapid change as a normal, no-change condition. Perhaps this is a further indication of our large adaptive capacities – in both senses of that phrase: first, that modern social systems have been able to absorb new developments without permitting them to rock the social order and, secondly, that we must *believe* that change is no-change, for to believe otherwise would itself upset our perceptions of social order. However, even if true

WEBBER, MELVIN M. (1968) 'A New Concept of the Future', from 'Planning in an Environment of Change', Part I, in *Town Planning Review*, vol. 39, no. 3, 179–81.

in the past, this is not likely to go on. Knowledge of physical, biological, and social systems is expanding at such a fantastic rate that it is triggering off an equally fantastic expansion in the technologies through which those systems can be modified. These new intellectual resources are making it increasingly possible to anticipate future scientific discovery and technological invention and to forecast some subsequent social effects of discovery and invention. As social theory improves, we are likely to be better able to forecast social change too. In turn, better forecasts will permit us deliberately to plan our responses to those anticipated outcomes – even to select, in some fields, those of the possible outcomes that we happen to prefer. This is to say, in effect, that among the consequences of the knowledge explosion is the emergence of a new way of thinking about the future. That conception is the derivative of our new capacities for prediction, our new images of our powers for controlling future events and, hence, a new outlook suggesting that, to a considerable degree, maybe we really can invent the future.

This new concept of the future represents a remarkable change, a change that is potentially as important as any of the developments that are now building up in the developed world. Let me here simply state my thesis.

Pre-industrial societies around the world all seem to be marked by a common perception that the future lies outside the field of vision and certainly outside control. The accomulating studies of peasant and primitive societies are revealing a common fatalism in virtually all of them. Some (the Sioux Indians are one example) do not even have a word for 'future' in their languages. Others that do conceive of future time see its events as in the hands of the gods.

With the coming of industrialization and the commercial economy, possibilities for forward scheduling of production and the requirements for monetary credit provoked a different image of the future. Within the short-run, managers found they could shape the institutions under their control. Observed and anticipated stability in growth rates permitted banks to make loans, with the prospect that they would be repaid. Population forecasters could extrapolate trend lines with some confidence that whatever determined birth and death rates in the immediate past would probably continue to affect them in the immediate future. Indeed, a large insurance industry was in fact built upon the actuarial estimates of probabilities that grew out of these measurements of system stability. For that matter, the whole of the industrial structure was built against the conception of the future that saw a sufficient degree of stability in the short run to justify investment. To account for those future changes that were not or could not be anticipated, the market system developed to feed information on change back into decision centres, so that managers and consumers could then adjust their predictions.

In brief, in the vernacular conception of the industrial age, the future was seen as closely resembling the present; where conditions and events would depart from the present, the response was to *accommodate* to those conditions and events.

The big change is the current shift away from that image of stability and accommodative response. With the emergence of the post-industrial stage of development, the future is being seen to depart drastically from the present, and it now looks as though men will be seeking more directly to design the future. If we can characterize a single distinguishing difference between the outlooks of the industrial age and of the post-industrial age it is this: that industry and government in the recent past had to respond to change after the fact; in the post-industrial age they will be intellectually equipped to respond before. That is to say, that the coming style for confronting the future will be forecasting and planning.

We are already seeing the signs of this new post-industrial outlook in the rapid rise of the new quasi-science of futurism and, in parallel, the rise of a large number of new kinds of planning institutions. These signs are seen in the projective work of such groups as Resources for the Future in Washington, Professor de Jouvenel's Futuribles group on France, The American Academy of Arts and Science's Commission on the Year 2000 and its several committees on the next ten years. In London, there are the Social Science Research Council's project on The Next Thirty Years, and the Centre for Environmental Studies' group on Developing Patterns of Urbanization. There are more. By now there is a literal flood of new institutes on the future being organized in America and elsewhere. Their counterparts are the new planning institutions with such unlikely names as CONSAD Research Corporation, the Rand Corporation, Systems Development Corporation, and even more unlikely names Lockheed Aircraft Corporation, Aero–Jet General, Litton Industries, and so on.

The best of the new students of the future are trying to foresee latent qualitative consequences before they become manifest – in effect, to develop an early-warning-system that might signal impending disasters, as well as potentially beneficial outcomes that might be exploited were appropriate action to be taken soon enough. Most important, they are attempting to trace out the alternative future histories – particularly the social and economic histories – that would be shaped by plausibly foreseen uncontrollable events and by deliberately designed ones.

Despite the excitement and fashion that is marking this activity, this is probably no fad. Had we been in the forecasting business before, the rise of futurist studies might have been foreseen as a deterministic outcome of the current knowledge explosion. More knowledge, better theory, and improved methods were bound to make conscious confrontation of emphatic and rapid social change inevitable.

Of course, neither students of the future nor practitioners of planning are new phenomena in our midst. There have been individual prophets and forecasters at work for a long time, but these men have typically been aberrants within the world of scholarship. Although scholars generally agree that the test of a theory is its capacity to predict well, theorists in the social and behavioural sciences have traditionally eschewed projective modes of thought in favour of observational modes; and they have done so just as firmly as they have declined normative interpretation in favour of positivistic accounts. The thing that is new is the emergence of a legitimate and organized activity, explicitly devoted to systematic and normative interpretation of potential future histories.

33   Predictions

Bertrand de Jouvenel

'Proference'

Man draws assertions about the future out of his present knowledge. If the reader studies himself reading a newspaper, he will notice that he often formulates *futura* which seem to be 'promised' by the facts in the articles. By an unconscious precedure, he 'deduces' a future aspect from a present one: but the term 'deduction' suggests a rigour of which the procedure is devoid. The action of going from present data to an assertion about the future is *sui generis*; it lacks a name, and so I propose to call it 'proference'; this suggests the action of carrying forward and will serve us more or less adequately.

The purpose of the quotations gathered below is to illustrate the elementary modes of proference. The mind spontaneously uses certain tricks for transforming present knowledge into 'pseudo-knowledge' of the future. We shall see them employed. Observation and introspection both confirm that the mind uses these devices. A little reflection will show that we have no reason for assuming an exact correspondence between the process of proference and the process of history. On the one hand, I derive my view of the future from my view of the present; on the other, the future state of affairs comes out of the present state of affairs. The two processes are of a quite different order. To improve forecasting is to bring the intellectual process closer to the historical process.

We obviously need to acquaint ourselves with the modes of proference, and to start with, it is worth considering the elementary modes, as the more elaborate ones may well turn out to be combinations of the simple ones.

I have said that the predictions assembled below illustrate the simple modes of proference. And indeed, the predictions were not the result of a conscious effort to forecast the future, even though they were made by eminent thinkers. Some of the predictions – as, for instance, Rousseau's – were tossed into a text quite incidentally; others – as, for instance, Condorcet's – were used as postulates in a discussion dealing with something

JOUVENEL, BERTRAND DE (1967) 'Predictions', in *The Art of Conjecture* London, Weidenfeld and Nicolson, 59–81.

quite different. And since these forecasts were not 'careful' ones, they prove nothing about the impossibility of making better ones. Somebody might object to my picking forecasts so little valued by their own authors. But I did not say the authors attached no value to them. Quite the reverse. If the predictions were not carefully 'worked out', the reason was that they seemed perfectly evident to their authors. Thus Rousseau says 'it is very easy to foresee that . . .'; Condorcet speaks of 'the great probability that . . .'; and Maistre says 'the odds are a thousand to one that . . .'.

Those men thought their pronouncements were *evident*. Simple, naïve modes of preference, which make a particular future seem evident, sometimes go wrong. This is one of the lessons that will emerge from the examination we are about to conduct, and it is a most useful lesson, for nowadays forecasts often seem very powerful because of the mathematical tools employed in them, but are really based on perfectly naïve modes of preference.

Our scrutiny of past predictions will enable us to make an inventory of the mind's natural modes of preference. It would be a great mistake to think that these simple modes are scorned in systematic forecasting, although their use may be regulated.

Prolongation of a tendency

We generally imagine the future scene in terms of differences relative to the scene we now know. We naturally tend to think that elements of the scene that have remained unchanged will continue unchanged. This can be put so as to correspond more closely to the psychological reality: it is natural for us *not to think* of changes in parts of the scene that by standing still have left us unaware of their mobility. We are alert to future change only in parts where previous changes have made us aware of mobility. If the unchanged parts of the scene are important, the future validity of the 'Map of the Present' is by so much the greater. The unconscious purpose of primitive institutions is, it seems, to provide an assurance of continued validity. We ourselves are far removed from such a 'stationary state'; we are vividly aware that many things have changed, and admit that they, these same things, will go on changing. But in what way will they change? The simplest idea to suggest itself is that they will change in the same direction and even at the same rate as in the past. In a supposedly stationary state, we postulate that tomorrow will be the same as today; likewise, when we are aware of movement, we assume that tomorrow will differ from today *in the same way as* today differs from yesterday. In doing this, we simply apply the postulate of inertia to moving things instead of to stationary things.

This simple idea exerts a strong sway over our minds. The lifespan of man has become longer; it will become still longer. The number of work hours in the year has decreased; it will decrease yet further. The standard of living has risen; it will rise even more. Whatever the precise reasons given to justify each assumption, they are brought in only to justify this immediate and spontaneous conviction – things will go on *that* way, for they have already gone *that* way. The sharper our awareness of a past movement, the stronger our conviction of its future continuation. A comparison of French and American forecasts of economic growth shows how persuasive past change is felt to be: American experts say that the standard of living in the United States will go up 50 per cent during the next twenty-five years, while French experts say theirs will go up 150 per cent. Yet we can find no reason for this enormous difference except in the past rates of growth of the two countries. (In the case of the United States, it makes no difference whether the 'past' used as a basis for the projection is a short past, extending back as far as the end of the Second World War, or a long past, stretching back into the nineteenth century. Whereas the French figure is based on the short past alone, the long past would lead to a lower figure than for the United States.)

Because prolongation of present tendencies plays such an important role in our anticipations, it is not surprising to find that this mode of proference was also important in former times. Thus, on the basis of the political evolution of the nineteenth century, Émile Faguet made this prediction for our own country:

> The chances are that from now on history will be less filled with vicissitudes, less colourful, and less dramatic. The great conqueror, the great reformer, and the great statesman will become increasingly rare (Faguet 1899).

He was convinced – fifteen years before the First World War, eighteen before the advent of Lenin, and twenty-three before that of Mussolini – that nations would no longer be ruled, but would govern themselves in a 'spirit of peaceful conservatism, economy, timidity, and preservation of the status quo'. He was so confident of this progress that he even allowed himself to strike a note of regret for the disappearance of men of great ambition.

A century earlier, Condorcet committed the very same error. In 1784 he spoke about

. . . the great probability that we have fewer great changes and fewer large revolutions to expect from the future than from the past. The progress of enlightenment in all the sciences throughout every part of Europe, the prevailing spirit of moderation and peace, the sort of disrepute into which Machiavellism is beginning to fall, seem to assure us that henceforth wars and revolutions will be less frequent (Condorcet 1784).

'Fewer large revolutions . . .' five years before the French Revolution; 'less frequent wars . . .' eight years before Condorcet himself called the nation to a war which was to ravage Europe for twenty-three years; 'the spirit of moderation and peace . . .' less than ten before he died a victim of the Reign of Terror.

Yet it is very natural to count on the persistence of a tendency. Look at what J.-P. Rabaut, a Protestant pastor, wrote (in 1791!):

Everything announces an age in which that madness of nations, war, will come to an end. The fury of the primitive hordes has already abated . . . wars are less wholehearted than among ignorant peoples; legions clash with one another with civility; heroes exchange greetings before slaying one another; soldiers from opposite camps visit one another before giving battle, just as men dine together before gaming. Neither nations nor even kings fight any longer, but armies and paid men. It is a game with limited stakes. War, once a frenzy, is now no more than a folly. (Rabaut 1791).

Wars have become gentler, therefore they will be gentler yet! What happened was quite the reverse. Attacks in column formation – advocated half a century earlier by Folard (1753) and always rejected as too deadly by the generals of the *ancien régime* – were adopted by the generals of the Revolution, who were not restricted to 'paid men' and were abundantly supplied with 'cannon-fodder' now that the 'nation was fighting'. I use Rabaut's own terms to emphasize the reversal of the tendency in which he had so much trust.

The trouble with prolongation of a tendency is that the reversal of the tendency is not anticipated. This comment is not intended to condemn extrapolation,[1] but only to serve as a warning.

1   The use of 'extrapolation' as a name for this mode of proference is now general, and I shall conform to this practice. Strictly speaking, an extrapolation involves treating a relationship between variables as valid outside the limits between which it has been observed. Different types of extrapolation are used in forecasting: it is an extrapolation to say: 'When the average income attains so much, the expenditure on cars will attain that much' (this is based on previously observed relations between the growth of income and the expenditure on cars); it is a different type of extrapolation (with time as the independent variable) to say: 'The average income will attain so much on such a date' (this is based on a previously observed rate of growth). In a loose and broad sense, people speak of 'extrapolation' when they assume that a future movement will be a continuation of a past movement. But we must remain aware of the nature of our assumptions, and of their frequent complexity.

Analogy

No procedure comes more naturally to the mind than looking for analogies. All science begins with classification. We would never have learned anything if we had never thought: 'This object resembles this other, and I expect it to manifest the same properties.' Even the savage who kept his fire burning had to think: 'This *too* is wood and it *too* will burn.' The classification of objects involves a prediction of how they will behave in given circumstances, and hence the classification of objects is associated with the classification of situations. Just as two objects recognized as similar should behave in the same way, so two situations recognized as similar should evolve in the same way. Rather than two ideas, we have here two aspects of a single idea, which is essential to any advancement of our knowledge. Taxonomic knowledge implies prediction: I saw that the conjunction of A and B gave rise to event C, and if I recognize two new elements as identical to A and B, I expect their conjunction to give rise to an event identical to C. Such a prediction is implicit when a new case is assimilated (justifiably) to a previous one. For example, in France at the time of the Directory, people began to realize that revolutionary fervour had exhausted itself and that, with the failure of new institutions to foster security or command respect, the republic lacked a foundation on which to settle. They saw in this situation a resemblance to the events of the English revolution after the death of Oliver Cromwell and recalled the outcome of that situation in 1660 – the restoration of Charles II by General Monk. Same situation – same outcome. This idea haunted the royalists, who thought they had a Monk in Pichegru. The coup d'état on the eighteenth of Fructidor of the year V removed their man, but it seemed to them that the unavailability of a particular man could not stop an 'objectively necessary process' (although this term is an anachronism here, their thinking resembled that of 'historical materialists' later on). And after the thirtieth of Prairial of the year VII, when it was the turn of Sieyès to look for a general, the royalists had no doubt that this general, whatever his own intentions, would eventually play the same role as Monk.

The republicans were no less aware of the analogy. But since they rejected the event it foreshadowed, they drew from the analogy a warning rather than a prediction. For instance, in his pamphlet *Des suites de la Contre-Révolution de 1660 en Angleterre*, Benjamin Constant tried to make the prospect of a restoration appear frightening by describing the punitive measures that followed the Restoration in England (his pamphlet appeared in 1799, not long before the coup d'état of Brumaire).

We see here the two uses to which an analogy lends itself: on the on hand, to predict what *must* happen;; on the other, to foresee what *ma* happen. I regard the latter course as the only advisable one in human affairs although man tends to adopt the former course when the analogy fore shadows a pleasing event. Thus, a little more than a quarter of a centur later, the French liberals were strongly inclined to assume that 'histor repeats itself': for the analogy between the restoration of the Bourbon and that of the Stuarts, between Charles X and James II, now pointed to a event they desired – the replacement of the Bourbon dynasty by the libera dynasty of the Orléans. In 1830 the awaited event took place.

Analogy is more rational than extrapolation. To anticipate by extrapola tion is to take things as they come – the intellectual effort involved i minimal, whereas a prediction by analogy presupposes that the mind ha sufficiently delineated the present situation to find some analogues for it judging the resemblance to be fundamental enough for the same sorts o events to follow as in the reference-situation. Consider this example. At th end of the Second World War an American economic forecaster sees certair analogies with the situation at the end of the First World War: but are they sufficient to warrant the prediction of a depression like that of 192 (Schoeffler 1955)? And similarly, the French political forecaster of 196: sees an analogy in the conflict between Parliament and the president o the Republic with the situation in 1877: but is the resemblance sufficient t make the same outcome likely?

In asking whether the resemblance is sufficient, we raise the questior of determining factors. Unless two situations resemble each other in respect: that are causally significant, we can hardly expect the same effects to follow It is obvious that in spite of causally significant points of resemblance, tw situations will differ in other respects, which may also be causally signifi cant. What is important to emphasize is that the effort of analysis require in the analogical method is commendable and conducive to progress, ever though practical conclusions may remain uncertain owing to the com plexity of real situations.

The 'railway'

In the previous section I mentioned two instances in which situations in France were interpreted in the light of previous situations in England; the idea underlying both these analogies was that a short sequence of events would conform to the same pattern as an earlier one. An idea of a much more ambitious nature is that history is repetitive in its general course, and not merely in short runs. That is to say, the secular sequence of important events in one country is 'signalled' by the secular sequence of such events in another country.

According to this conception, a nation is like a train travelling some distance behind another down the same track. The same railway station may lie in the 'past' for the passengers in the first train, but in the 'future' for the passengers in the second. The latter see the same scenes go by as their predecessors, and see them in the same order, and consequently can obtain prior knowledge of the scenes.

The idea is a queer one, and yet forecasters have made use of it. In particular, French minds were obsessed by it during the restoration of the Bourbons. By way of example, consider this passage written by Madame de Staël's son in 1825:

> When I let my thoughts run over the history of the two countries [France and England], I am struck by a remarkable parallelism; in one and the other I find series of almost similar events, and each phase of the history of England precedes the corresponding phase in France by a century and a half.
>
> In 1215, the English barons exacted from King John the Magna Carta, which the English still revere as the foundation of their liberties. One hundred and forty-one years later, the Estates-General of 1356 took advantage of the captivity of John II of France to insist upon guarantees to the nation as the price for the subsidies they granted his son.
>
> After the War of the Roses, the nobility were mutilated and exhausted; Henry VII and Henry VIII availed themselves of the opportunity to institute despotism by encouraging the commons. One hundred and fifty years later, the wars of the League over, Richelieu achieved a like but much more extensive success by pursuing a similar policy.
>
> The age of Elizabeth offers a striking analogy with that of Louis XIV. During both reigns, the greatness of the monarch (more real in the case of Elizabeth), the victories abroad, the splendour of the court, and the brilliant state of the letters – consoled the subjects for their lack of liberty.
>
> In 1640, the Long Parliament began the struggle of the English against Charles I. One hundred and forty-nine years later, the Estates-General were summoned to Versailles.
>
> One hundred and forty-four years lie between the death of Charles I and that of Louis XVI.
>
> Lastly, the restoration of Charles II came one hundred and forty-four years before that of the Bourbons. And if we read the history of the two revolutions side by side, countless astonishing similarities in the order of events and ideas, and even in the smallest circumstances, strike the eye. (Staël-Holstein 1825, pp. 23–5)

Implicit in this passage is the prediction that the Bourbons will be dethroned a second and final time, giving way, as in England, to a Whig monarchy. This prediction was verified (1830 minus 1689 equals 141 years). But no less implicit is the prediction that the French liberal monarchy will endure a long time, just as in England. But this did not take place. The 'railway' perspective gives no forewarning of the revolution of 1848 or of the coup d'état of 2 December 1851. Nor does it suggest the pattern of French history after 1848 – an oscillation, now slow, now rapid – between a parliamentary republic and a personal power far less restricted than that of the old kings.

This way of contemplating the future has so little foundation in reason that it would not even deserve to be mentioned here if it did not frequently function as a hidden assumption in forecasts. Indeed, in our day such an assumption subtends many predictions about the 'developing nations'.

The United Nations graph on which different countries are ranked on a dollar scale according to their national per capita income is ideally designed to foster the 'railway' outlook. This way of comparing countries makes us commit two serious errors: first, thinking that two countries at the same income level are in analogous situations; second, thinking that the present state of a country with a low income is analogous to a past state, more or less remote, of some other country with a high income. When, one may ask, was the American nation at the 'stage' which is currently that of China? These errors can too easily give rise to the conviction that the 'developing nations' will undergo the same evolution as the developed nations (hopefully at a faster rate), and will thus pass through the same stages.

Causality

Find a cause which will continue to act, then specify its necessary effect. This is a method of prediction based on a very sound principle. But its practical application can be badly defective, as is borne out by a passage which Rousseau wrote in 1760:

> It is, for example, very easy to foresee that England, for all its glory, will be ruined twenty years hence, and will, in addition, have lost what remains of its liberty. Everybody asserts that agriculture is flourishing on that island for my part, I wager that it is in a state of decline. London grows bigger every day, and thus the kingdom is being depopulated. The English wish to be conquerors, and therefore they will be slaves (Rousseau 1760).

Consider the sentence 'London grows bigger every day, and thus the kingdom is being depopulated'. The first proposition is true, the second false. The period designated by Rousseau was characterized by an accelerating growth of population – an acceleration which was to become more pronounced in the following century, Reliable statistics for the nineteenth century invalidate his claim that the growth of London is related to a decline in the population of the kingdom; during the first forty years, the population of London doubled, and so did the total population of the land; over the entire century, the population of London increased 5·9 times, and the total population about 4·7 times. Coming at a time when the population of England was beginning to soar, Rousseau's prediction was particularly unfortunate.

Let us learn from the errors of great men. How did Rousseau derive from his well-founded forecast about the expansion of London his erroneous conclusion that the total population of England would decline? The fact that birth rates were lower and death rates higher in large cities than in the countryside was then being widely discussed. From this fact it could readily be inferred that, as the proportion of the total population concentrated in the capital increased, the unfavourable population rates of the capital would weigh increasingly upon the national-average rates. Now if Rousseau had sought to 'quantify' his assumptions, deciding on some rate of increase for the rural population and some rate of inflow into town, he would have found that however high he chose to postulate the rate of population wastage in town the growth of total population would not be brutally reversed, but instead would be progressively braked over quite a number of years. Such a model would not have been a trustworthy predictor, since population rates are not stable over long periods. But at least it would have brought home to the author (this is a major function of mathematical models) what really followed from his own assumptions.

How foolish it would be to reproach Rousseau for not having used procedures foreign to his time! It was quite natural that he should use causal relationships without quantification. But perhaps we can blame him for confusing moral evaluations with positive estimates. This reasoning seems to have been as follows: He felt a strong moral disapproval of life in towns; he also strongly felt that a good social state necessarily had a growing population, and a bad social state a declining one; hence, postulating a perfect correlation between quality and quantity, he held that the badness inherent in urbanization would be translated into a declining population.

A discussion of Rousseau is not to the point here or else we could show how his use of the quantitative criterion often works against his qualitative judgments. What we must note is the intervention of a personal qualitative judgment in what purports to be a necessary causal relation. And Rousseau's case is by no means unique.

Causal relations in the social order lack simplicity and clarity. Which historian will attribute the course taken by such and such a phenomenon in the past to a clearly identified cause? And for each historian who does so, how many other historians will contradict him? We cannot deny the presence of a subjective element in our choice of explanations of the past. Likewise, in making a prediction, we use some 'preferred' causal relation.

War provides a convenient example. It is a phenomenon with relatively clear demarcations, which has long exercised the minds of men. When we consider, however, the explanatory theses which have been eagerly embraced in the course of the past two centuries, we see that they all attribute the detested phenomenon to a cause that men wish to rid themselves of for independent reasons. When monarchy grows unpopular, war is explained by dynastic ambitions. When the nobility from whom the officer corps is largely recruited falls into disrepute, war is explained by the pride of the military caste. When the capitalist system is denounced, conflicts are explained by the struggles of entrepreneurs to further their own interests. Man finds such explanations pleasing, for they enable him to predict that an evil odious to all will be eradicated when his fight against some hated institution or social category is brought to a successful close. However childish these views, we are less prone to recognize their nature to the extent that we are more affected by the passion animating them.

But surely we can find some calm, dispassionate thinkers. What about Émile Faguet? No preference seems to have prejudiced his judgment when he extrapolated into the twentieth century the progress made in the speed and ease of transport and communications during the nineteenth century (doing so with good reason) and then concluded that as a result a tendency toward large political agglomerations would appear. He was too conscientious an observer not to notice the awakening of strong feelings of nationality, seeing very clearly that they were opposed to the agglomerative tendency even though they might sometimes appear to coincide with it:

> During the whole of the nineteenth century, talk about the principle of nationalism has never ceased. The history of the principle is an interesting one: it is the history of a misconception. Different peoples felt a need to be strong, and thought they felt a need to group themselves by racial affinity. They spoke of Pan-Germanism, Pan-Slavism, Pan-Italism, and Pan-Hellenism giving to these confused aspirations the name of Nationalities. At heart they wanted to form large peoples, and that is something quite different.

In fact, the two aspirations are contrary. Nationality and agglomeration are not two different aspects of the same idea, but two mutually irreducible and conflicting ideas. Nationality is alive and intense only in a small people. Instead of championing large agglomerations, true nationalism is particularistic. The Belgian Revolution of 1830, which led to secession, and the formation of two small states in the place of one large one, was a true nationalist movement. That is to say, the Belgians were patriots rather than agglomerators, and preferred autonomy to power. Likewise the Irish would prefer to be weak in their own land, rather than boast of a powerful foreign landlord.

After pointing to the opposition between the nationalist and the agglomerative tendencies, Faguet went on to express his confidence that the latter would prevail in the twentieth century. But during the sixty-three intervening years, nationalism has manifested itself more frequently and with greater strength than the tendency to agglomerate and has led to the dismemberment of the Ottoman Empire, the destruction of the Austro-Hungarian Empire, and the abolition of the colonial empires. The chief fact in history of the nineteenth century possibly is German unity. To date, the chief portent for the history of the twentieth century appears to have been the triumph of Irish nationalism: a prototype early in the century followed by many other examples. Although it is conceivable that the agglomerative tendency may yet prevail, the fact remains that Faguet's prediction would have provided us with poor guidance during the times through which we have lived. And in the confidence of his pronouncement, we may read the choice of a man more sensitive to the general than to the particular, and more responsive to order than to emotion.

Systems

A system can be defined as 'a group of material or non-material elements which mutually depend on one another so as to form an organized whole'. Every social group constitutes a system; it is a tautology that the future states of a system can be known if its dynamics are completely known. In science we often have *macroscopic* knowledge of the dynamics of a system, and hence of its future states. The idea that a system-based mode of prediction is the right one was broached by Saint-Simon, developed by Auguste Comte, and triumphed with Marx. The hold of Marxism on our minds is comparable to the hold Aristotelianism once had, and its effects on our actions are even greater – this whether we have read Marx or not and whether we acknowledge him or dispute him. I have often been struck by the unconscious Marxism of American students.

Let us see how this powerful thinker predicted. He fastens on one central concept – the transformation of the mode of production – and uses it to give the history of the human race a new coherence. The efficiency with which labour is utilized when its energies are directed on the materials of nature differs considerably in different periods of history: for the efficiency to increase, great social changes had to occur. Quite so. Marx emphasizes that progress cannot occur unless capital is accumulated and that capitalists animated by selfish interests are the necessary historical intruments of this socially beneficial process. As the accumulation of capital continues, says Marx, the number of salaried workers and the production per worker will increase. True again. The increasing production has to be consumed – as the population is transformed into salaried workers, the latter constitute an ever-increasing proportion of the total number of possible consumers, and it is therefore necessary for the workers to raise their consumption if the increased production is to be absorbed. All of which is a matter of course.

At first sight, nothing in Marx's general account points to the inevitable downfall of capitalism and to a violent social revolution. Why, then, did he make these predictions? He took it as certain that the capitalists would oppose salary increases and that a subservient state would help them to resist. By keeping salaries down, the capitalists would inevitably produce stagnation and an economic crisis. The resulting misery and the scandalous failure to utilize the means of production would provoke a social revolution in which capitalism and the coercive machinery of the state would be overthrown. But why should the capitalists act against their own interests? A subjective judgment based on contemporary evidence encouraged Marx to think they would. However, in his sytem of thought, the attitude of the capitalists had to be a matter of objective necessity, rather than of mere probability. The way in which he made it so is described below.

It is not the least of Marx's achievements that he was the first to stress the concept, now basic to national accounting, of 'value added in manufacture'. To put is very roughly, the *value added* by a firm's operations is the difference between the financial receipts from its sales and its current expenditures (not including the acquisition of new capital items) on goods and services outside the firm (thus payments to its own employees are excluded). This added value is 'gross' or 'net' depending on whether it is taken before or after deduction of an allowance for capital 'consumed'. Marx considered the 'net value added'. This then is a net financial product of the firm':

operations, out of which both employed labour and employed capital are rewarded. By dividing it by the number of employees in the firm, one obtains the 'value added per man'. The increase over time of value added per man is the simplest expression of productivity gains with which we are familiar and which Marx expected. Now assuming that the value added per man is shared in unchanging proportions between worker and capitalist, both benefit: the worker's wage rises with productivity and so does the profit per man employed. Why then did Marx prophesy that the capitalist would eat more and more deeply into the worker's share, bringing about an ever sharper class conflict, impoverishment of the workers, and economic crises? His prophecy was entirely based on the supposition that increases in the value added per man would be brought about by increases in the capital investment per man, but that the increases in the value added would be less than proportional to the increases in the investment. Thus, if it was shared in unchanging proportions the reward of capital per man employed would go up as fast as productivity, but not so fast as the amount of capital invested per man, which would mean that the return per unit of capital, or rate of profit, would successively decline. In order to counteract this fall in the profit rate, the capitalists would seek an increase in their share of the value added, thereby bringing about conflict, impoverishment, crisis, and finally revolution. The whole intellectual construct is admirably built, but on a quite erroneous foundation: in fact, value added has increased faster, not slower, than capital invested (Jouvenel 1962), and this has been enough to do away with the 'historical inevitabilities' pointed out by Marx.

According to the dynamic model built by Marx, social revolution arises out of the actual development of capitalism and should therefore have proved very different – the first momentous revolution took place in Russia, and even more surprising in terms of the theory, the next in importance has taken place in China. It is worth trying to imagine how fundamentally different world history would be if Marx's prediction had come true.

We may then suppose that the revolution took place in the United States and in Great Britain, and since we are writing another Uchronia, we are free to choose our dates: say 1900 for the United States, the time of great agitation over 'trustification', and 1906 for Great Britain, the time of a great defeat for the Conservatives. Here then we have two Communist states at the beginning of the century. I can hardly help thinking that communism as translated into English would be something very different from Russian communism, and would come much closer to Marx's conception of it.

The 'centralized power of the state' of which Marx (1953, p. 39) spoke so critically, had long been the object of hostility in these countries – a favourable circumstance for action on his appeal to 'smash the bureaucratic and military machine'. The habits of local self-government and the practice of the Anglo-Saxon' in running orderly meetings would have helped the 'soviets', or councils, to function. Without claiming that the state would have withered away, I can see no reason why communism would have strengthened the state in English-speaking countries (and therefore, through rivalry, would have produced the same effect in other countries).

Since, by hypothesis, communism would have established itself in the most advanced countries, it follows by definition that these countries could not have set out to 'overtake' the level of economic development of another state. Nothing would have paralleled the Soviet obsession with overtaking the American standard of living; the need to 'force' national economic growth would not have arisen in the Communist states, and the harsh discipline introduced to this end in the Soviet Union would not have existed.

Moreover, according to the hypothesis, the new regime would have been installed in states that happened to have good natural defences (at a time when aircraft did not count). A harsh discipline could not have been needed, therefore, for reasons of security. In short, the Communist social regime would have assumed a completely different political complexion.

It is tempting to pursue this hypothesis and to depict a Western 'Communist world' instead of an Eastern one. But I have said enough to indicate how different history would have been if Marx's views had been verified in their role as predictions through the communization of advanced countries, instead of being adopted as normative doctrines first in Russia and later in China. In relation to Marxian dynamics, the victory of October 1917 is an 'accident' – but of what moment! And that an accident should be able to thus change a systematic anticipation of a course of events is something that must put into question all system-based prediction in general, even more than just this particular system-based prediction.

References

CONDORCET, MARQUIS DE (1784) Memoire sur le calcul des probabilités Histoire de *l'Academie Royale des Sciences*.

FAGUET, E. (1899) Que sera le XXe siecle, an essay published in *Questions politiques* Paris, Armand Colin. Reprinted in *Futuribles*, no. 232.

FOLARD, R. (1753) Commentaire sur Polybe. Supplement to l'histoire de Polybe translated by Thuillier, Dom V., 1727–30.

JOUVENEL, B. DE (1962) Le coefficient de capital. *Bulletin SEDEIS*, 1821, supplement 1, 20 May.

MARX, K. (1953) *La guerre civile en France* Paris, Editions sociales Internationales.

RABAUT, J. P. (1791) Reflexions politiques sur les circonstances presentes, *Pensée*, vol. 4, chapter X.

ROUSSEAU, J. J. (1760) Extrait du projet de paix perpetuelle.

SCHOEFFLER, S. (1955) *Failures of Economics: a Diagnostic Study* Cambridge, Mass., Harvard University Press.

STAËL-HOLSTEIN, A. DE (1825) *Lettres sur l'Angleterre* Paris.

Index

Index